THE GENTLE TASADAY

JOHN NANCE

THE GENTLE TASADAY

A STONE AGE PEOPLE IN THE PHILIPPINE RAIN FOREST

Foreword by
CHARLES A. LINDBERGH

A Harvest Book

New York and London
HARCOURT BRACE JOVANOVICH

Printed in the United States of America

All photographs are by John Nance—Magnum except "Panamin troopers on either side of Robert Fox, Elizalde, and Lindbergh," used by courtesy of the Minnesota Historical Society, and "President Ferdinand Marcos signing Tasaday reserve proclamation, with Manuel Elizalde, Jr., and Imelda Marcos," used by courtesy of Panamin.

The tape transcriptions are used with the permission of Manuel Elizalde, Jr.

Library of Congress Cataloging in Publication Data

Nance, John, 1935–
The gentle Tasaday.

(A Harvest book; 357)
Includes index.
1. Tasaday (Philippine people)   I.   Title.
DS666.T32N36   1977   959.9   76-40221
ISBN 0-15-634712-1

First Harvest edition 1977
A B C D E F G H I J

For Joyce

Contents

IV · FULL CIRCLE

*Photographs are between pages 82 and 83, pages 178 and 179,
pages 306 and 307, pages 402 and 403.*

Foreword

Alifetime closely related to fields of aviation has left me familiar with traveling through space. Jumping onto a treetop platform in the Tasaday rain forest gave me the strange but similar sensation of traveling through time. One moment, I was sitting in a modern helicopter looking down on the spongy-green cover of jungle ridges and valleys. The next, I was clinging to poles lashed to high branches and a tree trunk swaying over a precipice's edge.

In seconds, my environment had transformed from that of civilization to that of a stone-age, cave-dwelling culture. I felt that I might have been on a visit to my ancestors a hundred thousand years ago. Some seventy feet below me was a sharp mountain ridge. Out of sight across a deep, thorny, rain-soaked valley were the Tasaday caves—the home of a quick, intelligent, laughing people.

John Nance, in these perceptive and fascinating chapters, takes the reader down from the treetop landing, across the valley with its rushing stream, and up the steep mountainside to the high, conglomerate-rock caves. One sees the daily life of primitive cave man, watches his reaction to modern technology's miracles, listens to his secretly taped discussions after visitors have departed for the night.

These are chapters that teach us to know ourselves in basic human form. Here is man, shorn of all his civilized accouterments. But if one feels that the Tasaday are still living in a Garden of Eden, one sees that they have now bitten the apple of knowledge. A few metal blades, a few strips of cloth, and a modicum of medical attention quickly created in them the desire for a continuing supply. It is the old and constantly repeated story of civilization's impact on primitive man—except that primitive man is now impacting on civilization as never in the past.

Sitting on a dry, stony hump in the living cave, cook fires behind me and the morning sun streaming in through mists and hanging vines, I thought of what qualities were missing in the ways of civilized men. Qualities of the senses manifest themselves in tribal areas—the feel of earth and bark and leaves, the taste of rushing water, the smell of embered chips, the sound of wind. A mother nurses her babe. Naked children play along cliff ledges. Youths climb up from the stream with fish, crabs, and frogs.

My tyrannical intellect grew aware of the sensate values it had been suppressing—of how greatly these values could enhance my twentieth-century life. Somehow I must strike a balance between the civilized and primitive. It was a balance that both the Tasaday and I were seeking from opposite directions. In achieving it, I did not want to renounce my civilization, and they did not want to renounce their cave-centered culture.

Years before, the search for this balance had diverted my attention from the progress of aviation to the plight of primitive life. During decades of civil and military flying, I had watched tremendous changes take place on the surface of the earth. Slowly at first, rapidly later, forests disappeared, hills eroded, smoke polluted air, and wastes polluted water. Plants and animals that nature spent aeons in perfecting vanished, and men began crowding themselves into megalopolized cities that spread like scabs over the countryside.

Obviously, an exponential breakdown in our environment was taking place; and, just as obviously, my profession of aviation was a major factor in that breakdown. Aircraft had opened every spot on earth to exploitation, carried developers into wildernesses that had been inaccessible before. I realized that the future of aviation, to which I had devoted so much of my life, depended less on the perfection of aircraft than on preserving the epoch-evolved environment of life, and that this was true of all technological progress. Man's creations would have negative value in the future if they destroyed the surface of the earth from which they came.

I wanted to take my part in preserving our natural inheritance. To do so effectively, I concluded, would necessitate an intimate relationship with it. I began working with conservation organizations in America, Europe, Africa, and—later—in the Philippines. My work in the Philippines soon brought me into contact with Secretary Manuel Elizalde, Jr. and his PANAMIN organization. Elizalde carried the responsibility of assisting the tribal groups of his country in their adjustment to civilization. Through him, and as one of the directors of Panamin, I met and lived with several Philippine tribes, the most primitive of them being the Tasaday.

There is a wisdom of the past to which primitive man is close, and from which modern man can learn the requisites of his survival. It is the instinctive wisdom that produced our human intellect by evolving life through epochs. Before the impact of the human mind, life developed in beauty, variety, and fluctuating balance. One sees that in the few virgin wildernesses remaining—the perfection of their animals, the magnificence of their trees, plants, and flowers. In them, life and its environment interweave a pattern to which man has ascribed the term "divine." Only thereafter did the breakdown of heredity and environment begin, and only in our present generation has that breakdown assumed catastrophic form.

At what stage in his development did man start to lose the balance with his environment essential to survival? The Tasaday still had that balance before they were discovered by the wandering hunter of another tribe— or did they? Could any life group have balance in the midst of abundant food and isolated from all enemies? Is not physical competition, with its ensuing selection, essential for environmental balance and evolutionary progress? One finds such competition and selection in primitive nature, but does it anywhere still exist in man? Has the intellect enough wisdom to replace it?

President Marcos proclaimed a reserve around the Tasaday. Panamin told them they have freedom of choice in deciding their future, that they can maintain their rain-forest culture or merge with civilization according to their desires and abilities. At first they said they had lived in their caves since time began and liked them so much they never wanted to leave. A few months later, they had become so curious about the outside world that several of them wished to see it.

There will be much for us to learn from the problems the Tasaday encounter and the balance they achieve with passing years. This volume, based on Nance's on-the-spot experiences, describes the interaction of the ultraprimitive and ultracivilized under circumstances unique to our time. It captures the wonders and emotions of the first meeting on the forest's edge—the stone axe on the one side, the helicopter on the other. Then, gradually, you come to know Balayam, Mahayag, Dul, and Lobo as though they were neighbors of your own. At the end, it leaves you pondering the future for both cave and twentieth-century man.

CHARLES A. LINDBERGH

Hana, Maui
Hawaii
April 7, 1974

Preface

THE following account focuses on the discovery of the Tasaday and their first three years of intermittent contact with modern society; it is also about the outsiders who constituted that "modern society" for the Tasaday, and who got to know something about other Philippine tribes and the Philippine frontier as well. The story is based on my own firsthand knowledge and experiences—except for the events described in the first chapter and a few scattered incidents elsewhere for which I was not present. The text makes clear my absence on these occasions, and I have relied on the participants' accounts—in written records whenever possible, but usually in verbal interviews—to reconstruct events.

This book is a reporter's chronicle of the beginning of the Tasaday's recorded history; it is not meant to be taken as the final word on this period; much remains to be learned about the people and their way of life. In addition, I am not a social scientist; thus this is not a scientific report. In linguistics, for example, to mention just one of the exacting disciplines involved in learning about and understanding the Tasaday, I have relied upon professional linguists for the spelling, pronunciation, and meaning of Tasaday words wherever possible. However, the professionals have not always agreed, nor was one always present when I was with the Tasaday. Consequently, I have often relied upon my untrained ear to record the sounds and spellings as best I could. In linguistics and other complex fields of investigation, most of the social scientists mentioned in this book have prepared or are preparing reports. And more study must be undertaken if we are to answer many of the questions the Tasaday and their way of life present. The coming years will produce fresh analyses and insights, and the collection of new information may alter some data and inferences provided here.

This will take time. The policy of the Philippine government and the Panamin Foundation has been to limit visits among the Tasaday so as not to innundate them with foreigners who would overwhelm their social order. This being the case, nobody—government or Panamin official, anthropologist or linguist—has spent lengthy periods with the Tasaday. My own time with them, which is approximately as long as any nontribesman and much longer than most, totals about seventy-two days spread over three years.

Although as a reporter I may have wished for more time with these remarkable people, I respect this protective policy of benign restriction and deeply appreciate the commitment of Manuel Elizalde, Jr., the Panamin staff, and the Philippine government to the Tasaday and to many other Philippine tribes whose life ways are threatened by the encroaching modern world. Indeed, without Elizalde's commitment to the tribal peoples most of the events reported here would not have taken place; and without his assistance and co-operation I would not have been able to gather the information and take the photographs in this book. I am deeply in his debt. This is not to say that we always agree, however, and this book is not an official history of the discovery of the Tasaday and their situation. Moreover, it offers views for which I alone am responsible.

I am indebted also to Charles A. Lindbergh, whose commitment to endangered people and other natural resources of the world was an inspiration; and whose encouragement, observations, and suggestions significantly aided the development of this book. Lindbergh's enthusiastic concern for the Tasaday and other tribes, for Elizalde and Panamin, was unflagging. Only a few weeks before his death when I visited him in a New York hospital, he spoke of them fondly and at great length. He was in excellent humor and gave no indication of the seriousness of his illness, saying that as soon as he was out of bed and back in form he hoped to visit the Philippines. His death was a deeply felt loss by the many there who knew him to be a good and loyal friend.

To the Associated Press and Wes Gallagher, the general manager, I must express thanks for having granted the leave of absence that allowed me to undertake this work, and for having assigned me to Asia in the first place.

My appreciation goes also to the social scientists who shared with me their experiences and wisdom in countless hours of discussion—Carlos Fernandez, Robert Fox, Frank Lynch, David Baradas, Carol Molony, Teodoro Llamzon, Hermes Gutierrez, Irenaes Eibl-Eibesfeldt, and others, who are mentioned in the text. Special thanks and appreciation must go to Douglas Yen for the excellence of his insights and conversation, and for reading the manuscript; his suggestions improved the degree of accuracy and clarity.

I wish to state my gratitude for invaluable support from so many people that they cannot all be named. However, let me mention Mai Tuan and his brothers, Fludi and Dad, Igna, Oscar Trinidad, Ching Rivero, Dr. Saturnino Rebong, Dafal, Sol Sulan, Lucy Espino, José Torres, Severino Bartolo.

To many other friends and colleagues who have read all or part of the manuscript and/or helped in other ways through suggestions, criticism, and encouragement, I am also indebted—Jack Glattbach, Martha Jean Rutherford, Sam Udin, Dan Dixon, Tom Buckley, Tony Escoda, John Bell, Jack Reynolds, Bruce Bassett, Robert Reynolds; to William B. Goodman, my editor at Harcourt Brace Jovanovich, whose understanding and patient guidance have been immensely helpful; and to Gloria Hammond, whose concerned and judicious manuscript editing made many improvements.

Thanks also to my parents, John and Virginia Nance, for encouragement in many endeavors over the years.

To my wife, Joyce, goes my appreciation for her countless hours of reading, discussing, and typing that helped this book to completion, and my deepest affection for the unstinting enthusiasm and support, so lovingly given, that sustained me throughout.

I

AT THE EDGE
OF THE FOREST

I

First Encounter: A Reconstruction

ONE gray day in the early 1960's —the exact date will never be known—a barefoot hunter named **Dafal** took up his bow, poisoned arrows, and long-bladed bolo and headed for an uncharted tropical rain forest in the mountains of southern Mindanao. It was to be a routine hunting and herb-gathering foray for Dafal, one of the few who ventured far into that wilderness; many tribesmen in the surrounding hills shook their heads and rolled their eyes at the prospect of arousing the legendary spirits and savage creatures who, all prudent men knew, lurked in the vast forest's shadowy depths.

The frill of shrubby ferns and grass at the edge quickly became swallowed in tangles of vines, bamboo, rattan, palms, acacias, and tree ferns over which towering mahoganies and oaks cast a ragged, sun-shielding canopy. The moist jungle sprang up sawtooth slopes and down into ravines, across limestone cliffs and broad plateaus, climbing 5,000-foot peaks before it slanted onto the sandy shores of the Celebes Sea. The forest, squiggling like an ink blot, with long fingers streaking out into plains and valleys, covered several hundred square miles. Viewed from outside it stretched out of sight—as if a dark-green ocean flowed, soared, above the lowlands—and for the tribal folk the silver-gray clouds hanging in high hollows and mantling jagged peaks heightened the forest's aura of mystery.

But not for Dafal, a wily, stork-legged wanderer with a body as slender as bamboo and a nearly toothless, bulb-cheeked, strangely elfin face. He regarded the forest with more affection than fear, had hunted its environs most of his thirty-five or forty years, and even confided to a few friends that inside the forest, deep inside, he had been born.

Dafal, however, told such extraordinary tales that his listeners were not always convinced. They knew, though, that he did roam the forest and the seacoast and Mindanao's rolling plains and mountains. He brought back wild pig, deer, monkeys, birds, special plants for medicines, and vines to mix with betel nut in the astringent chew the mountain folk liked. Some said Dafal seemed to travel at times for no reason, just walked, hunching his skinny body into a flap-footed, elbows-out gait that looked comically awkward but which produced such speed that he was known as "the man who walks the forest like the wind."

Wherever he went, to settlements and towns far north or to the advancing frontier camps of ranchers and loggers carving niches in ancient tribal lands, Dafal was always lured back to the wilderness. Mountain people never knew when he might amble into their midst with his tall stories and loud songs and shrill, cackling laughter. And then, as suddenly as he had come, he would be off again, perhaps a wooden shield and a bow tucked under his arms, a tattered hat slapped on his head. He made homes in scattered places and had sired children who lived at different settlements of the Manubo Blit and Ubu tribes.

Dafal was shrewd, comic, and daring; to some he was irresponsible, to others adventuresome, and to still others a wraith, an untamed spirit whose eyes—small, dark, deep-set, bright, sometimes beady eyes—shone with secret knowledge. Or was it cunning? Even when he spoke most earnestly his eyes flashed a glint.

Despite his periodic needs for society, Dafal went his own way. And so it was that undated day in the 1960's that he set out alone from his home of the moment among the Manubo Blit,* at the edge of the great rain forest, and entered the dimly lighted jungle.

He had been gone for a day, or perhaps several, he doesn't recall, setting his *balatik* traps—saplings arched back into spring tension, armed with bamboo spears, and fixed with vine trip lines—when he spotted unfamiliar footprints. Human footprints.

He followed them deeper into the forest. Cautiously. Peering into shadows and pockets of light, listening for human sounds among the jungle music of birds, insects, a gurgling stream. Then, below him on a slope, brown skin flashed in green foliage. Dafal crept closer and saw three men with a stick digging for roots in the hillside. They wore only leafy pouches at their crotches and had no visible weapons.

One looked up, spotted Dafal, and shouted. Instantly all three men leaped to their feet and darted away like startled deer. Dafal bounded after them over rotting logs and slippery rocks, threading stands of rattan and bamboo, clambering up slopes, shouting all the while "I come as a friend. I am a friend. I mean no harm. Stop! Stop!"

---

* Blit is the name of the people—the Manubo Blit—and also of their language, and of their main settlement.

The men moved with animal quickness and Dafal strained to keep up. He lost sight of them most of the time, catching only glimpses here and there as they glided into splotches of sunlight. He continued shouting as he ran up a swift-flowing stream, and then, rounding a bend, they had stopped and waited, wary, trembling, staring, blinking, as he approached.

In hindsight the meeting was momentous, but at the time, to hear Dafal tell of it, there was nothing of great import: a mere chance encounter in the forest. The men indicated that they had stopped fleeing because they understood some of Dafal's shouts as friendly, but their ability to converse with him was extremely limited. They were scared, Dafal said, but tried to talk, though only a few words could be found of mutual understanding. He gave them bits of food from his woven sack and they gave him a succulent *bui* vine for his betel-nut chew. Dafal asked who they were and where they came from. They merely said they lived in the forest. They did not ask, or perhaps Dafal had not understood, where he came from, who he was, what he was doing. It was a short-lived meeting. Dafal assured them of his friendliness and returned to his trap setting.

Though the meeting was not a great event in Dafal's eyes, he did remember the forest people as thin creatures with few possessions and insufficient food who had given him some of the choicest *bui* vine that he had ever tasted. As for the date, Dafal, who reckons time by his own personal calendar, relates it to the period in which a child was born to his wife at Blit, but says he can't remember whether the meeting was several seasons before or after.

Months or possibly even years after his first contact with the forest people, Dafal returned to the meeting place in the stream. He shouted and waited, shouted some more. Eventually two of the leaf-clad men he had met before came, bringing other men and boys. Over the ensuing years he returned sporadically—five, ten, fifteen times? nobody counted —and each time the people came to the stream when he called. They provided him with *bui* and edible roots and he gave them a variety of items.

In May of 1970, a series of events occurred that would have powerful impact on the lives of the forest people. The focus of these events was a settlement of the Ubu tribe atop a high ridge called Datal Tabayong ("home of the clouds") some thirty miles northeast of where Dafal had entered the great rain forest.

Dafal was spending more time these days with the Ubu, with whom he had a teen-age son, than with the Blit. The leader of the Ubu was Ma Falen (sometimes called Datu, a title borrowed from Malay immigrants who had first come to Mindanao in considerable numbers in the fourteenth and fifteenth centuries). Ma Falen, a stern-looking, leathery-faced man who wore shining brass earrings and tied his long hair in a bun, was trying to organize various Ubu groups against invading frontiersmen. Dafal had known these Ubu ever since some had lived in the foothills to the east, before settlers forced them to the high slopes. He was a close friend of Ye Elen, Ma Falen's No. 1 wife, who prized Dafal because he provided her with choice herbs and vines and told amusing stories.

The Ubu were among the dozens of Philippine tribes whose claims to the land went back many centuries, long before records were kept. They had steadily lost ground as immigrants and entrepreneurs pushed into the hinterlands. And now, in 1970, Ma Falen's Ubu were making a stand on the ridge. One morning in early May, months of scattered troubles culminated in a bloody raid on Ma Falen's settlement. Attackers, presumably sent by lowlanders to stop Ma Falen from organizing resistance to their expansion, struck just after dawn—rifles and machine guns exploding in the faint light. The shocked Ubu responded quickly, using spears and homemade shotguns and their intimate knowledge of the terrain to kill four intruders. But the first blasts of gunfire had riddled the house of Ma Falen. His eldest and favorite daughter was killed as was the infant child of a visitor.

The attack was apparently meant as a prelude to even bloodier fighting. Within two days, more than a hundred armed men were reported massed in foothills below the Ubu, waiting for clear weather and a signal to advance. The outgunned tribesmen set deadly spear traps around their ridge and waited for the next move from below.

Then one morning a helicopter whirled through driving rain and fog and cross winds. The pilot, persuaded by a promise of 10,000 pesos (about $2,000) to brave the foul weather, landed on the point of the ridge near Ma Falen's house. Four men jumped out and raced for cover.

In the lead was a young-looking man with several days' growth of black whiskers on his pale face and a battered cream-colored yachting cap on his head. A mob of Ubu rushed through the rain to greet him, clawing at his clothes, hugging and kissing him. He was Manuel Elizalde, Jr., thirty-four years old, the Harvard-educated eldest son of a millionaire Filipino industrialist. Elizalde pushed through the mob to where Ma Falen and other Ubu leaders stood in the doorway of a long house on stilts. They were quickly joined by a barrel-bodied, mustached young man named Mai Tuan, a leader of the Tboli, the largest tribe in the area. Mai Tuan, who also had come in the helicopter, translated for the Ubu and Elizalde. As Ma Falen was describing the recent events, his wife, Ye Elen, pushed into the group. Her hair, usually combed into elaborate parts and ringlets, was lank and disheveled. Tears streamed down her face. The group fell silent as she told how her teen-age daughter, Kining, had been asleep when the machine-gun bullets ripped into their house. The girl apparently had sat up and thrust her arms forward protectively. A .30-caliber slug slammed into her palm, ripped a path up her arm, and lodged in her shoulder. In the confusion of screams and gunfire the girl crawled from the shattered house. Ye Elen found her later, hiding in some brush in a pool of her own blood, so weak she could barely murmur. The girl tried to raise her mangled hand. Her brass and ebony rings were coated with crimson. "I hurt," Kining whispered. "Why have they done this to me? I hurt so. Why . . . ?" She was dead.

Ye Elen's voice broke with sobs as she recounted the story. Then she tearfully pushed the slain girl's rings onto Elizalde's fingers. "Tau Bong," she said, "wear her rings . . . you must wear them always. Remember Kining. Remember . . . and tell your world that justice belongs also to the innocent."

Elizalde pulled the sobbing Ye Elen against himself and kissed her hair. "I won't forget. Tell her, Mai. Tell her I won't forget."

Ye Elen leaned into Elizalde and then other hands were laid on the pair of them, many hands, many arms, many bodies, encircling, soothing, binding all into a grieving knot.

In the center was Elizalde, the wealthy polo player's son; he who only a few years earlier spent his energies in prankish escapades and sulky outbursts of temper and a steady affair with Scotch and gin that was running up to a quart a day. Manda, as he had been nicknamed since childhood, was known among circles of Manila's elite, with head shakes and knowing chuckles, as "a playboy—a wild guy."

But now, among the tribes, he was known as Tau Bong, which meant "big man" or "big brother," and thousands had come to count on him. He had been made a government official—Presidential Assistant on National Minorities in the cabinet of President Ferdinand Marcos—and was head of the PANAMIN (Private Association for National Minorities) foundation which he had established in 1968 to help tribes deal, as its publications said, with encroaching civilization by "research, medical and legal assistance, and socioeconomic development projects among the cultural minorities of the Philippines." The foundation was a nonstock, nonprofit corporation. "Cultural minorities" applied to more than sixty different groups who lived in scattered, usually remote areas, and retained their traditional—often ancient—life ways. They numbered about 4,000,-000 of the Philippines' 39,000,000 population.

The Ubu lived in South Cotabato Province of Mindanao, one of the last great frontiers of that rich and fertile island. Elizalde had first come to Cotabato two years earlier and worked with the Tboli, whose lands were adjacent to the Ubu's, and had aroused bitter criticism. Several local officials accused him of needlessly stirring up the peaceful tribes-people, and some claimed it was to cover secret prospecting and land acquisition for an Elizalde family mining company, which listed him as vice-president. Others, both in Cotabato and Manila, saw him grabbing for publicity to start a political career. And a few old friends viewed his adventures with the tribes as just another kooky playboy fling; when the hobby ran longer than expected, some speculated he had acquired a Great White Father complex or was performing some kind of penance for his past. There was praise for his activities, but more often the reactions ranged from anguish and skepticism to amusement and puzzlement —"What's Elizalde up to? What's he doing?"

The tribes, however, did not question his motives and gave happy, childlike acceptance and appreciation.

Following the death of Kining, Elizalde and Panamin worked to prevent more bloodshed at Datal Tabayong by providing arms and support for the Ubu, causing the gunmen in the foothills to be withdrawn, and arranging for Ma Falen to be flown to Manila to meet President Marcos. A lowland court had charged Ma Falen with murder, a charge that failed to note that the killing occurred when machine gunners attacked his house. Ma Falen was asked about the trouble and the murder charge, and he, in turn, asked Marcos: "What would you do, Datu President, if someone killed your daughter?"

Marcos dismissed the charges against Ma Falen and proclaimed the Ubu's mountain lands forbidden to loggers, miners, ranchers, or others who would encroach upon it.

Panamin established a settlement project at Datal Tabayong, and when Elizalde visited early in 1971, the usual mob of welcomers included a man who had walked two days from the village of the Blit, a people and a place unknown to Panamin. The man invited Elizalde to visit. "There is no trouble there," he said, "but come. The Blit have heard of you and want to know you."

Ye Elen summoned Dafal, who gave a colorful description of the Blit, saying that there were mostly well-off people on a plain and poor people in a nearby forest. The poor people were cited merely in passing and granted no significance. Ye Elen did remark, however, that she had heard of people living in the forest, the eastern edge of which undulated within sight of Tabayong, but she considered them to be either outlaws hiding or the fruit of a storyteller's imagination.

Elizalde agreed to visit the Blit and invited Dafal to come along in the helicopter. The Blit gave them a warm welcome. Dafal led the singing and dancing and told his stories, mentioning again the poor people in the forest. Mai asked for more details but Dafal was vague, insisting that these were true forest people, not outlaws hiding or savage spirits. He pointed toward the forest only a few hundred yards away.

Mai inquired around but none of the other Blit, including the headman, Datu Dudim, knew more than fragments of information attributed to Dafal and an elderly blind man who lived beyond their settlement. A couple of Blit told tales of hunters disappearing in the forest, presumably snatched by savages or ghosts or witches, possibly the strange people

Dafal talked about. The Blit were a gentle, simple folk who farmed and hunted in quiet seclusion, only learning of troubles on the distant frontiers from travelers, like Dafal, who also brought trade in arrowheads and brass and knives and clothing. Though some Blit still wore loincloths, most men had acquired at least one old shirt and tattered trousers and the women a wrap-around skirt.

Mai told Elizalde about the forest people, but there were many tribes asking for help and the story was temporarily forgotten. For the next few months Elizalde worked out of the main Tboli settlement, named Kematu but always called simply Tboli. Elizalde bought a helicopter and his close aide and airplane pilot, Inocente "Ching" Rivero, was trained to fly it. On a trip to Blit, Ching passed over a corner of the sprawling rain forest and thought he saw smoke curling up and what might have been a man in a tree. He recalled Dafal's story about forest people and told Elizalde what he had seen. They planned to investigate but soon after that the helicopter crashed. Ching was not seriously hurt but the aircraft was ruined. A French-made turbine jet helicopter was purchased and Severino "Bart" Bartolo hired to pilot it, with Ching as copilot. In mid-May they took Elizalde on a wide-ranging survey of the forest. They did not cover it all but what they did see was spectacular—"probably the densest, largest unexplored area left in the Philippines," Elizalde said. They spotted no fires or people, but did see three logging roads cutting across lowlands toward the forest, each approaching from a different direction.

Elizalde was intrigued by the story of the forest people. But, he told Dafal, any people in the forest faced trouble. Loggers would not be gentle, and behind the loggers would come miners, hunters, settlers, exploiters of all kinds. It was the usual pattern in Mindanao timber country. "If you can find those people again, see if they'll come out," Elizalde told Dafal. "Tell them we'd like to meet them."

In late May Dafal hiked into the forest and at the stream called for the people. He told them a man named Tau Bong wanted to meet them and that they would have to walk a long way to the north, but that it would be worth it to see the man, whom he described as a special person, a very good man.

The forest people were surprised at Dafal's request. Several were reluctant and some seemed alarmed. They said they would think about it. While Dafal checked his traps, the people gathered privately and discussed the proposal. When Dafal returned, they said they would go with him.

"Some, particularly the women, were very afraid," Dafal later told Mai. "They were shaking and scared, saying they might die. But they had decided that everyone, even the children, would come with me to see the good man."

Dafal sent word to Elizalde that the forest people were willing to meet him and that he would clear a place for the helicopter to land inside the forest, because he did not think the people would come outside. The helicopter flew over to check the site, but it was on a hillside, too small, surrounded by tall trees. Landing was impossible, and Fludi Tuan, Mai's younger brother, was sent to help Dafal clear a spot at the forest's edge. They picked a low, knobby ridge that jutted out of the jungle, cleared its tip, then made lean-tos of saplings, bark strips, and leafy branches to shelter themselves and the forest people when they arrived. Throughout this work, Fludi says, he never saw the people.

On June 3, Elizalde received word at Tboli that everything was ready.

The helicopter flew to Blit the next morning, circling en route to locate the landing place. Elizalde and Mai saw Fludi waving from the clearing; and they saw people darting through the foliage behind him, inside the forest. They discussed this with Datu Dudim when they landed at Blit to pick him up. He was to serve as translator, Dafal having indicated he could not converse well with the forest people. The fleeting movements of unknown people in the forest added to suspicions that they might be outlaws or some other group in hiding and would cause trouble. Dudim was distressed, so Mai flew in alone first to check if everything was all right.

Meanwhile, Dafal was trying to organize the forest people—the helicopter, although barely visible from inside the forest, had upset several of them. Eventually Dafal calmed them and started into the clearing. But the first sight of the ridgetip and the open plain beyond alarmed the group. All fell back; some hid, others ran. Dafal sought to calm them again, but was able to convince only three men and two boys to come into the clearing. They walked stiffly, with tentative steps and blinking eyes, staring at the flatland and the distant blue-gray horizon.

Dafal said they would wait here for the good man. It was a cloudy, blustery day and the men and boys began to tremble and shake. They wrapped their arms around themselves, breathed noisily, shook their heads. The teen-agers huddled inside a lean-to. The men—two with long, flowing hair in their twenties or thirties and a balding, wrinkled man in his fifties or sixties—shivered with greater intensity as a light rain began falling. One of the younger men perched on a log, one hand over his mouth, staring. The other walked in circles, then squatted with his bow and arrows at his feet. The old one lowered his bony buttocks onto his heels, fastening his eyes on the ground and curling his arms around his knees.

They had looked nervously at Fludi, but when Dafal said the good man was yet to come they paid Fludi only passing glances. Fludi tried to talk with them but they did not respond and he thought they were *tau muloy* (wild men). The man perched on the log suddenly rose and headed toward the forest. The other young man saw this, joined him, and they began to leave. Dafal hurried over, talking softly, saying not to worry, not to be afraid, the man was coming, it would be good, wait and see. They mumbled, looked long at each other, and stayed.

Soon the helicopter appeared in the distance and Dafal pointed as it approached. The forest men spotted the tiny dark dot in the gray sky and watched it grow. Dafal kept up a steady chatter but soon his voice was drowned by the roar of the machine. Wind from the rotor blasted down as the aircraft hovered directly overhead, darkening the sky and wobbling as it descended. Leaves and twigs showered down. Tall grass was whipped flat. Dirt and debris flashed across the ground and swirled crazily in the air. The screeching roar of the engine became deafening as the helicopter settled on the ground in front of the men, its huge silver blade flashing as it spun.

The forest men cowered and threw their arms over their heads. Then one leaped to his feet, eyes wide with terror. He tried to turn toward the forest. Hesitated. Froze. Shuddered and plunged forward, sprawling face-down on the wet earth.

Mai hurried from the helicopter to talk with Fludi and Dafal, frowning at the contorted, nearly naked men lying beside them. Told that everything was satisfactory, Mai ran back to the chopper, whose engine had idled into a low rumble punctuated by the *ka-whang, ka-whang* of the steel rotor blade slicing the air. The noise erupted into a scream again as the helicopter rose and flew away.

The men remained immobile as Dafal assured them everything was fine. They uncoiled slowly, and the boys peeked out of the lean-to with frightened-deer eyes. The man who had fallen stayed on the ground the longest, then stirred and rose shakily to his feet, blinking rapidly and rubbing his hands nervously over his body. Dafal kept repeating, "Soon now, soon. The good man is coming . . . will be here . . . soon . . . only a little longer . . ."

In a few minutes the helicopter circled and descended again. The men cowered and turned away, hair flying and bodies pushed off balance, but they did not run or hug the ground. This time the engine whined into silence and Elizalde walked forward in his battered cap above a whiskery face, a holstered .45-caliber pistol strapped to his hip. Close behind him came his chief bodyguard, Felix Silvestre, with an automatic rifle poised, Datu Dudim, Mai, and Ching.

The forest men's trembling worsened into uncontrollable shaking. They sat or stood awkwardly, darting peeks out of the corners of their eyes. Elizalde approached slowly, noting the bow and arrows. Mai, also carrying a pistol, and Felix scanned the edge of the forest for sign of an ambush.

Dudim was worried. He grew increasingly nervous as he moved toward the men. They are weird, he thought. He remembered the tales of Blit hunters mysteriously disappearing in the forest.

Elizalde and Mai spoke to the men, but they seemed not to hear. Elizalde touched one or two and they dropped their heads. He called Dudim over and, through Mai, asked who these men were and where they came from. Dudim stuttered out several questions, which went unanswered; then his nerves gave out and he also began to shake. Dudim told Mai he couldn't talk to these people, he didn't know their language and could do no good here. He said that Igna, a Sduff tribeswoman who stayed with the Blit and was gifted at languages, would do better. Elizalde sent for Igna, returning Dudim to Blit. Dafal went also—he loved to ride in the helicopter.

While they waited for Igna, Elizalde and Mai studied the men. Their golden-tan skin was dirty and they were thin, but healthy looking. They had a longbow taller than they were and arrows with the distinctive markings of the Tboli at Lake Sebu, brass earrings, scraps of loincloth, a woven basket. Their appearance and possessions were similar to other primitive Filipinos, the Tambuid of Mindoro, the Agta of Luzon.

Mai and Elizalde tried words and met shivering silence. They offered a cigarette, but no one responded. Too shy, Elizalde thought, so he lighted a cigarette himself and put it to the elderly man's lips. He stiffened, raised his wrinkled face slightly, and received the white stick. It dangled limply as smoke curled into his squinting eyes. They tried the cigarette with the two other men. Neither knew what to do with it.

Igna arrived with a Panamin doctor, Saturnino Rebong. She was cautious, her chubby face and body tense. Dudim was right, she thought, these are strange people. If I were alone I'd run.

Prodded by Mai and Elizalde, Igna began to ask questions, translating their words—which Mai put into Tboli or Blit—into various Manubo dialects. There was no response, but Igna nervously and slowly persisted. "Who are you? Where do you come from?" The man in his twenties caught some words and responded, but Igna caught only a fragment. After another exchange with him she reported that they lived in the forest "near a mountain they call Tasaday." Apparently he said they called themselves the "Tasaday" (pronounced Taw-saw-dai), but she was not certain. The word kept occurring, however, and henceforth they were always known as the Tasaday.

Attention turned to the eldest man, because he might presumably be the most knowledgeable and important. But Igna could not extract any verbal response from him. He sat curled into a knot and stared at the ground, quivering and shaking.

The Tasaday appeared ready to flee into the forest, so Elizalde draped necklaces of bright red-blue-orange Tboli beads around their necks. The men looked down and fingered them with wonder. They seemed pleased.

Rice, always an effective gift to mountain people, was brought in a bag and Igna held out a handful of uncooked grains. The men stared dumbly at it.

"Oh, c'mon!" Elizalde said to Mai. "They can't be that scared. Give them some rice."

Igna thrust her hand forward, but the men recoiled. She said something and one hesitantly extended his hand and she dumped in the hard grains. He looked at them wonderingly and Igna said it was food, making a hand-to-mouth gesture. He hesitantly put a few grains in his mouth. His face immediately screwed up and the rice dribbled between his lips and fell to the ground. The young man grimaced and looked as if he might become sick.

"He's afraid it's poisonous," Igna said, and giggled.

For the next hour the Tasaday barely changed positions. They were offered corn, *camote* (a kind of potato), taro, and cassava. They apparently had no names for these things—staples among nearby mountain people—and indicated they had never seen them before.

The same was true of salt. Igna told them it was to be eaten with other foods. Another sample of rice, cooked this time, was provided but they did not understand. Igna sprinkled salt on the rice, explaining that they should not use equal amounts of salt and rice.

The young man who had earlier toppled over with fear was the only one to respond with more than sighs and murmurs, and Igna had difficulty understanding even half of the words he uttered. He was perhaps twenty or twenty-five years old; his long hair was tied back with a vine, and he wore a half dozen brass rings in each ear. He said his name slowly several times—Balayam, Ba-lai-yum—until Igna repeated it satisfactorily and he nodded. The old man, he said, was Kuletaw and the third, possibly in his mid-thirties, was Bilangan. The boys remained in the lean-to.

Balayam relaxed somewhat and Bilangan also began to say things, but Kuletaw remained in his silent ball. Balayam and Bilangan said more Tasaday were in the forest, though some might have run away. Mai was certain at least a few were there because of the nervous growling and yapping of a dog, which presumably was theirs.

As the day wore on, Elizalde worried not that these people would fight or cause trouble, but that they would run away when they were left alone. He had Igna ask them what they wanted. "Nothing," they said. Then what did they need? "Nothing." He gave a bolo—a long broad-bladed knife—to each man. He asked Igna to tell them that he and the others would leave and return the next day. Dafal would be sent back to spend the night, and tomorrow there would be more gifts. The Tasaday seemed to understand.

That evening at Blit, Elizalde, Mai, and Ching puzzled over the meeting. These people, the Tasaday—so scared and shy—what were they doing in the forest? How many were there? Where had they come from? Whom did they know—they evidently traded because they had cloth and brass. And bows and arrows—whom did they fight? Bows and arrows were common among the surrounding peoples, but less as tools to hunt food than as a weapon against human enemies.

But these forest people appeared so extraordinarily timid that it was hard to imagine them in battle. Elizalde questioned Dudim and other Blit hunters about their stories of Blit being captured in the forest. They repeated the stories, but when asked for details they could not provide a single specific incident or the name of anybody who had actually disappeared.

Elizalde and his party flew to the clearing early the next day, worried that the Tasaday might not show up. But Dafal waved as the chopper landed and the same Tasaday came out of the forest with two more boys and three more men, one carrying a child perhaps three years old with light-brown hair and almost white skin.

The fair-skinned child was a shock. Crusty scales nearly closed his eyes, his face was puffy, and many open sores scarred his body. The visitors asked questions about the strange-looking boy but learned only that it was his father who carried him and that his mother was either away somewhere or dead.

All the others appeared healthy, though skinny, with hollows around their collarbones and ribs showing. The adults stood slightly above five feet, nearly as tall as the average Filipino. Most were covered by ragged cloth G strings, though at least one wore merely a leaf drawn tightly under his crotch and tied at both ends to a waist string or vine. Their dark hair was in varying lengths, in some cases so long that if the vines holding it in a bun or ponytail were undone it would fall to their hips; others had cropped it short. Their skin was tan, but not the dark coppery color common to the people of the region; presumably it was lighter because they stayed in the shadowy forest.

Balayam was again the best informant and said their women and other children remained in the forest. Most of the men trembled, clasped their arms around themselves, darted their eyes—continuing the impression they might suddenly dash into the foliage and disappear.

Food was offered again. Sugar startled them and they gagged at the taste. They spat out bread sandwiches filled with guava jelly.

Questions were asked them as a group and individually, but answers were hazy because of their timidity and the language difficulties—relaying from English and Tagalog to Blit, then to Igna's faulty Tasaday, and back the same route. Dafal was asked to help and occasionally amplified certain points.

Out of this maze of translators' and informants' voices came bits and pieces of information. The Tasaday all lived near the mountain called

Tasaday and they totaled somewhere between fifteen and thirty persons. At one point they referred vaguely to other people in the forest, but at another said they never saw other people. They had never been out of the forest, made shelters of wild palms propped up with small limbs but had no permanent houses, and roamed, sometimes sleeping on shallow rock ledges. They apparently had a base area to which they regularly returned near the confluence of some streams. They indicated that everything they had, from articles to skills and beliefs, was handed down from their ancestors. The bits of cloth in their G strings were carefully preserved over the years and used only at special times because they did not know how to acquire more. They displayed one old bent bolo with a wooden handle about six inches long and a curving blade of about ten inches.

They admitted to no medical charms, practices, or ceremonies, and said a sick person was left to die alone. There was a hazy reference to sickness, which, after exchanges among the translators, came out as a dreaded epidemic disease that frightened the Tasaday and had caused their ancestors to flee from someplace and, perhaps, into the forest. Dafal and Igna enlarged upon this, saying that the Blit and other peoples talked of such an epidemic that in the distant past had scourged the countryside. Mai and Elizalde also had heard folk tales about a pestilence that had destroyed and terrified large segments of the population.

The Tasaday mentioned a legend handed down by their ancestors that someday a good man would come to them, a kind of Messiah. Dafal amplified, saying he had heard them talk of this, and that he had emphasized Elizalde was a good man when he asked them to meet him. Asked about it, the Tasaday nodded and glanced at Elizalde. Asked what this good man was expected to do, Balayam replied that they did not know; their ancestors had not predicted what he would do, only that he would help them.

Communication was exhausting, and from time to time Elizalde clowned to break the tension. He gulped whole sandwiches in one bite, pretended to gobble beetles or wriggly caterpillars, plopped a cracker tin on his head as a hat. Some of this coaxed smiles from the Tasaday— the first friendly cracks in their pinched expressions.

Elizalde had to return to Tboli that evening, and told the Tasaday he would come back the day after next. Would they wait here for him? Yes, they said; and yes, they would bring their women to meet him. He gave them a sack of rice, salt, five pieces of cloth, and more bead necklaces. Then he laid knives on the ground as an offering. Each man who had not received a bolo the day before stepped forward and picked one up; one was left.

Elizalde, who described this later with amazement in his voice, then had Igna invite them to take the last one. There was a confused exchange of words and she said, "They say they all have a knife now."

"But they could take this last one in case one breaks or is lost," Elizalde replied.

More words were exchanged and finally Mai shrugged and said, "But they say they all have one now . . . they don't seem to want it."

Elizalde had never seen mountain people turn down a knife, no matter how many they had. But to these people the idea of storing one, or of anyone having two knives, seemed incomprehensible.

"I couldn't believe it," Elizalde recalled.

The Panamin group returned to Tboli, where Elizalde attended to various concerns, including a National Geographic Society crew that already had spent one month shooting a documentary film about the tribes and had another month to go. Late that night Elizalde talked with Mai and they agreed the Tasaday were unique and possibly very significant. Mai said the Tboli had never heard of these people; nor had any other group he knew.

The next morning Elizalde radioed his Manila Panamin office, outlined the situation, and asked for guidance, particularly from Dr. Robert Fox, a fifty-three-year-old American who had lived in the Philippines for more than twenty years. He was head of Panamin's research department and the best-known anthropologist in the country.

The message, marked "Rush," read in part:

In extremely isolated region about 25 minutes by chopper from Ma Falen's area have found extremely primitive people who can in fact be called a "lost tribe." By comparison much more primitive than Batangan Taong Buid or interior Agta although by appearance much healthier. [He then listed various aspects of the visit and concluded:] No Tboli or Ubu from Ma Falen, Lake Sebu side down to Tboli settlement, have ever heard of this group except for one Ma Falen hunter [Dafal]. People closest to them, the Blit, are a pretty wild bunch themselves, 95 per cent of whom have never even seen a motor vehicle except for high-flying airplanes and now a helicopter. Biggest problem with this group —which we should refer to as Tasaday, which is high mountain around where they are from—is communication as even Manubo Blit can hardly communicate.

He added that the National Geographic wanted to include them in its film and asked the joint views of Fox and three other Panamin officials on what course to take. He signed off with his code name, "Soda."

The Panamin executives were impressed but uncertain. Fox was conducting research at a remote archeological site believed to hold remains of elephants, animals not living in the Philippines for centuries. The Panamin officials offered various ideas. One advised Elizalde to bring some Tasaday to Manila to meet the press. The other two counseled a go-slow approach and said they would try to reach Fox.

Elizalde was convinced that this was an important discovery, but he needed scientific support. He waited all day for his Manila staff to suggest more than a press conference and words of caution, but nothing was heard. He then fired off a series of terse, insistent messages, including anthropological questions and demands that Fox be got hold of immediately, even if it meant chartering a special plane. Elizalde was still afraid the Tasaday would disappear into the forest and not come out again.

Efforts to reach Fox failed, however, and the next day Elizalde messaged his Manila staff: "Fox is not the only anthropologist in the world. Get me an opinion!"

No record is available and recollections are hazy, but Oscar Trinidad, Panamin executive director, says that either at this point or shortly after the contact was announced publicly three of the best-known Filipino anthropologists were invited to participate in the study of the Tasaday. None could or would accept.

Finally, on June 8, a cable was sent Elizalde saying that in Fox's absence an associate of his at the National Museum, where Fox was chief anthropologist, had provided guidelines for "authenticating the lost tribe."

The message was brief and lukewarm. "Technically there is no such thing as lost tribe but only more isolated than other known tribes," it began, and recommended that a known tribe identify this "alleged new group." Then the Tasaday should be interviewed "to determine whether they are lost or not by going to their literature, customs and traditions." Additional suggestions were to make a comparative study of their language, their kinship structure, and "the way they live, more particularly if they eat in the morning, in the evening, like us."

That was all the eagerly awaited message said. Elizalde, anxious for more specific guidance, was frustrated, uncertain what to do, and angry with his Manila staff.

He was fuming as another message arrived later that same day from Fox, who had finally been reached. He said, in cablese (some punctuation added):

Soda—New group of great importance anthropologically. Have been expecting that you and chopper would find such group. Lost tribe simply means new tribe. If they are truly food gatherers with no agriculture [they are] among worlds rarest people. Two most widely diffused articles in modern times since Age of Discovery 15th Century A.D. are tobacco and sweet potato. If they do not know tobacco incredible discovery . . . If Ubu, Tboli, Tirruray, Blaan cannot speak easily with them a new language is likely and highly possible. Obtain estimated numbers by families. Check marriage arrangements and local leadership. The group may be small but still of great significance. Check economic base; what are they living on—wild yams? Pith of palms? Shoots of bamboo and rattan? Ferns? Edible flowers? etc. What proteins—bats? pig? deer? fish? crabs and shrimp? Check type of shelter—caves? Bark of trees? Wild palm leaves? Group's isolation of great interest. Estimate extent and pattern of extra group contacts. Ask them names for other people they have heard of—whites? Chinese? Moros? Tboli? Ubu? etc. What are their basic tools—iron? Stone? Extent of iron tools. Only bolo or others? Do they have bow and arrow complex? Spears? Type of traps? Try to get something on their world view and the world that surrounds them and their relationship with environment. If you think they are a distinct group, and they must be if food gatherers, you will know with your familiarity with Mindanao groups. There must be lost groups in Mindanao and any such discovery repeat of great importance to modern world. If you need me I am standing by working on project studies. If you want me in Mindanao I can fly at once or perhaps handle by radio. Please advise. Fox.

Elizalde was exuberant and the next day, presumably June 9—the date is not recorded—he flew with the National Geographic film makers to another meeting with the Tasaday. Also along was Juan "Johnny" Artajo, the Panamin director for southern Mindanao, who lived at Tboli, and Ramon Talusan, who had been sent from Manila to photograph for Panamin. The helicopter circled to signal its arrival and soon after it landed Dafal emerged from the forest with the Tasaday.

The men and boys came forward first, timidly but willingly, and three women holding children squatted nervously at the edge of the clearing, keeping one foot virtually inside the jungle. All looked quizzically at the men with cameras.

Igna was more comfortable this time, and Dafal sat next to her to help with translating. He looked uncomfortable; clearly he would have preferred to wander into the forest or to a stream below the knoll to fish. He displayed little desire or ability to speak more than a few simple Tasaday words and after half a dozen questions looked painfully bored.

The women were invited to join the group and did so, hesitantly, but stayed in the background. In addition to the three women in their twenties or thirties with children, there was Kuletaw's elderly wife, with curly gray hair. All wore only faded cloth wrapped around their hips. Brass rings dangled from their ears, and their teeth, like the men's, were stained red and the frontal crowns were flat, apparently filed with stones.

A mirror was held up and the Tasaday looked in it with puzzled frowns. Foods were offered and the women nibbled warily.

Dafal took over most of the interpreting about the Tasaday's metal-tipped arrows and traps. The arrows had come to them by trading *bui* vine, he said. Their monkeytraps employed thorny branches that clamped on a monkey when it grabbed banana bait. Their bamboo-spear traps sounded similar to Dafal's *balatik,* though the Tasaday called them *balawang.* And they had traps for rats, wild chickens, civets.

The mood relaxed slightly when Balayam brought out and played a bamboo mouth harp, similar to a jew's-harp. He said it was their only musical instrument and that he was the only Tasaday who could play it.

Tasaday left the gathering from time to time, walking into the forest for something to eat, to relieve themselves, or possibly just to get away for awhile. Some would return with fruit or an undistinguishable edible, which they would chew along with chunks of root taken from leaf wrappers.

They said all the Tasaday were present, but it was difficult to keep track with the comings and goings. Someone from Panamin made a count of twenty-two Tasaday, including ten children, who seemed to range in age from one to ten years.

Elizalde and Mai tried more questions with varying success. When they asked about other people in the forest, the Tasaday's tension increased, several becoming extremely nervous and agitated. A question of whether any of them had come from other groups brought a response from a young woman that translated to the effect that she had been "found" in the forest by her husband's father. This caused even more agitation, and it was impossible to pursue the subject. The Tasaday looked away, frowned, gave unintelligible answers. Because some tribes practice bride stealing or bride capture, it was suspected that "finding" this woman meant the Tasaday had stolen her. But nothing was conclusive. The only point established was that she had joined the Tasaday from another group. Why, then, had they said they saw no other people in the forest?

Balayam said forlornly that they used to see other people and that their women came from them, but that this was no longer true, and now there were no women available. He said that he, Balayam, was an orphan and the only Tasaday without a mother, father, wife, or children. He repeated that no women were available now and indicated by a pained expression that he was desperate for one. Elizalde replied with a remark suggesting he could help Balayam acquire a woman. Elizalde recalled later that he had not given much thought to what he said; it was a casual, almost joking comment to the effect that if he ran across a lovely forest maiden, he surely would introduce her to Balayam. Whatever he said was translated—and Balayam never forgot.

Because of the possibility that they had stolen women, and that virtually all minorities in Mindanao were battling somebody, Elizalde had Mai ask the Tasaday who gave them trouble. Balayam and others looked blank. The question was repeated several different ways and finally Mai said, "We cannot find words for enemies or fighting or war or anything like that."

"What about weapons?" Elizalde asked. "What kinds of weapons do they use?"

Mai, Igna, and Balayam exchanged more words and Mai said, "They just don't seem to understand what we are talking about . . . don't seem to know what we mean. They don't have any weapons."

"Aw, c'mon! What about the arrows, and those traps they make?"

More talk, then Mai said, "Yes, but they say they never shoot arrows at a person—they hardly ever shoot them at animals—and the traps are only for animals. They don't make mantraps like the Ubu or Tboli. Boss, they are becoming very upset by these questions. They don't seem to understand about enemies and say the people they used to see were friendly. And they keep insisting that they have not seen them for a long time and that they do not know where they are or what happened to them."

The subject was dropped for the time being. But a little while later Balayam asked Igna and Mai what was meant by the questions about trouble with other people. Mai called Elizalde over and told him that Balayam, looking deeply concerned, had seemed to be saying "You ask about trouble with people, does that mean people where you come from are not good?" What should Mai say?

Elizalde suggested that Mai tell him there were good and bad people. Mai started to explain this through Igna, but then turned to Elizalde and said, "I don't think this is good to say. They will not understand and will think we have devils or evil spirits. It will scare them." Elizalde agreed and that subject, too, was dropped.

The Tasaday were willing to talk about their foods (roots, fruits, tadpoles, frogs, palm pith) and their home in the forest ("a special place with a mountain and a stream, where the Tasaday have always lived").

Although Igna was learning more words, communication continued to be difficult. By midafternoon everyone was tired and it was time to leave. More gifts were given, probably including a flashlight (although no record was kept). The Tasaday were told that the Panamin group would go away for several days but would return as soon as possible. They were asked to come to the clearing if they heard the helicopter circling over the forest. They nodded.

The Tasaday were now calling Elizalde both Tau Bong, learned from Dafal, and Momo Bong, as Igna and the Blit called him; it meant about the same thing—"big brother" or "great man." The Tasaday called the helicopter *manuk dakel* (big bird).

A day later Elizalde flew to northern Mindanao to see the Higa-onon tribe so that the Geographic team could film their unusual houses high in trees. While there Elizalde wrote a twenty-three-page summary of the contact with the Tasaday and drew sketches of the Tasaday's old bolo—the only metal, except earrings, they had shown—and their monkeytrap.

Meanwhile, Fox had left the archeological diggings and joined Elizalde when he returned to Tboli. On June 16 a group flew to meet the Tasaday. Dafal, sent ahead into the forest, brought them out soon after the helicopter landed. Several, including aging Kuletaw, who had been among the most timid, greeted Elizalde warmly and put their arms around him. Their general attitude, however, was uneasy, most likely because they were not yet used to the exposure of the clearing or the strange people, things, questions.

Fox, white-haired and white-bearded, sat with Elizalde on the logs near the lean-tos, whose leaves had turned brown and crackly; he initiated systematic information gathering through Igna and Mai that continued off and on for the next two days.

The anthropologist constructed a tentative genealogy showing that the Tasaday had four married couples, one widower, and one bachelor, Balayam. There were fourteen children—ranging from perhaps one year to middle or late teens—of whom at least ten were boys. Later it was thought possible that another child had not been included, so the total population was put at twenty-four or twenty-five. Names were recorded for eighteen; at least four of the youngest children had not yet been named. Names were listed also for the wife of the widower and for the dead parents and sister of Balayam.

The largest family was that of Bilangan and his wife, Etut, who had four sons. The widower, named Lefonok, had a daughter and two sons, including the fair-skinned child. The visitors now considered him a retarded albino whose skin rash and other ailments would leave no chance of survival. One Tasaday said this boy's mother died "after a witch bit her on the breast."

The genealogy showed that at least three of the five adult women and some of the men had come from other forest groups, named the Tasafeng and Sanduka. There were other names, two of which were Talili and Lambong, but whether they referred to other places or still other people was not clear.

Discussion of the women's groups made the Tasaday visibly upset and they repeated their previous statement that they had not seen those people for a long time—that they had not seen any other people for a long time. It could not be determined if the Tasafeng and Sanduka once had a close relationship with the Tasaday or were separate. The informants indicated that the other groups had been slightly more numerous, perhaps thirty or forty persons each.

Fox concluded that the Tasaday spoke a unique dialect, related to that of the Blit. It was part of the Malayo-Polynesian family of languages, as are all the scores of dialects spoken in the Philippines, and was closely linked to various Manubo dialects found throughout eastern Mindanao. The anthropologist was able to list more than one hundred Tasaday words, their English equivalents, and, in most instances, the translators' equivalents in Tboli and Blit—a tricky job because of the complexities of multiple translations. And also, even in the short period of contact, the Tasaday had learned new words. Rice, for instance, they called *bigas,* a Tagalog word, not *begas,* as in many closer dialects.

No Tasaday words could be found for Philippines, Filipino, Mindanao, Manubo, Ubu, Blit, Tboli, or any other islands or peoples; no words for boat, ocean, sea, or lake—although the Celebes Sea was less than forty miles south of where they were sitting, and Lake Sebu was some thirty miles east; no words for many common local foods; none for clearing, plain, or flatland—although apparently new phrases were noted for the land beyond the clearing: "the place without up and down" and "where the eye looks too far."

Every Tasaday interviewed said he had not known such a place existed, had never been outside the forest, and never met anyone from outside except Dafal, and none of them knew where he had come from. Dafal said they never asked about his home or anything else; they simply accepted what he brought without question. The Tasaday said they lived in the forest, their ancestors had lived in the forest, and that was all they knew.

They expressed no knowledge of planting or cultivating crops, and the only activity even faintly verging on agriculture was their planting of the leafy top of an extracted root so it would grow again. These starchy, potatolike tubers, which they called *biking,* were one of the varieties that gatherers traditionally found to be excellent foods.

In addition, the Tasaday ate various fruits and many other forms of plant life including rattan and bamboo shoots. Ferns, most flowers, and wild banana were available but evidently not desirable, unusual because many primitive Filipinos ate them. Streams provided small fish, frogs, tadpoles, and crabs. The Tasaday were ignorant of any kind of fishtrap, a surprise to Fox because virtually all Philippine people used some kind of device for trapping fish. The Tasaday did say, however, that Dafal taught them to dam streams with sticks and rocks to make gathering easier. They prized monkeymeat but did not discuss trapping game or eating meat in detail. Fox concluded that crabs were probably their most important source of protein.

The Tasaday revealed three more fragments of metal during these sessions: part of a knife, apparently broken off from the bolo seen earlier; an awl made of wire; and a short metal rod used for mashing their betel-chew mixture. Questioning about these items eventually disclosed that all of them, including the bolo, had not been handed down by ancestors or acquired through trade, but had been supplied by Dafal.

This was startling. Further questioning brought out that Dafal had also provided a piece of crystalline quartz used as a strike-a-light to make fire. They called it *tik-tik.* Before knowing Dafal, they started fire by twirling a round stick in a wooden base. They still used this method, uncommon in the Philippines, and demonstrated it.

Names for ten different types of arrows were listed; then it was claimed that all arrows had come from Dafal.

In rather quick time Dafal emerged as the dominant figure in their technical history. Elizalde demanded to know what else had he given them! Dafal was summoned from wherever he had wandered and Mai questioned him. He immediately acknowledged supplying the Tasaday with all their metal, the bows and arrows, and the strike-a-light.

And what else? Their cloth? Yes, Dafal said, and also their brass earrings.

"Damn it, why the hell didn't he say so?" Elizalde shouted at Mai.

Dafal replied that nobody had asked him.

Elizalde fumed, telling Mai that he must get a complete list of everything Dafal had given. The hunter was interrogated on many aspects of Tasaday life. If, for instance, he had provided all their metal, then what had they used as tools before meeting him?

Stones. The Tasaday then described making stones into scrapers and pounders and imitated how they used them. Fox, who had been increasingly excited by what he was learning, was now astounded. He knew of no record of any living Filipino peoples' using stone tools; stone arrowheads, yes, but even that had been more than three centuries ago!

The Tasaday had no stone tools with them, but they answered Fox's questions knowingly. He had broad knowledge of stone implements; he had directed the excavations of the Tabon Caves on Palawan Island, west of Mindanao, that established the presence of stone-using men in the Philippines forty thousand years ago. The Tasaday's comments convinced him that their practical knowledge of these ancient implements was genuine. They apparently used them to make secondary tools of bamboo, which Fox saw as vital to their survival in the forest.

Dafal said the Tasaday made cloth by pounding the bast, or inner bark, of a tree with river cobble. Fox determined that the tree was a fig.

Elizalde and Fox found the extent of Dafal's contribution to Tasaday culture almost beyond belief, but they could find no evidence against either his claims or those of the Tasaday. None of the trade objects, for instance, could have been made by the Tasaday, not even the bows, which were all of a type made by the Ubu and Tboli from bamboo deliberately cultivated in the lowlands and not likely to be found in the Tasaday's forest.

Scant data was gathered during the two days about Tasaday religion or mythology; all they had had come to them from their ancestors, apparently called *fangul*. One man said he understood from his forefathers that a godlike man named Bebang was the first person on earth and that he had two wives named Fuweh and Sidakweh. They were Tasaday, had lived in the present Tasaday's special place in the forest, and had vague, perhaps superhuman, powers.

As for the Tasaday view of the world, it was bounded by the forest. A hazy reference to treetops, where souls of the dead resided, suggested that the scope of their world view included the idea of an afterlife.

The story of the great dreaded disease, or plague, was difficult to trace, and only through Dafal was a Tasaday name given it, *fugu;* its era was the misty past.

The interrogators' renewed efforts to discuss women were again frustrated by the Tasaday's reluctance—or what was taken as reluctance; it may have been that the questions or translations made no sense to the Tasaday. They did indicate that parents arranged marriages, and that part of the arrangement involved a dowry of food. No reference was made to women being "found" in the forest or stolen from other groups.

They repeated again that no women were available nowadays. A man had one wife and a woman one husband—strict monogamy. They apparently had no knowledge of polygamy—or polyandry, which would have been more likely in their women-short group. Fox was puzzled at their adherence to monogamy, because their mythology included Bebang's precedent of two wives, and many native groups in the islands practiced polygamy. Mai, for example, was continually teased about his wives, who were among the most beautiful women in the tribe.

Balayam grew deeply serious during the discussion of women and afterward cited Elizalde's earlier remark that he would find him a woman. Elizalde had all but forgotten it, but Balayam made it clear that he was counting on Elizalde. The "good man" must help him, he insisted.

Questioning elicited no sign of a hierarchical structure or of leadership roles for any Tasaday, which made it in anthropological terms a group, not a band or tribe, both of which have such political or organizational features. Tasaday decision making apparently was based on discussions in which men and women expressed views equally, with age and experience determining degree of influence.

Before meeting Dafal and acquiring pieces of cloth, one Tasaday said, they had worn only leaves. (Fox collected a specimen, which a botanist identified as a ground orchid.) The man told Elizalde that they covered their genitals in order to protect them against witches. The witches were not further identified or described. But another man said the covering was chiefly to ward off insects, leeches, thorns, and raspy vines that caused serious discomfort to the genitals.

By midafternoon of the second day, everyone was tired and the Panamin group prepared to leave. More gifts were presented—at least fifty arrows, one Tboli bow, one Tboli bolo, one Tboli spear, a sack of salt, two sacks of rice, two pieces of cloth, three empty rice sacks, dried fish, and tobacco. The Tasaday made a point of returning the tobacco, took some items with them, and put the rest in a lean-to.

They were shown how to cook rice by stuffing grains into sections of bamboo, adding water, and sticking the tube into a fire. Dafal said he had already taught them to use such tubes for cooking small creatures found in the stream. They said they ate their root food either raw, baked inside leaf wrappings, or roasted in the hot coals.

The later sessions were more relaxed, but most Tasaday continued to be nervously shy and the women and infants favored the seclusion of the lean-tos. This was in sharp contrast to the intimate affection they showed each other. Younger children were constantly carried, held, nuzzled, caressed; older Tasaday spoke together warmly, touched gently, shared food and shelter with no trace of friction.

Smiles for the visitors were rare, however; only Balayam was consistently talkative, although several other men, notably Bilangan, participated in conversations. Perhaps because of his need of a woman, Balayam also made the greatest fuss over Elizalde, embracing him and cooing words and nuzzling. Others also touched him and looked at him with reverence, apparently having accepted him as the legendary good man of their ancestors' prophecy. They also showed special regard for Mai, touching him and putting their cheeks and lips to his cheeks and sniffing, in a sort of kiss.

In general, Elizalde was encouraged by the Tasaday's attitude. True, they had not asked a single question about their visitors' homes, origins, or intentions, but they had come to the clearing when invited, were slowly but steadily shedding their fears, and seemed to welcome more meetings. Even the helicopter—the big bird—no longer terrified them. Sekul, Kuletaw's wife, had held her head and groaned long after seeing it the first time; Rebong thought she suffered a severe headache, but it was simply fear of the machine. Now she tolerated its coming and going with barely a wince. Sekul was particularly susceptible to loud noises and when a member of the Panamin group fired a shotgun at a *kalaw,* a big-beaked bird also known as a hornbill, she collapsed in shock for several minutes. The sudden blast had frightened all the Tasaday, and Elizalde ordered that henceforth nobody was to fire without clearance from him or Mai.

Elizalde and his party had to return to Manila and informed the Tasaday that no meetings would be held for many days, that they could go to their place inside the forest and would be signaled by Dafal and the helicopter when it was time to meet again. Some Tasaday nodded and pointed in the direction of their place, possibly so the "big bird" would circle there.

Back in Manila, the Panamin group was exhilarated. Fox termed his experience and the Tasaday as "startling—even for an anthropologist." Elizalde was happy and excited. The Tasaday held great potential—as subjects of scientific study, as a means of dramatizing the cultural minorities of the Philippines and their problems, and as a way of publicizing the work of Panamin and its personnel. And the Tasaday themselves? What would happen to them? What could, should be done with them, for them? They needed protection and careful treatment. Elizalde discussed it with Fox and both men pondered the next steps.

Fox worked on his own notes and Elizalde's field reports. It was impossible to know to what extent information from the Tasaday had been colored or changed by translators, and much was tentative—but much also appeared solid: their distinct dialect; their account of stone-tool usage; their isolation; the absence of agriculture and a variety of foods; the lack of tobacco, metal, and other material items common to neighboring peoples.

Fox and Elizalde worked virtually all of the known significant information on the Tasaday into a thirty-two-page report, complete with a genealogy, one hundred and ten Tasaday words, and a list of material items provided the Tasaday by Dafal and Panamin. The report, titled *"The Tasaday Forest People*—A Data Paper on a Newly Discovered Food Gathering and Stone Tool Using Manubo Group in the Mountains of South Cotabato, Mindanao, Philippines," offered tentative theories about why the Tasaday were in the forest (a splinter group that got separated from a larger Manubo group; remnants of a people who had fled into the mountains to escape a plague), and how long they had been there (probably more than four hundred or five hundred years; possibly, "it was tempting to argue," they were descended from a people whose separation from a larger society had occurred some fifteen hundred to two thousand years ago). Dafal was reported to have first met them in 1966 or 1967.

The Tasaday, described as a "symbol of Man's variability and adaptability and of his universality," provided an unparalleled opportunity in the twentieth century to "more fully understand Man's culture and behavior before the appearance of agriculture and the domestication of animals; before the appearance among 'modern' man of a highly complex technology based upon metals which is devastating the natural environment upon which the Tasaday still depend and upon which Man everywhere once depended."

The paper went on to say that the Panamin research staff, directed by Fox, would live among the Tasaday and study them: "In this Age of Space Exploration, their discovery provides us with the opportunity to query again the essential stuff of Man's nature . . . to study the relationships between Man's technological developments and his institutional arrangements and to study the qualities of human-ness, the so-called cultural universals which all men share . . . to better understand ourselves and the problems which we have created.

"The survival of these singularly unique people," the report continued, "is being threatened by plans of loggers to drive roads into their great forest sanctuary. Annually, the neighboring slash-and-burn agriculturists are destroying thousands of square hectares of the climax tropical forests in which the Tasaday roam." The Tasaday's present isolation was only temporary; and logging roads, farmers, other tribes will inevitably reach the Tasaday—"today, tomorrow, a year from now"—and such contact could be "disastrous for the Tasaday."

The paper proposed establishment of large forest reserves for the Tasaday and other mountain peoples that would stop "the rape of our land, its natural resources and its people." Panamin called for new and fairer systems of land allocation throughout Mindanao, and for improved programs of land utilization. It affirmed the rights of cultural minority peoples to retain ancient beliefs and values, their own religions and languages, and to adapt to outside influences "with dignity and their own choice."

The authors expected an enthusiastically favorable response, but also some skepticism—their report admittedly was based on only a few days at the forest's edge, where the Tasaday were uncomfortable and the communication problem formidable. And, surely, they anticipated raised eyebrows and criticism from those who would ask "What is Elizalde up to now?"

2

Managing Skepticism

THE first public mention of the Tasaday appeared July 8, 1971. It was a muggy rainy-season afternoon and I was at my desk in the Associated Press bureau in Manila, leafing through the first edition of the *Daily Mirror*. A brief story in the middle of page 14, almost buried by other reports, stopped me. The one-column headline in small letters said: LOST TRIBE FOUND IN C'BATO.

The story reported the discovery of "a hitherto unknown tribe believed to have lived in virtual isolation and under paleolithic conditions for more than 500 years."

These "vanishing tribesmen" had been found a month earlier in a remote rain forest, the newspaper said, adding: "Ostensibly described as food gatherers and trappers, the so-called 'lost tribe' of Tasaday Manubo has puzzled anthropologists for having survived in that forbidding forest area with virtually no contact with the outside world."

The only outsider they had known before was a primitive hunter from a nearby mountain tribe, the *Mirror* said, and their first contact with the civilized world came on June 7, when they met Manuel Elizalde, Jr., and a Panamin land-survey team. This reportedly took place within about fifty miles of the town of Surallah, some six hundred and fifty miles south of Manila and only a few miles inland from the Celebes Sea on Mindanao's southern coast. I had visited the area with Elizalde the previous year and had seen its dense jungles and rugged mountains.

"What is more amazing [than their physical isolation] is that the Tasadays have not known rice and other cultivated plants and have never tasted salt or sugar or smoked tobacco," the *Mirror* asserted. Well-known

28

anthropologist Dr. Robert B. Fox reportedly said "it is possible that the Tasaday are among the few, if not the only people in the world today, who do not know or use tobacco."

Near the end of the story, Elizalde was quoted as saying the Tasaday's technology was still based on stone tools and that the discovery of the people was of "great scientific interest."

It was indeed of great interest and my first reaction was to write an account for the AP news wire—but was it true? Several questions nagged. Why was the story buried on the *Mirror*'s fourteenth page? Why no photographs and so few details when the discovery reportedly occurred four weeks ago? How many Tasaday were there? What language did they speak? What did they wear? Why was the announcement delayed? Why had the editor put quotation marks around lost tribe and used such qualifiers as "so-called" and "ostensibly described"—did he doubt the story?

I grabbed Manila's other major afternoon newspaper, the *Evening News,* certain to find a story about the discovery because it was owned and published by the Elizalde family. But it had not a word about the Tasaday.

A check of all the larger-circulation morning papers also turned up nothing. The news desk at the *Mirror* had closed for the day and could give no help. None of the AP editors or reporters had heard about the Tasaday on the radio; neither the government nor Panamin Foundation had issued news releases.

This was odd. Manila had a superabundance of news media and re-porters—sixteen daily papers, more than a dozen magazines, at least forty radio stations, seven television stations. The intensely competitive media normally would give such a story considerable coverage. Perhaps the *Mirror* had simply beaten them all? But that would be more reason to play it up prominently, not bury it in back pages.

I reread the *Mirror* account to see if it was based on anonymous sources. No, Elizalde and Fox were clearly quoted. Then I noted at the end the initials "PNS," Philippines News Service, which gathered and distributed news to all newspapers and major broadcasters by teletype. Others must have the Tasaday story, including the Elizalde newspapers and radio and TV stations. Why had they refused to use it?

Several years as a newsman had conditioned me against the ploys and entreaties of politicians and various kinds of promoters when they wanted something publicized. I began to wonder if the historic discovery was a mistake or a hoax. The more I thought about it, the more suspicious I became—a people isolated for centuries from towns and civilization only forty or fifty miles away. Incredible!

My growing skepticism also was abetted by my experience with Elizalde. In several meetings in Manila and on a week-long trip in Mindanao, his attitude had fluctuated from a self-conscious aloofness verging on arrogance to easy friendliness, from spoiled cockiness to selfless idealism. He was complex and enigmatic, difficult to figure out; but I thought I saw at least one characteristic clearly: a penchant for publicity.

I tried to reach him by telephone to discuss the "Tasaday discovery" but secretaries at his offices and home said he was not available. I then tried to phone Fox, who had been talkative and amiable both times we met. I knew of his work at the Tabon Caves and his research on the Pinatubo Negrito people of Luzon, and that he had worked with Elizalde on various projects in recent years. But Fox was not at the National Museum or the Panamin office.

As hours passed, my skepticism was pricked by selfish annoyance. If the story was true, why hadn't I been told? In addition to the week traveling with Elizalde, I had spent most of my last vacation in the mountains near Tboli gathering material for a children's book on the Ubu of Datu Ma Falen, to whom Elizalde had introduced me. I was interested in and sympathetic to the plight of the tribes and maintained closer contact with Panamin than any other reporter I knew.

Late in the afternoon I finally reached Oscar Trinidad, an attorney and assistant executive director of Panamin, who was a close aide of Elizalde's and particularly concerned with public relations because he had been a newspaperman. Trinidad said apologetically that there had been a still-unexplained mix-up in releasing the discovery story and a publicity firm handling it apparently had given the news only to the *Mirror* or PNS, too late for the morning papers. A lengthy Elizalde-Fox data paper was supposed to have been provided to all the major news media at the same time, Oscar said, promising to send me a copy at once by messenger and hinting that if I wanted to see Elizalde I should hurry to his house.

The huge two-story house was in a once fashionable but now fading suburb. I got through the gate in the seven-foot-high wall easily, probably because Trinidad had phoned ahead, and was ushered to the main door by a uniformed armed security guard, a common figure among Manila's well to do.

Elizalde and Fox called out cordial greetings from their seats at a long table in what must have been, decades earlier, the ballroom of the Club Filipino, onetime gathering place for the social elite. Roughly the size of a basketball court, the ballroom now served as the living room. Cut-glass chandeliers hung from the high ceiling, and dark woods paneled the walls. Four or five overstuffed chairs and sofas were clustered at the far end of the room. Sung and Ming porcelain plates and jars, burial urns, wood carvings, bows and arrows, spears, and other artifacts stood on small tables and the polished hardwood floor. It was a handsome room, but far from elegant; the dominant impressions were of bigness and old age. The only quickly noticed modern objects were the expensive glass-and-chrome table and black leather swivel chairs occupied by Elizalde and Fox.

Aides hovered nearby and housemaids in white-aproned uniforms slipped silently in and out with iced tea, bowls of nuts, fresh ashtrays. I tried to conduct an interview with the two men but was frequently interrupted by the aides, visitors, and telephone calls. During these breaks I read a copy of the Elizalde-Fox report on the Tasaday. It gave a much more solid cast to the whole affair, but I still had some questions and tried to squeeze them in whenever possible.

Elizalde said that when he first met the Tasaday, "we thought they were just some ragtag band that had gotten lost or was in hiding or something. We even suspected they might try to ambush us or make trouble." This mistaken view, the difficulty of language communication, and the tense timidity of the Tasaday had caused considerable delay in realizing their significance, he said.

Fox observed that while "lost tribe" had a nice ring to it, these people were not lost; the forest had been their home as far back as any of them knew. Elizalde added, "It would be more reasonable to say that everyone else was lost and they had stayed where they belonged."

My anthropological background was meager and I probed for a layman's explanation of the significance of it all. Fox stressed that there was a great amount of study to be done before the ramifications would be fully known, but he joined Elizalde in proclaiming that it seemed beyond doubt that this was an extremely important discovery scientifically.

It sounded extraordinary, I agreed, but if it was as significant as they claimed, why had it been disclosed so haphazardly? I mentioned that, apart from the documentation a scientist would need, even a layman would want substantial evidence to give such unusual claims credence. But the way it had reached the public cast doubt upon the whole story.

"Okay, okay," Elizalde said impatiently, grumbling that he was fully aware the announcement had been fouled up. An aide said that the data reports were being distributed at that very moment and that photos would be available later in the evening.

"What's wrong? You don't believe the story?" Elizalde asked. "Okay, what don't you believe? What? Go ahead, what do you want to know?"

I asked several questions aimed mainly at establishing credibility for what was in the data paper, and Elizalde said, "Look, most of what you are asking is right there in our report—it's true, we put our names to it. What more can we do?"

He added that they hoped to gather more data and planned another expedition to the Tasaday forest soon. I spoke up immediately, saying I would like to go along.

"Why, sure, of course," Elizalde said expansively. "Done. Consider it done."

I assured him I was serious, eager to go; and he assured me that he was serious, too, and would "personally" see to it that I would be invited to join the first group to accompany him.

Soon after that I left, with the promise of the visit to the Tasaday firmly in mind. I then reread the data paper, and, although there were nagging questions, it did provide ample material for a news dispatch. There were also several points that stuck out from our conversation, particularly a claim by Elizalde that the Tasaday did not have any enemies or weapons —or even any words for fighting or war. This sounded dreamily romantic, but Elizalde insisted he believed it.

It was impossible to judge such claims, but the official status of Elizalde and Fox gave their statements authority. I wrote a story for AP, quoting our conversation and their report throughout. Late that evening, Panamin released photographs of the Tasaday, two of which were distributed over AP wires.

Early the next morning, messages began arriving from widely scattered places—Australia, Turkey, the United States—asking for more information, more photos, more anything about the Tasaday. Other news agencies were carrying the story, too; it was stirring interest around the world. All the morning newspapers in Manila played the story prominently, which indicated that it had been a mix-up the day before, not a deliberate blackout.

The immediate general reaction was approval, but expressions of doubt soon began to circulate. Most of these were to be expected—particularly that conclusions were being reached about the Tasaday without sufficient study—but some were unexpected, in both bitterness and cause. Among the strongest negative comments I heard was one from a Filipino public relations woman who had been in Tokyo promoting tourism when the story appeared. She returned to Manila furious.

"It was disgusting and embarrassing," she said. "It makes the Philippines look so primitive." She was most angry about a photograph we had distributed showing a Tasaday girl with her father combing his hands through her hair. I thought it conveyed an intimate relationship and also showed their handsome features. But the PR woman, a university graduate who had once worked at the United Nations in New York, thought it was ugly and degrading to show the father picking lice from the child's hair. I argued that few Western people would even realize that that was what he was doing and that it was not the point of the picture anyway.

"Perhaps not," the woman said through tight lips, "but of course the whole world is going to think *all* Filipinos are like that—dirty backward creatures in the jungle!"

I heard this a few times, but the most common reactions were curiosity, excitement, and concern about what would happen to the Tasaday.

I was eagerly anticipating joining Elizalde's next expedition, as he had promised, hopeful of answering some of my own questions. I phoned Panamin daily, and on July 16 was told that late the following week I would be in a small party of newsmen and scientists. I would be informed of the exact date well ahead of time.

But I was uneasy about it and two days later double-checked. A secretary at Elizalde's house said he had left for Mindanao early that morning with several aides and a writer for *Reader's Digest*. I phoned Oscar Trinidad, who confirmed this and added that an American television news team was to join Elizalde in Mindanao the next day, Monday, and then all would meet the Tasaday on Tuesday. I was listed in a group of more than a dozen newsmen scheduled to arrive about Friday, if everything worked out.

Trinidad said he had no idea why I was going last instead of first as promised. I grumbled for a while, then drove to the airport and bought a ticket on the first flight to Mindanao. At dawn I was on the plane with field gear and cameras. The plane landed at Davao City, a sprawling port town of about 400,000 people, the largest city on the island. In the airport I met Jack Reynolds, who had come from Tokyo in charge of a three-man television team of the National Broadcasting Company. He squeezed me aboard a small plane that had been chartered for them and we flew one hour southwest to the frontier town of Surallah, whose Allah Valley Station was the closest airstrip to Panamin's main settlement project among the Tboli. We rode a Panamin jeep for another hour to the secluded valley settlement, where Elizalde was supposed to be waiting.

There was no telling how I would be received. I was not expected, and presumably not wanted, but I had taken Elizalde's invitation seriously.

At the Tboli settlement we found Elizalde on the porch of a hilltop staff house. He wore a crumpled yachting cap and a stubble of whiskers, and was surrounded by Panamin staff members and tribespeople in their traditional clothing of heavy woven cloth. The men wore long knives on their belts, the women colorful hair combs, many bead necklaces, and bright brass earrings.

Elizalde spotted me, frowned, half chuckled and called out, "Well, well, look who's here! What brings you, Nancy?"

I tried to smile and replied that I was grateful for his assurance that I would be among the first newsmen to see the Tasaday, so here I was, ready to go.

"Oh, yeah, yeah . . . right," he said with a blink and a shrug.

A few more sarcastic comments was about all we said of my unexpected arrival.

We ate dinner and chatted on the porch as the sun shot its last rays into the valley, glazing brown thatched houses with gold. The red-orange sky had piles of big pillowy pink clouds. Steep green slopes rose from both sides of the flat valley floor, where about two hundred Tboli houses

on stilts stood in a neat long rectangle. The valley's open end flowed into
a rolling plain of farms and ranches that ran for miles. The other end was
closed by low foothills that rippled back into another enclosed valley and
then climbed upward in a series of steeper, stairlike slopes that melded
into a mountain forest.

A swift-flowing river wound through the settled valley, where there was
a reservoir, meeting hall, medical clinic, marketplace, children's play-
ground. There was enough electricity to light the lanes between the
houses. Rice was grown on the hillsides and in the other valley, and each
house had a small vegetable plot.

I remarked on the beauty of the setting and Elizalde, gazing out into
the valley, said, "Yeah, and you should have seen what we . . . the
Tboli . . . went through to get it. When we got here there was nothing,
zero! This house we're in now was just a shack for the goons guarding the
place. The rancher who claimed this land had gunmen up here, over there
on the opposite hill, and down there where the main road comes in. And
now it's this. And the Tboli did it. We helped, of course, but it was really
them. Great people. Just give 'em a chance . . . they'll do it, do anything. This was Tboli land in the first place!"

Elizalde talked on; a dozen people gathered. The mood was relaxed
and warm, with the camaraderie of a bunkhouse or athletes' clubhouse.
Two of Elizalde's closest Panamin aides were there, as was the most powerful Tboli leader, Mai Tuan, whose barrel body and drooping black mustache made him look as if he could snap you in half with his bare hands,
but whose voice and manner were gentle. He and the others nodded and
laughed knowingly as Elizalde recalled times past.

His stories sounded like tales from the Old West—gun fights in the
night, kidnapings, ambushes and shootouts in the roads and hills, con-
niving between frontier lawyers and politicians, settlers and police. He
obviously relished the telling, usually with himself and the "Panamin
boys," and Mai Tuan and his tribal warriors in the forefront of the action.
Occasionally an exaggerated he-man ruggedness took over, but always the
tales were exciting and Elizalde was an engaging and enthusiastic storyteller.

This was a relaxed and amusing Elizalde I had never seen in Manila,
when his guard was up. I wondered if these stories, some of which I had
heard on my previous trip with Elizalde, were as true as they were fascinating.

The storytelling was ended this evening by whisperings in Elizalde's ear
—there always seemed to be a lot of whispering and muffled exchanges—
and he went to a table in a corner to join a group that had assembled unnoticed: a couple of nervous-looking tribesmen, Johnny Artajo, and two
other Filipinos, one a husky crew-cut man with eyeglasses, a potbelly

bulging over his belt, and a pistol in his back pocket. They settled down to a serious and obviously private conversation.

Later that evening, Ching Rivero, who handled transportation, told me I would be on the first helicopter flight in the morning to Tasaday country. It would include Elizalde, Christopher Lucas, of *Reader's Digest,* Mai Tuan, Bart Bartolo as pilot, and Ching as copilot. The second flight would carry the NBC team, Robert Fox, and Jesus Peralta, a Filipino archeologist for the National Museum. The National Geographic crew had rented a chopper and was headed elsewhere.

I went to bed excited—in a few hours we would see the people who supposedly had lived for centuries in the Stone Age and had never known war or enemies. Hard to imagine; harder to believe.

All that I could remember reading or hearing about the Tasaday went through my head that evening. And seeing the Tboli settlement, hearing the adventure stories, and having narrowly avoided being left behind brought to mind my first visit to Mindanao with Elizalde.

Beginning in 1969, I had been reading the Manila news items about his activities with the tribes. It sounded admirable and I was interested in doing a story. I had heard various explanations about his motives, some imputing unflattering self-interest—that he was prospecting for minerals, merely adventuring, or seeking attention—and decided I should meet him and make up my own mind.

The first time we met, at a large cocktail party, Elizalde's appearance surprised me—much trimmer, harder-looking than I had expected. He was shorter than I had thought, about 5 feet 6 inches, and had somewhat brooding eyes in a sharp-featured, serious face. Newspaper photos a few months earlier had shown him curly-haired, chubby, and double-chinned, rather soft. In response to my inquiry about a story, he said, "Yes, yes, of course. That would be fine." But he was stiff and seemed to be half listening, only artificially interested, as he darted his eyes over my shoulder around the crowded room. He then referred me to an aide and walked away with the air of an extremely busy and important person who did not discuss such matters himself. I talked with the aide and expressed my interest in joining a Panamin field trip. He told me I would be welcome and would be called soon. I never heard another word about it.

A similar experience several months later did not encourage me to pursue a story, but I was curious about Elizalde's response; it was not in keeping with reports that he wanted publicity. Then, in May of 1970, I learned that Charles Lindbergh, the famous American pilot, was again in the Philippines and I saw the possibility of combining a story on Elizalde and his tribal work with a story about Lindbergh. I had met Lindbergh once at a meeting of Filipinos who were organizing a wildlife-conservation program. He was there to spur efforts to save the tamarau, a wild buffalo found only on the island of Mindoro, and the monkey-eating eagle, a large awesomely fierce bird believed to exist only in the Philippines. Authorities said both were nearing extinction. While working on these projects, Lindbergh learned of Panamin's activities with the tribes, which was essentially to save people from extinction. He was intrigued and made several trips with Elizalde, lending his name to Panamin's efforts and becoming the hardest-working member of the Panamin Foundation board of directors.

Lindbergh, however controversial in the past, had remained one of America's legendary figures—a folk hero to a generation that still vividly recalls that in 1927 he made the first nonstop flight between North America and Europe. For the past two decades he had stayed out of the public limelight, avoiding interviews with newsmen and appearances on television. I had first seen him when he visited Vietnam in 1967. He refused to talk to newsmen, brushing past us where we stood outside his hotel.

In the Philippines, however, he was sometimes willing to let down the barriers in circumstances involving him with wildlife and the tribes. Twice, in fact, Alden Whitman, of the New York *Times,* accompanied him. During one visit Manila newspapers printed vague accounts of Lindbergh, Elizalde, and their party having barely escaped an ambush one night on their way to the Tboli settlement. Their bus was halted on the road and guns were cocked on both sides, but a bloody shoot-out was narrowly averted.

When Lindbergh arrived at the Manila airport a few days later, I introduced myself as a reporter. He put down his bags, smiled cordially, and shook my hand. Lindbergh would talk about the tribes, but refused to answer questions about the reported ambush, saying it was the concern of Panamin and Elizalde and not his place to comment.

The Manila rumor mill, which was always hyperactive, subsequently churned out several versions of the incident, some contending that the ambush had been set up either to kill Elizalde or frighten him from continuing his work with the tribes. Another version said it was merely a minor confusion on the road; the most bizarre account said the ambush was faked, staged by Elizalde to impress Lindbergh and the American newsman.

Lindbergh left the Philippines shortly after that, but returned a few weeks later. I telephoned Elizalde and proposed a story on Lindbergh and Panamin and the tribes. "I don't know," he said. "You'll have to talk to Charles about that."

A luncheon was arranged at Elizalde's house, the renovated Club Filipino where he lived with his wife and three young children. It was also home for a crowd of other children and older people in various styles of tribal dress. Oscar Trinidad told me that the children were among fifty-one orphans Elizalde had adopted over the years, most of whom stayed with him while attending Manila schools. "There's usually at least forty people living here," Oscar said.

Lindbergh was there when I arrived. He wore a gray suit and looked very tall as he spoke softly with a group of Filipinos. He listened with his head cocked down, partly because of his superior height and partly because of a hearing problem. He smiled and shuffled his feet a lot and appeared determinedly modest. I had the momentary impression of watching Jimmy Stewart playing Charles Lindbergh—or vice versa.

Observing him in public often during the next several months, I realized that it was a consistent manner, even with the gray-haired grinning strangers who approached him in hotel lobbies and airport terminals, introduced themselves, and then related what they had been doing when they learned Lindbergh had landed safely in Paris nearly fifty years ago. "Everybody tells me that," Lindbergh once said with a half sigh and chuckle. "I must have heard it thousands of times." He showed considerable attentiveness in these instances, but if the stranger hung on too long, Lindbergh usually excused himself and departed with a smile-nod and a half bow.

It did not seem to be shyness or exaggerated humility, but a low-key politeness. In less public situations he was an enthusiastic conversationalist and could talk for hours, choosing his words thoughtfully, frequently finding ways to turn a discussion to conservation, the environment, and the dangers confronting all forms of life. He seemed indefatigable on the subject.

He was formidable in anger—head and body erect, eyes flashing, voice authoritative as he addressed his adversary with firmness, brusqueness, or exasperation, depending on the degree of his annoyance.

There was firmness, but no brusqueness, at lunch when I proposed the news story to him and Elizalde: "That's out," Lindbergh said. After some discussion he said he would not object to being included in a story about Panamin and its work with the tribes. I said that had been my intention, but that it would be unrealistic to treat him as merely incidental—"By the way, Charles Lindbergh was also among the party." He necessarily would be prominent in a story focusing on the tribes.

"Well, if it'll help Manda and the foundation, then I'm agreeable," he said. "But Manda knows how I feel about these things and I'll let him decide."

Elizalde said he thought it would be worthwhile. It was agreed that we would soon depart for northern Mindanao, accompanied by a leader of the Higa-onon tribe, Datu Mampatilan. For several days the newspapers had carried pictures of this wrinkled, giggling, snaggle-toothed, tough old man with President Marcos at the Presidential Palace.

He was the most powerful known leader of the Higa-onon, Elizalde explained, a loosely organized tribe of possibly tens of thousands scattered over Mindanao's northern provinces. For several months Mampatilan had been chased by police and armed gangs. Elizalde learned that two of Mampatilan's nieces had been raped and murdered by a crew from a lumber company; one of his sons was shot and wounded; a nephew was kidnaped, stuffed into a burlap bag, and used for target practice long after he was dead. A vengeful Higa-onon band armed with knives, spears, and an assortment of guns swarmed over the lumbermen's camp one night and left seventeen men dead or dying.

Local authorities mounted a hunt for Mampatilan and other Higa-onon warriors hiding in the mountains. Higa-onon in the lowlands were harassed. Elizalde dispatched a three-man team, with a single-side-band radio, and after a week of hiking, they found Mampatilan and radioed the location of a nearby dry stream bed in which a helicopter could land. Elizalde flew in accompanied by a news photographer, convinced Mampatilan that Marcos would help him, and offered to remain as a hostage if Mampatilan would go to Manila. The *datu* was flown to meet Marcos and received amnesty for his people on the grounds that they had attacked the loggers in self-defense. The President ordered the tribesmen and loggers to stop battling or he would send in military troops.

Elizalde was then brought back to Manila; he would take Mampatilan to his mountain home as the first leg of his trip with Lindbergh and me. We flew to Butuan City, in northern Mindanao; we were to take a helicopter into the mountains where the Higa-onon were awaiting Mampatilan. The rotor blade of the chopper was already turning when we landed, apparently alerted by radio to be ready to go. Elizalde had decided that I was to go on the first flight so I could photograph the arrival of Mampatilan, which would be tumultuous. The only other passenger was a radio operator, carrying fresh batteries for the single-side-band radio. I carried only my camera bag, leaving behind a larger bag with clothes and field gear because Elizalde said the pilot wanted his load as light as possible on the first trip.

The small helicopter twisted up and flew east over thickly wooded mountains. Twenty minutes later we circled and circled, and finally descended among towering trees onto a narrow pebbly stream bed that knifed through the forest like an alley among skyscrapers. The pilot took off immediately after we alighted; presumably he would return at once with Mampatilan, Lindbergh, and Elizalde. Other members of the party, plus my belongings, would come after that.

About eighty mountain people had congregated, but the only people I could talk with were the radio operator and Al Spileski, one of the men who had hiked in to find Mampatilan weeks earlier and was still in the forest. Spileski, a stranger to me, was about forty, a rugged-looking six-footer with a raggedy, reddish stubble of whiskers. He beamed a jagged-toothed smile at me as I climbed from the helicopter.

Spileski said he'd been longing to get out of the mountains, but could not move until Elizalde said so. "I dunno. We figured it'd be any day now, but, you know the boss" (as many called Elizalde). "Geez, we may be stuck here for weeks yet," he said with a wheezy laugh. He explained that he did not exactly work for Panamin or Elizalde, but he did do odd jobs like this "for the boss" from time to time, had been for years. "I'm crazy, I guess." He chuckled.

Spileski said he had been all over the Philippines working at various jobs, but what he liked best was to go prospecting on his own. As we talked he occasionally shouted into the radio to try and raise the helicopter or Elizalde's party. More than three hours passed and we received no sign of them. It began to rain.

"Christ, gotta get outta this place—stream bed'll fill up in no time. It is gonna pour," Spileski said, motioning for me to grab my camera bag as he headed off into the brush and up the mountain.

It looked nearly straight up. The tall trees shut out the light and the undergrowth was thick and tangled, so we guided ourselves along a rain-swollen creek. Of course, my boots were in the baggage to come later. The leather shoes I wore slipped off the wet, mossy rocks like skates on ice.

Foolishly turning down offers of aid by several Higa-onon, I insisted on carrying my camera bag, which weighed about forty pounds and swung awkwardly from my shoulder as we slithered up the slope. The rain was a tropical torrent. A barefoot Higa-onon girl, who looked about twelve years old, bounded up, grabbed my bag, fitted the strap around her forehead, so that the case dangled down her back, and darted up the mountain—flashing a grin over her shoulder! I stuck with the radioman, who had made this trip before, and we straggled into a hillside settlement an hour later, cuts on our hands and legs, streaked with mud, soaked and shivering. It was more than five thousand feet above sea level and the rain was cold.

I passed the time talking with Spileski and the radio operator, trying to learn something about the Higa-onon. I also made several efforts to photograph the settlement, although it drizzled or poured rain so often that my slippery shoes made it almost impossible to maneuver. The barefoot Higa-onon just dug in their toes. I tried that, but the hillsides sloped down sharply and the grassless rain-soaked soil around the houses was like grease. I fell at least twenty times the first day—my feet suddenly shooting out from under me in a stuntman's comic pratfall.

Elizalde radioed that he had not come because the pilot refused to land again in the stream bed: "He says it was too dangerous—the cross winds were wild, air too thin at that altitude. Claims he almost crashed trying to get in and out of there."

Spileski and a Higa-onon crew cleared a spot nearer the settlement. The chopper flew over and departed; the clearing was too small. The third day, on a ridgetip a couple of miles north, a house was knocked down, trees felled—plenty of room. Several hundred Higa-onon lined the ridge back into the forest. The scene promised to be spectacular—Mampatilan, Lindbergh, and Elizalde surrounded by exultant tribesmen on the rim of a sweeping ravine.

The helicopter zoomed in, landed, and out climbed Mampatilan. The pilot waved to me. "You the newsman?" he shouted above the engine's roar. "Get in. I'm supposed to pick you up."

"But where are the others?" I asked.

"All I know is that I'm supposed to get you," he yelled.

I took a few photographs and climbed aboard the helicopter. We arrived shortly at the foothills town of Salug, and I was directed to a ramshackle house where Lindbergh was sitting on the porch with Elizalde, who sported wrap-around dark glasses and had his feet propped up on a table as he sipped ice-cold soda. "How ya' doin', champ? Get some good pictures?" he called. "We got kind of tied up. Got to go south now. Want a Coke or anything?"

I just looked at him—feet up, yachting cap at a jaunty tilt, grinning under the big dark glasses. At first I was just surprised; then I got angry. I was to spend five days on the trip, three were already gone and I had seen Mampatilan with the Higa-onon for no more than a couple of minutes, had not seen Lindbergh with them at all, and now was staring at an indifferent Elizalde, sipping iced soda and smirking. The rain had prevented my making decent pictures of the Higa-onon, my clothes were never completely dry, I had slept rolled in newspapers, ate only baked roots and canned sardines, and had little to show for all the trouble. It was ridiculous.

I glanced at Elizalde, who made an amused remark about my bedraggled appearance, and sat glumly at the end of the porch, ruminating upon all the uncomplimentary things I had heard about him and adding more of my own.

Finally I said loudly to no one in particular that it had been a spectacular scene at the landing site—the ravine, the crowd of jubilant tribesmen—and with Lindbergh, Mampatilan, and Elizalde it would have made spectacular photographs, certain to be on front pages all over the world. "Chief returned to his people—Lone Eagle and Filipino humanitarian land in the mountains," I said. "Terrific!"

Brief silence. "Hm, really," Elizalde said, sitting up in his chair. "Big crowd, huh? Well . . . well . . . What do you think, Charles? Should we go in? Wanna go? We can't just stay a few hours, though, you know. We'd have to spend the night. Can't just pop in and pop out like politicians. If we go we have to stay awhile."

"Up to you, Manda," Lindbergh answered. "I'm always ready."

Elizalde had a muffled discussion with his aides and began shouting orders. People scurried in all directions, making ready to fly in to the mountains. I said I preferred to stay behind.

"You can't do that," Elizalde said. "This is what it's all about."

I said I'd already been there for three days and that was enough, thanks anyway.

"That's no way to be. You mad? We couldn't help it—got tied up in town, had to meet the mayor, all kinds of problems. C'mon, it'll be good this time, you'll see. You can't stay here anyway. When we leave, there won't be anybody here."

There was no choice really, so of course I agreed to go, planning to use every opportunity to expose Elizalde as a phony. A half hour later we were flying back to the cleared ridge, Elizalde having radioed Spileski to hold the crowd and Mampatilan there.

When Elizalde stepped from the chopper they mobbed him. After several minutes we began the one-hour hike to the settlement. It was a grueling trip—up and down over root-snarled ridges, steep slopes, sharp cliffs. Elizalde went first, picking his way along a narrow trail. Lindbergh, turning away assistance, carried his own bags and bent his seventy-year-old body to the job, once crawling on his hands and knees over a slippery, mushy log that bridged a deep crevasse.

At the settlement, people followed every step Elizalde took, hugging him, leaping on him. I watched closely for things to criticize. For two days he talked, lectured, joked, telling the mountain people to be proud of being Higa-onon, to work together, to be strong together. More than once, as his words were translated, several old men wept.

We ate off banana-leaf plates—roots and corn, and chunks of deer and pig roasted especially for him. We slept on the floor amid a tangle of thirty or forty people.

Then we hiked out, caught the helicopter, transferred to a logging truck in the foothills, and rode a couple of hours to a river. We crossed it in a beat-up launch and boarded a bus of the La Fortuna line that looked and sounded as if it were made of rusty soup cans.

The rickety machine clattered southward for the next thirteen hours. We reached a border town of South Cotabato Province about 1:00 A.M. and stopped at a dingy restaurant-nightclub, the only place open. The proprietor appeared, greeted Elizalde effusively, and woke up his staff. Within a few minutes two sleepy-eyed guitar players and a pianist were performing on a small stage illuminated with strings of blue and red

Christmas-tree lights; a cook shuffled into the kitchen; a waitress and bus-boy arrived rubbing their eyes; and word got around that a few "host-esses" would be available upstairs if any of the party were interested.

Our group now numbered more than twenty and most carried guns. Men with rifles maintained a watch outside and two inside followed Elizalde with their eyes wherever he went. He spent much of the time conferring privately with the proprietor at one of the tables. After a meal of fried chicken, rice, and warm Coca-Cola, we reboarded the bus.

The proprietor was an old and good friend of Elizalde's who had helped him and Panamin in times of trouble. In addition to owning the only res-taurant-nightclub in town, he also ran the only brothel, the main gas station, and was the mayor. He was tough and wild, probably had to be to deal with the problems of the frontier. "Some of the mayors and police chiefs around here are criminals wanted for crimes committed on other islands," Elizalde told me. "This area is the country's greatest source of hired killers and thugs. They export them all over the islands."

As we headed toward the Tboli settlement, which was named Kematu but always called simply Tboli, the mood inside the bus became tense. Elizalde shuttled the men around, issuing gruff commands like a novice infantry commander. Lindbergh stationed himself in a rear seat, fingering a Swiss submachine gun and peering out an open window. Elizalde was up front with a white-handled .45-caliber pistol and another submachine gun. Among the rest of the party—which included a squad of bodyguards headed by Felix Silvestre, Ching Rivero, Dr. Rebong, two cooks, a lawyer, and two men carrying dark briefcases—were at least ten M-16 automatic rifles, two M-14's, a grenade launcher, a rocket launcher, and assorted pistols.

All weapons were made ready as word circulated that we were ap-proaching the place in the road where a few weeks earlier a group of armed men had suddenly loomed up in the darkness. There were at least a hundred of them, Elizalde said. "It was an ambush all right, but maybe just to scare us. I really don't know why they didn't open up. Must've seen that we had plenty of guns, too."

Why did they want to attack him, I asked.

"Stick with us and you'll see," he said. "The Tboli refuse to be pushed around down here since Panamin arrived. They fight back now and the local guys don't like that. They're used to having their way with the tribes."

I remembered the rumors in Manila that the ambush was merely a minor confusion, perhaps even staged. I mentioned this several times, and, months later, Lindbergh wrote me his account:

"The facts of the ambush are as follows. Elizalde and his party often traveled from Davao to Tboli on a chartered bus. A considerable amount of fighting was going on in various areas of Mindanao, and as a matter of policy almost every man on the bus was equipped with either an automatic rifle or a submachine gun. The most dangerous area for Panamin was in the vicinity of the city of Surallah, where opposition to the organization was high, and where passage was often by night. A feud was going on between Elizalde and the mayor of Surallah. I heard rumors to the effect that a 50,000-peso-reward (then about $10,000) had been offered for Elizalde's death.

"On all bus trips in which I took part, shells were chambered and guns kept in hand as we approached the Surallah area. On the night of the ambush, I was sitting on the left side of the bus, armed with a 9-mm. Swiss HK submachine gun. On this night, the Panamin group was larger than usual, and we were in two buses. Elizalde and I were in the forward bus, he on the right-hand side. All windows were open.

"As we passed through Surallah, we noticed that the streets were unusually quiet. A few miles farther on, we came to a village and saw in front of us a truck drawn across the road to form a block. The night was dark. When we stopped close to the truck, we saw vaguely on each side of the road men armed with rifles, and we heard the rattle of gun bolts behind the figures we could see. (We were later informed that over a hundred men were at the ambush.) We were not only greatly outnumbered; we were excellent targets in the bus, although all interior lights had been turned off. Probably our greatest asset, in case shooting started, lay in the second bus, which was well armed, and which had stopped about fifty yards behind us.

"Obviously, the situation was tense, with fingers on triggers on both sides. After what seemed a long time—probably only a few seconds, though—our bus driver opened a door and a young member of the Philippines Constabulary, in uniform, jumped out with his automatic rifle into the nearby group of armed men. About the same time, the truck that had been blocking the road moved slowly off. Our bus driver then moved slowly forward. The second Panamin bus moved up and picked up the young Constabularyman. Thereafter, we drove on to Tboli.

"I am under the impression that the incident involved a 'show of force' on the part of the Surallah group, and that no shooting was intended. The main danger in a situation like this is that by accident or through excitement one gun may fire and trigger off shooting on both sides. Just one shot could have triggered a blood bath."

Memory of this incident must have been a large part of the reason for the high tension in the bus the night I made the trip. The vehicle ran with its lights off for several miles. Then a Jeep approached and stopped in front of us on the road. It had a .30-caliber machine gun mounted on its hood.

It was a government army unit based at the Tboli settlement that had driven out after a message that Elizalde was near had been relayed from the small border town. The Jeep drove ahead of us the rest of the way and the steaming old bus chugged into the Tboli settlement without incident about 3:00 A.M. Most occupants of the bus had fallen asleep, but Lindbergh maintained a constant watch out his window.

He and Elizalde spent the next day touring the Tboli project with tribesmen, and then Lindbergh suggested that he and Elizalde should arrange to have lunch with Surallah's mayor, José T. Sison. Ever since the ambush incident a few weeks earlier, Lindbergh had been worried about future danger to Elizalde. He felt that if the feud between him and the mayor continued, bloodshed would be the eventual result. In spite of the fact that the Panamin security organization was uneasy about the idea, the luncheon was arranged.

The mayor and his chief of police, both well armed, arrived in a truck at Tboli. During their discussions, Sison invited Lindbergh to visit his pig farm. Lindbergh climbed into a truck with the mayor, and later gave this report of the trip:

"As we passed through a village, I said: 'Mr. Mayor, is this where the ambush took place?' (We were on quite good terms by that time.) He looked at me seriously for a moment, then laughed and replied: 'No, but I'll show you where it was. It wasn't really an ambush.' (He didn't elaborate on that statement.)

"When we came to another village, he pulled the truck over to the side of the road and said: 'This is where it was. I was standing there' (pointing). I recognized the front of a building I had seen vaguely on the night of the ambush. The mayor had no idea I was aboard the front bus, and I didn't tell him that where he said he had been standing was almost exactly where I had planned on firing my submachine gun if shooting had started."

By this time, Panamin vehicles with Elizalde and guards had joined them, and all proceeded to the mayor's pig farm. It turned out to be an excellent farm. The mayor conducted a tour of the pens and stalls, and ordered that a pig be presented to Panamin at Tboli. Elizalde, in turn, invited the mayor to fly by Panamin helicopter the next day to Lake Sebu for a ceremony and reception.

"Obviously," Lindbergh recalled, "the mayor was hesitant about the invitation, and for reason. In the Lake Sebu area, 'Christian' settlers had been encroaching on lands that tribal groups considered to be theirs.*

---

* There were several ways for tribes to lose their land; one revolved around the frequent complaints of the Christian farmers and ranchers that their cows and water buffaloes were being stolen. Sometimes they were; sometimes they had merely wandered away from the grazing area and turned out not to be missing at all. Invariably, however, the "natives" in the hills were accused of cattle rustling, and

Fighting and house burning had recently taken place, with killing on both sides. Many Ubu and Tboli looked on the mayor as a deadly enemy. Except as a guest of Elizalde, it could have been extremely dangerous for the mayor to visit certain areas around Lake Sebu."

Lindbergh encouraged the mayor to make the visit and then stayed with him throughout. Eventually everyone relaxed, and in the beautiful setting at Lake Sebu the congenial mood gave hope of better Christian-tribal relations.

For a time, at least, better relations did result. At a ceremony in the mayor's office in Surallah a few days later, Lindbergh was made an honorary citizen and honorary chief of police of Surallah. Elizalde purchased several pigs from the mayor's farm for Tboli, and the mayor accepted a position on a Panamin committee that would deal with Christian-tribal relationships in the future.

From Lake Sebu, Mayor Sison returned to Surallah and the rest of us flew to Datal Tabayong, an Ubu settlement high on a ridge, home of Datu Ma Falen. Elizalde and Lindbergh were spending the night, but I had to return to Manila, and after an hour prepared to leave. Lindbergh stood on a hillside, waving as the chopper flew me away, his submachine gun (which he carried much of the time) slung on his shoulder. On his head was a cone-shaped papier-mâché hat presented as a gift by a crowd of tribesmen at Lake Sebu. He had grimaced slightly, then grinned and wore it uncomplainingly as I took photographs of him. This was especially amusing because he had remarked only two days earlier that he always had great sympathy for celebrities who got into situations in which they had to wear odd-looking hats.

Elizalde was off somewhere, surrounded by Ubu, enjoying himself. He had told me that he thought Lindbergh liked these trips because he could do what he wanted without constant bothering by people who never forgot he was *the* Charles Lindbergh.

Time had passed quickly since the party flew into the Higa-onon's mountains. I had then a strong impression that Elizalde had decided to go because I had talked of photographs making front pages around the world. But the Higa-onon visit was more than just show. He worked hard; he preached to the Higa-onon that if they hoped to survive against the encroaching modern world, they had to do it themselves—nobody could

---

armed gangs went after them. If any were caught, and not killed in the process, they often wound up in jail, virtually automatically, guilty or not. If the gangs failed to catch a suspect, they kept on hunting, battling whoever ᵃot in their way. There was loss of life and property on both sides. Lowland courts issued warrants for the arrest of tribesmen, making it impossible for them to go near their land without having to fight or be captured. Their families were harassed, the women often raped. Mai Tuan and his brothers were among those wanted on several warrants and were under indictment for murder. They had no choice but to fight or flee.—JN

do it for them. They had to be strong and proud of their heritage, but they also had to learn how to deal with the modern age—if they did not, they would be destroyed. He and Panamin would help them, if they wanted help, but Panamin would not, could not, tell them what to do. The Higa-onon must decide.

He took the same line with the Mansaka, the Blaan, and others who trooped into the Tboli settlement to see him.

Elizalde told me that these had been his major themes since starting work with the tribes. "Look, they'll be destroyed—they *are* being destroyed little by little every day—and it can't be stopped unless the people themselves want it to stop. The big difference between us and everybody else in this kind of work is that we don't *tell* people what they should do, we *ask* them what they want. Everywhere else people are telling minorities they should do this or do that, and they haven't the slightest goddamned idea what the minorities themselves want. That's ridiculous. It'll fail every time. We find out what they want and then try and help them get it."

It sounded fine. And, from what little I had seen, it looked fine. But how far did it go? The problems seemed difficult beyond measure.

And what about Elizalde himself? What was driving him? He was wealthy, could go anywhere, have or do almost anything—why was he charging around in the jungles? Was he poet, adventurer, philanthropist, eccentric playboy, publicity hound, humanitarian, power seeker? What? And there was that aloofness he occasionally slipped into—was it arrogance, or a defense? I discussed this with Lindbergh as we sipped steaming coffee one cool dawn among the Higa-onon. When I questioned Elizalde's motives, Lindbergh said, "Well, I guess I've been around quite a good deal over the years, and I've never seen anyone with the missionary zeal that Manda has, but without the missionary dogma—without the insistence that things be done a certain way.

"I think he's an extraordinary person. And I'll tell you, I think you've got to be very careful, *very careful* about looking into motives. Why does anyone do anything? If you ask too many questions about this you begin to be compelled to find an answer, produce one—whether it's the right one or not. But it's very rare that you can say accurately what is going on inside another person. I have my own ideas, of course, but I don't *know* what motivates Manda. And it doesn't really concern me much. What does concern me about a man is the kind of job he does. And I think he does an excellent job. Yes, I have no doubt, an excellent job."

That closed the discussion. I saw Elizalde a few times in ensuing months. Once, when I told him I wanted to do a children's book on the Ubu, he arranged for Panamin guides to help me reach their settlement. But he remained an enigma; I could not drop my curiosity about his motives and where all this was heading.

These, then, were some of my thoughts that evening more than a year later, July 19, 1971. The next day we were to fly to the Tasaday's forest. Much that went through my head was inconclusive, puzzling.

And just ahead was the biggest puzzle of all, the Tasaday.

3

The Reality of
the Tasaday

WE headed for the Tasaday about eight o'clock the next morning. It was gray and cool as the helicopter took off across the valley's open end, passed Tboli foothills, rose over a ridge bordering the great plain, and entered forested mountain country.

Here and there a house on a slope or peak was a speck of brown stuck into the green, like a rowboat on a choppy, dark sea. After flying half an hour over this rugged terrain we approached a broad stretch of rolling flatland, where some three dozen houses near a stream formed the main settlement of the Manubo Blit tribe.

Less than five hundred yards south of the houses the earth faded into a ravine, started out of it, and ran against the edge of a magnificent tropical rain forest. The jungle climbed a row of cone-shaped mountains, dropped behind them, climbed and dipped again, then rose steadily in waves of green, blue-green, black-green that undulated over mist-tipped peaks far into the distance.

The helicopter landed at the settlement, but only Christopher Lucas and I climbed off. Igna, the chubby woman translator who lived with the Blit, took a seat and the chopper flew toward the forest, disappearing behind intervening trees. Dafal had walked in a day earlier to bring the Tasaday to the forest's edge. About twenty minutes later the helicopter returned and picked up Lucas and me. The forest looked forbidding as we approached; wispy clouds floated in over the upland valleys.

Within two or three minutes of our departure from Blit the helicopter landed on the cleared tip of a knoll jutting out of the forest, let us off, and flew to Tboli to pick up Jack Reynolds, his crew, and the scientists, Fox and Peralta. Panamin's Dr. Rebong and others would follow. We eagerly scanned the landing site for the Tasaday, but saw only two lean, tan-skinned men sitting on a log beside Elizalde. He told us that most of the Tasaday had gone with Dafal back into the forest and we would meet them there—it would be a more realistic setting for us, and more comfortable for the Tasaday. We had already been cautioned to behave gently and not upset them. Elizalde asked us to wait for the next load of visitors so that we all could be guided in together. He then called to Mai, and they started down a trail past four lean-tos made of saplings and branches. The tan-skinned men on the log and at least two more people, who emerged from the shelters, hurried ahead of them into the forest. Apparently they were Tasaday, although there had been no chance to really look at them. They had averted their eyes and turned their bodies away during the brief time we had been there.

I was curious that Elizalde was going ahead like this. Why the change? When I asked Ching, he only shook his head and said he guessed the boss had plans. A muscular man in his thirties, with a crew cut and bullneck, Ching was rugged-looking but extremely charming when so inclined. He smiled warmly and said, "Well, don't worry. We'll all be in there soon. I'm sure everything is fine." He then changed the subject, but I continued to wonder why, if the Tasaday had been here just a few minutes ago, we were going into the forest.

About an hour later the helicopter arrived with Fox, Peralta, Reynolds, cameraman Lim Youn Choul, and soundman Detlev Arndt, and we followed guides into the jungle.

It was moist inside, humid. The light dimmed with the first few steps and grew steadily darker as we stumbled through tangles of rattan, bamboo, and vines. We edged between saplings and large oaks, slipped on the damp rug of dead leaves covering the mushy earth, tripped over ankle-high roots.

The thin trail—no trail at all, really—took us up and down slopes for about half an hour, and then along a mound that dipped and turned, leading finally to a stream, about six inches deep, that rippled and sparkled across a bed of rocks, pebbles, and sand. Sunlight streamed down in white-yellow shafts where the stream cut a path through the jungle foliage. The sky was visible in patches above the jigsaw edges of several layers of leaves.

We followed the stream around a bend and there, about fifty feet upstream, were the Tasaday. A few sat on a log beside Elizalde; others clustered around a fire that sent up long curls of blue-gray smoke. Two women with babies in their arms perched on rocks in the stream.

Their amber bodies were partly covered by shiny green leaves, which created an instant visual link with the forest. The men's leaves passed between their legs and were folded front and back into a vine encircling their waists. The women wore leafy skirts. The children were naked. All sat silently in and around the rippling water as sunlight sifted softly down upon them.

To turn that bend in the stream had been like having a curtain go up on a dazzling scene. I felt as if someone had unexpectedly poked me in the stomach—not hard enough to hurt, but enough to cause a sudden gasp for breath. When the surprise and delight subsided a bit, I began to wonder if Elizalde, who sat proudly, grandly, in the middle of the Tasaday, might have carefully selected this spot and arranged our introduction for maximum impact. It was too perfect.

We approached slowly and the Tasaday did not stir. When we reached Elizalde, I asked what had happened to their cloth. Several wore cloth in the photographs we had seen.

"We asked them this morning to dress like they used to before they met Dafal or us," Elizalde said. "And when we got down here a little while ago, this was it—leaves. They must have left the cloth scraps upstream somewhere."

The Tasaday hardly moved. They did not talk, just watched us. Some dropped their heads onto their arms. The admonition for us to be well behaved did not need restating; the mood was so still and the people so delicate-looking that we virtually whispered to one another as we stood near them. None of the Tasaday smiled, although when I caught the eye of any I would nod and smile, a reflex gesture on my part, perhaps silly in their eyes.

A woman appeared around a bend upstream, one child on her back with its hands clasped in front of her neck and a small infant cradled in her arms, nursing at her breast. In many years in Asia I had never seen such an arrangement. The woman waded toward us, then stopped about thirty feet away, squatted, and was still. The children stayed in position, so that in the shadowy light they looked like a strange monolithic sculpture of heads, arms, and legs. Then the child on her back slid off into the stream and a slender young man walked out of the forest and stood beside them. He dug pieces out of a large brown fruit or vegetable and handed chunks to the woman and children. They popped them into their mouths.

Four young boys sat on a fallen tree beside the fire, their arms and legs golden against the blackish bark. They stared at us. The dark eyes of one gazed more boldly than the others and his face was so finely formed we thought he was a girl—a mane of black hair fell below his shoulders and framed high cheekbones, large eyes, chiseled nose and chin. Later we learned he was Lobo, a boy of about ten or twelve.

Various Tasaday eventually stirred and walked about, disappearing up- or down-stream or into the thicket, apparently to get food. I counted at least twenty-two, but I may have missed some. There were always at least fifteen who squatted and watched as we took pictures and chatted among ourselves.

Suddenly, from a cluster of people, Fox shouted "My God! Look at this! Stone tools!" Fox's cheeks grew rosy above his white beard and his eyes widened as he fingered a stone the size and shape of a hen's egg bound with rattan laces to a six-inch-long wooden handle.

The Tasaday showed us three stone implements—the egg-shaped one, which Fox called a hammer ax; a long, flattish stone the size of a folded pocketknife with a protrusion on one edge that had been ground sharp, and also laced to a haft; and a flat flake the size of a man's thumbnail with a sharp-ground edge, which Fox called a scraper.

The Tasaday were asked to demonstrate the use of these tools; one of the men—Bilangan—picked up the stone with the protruding cutting edge. He palmed it so the cutting edge poked between his thumb and forefinger, the handle laying inside of his wrist. Stroking away from his body, Bilangan cut a piece of rattan held in his other hand. He rocked on his feet, which were planted among pebbles at the stream's edge, and his long flowing hair swayed rhythmically against his hips as he worked. He shaved off long strips of rattan, looking up from time to time, his lips compressed in a satisfied almost-smile.

Fox and Elizalde sat on the stream bank and talked, through interpreters Mai and Igna, with any willing Tasaday. Bilangan and a couple of others were willing, but most of the talking was done by a young man named Balayam. He had an expressive face and gestures and stayed close by Elizalde most of the time. Seven brass rings dangled from each of his ears.

Dr. Rebong asked Igna if any Tasaday had cuts, sores, or other ills that needed treatment. Igna inquired, and Balayam said he had a bad feeling in his stomach, which he rubbed in circles. Rebong pressed Balayam's belly and then listened to his chest with a stethoscope as the patient tucked in his chin and peered curiously down his nose at the doctor. Rebong gave him a pill and acted out how Balayam should open his mouth, put in the pill, and swallow.

Balayam studied the red pill, opened wide, and popped it in. But it wouldn't go down. He swallowed several times but the pill stuck in his throat and his eyes looked worried. He was advised to drink water. He snapped a leaf off a branch, swirled it into a cone cup, and scooped water from the brook. He drank, the pill remained stuck. He drank again, down went the pill with a gulp. Balayam waited a moment, knitted his brows, looked around at the group that had assembled, then nodded several times to indicate everything was fine. He climaxed it with a little yelp and smile.

By this time our eyes had become accustomed to the dim light and the shadows seemed to be in constant motion: butterflies, orange and purple and blue-black, with wings as big as playing cards, fluttered in the humid air; tiny insects flitted and flew and seemed to pop constantly on and off leaves and skin; the undergrowth was luxuriant with vines twined around tree trunks, leaves curled into other leaves, branches arched into shimmering green-yellow arbors.

The Tasaday maintained a timid wariness but did not seem frightened or excited. I was eager to get some idea of what was going on inside their minds and asked Mai. "How do they feel about what has happened to them the last few weeks? What are their feelings about all the new things and new people they have seen?"

Mai called Igna. They addressed Balayam, and, as the question passed from Mai to Igna and into Tasaday, a frown crinkled across Balayam's forehead. He put his fingertips to his cheek and blinked and held them there for several seconds before saying, in a soft, clear voice:

"It is like lightning." And then: "It has come to us without warning."

Balayam said no more and sat looking at us. For a moment the simple power and eloquence of his response befuddled me. I realized he had said in four words a stunning amount, more than I had expected—perhaps more than I wanted to know. I became aware of a nagging apprehension I could not identify, but I knew it had to do with guilt. What right had we, I, to inflict ourselves on these gentle people, peer at them, poke our cameras at them?

I had previously thought of the Tasaday with sympathy and concern, but these were rather vague, general responses. Until this morning they essentially had been anonymous objects of curiosity. This realization was unsettling: I, who was so suspicious of Elizalde's motives, had my own selfish interests. But, I assured myself, I had never claimed otherwise; reporting was my job. Besides, I intended no harm, would tread carefully, respect their sensibilities, seek truth, serve the public interest. . . . But as the Tasaday became people with names, faces, feelings, it all became more complicated.

None of this was clear in my mind at that very moment, but I was aware of a deepening response to them as fellow human beings. It was my first true sense of their vulnerability.

I intended to ask if the lightning was still striking, or had passed. But before I could phrase the question, a barely perceptible sound floated down—tap, tap, tap—as raindrops splattered onto the higher leaves. Then the sound was around us, upon us. Gently at first, then stronger and louder, until the sound and presence of water was everywhere. The air seemed alive with water. We sought cover under trees, ponchos, tarpaulins, jackets.

Water pelted leaves with a steady crackle. Water rose quickly in the stream, turned muddy brown, gushed over the rocks. Water streamed down tree trunks and poured from the creases of palm fronds. Water bent filmy ferns and saturated bushy plants. The ground became slick where it was hard, mushy where it was soft. Footprints became instant pools.

The raindrops felt cool, yet it was warm and heavy and steamy as we huddled under cover. We shuffled and shifted, trying to escape water down our necks. Shoes were soaked, and clothes stuck to flesh—if not wet from rain then from sweat.

The Tasaday had hardly moved. A balding, wrinkled old man who had been sitting on his heels didn't shift his feet an inch. He twisted his torso, stretched out a bony arm toward a stalk of wild banana tree, and pulled a five-foot-long leaf down over himself and his woman. Two Tasaday mothers with children joined them under this umbrella.

Another Tasaday man moved swiftly to a palm and tore off huge leaves, which he passed around. Bilangan joined several boys in the stream and squatted with them on a log under a leafy awning. Another man curled himself around his young child—the boy with strangely pale skin and running sores all over his body—and sat against the trunk of a tree. The motherless boy was mentioned in the Elizalde-Fox report as probably an albino with a mortal illness. His face was puffy, his eyes running with mucus; he was carried everywhere. There was no explanation for his condition.

The rain poured down for half an hour—the Tasaday sitting contentedly throughout and seeming settled for the whole day if necessary. Then the rain lessened and finally was gone; we could hear it moving away through the forest like a locomotive.

The Tasaday flipped off their leaf roofs and stretched. The bodies of several looked partly painted: elbows and knees that had stuck out into the rain gleamed where a film of dirt had been washed away. Wet streaks crossed chests and backs where a leaky leaf allowed water to dribble down.

The wetness seemed to call out even more insects, and the ground had become a marsh. Elizalde announced that we would return to the clearing. We slithered away lugging soaked bags. The return trip was more difficult because the rain had made the soft forest floor slick and it was uphill most of the way. I plodded ahead—when not slipping sideways or sliding backward. Hunched over, head down, I wrestled two camera bags, occasionally losing one of them or my eyeglasses when a springy branch snapped past.

The Tasaday zipped ahead, lifting their knees high, prancing up the sharpest inclines, gliding across the flat stretches. They twisted a shoulder here, a hip there, picking their way smoothly and swiftly through the jungle's tangles.

At one point, grappling with a camera bag that had wedged itself among branches of a fallen rotting tree, I became aware of feet trotting past me. I looked up from my labors and saw a Tasaday man springing, I mean *springing,* up the hillside, back straight, head high—and on his shoulders a child of about five. They were out of sight in seconds.

My sympathy for the Tasaday took a sudden downturn—toward self-preservation; *they* should worry about *me.* At the clearing I gaped at a couple of Tasaday teen-agers sitting contentedly on a log as I puffed and staggered in and flopped down my bags. They looked cool, as if they had merely strolled across a meadow, although I noticed blood rolling down one boy's calf and oozing from two spots on a man's ankles. Leeches. The Tasaday scratched them out with their fingernails and flicked them into the grass. Elizalde removed a leech from his leg by holding the glowing tip of a cigarette against it. The slimy sucker backed out and curled into a blood-gorged ball. In Elizalde's open palm it uncurled, raising the tip of its half-inch-long body and wavering to and fro like a tiny cobra.

It was much fresher in the clearing; after the forest interior it was as if the curtains and windows of a dark house had been opened to the air and light.

But the Tasaday did not find it so pleasant. Many squeezed into the lean-tos. Mai said they disliked the clearing because it was either too windy and cold, or too sunny and hot. The loud and unfamiliar noises that reached the knoll added to their discomfort. A few of the men stood hugging themselves. They seemed cautious and confused, their movements tentative and awkward. They jerked their heads around at strange sounds like illiterate arrivals in a strange country.

Raisins and a tin of ladyfingers were passed. The Tasaday reached out tentatively, as if a trap would snap across their knuckles. They nibbled at the cookies and one man suddenly wheeled and turned away. Mai said later that the man had vomited.

Balayam came forward rather confidently, however, and demonstrated the use of the hammer ax, pounding a chunk of palm to loosen edible pith from the bark. Pith and roots were supposedly their main staple foods. A man named Mahayag showed how they used the small scraper, smoothing a strip of bamboo that he held flat with his toes as he squatted.

By midafternoon NBC had filmed these and other activities and was interviewing Fox on camera when Elizalde advised that the Tasaday had gone through enough for one day. Reynolds and his crew had completed their work, and were excited about it. It was to be edited and given a script, and would then be shown in the United States. Fox and Peralta returned to the Tboli settlement that afternoon with Reynolds's team and Lucas.

Elizalde told the Tasaday that the rest of us would come back the next day, and we climbed aboard the helicopter for the Blit settlement. The Tasaday stared at us as we waved good-by.

It had been a physically and mentally tiring day. During the evening's relaxed conversation, I took advantage of the easy atmosphere to bring up to Elizalde my various doubts about him and Panamin. I said my general skepticism had been increased by the feeling that our meeting inside the forest had been set up—his sitting in the midst of the people at the stream and the switch from cloth loin coverings to leaves.

Grinning, Elizalde said there had been no gimmickry or staging intended; it was simply that the people did not like the clearing and he hoped that their introduction to newcomers would be more relaxed and pleasant in surroundings they preferred. The cloth had been eliminated because it was dirty and ragged, was not their traditional dress, and it looked terrible in photographs—which caused many people to think the Tasaday had a system of barter or traveled outside the forest. "The cloth contradicted much of what we were saying, things we knew to be true, but which the cloth made seem doubtful. But anyway, we didn't tell them to put on leaves or anything else. All we asked this morning was would they please dress the way they used to, the way their ancestors always dressed, before they met Dafal. And it was just as much a surprise to me as anyone to see them wearing the leaves that way. Of course, I thought it might be something like that, but didn't really know."

There was a pause and then Elizalde said, "So, you don't believe it? You think this is all some kind of trick or hoax?"

I said I really did not know what to think. The experience today had been fascinating and the people surely were extraordinary. But some aspects of their story were extremely difficult to believe, even if 100 per cent true; I cited my experiences with him as cause for skepticism—all the whispering and the air of suspense common to Panamin activities.

"Yeah, well, we've got a lot of things going on all the time, tough things. You think this is some kind of fun and games down here. We are always fighting somebody, usually crooked policemen or politicians or ranchers—we've got a lot of enemies. I've told you this before, but you just won't believe it. So we behave in some odd ways, I guess, that you so-called civilized people wouldn't understand."

Then I related in detail my version of the trip with Lindbergh; my being shoved on the chopper and put out of the way for three days; the return to the mountains, which, I emphasized, came only after I said the photos would bring a lot of publicity. Then there were the rumors of his mining interests and political ambitions. And capping everything was his invitation to me to join the first group to the Tasaday and then, after I had checked repeatedly and been assured of it, he had gone ahead with instructions that I was to come last.

He was wildly amused by all this, laughing almost constantly. When I finished, he said, "Well, what the hell, you're here, aren't you? What're you complaining about?"

"No particular thanks to you."

"Ah, well, maybe. But it seems you do okay. You got your stories—

better stuff on Lindbergh than anyone else has gotten—and now you're here, ahead of other reporters, which is a big thing to all you guys."

Ching arrived to say that dinner was ready, and we walked in the cooling dusk to the long house of Datu Dudim, the Blit leader, and ate roasted chicken and wild pig off bamboo skewers. The visitors included Ching, Mai, and Edith Terry, an anthropology student at Yale, whose family lived in the Philippines; she was working with Panamin during her summer vacation. Elizalde insisted I tell them the story about the trip with Lindbergh and him, reminding me whenever I left out anything and laughing harder than anyone.

We slept on the floor, jammed together with a dozen Blit adults, another dozen children, half a dozen mongrel dogs, and hordes of insects.

We flew to the clearing the next morning as soon as the helicopter arrived from Tboli, where it always stayed at night. The rest would come later: Peralta, Fox, and an American dentist friend of his, Dr. Norton Winters, who had his practice in Manila and was seriously interested in anthropology.

I wanted to find out the Tasaday's reactions to their new experience, beyond its being "like lightning." Elizalde agreed and soon after reaching the clearing we assembled near a lean-to in which at least six Tasaday nestled. Peering into the darkness, we could see only the balding old man, Kuletaw, and his gray-haired wife, Sekul, and a young woman with a nursing child, and two older children. Balayam came over, followed shortly by Bilangan, then Lobo and some other boys.

The following report takes only a few minutes to read but covered nearly two hours of conversation. Mai translated questions from English into Blit for Igna to translate into Tasaday. She said she was able to understand more than half of the Tasaday's words by this time, and occasionally could relay whole strings of sentences with seeming fluency. But sometimes our questions would bring no answers, only blank stares—not only from the Tasaday, but from Igna, too. Other times an answer came back to us with no relation to the question; then we all looked blank. I should note that Mai and Igna undoubtedly smoothed off the rough edges of the questions and answers—this is unavoidable. So, too, did I smooth out some of Mai's words as I took notes, but only in cases where I thought it would more clearly convey what he said. This accounts for the paraphrased, rather than directly quoted, information that occasionally appears.

Mai and I asked most of the questions, though Elizalde stayed nearby and put in a query or remark once in a while. It was extremely difficult at times, one of the hardest things being their apparent lack of certain ideas and concepts that we regarded as commonplace. Balayam was the most frequent respondent, the Tasaday spokesman in a sense, but often he would confer with Bilangan and a man named Udelen, or with some of the boys.

After amenities and small talk, the conversation began in earnest.

"You say that it is like lightning to see us and see our things, does that mean it is bad?"

Balayam: "It was before, but it is not now. It is all right now, it is good."

"Why is it good?"

"We know now that Momo Bong* is the good man our ancestors said would come to us. The things and people he brings to us must be good also."

Elizalde advised Mai to tell them that the reason all of us came was because the Tasaday were so beautiful.

Balayam responded seriously: "And we are happy to see so many coming to us. People coming with Momo Bong are good."

"What was this good man your ancestors spoke about supposed to do?"

"We didn't know. Just that he was coming and he was good. And he helps us . . . he gives knives to find food . . . other things . . ."

"But what did your ancestors tell you about this man?"

"They said we would always have to live in our forest and suffer [this word was uncertain; Elizalde insisted it was one of Igna's or Mai's] until the good man came to us."

"Why didn't you leave the forest?"

"We can't go out of our place."

"Why?"

"We love to stay in our forest. We like it there. It is a quiet place to sleep. It is warm. Not loud."

"But you could have come out if you had wanted to?"

"We never knew of a clear place like this. Everything we know is in our forest."

"You say you 'suffer' in the forest. What does that mean?"

"To gather roots, search for roots, the pith of trees. Look for food." (This suggested that suffer meant to toil or labor, but it was still not exact.)

"What did you think the first time you saw Dafal with metal knives, with cloth . . . all his things?"

"We were surprised there was another kind of people. We were afraid

---

* A name for Elizalde, learned from Igna, which at this stage they interchanged with Momo Dakel Diwata Tasaday. The latter, of uncertain origin, eventually became their only name for him. It was loosely translated as "big, or great, man-god of the Tasaday," which took *diwata* to mean "spirit" or "god," as in some Philippine dialects where it derives from the Sanskrit *devata*, "divine beings, divinity." Later, however, Elizalde insisted that *diwata* was a word of Dafal's or a translator's, not a Tasaday word.

of him and ran away. Dafal [whom the Tasaday called Da-isuk-lawa (small body), a name apparently given after seeing larger outsiders] kept following us and shouting 'I am good . . . I am good!' and finally our people stopped to see."

"But did you know of other people in the forest? Do you have enemies there, people you are afraid of in the forest, that you fight with?"

Balayam conferred with the others, then said, "We have never heard about such things from our ancestors."

"But there are other people in the forest?"

"The Sanduka. But we have not seen them for a long time."

"How long?"

"Very long."

"But how long is that?"

"Very, very long."

"Do you measure time in some way? Do you have a way of counting weeks, months, years, seasons?"

No reply. Confused, blank looks.

Pointing to a boy of perhaps three years: "Well, then, have you seen these Sanduka people since the birth of that child?"

"No."

"How long before his birth?"

"Long. Very long."

Back where we started on this. We decided to change the subject: "What is the most beautiful thing in the forest?"

"Finding *biking* [their root food]. You must dig deep to find it, and the deeper you dig the better the fruit." They usually dug with a stick, deer-horns, or their hands.

"What is the worst thing in the forest?"

"The big word is the worst thing. We are afraid of it. Our ancestors also were afraid."

This was puzzling. Mai, who could readily convert metaphorical language into common terms, smiled and said, without asking them, that the "big word" was thunder—the worst thing in the forest was thunder.

"What do you do when the big word comes?"

"We stay in our places and some of us put our hands on our ears."

"Where does this big word come from?"

"We don't know . . . we don't know."

"Do the Tasaday have any idea of a heaven or heavens?"

"We don't know about such a place."

"When Tasaday die, do their spirits [which Mai translated as "inside feelings"] go someplace?"

"We don't know of any place they go."

This exchange stalled on the matter of spirit and soul and seemed to confuse the Tasaday, so we changed the subject again: "What do you think of the helicopter?"

"The flying thing? That big bird? We were afraid, very afraid at first, but now we see that it is used by Momo Dakel Diwata Tasaday. He is good and his big bird must be good."

"Well, then, what do we [other people] look like to you?"

"You look good, too . . . but [a short conference] we would not like those black eyes [my dark glasses] you have."

"Do you like our food?"

"Uh . . . we like our food better."

"Do you want to go back to your place in the forest?"

"Oh, yes. Yes. We love our place. It is far inside the forest and there is a stream and we go all around and find food."

"Why is that such a good place?"

"It is our home! Where we have always lived. Our ancestors lived there. We were children there."

"And is anybody there now, right now?"

"No, everybody has come here. This is all of our people."

Elizalde, Fox, Dafal, and Mai had reported that the Tasaday had not expressed curiosity about us or the outside world (with one exception: Elizalde mentioned that following the earliest queries about enemies or trouble in the forest, Balayam asked about people in our world—were they not good?). So now we tried encouraging them to ask us questions.

"When we are gone, when Momo Dakel Diwata Tasaday is gone, do you talk among yourselves about all this, about all that has happened?"

"Yes, we do. And, when Momo Dakel Diwata Tasaday and his friends are gone, we feel sadness inside of us."

"Do you wonder about him, about us? Do you have any questions? Would you like to ask any questions?"

"We want to ask, but . . . we don't know . . . would it be all right?"

Assured that questions were welcome, Balayam went ahead. "Where do you come from? Where is the place you live?"

"A place called Manila."

"Is it far away?"

"Yes, very very far."

"And how do you go there?"

We discussed this before answering and decided it would be less confusing to say we traveled by air, because they had seen the helicopter, and not mention being on the water, because they supposedly had no knowledge of the sea or of boats. So Mai told them we traveled in a bird bigger than the one they had seen us come in, and that it passed high in the sky, beyond the clouds.

"Ohhh. . . ." They looked at one another. "But you do not die?" Balayam asked.

"No, because we have the special bird."

They became confused, and we were afraid that we had frightened them, so we rested a bit. Then someone asked the Tasaday if they had thought of going to our place—did they want to go?

"No. No. But we might like that later. Not now. We might sometime like to see where Momo Dakel Diwata Tasaday lives."

We remained silent for a minute or two, but the Tasaday did not ask any more questions.

"Is there anything else you would like to ask?" we finally prompted.

"Yes . . . We would like to know . . . but perhaps we should not ask . . . we do not know how to ask . . . It's about those things you have [pointing to clothes, shoes, cameras]. We don't know what to call them. What are their names? What are they?"

Elizalde, several feet away but listening intently to be sure the Tasaday were not upset or browbeaten, interrupted and said,"Be careful with this now. Watch what you say. Don't make them feel inferior or backward. Mai, you better tell them that we have special people who make these things for us—we ourselves can't do it. And then you better tell them that these things we have are not so important, but that people like the Tasaday are important. Yeah, tell them that the Tasaday are the most beautiful people we have ever seen. We couldn't live in their forest, aren't strong enough, not smart enough, but that they live there and are happy."

Mai and Igna translated this and Balayam quickly responded.

"Oh, yes, you could live in our forest. It may be hard *now,* but when you have lived there for some time it is not hard. Your legs become strong and you learn to walk like this." Balayam stood, swung his arms freely and lifted his knees high, strolling back and forth to demonstrate the proper walking technique in the forest.

Elizalde told Mai to have Dafal imitate that and then take a pratfall. Dafal did and the Tasaday roared with laughter, some until they had to hold their sides. It was the first time I had seen them laugh and their exuberance took me by surprise. It was hearty laughter from deep inside them, rich and free. Throughout this session the Tasaday showed interest, leaning on one another as they watched and listened, linking their arms and legs together, talking softly. They held small children in their arms, nuzzling them and cooing.

After the eruption of laughter, the Tasaday seemed to lose the desire to ask more questions and sat silently. A couple of boys and a man wandered off, as some had done from time to time during the conversation. Most stayed nearby.

"You say there are no unfriendly people in the forest," we asked Balayam, "but what about unfriendly animals?"

"Yes," he said. "There are those we are afraid of. Snakes . . ."

"What do you do about snakes?"

"We run."

"Has any Tasaday ever been bitten by a snake?"

"Yes," Balayam said with a troubled expression, "my mother. She died of the bite of a snake."

Balayam looked so sad and upset that we changed the subject: "Have the past few weeks changed your life?"

"We always want to stay in our place. The biggest surprise [or perhaps change] was in coming out of the forest to see this clearing. But we could not stay in a place like this for long."

Then Balayam used his fingers to indicate that five days would be the limit of their stay. "It is cold and windy here, not like inside our place where it is warm." (The use of his fingers and hand to count was not all clear to me. He pointed to his fingers and then bent his hand back from his wrist and swung it forward—meaning the sunrise and sunset, Mai said —and then he made some kind of measurement up his left arm with the spread between his right little finger and thumb.)

Recalling that Fox said they referred to the sun as "the eye of the day," I wondered if natural objects and phenomena had a special meaning for the Tasaday. The Ubu, for instance, would ask the spirit of the mountain to allow them to plant on the slopes and would assure the spirit they meant no harm and would use the land only temporarily.

"Do the Tasaday talk to the rocks and streams and mountains or other things in nature?"

Balayam and others looked puzzled, as if to say "What? Talk to rocks? Do *you* talk to rocks?" Of course, I did not know how the question had been translated to them, but Balayam indicated the answer was no.

"Well, then, what about the moon?" (The Ubu and Tboli had marvelous and exciting legends involving the moon. In one, the full moon was under attack and partly swallowed by a huge serpent, leaving visible only a yellow crescent. The Ubu banged on their plates to call the god of the sky who fought the serpent. The god eventually won and sliced the serpent to pieces with his long bolo, thereby freeing the moon, which was then whole again.) "Does the moon have any special meaning for the Tasaday?"

They seemed confused. None responded.

"Well, what do they think about the moon? Does it do anything?"

More confusion ensued and the question was repeated. Balayam finally said, "No, not that we know of. We didn't even know that thing stuck up there . . . until we came to this clearing."

We puzzled over this reply and checked Igna to be sure her translation was correct: "Did he say they didn't know the moon was up there? What does that mean? Can't they see the moon from the forest?"

Igna confirmed her translation and then passed on the new questions to Balayam. He said, "Inside the forest we can't see that thing's body. We can see the light from above the forest at night and our ancestors told us it was just the night brightness of the sky."

"Why that's ridiculous!" Elizalde blurted. "I don't believe it. We've known a lot of forest people and *nobody* ever said they hadn't seen the moon. Let's wait awhile and then ask them about it again, but ask in a different way. They probably didn't understand, or else the translation is screwed up somehow."

So we asked, "What about the bright light in the daytime? Do you see that in the forest? Do you see its body?"

"Oh yes. That is the sun [*fuglaon*]. We see that . . . and we wonder who owns it."

"Does that mean someone owns the forest?"

"Our ancestors said a person came to them in their sleep and said he was the owner and that our mountain is Tasaday mountain. He owned the mountain. He told that to our ancestors and they told us."

"Do the Tasaday worship dreams or people who come in dreams, like the owner of the mountain? Do they worship anything?"

Blank stares. The question seemed to confuse everyone, including Igna. Apparently a word for worship was causing the trouble; a suitable term in Blit could not be found. The Tasaday spoke together and Mai thought he heard words that might refer to something like a cave, but he could not make sense of it. We returned to the moon.

"Ask them," Elizalde said, "what shape the moon is."

Balayam made a circle with his thumb and forefinger.

"You see," Elizalde said, "he has seen the moon. It was just a mix-up."

We asked Balayam if the moon was always that shape. No reply. He looked frustrated and shook his head. Then he said, "But we don't know . . . we never saw it up there before. We didn't know that one sticks up there."

Elizalde shrugged. "I don't know. That's pretty hard to believe. But he's not lying, of course. Strange."

Someone suggested that perhaps the forest was so thick that unless the moon just happened to pass a crack in the foliage they might not see it.

"Yeah, well that's pretty farfetched," Elizalde said. "But, then, after the past few weeks, I guess that anything is possible—but we better not keep after them on this. They look worried about it already."

A few Tasaday had simple tattoos—X's and oval shapes. We asked if they symbolized anything. Bilangan said there was no particular meaning to them or reason for having them; some people did, others did not. He said he had watched his ancestors make tattoos with a substance taken from a tree (probably resin), which they mixed with something like ashes or soot and applied with a thorn. Bilangan said he had imitated this and made tattoos for those who wanted them.

Asked about earrings—not the brass hoops, which, we were told,

Dafal had brought, but their own—Bilangan said that they had learned to make them from their ancestors, too. The explanation was complex; all that we could make out was that a piece of rattan fruit was used to somehow pierce a hole in the ear lobe. "Dafal taught us to make many holes and brought the round shiny things," Bilangan said.

Dafal said later that he brought the metal hoops because the Tasaday had used berries to decorate their ears and he did not think they were attractive.

Among many other fragments of information gleaned from the questioning was that the Tasaday's ancestors had taught them to make stone tools and had been the source of all knowledge until Dafal came.

The arrival of the helicopter ended the session. Throughout it the Tasaday spoke softly and intently. The rhythm of their language varied smooth melodic passages with sharp staccato phrases, and the words themselves reflected that contrast—melodic in multisyllabic words like *selatal* (far) and *fuglaon* (sun); staccato as in *akun* (*I*) and *dakel* (big). The *a* sound was frequent and broad, as in dawn; thus Tasaday was pronounced Taw-saw-dai. The *l*'s, *k*'s, *d*'s, and *f*'s were pronounced firmly and sometimes had a hard edge. Emphasis frequently came on the second syllable, or so it sounded to me. The language was not musical but did have a pleasant flow.

Partly because of our inexpertness in asking the questions, but mostly because of the difficulty of going back and forth through three languages, particularly in regard to ideas or abstractions, many questions were rephrased or repeated. Much of this has been omitted as confusing and tediously repetitious. We had tried to keep our questioning on a conversational level, although we did verge on interrogation occasionally. Elizalde interrupted when he thought we pushed too hard or too far. We had much more to ask, of course, but the procedure was tiring and the Tasaday and Igna finally became restless.

The women huddled inside lean-tos with their children as the helicopter approached, but several of the men stood bravely in the open, watching the machine until the rotor's wind blast forced them to turn away.

The passengers were Fox, Peralta, Manuel Santiago, an artist of the National Museum, and Dr. Winters. Shortly after they arrived, a second helicopter brought in the National Geographic team; they had decided to film additional material on the Tasaday.

Pockets of activity developed around the clearing as a light rain fell, occasionally chasing all the Tasaday inside the lean-tos. Udelen was photographed making a monkey trap, Balayam using a stone tool, Lobo tending a small child. The scientists observed, took notes, asked questions.

The Tasaday were alert and watchful, but still looked uncomfortable and sometimes apprehensive, shivering and wrapping their arms about themselves. Some moved tentatively, a hint of fear in their eyes, and seemed like bright, sensitive children in a strange and forbidding garden. Others had the lost-immigrant look. I had an urge to put my arms around them when they stood close by, but decided not to, stopped by the feeling that they should make the first such move. Some visitors did try draping an arm across their shoulders to give a friendly hug, but the Tasaday invariably escaped, some dodging quickly, others edging away slowly. They did not react this way with Manda, Mai, or Dafal, but I noticed that they rarely put their hands on the Tasaday. So I restricted myself to nods and smiles, which I continued to consider a universally friendly gesture, but which brought only downcast eyes, blank stares, or, at best, barely discernible twitches at the corners of a few mouths.

After Balayam and Bilangan, the most outgoing Tasaday was the handsome Lobo. He scampered around the clearing, peeking curiously into this group or that. But he never smiled; if he became aware of strange eyes watching him, he frowned and withdrew, seeking the companionship of two or three other boys who looked his age, but whose hair was chopped shorter than his.

Some of the Tasaday trimmed their hair with metal knives because, apparently (the translation was confusing), long hair got tangled in branches and vines. The Tasaday hair types varied from straight and thick to soft and curly, almost frizzy when damp, to wavy and coarse, and was either dark brown or black except for the elders', which was steely gray. The fair-skinned child had straight, thin, straw-brown hair.

The men's faces were essentially hairless, although around the upper lip and chin of some were a few short whiskers. Presumably, those would be trimmed or plucked when they became longer.

Lobo crawled under a mound of branches and rotting leaves the size of a small car—its moist black innards must have teemed with insects—and emerged shaking bits of leaves from his mass of hair. He had set a snare for a mouse and was checking it. Empty.

Soon after this, Balayam began playing his bamboo jew's-harp and the scientists and film makers excitedly prepared to record his twanging music. But when they were ready, Peralta began to wonder aloud how the Tasaday had got such an instrument. True, the harp was known throughout the world, including many remote areas, but this one was made of lowland bamboo, which was found in country like this only if deliberately transplanted.

When Balayam was questioned, he said that Dafal had given it to him and had also taught him to play it. Dafal confirmed this. When he met them, he said, the Tasaday had no musical instrument.

"But why in hell didn't he tell us?" Elizalde said. "We've asked him over and over to tell us everything he gave them or taught them."

Mai translated and Dafal sighed. "I forgot," he said with a shrug that asked what possible difference it could make.

"We've got to talk with Dafal again," Elizalde said. "Every damned day we find something else of his we didn't know about."

Fox chuckled and commented that Dafal himself could be the subject of a major scientific study on how a single man had affected the life ways of an entire people.

By midafternoon most of the Tasaday men had joined the women inside the shelters. From one lean-to came the sporadic growling of a dog I had not yet seen; it stayed in a corner, behind an old woman. A young woman sat near the entrance, chewing betel nut as her chubby baby tugged and sucked at her breasts. He interrupted himself occasionally to fondle the only visible toy, a small monkey skull.

The mother and son were smudged with ashes and dirt. The child had skin sores—insect bites and infected scratches—but otherwise looked healthy. The mother looked healthy, too, and was rather handsome—except for her teeth, which were filed and stained red from betel-nut chew, droplets of which had dribbled down the front of her body. The woman, Dul, sat with quiet dignity, never looking directly at me as I snapped photographs. She switched the child from one breast to the other and then matter-of-factly spat a large red glob of betel chew near my feet. I thought this might have been a hostile gesture, but Dul did nothing else to support that; she continued to sit there, with watchful eyes, occasionally cooing to her baby, who was content with the monkey skull and breasts and paid me no attention.

Elizalde shouted that it was time to leave. He was going to Blit; the rest of us would go to Tboli, and I had to return to Manila. My time with the Tasaday was ended.

Note taking and photographing had kept me so busy that I had not thought about leaving; nor had I pondered deeply the experience of the past two days. But now it hit with unexpected force.

I was excited at having the story and eager to report it, yet I did not want to go. Many feelings rushed over me at once—joy and sorrow, excitement, frustration, anxiety, puzzlement, wonder—feelings I could not sort out.

Exhilaration was dominant, but the other sensations tried to drag it down. They did. I was aware of knowing more about the Tasaday in one sense, but also of knowing less because unanswered questions were no longer merely theoretical; they involved events and people now real to me. And I had so many *more* questions now.

All my thoughts were infused with a haunting, awesome sense of the people, the Tasaday. What was it? Their mystery? Their purity? Strangeness? Delicacy? Their kinship with the forest? Extraordinary as it was, I believed them—at least I wanted to—when they said they had never been outside the forest, that it was their world, their universe since their knowledge of time began. How could an outsider comprehend what that forest meant to them? Impossible. They were part of it; it was part of them. And now with their discovery of a world beyond the forest—of people and plains . . . wheels . . . shoes . . . helicopters!—what unimaginable, staggering thoughts must be going through their heads. Astonishment beyond measure. "Like lightning," Balayam had said. Yes, it must have been—like fantastic lightning.

If they had been dull and stupid, their experience would have been frightening enough, but obviously they were sensitive, intelligent, loving, gentle people. Enormously vulnerable. What defenses had they against modern man? Against us? They had the forest, but loggers were reportedly on the way—the Tasaday's sanctuary could be destroyed, perhaps them with it. And if not loggers, then people like me, probing, seeking, challenging. What would happen to them?

And could they truly be considered as living in the Stone Age? They contrasted sharply with the popular vision of Stone Age man, hulking and grunting, crude and dull. How long had they really been in that forest? How did they live?—we really had not seen that. And why were they there in the first place? Why were there so few? What about the other groups? How many were there?

Was all this true—was the Tasaday's simple beauty, their mysterious purity true? It seemed so, but what did we *know*? How much of this was my romanticizing? Was it really mysterious or did ignorance merely make it seem so?

I knew that just beyond the brink of emotional awe was thought more rational—skepticism again?—waiting for its chance. It would seek to put all this in perspective, to make it more believable, less dreamy. It would argue that I had seen the Tasaday only briefly, a glimpse of players on an exotic stage. Reason would insist that they were, after all, human beings with hate and love and jealousy and competition and curiosity. They could not be as innocent as they seemed.

I would struggle to find balance, to settle on a comfortable truth. But it would be impossible to know. One could only report what he saw and heard and felt, and leave conclusions out. Keep the door open for later knowledge to lead wherever it would.

A chill rain began to fall and mist and clouds settled into the plain beside the forest. The helicopter had to leave immediately to make Tboli before dark. Elizalde and his party went to Blit, and then Bart and Ching navigated the rest of us brilliantly through heavy wet clouds, slipping between half-hidden peaks as gusts buffeted the machine and water washed in tiny waves over the curving plexiglass windshield.

The excitement of the flight had distracted us from the Tasaday, but, safe on the ground at Tboli, they again pushed all else out of mind. On the staff-house porch, an artist from the National Museum put finishing strokes to sketches of their stone tools. Winters, staying another day with Fox, was anxious to inspect the Tasaday's teeth and, with Dr. Rebong, make other physical examinations. Fox and I talked for hours.

He and Elizalde had been involved in many activities for several years, from the excavation of ancient pottery to the preservation of ancient life ways. They seemed to have a solid working relationship and mutual understanding that had seen them through varied and occasionally difficult times.

Fox was exuberant about the Tasaday and talked repeatedly about their stone implements. Peralta, involved with a study of Paleolithic stone-flake tools found in Philippine caves, said he was amazed that the Tasaday were using them. "I had some doubts before I came here," said the slim, bespectacled scientist. "But I see now that these are authentic— no question of it!"

They both described the scraper as the basic tool in the Tasaday's "technological kit." The example we saw was of opalized quartz, 21 mm. by 14 mm., and had a high-angled working edge. Fox said it was used to scrape and shape bamboo into knives, projectile tips, piercing implements, and so on, and added that the only known historical reference to scrapers being used in the Philippines was by an Italian scientist, Giovanni Camelli Careri, who visited the islands during a world tour between 1693 and 1697. Careri wrote that Negritos of the northern Philippines used scraperlike stones as arrowheads.

"These tools are simply incredible," Fox moaned, with a shake of his head. "Every time I see that edge-ground scraper I want to faint. Fascinating. You see, the scraper is so fundamental that without it man could not survive. It's the primary tool for working bamboo or any wood. We've found thousands in Philippine Paleolithic sites, tens of thousands of years old—but this is the first scraper ever discovered here actually *in use*."* He added that the scraper dated from the beginning of the Neolithic period, usually appearing at the end of the Paleolithic. I realized that we were probably about to launch into scientific waters out of my depth, so I asked the significance of all this to the layman.

"What does all this mean?" Fox repeated. "Oh, God . . . who knows at this point. We've got a couple of years of research here."

I pressed him, though, for his specific reactions at the moment.

He began by pointing out that the acquisition of sample tools could add measurably to the study of man's reaction to his environmental needs. The Tasaday tool kit included thorns, pebbles, and cobble from the

* Unfortunately the scraper was lost, not accounted for after this visit. The other two stone tools of the Tasaday—the long, flat, hafted stone with the sharp-ground protruding edge and the egg-shaped hammer ax—were presented by Panamin to Imelda Marcos, the President's wife, who had long supported Panamin work, to be used in cultural exhibits.

stream bed, which they used in making bark cloth. Stone was used by many cultural-minority peoples to file and chip their teeth; the idea was to improve their appearance by making their teeth unlike the sharp white fangs of animals. The use of the nut of the betel palm was widespread and ancient also—it was thought to combat intestinal worms and assuage hunger pangs; containers for the lime that was mixed with the chewable preparation dated back more than four thousand years.

But such data accounted for only part of Fox's excitement. He said that even the little learned so far raised questions about the traditional concepts of the stages of man's cultural development. He had obviously thought about this matter for some time. It was technically correct to speak of the Tasaday as having a Stone Age culture, Fox asserted, but still they did not fit the classic description of Stone Age, Metal Age, or whatever titles were used. Such terms described cultural history, but they relied on the types of materials or tools people used, and "this ignores such criteria as the absence or presence of agriculture, for instance, which may be much more significant in describing man's development." He indicated that there were increasing scientific challenges being made to those long-established classifications, but that more research was required.

If the Tasaday could truly be said to have a Stone Age culture, then they were certainly a formidable challenge indeed to one popular notion: the comic-strip concept of Stone Age man. Scientists perhaps knew better; but for many laymen Stone Age man was that muscle-bound, hairy creature with apelike arms and a lantern jaw who lumbered around, grunting and smashing his women over the head with a club. The Tasaday were not like that; they were gentle and loving, innocent.

4

Withdrawal Symptoms

BACK in Manila certain aspects of the visit with the Tasaday gained clarity, became even more vivid in memory than in reality—their slender soot-smudged bodies and shy eyes, timid but bright; their awkward discomfort outside the forest and confident fluid grace within; and the forest itself, unknown and menacing to a stranger, but to them home.

The Tasaday's vulnerability loomed greater than ever. Despite having apparently overcome some fears of the outside world, they had no knowledge of the real dangers it posed.

My doubts that they were an extraordinary people had faded, but I did not know, nor did anyone, the extent of their significance. Mysteries remained, questions multiplied, curiosity intensified. Hindsight kept reminding me that I had had only a glimpse of the Tasaday. But it was unforgettable. Would there be another?

What would Elizalde do? He had been friendly and accessible during the visit; after I had confronted him with criticism of his behavior about the Higa-onon visit he was not upset or embarrassed but delighted, asking me to tell the story to others. Had I misread him in the first place? I also now detected his genuine concern and affection for the Tasaday, and they for him. The nature of their special regard was unclear, however; did they truly consider him some kind of god? The fulfillment of a messianic legend? This had disturbing portents.

Also potentially disturbing was the number of visitors the Tasaday were receiving. Three days after the National Geographic and NBC teams, Fox, and I had left, more than a dozen local reporters and photographers, a few foreign newsmen, and at least two more scientists had visited. After they left, Elizalde stayed two or three more days, then returned to Manila, where aides presented him the beginnings of what would become a small mountain of news clippings and letters. Most of the latter were from Europe and the United States, and expressed concern about the Tasaday, urging that they be protected; some said they should be left alone completely, by everyone, including Panamin and Elizalde.

Near the end of July, I telephoned Dr. Winters and asked about his experience with the Tasaday after I had gone. Winters, an outgoing man about fifty, related how he had looked first into Elizalde's mouth to show the Tasaday that the examination would not be harmful. But "they were a little reluctant, so I didn't get to examine many teeth . . . they seemed pretty scared."

In three of the men he found all their teeth had a filmy coating of plaque but no cavities. Two had virtually perfect teeth; the third man, who, Winters estimated, was in his early forties, was missing five and several others were loose. All the men had filed teeth—some to the gumline —apparently done with sandstone, and the enamel had been blackened with pitch or charcoal.

"The biggest surprise, though, was that lack of cavities—not a single one. Even a guy with gum disease had no cavities," Winters said, adding that the Tboli and other tribes had plenty of cavities. The Tasaday's diet of raw vegetables and the lack of sugars may have accounted for the difference, he said, noting also that the betel nut the Tasaday chewed might protect enamel. Winters again mentioned the terrific amount of plaque and salivary calculi, and said he suspected the Tasaday also had some abcesses, and that it "would be interesting to take in a portable X ray. There really wasn't enough time, so I'll go down again and check in more detail. I decided not to press it this last visit, it was too hectic."

I wondered if Elizalde and Fox, who was reportedly at work on a revised data report that would include a detailed research plan, would permit such things as X rays.

Meanwhile, an article was published in the newsletter of the Institute of Philippine Culture (IPC) by Professors Frank Lynch and Teodoro Llamzon, who had been in the most recent party of visitors to see the Tasaday. Lynch, an American Jesuit and project director of the IPC, was a professor of anthropology at Ateneo University, one of the Philippines' most prestigious schools, and held a doctorate in anthropology from the University of Chicago, as did Robert Fox and several other scholars in the Philippines. Llamzon, a Filipino priest, was professor of linguistics at Ateneo.

The article made clear that the authors were impressed by the Tasaday, although they qualified their data as "extremely tentative." They were more cautious in some aspects than Elizalde and Fox had been in their report, pointing out that the poverty of information about the Tasaday was at least partly due to the fact that it had been gained not from "lengthy participant observation, but from the answers to questions asked during limited contact with the Tasaday, away from their usual habitat." They hoped that future meetings would be "less artificial," more leisurely, and inside the forest, where the Tasaday were more comfortable.

Lynch and Llamzon pointed out that despite great cultural differences between the Tasaday and the Blit, remarkable likenesses suggested a common ancestry: "Most obvious, perhaps, is their physical similarity, for the Tasaday and the Blit seem to have approximately the same nature, skin color, eye form, and straight-to-wavy hair. Take away a Tasaday's shyness, clothe him as a Blit and he could pass for one in a crowd." They believed that the Blit also provided a clue to the duration of the Tasaday's isolation: prelminary data indicated that the Blit and Tasaday shared about 82 per cent of words for non-cultural items. This approximately 20 per-cent loss of shared words would, under Robert Lee's widely used statistical formula, suggest that the split between the common ancestors of the two groups occurred somewhere between seven hundred and nine hundred years ago.

Speculating on the Tasaday's lack of agriculture, Lynch and Llamzon felt that it was unlikely the Tasaday's ancestors knew how to plant and then forgot it, but, rather, that they never knew it. The same applied to the use of bows and arrows and of iron. They conjectured that a vast area surrounding the Tasaday's present homeland was once populated by forest people like the Tasaday, and, as outsiders moved in with iron and agriculture, some of these people became acculturated and others retreated into the rougher, higher terrain. Lynch and Llamzon concluded that "the Tasaday may well emerge as one of the few known groups in the world who live purely by means of a hunting-and-gathering economy."

Portions of this report later appeared in a Philippine academic quarterly magazine along with an article written by an outspoken Filipino historian, Z. A. Salazar, who also held degrees in social sciences and linguistics. The article was critical of the research on the Tasaday, of Elizalde, Fox, and the news media for a "spate of sensational newspaper reports." He was skeptical about claims being made, insisting that the linguistic data was superficial, and that all data would remain inadequate until a scholar learned the Tasaday language.

Some social scientists were upset that a Filipino anthropologist was not in charge of the research. And there was the inevitable criticism of Elizalde—that he stage-managed the whole affair, perhaps planning to run in congressional elections in November, and that had led to too much publicity about the discovery, too many newsmen bothering the Tasaday, too much of a circus atmosphere. A few scientists said no newsmen should have been allowed; scientists should be free to conduct research without reporters and publicity.

I did not want a circus atmosphere either, and I recognized the researchers' desire to work in peace—but, of course, I did not agree that *no* newsmen should be allowed.

In late July, 1971, the Associated Press headquarters in New York asked me to investigate the possibility of a book being done on the Tasaday, and so I began to pull together as much information as possible. Although Panamin granted me access to its files, there was little recorded of the first meetings with the Tasaday, and some of that was contradictory. For instance, the Elizalde-Fox report said that Elizalde's first contact with the Tasaday had been June 7, but other data indicated that it had been a few days earlier; and there was uncertainty about the number of subsequent visits, how long they lasted, and on what dates they occurred.

Hopeful of learning what was ahead for the Tasaday and of discussing the possibility of the AP book, I went to Elizalde's house the evening of July 27. Several visitors were around the sleek table in the big living room. Elizalde, asking as many questions as he was answering, seemed uncertain about the next steps. Someone suggested bringing in an internationally recognized scientific organization, museum, or university; another said Panamin should try to get a spread in a major magazine like *Life*. The general criticism was that there had been too much publicity already, too many newsmen, photographers, and scientists gathering bits and pieces of data without over-all direction.

Elizalde admitted that the large group of news reporters had been disturbing. A few had been excellent, he said, but several reporters had no idea of the Tasaday's significance and merely viewed them as oddities. He said two local women society-page reporters had worn spike heels and cocktail-party pants suits. "It was ridiculous. We walked a ways into the jungle and you wouldn't have believed it. Those two stumbled all over the place. And some others just gawked at the Tasaday, giggled, asked stupid questions. How did I know it would be like that? Ah, well, the stupid ones were anxious to leave, so we got them out of there in a few hours and the Tasaday couldn't have been too upset."

After a couple of hours everyone had left except me and the regular occupants of the house. Maids flitted around; youngsters scurried in and out of the TV room; an occasional tribesman passed through. Elizalde's own three children gave him a kiss and a hug before being led upstairs to bed.

Although it was after ten o'clock, the temperature was near 80 degrees. The air was damp, humid. Elizalde ordered another iced tea for himself, Scotch and water for me. He was wound up by this time, and started to talk—by turns in anger, enthusiasm, defensiveness.

"Okay, okay," he said when I remarked that some of the criticism seemed valid to me. "Sure. It probably would have been better to have completed more scientific study, but that could take more than a year. The logging roads could be in that forest before then. And how could we expect the government to declare the forest a preserve unless it was established that a special people were really there? So now we've got to go into the forest and spot their particular area on a map. That forest is absolutely unbroken jungle—the thickest I've ever seen. From the air you can't spot a thing. We can't ask that whole damned forest to be made a reserve. Lumber companies already have claims on all of it.

"And remember, we didn't rush in there, as some people are saying. We had known of them for about eighteen months—since we first met Dafal. And the reason we went in at all was the logging roads. One gigantic ridge has a road coming straight over it . . . that has happened in just the past three weeks! That ridge overlooks the beginning of the Tasaday forest. I'm telling you, the settlers who come in with the roads are tough sons-of-bitches. They'll chew up the tribes, chase them right back into the Tasaday's forest. That one road alone coming over the ridge justifies everything we have done. It's heading straight for the Tasaday."

He slumped back in his chair and puffed on a mentholated cigarette. "As far as I'm concerned the best thing would have been to leave the Tasaday alone . . . leave them alone altogether," he said.

Did he really mean that? Why then did he invite so much publicity?

Perhaps there had been too much, Manda said. He did not object to publicity; funds could not be raised without it, nor could the public appreciate, or even know about, the plight of the tribes. "But publicity was not the reason for meeting the Tasaday, and we are not going to let this become a carnival sideshow. Whatever we do, the Tasaday will come first. We've got an obligation to them, to protect them—just read all the letters we're getting that support us—and that is more important than anything else, including science."

What about science?

"Yeah, well, we've got to round things off with a scientific team, but I'm not exactly in favor of that. Of course, without it we'll just get more criticism, but we'll get that anyway. The scientists who have seen the Tasaday have different and guarded opinions, conservative. Okay, that's the way they think they have to be. I guess we need to form some kind of scientific board to establish a good program."

He stopped talking long enough to call for a glass of iced soda, then resumed talking with the announcement that present plans called for entering the Tasaday's forest about mid-August. The mistakes that had been made in dealing with the Tasaday, he said, were not disastrous mistakes. "Our major job in studying them is not to disturb them or hurt them. But we've still got to go into their forest, where they live."

He stopped and leaned forward, smiling confidentially. "And I'll tell you something else. Foisie [Jack Foisie of the Los Angeles *Times*] got me to really thinking about that place of theirs. Foisie's sharp—he kept asking about that valley. So, after the reporters left, I started talking with the Tasaday . . . it must be an incredible place, beautiful. They say it is a one-day walk for them, and that probably means at least three days for us—*if* we can make it. Let's face it, they can do things in that forest we could never do. Anyway, somewhere in the forest is a valley that is so isolated no outsider has ever been there. Not even Dafal. They say water flows down the mountain and their place is way down; you have to climb down vines and roots to reach it. They have shelters in ledges—sandstone, apparently—and in the roots of those tall trees with the buttressed roots. There are no huts or lean-tos—Dafal showed them how to make lean-tos. Can you imagine that place? Like some kind of Garden of Eden . . . Jesus! It must be incredible!

"But if we aren't careful, they are going to get one helluva terrible shock from our world. They might run away, disappear. And do you think we could find them in that forest if they didn't want us to? Not a chance."

We talked about the danger of upsetting or frightening the Tasaday.

"Oh, that reminds me," Manda said. "After all the newsmen and scientists left last time, the Tasaday told me they were terrified of something. Mai, Igna, all of us, tried to figure out what it was. They said they didn't like 'that little black man.' Mai asked them who they meant and they made a small shape with their hands and said, 'That one who takes the voice of the Tasaday.' "

Elizalde paused to let that sink in, but before I could say anything he exclaimed, "A tape recorder! Somebody apparently played it for them as a joke or something. Some people are just stupid. I don't care if they are scientists or journalists or what they are."

This kind of behavior was a continual problem in dealing with tribal groups. "Some people are crude," he said, "poking around and prying, asking questions about anything, everything . . . about their sex lives . . . and then giggling and smirking. Really. I mean there are tribes we have gone back to see years later and they still have unhappy memories of how somebody we had brought in measured their heads and all that stuff."

He said the Tasaday had been troubled by the dentist on the most recent visit. "They were really upset. All that poking around in their mouths. We had to stop it after two or three. They told Mai that they just wouldn't stay around for that; they were going to run into the forest. So you can't have that kind of stuff. But if I say no, then I'm the bastard and everyone says I'm un-co-operative. Aw, what the hell, they're going to say that anyway. I don't give a damn. I've told some scientists so and they don't like it, of course."

I said I thought he and Fox got along very well.

"Yeah, well, Fox is different. We've been together a long time on this and that. But still, you know, he's a scientist. . . ."

It was well after midnight by now. I was getting weary, but Manda was going strong.

"Listen. These are incredible people. We can learn from them. They are simple, absolutely honest people who have found a way to live happily in their environment . . . no greed, no selfishness. Everyone goes around talking about people being bad because that's human nature. Well, I say that is crap. When you see these people, you have got to say, 'No, man is not basically evil.' At Harvard, for instance, I never heard it said that man was basically good. No. Man has always had to prove that he was good, had to overcome sin or find lost goodness or something. But the Tasaday—good. There's no greed. They share everything. If everybody doesn't eat they aren't happy. If some eat and others don't they are not happy. That's true!"

I admitted that although it sounded impressive, I rejected the Garden of Eden idea as too romantic a conclusion, drawn without seeing the people over a long period of time or even once in their own place. Furthermore, there were too few of them to justify making conclusions about human nature in general that were based on their behavior. And they were human beings, after all, so how could they talk about good and not have a concept of bad? How could there be one without the other?

"If you mean do they have a sense of good and evil," Manda said, "we don't know. But we do know that when we asked them if they had enemies—if they killed people, and so on—they didn't understand. We tried and couldn't find words to get the idea across. Then it hit us: *These people don't know what we are talking about. They don't know about killing, murder, war! Never heard of them.* Do you realize what that means?"

I agreed that this sounded marvelous, but there was so much that was not known. Furthermore, with all the difficulties with the language, they simply might not have understood the words being used; maybe they had different words for killing?

"That's the trouble with you. You're a goddamned unbeliever. You have to pick and poke and screw around with being intellectually critical and all that. Everything has to be proved to you, and then you're probably wrong anyway. I am telling you that the Tasaday do not know about war or killing or things like that. Just look at them! Look! Can't you see? I've never encountered such a thing and we've been running around the mountains a long time and have seen some pretty far-out people. I tell you, if the Tasaday say it has been like lightning for them to meet us, then it has been like lightning for *us* to meet them. All the other people we've met have had problems, problems because they've had contact with the outside world, but not these people. For the first time we have a chance to stop trouble before it starts. And that is really something."

But what about their women, I asked, citing a reference in his and Fox's report about bride stealing, which would suggest they did have problems with other people.

"That was wrong. We were completely wrong about that. They simply wouldn't steal women. They don't even kill animals, or at least they didn't used to. I bet if they met a deer in the forest they would just say, 'Hello, deer,' or something like that, and go along their way. And this palm pith they were supposed to have gotten. Naw. They told me that Dafal taught them to get that, after they got metal. And this was very important because they had to go out in groups to get it, mash it, and so on. But their main food is, or was, roots—the sort of thing a guy can go out alone and get by himself."

But. . . .

"I know our first report said they got pith. But that was wrong. Look, that was my fault and also the scientists. It's hard to tell most scientists anything. They've got preconceived ideas. But if you want to learn anything, you have got to listen and look and stop trying to fit the people into a niche. If we would just stop thinking and theorizing and talking so much ourselves, we could learn from these people. Just sit, watch; be quiet with them. I saw a Tasaday guy climb a tree—no, he didn't climb it, he *ran* up it—then he leaped to another tree, slid down on a vine to the ground, and was off. Mountain people never use vines that way— that's for Tarzan movies—they're afraid the vine will break or the whole top of the tree, or a branch will crash down on their heads. But the Tasaday *know,* by instinct or by the first feel, which vine is okay and which one isn't."

We were interrupted when a telephone call to the U.S. that Manda had placed earlier came through. He spent about twenty minutes talking to Dr. Harold Conklin, the head of Yale University's anthropology department and author of major studies of Philippine groups. Elizalde had wanted to confer with him about the Tasaday. Afterward, Manda reported that Conklin thought the Tasaday were important, but that he could not get involved because he had too many projects already. "I told him our problems and that the people come before science," Manda said, "and his reply was to 'do your thing . . . protect them . . . no exhibitions . . . no roadshows.' Okay. That's right. We've taken on the burden and we can do it."

It was approaching 2:00 A.M., but I couldn't leave without getting onto the subject of Manda's using the Tasaday for publicity in preparation for entering politics.

He denied it, not without muttering a string of obscenities. I reminded him that months earlier he had acknowledged that associates were advising him to get into politics, and that his name was being mentioned in the news as a senatorial candidate.

He replied that he was too busy, especially since the discovery of the Tasaday, to even think about politics. But he admitted that the pressure for him to run was increasing. Then he asked what I thought about it. I said it would be a mistake for him to enter politics, adding, only half-jokingly, that I was having enough trouble trying to figure out what he was up to already and politics would only complicate matters.

I left soon after that, and Elizalde saw me to the door.

"You really are a suspicious guy, aren't you?" he said, with a half smile. "Really suspicious."

On my way home, I found myself musing on the subject of Philippine politics. As in many countries, it was the national pastime. Filipinos boasted that theirs was the freest and most open government in Asia, and every two years they set about their national election campaigns—complete with vote buying, massive spending, coercion—to prove it.

Those who were particularly concerned that Elizalde not run probably sensed that one particular aspect of politics—rising to stardom, as in athletics or show business—might be tempting for a personality like his. Then, too, there was the familiar danger of the candidate's becoming the servant of private, rather than public, interest. Often the people already on top in this land of few rich and many poor maintained their extraordinary privilege and power through intimate ties with politicians.

A day or two after my long conversation with Elizalde, Oscar Trinidad telephoned to report that Manda hoped to enter the forest in about two weeks to pinpoint the Tasaday's home, and that I would be invited.

On August 2 news reports said Elizalde had definitely been nominated as one of eight senatorial candidates of President Marcos's Nacionalista party. I phoned Trinidad and he said blandly that it was true; Manda had been "drafted" by the party. He then read a prepared statement to the effect that Elizalde had acceded to the demands of the people and would seek to provide congressional representation for the millions of have-nots in the country, just as he had been a voice for the downtrodden tribal minorities, et cetera—a patently political statement with the usual clichés.

I asked what this meant for the Tasaday and Oscar said, in a rather official voice, that campaigning would prevent any lengthy visits with the Tasaday but there was a possibility that Manda would squeeze in a short visit and lead a small party in search of their homesite so it could be included in an area Panamin would seek as a reserve.

I was disappointed. If Elizalde did not visit the Tasaday soon then it would not be for many months; if he did visit them now it would have the effect of making them a political gimmick. Perhaps it was true that all his efforts had been part of a plan to gain publicity and enter politics. It was disturbing to think that I might have been used; some of my stories on the Tasaday had been printed in Manila, and, while none praised Elizalde, he was a central figure. My old suspicions rose again.

The AP book project appeared to be out, but I was determined to join the trip to find the Tasaday's homesite. If they were to be trotted out as campaign toys, I wanted to report it firsthand.

But there was no trip, no meeting with the Tasaday.

Elizalde, outfitted in rainbow-colored mod shirts and pastel bell-bottoms, campaigned constantly during the next three months. I saw him twice, each time for about fifteen minutes. The first was at his house; I wanted to know if he planned to visit the rain forest. Elizalde said it would be impossible, that he was too busy, and it would be several months before he would see the Tasaday again. Perhaps aware of my suspicions, though I didn't voice them, he said that the Tasaday were not being mentioned in his campaign.

The second time I saw him was at his younger brother Freddie's house in Forbes Park, at a posh party complete with imported cheese and caviar and scores of Manila's most glamorous and powerful figures in business, politics, and high society. Manda stayed in an upstairs den most of the time and left about ten o'clock, winding his way downstairs and through groups of chic women and elegant men. In his politicking outfit—lavender slacks and yellow shirt—he looked ill-at-ease as he and a retinue of aides and bodyguards walked through the main party room, pausing here and there to shake hands and talk briefly. We chatted a few minutes. He was happiest talking about the tribes and mountains, but he did say that campaigning was going well and that according to the polls, he had a good chance to win one of the eight available senate seats.

His decision to run was seized upon by some Filipinos as proof that he had been insincere about his work with the tribes. A few contended that Panamin's work was spectacular but disorganized and without substance, providing merely temporary stopgaps to problems; Elizalde's entry into politics confirmed that something was amiss.

Most troubling was the future of the Tasaday. I asked about them both times I saw Manda and he said there was no news, nothing had been heard of them since the last contact, in July. It struck me as odd that people who had seemed so important to him could so easily be put aside —nobody sent to check on them or explain why he had not returned, no new information obtained about the logging roads, supposedly nearing the forest at a fast clip, that would "inevitably" destroy the Tasaday's place.

What were the Tasaday thinking? For six weeks they had had stunning experiences, then it all stopped. Stopped as abruptly as it had begun. No explanation. Elizalde left one day and said he would return, but he never did. Were they puzzled, worried, frightened? Now that they knew the way out, would they venture from the forest on their own?

They were at a crossroads in their lives and the man most responsible for putting them there was too busy for them. I had nearly become convinced he was playing it straight; but now doubts began to creep in again. I searched my mind for what I knew of Elizalde's background. Perhaps there was something in it that would help explain his behavior.

Manuel junior, "Manda," was the oldest son, second of three children of Mary Cadwallader Elizalde, of American descent, and Manuel Elizalde, a polo-playing millionaire of Spanish descent who was fond of white suits and whose business interests included sugar, steel, rum, rope, insurance, mining, paint, newspaper publishing, and radio and television broadcasting. Elizaldes had been influential for decades in the Philippines, one serving as ambassador to the United States, and were firmly entrenched among the social elite. In 1969 the family was the country's sixth largest taxpayer.

Manda liked the outdoors as a youngster, studied little, played a lot. After graduating from a private high school in Manila in 1954, the family sent him to the U.S. and he enrolled at Harvard, joining several clubs and settling down, by his own description, to a period of playboy antics usually abetted by booze. He recalls at least twenty traffic accidents and driver's-license suspensions in Massachusetts, Connecticut, and New York. There were holiday trips to Europe and the Caribbean, and countless weekend junkets to Harlem, where he would stuff his cash inside his socks and sit all night drinking and talking in bars and nightclubs. More than once he bought every seat in a railway parlor car from Cambridge to Manhattan and lounged grandly, drinking and swapping yarns with a couple of buddies. Once, he set his books on fire in the courtyard outside his campus quarters and the police chased him through snowdrifts in his underwear.

He graduated from Harvard in 1958, near the middle of his class, with a degree in social relations. He went to Manila, Spain, back to Manila; by his twenty-second birthday that year, he estimates he had traveled around the world more than twenty times. Two close calls in the air—one aboard a beat-up, chartered DC-5 lurching through a lightning storm with the crew panicking in the aisles—implanted an enduring dread of flying. For years he quelled the tremors with Scotch.

He brushes aside the immediate postcollege years as insignificant, chasing around, working haphazardly in family enterprises. Then, in 1964, to the relief of his parents, he married an attractive blue-eyed Manila girl of Spanish ancestry. Manda was twenty-seven, expected to finally settle down, take on responsibilities. His public relations men once told how he took his bride on a honeymoon to the island of Palawan in the southwestern Philippines and began to find himself: the inspiration of the lovely bride and the beautiful island supposedly had triggered mistily romantic leanings toward self-realization.

But the marriage broke up in 1971, and he took custody of the three children. The couple had grown apart as he spent more and more time in the hinterlands. "There's a lot more to it," he says, "but I guess you could say this work cost me a marriage." He sloughs off further questions about it. Whatever the reason, he first started spending considerable time in the wilds in 1964.

He got to know the Batak people on Palawan, and then the Taong of Mindoro. The excursions may have begun as fun, adventure, escapes from business, but they soon became a serious hobby, then a vocation. In 1966 Elizalde outfitted an old fishing boat as a hospital and toured the islands with doctors and college-student volunteers. During the next four years, they conducted medical missions, which, by Panamin's count, treated more than 1,500,000 people. "For sheer pleasure those missions were the greatest work we've ever done," Elizalde says.

He learned that many tribal patients had grave problems beside illness: they were losing their ancestral lands by legal means, by trickery, and at gunpoint. Elizalde set up a legal-aid program with lawyers from his family's companies. This helped, but it could not solve the tribespeople's most fundamental problem—lack of power. They did not vote, and so held no interest for politicians, were unarmed, uneducated to modern ways, and spread all over the islands in disorganized and disintegrating groups.

The frontiers attracted ambitious settlers and entrepreneurs, and also gunslingers, fast-talking lawyers, crooked judges and politicians. Tribal leaders were put down, forced to crawl into the hills and bear their helplessness, or be jailed or killed before the eyes of their women and children. And some tribal leaders were crooked themselves, selling out their own people.

Most of urban society either did not know about the cultural minorities' plight or did not care. To many the tribes only hindered progress; they were "savages" with no education and no civilized religion. Christian missionaries cared, but usually preached turning the other cheek and concentrated on convincing the people to wear more clothes, forget their own religions and adopt Christianity—to be "saved" spiritually if not physically. This further shamed the people, making them confused, meek, embarrassed by their own heritage.

There were parallels with the American Indians, who had also been among the original peoples of their lands, had rich, colorful customs and beliefs, an intimate, sometimes mystical rapport with the natural environment. Elizalde relished the idea of helping the underdog and attacking the establishment. It combined adventure, excitement, a Robin Hood sense of romanticism and justice, maverick iconoclasm and idealism. On top of everything, it was fun—and the tribes needed him, even more than he needed them.

In the early days there was usually no shortage of liquor, although on one expedition to Mindoro—according to a widely circulated story that Elizalde does not deny—it did run out. A helicopter was summoned and it lowered supplies of Scotch and ice into the jungle by cable.

As he and his fledgling organization took on increasing tasks, Manda decided to stop drinking. He joked about the drunken sprees of the past and did not seem to mind if liquor was all around, but he never took a drop. Instead, ice chests of soft drinks, usually including plain soda water, were carried wherever he went, always, no matter how far into a jungle or up a mountain. He often downed a dozen bottles a day.

"I could take a drink right now if I wanted to without going off on a drunk," he told me. "But what's the use? If I'm going to drink, I'm going to drink big—I don't like to do anything in little bits. Do it big or not at all. Besides, I don't need the booze any more. I get my kicks other ways now."

The work with tribes grew. President and Mrs. Marcos called him to the Palace in 1967 and urged him to expand it, "to do it right," he says. He was made a special adviser on minority problems and the next year joined the cabinet with the title Presidential Assistant on National Minorities. Shortly after, the Panamin Foundation was created. In 1968 it moved into Mindanao and began work with the Mansaka of Davao, the Samals of Zamboanga, the Higa-onon of Agusan, the Blaan of Cotabato. That same year two Protestant women missionaries of the Summer Institute of Linguistics told Elizalde that the Tboli, with whom they were working, had serious troubles.

The Tboli numbered perhaps 100,000; they were scattered and on the run. A Panamin report says they had lost more than 75,000 acres of ancestral lands, much of it in the rich plains, and were steadily being pushed deeper into the mountains. Tboli men were being murdered, women raped, families destroyed. Some Tboli tried to co-operate with the newcomers but usually wound up being tricked and ridiculed. Shamed, they took Christian names, and traded their earrings and colorful clothing for anything that would make them look less different—raggedy T shirts, tattered jeans, tennis shoes.

In August, 1968, Elizalde met Mai Tuan, who was helping the Summer Institute women translate the Bible into Tboli. Mai, whose father had been a strong figure in the tribe, had finished high school and planned to attend college and study law. After Elizalde talked to him, Mai postponed his plans for school, stopped translating the Bible, and, with his brothers, Fludi, Yanni, and Dad, provided a nucleus with which Panamin started work. The valley called Kematu had belonged to Mai's family but had been taken over by a rancher; it was selected as the place to start a major Tboli settlement, the place to make their stand.

In October Elizalde held his first meeting with a crowd of Tboli. With Mai translating, he accused today's Tboli of being cowards. He praised their ancestors, who had not succumbed to the Spanish, the Americans, or the Japanese when they conquered the islands. Why, then, were the Tboli now being beaten by thugs and gangsters? He told them nobody could help the Tboli but Tboli, and unless they did it soon, it would be too late. He implored them to be proud of their ancient customs, their dress, their dances, their art, their names, to stop selling out Tboli greatness for the newcomers' hand-me-downs. True, the modern world had things to teach them, but they must not bow and scrape before it; they must be selective and wise. "You must remember your Tboli greatness," Elizalde concluded. "Remember it or you die!"

Mai, recalling the speech four years later, had tears in his eyes. "The old men and the young all leaped to their feet, shouting and weeping. I had never heard such a thing before. They all began to shout together, over and over, 'Tboli, Tboli, Tboli, Tboli. . . .' It was a great day for us . . . it changed our history. None of us who were there can ever forget it."

The ensuing months saw ambushes and pitched fights, espionage and court battles, political finagling and nightlong planning sessions by candlelight in mountain hideouts. And the tribesmen, formerly armed only with spears and poisoned arrows, were provided guns to match the weapons of their enemies. The valley was finally won, and then nearly ten thousand acres more were acquired through purchases and government land grants.

Of course, the tribe's success was not to everyone's liking. Rewards were offered for the capture or killing of Mai, his brothers, and several other Tboli. Elizalde was charged with crimes, too, and a frontier court issued a warrant for his arrest.

His opponents insisted there had been no serious problems between them and the tribal people until Elizalde arrived. They accused him of stirring up Tboli to a point where the most peaceful farmers felt threatened. Elizalde, they said, was after minerals, land, lumber, power. His position in the cabinet was a major weapon, however, and his direct line to the Presidential Palace compelled opponents to move carefully.

By late 1970 the valley had become a model settlement. About one-tenth of the estimated 100,000 Tboli had been touched directly, and many more thousands shared in the Tboli resurgence, as did other tribes, who sent representatives to see the settlement, discuss their own problems, seek help. One of the toughest problems was finding ways for the people to live on less land and establish a dignified, self-sustaining place in the modern world.

Projects were set up deeper in the mountains with other Tboli and the

The rain forest of the Tasaday

The main settlement of Manubo Blit, beyond which lies the Tasaday's "place";
Dafal standing beside a group of Blit, Datu Dudim directly in front of him; Dafal

Logging road cutting toward the Tasaday

Clearing where Tasaday first met outsiders

Elizalde embracing Kuletaw during July, 1971, meeting at forest's edge, with Bilangan, Balayam, and Mahayag watching

Tekaf grimacing at chopper's rotor blast

Tasaday men beside the "Big Bird"

In Mindanao mountains, Panamin troopers on either side of Robert Fox, Elizalde, *center*, and Lindbergh

A grinning Mai Tuan

Datu Ma Falen, Charles Lindbergh

Igna

Oscar Trinidad

Lobo getting attention from Ching Rivero, Lucy Espino, and Mila Asion

David Baradas and Carlos Fernandez taking notes as Udelen watches

"Bart" Bartolo

Father Frank Lynch

Lobo, Lolo, Bilangan, and Balayam escaping rain-forest shower beneath palm-frond umbrella. *Opposite,* Lefonok holding Sasa; Etut and two sons huddling in stream; Lobo, peering into treetops, and Ukan; Kuletaw with stone pounder

Holding Maman, Udelen watches chopper take off, while, *below,* roto blast raises Lefonok's hair. Lobo clinging to Mai and Manda (not seen) in back seat of chopper; Balayam leading rush from chopper after flight

A pensive Lobo after flight with Bilangan, Adug, Balayam;
Adug, face in hand; Balayam recounting the wonders of flight

Dul offering Maman monkey-skull toy

Mahayag shaping bamboo tool with tiny stone scraper

Balayam playing bamboo jew's-harp, with Lobo and Ukan listening

Doc Rebong applying stethoscope to Balayam

Lobo and Bilangan showing the tense expressions common among the Tasaday during their first visits to the forest's edge

Vine-swinging Elizalde losing control, helped down by Balayam

Balayam demonstrating proper vine-swinging technique

Elizalde stung by a bee; recovering to the laughter of a Blit girl, Igna, and Balayam

Balayam in an inviting pose for the benefit of the Blit girl, who, he hopes, has been brought to meet him

A relaxed mood marked by nuzzling between Elizalde and Balayam

Lobo in a moment of puzzled wonder

Adug and Lobo laughing at Elizalde's clowning

A boy demonstrating how the Tasaday reach their mountainside
cave, which is higher than the tree Balayam points to

Ubu. By mid-1971 Panamin had twelve settlements, was maintaining a radio network, and had administrative offices in Manila. The organization numbered more than fifty fulltime staff members, but it relied on Elizalde for direction, decision making, fund raising, almost everything. So it was that Panamin became known as a "one-man show."

In the early days this had been almost unavoidable. Panamin says that from 1967 through 1971 the Elizaldes provided roughly half a million dollars. In the next three years government allocations more than matched that, and a fund-raising drive, with the President's wife, Imelda Marcos, as the honorory chairman, pushing collections among the well-to-do, raised the figure substantially.

Some company executives of the Elizalde enterprises resented the fact that they struggled to bring in money that was promptly put into Manda's private project. And it was not just his spending that aggravated them; although he was first vice-president of the parent company and an officer in several others, he paid scant attention to them and was cocky about it.

I once met a company executive at a dinner party, before I knew Elizalde, and I innocently asked him about Manda's work with tribes. The man changed the subject; when I returned to it he braced his shoulders, shut his eyes, and sighed. Then he muttered, in a low, quivering voice, "I don't know what he is doing except throwing away money. Absolutely throwing it away. God! If his father doesn't stop him he may ruin us all. Don't talk to me about Manda!"

Obviously, what family and friends had once dismissed as a lark had got out of hand. But asking him to give it up, as some did, only seemed to drive him into it more deeply. At the same time, the rumors concerning his motives increased. Manda enjoyed the attention and the puzzlement but dismissed all the speculation as completely wrong. He said he did not want to enter politics; nor had his tribal work anything to do with mining or logging claims. And it was too much sweat over too long a period to be just fun and games for a bored playboy.

The first time I asked him about his motives Elizalde went into a standard exposition about the problems of the tribes. I pressed him further and finally he flared up. "Look, for Christ's sake, I'm doing what I like to do. Okay? That's enough motivation! That's all the motivation I need. I don't ask you why the hell you do what you do. What right have you to question me anyway? None. You have no right!

"All this talk about why I do things is ridiculous. The reason is simple. I like it. I love it. I get a tremendous kick out of it. Making people happy gives me more pleasure than anything I can think of."

"Must be like Santa Claus," I said.

"Yeah. Right. I knew you'd understand. And I'll tell you something else, if you can somehow grasp the concept and stop asking why I blow my nose or why I am so handsome. For the first time, these people are being asked what they want, not *told* what they should have. Now that is extraordinary."

But not long after that, he ran for the senate, after steadfastly insisting he wouldn't, and put all his energy and large amounts of cash into the campaign. For the Tasaday and the other tribes, suddenly there was no time.

The election was held November 7 and the ruling Nacionalista party suffered an overwhelming defeat. Their cause had been drastically hurt in late August, when terrorists hurled two hand grenades into a rally of the opposition Liberal party. The grenades shattered the speaker's platform, wounding all but one of the Liberals' senate candidates, killing a dozen onlookers and photographers, and injuring scores in the huge crowd. Two of the top Liberal candidates were maimed and could not campaign, and other candidates stumped in casts and bandages. The grenade throwers were not caught, and the Liberals won widespread sympathy.

Only one of the first seven senate seats went to the Nacionalistas. Elizalde fought for the eighth and last seat with a member of his own party, incumbent Senator Alejandro Almendras, who edged slightly ahead in the final tabulations. Since both candidates claimed the other had rigged, bought, and coerced votes, the fight dragged on through February of 1972. It could go on for many more months.

The AP had granted me a leave of absence I had requested to finish a book on the Ubu, and I had held out a slight hope that Elizalde might make contact with the Tasaday during this time. It did not seem likely now as he waded into the long court fights with Almendras. In early February I found I needed another visit with the Ubu to reshoot some photographs, and so I telephoned Oscar Trinidad to ask for Panamin guides to help me. The next day Manda called and asked me to come by for a visit.

He was restless and unhappy about the court cases with Almendras. "A lot of my lawyers say I should keep after it, but I'm sick of it. I just want to get out of here. It's awful. My big worry is that old saying that if you lose once in the Philippines you're always known as a loser—whatever you do. The lawyers insist I've got to stay in town all the time for court appearances, the commission on elections, all that. It's miserable. I can't do anything. Can't go anywhere."

I asked if he wanted to win. "Of course—what the hell did you think? We never quit anything we start . . . give it our best effort, all the way. The thing is, though, this is painful just sitting around, drives me right up the wall. I don't even know what all the lawyers are doing. . . ."

When he said he wanted to visit the Tboli and other groups and to pick up again with the Tasaday, I mentioned that the Tasaday must have been confused to have had their traumatic experiences of June and July suddenly stop. Manda said he did not think they were upset. Dafal and Igna's husband had recently walked into the forest and called for the Tasaday, who came running. Everything was fine, the Tasaday said; they asked when they would see Momo Dakel again.

In early March I flew to Mindanao and Panamin helped me reach Ma Falen's hilltop settlement. I had spent four days with the Ubu when José Torres, Panamin's resident staffman on the project, received a radio message asking if I would like to come down to Tboli—Elizalde was there, and "Nance might find it interesting."

Three hours later the helicopter picked me up. At Tboli I found Manda slouched in a chair on the front porch of the staff house. He waved, smiled, and without preamble asked, "How'd you like to go and see the Tasaday with us?"

"Of course. When?"

"Oh I dunno," he said. "How's tomorrow morning sound?"

5

Toward the Rain Forest Sanctuary

BEING stuck in Manila had become intolerable, Elizalde said, so he left his lawyers to worry about the election and flew to Mindanao, spent a day at Tboli, then visited Blit. Dafal was sent to find the Tasaday.

When the helicopter landed at the forest's edge the next day, nobody was there, Manda said. They waited three hours and then, with rainclouds threatening, reboarded the helicopter. As it rose, they noticed a man running through thinning foliage toward the clearing.

The helicopter landed again and by the time its occupants were on the ground, the figure had emerged from the forest and was racing toward them. "It was Balayam, running as fast as he could go," Manda said, "and carrying some deerhorns and a wild chicken. He ran up to us, sweating like crazy and gasping for breath, trying to talk, dancing around all excited. He shoved the horns and chicken at me and started hugging me and laughing and crying all at once—tears were running down his face. He babbled constantly but I didn't know what the hell he was saying, only that it had to be important."

When Balayam's excitement subsided, Mai translated: he was elated to see them, and other Tasaday were coming with Dafal but he had run ahead. He resumed hugging Elizalde and talking, and then Mai reported that Balayam wanted a wife—he *must* have a wife! The chicken and horns were gifts to help acquire the bride.

"We talked and waited," Manda told me. "But nobody else came before it started to rain hard and we had to get going. We promised Balayam we would see him very soon. After we got back here, Blit radioed that Dafal had arrived and said all the Tasaday were fine and wanted to see

us. We told him we'd go back to the clearing in two days. That's tomorrow
. . . you sure you wanna come along?" He chuckled.

We all discussed the impending visit for the rest of the day—Mai,
Ching, and Johnny Ugarte, a relative of Elizalde's who had worked in the
election campaign and then joined the Panamin staff—and agreed not to
question the Tasaday on matters that made them uncomfortable, such as
the Sanduka and Tasafeng or how they acquired women, not to use tape
recorders or do excessive camera work. I would use only one camera, instead of the three or four I often carried, and if that bothered them I
would stop photographing completely. We would try to match our pace to
theirs, aiming above all to keep them feeling at ease.

The sky was overcast the next morning as we left Tboli, picked up
Igna at Blit, and turned toward the rain forest. The helicopter hovered,
then dropped swiftly like an elevator, making the forest seem to shoot up
and away from us. The clearing was empty.

Perhaps the Tasaday won't come, I thought. Anticipation that had lain
dormant for months had in the last few hours grown into nervous tension.
It was March 9, 1972. Except for the brief meeting with Balayam two
days earlier and a couple of meetings with Dafal in the forest, the Tasaday
supposedly had not met any outsiders for seven months. Would they be
different? Had the "lightning" changed their lives? Were they sorry they
had come out of the forest before? Would they come at all this time?
There was no sign of them on the ground.

We walked a narrow trail down the hump of the knoll toward the forest. Up ahead of us, standing in a dip, was Balayam. Behind him were
half a dozen men and boys. Balayam shouted, bounded forward and put
both hands on Elizalde's shoulders. He cooed through pursed lips and put
his cheek against Manda's. The other Tasaday closed in, murmuring, and
petted Manda.

Igna, Mai, Ching, Ugarte, and I followed the cluster of people into
the shadows of the first row of trees. They sat on a log near the old lean-
tos, which had been repaired and were occupied by huddling Tasaday
women and children. We passed an open-sided shelter made for Panamin's visitors the previous year. Inside were a full bag of rice and several
other items, including a case of soda, blanketed with dry leaves.

The women peeked nervously out of the lean-tos, but the Tasaday men
and older boys had shy smiles and shining eyes. Balayam cuddled next to
Elizalde on the log. Bilangan stood beside them with quiet composure.
We exchanged glances and I nodded. He said, "Bilangan. *Akun* Bilangan
[I am Bilangan]." I repeated his name but messed it up, and he said,
"Bee-lawng-awn." Again I mispronounced it and he shook his head, say-
ing it slowly and emphasizing each sound. I tried again and he made a
quick affirmative nod and said, *"Oh-ho."*

Balayam told Igna the Tasaday were glad to see Momo Dakel Diwata

Tasaday, carefully pronouncing the full name several times during a short speech that had the tone of an official welcoming statement.

Asked if life had been as usual since the last meetings, Balayam said yes, adding, however, that strong rains and winds had toppled trees and branches in the forest and smashed their shelters. Nobody had been hurt, he said. We asked if all the Tasaday had been well and he said everyone was fine, no illnesses or deaths. Balayam said they had looked for food as always and had waited for Momo Dakel Diwata Tasaday to return; sometimes they heard a big bird flying over and rushed to a mountaintop to see if it was *the* bird, but it never came. "We want Momo Dakel Diwata Tasaday to stay with us always," he said, flopping his head onto Elizalde's shoulder.

We asked whether the storm-damaged shelters were the buttressed tree roots and rocky ledges mentioned previously. The question brought a confused response that we took to mean that they were a kind of shelter made to be used when they were too far away from their natural places.

"Are these natural places bigger than these [the lean-tos, which were about four feet in width and height and five feet long]?"

"Oh, yes. Much bigger."

"Could many of these huts here fit inside one of them?"

Balayam looked puzzled.

"Could we stand up inside?"

"Yes. It is high inside."

"How many people go inside at one time?"

"Everybody—all of us."

Mai, Elizalde, and I looked attentively at one another . . . "Is this place in the side of your valley or of a mountain?" Mai asked. "Does it go back inside?" He made a half circle in the air with a cupped hand.

"Yes, that's right," Balayam said, nodding.

"Caves! They live in caves!" we exclaimed.

The Tasaday blinked and looked at us as we babbled to each other.

"Of course . . . of course," Manda said. "We never asked them . . . why didn't we think of that? Caves! In their valley. Sure. Perfect. No wonder they say they are safe and warm there."

Our excitement must have puzzled the Tasaday, but then much of our behavior must have seemed odd. They watched quietly as we marveled back and forth. Mai tried to find a Tasaday word for cave but got only a description of a place back inside a mountain. Then:

"Are these places high up the wall of the valley you talk about?"

"Oh, yes, very high," Balayam said.

"Higher than that tree?" I asked, pointing to a white-barked trunk that rose perhaps one hundred feet.

"Yes."

He stood up and said they were higher than *that* tree, pointing to one whose tip rose almost out of sight above branches and leaves. It was at least one hundred and fifty feet tall.

Balayam said they reached the caves by climbing on vines or roots. Women turned their infants over to the men for this, he said.

We looked interested, and one of the men stood up, seated a boy of about three astraddle his left hip, crooked him in his left elbow, and put his left hand on the trunk of a slender tree. He slapped his other hand higher up the trunk and began to climb—pulling with his hands and pushing with his legs and feet, which curled around the trunk. Up the tree they rose.

We tried to think if there were any people in the world now living in caves, but the ones that came to mind used caves only sporadically. Palawan Filipinos had—but that was tens of thousands of years ago.

"Do you make marks on the cave walls—draw with charcoal, pitch, anything?" Elizalde asked. The question took some explaining by Igna and brought quizzical frowns and a no from the Tasaday.

We talked about the caves for the next hour. They said a shallow stream flowed somewhere below them, and that after Dafal had taught them to extract the pith from palms they sometimes built lean-tos beside the stream while preparing the pith food, called *natek*. Balayam said they usually did their cooking in the caves and almost always slept there at night.

Balayam said that before Dafal showed them how to cut bamboo sections to use as containers, which they called *naf-naf,* they did not carry water to the caves from the stream, since they had no way to. They did not use much water anyway, he said, drinking perhaps once a day if they happened to pass the stream.

One cave was about as long as "from here to that tree" (roughly fifty feet away), Balayam said. It had a wide mouth protected by two large rocks that were "good" because they "prevented falling." When thunder, the "big word," was loud, some Tasaday lay on the floor of the cave.

Their ancestors had lived in these same caves. As children they were told that they could go into the forest in daytime, but must return home every night. Now, however, they sometimes went food gathering overnight.

Asked if Momo Dakel would be able to climb to the cave, Balayam said it might be too difficult. Elizalde looked pensive and Balayam added, "You may think we don't love you because we can't talk and say so, but we do." He smiled and put his arm around Manda's shoulders. "You should come to our place, but maybe you cannot make the long walk. But if you are very strong inside, I think you can. . . ."

During this conversation, Lobo became restless and ambled around, poking into this and that. He climbed about thirty feet up a sapling, leaped to another one, and slid down. Then he ducked under a pile of rotting logs and branches and peeked out with a broad grin.

The others sat in seeming contentment. Their bodies looked heavier than before; a couple even had beginning curves of fat edging over the cord holding up their G strings. They all wore leaves; the old pieces of cloth had not been restored. The fair-skinned boy appeared slightly healthier—at least his skin ulcerations and runny eyes, which the doctor had treated the previous year, seemed no worse, possibly better. And he now sat up alone, instead of being cradled in the arms of his widowed father.

We counted nineteen Tasaday; the rest had not come because they were making *natek* and could not leave it or the pith would spoil.

Asked if they had seen any other forest people, the Tasaday said they had seen nobody except Dafal and Sut, Igna's husband. The gifts they were given last time had been kept in the cave. They liked the knives best, but other things were good, too, because they were gifts from Momo Dakel Diwata Tasaday and reminders of him.

Elizalde asked if there was anything they needed or wanted now. Balayam said no, then paused, put his hand to his mouth, and looked up toward the helicopter. After several seconds he said, "Aah . . . I wonder what it is like inside the big bird."

"Would you like to ride in it?"

Balayam took a breath and said yes, he would.

"But wouldn't you be scared?"

"Yes, but if Momo Dakel Diwata Tasaday went, and others went . . . I would like to go in it."

Did anyone else want to go? The Tasaday men looked at one another and Bilangan told Igna that if Balayam was going then he would go also. Lobo danced around and said he wanted to go, and an older boy with his hair tied behind his head nodded that he should be included.

"Okay," Elizalde said. "Let's go."

As we walked up to the clearing, I suggested to Elizalde that perhaps this was going too fast; we were introducing something they could not understand or might be afraid of, like the tape recorder.

"Yeah, but this was their idea, not ours," he said. "They're curious about that big bird. They were scared of it before and now they want to try it. It's quite a step, takes a lot of courage. Don't cheat them of that. They want to go, it'll be okay."

Everyone walked to the clearing except the women and infants. Bart climbed into the pilot's seat and Balayam was belted into a space next to him. He sat on the edge of the leather seat, his head and neck poking timidly from between his hunched-up shoulders like a turtle peeking from its shell. His almond eyes were wide and bright, his lips curved into a slightly impish smile. He clutched a woven bag made of plant fiber in his lap as a child would a teddy bear. In the back seat, Mai and Manda secured Bilangan and the two boys. Bilangan maintained a stolid dignity but the boys looked scared.

Bart snapped levers and clicked buttons and the rotor blade began to turn slowly. The engine whined into a roar and the rotor flashed faster until it was a silver circle. The helicopter wobbled up, dipped its gleaming nose and swooped out across the plain, veered toward the Blit settlement, climbing and circling, and disappeared behind dark-green trees, taking four Tasaday into the sky, over a new world—farther north in a few seconds than they had gone in their lifetime.

The Tasaday on the ground watched in fascination, their mouths open. When the helicopter flew out of sight they gasped, looked at each other nervously, and craned their necks to scan the sky. Then a moving dot flickered behind treetops and the helicopter appeared once more over the forest. The men let out little cries as it circled and came back to them.

Balayam led the Tasaday from the machine in a crouching run, like soldiers dashing across no man's land. A crooked smile creased his face and he hugged his fiber bag to his chest with both hands. The four fliers scampered down the trail and sat on a log, panting, shaking their heads. Both boys frowned; the oldest anchored his chin in his hands and stared, speechless.

Balayam and Bilangan said they had been frightened but it was all right now, it was good now. Their chests heaved as they spoke. Then Balayam sat up and raised his hands before him. "I am surprised . . . everything so flat. And all those lean-tos [the Blit settlement] where the ground was so flat! Flat all around! We didn't know . . . hard to believe. Flat! We thought that everything was up and down [see-sawing his hands in the air] like our place." Then he sagged back onto the log.

Everybody sat quietly for a while and *natek* was produced from bark packets. Balayam described the flight to them without words. He stretched his hands in front of him and imitated how Bart had pressed the buttons and gripped the navigation stick. Then he put one hand above his head and twirled one finger—the rotor turning—and slowly stood up. He peered over one shoulder—looking at the earth below—shuddered, and sat down, peeking now and then over that shoulder. Then he laughed as the Tasaday exclaimed and shook their heads.

Our group retired to Panamin's shelter, about one hundred feet from the Tasaday's lean-tos, to lunch on the chicken and rice wrapped in leaves that had been brought by Dafal and a teen-aged girl from the Blit settlement. Balayam wandered up half an hour later and immediately noticed the girl. She sat shyly; Balayam could not keep his eyes from slipping back to her every few seconds. Holding himself in a formal stance, he addressed Elizalde in solemn tones: "We are happy to see Momo Dakel Diwata Tasaday and welcome him. . . ."

Balayam delivered such set pieces several times through the day. His voice was clear and loud, his manner confident, somewhat like a well-prepared schoolboy reciting. It was a sharp contrast to his manner when a question touched an area he was uncertain about or did not want to discuss. Then his voice faded into a barely audible mumble, his head drooped, and his eyes darted evasively.

But now Balayam was on stage, smart and snappy, beaming smiles at Elizalde and then at the girl, who stared at the ground. Balayam had sized her up and found her fine. Manda finally told Mai to introduce the girl, who was probably about fifteen. She refused to look up, but Balayam said, *"Oh-hooooo,"* with arched eyebrows and a broad grin. *"Akun* Balayam. *Akun* Balayam." The girl cowered behind Elizalde, but Balayam's smile, which was beginning to look silly, stuck on his face.

Manda got Balayam's attention by asking how long it took the Tasaday to walk from their cave to the clearing. Balayam opened his hand, palm up, and then flipped it over, indicating sunup to sundown, one day.

Was it a difficult walk?

Yes, they walked hard all day.

And fast?

Yes, they kept moving to make it before dark.

"How long would it take us?" Manda asked.

Balayam spoke to Igna while repeating the hand-turning movement a few times: four days, three nights.

"Yeah, that's what I thought," Manda said. "It'll be tough—if we can do it at all." Then he asked Igna to find out why he could not do it in one day if Balayam could.

Balayam chortled and said that, from watching Momo Dakel walk, it would take much longer. Then he showed how it should be done: a swift, loping stride that seemed to skip across the ground. After the demonstration, he said, "It may be hard for you, but if you are strong inside you can come . . . and then we'll always be together."

"Hah!" Manda replied. "We'll see about this. Tell Balayam to watch closely."

Elizalde strode to the top of a sloping hillock, let out a Tarzan yell, and charged down, hurdling a stump at the bottom and grabbing a small tree to stop himself. "Now," he said, "ask Balayam how long it would take at *that* speed."

Two days.

Elizalde returned to the top of the hill and ran down at full speed. "Now how long?"

Balayam cupped a hand over his grinning mouth and said maybe one day.

"Maybe!" Elizalde shouted. "Watch this!"

He again hurtled down, shouting, pumping his arms, leaping the stump, stumbling over two Tasaday boys who had come to watch, and plowing into a clump of thick brush.

Now sweating and puffing, Manda turned to half a dozen giggling Tasaday: "Now, how about that?"

One day, Balayam finally agreed, smirking.

"Hah," Manda retorted. "He doesn't believe it. Mai, you tell them that I am one of the great forest walkers of the world. Come on!"

He walked a short distance into the forest and found a vine dangling from a tree on an overgrown slope. He tested the vine with a few jerks, backed up the slope, and then leaped forward, swinging out rather neatly about twenty feet. But then his grip slipped and he lost control, twirled, bounced off a sapling, and slammed sideways into the trunk of the tree.

Balayam frowned and looked concerned.

Elizalde shouted for a bolo and cut off the bottom of the vine, which he said had thrown him off balance. He swung out again but was jerked to a stop at the apex of the swing when his pants leg caught in some thorny vines; he kicked himself free, only to slam into a rotten stump, which whacked him in the groin. Groaning, he spun into a thorny bush and finally sagged to a halt. He was half lying on the bush, still clinging to the vine, when a bee stung him behind the ear. He cursed and slapped at it, sinking deeper into the bush that had imprisoned him. Balayam helped him out and, as he limped away, torn pants leg flapping, Balayam leaped onto the vine, swung out and back, and slipped gracefully to the ground with a grin.

Elizalde, seeing this as he alternately rubbed his battered crotch and bee-bitten neck, laughed and grabbed the bolo again, slashed another chunk off the bottom of the vine, and swung out and back, awkwardly but without a hitch.

"Now! Now, ask him," Elizalde said to Mai between breaths, "how long to make it to the cave?"

"You will not make it!" Balayam said, shaking his head.

Elizalde stared at Balayam, as Mai, letting out laughter in little snorts, said never mind, the Tboli could not swing on vines either.

As Igna worked to remove the bee's stinger, Manda told Dafal that he had felt beautiful on the vine, "just like a bird."

Dafal translated and Balayam choked with snickers. "Like a baby bird," he finally said.

All the Tasaday were laughing by now. Almost out of control, they roared and giggled, rocking back and forth. They waited expectantly for Elizalde to perform again, but he decided to change the subject. He asked Balayam about the Tasaday's original earrings, before Dafal gave them the brass rings.

Balayam said their ancestors taught them to wear only one ring, made from a tiny doughnut-shaped section of a rattan seedling. The ring was separated in one place and the two facing tips were bitten or scraped into points. The tips were then pried apart and the ring was attached to an ear lobe. After several days the ear lobe was pierced by the sharp tips' pressing to meet each other. Balayam winced and said, "It bleeds and is very painful." Berries were then tied on the ring with a vine thread.

Just then Balayam spotted a hornbill in a tree about one hundred yards away, picked up his bow, fitted an arrow to it, and took aim chattering all the while. It was an impossible shot for an expert—the bird was a distant speck through leaves and branches. But Balayam confidently planted his feet, drew the bowstring, and let go. The arrow went about twenty-five yards, wavered, and plopped into a wooded gully. Balayam tossed aside the bow, rubbed his shoulder, and shrugged. "Bird was too far," he said to Dafal with a laugh.

"They do not know the bow and arrow," Mai said. "Balayam just left his arrow where it fell. No forest man I've known would forget an arrow —they are too valuable. And no hunter would ever take a shot like that!"

A midafternoon breeze stirred the trees and the sky darkened. "Let's see if we can beat the rain to Blit," Elizalde said. We gathered our things together and told the Tasaday we would return the next day.

Before we left, Balayam told Igna and Mai that the Tasaday would like Manda to see their place in the forest. "If he is strong inside, I think he can make it. We will help him."

At Blit several dozen tribesmen rushed to greet the helicopter, as they always did, whether Elizalde had been gone thirty minutes or three months. And the rest of us were also welcomed warmly: the Blit came forward in waves, touching, hugging, kissing hands and cheeks, sniffing to breathe us in, slipping arms around us. Each visitor was surrounded— four and five abreast in front, behind, and on both sides. We walked slowly so as not to crunch bare feet or knock down the tiny naked children who mingled in the moving mass. The men beamed smiles. The women hummed a high, soft, nasal oooh sound. The effect was of light, delicate music alternately wavering and swelling somewhere overhead.

No matter how often I experienced this greeting, it always produced a happy, glowing response inside of me. More than once, I saw visitors who were unprepared for the welcome become smothered in the tender warmth, smiling uncontrollably and with tears in their eyes.

Minutes after we settled inside Datu Dudim's long house, the rain came, slapping the thatched roof in a loud, steady drumbeat. In the waning light I scribbled in my notebook, trying to remember everything that had happened. I had made only sketchy notes among the Tasaday because writing was so distracting. At first I had passed up opportunities to photograph them, or had simply shot blindly from my chest or waist without putting the camera to my eye. But after a short time they paid little attention to the camera. They had no idea of its function and were not self-conscious.

In the evening darkness, we discussed the day. Mai was concerned about visiting the Tasaday's cave, afraid of what it might mean to them: "Once they have footprints in their hidden place they will learn to fear for their safety. At first they may not be afraid, but then, after we've gone, they will see those footprints and know that outsiders know where they live. They may fear that other outsiders will come and hurt them. Then they will have to leave their place, find another."

"But," I said, "if they've never known unfriendly people, as they say, and if the outsiders who deal with them behave properly, what will they fear? If it's the unknown they fear and if the unknown we represent becomes known as good, then they won't fear it."

"But this could become a danger itself," Elizalde put in. "If they are confident that all the outside world is good, they might just blunder into trouble with loggers or hostile tribes or any number of things. It's a fantastic problem—we've never had anything like this before. We're thinking about trying to protect them from dangers they don't even know exist. If we try to explain the dangers, they wouldn't understand and we'd just confuse them or frighten them. We can't ask their opinion, they don't have any. It's Panamin's decision and we've got to be careful."

Later in the discussion, Mai again expressed his worry. "No matter what we do, we already have started them thinking—about us, about the outside—and two things will happen: they will learn fear and want." He emphasized that originally the Tasaday had said they did not want or need anything. They still said that; but they also said they liked knives and cloth. And now that they were happy with metal, could they get along without it? Each man has a knife, but what will happen when it breaks or is lost? The Ubus ask for cloth and salt and bows and arrows; the Tasaday ask for nothing because they have never had anything. "But they are beginning to see a difference, to see strangers in their world, to wonder . . . the helicopter ride . . . perhaps they will talk all night about that. And as they keep seeing people in clothes they may become ashamed, may want to cover themselves."

The talk centered on alternatives: leave them alone completely; forget the cave and meet them only at the clearing; go to the cave but under certain conditions.

Certainly a better understanding was needed of the Tasaday's own wishes. "At least we've got to try and find out what they think at this point, what *they* want," Manda said. But no one knew if all the Tasaday wanted what their chief spokesman Balayam wanted. Perhaps, said Mai, when Balayam tells us to come to their place, "the others are saying to themselves, Stop, stop, Balayam. You are telling all of our secrets. You are giving us away.

"Maybe they will kill him. The distance from pointing a bow in the air at a bird to pointing it at a man is very short. You are looking up and then you look down. They may think of that one day . . . Ah, but to see Balayam with that bow today! He shot the arrow good-by—so they have no fears or dangers that they need arrows for. The Ubu of Ma Falen shoot only when they can see the eyes of the enemy."

Balayam's woman problem was getting worse, Manda said. "What the hell are we going to do? He thinks I'm going to get him one. I never thought of myself as a pimp before."

Mai said Igna had confided that she might be able to find someone for Balayam, "a volunteer . . . a Blit or a Sduff woman, I think."

"I don't know . . . that could get pretty messy," Manda said.

"That's right, sir. And also I don't know what Igna has in mind," Mai said. "Maybe they want a kind of spy in that forest. You never can tell. Sut is a clever man." (Igna's handsome, smooth-mannered husband was better dressed than most Blit or Sduff and had a reputation as a cagey operator involved in shady affairs.)

Manda returned to the subject of going to the cave. Perhaps the Tasaday's repeated mention that the route was difficult was a veiled way of saying they did not want him to come, and that the reason they kept inviting him was simply politeness—and a desire to keep seeing him and receive presents. But moments later he dismissed this notion. "Of course they want me to come. They've never seen anyone so handsome, so beautiful . . . how can they resist me?"

The fact remained that reaching the cave would be difficult. Outsiders would have a hard time in the forest and would need supplies and support for at least one week each way, in and out. And bad weather would mean more time each way.

Near midnight I fell asleep hearing Elizalde make his favorite promise to Mila Asion and Lucy Espino—two young staffers who cooked and handled all manner of travel and camp chores—that if they brought his cold soda and bug repellent quickly, they would be sure to go to heaven.

Sunlight filtered into the house about five-thirty, revealing two dozen Blit and visitors asleep in various twists and curls on the floor. By seven Mila and Lucy had laid out a breakfast of hardboiled eggs, crackers, guava jelly, and steaming cups of coffee.

Talk resumed on the need to get broader Tasaday opinion about going to their cave. I wondered aloud if all this talk might only be an exercise—that Elizalde already knew that he would go into the forest, that he could not resist.

"If we don't need to go in, then we shouldn't," Elizalde replied with a frown. "If they don't *want* us, we sure as hell won't go. But the logging roads may have made the decision for us. If we really want to protect them we probably have to go in."

When I asked if the roads were really that close, Ching replied that the one on this side of the forest was about ten miles from where we were. "In five years, maybe only one or two, the roads will be in the forest," Elizalde said. "And what the hell do you think that means? The Blit— they've been spared so far—will be right in the middle. The timber cruisers will run right through them, and they'll be backed right into the forest with the loggers and everybody else right after them."

Shortly after nine o'clock we landed at the clearing; Bilangan and three other men arrived seconds later. As we walked the path to the lean-tos, Balayam hurried up, greeted Elizalde, and then began darting his eyes through our group as if to be sure he had not missed someone. He was apparently looking for the girl from yesterday.

Elizalde, Mai, and Igna sat together on the log facing the lean-tos. The Tasaday women were inside and the old man, Kuletaw, perched just outside. The only hostile note came from a dog, still unseen, whose nervous growls rumbled sporadically from within a lean-to. A chubby boy of about two sat beside a tethered rusty-red wild chicken that was a gift for Elizalde.

After welcoming exchanges, almost like diplomats making ritualized salutations before getting down to busines, Elizalde asked Mai to tell them we had been thinking of their invitation to go to their place and were wondering if they really would like that.

"Yes!" Balayam replied at once. "If you can make it."

Balayam sat beside Elizalde, who asked Igna to direct questions to the other Tasaday. She apparently responded by telling Balayam he was not to answer, because he looked pained, blinked, and moved his head in jerks like a rooster.

"No, no," Manda said. "Mai, tell Igna to let Balayam know that he is welcome to answer but that we would like to hear from other Tasaday, too. Ask the old man a question, for instance."

Igna said something to the old man, who nodded and then uncoiled his creaky body, stepped up to Elizalde, and squatted at his feet.

"No," Manda said. "He doesn't have to do that. She shouldn't tell anyone to sit anywhere, let them stay where they are. Just ask them questions generally, let anyone answer."

Igna apparently then told the old man to go back to his place, because he looked bewildered, started to rise, and then squatted again, peering nervously behind him.

"C'mon, Mai, c'mon." Elizalde sighed. "Look, you tell Igna to just let them be. Don't bother them. Let them do what they want."

The original question was asked again. After many seconds of silence, a man sitting on the log said, "Yes, we want you to come if you can." Then Dul, the young mother, said, "We would like to see Momo Dakel

Diwata Tasaday in our place. We would like him to see it, if it is not too difficult for him."

Elizalde said, "Mai, we've got to find out if this business about its being so difficult is really a way of saying don't come. Ask them if they would rather meet us at their place or here at the clearing. Tell them we could just come here and they could visit us whenever they wanted to."

A few Tasaday discussed this, and then one said, "Either place. Where do you like? We could come here if you want us to."

"Yes, but which do you prefer?"

"Either one. We could come here, or you could go there."

Manda said to tell them that if he went to their cave it would be only for a short visit, not to stay permanently, and that he would bring several friends with him. In view of this, if they would rather meet at the clearing, it would be fine.

The response was as before: "Whatever you like best."

This went on for several minutes; it was decided to change the subject. "Ask if there is anything we could do to make them happy."

"We are happy. When we were alone we were happy, and now we are even more happy."

"Well, then, do you want anything from us, or need anything?"

"No," Balayam said, "we don't want anything. We don't need anything —at least we don't know any things we want or need."

"But what did you like from our other visits? Anything you want more of?"

"All things Momo Dakel Diwata Tasaday gives us make us happy."

"Okay." Manda sighed. "Ask them to tell us more about the cave."

Balayam said how much they liked it, and again described the rock they must climb over that kept them from falling, and how "my father's father told my father, and my father told me, that we can roam in the forest in daytime, but must come back to the cave at night. It is always safe there."

"Safe from what?"

"Safe from rain, from snakes, from . . ." He shrugged as if to say "I don't know, just safe."

There was a rustle of activity in one of the shelters as an infant moved his bowels on the floor. His mother whisked him outside and grabbed soft leaves to wipe up the mess, finishing with splashes of water from a bamboo tube.

While this was going on, Manda found a fuzzy, black, white, and yellow centipede about two inches long and asked Balayam its name. *"Kolowan-tanna,"* he replied.

Elizalde laid it in his open palm and prodded it with a fingertip. The centipede curled up and Manda leaned his head down and pretended to take it in his mouth and swallow.

"Aaahh! Ooohhh!" the Tasaday chorused.

Then Manda opened his hand and there was the centipede. Tasaday eyebrows rose, eyes widened. He grabbed the jawbone of a wild pig and held it up to his chin and snorted, then pushed the bone's tip into Balayam's chest. The Tasaday snickered. A bird sang in the forest and Elizalde whistled back. The bird sang again. Elizalde stood up, shook his fist furiously in the air, whistled again, and sat down. After a few seconds the bird whistled and Elizalde leaped to his feet and shouted in mock anger. Once more the bird whistled, and the Tasaday erupted with laughter. Elizalde, defeated, sat down and then, deliberately, fell backward off the log into a bush. Balayam helped him up as the laughter, which had grown almost raucous, reached a fresh crescendo.

The Tasaday were asked if they imitated birds. Not that particular bird, they said, but they did call *le mokan*. It was as big as a hand, with a brown body and white head and tail. If *le mokan* sang or appeared when they were preparing to go somewhere, they sat down and waited. If it was morning, they delayed their trip until afternoon; if afternoon, until the next day.

Lobo, who had been cavorting since we arrived, crawled from under a pile of debris, picked up a younger child, balanced him on a stump, put the child on his shoulders and paraded, batting his eyelashes at us. He swept his long hair up on top of his head like a turban, dropped it, grabbed someone's ponytail and fanned it out with long sweeping strokes. He obviously enjoyed being watched, for, when we turned our attention to a woman holding an infant and gathering bright-orange flowers, Lobo ran to join her. (We learned later that she was his mother, Etut; his father was Bilangan.) The woman stood waist deep in foliage, plucking soft petals from the flowers and holding them out to the baby. He flicked out his tongue and lapped them from her fingertips, as if he were eating an ice-cream cone. Lobo then ate several petals, and when the mother licked petals and stuck them on the baby's face, Lobo did the same to himself. Both children soon had petals on their foreheads, cheeks, chins, nosetips. When I took photographs the woman paid no attention, but Lobo preened and grinned. We asked why they put flower petals on their faces, and they said it was for fun.

Elizalde again asked the Tasaday if they would prefer the next meeting here or at their place inside the forest.

"It would be good if Momo Dakel Diwata Tasaday could see our home. We would like to leave him there," Balayam said.

Elizalde explained that if he went there it would mean that friends of his would go ahead to try to find a spot near their place for the big bird to land. Would that be agreeable?

Yes, they said, but added that there was no open space in the forest for the bird to land.

What if his friends took in a huge bolo that made sounds like the big bird (a chain saw), and cut down trees so the bird could land? What did they think of that?

"We would like to see Momo Dakel Diwata Tasaday at our place. Any way he likes to do it is fine," said Kuletaw. It was the first statement any of us could recall him making spontaneously.

The helicopter then arrived with a hot lunch from the Blit settlement, delivered this time by Lucy and Mila. The Blit girl who had come the previous day stayed home; Balayam's attentions had made her nervous. Balayam saw the girls and bounded up to them.

"*Akun* Balayam," he repeated over and over, standing before them with a smile. He learned their names and then kept saying, slowly, "*Akun* Balayam—*niko* Usi [you are Lucy]" and "*Akun* Balayam—*niko* Miya."

The girls were pleased by this attention; they did not realize Balayam thought they were candidates for the girl Momo Dakel would provide for him. They were even more thrilled with Lobo, who edged near, rolling his eyes shyly. They immediately began to fuss over him. He stood quietly as they petted him, stroked his hair, teased him. He clearly did not mind.

Balayam shifted nervously on his feet, clucking and chuckling to himself. Finally he stretched out seductively on a bark platform a few feet away, with his head propped in his hand. "*Akun* Ba-lai-yam," he said.

His intention was straightforward—to get a woman—but there was also something whimsical in his manner. He seemed to be amused and delighted with himself. There was nothing brazen or crude in his manner. Instead, he was rather coy and teasing as he sent out his signals. The sight of him displaying himself—his body running a shade plump, smudges of ash and dirt on his face and knees—was both comic and touching. It was hard not to laugh aloud and several people stuttered with half-suppressed chuckles. Balayam looked at them, then joined in with a big laugh of his own and continued to lie there proudly.

A sharp crackling sound from the north distracted us. Ching walked to the clearing to investigate. He reported that three fires were blazing within two hundred yards of the knoll—Blit farmers preparing hillsides for planting.

"Mai, we've got to tell Dudim again that the Blit must stop that. It is too close, practically into the forest," Elizalde said.

The crackling grew louder through the afternoon. We asked the Tasaday if they had heard that noise before (they could not see the fires, which were visible only from atop the knoll); they said they had not. "It sounds like wind in the trees," Balayam said.

The visit ended in midafternoon with assurances that Elizalde would return after several days. Dafal would enter the forest beforehand to tell the Tasaday, but he would not go to their cave; nor would any of the men Dafal would bring later. If they heard strange noises, like the big bird, they should not worry because it would be the big bolo at work; but they should avoid anyone who appeared without Dafal's warning. The Tasaday nodded and said they would be waiting. Balayam kept smiling and watching Mila and Lucy, but he was more subdued. Igna had apparently informed him that these girls were not intended for him.

Before we left, Elizalde gave the Tasaday a piece of white cloth, salt, rice, and a whistle. We then learned that Dafal had given them a brass box inlaid with ivory to keep betel in, two knives, a comb, and a woven basket. Elizalde was furious. "Dammit!" he said to Mai. "This guy has got to stop giving them stuff. We never have a record of it and it just keeps popping up. An inlaid brass box, for God's sake! A comb! That kind of stuff will confuse everybody. Bring Dafal to Tboli. We better get this straightened out once and for all."

In parting, the Tasaday embraced Manda and Mai and Balayam made a small speech proclaiming the Tasaday's eagerness to show Momo Dakel their home—after which he slipped in a brief reminder about his need for a woman.

As we flew away, I thought again how little knowledge we had of the Tasaday. Questions such as where they had come from, how long they had been in the forest, and why they were so few represented only one aspect of our ignorance. Even more confounding was their seeming lack of adventure, curiosity, competitiveness; I had thought these were in some degree basic elements of human nature. Could anyone be so innocent? I still felt skeptical—perhaps I feared being taken in by a fairy tale. It was too romantic, too perfect: beautiful, gentle people in a Garden of Eden, hidden valley, Shangri-La.

Back at Tboli, Elizalde immediately began to plan the details of the cave expedition. Mai repeated his worry that footprints in their forest might upset the Tasaday by reminding them that strangers knew their secret place, but Elizalde had made up his mind. "We've got to go in if we want to get the land reserved," he said, adding that as soon as Panamin had established the location of the Tasaday homesite, President Marcos would proclaim it a reserve. It would not be a reservation in the popular sense, however—Elizalde was emphatic about that. He wanted to avoid any suggestion of similarity between the Tasaday reserve and American Indian reservations.

Elizalde hardly mentioned the senate elections; the court cases continued and his opponent had held on to a slight lead in the most recent re-count. All his attention went toward deciding who would go into the forest and how best to get there.

He was looking forward to briefing Lindbergh, who happened to be passing through Southeast Asia and had messaged that he would visit

Manda. He arrived the next afternoon and joined Manda and others of us in Manila, where arrangements for the expedition were being taken care of. Lindbergh was eager to participate. As a Panamin director, he was concerned with formulating an over-all policy toward the Tasaday that would ensure their safety; he questioned Elizalde closely about such things as financing and the size of the hoped-for reserve.

Scientific aspects of the expedition were as yet unsettled. Elizalde and Robert Fox had had a falling out—exactly why was not clear, but they had had disagreements about the Tasaday. Frank Lynch, professor of anthropology at Ateneo University, first declined, then accepted an invitation to join the expedition, even though another commitment would make his stay brief. A Filipino anthropologist, Carlos Fernandez, who was working toward a doctoral degree in anthropology from the University of California at Santa Clara, would accompany Lynch and stay on after he left. I asked Lynch if he knew of any contemporary cave dwellers. He knew of one group, the Toala, discovered early in the twentieth century in a remote valley on the Indonesian Island of Sulawesi (Celebes). There were about one hundred, the eldest of whom said they had once lived in caves, but had moved into small huts many years before their discovery. By 1913 the ruling Netherlands government had completed relocation of all the Toala to a village, where they underwent a rapid change in life style. There was still an identifiable Toala language in the 1960's, but the people were so widely dispersed throughout the island that anthropologists predicted they would vanish as a distinct group.

Elizalde was pleased to find that Kenneth MacLeish, a senior assistant editor of *National Geographic Magazine,* would be available. Early in 1971 he had spent several weeks among the Philippine tribes preparing a long article that became the basis for the Geographic Society's documentary film. Both the article and the film had elicited widespread enthusiasm for Panamin's work. John Launois, a free-lance photographer based in New York, would do the pictures for the *Geographic.*

My chief responsibility on the expedition would be to document it, both for Panamin and for any news articles I would be able to prepare.

After long discussions on how to get into the forest, it was decided that a helicopter would be best. The main objection to that method had been that cutting a clearing in the forest for a landing place would provide a convenient landmark that anyone could find, but Norman Certeza, Panamin's executive director, suggested building a treetop platform onto which we could either jump directly from the hovering helicopter or be lowered by cable. It sounded deceptively simple. According to Ching Rivero's estimate, the landing place would be about four thousand feet above sea level; the probable mountain cross winds coupled with the rotor blast would certainly test the platform's stability. Lindbergh, recalling his experiences as a stunt pilot, warned that jumping into the treetops would be risky, and landing by cable could be even more dangerous; he recommended walking in or else clearing a landing place on the ground. But Elizalde, Ching, and Certeza felt that, with careful planning, the treetop platform would work.

Lindbergh, who was leaving the next day for the United States but planned to be back for the start of the expedition in about ten days, chuckled and shook his head during the discussion of the treetop landing. "However you decide to do it," he said, "I wouldn't miss it for the world."

II
INSIDE
THE FOREST

6

To the Caves

NINETEEN Tboli from Kematu, led by Fludi, walked to the Ubu settlement, collected six more men, and proceeded to the Blit settlement, where they were joined by Al Spileski. Inside the jungle they met a smaller party led by Dafal. They had packed coils of rope, tools, chain saws, food, and weapons. By the time a week had passed, the advance party had reached the general vicinity of the cave and a landing site had been selected for the rest of the expedition. The platform would rest upon a tree about one hundred feet in the air.

The morning of March 23 dawned misty and gray but cleared after breakfast. The party was to enter in three flights; on each the jet helicopter would carry four passengers and essential personal gear. We were to jump one at a time as Bartolo kept the chopper hovering over the platform.

Elizalde, Launois, MacLeish, and I went on the first flight. The helicoter rose and swept away in a long low dip, then started up over the forest. Bart flew straight at the closest mountains, arched over the smallest one, and veered toward a higher peak on the right. Then he slanted down between two peaks, and green walls suddenly towered above us. After a minute or so a valley appeared below, the sides like giant green washboards standing against a hill. Bart turned up the valley, staying north of a wedge-shaped ridge that jutted up a few hundred feet from the valley floor and ran for almost its entire length.

Suddenly two red flares burst in the air to our left and Bart veered the chopper sharply, nosing down toward the ridge. Perhaps a thousand feet away and barely visible in the top of a spindly-looking tree was a tan dot.

Bart made the helicopter seem to float down. The platform grew to the size of a Ping-pong table . . . and then we were hovering at its edge. We could see Fludi and Fausto, an expert Tboli carpenter, waving in the chopper with one hand and holding onto the lashings with the other as the rotor blast slapped at them. Bart tried to keep the chopper to within five feet of the platform's surface.

Elizalde leaped first and Fludi grabbed him. Then Launois . . . and MacLeish. I slid toward the door and poised to jump, but a helicopter wheel got caught in the rope fence around the platform. Bart wrestled with the chopper a minute, soared upward, and patiently maneuvered in again. I could see Launois and Elizalde gesturing wildly. MacLeish was already talking into his tape recorder! I leaped and felt hands grab me as the downdraft buffeted the platform. The helicopter soared away, leaving the air suddenly still and the platform wobbling. I peered over the edge and saw a sea of green twisting away far below. It was about seventy-five feet from the platform to the narrow ridgetop, but each side of the ridge slanted down abruptly for another three hundred feet to the valley floor.

We descended by way of a trapdoor and a rope ladder attached to a tree trunk. Fludi and Fausto remained on top to remove the rope railing. The flight had taken only about five minutes, less time than expected.

Dafal emerged, grinning and babbling, from the advance party of Tboli, Ubu, Blit, and Blaan, who cheered as Elizalde came down the tree ladder. Dafal reported that they had seen only one person in the forest, Balayam, who had come one afternoon and talked to Dafal. They had seen footprints of other Tasaday, and Dafal thought their homesite was not too far.

Within fifteen minutes the helicopter returned, with Mai, Elizalde's bodyguard Felix, Igna, and her friend Sindi, a slender, sad-eyed Blit widow. Soon after it departed for its third delivery, Balayam appeared on the ridge, slipping out of the jungle perhaps one hundred yards away. He searched with his eyes for a moment, then with a smile bounded toward Elizalde, brushing past the tribesmen, and threw his arms around him. Balayam beamed at Elizalde, then squinted his eyes to watch the returning helicopter deposit Dr. Rebong, Ching, Mila, Lucy, and Onto, a Higa-onon girl lately added to the kitchen staff. Onto was used to the Higa-onon tree houses and was completely at home here. As I watched her nimbly descend from the platform, I realized that she was the girl who had raced up the mountain with my camera bag on my first day with the Higa-onon more than a year earlier.

Balayam stayed close to Elizalde while baggage was lowered by rope from the platform. Several tribesmen carried up clusters of large orchid plants which were thrown onto the chopper to be traded or sold by the Blit.

Elizalde instructed Mai to have the tribesmen prepare a camp on the ridge, which Spileski would supervise. "And pick four or so of your best boys to come with us," he said. "No one else is to come farther on unless specifically told to do so."

Elizalde asked Mai to find out from Balayam how far it was to the cave. "Not so far," Mai reported.

"Well, tell him we are ready whenever he wants to go—and not to go too fast."

Balayam nodded and set off down the ridge, Elizalde right behind him, MacLeish next; Mai, Igna, and a line of others joined the file. Launois and I waited near the tree ladder to take pictures as they passed, but one step beyond the ladder Balayam turned, made a quick hop-step to his left, plunged into the foliage and straight down the side of the ridge. There was no trail.

"Here we go!" someone yelled as the line of people bounded after Balayam and sank up to their waists in green. Seconds later the front of the column was out of sight; only Elizalde's white cap and MacLeish's head were visible.

Launois and I joined Ching at the end of the line and crashed down the slope. A slight trail had been broken by those ahead and their footwork made the damp earth slippery, but the resistance of the dense foliage made it like walking through neck-deep water. When we reached a sparsely grown patch, we all plummeted out of control, even the Tboli. A grab for support might produce assistance from a sturdy branch or a ripping tear from a thorny vine.

Within an hour we were on the valley floor. A stream flowed swift and clear over pebbles and around rocks and boulders. It was less than a foot deep in most places and rarely more than ten feet across.

Elizalde and MacLeish had stayed close to Balayam, scrambling as best they could as he flashed smoothly along, using his arms as much as his legs to travel—swinging and sliding on vines and branches, vaulting rotten stumps, scooting on top of fallen tree trunks. At the stream Balayam danced from rock to rock for a quarter of a mile or so, then swerved into the forest, heading up the face of a cliff that Elizalde thought would be impossible to climb. He shook his head, indicating he and MacLeish could not go that way; Balayam moved farther on then, up a steep but negotiable incline.

We followed, hooking fingers under roots and around slender trees, digging toes into the slick earth, clawing and pulling our way. After a few minutes our breath came in rasps and mud glazed our knees, elbows, boots. The physical effort prevented much looking around; sweat-stung eyes searched the ground for the next root to grab or niche to use as a foothold. It was noontime but dark as dusk, except where shafts of sunlight pierced the forest and spangled leaves and ferns with yellow. We reached a shelf in the mountainside, gave a shout, and paused to rest.

"Here! Up here. Come on!" a voice called back.

We saw only more forest, but the voice sounded straight ahead and near. We clambered over slabs of rock and huge ferns, stumbling among exposed roots and rattan. Then, at the top of a rise, a growth of bamboo was silhouetted against a soft yellow light. Ducking through a curtain of leaves, I stopped in a half crouch, staring upward into an airy space. It was as if I had emerged unexpectedly from a dark cellar into a huge well-lighted room. Colors, shapes, sounds swirled into my consciousness as I wiped sweat from my eyes and stepped slowly forward. It seemed as if I were floating within the frame of a gigantic painting that had been hung on a mountainside. We had reached the caves.

Several Tasaday stood quietly, smiling, their bronze skin gleaming against a background of gray rock roughly one hundred seventy-five feet across and seventy-five feet high. This rectangle was etched with jagged ledges, niches, archways. The broadest arch curved directly above and behind the Tasaday and formed the yawning mouth of a cave. From there, a dusty path rose over a smooth ledge and angled upward to the left, running beneath a ragged overhang of rock. The overhang partly hid the mouths of two more caves, one slightly higher than the other, at least twenty-five feet above us. Bright sunlight struck the rocky expanse between the lower and upper caves, coloring it yellow-amber. Vines, grass, and rattan fringed the cave mouths and laced the open spaces in front of them. Leaves in a dozen shades of green reflected light in pale shimmers. The air was cool and still, except for the sound of birds and a waterfall.

The first words I heard were from Manda. "Unbelievable . . . unbelievable . . ."

Half a dozen Tasaday clustered around him and MacLeish, who sat on the ground and held the hands of the Tasaday nearest them. Faces appeared at the entrances to the two upper caves, and a boy ran down the path, his body flashing in the sun. Lobo suddenly appeared on the apron of the middle cave, jumped onto a white-barked sapling, shouting "Momo Daa-kell!" as he slid twenty feet down the wavering tree to the ground and bounded toward us, black hair flying.

By now eight more Tasaday had joined the group around Elizalde, some wide-eyed, others laughing. I was overcome by a combination of exhilaration and sadness. I wanted to laugh and shout "This is it! This is it!" but instead stood speechless, staring at the caves and the Tasaday.

We spent a half hour on an earth mound in front of the lower cave. Nobody said much; words were inadequate. Kuletaw rested a hand on MacLeish's arm; Balayam snuggled happily against Elizalde. The other Tasaday sat on the ground or stood chatting among themselves. One of the two women holding children was wearing a faded cloth around her hips. All the other Tasaday were wearing only leaves.

Manda suggested that we take a few photographs and then go back downhill to set up a camp. As we worked our way down, we found our speech again. It had been like sailing backward in a time machine, Mac-Leish said. "That scene was not Neolithic, it was Paleolithic—seventy-five thousand years ago!" Launois agreed. "It was out of a history book . . . a museum."

About one hundred yards below the caves was a knobby shelf, where the trees were not dense and the slope was gentle. A gully alongside the shelf carried the creek created by the waterfall at the caves to the stream another hundred yards below. The shelf was out of sight of the caves, about halfway between them and the stream.

Within an hour, four shelters were under construction. Sheets of heavy salmon-colored plasticized canvas were stretched and tied to trees and propped up with cut limbs. The sides were left open to make them as airy as possible. Years of experimenting had shown that this was the best style of tent for the jungle. "You must have breathing room or jungle fever will get you," Elizalde said. "I've seen it. Everybody packed in, snarling at each other—especially if you're trapped by a lot of rain. It could drive you crazy."

Three Tboli boys worked at making flat terraces for sleeping and a place for a kitchen, which Mila, Lucy, and Onto began setting up. After about two hours the basic accommodations were set. A tent was erected about fifteen yards above the main shelter for Dr. Rebong, Felix, and the radio operator, a Blaan youth named Delfin Lawa but always called Dog Love, his radio code name. The first message received on his single-side-band radio said that the weather outside was rainy and gusty, meaning the anthropologists would not come in until the next morning.

The camp was surrounded by plants and trees of all shapes and sizes: palms, rattan, bamboo, ferns; giant oaks that rose more than two hundred feet; air plants that hung from branches and orchids that clustered in the treetops. Vines drooped through the dim light, some as thick as a man's leg and at least one hundred feet long. Ragged patches of sky were visible through three and four canopies of leaves.

Balayam and Bilangan visited the camp in the early afternoon and watched all that was going on. Balayam walked over to Igna and Sindi, who took a chew of betel nut from a small packet and tapped Balayam on the leg, offering it to him. He took it, smiling, and cautiously inserted it into his mouth, chewed, screwed up his face slightly, and nodded. Balayam stood quietly for about a minute, then began to stroll around, looking at this and that, until he reached the edge of the tent. He peeked over his shoulder, saw that Sindi was not watching, plucked the chew from his mouth, and flicked it away. Then he resumed his stroll.

Presumably the mix had not met his standards. According to Dafal, the Tasaday used the rare *bui* vine in their mix, combining it with pieces of betel nut, betel leaf, powdery lime made from snail's shells, and wrapping all in a soft leaf.

As the final touches were being put on the shelters, the sound of approaching rain joined that of the rushing stream. The forest darkened and suddenly water seemed to be everywhere—in rivulets and pools, streaming from tent folds. Curtains of rain enclosed the tents. The seams began to drip, and, as we worked to repair them, we heard Balayam laugh at something Bilangan said. "He advises us that their caves don't leak," Mai reported.

The rain lasted for hours. As we sat looking out into the darkness, a message was handed to Elizalde. He read it and frowned. "Okay," he said. "I'm glad it's over . . . just as well." The Senate Electoral Tribunal had ruled against his appeal; unless he chose to fight further, the last senate seat would go to his opponent. He shrugged it off by sending a message of congratulations to Almendras.

Mahayag, who had demonstrated the use of the small scraper on a previous trip, stopped in briefly. Then he and Bilangan said good-by and returned to the caves. Balayam stayed for a while and, through Igna and Mai, talked to us. He said the Tasaday had always lived in these caves. "Our fathers and our fathers' fathers lived here. We never heard of Tasaday living anywhere else."

"Where did the first Tasaday come from?" we asked.

"I don't know. Our ancestors said never to leave this place. They had a good dream that said if we stayed we would not get sick. We have a little sickness—like coughing—but nothing bad."

After he left, Dafal and Fludi came in, carrying a Tboli spear and several arrows that had previously been given to the Tasaday. Fludi found them near the edge of the forest. "I wonder if this is some kind of rejection of our ways," Manda said. "They may be fed up with us already."

He instructed Mai to have Dafal ask the Tasaday to live as they had before meeting outsiders—the woman with the cloth skirt could go back to leaves like the others, and items such as beads should not be brought out for a while.

We ate roasted chicken and rice for dinner. The rain stopped by eight o'clock, and a cool wind fluttered the tenting. We unrolled our bedding and slept early our first night in the Tasaday's forest.

Sunlight eased into the jungle shortly after five. Three hours later seven of us were making the first visit to the caves by outsiders. The lower one, where we had been the day before, was empty. We mounted the rounded ledge to the left of it and walked up the path, which was still dusty despite the rain because the overhanging rocks jutted out several feet. A Tasaday appeared in the mouth of the uppermost cave, calling out as we approached. We climbed a rocky ten-foot incline to a ledge about four feet below the cave's lower lip. We looked inside to a vision of time flung backward.

About twenty Tasaday were seated beside fires or on rocky shelves around the rear of the cave. Their eyes, reflecting light from the fires, blinked out of faces coated with soot and ash. Limestone and conglomerate rock walls and ceiling caught reddish highlights when the flames blazed up. From the middle of the back wall an outcrop of rock protruded a few feet, forming a divider; to its left Bilangan, his wife, and children sat around a small fire.

We hoisted ourselves directly into the cave from our position on the ledge, although the main entrance appeared to be about fifteen feet to the left, where the lip curved in and a large slab of rock sloped up, forming a ramp. The chamber was about thirty feet from the front to the deepest point in the curving back wall and roughly fifty feet across at its widest point; the concave ceiling was ten feet from the center of the floor. The walls and ceiling were a glistening dark brown; directly above fire sites the ceiling was like shiny black coal. The smoke had left a glazed tacky coating, as if the surfaces had all been recently shellacked. A Tasaday man showed me a chunk of rock that had apparently broken off from the wall. I could see that the smoke glaze had built up to a thickness of one eighth of an inch.

There were several small, natural niches in the rock wall. One held firewood, another several deerhorns, another an empty cracker tin salvaged from a visit to the clearing, and still another three stone tools. As we glanced around the Tasaday looked frightened; none but Balayam smiled and the whites of their staring eyes were accentuated by the smudges of soot on their cheeks. Manda wondered if we were upsetting them. He picked up the cracker tin, put it on his head, held some deerhorns above his ears, and snorted around the cave teasing the children. Several Tasaday laughed.

Balayam, Mahayag, and Udelen began to make a fire. They hunched over a slim foot-long stick of wood, round like a dowel, whose tip fitted an indentation in a thicker stick about the same length. Udelen began by rotating the drilling stick between his palms as his hands slid downward. When he neared the bottom, Mahayag immediately placed his palms around the top of the stick and continued the twirling. When his hands reached the base, Balayam took over. They huddled over the drill with intense concentration. After each man had had three turns a wisp of smoke appeared and Balayam quickly applied a handful of fluffy dry moss. The men murmured as the moss began to smoke. Balayam lifted it and blew gently—then a tiny orange dot burst into flame. Balayam handed the burning material to Mahayag, who held it proudly for a small boy to see. The men rocked back on their buttocks and laughed. *"Yeeah! Yeeah! Yeeah!"* they said, their eyes shining.

Their delight was contagious and we visitors laughed, too, suddenly feeling that we had shared in a great event. I reflected on the fact that a few days before, we were in Manila with honking buses and skyscrapers; yesterday we had leaped from a jet helicopter, and now we sat in a cave rooting for people as they made fire!

A baby cried, and was given a piece of *ubud* (moist palm heart). They said that *natek* (mashed and cooked palm pith) was their favorite food, followed by *ubud,* and then *biking* (wild yam). *Natek* was hardest to obtain. The Tasaday said that they did not know how to extract palm pith until Dafal showed them and provided the metal tool.

Still, they were proud of their stone tools; Balayam brought out the three that were cached in a wall niche. One was flat and round like a saucer, another triangular with a sharp point, and the third was oblong. All had handles tightly wrapped with rattan strips and were similar to those seen at the edge of the forest, which were given to Imelda Marcos. These tools were prized heirlooms, made by their ancestors, Balayam said. They called a stone tool *fais batu* (striker made of stone), pronounced faw-ees baw-tu; a metal knife was simply *fais.*

Manda, sitting on the cave floor, asked Mai and Igna to explain that we would stay in the forest for several days, and that we were strangers and might make mistakes—the Tasaday must speak up if we did anything wrong or bothered them.

They nodded and said they would. When asked specifically if there were things we should do or not do, the young woman named Dul said something to Balayam, who nodded and told Igna: "We do not remove the vines or branches in front of our place here. They are beautiful and we love them. They should not be cut." They were aware of the cutting we had done the day before to prepare our camp.

"Tell the boys, Mai," Manda said. "No cutting unless absolutely necessary. And absolutely *none* at the cave site. Anybody who does will walk out of here immediately."

He then asked about rattan earrings. Balayam grinned and pulled back the hair covering his ears. The metal hoops were gone—as they were from all the Tasaday. He wore only a tiny wooden ring made from a rattan seedling.

Launois asked if it would be all right to use his strobe lights to photograph the Tasaday in the back of the cave. Mai explained the lights to Igna and asked her to find out if the Tasaday objected. Balayam indicated it would be agreeable. But when Launois flashed them a few times experimentally, the Tasaday flinched. Manda told them that the cameras were collecting memories, and then he clowned to distract them while Launois worked. The Tasaday looked away when the lights flashed. As Launois hurried to finish, Frank Lynch and Carlos Fernandez arrived at the caves with Johnny Ugarte.

The Tasaday said that all of them slept in the uppermost cave except Balayam, who used the smaller one next to it, reaching it via a twenty-foot-long honeycomb of niches. Asked why nobody slept in the large lower cave, Balayam said, "We just don't." No reason was given.

The caves faced the east, toward the stream, which was not visible. The slope was much steeper and more sparsely grown over in front of the upper caves and the sun's rays hit them directly in the mornings. The lower cave, fronted by flatter land and much heavier growth, was in shadow most of the day.

After another hour we returned to the camp. Lynch was impressed with what he had seen, but the cleanliness of the cave bothered him. There were few accouterments of life, like scraps of firewood, or gifts received in the past several months. He thought the caves were perhaps temporary shelters and that the Tasaday lived elsewhere.

What with every conversation requiring double translation, it would be easy to misunderstand; or they may have said they always lived here in order to mislead us for some reason. The fact was that the caves were just too empty.

He made such a strong point about it that we pondered throughout lunch, until somebody remembered that Dafal had been instructed to ask the Tasaday to show how they lived before meeting outsiders. Dafal told us that the Tasaday had willingly complied. Early that morning they had removed everything, although there wasn't much, Dafal said.

"What did they do with it?"

Dafal shrugged. "I don't know. They just took it away."

Balayam visited the camp later and we asked him if they had taken things out of the cave. "Yes," he said. "Dafal told us that Momo Dakel Diwata Tasaday said we should."

He was asked where they had put their things. He said only that they were nearby, in a safe spot.

Lynch asked what they called this place.

"Tasaday. This is the home of the Tasaday," Balayam said.

"And what do you call the stream?"

"It is the Tasaday stream."

"Do you go far from here?"

"No. The longest I have been away was three nights. And not often."

"Are there other caves like these?"

"No. No other place like ours."

"What do you do when you see other people in the forest?"

"We don't see other people."

"What about the Sanduka? Where is their place?"

Balayam pointed south, away from Blit, deeper into the forest.

"Do you see the Sanduka?"

"No. I was at their place only as a child, with my father. He told me they were good people. Their place is near a stream, but not the same stream as ours."

"You see no other people?"

"We don't see any. I don't know if there are any."

"Do you still use the things Dafal and Momo Dakel gave you?"

"Yes. We use them for cutting, for getting food. Before, we used deer-horns and sticks. Now, we use knives to get *biking* and to make *natek.*"

"And where are the bolos now?"

"We keep some by the smaller creek where we make *natek.* We keep all of our belongings in their places, but some are in a new place . . . Dafal asked us to move them."

He said they had moved betel nut, fruit, *bui* vine, and then added, possibly with a touch of defensiveness, "This is the only place to live in the forest." I wondered if he said this to assure us, for whatever reason, that they did not have other caves.

Asked how often they found edible roots, Balayam said frequently but not always; when they did not get roots they would get palm pith instead, or tadpoles or crabs from the stream. He said everybody helped—if one group went fishing, another went for roots or *natek,* and everyone shared what they got.

"What if nobody gets any food?"

"But we must get some."

"But if you have very little food, what happens? Who gets to eat it?"

"We divide it among the smallest children."

"What do you think about the visitors coming to your special place?"

"We are not afraid because Momo Dakel Diwata Tasaday is with you. But if he were not here, and we saw you and others—that man who covers himself with the bright things—we would run." (He may have meant Johnny Ugarte, who was wearing a scarlet shirt.)

"Is there anything else that bothers you?"

"Those flashing lights [the strobe lights]. We don't know what to think about them."

Balayam had been answering all questions patiently, some for the second and third time since he had first met outsiders. Now he was beginning to show fatigue: pausing and looking away between questions, sighing, squirming, and darting his eyes toward Manda, who was sitting a few yards away.

He was asked who is the most important Tasaday, the headman. "Nobody. Bilangan is good for fishing and for *biking.* Others are good, too."

"Who decides who does what?"

"We do as we like."

"Well, when Dafal asked you to come and meet Momo Dakel it must have been a big decision. How did you decide it?"

Balayam's interest sparked again. "When Dafal asked us to come out, he said there was a big man to see us. So we went to see him. Some Tasaday were scared, but we all came. We told each other to come so all of our eyes could see."

"But why did you come out? What did Dafal tell you about the big man?"

"That he was a great man who would love us. And he does—he gave us knives, and that thing we don't know the name of [making a forward-back motion with his thumb, indicating the flashlight]."

"Did Dafal tell you the man would give these things?"

"No, he didn't say so. But he did say the man would have pity for us."

"What do you mean by pity?"

Balayam repeated the word for pity, *widiwan,* which Mai said was like the word for love and described the feeling for children, friends, relatives, mates.

Because the decision to come out was probably the most important of their lives, we asked more questions about it, but Balayam added only that they "gathered together and some did not want to go, some did. I, Balayam, urged them to go. [He smiled toward Elizalde.] It was not a long meeting. We just met and decided that we would all go."

"Are you sorry you went?"

"No."

"It doesn't seem so far to that clearing. Why did you not go there before?"

"Our ancestors told us not to leave this place. Someday, they said, a god of the Tasaday will come to you."

"What would he do?"

"They said that when he came nothing would be bad and we would get something good."

"What would you get?"

"We didn't know—maybe he would give us something and stay forever in our place."

"And now the rest of us have come also. What about that?"

"I am happy to see you. You have shining faces."

Balayam was again clearly weary of the questions; he sighed deeply and loudly, crawled over to Elizalde, and hugged him.

Bilangan arrived and began to chat with Mai and Igna, telling them that the flashlight given them previously did not work. Mai inserted new batteries, switched the light on and off, and handed it to Balayam, who could not turn it on. Bilangan took it and pushed the switch forward: light. "Aaah . . . yahaa," the men exclaimed.

They passed it back and forth, switching it on and off. Bilangan put it to his lips and blew on the lens. He shook his head. Then Balayam blew on it. "This is not so good," Bilangan told Mai. "It cannot make fire."

Then, with a hug for Elizalde and a nod to Mai, the men pointed toward the caves and departed.

There was work to be done at the camp, so we decided not to visit the cave in the afternoon. Lynch, Elizalde, and Fernandez discussed the reservation sought by Panamin. Elizalde insisted that Panamin did not want a reservation for the Tasaday patterned after those popularly associated with the American Indians. He said the intention was to leave the Tasaday to continue as they were, except that now they would be protected from outsiders.

Balayam sauntered into camp later on and sat on a bench the Tboli boys had made out of tree limbs. He seemed eager to talk, so we called Igna. The first question we asked was whether the Tasaday went out at night.

There was no need to go out at night, Balayam said. When it got dark, they went to the caves—unless they were gathering food too far away to get home before dark; then they built lean-tos or found roots to sleep under. And anyway the night was dangerous. "It has thorns, snakes, leeches, things you cannot see. And you might slide off a cliff or steep hill. In the daytime we can see these things, and our bird [*le mokan*] warns us; when it calls, we stay still. My father told me that. If you go out when the bird calls, something bad may happen—a branch may fall on you, or you may fall down yourself, or a snake may bite you." He mentioned again that his mother was bitten and died.

Balayam was just a boy when his father died. "He had a very painful chest while he was gathering food in the forest. And he died there." The body was left in the forest. If someone died in the cave, the body was taken into the forest; but there was not one general burial place, nor were the spots marked in any way. The body was merely covered with leaves.

"What about the soul of a dead person? What happens to it?"

Balayam did not answer—perhaps he had not understood the question, or did not want to understand it. Talking about his parents' death had made him uneasy. And it was always especially difficult to translate abstract ideas like soul. So Mai asked if the Tasaday had dreams. Balayam said yes and then apparently saw the connection between that question and the previous—or it may have been suggested by Mai or Igna—because he added: "The soul may be the part of you that sees the dream." He said the dream (or the seer of dreams) was called *lomogul*. "I dream," he said, "but I don't know where it ends or starts."

In an earlier meeting with the Tasaday, Robert Fox had picked up the names Talili and Lambong, but it had not become clear whether they referred to people or to places. Lynch now asked Balayam what they meant. He did not know about the first, but Lambong was a Tasaday place where a smaller stream connected with their large stream.

"How about the Tasafeng [another forest group]?"

Balayam looked hesitant, pointed one way, then another. Finally he said he was not sure, and gazed out of the tent into the darkening afternoon. He sighed, hunched his shoulders, and stood up. "Kakay [friend] Mai, I will go now," he said, and walked away toward the caves.

That evening, Lynch told us he was now satisfied that the Tasaday did make their permanent home in the caves. Determining the exact scientific significance of the Tasaday was not going to be easy, Lynch said. "We can't say yet. There's so much frustration in trying to get solid data. Take Balayam today, for instance. Just trying to learn what he knows was frustrating for him and us. The need is for an anthropologist to learn the Tasaday language and then get inside the head of Balayam and learn the great story he knows."

Carlos Fernandez hoped to learn as many Tasaday words as possible, but for the next week or two would concentrate on studying their foods, gathering and trapping techniques, and the range of their daily travels. He would later co-ordinate his research with Lynch, who had to return to Manila the next day.

Manda felt that the Tasaday proved the falseness of the long-held belief that food gatherers must be nomadic. "These people don't have to go far. They only stay away all night if they can't get home before dark. Maybe they stay a couple of nights if there is plenty of food where they are gathering, but it isn't a regular practice—even making lean-tos was learned from Dafal. These people simply do not travel."

After dinner, the others retired to their tents and Manda, Mai, and I talked. Around nine Manda said, "Shall we visit the caves? Come on, let's go up." The three of us and Ching, Igna, and Sindi picked our way toward the caves by flashlight. When Manda shouted from the lower cave, a welcoming shout came in return. We climbed up the path and rocky ledges, guided by the soft glow from the upper cave.

Bilangan and his family sat around a small fire to the left of the rock that protruded from the rear wall, and others were scattered around two fires on the other side. The children were huddled together; one was asleep under a ragged rice sack, two others on small thin mats of bark. The older Tasaday reclined on rocky ledges at the rear.

Balayam came over from his cave with the news that some Tasaday were staying out all night making *natek*. Mai asked who stayed in the middle cave with him, and Balayam said he stayed alone. He repeated he was the only Tasaday who had no family, no children, no mother, no father, no wife. Igna giggled and mumbled something about Sindi, who sat beside her, and then Mai, Igna, Balayam, and Sindi spoke together for several minutes. The other Tasaday, after a few greetings, had apparently gone back to sleep.

"Do Balayam and Sindi want to talk, to get acquainted?" Manda asked Mai. Mai replied that Balayam wanted to very much, and so did Sindi—

but she was too shy. "Perhaps we should leave them with just you and Igna, so they won't feel there is a crowd," Manda said. "Let's go look around."

Manda, Ching, and I worked our way back down to the lower cave and shone flashlights into it. It was by far the largest cave; the mouth slanted sharply back toward an inner chamber, whose entryway was marked with a line of boulders that looked as if they had been placed there deliberately. We ducked through the low, wide opening, which turned out to be one side of the triangular inner chamber. The other two walls were straight and flat, and about fifty feet long; the ceiling was roughly six feet high.

We could hear the waterfall that fell into small pools in front of the cave's mouth. Surprisingly, we could even hear the stream rushing in the valley below.

Bats hung by their tails from the rocky ceiling. Several squeaked and flapped their wings when the light flashed on them, then fluttered past our heads and out into the forest. Swifts darted around us; their nests were solid and showed signs of long use, indicating the Tasaday did not bother the birds or their eggs. We saw spiders—one huge, black and stripe-legged—a mound of rocks on the cave floor, some human excrement, signs of a fire or two; bat droppings crusted the floor and dusted rocks everywhere, and the odor was strong. We ducked into the arching mouth of the cave and breathed deeply of fresh air. The Tasaday apparently made little use of this cave. The upper cave was more habitable. Though smaller, its high ceiling made for better ventilation and a sense of spaciousness.

We had been gone about fifteen minutes when Manda called to Mai: "Ready to go?"

Mai shouted yes; then he and the women joined us. As we started toward camp, we heard "Momo, Momo Daa-kelll . . ." Balayam was singing good night.

7

In the Stone Age

THE next morning was bright and the air fresh as Fernandez, MacLeish, Launois, and I accompanied Balayam, Bilangan, and Lobo to the stream that wound through the valley about two hundred yards below the caves. The water rushed briskly toward us from around a bend upstream and disappeared beyond another bend twenty yards farther on. It bubbled and foamed over rocks and boulders, around grassy islands and soggy dark logs. Shrubby bushes, ferns, and several varieties of palm grew along both banks.

Lobo sat on a large boulder, holding a leaf twisted into a neat cone, as Balayam and Bilangan waded into the water. They worked slowly downstream, looking like high-hipped four-legged animals as they slid along searching with their hands and feet for the slippery prey. Every minute or two one of the men would shout and straighten up, dripping and smiling, with some morsel to deposit into Lobo's cone. After a quarter of an hour they had five shiny tadpoles the size of a child's thumb and two small pink-gray crabs with bodies not much larger than a bottle cap.

After working for about fifty yards, the men stepped into the forest to search for *biking* and *ubud*. Lobo bounded farther along the stream, poking around on the bank until he found what he wanted. He perched on a boulder, gnawing at pieces of reddish-brown wild ginger.

In the forest, Balayam spotted telltale leaves and tugged out a carrot-sized root, which he quickly replanted—too small. Bilangan located a mature *biking,* and the two men started digging with a pointed stick and a bolo, every so often lifting out chunks of root. They took turns scooping out the soil, until the hole was so deep that they had to lie on their stomachs. After half an hour they decided that they had got all they could

(there were enough chunks to have made one three-foot-long root).
Bilangan made a last probe of the hole as Balayam, smeared with dirt
from his forehead to his toes, stood up and began to sing happily. Fludi,
who had joined us, knew enough words to say the song was about the joy
of finding *biking*.

Next, Balayam found an *ubud* palm. Three strokes of his bolo topped
the three-inch-diameter tree. He then lopped off a section about three feet
long and pared away the bark until he held only the cream-colored heart.
He smoothed this with his bolo, looked it over, and bit into it, crunching
and smiling with a mouthful of pith. (We tasted it later; it was similar to
artichoke heart.)

Bilangan had gone in another direction. After Balayam had taken a
few more bites of the palm heart, he, too, bounded out of sight. Lobo
appeared occasionally, but never for long. Each seemed to have evapo-
rated into the jungle.

We walked toward the stream, catching glimpses of Balayam as he
darted over knolls and dips in the forest shadows. We finally saw him a
few minutes later, standing motionless beside the stream thirty feet below.
There was no evident trail down from the embankment. Bilangan suddenly appeared, a dozen yards away from us. He skittered down a fallen
tree, hopped off the end, bounced a few steps through greenery, and was
alongside Balayam. It looked easy, so we climbed onto the fallen tree.
The surface was round and slippery—it was like standing on a greasy
basketball. We decided to crawl out one at a time, but part of the rotting
trunk cracked and gave way under the weight of the first man. He crashed
into the foliage and on down the embankment. I straddled a thick branch
that veered off from the trunk and slid out to a stump, then grabbed hold of
a slender tree that rose beside the stream. The tree swayed and bent down
with my weight, so that I was dangling by my hands just a few feet from
the ground. I let go, expecting to drop neatly to a stand-up landing, but
the strap of my camera bag had hooked over a branch and I was jerked
cockeyed. For a moment I hung suspended; then the branch broke, and
I flopped noisily into pebbles and rocks, flat on my back.

Bilangan, who had been watching our progress as he wrapped chunks
of root in leaves, now gave me a little smiling nod as I lay there, hiked his
eyebrows in acknowledgment, and went back to work. He seemed to be
saying "Well, that's not exactly how I would have done it, but, of course,
it's up to you . . ."

Balayam came loping up as we reassembled around Bilangan while he
finished wrapping his packets of root. Around each he wound a vine and
made a knot, which he cinched in such a way as to leave a looping handle.
The packets looked like tiny green purses.

As we walked back upstream, Lobo rejoined us from the forest and
Bilangan picked up items he had cached along the bank—the leaf cone

containing tadpoles and crabs, a piece of *ubud* he had cut while alone. Balayam had nibbled about six inches off his stalk of *ubud* by now and tucked the rest under his arm like a riding crop. They accompanied us to where our path led up to the camp and continued on, apparently to take their regular route to the cave.

Later we watched them cooking. The tadpoles and crabs were wrapped in leaves and nestled among hot embers. The *biking* was tossed into the fire, unwrapped. The *ubud* was eaten raw.

Soon after we reached our tents, Lindbergh arrived, rosy-faced and sweating darkly through a tan shirt, but in high spirits. "Manda," he said, grinning and shaking his head, "you've outdone yourself. That landing in the treetop was spectacular, just spectacular. It's a masterful piece of carpentry, but I can't say I'd want to jump into it every day. Once is enough—but it was marvelous."

After a short rest, during which he sipped a glass of water from the stream, Lindbergh looked surprisingly fresh, especially for a man of seventy. He wore familiar khaki work pants and shirt and a floppy white cap with the narrow brim turned down all around. He had brown boots, however, instead of his usual black shoes.

"I had left my gear at our place in Hawaii, thinking I would stop off and pick it up on my way back," he said. "But your cable [that the expedition was ready to start sooner than expected] caught me by surprise, Manda, I must admit. I was in New York City and hurried over to a surplus store and got what I could—these boots, for instance—and rushed to catch the next plane coming out this way. I had only a few hours."

Half a dozen of us visited the caves in the afternoon. Lindbergh towered above the Tasaday as he quietly looked everything over. Fernandez, who had been walking around outside the top cave, called attention to a mound protruding from the ledge just below the lower lip. "Look. That's the midden," Carlos said. Ashes and bits of charcoal and other debris lay on top of the mound, which was grown over with leafy plants, bamboo, and rattan that rose higher than the mouth of the cave. The refuse heap was about twelve feet across and extended out perhaps ten feet from the cave. "It must go down about sixty feet." He pushed his glasses back up to the bridge of his nose in a gesture of nervous excitement. "See those ashes on top? They apparently just sweep everything out of the cave and that's where it lands. No wonder there is no debris pile inside—they just push it all out here." We frequently speculated thereafter about what the midden contained and how long it had taken to reach its present size; but it would take an archeologist to probe it and discover the meaning of what was inside.

This was the third day of the expedition; by now we were able to match quite a few names and faces. Dul and Dula were the young women, perhaps in their late twenties, who continually carried young children. Dul was dark tan and solid-looking, with plump breasts, round face, and a thick mass of long dark hair. She was the least shy of the women and sat confidently among us. Dula was slender and extremely shy, with peach-colored skin, and hair usually tied behind her head with a vine. She appeared fragile beside Dul. Her eyes flickered hesitantly when we were around, and I had never heard her speak.

But neither had I heard the voices of the three other women—Etut, Sekul, and Ginun. Etut was Bilangan's wife, Lobo's mother. She had delicate features, large, dark eyes, and long, wavy, almost curly, black hair. She was very handsome, but was thick around the middle and did not move as gracefully as the others. She often looked uncomfortable.

Sekul was the oldest woman, the wife of Kuletaw; both were in their sixties, at least. She had leathery-looking, tan skin, sagging flat breasts, and tousled curly hair with a streak of silver-gray in the front.

Ginun was rarely present. She was thin and quiet, and always had downcast eyes. Her straight dark hair fell forward against her cheeks, so that she had to peek through it to see.

Of the men, Balayam, Mahayag, Udelen, and Lefonok ranged from the mid-twenties to late thirties in age. Bilangan was probably about forty.

Udelen, Dul's husband, had a shy manner; when he laughed, as at Elizalde's clowning, he sometimes giggled out of control, holding his sides and covering his mouth. Lefonok, the widower with the fair-skinned son, often had a vacant stare and seldom laughed. Mahayag, Dula's husband, was sturdy and muscular, and said little.

The man we saw least was Tekaf, a stringy-bodied fellow, never heard to speak. He had bloodhound eyes that looked soulfully over a long nose. He was Ginun's husband, probably in his late fifties.

Of the children, Lobo was easily the best known. He was everywhere, climbing, laughing, teasing, showing off, enjoying attention. His older brother, Lolo, was also physically handsome, although he did not have Lobo's striking beauty and exuberance. Their other brothers were Natek, about four, another unusually good-looking child with chubby legs and big black eyes; and a boy not yet named, who was probably less than two years old.

Soon we learned the names of all the others. Adug and Gintoy were the teen-age sons of Sekul and Kuletaw—Adug with the lumpy beginnings of a goiter, Gintoy with ringworm and a fungus affliction that made scaly white patches all over his body. Widower Lefonok's children were Kalee, a shy girl of about nine; Udo, a thin boy who looked about the same age; and Sasa, the light-haired boy with fair skin, who was also called Mabulu-ulu (white hair, or white head). The children of Dul and Udelen were two boys, Siyus, about three, and Maman, about two. The children of

Dula and Mahayag were Siyul, a girl of perhaps six, and Biking, a boy of possibly seven. All the ages were guesses, with room for several years one way or the other in most cases.

This afternoon more than half the Tasaday were away but the rest seemed more relaxed than before. The older children took turns climbing on the rock outcropping on the cave's back wall. Four feet high and two feet wide, it made a perfect perch with a commanding view. A boy would sit or squat on top of this rock throne, feet curled over the edge, and gaze out into the forest or down at us. When he slid off, another boy would climb up. MacLeish noted that the top and front of the rock were glassy smooth, in contrast to the rough sides. After watching the boys slide on and off it for a while, we realized that over the years such buffing had worn away the roughness.

There were no deliberate improvements apparent—no steps notched into the entryways, no deepening of niches for storage. For us it was uncomfortable to sit for long on the rough floor and arduous to mount the steep incline to the cave. But the Tasaday obviously were not bothered; even the smallest toddlers got around more easily than we did.

And the sight of a Tasaday darting along the stream or gliding through the forest or easing up onto the rocky throne in the cave was visual pleasure. They moved like graceful animals: no wasted motions, no jerky stops and starts. When they ran, stopped, and sat, it was not in a series of distinct muscular actions but, rather, in one fluid movement.

Later, at the tent, Elizalde said he was more than ever convinced that the Tasaday did not travel far. "They are part of this place and they've got everything here. There is no need for them to leave. They are just incredible, that's all, incredible. They have no war, no fighting. Just look at them and you can see they disprove all the ideas about man being innately evil or a killer."

Lindbergh was certain that Tasaday had been isolated for many centuries. "This is Stone Age," he said. "I don't doubt it for a minute."

I remarked that the lack of competition from other peoples and of apparent dangers from wild animals, floods, droughts, and freezing weather must have played a significant part in their development. If what the Tasaday said was true, they had the forest to themselves with sufficient food, water, shelter.

"Yes, but the mystery—the big mystery," Manda interjected, "is the other people. Why don't they want to talk about them? Why don't they see them? Or go to their places? They are short of women—you'd think they could get very ambitious and competitive about something like that. Maybe this mystery is connected with their women . . .? I just don't get it."

That night Lindbergh joined us for another brief visit to the caves by

flashlight. Again three fires flickered in the upper cave, making it noticeably warmer than in the forest. Men took turns fueling them.

Sitting there, we suddenly remembered that there had been no sign of
the dog we had heard at the clearing. We asked about it.

"Ahhh. The dog," Balayam said, and looked at the other Tasaday.
"It died."

"But you had it only a few days ago."

"Yes. But coming back from our last trip to the clearing it . . . died.
We had to carry it sometimes and it died."

"What happened?"

"It just died. We were very sad inside. Nobody could look at it. We all
cried and looked away. We left it in the forest. We liked it very much."

They said Dafal had given it to them and they didn't know where to
get another. Manda asked if they wanted a new dog.

"Yes . . . yes. That would be good."

"What kind of dog?"

"Like before. Like that one."

Did they want just one dog?

Balayam looked around and said, "We all want dogs. See, Udelen
wants one. I want one. Bilangan wants one. The others, too."

"But what would you do with the dogs?"

"Feed them . . . take care of them. They are good to take care of."

"Do you want male or female dogs?"

"Both."

"But if you have both, they will have little dogs."

"We know that," Balayam said with a laugh.

We left shortly after that, but not before Mai, Igna, Sindi, and Balayam
had another chat together among themselves. It appeared that a court-
ship was being set up; I asked Manda, casually, if that were so. "What?
Do you think we'd do something like that? Why, we just brought Igna's
companion and this is what happened." It was dark and I couldn't see his
face, but he didn't sound surprised.

At the tents it was decided not to mention the dogs again unless the
Tasaday brought up the subject. Dogs might bring disease, fleas, and
other problems the Tasaday would be unfamiliar with; also, a multitude
of dogs could be a feeding problem.

By the next day we had fallen into a routine of sorts—a few hours
with the Tasaday at the cave or stream; our own three meals at the tents;
talking in the afternoons and evenings among ourselves; improving the
tents and kitchen during odd hours.

Rain often fell in the afternoons or evenings, but not every day, and
usually for only a couple of hours. A temperature recorder was hung in
a tree but was erratic after the first three days, during which it gave the

highs in the 70's and the lows in the 50's. Nights were chilly, especially when the wind blew.

Dawn broke shortly after five, the first rays of sun coloring the sky a faint silver behind the ridge—where we had landed—opposite our camp and the caves. By eight the sun was striking the brow of the main cave and beginning to shine into it. The valley in front of the cave was in sunlight until after noontime, when the sun slipped behind the mountain. By 5:00 P.M. the last of the sun was in the tops of the trees and by 6:00 it was dark.

Some mornings the dawn was spectacular. The silvery sky would turn pale yellow, and a pink cloud would occasionally glow through the trees. Half a dozen or more different species of bird welcomed the day with caw-caw and chik-chik, ooh-ooh-ooh and whooo-whooo, twee-eet and chee-chee-chee. A shrill eee-eee-eee occasionally rose in solo above this discordant symphony; sometimes the loud, rude honk-honk of the hornbill drowned out everything.

The first light leaked white-yellow into the treetops, then slid lower, so that great dark forms took on detail. Then, suddenly, a yellow streak descended, like a string dropped, as the light singled out a tall, white-barked tree and glazed its trunk. Then more streaks appeared—widely scattered—and odd shapes, yellow, gold, and green, where leaves scooped up sunlight. At ground level, plants and leaves were white on top, green-black underneath. Light showered when a spiny fern caught the sun.

Lindbergh awoke one morning in the corner of the main tent, pulled on his boots and hat—he slept in his shirt and trousers—and walked off into the forest. He returned two hours later and said the dawn had been beautiful, the forest was beautiful, and the stream was beautiful—but already it bore marks of the expedition! Tin cans, chicken feathers, film wrappers, and other debris littered the stream banks, stuck to rocks, swirled in the pools, not to mention the remains of a few small trees, which lay in the stream where they had been cut to provide construction material for the camp.

"Man is the dirtiest creature on earth," he proclaimed to nobody in particular. And then, with a sidelong glance at Elizalde, he continued, "I've always said that. Seen it everywhere. And now in this forest."

That afternoon Elizalde took Ching, Felix, and half a dozen Tboli and Blit to the stream to clean it up. In an hour they had gathered buckets of paper scraps, feathers, cans, cellophane, tinfoil, and other items we had brought.

Another morning, Balayam and Bilangan stopped by the tent and were asked if they would go gathering at the stream and take some of the women and children with them. They left and returned shortly with a group trailing behind.

At the stream, the men waded in, Mahayag leading the pack in hops and jumps upstream. The women stayed on the banks at first, wary of the strangers who were stumbling around on the slippery rocks trying to take notes and photographs, and watch everything at the same time.

Udelen, with Siyus on his shoulders, opened sections of reddish-brown ginger and chewed the tart seeds from the leathery skin. Siyus nibbled on orange flower petals.

After a while the women joined in the gathering. Three generations were represented—Sekul, the eldest and the mother of Mahayag; her daughter-in-law, Dula; and her granddaughter, Siyus, who was Dula's daughter. Etut was behind them with her unnamed youngest son; Mai had learned from Bilangan that she was with child. Bilangan said Etut was about halfway through her pregnancy. This explained the heaviness that made her leafy skirt flare out and the awkwardness with which she moved.

Dul and Dula led their children into ankle-deep water and splashed it over their shoulders. Then they washed their faces—squinting eyes and puckered mouths notwithstanding. The water rinsed away a coating of soot, and halfway through the operation the youngsters looked as if they were wearing dark, shiny coats over dusty-gray trousers.

Then Balayam and Bilangan demonstrated their stone tools, pounding ginger open and cracking the sections, then picking out clusters of the tiny berrylike seeds and popping them into their mouths. After an hour or two the Tasaday left, carrying cones filled with tadpoles and crabs, and armfuls of leaves and fruits.

Visits to the cave were increasingly relaxed; our discussions rarely touched on sensitive matters, and we avoided strenuous question-and-answer sessions. Talk generally revolved around whatever subject came up naturally and was agreeable to the Tasaday. One evening the moonlight had put a soft yellow glow on the valley, and a long silver patch of sky was visible between the jagged tops of silhouetted trees. The Tasaday were asked if the moon ever passed so they could see it from the cave.

"Sometimes," Balayam said.

"Oh, then you do see the moon in here?"

"Yes, we see it sometimes."

"But, Balayam, do you remember telling us at the clearing that you couldn't see the moon from in here?"

He was puzzled.

"Perhaps we misunderstood. We asked if you could see the moon from the forest and you said no. And after you saw it at the clearing, you said you didn't know it stuck up there."

"Yes, that's right," Balayam said. "We don't see it from inside the forest. We see it from the cave."

He added that it was true, they had not known the moon stuck up there —outside the forest—*too*. It was an example of the confusion that could arise from questioning through interpreters, from not being aware of the stress put on certain words or phrases, and from imprecisely worded questions.

What was still puzzling was that Balayam said they did not see the moon from the forest; we assumed that this was because, as he had said earlier, they did not go outside after dark.

During one of our evening visits Balayam spoke up about his fondness for Sindi and said he wanted her to stay with him. She admitted she liked Balayam and wanted to stay with him. Elizalde, however, insisted that, although Sindi was a childless widow in her late twenties, she had to go back to her parents, at least for a while, before she could stay with Balayam.

"Balayam can understand that, can't he?" Manda asked Mai.

Balayam said yes, but made clear that he was desperate for her to stay.

Perhaps, he was told, she would come back—she wanted to—but there could be no guarantee. She apparently was not in demand as a wife at Blit, but there was the possibility that her mother would object.

Balayam sighed and said he understood.

Meanwhile, he was told, they could get better acquainted, so long as both realized she must leave when the rest of the expedition did. Balayam said he understood that, and then seized the opportunity to have Sindi spend the night with him. He was so nervous that his voice quavered and cracked as he spoke.

Mai translated. "Balayam says he lives alone in the middle cave . . . he is the only Tasaday without a family, without a wife. He wants very much to be with Sindi."

Sindi said she wanted to be with Balayam. We decided it was time to return to our tents.

In one of the conversations about tools, we asked if the Tasaday used their stones for weapons or protection.

"No."

Did their ancestors ever talk about people who caused trouble?

"No."

Did they ever have disagreements among themselves?

"No."

A dozen Tasaday were sprawled in the middle of the cave during this session; they had just eaten. The oldest couples stayed in a corner, the children toddled about.

"You don't have disagreements, but does anything unpleasant come up among the Tasaday, anything that upsets some or all of you?"

"There is nothing not good," Balayam said.

"Well, then, what would you say is *least* good about the group or about living here?"

Balayam looked around, said a few words to someone, then replied, "We can't think of anything that is not good."

"Nothing you dislike about people?"

"Well . . . we don't like loud voices and sharp looks."

A fragmented exchange brought out that they had been bothered by two or three visitors who had come to the forest's edge during the meetings the previous year, and were particularly alarmed by one man, apparently a photographer. Elizalde then told us of an incident when an excited cameraman tried to pose some Tasaday, impatiently called out instructions to Igna and Dafal, and finally, in agitation, grabbed Dafal and some of the Tasaday by their shoulders and hands to steer them where he wanted them. Elizalde had intereceded immediately, gripping the photographer angrily and telling him to keep his hands off the people. The next time he misbehaved he would be put on the helicopter back to Tboli.

Elizalde assured the Tasaday that he, too, disliked such people, and that they should always speak up when anyone bothered them.

"Yes," Balayam said. "We don't like loud voices and sharp looks. Those things don't look good to our eyes." This disapproval seemed to cover all impersonal, brusque, or condescending attitudes and manners, as well as shouting and staring.

We asked the Tasaday if their children misbehaved. They did, but only when they were hungry and food was not ready to eat; then they cried. There was no punishment.

They said getting food was their most serious continuing problem—"Sometimes we get hungry . . . but if we get *very* hungry we can always get some food if we go out for it."

"What is the best thing you say about another person, another Tasaday?"

"We say he is good to be with; we like to be together. You feel good inside when you are together, and when he is away you feel lonely."

"Why do men and women get married?"

"To have a companion, to have someone to share food with." (It was not clear whether this meant sharing in the acquisition of food or in the eating of it.)

"When do a man and a woman get married? At what time in their lives?"

"When they are strong enough."

"What do you mean?"

"When a man's penis is strong and women are ready," Balayam answered and giggled, along with several other Tasaday, either at the question or at Igna, who was snickering and had to cover her mouth.

"Do you have any special ceremony, or do anything special for a marriage?"

There was no ceremony or celebration, at least as they understood the idea. "We all gather around the new couple and say good, good, beautiful, beautiful [*mafeon*], that's all."

"How long does a couple stay together?"

"Until their hair turns white."

We asked if there was any sharing of mates—if one member of a couple might sometimes stay with another person as a husband or wife. This caused talking back and forth among the Tasaday, but they seemed confused, and produced no intelligible answer.

Mai asked if, in view of their shortage of women, a woman might be shared as a wife. The Tasaday reacted rather sharply to this idea, frowning and waggling their heads. Balayam shook his head no. The expression on his face could have been read as shock, or merely confusion. We did not pursue the subject.

They were then asked where children came from. (Some primitive peoples are reportedly unaware of the relationship between sexual intercourse and childbirth, perhaps because of the many months between cause and effect.)

Balayam looked puzzled after hearing the question, cocking his head quizzically. Then he tried to suppress a laugh, but it still came out in sputters, along with the giggles of several other Tasaday and Igna. Balayam shook his head and looked at us as if to say "Don't you know?" It was not clear whether he thought we did not know or were teasing them. Igna pursued the question through the laughter; Balayam finally responded and Mai translated. "He says children come after a man and a woman play together."

Throughout this particular visit some Tasaday sat contentedly, others wandered casually in and out of the cave. Adug came back from a food-gathering mission. As he was settling on the rock throne, he untied the vine that held his hair in a sleek ponytail and shook it into a bushy mass that hung below his shoulders. Occasionally he turned his head to one side and pushed the hair back behind his ear so he could hear better.

Both men and women consistently tied their hair back when they went into the forest, evidently to keep it from snagging in thorns and vines and from dangling in their eyes.

Dul's hair reached below her hips and so did Bilangan's. Several had much shorter hair; they said they had started trimming it after Dafal introduced the knife. We asked if they also trimmed their fingernails and toenails. Bilangan said nails were not cut deliberately; they were kept short naturally by digging and walking. He nodded toward his own feet, which were scarred and calloused. The tough, wrinkled skin looked as if it belonged to an old man. "Sometimes," he said, "my nails get too short. Then it's hard to walk where it is steep and slippery."

Lobo seemed to be in constant motion, chasing after Ching, cuddling into Manda's lap, running down the path, waving for attention. Once he started out of the cave to climb up a vine growing in front of it, but Balayam called to him, pointing up and to the left of the entrance. Just outside, perched on a leafy branch, was a small dark-brown bird (probably a swift) only four or five inches long from head to tail. Lobo sat down and no Tasaday went out for about an hour. We thought it was the *le mokan,* the special bird that warned the Tasaday of trouble. No, they said, this was just a friendly bird, but it was best not to take any chances.

They called the *le mokan* one morning, after hearing its song from the forest. Mahayag squatted at the lip of the cave, cupped his hands together and raised them to his lips. He blew between his parallel thumbs, letting the air out of the cup by opening and fluttering his fingers. He warmed up, blew a few notes, then licked his lips and began in earnest: "Whut-whut-whuttle. Whut-whut-whuttle. Whut-whuttle-whuttle."

The Tasaday were quiet and watchful. Balayam joined in the calling, and then Adug squatted and called, too. They took turns and then called all at once. They stopped and waited.

From the distance came "Whut-whut-whuttle."

"Yaah," Mahayag said, and began calling again. After about three minutes he smiled and pointed. The Tasaday turned and several exclaimed softly. Mahayag and the bird traded calls and finally we, too, saw the bird—a golden-brown flash of color swooping into a tree about fifty yards away and disappearing. In a minute or so it arrived, fluttering its wings and settling on a branch just outside the cave. It was a jungle dove of some kind with a brown body, white head and tail.

As our stay in the forest progressed, the men—except for the two eldest, Kuletaw and Tekaf—grew increasingly open and friendly. Balayam led the way. Bilangan was more reserved but eager to communicate. Mahayag became an enthusiastic participant in gatherings. Udelen and Lefonok were quiet, but warm and responsive. Lobo performed as the star of the show, cavorting, teasing, and openly courting attention, which we could not help giving him. His feats were sometimes dazzling: hanging by his feet from a limb, dancing across fallen logs, climbing slender ribbons of rattan. Some visitors made a conscious effort to pay him less attention, but were not too successful. Perhaps he sensed this, because his antics became more insistent: snatching Elizalde's white cap and putting it on his own head, leaping onto Ching's shoulders, tying vines to the back of a visitor's belt without his knowing it. It was impossible to ignore him.

The other boys were much more subdued. The teen-agers were shy, and the younger ones scared. One afternoon three toddlers forgot our presence and scampered around the cave in a game like tag. They swiped at one another and ran, laughing, until one threw a handful of dust-dirt. Another volleyed back and they had an exchange of dirt throwing until one mother called out sharply and pulled a boy onto her lap. The boys had played right up to the cave's mouth, their tiny toes sometimes over the rocky lip, but they seemed oblivious of danger. The drop was four feet straight down to a narrow ledge, then a sharply slanted descent into the valley.

The women, except for Dul, remained generally uncommunicative. They warmed somewhat to Igna, Mai, and Sindi, and liked to sit next to Manda in a group, but looked away nervously or giggled when others of us were close by. Etut was the least responsive, even when Balayam or Bilangan would encourage her. Balayam eventually took it upon himself to apologize for Etut and asked Mai to explain. "We mustn't blame Etut if she doesn't look happy. Like all women when they are pregnant, she is happy but doesn't show it so well."

Sekul made a friendly gesture one morning by presenting grubs to Elizalde and Lindbergh. After they nibbled at them, she gave Elizalde a monkey skull to chew on. The men had gamely bitten into the grubs—light-brown sluglike worms found in rotting tree stumps. Elizalde said they tasted like "old, tough rubber" and were not as unnerving as some things he had eaten while visiting other tribes; the snakes were okay, pretty tasty in fact, he said, but rats and lizards were unsettling. He did not know some things he had eaten—and did not want to know. Lindbergh said the grubs were "not too bad . . . like an oyster, a very tough oyster."

The monkey skull—roasted, but several days old, rotting and rank—was supposed to be cracked open and the brain eaten. The Tasaday considered this a delicacy and watched proudly as it was given to Manda. He thanked them profusely and said he always liked to share such extraordinary foods with all of his companions—and it just happened that most of them were at the tents at this moment; he would take the food to them so all could enjoy the Tasaday's gift.

The Tasaday smiled happily as Manda handed the skull to Mai. Back at the tents it was given to Igna, I think, to eat or do with as she wished; in any case, it disappeared quickly, although the stench lingered on.

Day after day Carlos Fernandez was filling notebooks with observations and interview data. Most questioning was done informally in group sessions, but once or twice he was able to get Dafal, Fludi, or Mai to assist him with translating so he could pursue matters more systematically. He also joined the Tasaday on their excursions whenever possible, once accompanying three men to their traps. The traps were well placed—close by streams or watering places for pigs and deer—but were not well constructed and nothing had been caught. The largest traps were made of branches or saplings; it took two men to pull them back into spring tension. They were armed with sharpened bamboo, and a vine trigger was strung across a path, each side of which was lined with a fence of long leaves and sticks stuck into the ground to guide the animals.

Carlos also visited a Tasaday lean-to in which they had cached bolos and where they sometimes smoked meat, as taught by Dafal, so it would keep longer. No game was caught during our visit, however, and the Tasaday showed little disappointment. After all, meat apparently had been part of their diet only since Dafal had introduced them to traps—and then only an occasional part.

Fernandez, a soft-spoken native of Palawan Island, was sensitive and intelligent. The circumstances in the forest were not ideal for scientific research, but he seemed unbothered by the presence of a journalist and photographers, and we spent hours trading notes and observations, and theorizing about the Tasaday. Rarely more than three hours a day was spent with the Tasaday, so there was plenty of time for talking and reading.

He had grown fond of the Tasaday, and said he would love to spend a year with them were it not for previous commitments. The first two months would be concentrated on their language, which he did not think unusually difficult. He found the situation scientifically exciting and the Tasaday delightful.

Among many things I read during the visit, one book was particularly impressive: anthropologist Elman R. Service's *The Hunters.* "The most primitive societies," he wrote, "are the most egalitarian. Dispute was deemed exceptional at the band level because feuding was understood by all persons to endanger the whole group's survival." Service quoted fellow anthropologist Marshall Sahlins on the origins of society:

"In selective adaption to the perils of the Stone Age, human society overcame or subordinated such primate propensities as selfishness, indiscriminate sexuality, dominance and brute competition. It substituted kinship and cooperation for conflict, placed solidarity over sex, morality over might. In its earliest days it accomplished the greatest reform in history, the overthrow of human primate nature, and thereby secured the evolutionary future of the species."

The book went on to say much more about such men and their society than we could begin to suggest about the Tasaday—for one thing the book was about hunters and the Tasaday had only recently learned even to trap; yet the possibilities of comparison were tantalizing.

The most popular topics of our conversations were whether the Tasaday could validly be described as Stone Age men or true cave men; where they had come from; why they had remained isolated.

Fernandez felt that few scientists would quarrel with his belief that the Tasaday were the most significant anthropological discovery of this century—"and I think we could say of centuries, but at this point I would want to be conservative." The two immediate chief considerations, in his view, were to protect the Tasaday and to conduct significant studies while they were essentially still in Stone Age circumstances, even while shifting into an evolutionary phase through the introduction of metal.

Lindbergh described his visit as "one of the great experiences of life— I believe anyone would have to say that." He had joined expeditions among primitive tribes in Africa and gone deep into the Tumucamaque of Brazil, but none had equaled this experience. It was "extraordinary," he said, "coming from New York, where we were dealing with the supersonic jet and speeds by which people traverse the Atlantic in three hours, to people who have traveled no more than a few miles since their time began. And that step onto the treetop from the jet helicopter was like going through the looking glass—that tree was the transition—into a new world; you abandoned the modern world."

The tall pilot smoothed the snowy hair thinly covering his crown and shook his head. Asked what had impressed him most, he answered quickly. "No question in my mind, the most impressive thing yet is walking up that trail to the caves and seeing four or five Tasaday standing in the caves—that took me back through the ages. Second would have to be the groups standing around their fires. That is cave man. And, third, I'm puzzled by the lack of spirit of adventure—they've not made one single mark in improving their places, for sleeping, for entering. Why not make it easier? And don't they wonder what is beyond the next mountain? And why are there no more signs of inbreeding?"

I suggested that the Tasaday seemed to prove the adage that necessity is the mother of invention. They had not improved their caves or wandered beyond the next mountain because they didn't need to; they had all they required here and were satisfied. They were not pressured by wild animals or hostile men, the weather was tolerable, the caves excellent shelters.

Elizalde broke in. "They are simply creatures of this environment. They are natural conservationists and they are beautiful, loving people. They don't fight—that is fantastic in this age. The world is tearing itself apart, and yet these people exist in goodness. *That* is what is incredible."

"Well, I think I can understand those things," Lindbergh said, "but what still puzzles me is the lack of a sense of adventure. I have assumed that this was fundamental to man, had led him to travel, to discover, to invent."

In the lengthy discussion that followed, on instinct, will, emotion, intellect, Lindbergh recalled a theme I had heard him express before: the roots mountain people had in the earth and nature; the predicament of contemporary man who has been uprooted.

"The rise of intellect has coincided with the decline of natural life," he said. "The rate of change was at first very slow, but in recent times it has accelerated to the point where, if you were to plot it on a graph, the curve would make a long, low, slightly rising line covering eons of time, but then would turn rapidly upward. Modern man is at a place where the curve is almost perpendicular to the base line—and before it becomes perpendicular, it must bend or break. We must either change that curve or catastrophe will change it for us. Time is running out faster than most people realize. The human intellect's development of technology, with its insatiable commercial demands and fantastic destructive powers, has taken us to a stage where life itself is endangered, man included. We are destroying our environment through pollution, ripping up the earth to get at natural resources, cutting forests, spoiling lakes and rivers and oceans. Many forms of plant and animal life are on the verge of annihilation, and I think this is extremely serious and we have got to face it."

He paused a moment and then gestured toward the caves. "And, in simple terms, this is the result of having stepped from where these people are right now—or had been until they met Dafal. He brought the apple and they bit it, no question about that. Now there's no turning back, but great care can be taken in seeing that the Tasaday are not destroyed or allowed to destroy themselves."

(Robert Fox had once talked of Tasaday history as falling in the phases B.D.—Before Dafal—and A.D.—After Dafal. Fernandez noted that Lindbergh's apple symbolism suggested a new meaning for A.D.— "After d'fall.")

One of the more fascinating aspects of the Tasaday's development was that some of them displayed a sharp intelligence, which, when their great physical agility and manual dexterity was taken into account, indicated that something aside from mental or physical limitations had kept them from making technological or economic progress. Some scientists contend that food gatherers were constantly on the move in search of food, and that this struggle for mere subsistence left no time or energy for inventing. But the abundance of the Tasaday's forest seemed to allow them to fulfill their food requirements in a few hours a day. Fernandez, using a phrase from Marshall Sahlins, referred to them as "the original affluent society."

Dr. Rebong said their health appeared to be excellent. He was called upon from time to time to treat various minor ailments, usually skin infections, cuts, and bruises, and noted that Sasa, the light-haired boy previously thought to have fatal skin ailments, had improved markedly and was walking around on his own.

Rebong had counted three cases of goiter, apparently caused by lack of iodine; two cases of conjunctivitis, which were bacterial and not communicable and lasted only a few days; scattered skin problems, including one case of scabies, Gintoy's case of ringworm complicated by a fungus, and Kalee's less serious case; a few minor colds or respiratory problems among children, caused by night chill and dampness; and one potentially serious bronchial problem in Kuletaw, who often had difficulty breathing after physical exertion.

The worst single physical problem was Mahayag's hernia. It swelled from his groin to the size of a golf ball. Rebong was concerned, but Mahayag said it did not bother him. Rebong said it might cause no difficulty for years, but on the other hand, it could strangulate under stress, become excruciatingly painful, and probably fatal without medical attention. It was the cause of considerable debate in the months ahead.

Rebong suspected that the slightly swollen bellies in some of the children were caused by the internal parasites common throughout the Philippines. The Tasaday were constantly exposed to them because of their bare skin and high intake of raw foods.

The lack of serious health problems, however, was amazing. Malaria was endemic to the area, but none was noted. There was no tuberculosis, which afflicted as much as 90 per cent of some Philippine mountain tribes and was present in all tribespeople Dr. Rebong had seen; no apparent cases of malnutrition, from which a few million Filipinos suffered; no yaws; and no schistosomiasis, common in many Asian countries, where it is known as snail fever. Admittedly, Rebong had made limited observations, and had not thoroughly examined each individual, but from what he had seen so far, he felt the Tasaday were in "better health than any group of minority people—and many urban people, too—that I have ever seen." The thirty-five-year-old general practitioner had been working with Panamin for four years and had traveled throughout the islands.

The skin on the Tasaday's knees, hands, and feet, the thickest Rebong had ever seen, afforded good protection. He was particularly impressed with their cleanliness: the caves were swept regularly with branch brooms; there was no sign of fecal matter in or around the dwellings because mothers immediately cleaned up after an infant who defecated or urinated, and older children would do the same if their mothers were absent.

The apparent lack of salt in their diet was puzzling. Rebong said the total absence of salt means that the body tires quickly, becomes prostrate, and eventually dies. The speculation was that the Tasaday got the necessary amounts of sodium chloride from plants. We knew that they ate many more fruits and plants than we had been shown so far. Elizalde could offer no certain explanation, but he believed that nothing was impossible regarding the Tasaday. "Who knows exactly how or why they function so well in here? This is a new ball game. You've got to open your minds and treat everything as new. It's the only way you'll get anything more than surface understanding. Maybe they don't need salt."

One day Bilangan found a tree with *natek*—a fishtail palm, so named because of its large spiny, fan-shaped leaves. Not all such palms contained the makings of *natek,* but Bilangan had learned from Dafal how to tap the trunk to detect the sound that meant the right kind of pith. Next,

Bilangan wrestled a three-foot-long section of the palm's trunk end over end onto a grassy spot beside the stream. The trunk was heavy, as big around as a basketball; Bilangan halved it lengthwise by bolo-slashing niches into which he pounded wooden wedges with a boulder. He laid one half of the split trunk on a blanket of banana leaves and Bilangan went to work with an L-shaped pounder made of bamboo and rattan, hitting the moist pale-yellow core repeatedly. The blows made contact about an inch short of his foot, which he used to hold down the pith. Shreds looking like sawdust flew through the air, as Mahayag and Udelen took turns pounding; after another section of trunk was split, all three men worked at once.

Meanwhile, a few feet away at the stream's edge, Lefonok and Balayam assembled the complicated device used to extract the starch from the pith. A square stand about two feet high was constructed of sticks tied together with vine. The ends of two saplings about six feet long were placed on top of the stand with the other ends on the ground, and a long sheet of soft thin bark folded to look like a canoe was fitted between them. Four layers of ferns and leaves were stacked on top of the stand, each layer separated by pieces of bamboo. A hollow banana stalk was cut in half lengthwise and inserted halfway into the bottom of the stack of leaves and ferns, making a small canal.

Bilangan fashioned a piece of thin bark into a scoop and tied it to a long stick. He climbed on top of the layers of ferns and Mahayag laid an armload of the mashed pith at his feet. Bilangan dipped his scoop into the stream and ladled water onto the pith. Then he trampled on it, running in place. Within a minute or two a thick yellow-orange soup began trickling out of the banana stalk canal and into the canoe-shaped trough. Dafal, who had appeared to supervise for a while, saw too many mistakes; he put aside his hat and joined the work, making a few adjustments here and there. The trickle became a steady stream. Pith was continually heaped on the press, and other men took turns treading. After an hour, the bark trough was filled with the pith soup.

Dul and Dula, each carrying an infant, and several children arrived. A happy mood prevailed, and Udelen even made a little rhythmic music; while the three men were pounding loose the pith, Udelen leaned away and gave quick little stabs with his pounder on the ground—tumpa-tumpa-tump, tumpa-tumpa-tump—which made a counterpoint to the steady tump-tump-tump of the other two. Udelen grinned. Dafal had taught them this, along with the whole *natek*-making process.

Dafal confided that the Tasaday were not very good at this work— "And I showed them four different times how to do it. They just don't seem to get it right."

It may have been a disappointment to Dafal, but to the rest of us it was a marvelous device, as complicated and funny-looking as a Rube Goldberg cartoon.

I asked Dafal why he had taught the Tasaday to make *natek*.

"They were hungry," he said.

"Is that what they said?"

"No . . . but they didn't eat much. And they looked hungry—they must have been hungry."

"So you spent several visits showing them how to make this. You must care a lot about these people."

"Not especially. They're okay. They get me the best *bui* vine."

After the trough had filled with liquid, the pressing stopped, and the starch was allowed to settle to the bottom. Then one end of the trough was opened and the unwanted liquid drained away. The starchy pudding left at the bottom was wrapped in bark and put into a fire to bake. When it was done, the bark cover was opened and half a dozen men and boys squatted, dipping their hands into the warm *natek*. Most of it had baked into pasty-white cakes, which were broken or cut into pieces. But some was like honey-colored jelly and the Tasaday scooped this up first and crammed it in their mouths, licking their fingers and muttering with satisfaction.

They gave us samples of the cakes, which were dry in texture and tasted like unleavened bread. The first batch baked, they set to work on another. In the late afternoon, all the Tasaday left with bundles of *natek* except Bilangan, who stayed to work by himself. He had the largest family—four boys and a pregnant wife.

That evening the forest was cool and damp. The usual chorus of insects and frogs was interrupted by a loud crack, then another, followed by a slow creaking, a splitting sound, and a crash. A large tree had apparently toppled to the forest floor. The next day we saw its huge black trunk on the slope opposite the tents. Mai reported that it had rotted and fallen by itself. All the trees near the tents were then inspected. Mai said that "one of the great fears of forest people was falling trees." Three times during our visit we heard trees crack and crash down.

By the end of the first week, the Tasaday had coaxed Elizalde to spend one complete night in the cave. He said it was rocky but tolerable—for one night. The Tasaday were very happy he had stayed.

In general they were more relaxed than ever. Only a few remained shyly on the fringes of activity. When Manda lay down on the cave floor, the Tasaday swarmed on him, almost burying him with their bodies, touching, holding, nuzzling. And they showed signs of accepting the rest of us. Balayam, Mahayag, and Udelen would embrace us; Lobo would leap into people's arms, onto their backs. Names were given to all the visiting party, and Balayam would provide a sort of christening ritual. He would ask someone's name to be pronounced and repeated carefully, while he leaned forward, listening with furrowed brow. Then he would nod, stand straight and smile, and pronounce the name, always preceded by *kakay* (friend).

So it was Ting, for Ching; Shalo, for Charles (Lindbergh); Kalo, for Carlos (Fernandez). Elizalde, of course, was Momo Dakel Diwata Tasaday. Some names sounded almost the same in Tasaday and English, such as Ken (MacLeish), Dokoto (Doctor), Igna, Sindi. Others underwent strange transformations—either because Balayam had difficulty re-creating the original sounds, or because he simply liked to change them. Thus Mai was Mafoko, John was Jambangan—occasionally embellished to include the cameras and eyeglasses I usually wore, as Jambangan La'Fat Mata (John with four eyes). I suspected that Elizalde had suggested the embellishment, but Mai insisted it was Balayam's idea.

We wondered about the origins of the caves, which showed signs of water erosion. The texture of the rock was in some places like plaster, grainy and crumbling to the touch. The presence of minerals was indicated by glints of orange, ochre, green, and a gray-white. Lynch had speculated that the middle and top caves were primarily conglomerate quartzite and that the mass of the mountain was limestone—indicated by the lower cave's huge arching entry, sharply angled chamber, and round pebbles. The waterfall in front of this cave had made cups in the flat rocks where it landed. The Tasaday used these little pools for drinking and washing, except in a dry spell when the waterfall was only a trickle.

We asked the Tasaday if they would show us how they made their stone tools. They said they rarely made them any more, because they had metal knives, but agreed to demonstrate. Udelen, Lefonok, and Balayam took Fernandez, Mai, and me to the stream. Each waded along, picking up stones here and there for inspection until they found the right one. Then they each squatted before a flat rock that was occasionally washed by the stream. One edge of the selected stone was rubbed on this anvil, in a circular motion, first one side and then the other. They frequently felt the edges to see how they were progressing. While Udelen and Lefonok continued the grinding, Balayam searched for small branches, rattan, and a long, thin vine. When a stone was ready a branch was folded over it; the ends of the branch were brought together, and the vine was laced three or four times around the stone and branch together and then wrapped around and down the handle. The loose end of the vine was wedged tightly between the two halves of the handle and tied.

Lefonok finished his tool in less than twelve minutes. Balayam and Udelen took about fifteen minutes; their tools had slightly different shapes and handles. The honed edges of all three tools were sharp enough to saw through a vine; the heads were firm enough to serve as hammers or pounders for fruit or nuts, but would not do for heavy work.

Udelen quickly made another, smaller tool as we were preparing to leave, and all four were handed to us. Fernandez eventually took them to Manila for the Panamin Museum and for study by Lynch. The tools apparently were effective enough for the Tasaday's present limited needs, but were much less expertly made than the heirloom tools they kept in the cave. These old tools were bound with smooth rattan and the stones were harder, smoother, better shaped, and more sharply honed. Because of the uniform excellence of the rattan lacing, we suspected that it had been replaced after the Tasaday had acquired knives.

The tools we saw made seemed to have low priority for the Tasaday. The speed with which these implements were constructed suggested that they were used once and tossed aside. In any case, the vine lacing stretched as it dried, so that the stones loosened, making the tool unusable.

March 29, our seventh day in the forest, was the last one for MacLeish and Launois, who had commitments elsewhere. Their last evening was partly given to a discussion that had started two days earlier, when word was radioed that a television news team from NBC had arrived in Manila and wanted to cover the story. Accounts of the expedition released by Panamin and my own stories radioed to the AP had appeared on international news wires.

There was opposition to television coverage, however. Lindbergh, for instance, had little use for TV and felt that if any filming of the Tasaday was to be done, it should come only after various film makers had been allowed to bid for rights, arguing that it could run to a large amount of money for Panamin, possibly several hundred thousand dollars. Earlier, upon learning that the Geographic had not made any financial contribution in connection with its film or article, Lindbergh had told Manda that such a contribution would have been in order. "That's not unreasonable," Lindbergh said. "This is a development of major importance, Manda. Don't underestimate this Tasaday affair. And it is going to cost Panamin plenty of money. You need money, I know that. I've seen the records and I know!"

"Yes, of course," Elizalde had replied. "But . . ."

"Now, I think you've got to get it where you can, so long as it is reasonable and dignified. And getting contributions to the foundation for coverage of the Tasaday is a perfectly legitimate and reasonable way."

Manda was hesitant. "I don't know, Charles. I mean, wouldn't it look mercenary? You know, like we were using the people, or selling them?"

"Not at all. Why, this sort of thing is done all the time, and it is not mercenary. You are doing important and valuable work. I think you definitely should consider this. Why, I've been offered large sums for all kinds of wildlife things—movies, television, and so on," Lindbergh continued. "I didn't do them because I simply didn't want to get involved in films, but I didn't think it was mercenary. Nor was that the reason I turned them down. Many important organizations raise funds like this."

It was also possible, as MacLeish, Launois, and Lindbergh pointed out, that entry of a television news team into the cave area would jeopardize a later documentary film—there might not be enough fresh material left.

Elizalde was in the middle. He reminded them that whatever was done would depend on the Tasaday and whether they were agreeable. Television exposure now would give an effective push in the drive for the reservation. But he did not want to nullify a later film or monetary contribution. He asked my opinion.

I believed that limited TV news coverage now would enhance the possibility of a documentary, not hurt it; and that there was more than enough material for a full-length film. I was influenced by the knowledge that the team waiting to come in was the same one that had covered the Tasaday at the edge of the forest and had treated them with respect and appreciation. It obviously had been more to them than just another story.

The matter still was not settled by the next morning. Lindbergh, Elizalde, Ching, and I went on discussing it. Finally it was proposed that NBC be allowed in for one day only, to shoot in specific areas—not inside the cave, for instance—and for brief periods at a time. Two other conditions were that if the Tasaday objected at any time, NBC would stop filming; they would be allowed no more than a total of five minutes of broadcasting time on the Tasaday themselves.

The NBC team agreed to the conditions and was advised it could come in the next day. All the many other requests from newspapers, magazines, and television organizations were turned down.

I asked Elizalde if it would be possible after the NBC crew arrived to have the helicopter remain so that I could try to photograph a general view of the caves from it. He said it would be too dangerous that way, but suggested climbing one of the big trees about one hundred feet in front of the main cave. The trees had no branches for the first thirty feet, were as big around as a person, and slippery smooth.

I could not climb up, but Fludi and Fausto could. They strung ropes between two trees, making a ladder up to the first branches. It was still a difficult climb but worth every strained muscle, because it put me at eye level with the cave. The Tasaday reacted by laughing and pointing, at first. After that it was like watching a movie. Balayam got a stone tool and fondled it for a while, then pretended he was going to hit Dul, who laughed and pushed him away. Mahayag used a long staff to vault around the cave. (Later he said he used it to cross the stream when rain made it high. During storms the water rose suddenly several times its normal level and rushed down the valley, muddy brown and three or four feet deep.)

Udelen took a bow and practiced aiming arrows as Tekaf watched with absorption. Lobo and other boys crawled into niches between the main cave and the middle one. After half an hour or so, Balayam joined Sindi in his cave and they sprawled in its mouth like sweethearts on a private porch, nuzzling and caressing one another, she picking leaf chaff and small insects from his hair, and he teasing and tickling her.

That afternoon Lobo got hold of a small magnet that Lindbergh had given to Ching. He was shown how it attracted small pieces of metal, but when he found a leech on himself and tried to pull it out with the magnet, he was disappointed. Then he darted about, trying it on everything—lamps, knives, anything handy—seeing for himself that it attracted only metal.

The magnet was one of several items that randomly came out of Lindbergh's special emergency kit. The mosquito forceps (a scissorslike surgical instrument used to remove splinters and thorns), knives, and malaria pills were understandable items in Lindbergh's special kit, but, he was asked, what about the magnet? He laughed. "Well, I've always been fascinated with magnets—and when the word came about the expedition I just brought it along. No particular reason."

Lindbergh's general good humor and smiles gave way to a serious nononsense manner when the NBC crew arrived. He politely shook hands with Jack Reynolds and his crew, then sat silently, looking into the forest. Late that afternoon, however, he got into an animated discussion with Reynolds about conservation, in the course of which Lindbergh came to respect the correspondent.

During filming the next day, Balayam surprised and delighted everyone by suddenly impersonating some of the visitors. He did the doctor, struggling up the hill to the cave with his little black bag, stumbling, and sprawling on his back, and finally huffing and wheezing into the cave. He did MacLeish, murmuring into an imaginary microphone. He did photographers, putting both hands to his eyes, then bending this way and that into contorted positions; he reproduced the shutter sounds of different cameras—"tasuk" and "kazeek." He topped it all with a depiction of his helicopter ride—strapping himself into the seat, clicking buttons and switches on the instrument panel, leaning back to flip an overhead switch, and then rising—his hand above his head with one finger extended and twirling like a rotor blade. It was an expanded and superior version of the performance he had given just after getting off the chopper.

His repertoire was varied; he perceived the significant gestures and the small details that individualize character; he used a minimum of movement and facial expression. It was gifted mimicry—the Marcel Marceau of the tropical rain forest.

The Tasaday gathered food and showed us their lean-to where a tributary joined the stream at the place they called Lambong. Kuletaw was curled up asleep there on the grassy ground. Lobo ran along the stream; Balayam climbed a tree and stood in the V where the trunk branched. When we spotted him and waved, he laughed and began doing his imitations again, staying in the tree throughout. Balayam picked a twig, leaned back grandly, and puffed on the twig, in imitation of Reynolds smoking his pipe. But when he blew out the imaginary smoke, he was dissatisfied. He pondered a moment, then repeated the pantomime as last time—except that when he blew out, he put his fist in front of his mouth and then opened and fluttered his fingers as he extended the hand to arm's length: smoke.

We talked for a while and Mai tried to find out the Tasaday word for cave, but was unsuccessful. The closest he understood was "a place inside the mountain."

We noticed that Lefonok was missing the first joint of one index finger and asked what happened. He said it had been cut off by a sharp piece of a tree as he tried to bend it over to break it off.

"Did you treat it in any special way? Put Tasaday medicine on it?"

"No."

"Did it bleed a lot?"

"Yes."

"But didn't you put leaves or dirt or something around the finger?"

"No, I just held it with my other hand."

Some Tasaday stayed at the stream when we left; one of the women was starting a fire with a bit of mossy tinder and a glowing ember she had brought from the caves.

It had been decided to end the expedition and fly out of the forest April 1—our purpose, locating the caves, had been accomplished; supplies were running down; the Tasaday probably would like a respite from visitors; a reasonable amount of data had been collected. But on the evening of March 31, Bart sent a message that the helicopter was grounded. The entering edge of the rotor blade had come loose and it was risky to fly anywhere, let alone try to make it over the mountain forest. Materials for repair were being sought in Manila.

The next day, Bart radioed that the parts were not available in the Philippines and would have to be sent from the manufacturer in France, which meant a delay of probably two weeks. No helicopters were available for chartering.

The radio's batteries were low; only some canned goods and a small supply of rice was left, perhaps enough food for three days. "We could try to walk out, but damned if I know how long that will take," Elizalde said. "It will be very rough country and we might hit weather. Suppose it took us a few days to make Blit—if we could make it—we still would have to hike to Ma Falen's place and beyond before a vehicle could reach us. It could mean eight or ten days, maybe more. We'd have to hunt for food along the way."

Most of us would have been agreeable to stay where we were, but the dwindling supplies would make it difficult, and hunting for enough food to feed all of us for many days might have a disruptive effect on the environment around the caves. An air drop was a last resort because it would be risky and would also mean chartering a fixed-wing plane and pinpointing the area for strangers. Fear of revealing the location also ruled out trying to borrow a helicopter from a local logging or mining company, several of whom had little love for Panamin, anyway.

Panamin headquarters in Manila was asked to try to get a helicopter from the Philippine government or from the United States Air Force. A message came back that the U.S. would send a helicopter the next day from Clark Air Base, north of Manila.

There had been a conscious effort not to sound an alarm in our messages, but the word got out somehow that the party—with Charles Lindbergh!—was stranded and would be rescued. Oscar Trinidad radioed that he was besieged by news media wanting continuing reports on developments.

Elizalde was upset. Being rescued was embarrassing, for one thing, and he was worried that news of the air rescue would push all the positive aspects of the expedition into the background.

Still, there was not much to be done about it. Several of us prepared a report for Trinidad to release to the news media, stressing the lack of danger. I wrote a similar story for the AP, which was radioed to Manila.

Later that evening a message arrived that the air force helicopter would leave that night, pick up Bart in Surallah, and would reach us before 9:00 A.M.

The tribesmen who had remained with Spileski at the ridge camp had been working for several days to prepare a place so the Panamin helicopter would not have to discharge passengers into the treetop. So there was already a landing spot prepared, about one hundred yards south of the tree platform.

The Tasaday did not know about our departure. At dawn we went to say good-by. The orange sun was rising over the mountain and light streamed into the caves. Several Tasaday gathered around Elizalde, and he told them that we were leaving. Then the other Tasaday quickly joined the cluster. They frowned as Mai translated all the words, and tears appeared in many eyes, but no one spoke.

Elizalde, who looked sad himself, said: "Now look here, Mai, you tell them no crying. No tears. If they cry, then we will cry. But this is just the beginning, not the ending. We will come back."

A chorus of *"oh-ho"* came from the Tasaday and several tried to smile, but in vain.

Manda asked Mai if Sindi was ready. "She's coming with us, right? If she wants to she can come back, but this was understood. Tell Balayam she can come back but she must ask her mother and father first. Tell him that she doesn't want to go, but that's the way it is . . . Is Balayam crying?"

He wasn't, but looked on the verge. Mai told Manda, "He likes her, she likes him . . ."

"Yeah, well, just tell them again that the sooner we go and do this, the better for all. We want to make it good for Balayam permanently, not just temporary like this. It will not be good for her parents not to know."

Mai translated and Balayam smiled halfheartedly and nodded.

"Tell Balayam not to be sad when we are out. I'll be sad, too, if he is," Manda said. The Tasaday murmured *"Oh-ho"* and smiled.

"We don't want to see a lot of long faces. All right," Manda said, "let's change the subject. Now about the Tasafeng—they better not try to go out and find them before us, better wait until we come back. They might get sick on the way . . . besides Balayam can't walk like me in the forest."

The Tasaday laughed and shook their heads.

"Also tell them they mustn't cut down all the trees; only the ones for *natek* and *ubud* or there will be no more forest." The Tasaday nodded.

Mai, speaking in his husky near-whisper, told them that the big bird had gotten sick, so today we would be using a different bird, the father bird.

Then, as Dr. Rebong treated half a dozen minor scratches and tended to a fistula on Sasa's groin, Balayam and Mahayag began calling the sacred bird, *le mokan.* Perhaps they thought that if it came Elizalde would have to stay. Their calling was the only sound for several minutes and most of the adult Tasaday peered out into the valley. The bright sunlight made the leaves chartreuse and lemon yellow. The valley was a never-ending show for the Tasaday; every time we visited—morning, noon, evening—some of them would be gazing into it, seeing things we could not and sometimes pointing them out—a fluffy-tailed squirrel on a limb, a bird flitting from tree to tree. Considering modern man's thirst for fresh entertainments, it was amusing to think that the Tasaday had looked into the same small valley every day for decades and still seemed to find it fascinating.

Igna sat on a ledge and began to sing in a high, plaintive voice. The song's wistfulness was unmistakable; it was not necessary to know the words, which Mai said were about friends parting. Tears began to roll down Igna's chubby cheeks and her voice wavered and became so thin that it was barely audible.

I moved to the lip of the cave, seeing the yellow-green jungle in front of me and feeling the cave's smoky warmth. I felt happy and sad at the same time, and a nagging apprehension: The Tasaday seemed much less vulnerable inside their forest; yet their innocence and simplicity could not survive steady exposure to outsiders even here. Should it survive? Already they talked about not wanting people with sharp looks and loud voices; and of course they would develop more protective attitudes and devices— wouldn't they? What would be next?

As we said good-by the men embraced us, gently and with tenderness. They put their cheeks against ours, sniffed, murmured our names, looked into our faces with sad smiles and moist eyes. Unexpectedly, I felt tears starting in my own eyes and turned away, noticing as I did so that others of our group were blinking also, looking uneasy. The Tasaday did not try to hold back their tears, but let them flow; they made no effort to hide their feelings. Elizalde was buried under a mound of Tasaday who hugged and touched and wept and called his name.

We left the cave soon after that. The Tasaday had been asked not to come to the helicopter landing place, but many did straggle down to the camp as we finished packing. Manda was followed everywhere by Lobo and Balayam, who looked forlorn—Sindi had exchanged her newly acquired leaf skirt for her Blit clothes.

The hike back to the landing place was more arduous than the entry. It was sharply uphill most of the way and slippery. And there was not the excitement and anticipation to buoy tired bodies.

As we were catching our breath at the new landing site, I asked Lindbergh again about the visit—which he had described earlier as one of the great experiences of life—and wondered how it compared with his historic flight in 1927. "I couldn't compare them," he said. "They are so different. This one stands by itself."

Reynolds interviewed Fernandez as we waited. He felt it would be difficult to overestimate the significance of the Tasaday to anthropology— "They are at the opposite end of the spectrum of modern civilization." He said one great value was that the Tasaday might help civilized men to understand better what they had gained by knowing what they had lost.

Manda said he was sad to leave the Tasaday, adding that he was "very anxious to get this place reserved. With that we will have achieved all the purposes of the expedition. It was a warm, friendly contact and I only hope we didn't bother them."

About nine, a U.S. Air Force tanker appeared high above us. Then a big, dark-green Chinook helicopter arrived, three times the size of Panamin's. It circled repeatedly, lower each time, surveying the ground. A tall paramedic in a gray flight suit, white helmet, and black goggles stood in the doorway of the Chinook and waved as it flew by.

The landing place was a ridge hump, shoveled flat, about fifteen feet wide and thirty feet long. It descended like a ski jump on both sides. The helicopter finally came in but did not land—the ridge was too narrow—

hovering instead about four feet off the ground. Twelve of us climbed aboard and were flown to a field of high grass near the Blit settlement. As the helicopter returned to the forest we walked toward the houses. Blit was empty, not a person in sight.

Elizalde and Mai shouted repeatedly and finally Datu Dudim and two other men appeared. They said all the Blit had rushed to hide when the huge, strange helicopter came into view and that some of the men were ready with guns and spears to fight whoever was invading them. Now, discovering it was Panamin, they all raced joyously out of their hiding places to mob Elizalde.

The Chinook shuttled everyone out of the forest to Blit in four trips and then began ferrying us to the Tboli settlement at Kematu.

On Lindbergh's flight the chopper refueled in the air—tanker and helicopter hooked together in a long sweeping circle over the town of Surallah. Lindbergh urged Elizalde to fly with him to Manila, where he was to catch a flight to the U.S. the next day, but Elizalde refused. He preferred to stay at Tboli, to play down the "rescue" as much as possible.

As Lindbergh waited to begin the first leg of his trip we sat and talked. Near us were the disassembled parts of the Panamin helicopter's rotor. Lindbergh suddenly asked, "Did you ever wonder why that holds together?"

"What?"

"Metal, the metal in that rotor blade, for instance. Why don't the molecules just fly apart?"

I had to confess that I hadn't given it much thought lately, and asked Lindbergh if he habitually pondered such things. "Yes, I guess so," he said, "since I was a boy I've been fascinated . . ."

He didn't finish because the Chinook was landing with its last load. It kept its engines running and Lindbergh climbed aboard. Before taking off, the pilot of the chopper, excited to have the famous aviator as his passenger, shouted over the engine's roar that he had grown up near Lindbergh's home in Connecticut and had played with Lindbergh's son, Jon. Moments later they took off. It was forty-five years to the month since the "Lone Eagle" had become the first man to fly nonstop alone from New York to Paris; now he was being "rescued" from the jungle by a pilot who had been his son's childhood playmate.

8

The Tasaday on Tape: The Aura of Momo Dakel

ELIZALDE had worried about the Tasaday's response to visitors ever since the beginning of the visit and was only partly satisfied with their seeming tranquillity, even though discussions with the Tasaday elicited no serious complaints; they said repeatedly that they were happy he had come and brought his friends.

But the difficulties of communicating with them did nothing to allay his fears that they might be upset or confused and he would not know about it. He was especially concerned when their usual straightforward manner changed to awkward reticence in response to our mention of other groups in the forest or the original homes of their women. The Tasaday's reluctance to discuss these matters and their obvious discomfort suggested that they might be holding something back.

On the fourth afternoon of the visit Elizalde thought of leaving a tape recorder running in the cave when we were not there. He borrowed a small portable unit from Fernandez and put it inside a black leather bag with some clothes. Mai and Dafal took it to the cave in the evening and said they were putting Manda's wet clothing beside the fire to dry. Just before departing Mai switched on the recorder; its microphone rested against a small opening in the zipper. Mai fetched the machine later and then he, Igna, and Elizalde huddled for more than two hours over the thirty-minute tape. By midnight they had completed it, Mai and Igna translating and Elizalde writing everything down by flashlight. It was painstaking work and there were many uncertainties, but the results were fascinating. Elizalde immediately sent to Manila for a larger recorder and a supply of tapes that would record for two hours on each side. After they arrived, several hours of each day were spent rigging up the machine and transcribing what it recorded.

Elizalde risked criticism that this was spying on the Tasaday, bugging their cave, so to speak, because he believed it was in their best interest. They would be better understood and better accommodated in their wishes and needs. He vowed that the information would not be used to take advantage of them.

The ethics of taping the Tasaday did not trouble me excessively at the time, although I did think about it. The invasion of their privacy and the danger of information being misused was real, of course, but their whole relationship with the outside world was potentially perilous; they were so vulnerable that virtually anything could be used against them. Entering their forest and caves in the first place was an invasion of their privacy; the use of tapes, which took us deeper into their lives, could be helpful or destructive to the Tasaday, depending on the wisdom, sensitivity, and good will of the users. The protection of the Tasaday's rights was up to the visitors. Elizalde took the major responsibility for this, but I believe that everybody present felt the need to monitor themselves and each other to help avoid, however innocently, ultimately harming the Tasaday.

The tape recordings revealed things that would have taken hours to learn otherwise, if at all. Tapes were better than direct conversation because the Tasaday did not get tired, bored, intimidated, or annoyed by questions; and, of course, the recordings could be played again and again, to obvious advantage for the translators.

All but the last recording session was transcribed in the forest; as the information increased daily, it influenced our approach to the Tasaday. We came to know, for instance, that they had not seen the Sanduka or Tasafeng for a long time, and, as Dul remarked, had almost forgotten that their ancestors had even existed; that they confined themselves much more than usual to the cave because of Momo Dakel; that they were seriously troubled by questions about things they did not know; that they put considerable value on gifts, particularly knives; that Balayam, Mahayag, and Dul (clearly the most outspoken woman) exerted, to an unknown degree, some kind of leadership, Balayam at least partly spurred by his desire for a wife; and that Elizalde was a figure of such importance that he dominated their private conversations and affected much of their thoughts and activities. Worth special note also were the women's considerable interest in Igna's bracelets and cloth; the repeated warnings of mothers to children that strobe lights or certain persons among the visitors would come as punishment unless the children behaved; and the calls for unity, such as a statement by Mahayag that they must call all women one woman, and all men one man.

Elizalde, responding to this information, advised the Tasaday that they should go out food gathering as usual and not remain at the caves just because he was present; he also asked the Tasaday not to search for the Tasafeng and Sanduka, which they had proposed to do among themselves (because it might complicate efforts to get a reservation and mean new responsibilities for Panamin; he thought, too, that it would be valuable to accompany them on the search). He laid down more precise guidelines for visitors about questioning so that matters the Tasaday did not know about would not be continually put before them. Uncertain what to do about the religious-mythical aspects of his role, Elizalde decided to wait and see how it developed before taking action.

The material presented here is all of what was written down by Elizalde at the time of the original transcription. Some redundancies have been eliminated and some grammar changed to facilitate understanding. About 2 per cent of individual words were changed, but only because later information showed the initial translation as incorrect, or because clarification was necessary.

The conversations will perhaps suggest that the Tasaday have an extremely limited variety of experiences in their daily life. It must be remembered, however, that the impact of Elizalde on the Tasaday was monumental and pervasive; thus it can be safely assumed, I think, that their conversation and behavior during this visit did not reflect their typical way of life. By the same token, the mere presence of any outsiders at the caves—presumably one of the most exciting events the Tasaday had ever experienced—took up conversational time that might otherwise have been devoted to a greater variety of everyday topics.

The bracketed notes appearing throughout the dialogues provide information lacking as a natural result of the reader's being able to read the tapes but not hear them, or whenever there was confusion over who was speaking or what was meant. I have not, however, signaled subtle implications of certain remarks, because I feel that the reader has been sufficiently introduced to the Tasaday to be able to read between the lines. A good example is when Balayam refers to Sindi as being like a sister to him, which was decidedly different from his true view but may have arisen out of some delicacy of manner among the Tasaday. Some references are made clear later in the book; some are never understood.

Brackets are also used to indicate who is being addressed when the translators recognized them by minor utterances or other sounds (of children or of someone arriving), which, because they added nothing significant to a conversation, were not transcribed.

Some of the transcriptions are comparatively short, because sometimes long periods elapsed in which virtually nothing was said—either the cave was nearly empty or the people present were silent. This was true within single transcriptions as well. Most of these pauses were not marked in the original transcription; I was able to detect and mark only some of them, so there will occasionally seem to be an abrupt change of subject, when it was actually just a period of silence.

Of course, once scholars have more knowledge of the Tasaday language, these transcriptions may be corrected extensively, particularly word subtleties. Meanwhile, they remain one of the best sources of information about the Tasaday.

No more than three hours of taping were done after the first two cave expeditions ended, April 23, 1972. There were three reasons: a change in physical arrangements at the caves; improved understanding of the Tasaday; the Tasaday's willingness to speak out readily. On the second expedition there was an attempt to explain the recorder to them, in order to avoid the criticism that taping them was spying, and to encourage them to say things to Panamin on tape that they may have been too shy to say in person. They appeared to have grasped part of the idea, but whether they understood it fully was never certain; however, during several visits over the next eighteen months this candid recording technique was used on only two occasions.

The following was recorded between March 26 and April 1, 1972, in the upper cave.

Session 1   Evening of March 26

MAHAYAG: We are only *natek*-making people but now we have found a friend.

BALAYAM: We will concentrate our hearts to Momo Dakel Diwata Tasaday [abbreviated hereafter to MDDT].

MAHAYAG: We must not look up to others, only MDDT. Whenever we roam in this forest, we must never forget we have MDDT. Now that we have been here for so long we have to stay in this place of ours because we have him.

BALAYAM: Our ancestors said, "Do not leave this place," and their word came true with MDDT. Now that he has come this home should be his home.

MAHAYAG: It really is true that he has come to us!

BALAYAM: We also are grateful to Dafal because it was through him we found MDDT, and also to Mai. We must unite now in gathering *biking, natek, ubud.*

MAHAYAG: We will check our traps tomorrow, as we may have some monkey or deer.

BALAYAM: We are lucky MDDT has come to us. The way he looks at our place is very beautiful and we must never leave it.

MAHAYAG: We must believe all that is said by MDDT. When we go out, two of us can go but someone must stay home.

BALAYAM: If we go out, women must stay home. If MDDT comes up here [to the caves] and sees none of us, he may get discouraged.

MAHAYAG: All men and women: We must cling to MDDT by our right hand. We have been telling MDDT about our place and now he has come here despite great difficulties. To all of you women, keep that inside you.

DUL [who had been talking in the background to Etut, observing that because Etut was pregnant it was hard for her to wear the leaf skirt]: Let us not doubt, and concentrate our love in MDDT. Wherever you roam, carry with you MDDT. Even our children must be taught to love MDDT. If we had not seen MDDT we probably would have died in darkness, without seeing the prophecy of our ancestors. We can see how MDDT loves us, and he has eyes and ears with us even now.

BALAYAM: MDDT has shown us love by sending us Sindi, who is like my sister. MDDT really took us into his inside feeling [sometimes translated as "heart," but the word, probably a derivative of *widiwan,* was later thought to be Igna's] by giving me a wife who is the sister of Kakay Mafoko. The fruits we eat must not be forgotten and neither should our stone tools.

Session 2   Morning of March 27

BALAYAM: Good weather this morning.

MAHAYAG: Wake up now, Kuletaw. It is already morning. We have to gather together our feelings to look up to MDDT, who has given his whole feeling to us. If we go out looking for food we must come back before dark because MDDT might come when we are not here.

MAHAYAG [addressing Balayam]: With our knives given by MDDT we can get many, many foods, not like with the stone tools, which cannot cut the trunk of trees that the *biking* grows under.

BALAYAM: Mahayag, Kuletaw, Udelen, Tekaf—if MDDT doesn't love us very much he will not stay with us so long. So if we go out we must leave our women behind. MDDT has come to our home and when he was here he asked about the food we eat, like *se-fuk* [fruit of a tree]. He is so concerned about what we eat.

[Pause.]

BALAYAM [to Mahayag and some women]: I have the feeling that we will be given more knives by MDDT so that when we go out we can get more food and we can come home faster. It is very surprising that MDDT gives us so many things.

MAHAYAG: It is surprising MDDT gives to us and we have nothing to give him, and he asks for nothing.

BALAYAM: Instead, he is the one giving us so many things. I wonder why MDDT asks what we like when we do not know what we like—or need.

MAHAYAG: We don't know what we want because we cannot name things we don't know.

DUL: MDDT said he will bring us those things that go around our neck [beads].

BALAYAM: Mahayag, Udelen, Kuletaw, Lefonok, Adug, Gintoy, and Lolo—whenever we go out we must not just waste our time uselessly but come back. The old men among us must stay with the women. All of us are now sons of MDDT.

MAHAYAG: We are grateful for our knives because we can get more *biking*. We also have tasted the food of MDDT. [His intonation suggests the food was not so good.]

BALAYAM: We have tasted the *natek* of MDDT [probably rice]. Lefonok, where is your *balatik* [bamboo-speared trap for pig and deer] and monkeytrap?

LEFONOK: I have one *balatik* there and a monkeytrap there.

MAHAYAG: Let us not go our own way. We must wait always for MDDT. We have MDDT and his companions who are very good to children and to women. We must not leave this home of ours—we can go out but we must not stay long. We must come back right away.

BALAYAM: Yes. And we will show them how strong we are in making *natek* and how strong we are in digging *biking*. I will play my *kubing* [mouth harp] now. I really know how to play this.

[This is followed by music, then a pause and sounds of people coming and going.]

ADUG [teen-aged boy, to Dul, apparently following her asking him to the stream]: How long will you stay down at the stream?

DUL: I don't know.

DULA [addressing her daughter, Siyul]: Do you want to go to the stream?

SIYUL: Yes.

ADUG: Yesterday MDDT was always falling down by the stream. If we have much *biking* we will give some to MDDT.

SEKUL [Adug's mother]: Yes. And I left some betel chew where we make *natek*. Will you go and get it? We do not have any more here. I am somewhat scared of that companion of MDDT with white hair.

KULETAW [Adug's father]: Now that we are seen by many persons who come with MDDT, I cannot tell if we still have a hard time or a good time in the future.

ADUG: I wonder about that big bird of MDDT's—MDDT might have made it. I will go out to look for *biking,* but my head is painful. If you find a big tadpole, wrap it with leaves and bring it home [possibly for his headache?]. MDDT wants to go to the stream tomorrow to see *natek-*

making. [Pause, spurts of conversation, and then Adug continued]: I dreamed that I was whipped by MDDT. I cried and woke up and thought it was true. That was my dream last night and I dreamed also that MDDT went home and I cried to see him going. And because he saw me crying where I slept between the trunk of a big tree somewhere below, he suddenly came back to me and wiped his hand over my forehead . . . if we knew how to speak the words of MDDT we could talk to him . . . but we don't know.

KULETAW: That's true . . . MDDT loves this home of ours very much.

ADUG: What is this black thing [apparently the bag containing the tape recorder] we have here in the corner?

KULETAW: We must love MDDT very much.

ADUG: Why is it that MDDT does not sleep with us here in our home?

KULETAW: Even though I am old, I count MDDT as my father.

ADUG: We must not go out so much because MDDT comes up here often. We must not wander around and around so much we might die. We already have our father here in our home.

KULETAW: Yes. Our father below [MDDT] might have the feeling of not being near us.

ADUG: Even though there are many persons with MDDT, we will only look to him alone, because he is our father Tasaday [or some similar word meaning "god-spirit"]. I cannot be happy today because I have pain in my head.

KULETAW: If we leave MDDT and always go out, it means that we do not love him. We feel very happy because we have him and we have many things. We will make his eyes contented to look at us, even if we do not have anything to give him.

ADUG: MDDT asks what we want. We don't know what to name because we don't know those things he knows.

KULETAW: MDDT has given us knives and things to place around the neck [bead necklaces] and we don't know what other things he means. We have a hard time always before, but now we have many things given to us by MDDT.

ADUG: We must obey what MDDT tells us. And if we find other persons we must run from them—they might get our things away from us. . . . I will not talk more, because my head is painful. I will go out, near here, where I found a small *biking* yesterday.

KULETAW [following a garbled exchange]: Make your *asut* [leaf G string] nice. I am now very old; it is a fortune to see MDDT.

LEFONOK: We have good feelings now that we have MDDT, our father [again the word meaning "god" or "spirit"] of Tasaday.

ADUG [to younger children]: Do not urinate inside here. MDDT might smell it. Let's go out to get *naf-naf* [bamboo sections] to cook *ubud* by and by.

Session 3   Night of March 27

BALAYAM: Let us get together. Where is Mahayag? He must have gone for *natek*. [To Lefonok]: If you know that place Sanduka, let us try and make a trip there. This place of ours is the place of Panong and Salibuku, my father, and I am Balayam, his son. If you know that place let us try to travel there. If we are sure about the location of Sanduka we can get a wife, and also go to Tasafeng so that all of us can get a wife. Adug, Lolo, Lefonok are still single. We have to look for wives for these men. We know now very clearly from our ancestors that we have MDDT helping us now. Etut is a Sanduka, Sekul is from Tasafeng. We don't know if there are still people in Sanduka and Tasafeng. Now you women from Sanduka and Tasafeng, it would be good if there are still women there. All of us here now must have unity of feeling and always keep in mind what has been told to us by MDDT [this may have been a reference to Manda's suggesting to the Tasaday that they try to find wives as they had previously]. Long ago this place of ours was the dwelling place of our ancestors Fangul and Salibuku and this has been their home.

DUL: You must not forget your ancestors.

BALAYAM: We do not know where Fangul got his wife. The way I remember it, the brother of Fangul was Sambal [Bilangan's father] and I think now that we see MDDT that Fangul one day will come back also. Now we must wait for Mahayag and Udelen. Where did you get Etut, in Sanduka, Bilangan? Where did Sambal get Etut for you, in Sanduka?

BILANGAN: I got Etut in Sanduka.

BALAYAM: Kuletaw got his wife in Tasafeng. How I wish there were people still in Tasafeng and Sanduka. This we would like, there are still those among us who have no wives—Lefonok, Lolo, and Lobo. We have MDDT, who is kind in his help to us. We have to stay very good here. [Balayam may have been so openly solicitous about the other single men because he had just gotten a wife and wanted to avoid envy.] How we wish there were women in Sanduka and Tasafeng. Etut is a woman from Sanduka and Sekul a woman from Tasafeng. [To Mahayag, who has just arrived]: Is the palm tree that you cut down containing *natek*?

MAHAYAG: Yes, it has *natek*.

BALAYAM: This is all we know—to get *biking,* to make *natek,* and gather other food in the forest. But those questions, it is hard to know the answers. We do not know.

BILANGAN: That is true.

BALAYAM: We know of making *ketab* [mousetraps] and *balatik*. I will try to travel to Sanduka and Tasafeng when MDDT is not here, and then I will tell him if there are people in those places. We will tell him if we can find people there.

DUL: Try to find out if there are still people of my group.

BILANGAN: Long before, we had a hard time. Now that we have MDDT with us, it is not so hard. We will try to find that place after MDDT is not here so we can tell him if people are there or not.

BALAYAM: Yes.

BALANGAN: To us, we only know of making deer-, pig-, and monkey-traps and making *natek*. MDDT knows this.

BALAYAM: This is what we know only.

BILANGAN: Yes.

BALAYAM: Let's have some betel chew.

BILANGAN: Yes, and let us talk again when Mahayag returns. MDDT has big love for us. This coming of MDDT to our place is very good and we all are happy inside. I wonder why MDDT likes this big place [the upper cave]. We have big luck because we have MDDT here with us in Tasaday. We have big luck here in the big place of ours. Many always come up to us.

[Balayam and Sindi are murmuring in the background; from the few understandable phrases it is love talk.]

DUL: Don't cry, baby, we may disturb those below [at the tents?].

BALAYAM: We will make *natek* tomorrow. We will make much *natek*. MDDT stays long with us and we will make much *natek*. What MDDT said is that if we ever see any persons inside the forest that we have not seen . . . [obscured by baby cries and Dul talking to a child] . . . good if there is sunshine tomorrow.

DUL: The woman below [Igna] says *agdaw* [sun] and we say *fuglaon*. [Balayam and Sindi are talking in the background about going to sleep.] That fat woman [Igna] said *bulan* [moon], while we say *sebang*.

BALAYAM [to Sindi]: Teach me your words so I can teach you ours.

DUL [who has been talking with the child about leaves the adults wear]: Let us lie down together. This sister of Mafoko [referring to Sindi] may not know how to go in the grass or forest . . .

SINDI: I will make it.

BALAYAM [speaking loudly]: I want to sleep. [He and Sindi apparently retire to his cave. Children continue to play and Dul tells them to stop, tells the baby to stop crying and all of them to lie down.]

BILANGAN [speaking as if to himself]: I will look for a *natek* tree tomorrow.

Session 4   Evening of March 28

ETUT: Where are you going tomorrow?

DUL: If they want me to go to the stream, I will go. MDDT pitied me yesterday when I was at the stream, but I wonder why he seemed to have a heavy face there.

DULA: I think something was wrong.

DUL: Perhaps we women can also have a knife. Tomorrow we will go to MDDT again and he will be interested in what we are doing. We will go down again tomorrow so he can see us very often. Did you see, MDDT was not tired when climbing up here, so we must visit him also.

[Pause.]

DULA: Children, divide the *ubud* equally so you will not cry.

ETUT: MDDT may see that I am not too happy, but inside I am very happy . . . although it is hard for me to find leaves for my dress.

DUL: MDDT has said he will bring us things that the fat woman [Igna] wears. Did you hear when he was about to leave [the cave] and he asked what we wanted and I did not know how to answer him?

DULA: MDDT said, though, if he gives us that which she has [cloth] we should still wear our own clothes [leaves]. It is very nice to look at the three other women with MDDT [Mila, Lucy, and Onto]. Are they his daughters or not? [To a child]: Be careful . . . come over here or the man with a sharp look will get you.

[Long pause; Balayam arrives and begins playing his mouth harp.]

BALAYAM [perhaps to the children]: Don't bother me, because I'm playing.

DUL: Balayam always plays his harp now because he has a companion.

BALAYAM: I have a painful body today.

ETUT [to her second youngest son, who is about three or four]: Natek, do not push your little brother, he might fall down. [To Lolo]: When we go down to the stream later you will carry your little brother. When we are there we must not talk nonsense . . . only important things.

BALAYAM: When MDDT comes up here and calls we must answer immediately and look over the edge of the cave.

DUL: What do you want from MDDT?

BALAYAM: Knife.

LOBO: The same.

BALAYAM: We all will have one now.

SEKUL: Will you be able to get covering [cloth] for your wife?

DULA: It is night already so we cannot go out to get leaves.

[Lengthy pause.]

DUL [to her children]: Don't go where Balayam is because the way is difficult. [Balayam apparently has gone to his cave with Sindi.] We will go down now [to the lower cave?].

DULA: No, never mind, let's just wait for Mahayag and the others to come up here. Let's not talk so much because some want to sleep.

DUL: Tomorrow when we go down we will take fire with us so when we get *natek* we can give some cooked to MDDT.

DULA: And food we eat we will give some to him so he can try it.

ETUT: Why doesn't that other woman [Igna] want to sleep here?

DULA: Maybe she thinks that we are not so good.

ETUT: When there is time I would like to ask her if her companions are like us.

DUL: So would I, but I am shy.

SEKUL: I would like to go nearer to MDDT, but I am shy.

UDELEN: Don't talk so loud—they may be bothered below [at the other caves or the tents].

DUL [to Adug, who apparently just arrived]: What are you carrying? [Without waiting for an answer, she addresses Balayam, who has again come up from his cave]: Now that you have Sindi, I will let one of my children be under your care.

DULA [to Dul]: We who are somewhat light [not pregnant like Etut] will show MDDT where we make *natek*.

ETUT: That woman with MDDT [Igna] is very gifted in speech. There are many words of ours she knows.

DUL: I'll be waiting for the long piece [of cloth] from MDDT . . . Among those four women, we know only that one [Igna]. We cannot forget her. [To her son]: Do not waste your food. [Back to the subject of Igna]: The headpiece and leg pieces [beaded comb, ankle bracelets] on her are very beautiful. How do they make those? It is very nice to see. They must be made by MDDT.

UDELEN [Dul's husband]: Dul, do not seek everything you see, because even if you had those things you would not know how to use them.

DULA: If we have those things on our feet, perhaps our feet would be cut off.

KULETAW: Do not admire all that you see because that woman might laugh at you.

DULA [to a child]: Do not cry and cry, because if you do the tall man with MDDT will come up.

SEKUL [to Adug]: Find bamboo to cook the *natek* [rice] of MDDT.

DULA: We will go to the stream tomorrow so MDDT will see us look for our food.

BALAYAM: How do you like the taste of MDDT's *natek?*

DUL: Not so good.

LEFONOK [to children]: Don't waste the *ubud!*

DUL [to Dula]: When MDDT met us last time at the lean-tos [at the clearing] he asked about you and Tekaf, Mahayag, and Ginun [they were making *natek* and did not come].

DULA: You are better than I am—you always go. [To a child]: Don't go near the edge or MDDT will get mad. Besides, Sindi is over there [in the next cave] resting.

DUL: Did you see MDDT eating our *ubud?*

DULA: Imagine, he likes our food. [Laughter. To children again]: Don't be so noisy, because by and by that sparkling light [the strobe lights] will come again.

DUL: We have a wonderful home here. We must never go far from it. One day we will take MDDT to the top [of the mountain] and see if he can make it without falling down. Perhaps I will laugh and laugh if MDDT keeps falling down.

BALAYAM: Don't try it [defensively], because MDDT is a very fast walker.

DUL: When MDDT is here I will ask him for a knife so I will have one to look for food. Ah, the earpieces [earrings] of Sindi are very nice.

DUL [to children]: Do not waste the *natek* of MDDT or he may feel hurt.

DULA: If you want a knife, so do I.

DUL: The men received arrows, so we will ask for knives.

DULA: Roast some *biking* for the children.

ETUT [to Lolo, her oldest son, a teen-ager]: You go down to sleep with MDDT. [Laughter]

LOLO: No, I can't.

ETUT [to younger children]: Don't cry or we will send you down to MDDT.

DUL [whispering to Etut]: Do you think the woman [Igna] has a husband? [To Lefonok]: You must always hold your bow and arrow so that MDDT sees that you like it. [To Balayam, jokingly]: You must not sleep so late in the morning. Is that because you now have Sindi? [Laughter]

DULA [sings]: Do not cry my baby . . .

DUL: You sing now, but when MDDT hears you and asks you to sing you will be scared. [Jokingly]: I will call him now.

DULA: No . . . no. He might still be eating . . . but even if you call MDDT he will not understand you.

DUL: MDDT really loves us. How did he get here?

BALAYAM [proudly]: He came with me!

DUL: I thought that MDDT would take a long time before coming to visit us, but he came soon. If MDDT stays with us for a very long time, we will take him to where our husbands make traps and teach him how to walk properly. [Pause.] Our rock is very shiny. MDDT plays on this rock.

ETUT: I figure he already has come up here three times [apparently meaning at night].

DUL: How does he know how to walk at night? . . . the way to our place is being destroyed . . . it's different than before [trees broken, path muddy and torn]. [To a child]: You cannot eat monkey meat, because your father has no time [indicating he is so busy with the visitors he has no time to trap].

DULA: But even if the traps catch a monkey, let it rot, because MDDT is more important than any monkey.

DUL: If we get any meat, let us cook it in bamboo and let MDDT taste it. You, Mabulu-ulu [the light-skinned child], you are always playing. Your hair is like that of MDDT's companion. When you grow big, you can go with MDDT and Kakay Mafoko. When you come back, you will be a young man.

BILANGAN [to Etut, his wife]: I remember when I was a small boy I went to Sanduka. How would you like to go there for a visit?

ETUT: If you want to go I will try my best to go with you. It would be good if we can find some of my companions. We will tell MDDT about it. I can still remember that place of my mother and father . . . there is a mountain . . . The name of my father is Begung . . . and the name of my mother is Kuyong. If we go, we will make *natek* on the way. How about you, Dul, would you like to visit your place?

UDELEN: We will try to go there when MDDT is no longer down below. Well . . . we will if that is the wish of our wives. Let's try to go then. How far is it?

DUL: I don't know exactly how far it is.

SEKUL: How about you, Dula, would you like to visit our place [Tasafeng]? If we go to our place, shall we sleep there?

DULA: I don't know if we will or not. I will go and I know you will remember the way and the place because you are older.

SEKUL [to Etut]: If you go to Sanduka we will go to Tasafeng. We will tell MDDT if we can still find some of our companions. If we can find our place, even if we find no companions, we will take MDDT so he can sleep in our place. We will make *natek* on the way.

DUL [?]: As for us, if we can find our place in Sanduka, we will bring MDDT there so he can also sleep one night with us and try to taste *natek* there. But, Etut, I don't know if MDDT will be bothered by the cry of our babies on the way. MDDT has been asking about our place. Perhaps he wants to go and visit it.

SEKUL: We are from Tasafeng and you are from Sanduka. Let us see in which place MDDT will sleep first. Let us sit down and tell about our way before we let MDDT choose which place.

DULA: I can still remember that our place is very high. I remember that place . . . there is a mountain with hot water . . .

DUL [to Etut]: How about our place, what do you remember of it? [Possibly erroneous translation or identification, because Dul said repeatedly in later discussions with MDDT and others that she came from Tasafeng—although references to her as being from Sanduka appeared several times in this tape transcription. Or she might have deliberately changed her story.]

ETUT: The way I remember it down below is a creek, and our place, which is up from that creek, has few trees.

DUL: If we can still find that place of ours it would be good if MDDT can sleep with us there. But I love this place here more than there.

ETUT: If MDDT will come back again after [garbled] we will bring him right away to our place.

DUL [to Udelen]: When we go you carry Maman [their youngest child] so we can move fast. Children must be quiet now . . . we have thinking inside of us.

LEFONOK: When you go I will go to find *mamak* [*bui* vine].

ADUG: I will go when my mother goes, so I can see her place in Tasa-feng.

KULETAW [to Sekul]: Don't be lazy. Let's go find that place of yours so we will have something to tell MDDT.

DUL [to Etut]: When MDDT is not down below we will go and visit our place and come back right away . . . only now do we remember our place. If not for MDDT we would have forgotten it.

UDELEN: When we go, somebody must stay here.

DULA [laughing]: I even start laughing now when I think of MDDT try-ing to go with us [more laughter] . . . that long climb!

DUL: MDDT always loves to see the plants and vines in front of our home here.

MAHAYAG: Imagine his great love for us. He even talks about the things growing in front of our home.

DUL: Well, this is all we will talk about our places. When MDDT is not down there any more we will each go to our places.

MAHAYAG: So that MDDT may eat, I will gather *ubud*. We will let him eat the food we eat. I'll joke with him, I'll tell him to stay alone with us when the rest go home. I will be the one to look for his food and cook for him. I will cook *biking* and *natek*.

DULA: I don't know if he really likes our food.

MAHAYAG: He loves us, he will eat our food. I will look for worms [grubs] and he surely will like that. They are delicious! What do you think—will he be willing to stay behind with us?

LEFONOK: I'd like it very much. Wherever we go we'll bring him with us, and if he cannot walk I'll carry him.

DULA: Do not try to make him stay—suppose he cannot eat our food and dies here.

DUL: Now when he stays here you must give him the head of a monkey so he can cook it himself.

ADUG: I would like it also if MDDT stays with us. I'll let him watch me dig *biking*. If MDDT stays with us, perhaps those companions of his will continue bringing knives.

BALAYAM: It would be wonderful for me if MDDT stayed with us. I would take him up the stream to look for fruits.

MAHAYAG: I can imagine that MDDT would be very cold. He will have no cover and is not like us who do not feel cold here.

KULETAW: You try to talk to him and convince him to stay here. I will be the one to take him looking for palm fruit. We can put *natek* inside leaves and he can carry it in his hand.

LEFONOK: We will feed him our food. He will not be hungry. If he doesn't like *natek,* we will look for fruits.

BALAYAM: That is why we must keep on visiting down below, so we can convince him to stay.

LEFONOK: I have tried carrying him already. If he can't walk with us, I can carry him.

DUL: If he goes with us, we will find him tadpoles . . . and crabs and frogs.

ADUG: I'd like it if he stayed. I'll show him my monkeytrap—it's very high.

DULA: I could hardly believe it if MDDT stayed here.

MAHAYAG: Why not? He really loves us. I'll ask him if they make mousetraps in his place.

[Dula starts singing.]

LEFONOK: If MDDT stays with us we will get bark [to make a carrier of some kind] so he can have food with him always.

DUL: If MDDT tries to go home, I'll try to go with him.

ADUG: Don't go. If you go and get into that big bird of MDDT's you can't see anything any more.

MAHAYAG: Tomorrow we will work on the *natek* press that MDDT asked us to build.

DUL: If the men are working at the stream tomorrow, I'll go fishing.

DULA: So will I.

DUL: If MDDT asks what we want, I'll tell him knives.

KULETAW: I'm already old. MDDT is very kind, like when he showed kindness to Mahayag.

MAHAYAG: If MDDT will stay behind, we will give him a *fuyut* [basket] so he always has a place to put betel and become like us. When we go making *natek* we will always let him go with us so he can see and learn.

ADUG: If he stays, I'll teach him to make monkeytraps and pig- and deertraps.

KULETAW: We'll take him to the stream and teach him to fish. If he'll stay with us we'll make many traps so MDDT can see a round pig.

BALAYAM: We'll also ask Kakay Mafoko if he would like to join MDDT here. If MDDT will stay, maybe many of his companions will visit him always.

ADUG: I'll show him that big *biking* I saw.

MAHAYAG: If he stays I'll give him the sticky part of *natek* and cook *biking* for him with tadpoles and leaves. That is very good. He'll like that. Tomorrow we'll make *natek* so MDDT can see us make it.

ADUG: We'll sleep little tonight, because we will go early tomorrow. I don't know how to get MDDT to stay with us. We like our food . . . but I don't know if he does.

DUL: And we are different from that woman [Igna] who goes with MDDT. She has almost the same appearance as Kakay Mafoko. [Both are chunkily built.]

DULA: Look at our stomachs, very small. The stomach of that woman with MDDT is very big.

MAHAYAG: Don't look [too much?] at the companions of MDDT. They might not like it.

DUL: We will not sleep so soundly, because MDDT might come.

Session 5   Late Morning of March 30

[Babies are crying and Dul quiets them.]

ADUG [to the children]: Don't play with fire.

ETUT [to a child]: Don't tease your brother.

DUL: Let us try to stop the children from crying.

DULA [sings to her children, stops, and says]: Lobo, don't go down, the people below may be disturbed. [She resumes singing.]

DUL: I'm expecting my knife from MDDT—so I can get *ubud*.

[Udelen makes some remark to Lefonok about a knife.]

BALAYAM: Do you need knives, too, Mahayag? And you, Udelen?

UDELEN: If our knives get broken we should keep the pieces and show them to MDDT.

DUL: I'm also waiting for my knife from MDDT. I would use it for getting betel and palm-tree worms.

ADUG: The knife that I like is the one with *umbay-umbay* [decoration]. The one I had was broken when I cut a palm tree.

BALAYAM: Any of us who go out can take the knife here until each of us has one. I'll ask Igna if MDDT will go home and when. Then, when he goes, Mahayag, you and I will immediately try to travel to Sanduka to find the place and tell MDDT.

[Balayam apparently remained in the cave as others came and went during this session; he spoke with various people at intervals; there was no talk in between.]

Why are our companions out? They don't come home very early.

LEFONOK: They went to look for crabs.

BALAYAM: We have stable feelings now that MDDT has slept with us.

DUL: He slept with us because he loves us so much.

BALAYAM: Sindi, MDDT loves us here very much and now you are going to be my wife because he has loved us so much. Tell MDDT that all of us here are very good in our inside feelings.

[To Lefonok]: MDDT holds us now very truly with his right hand, because he gave us a woman to be my wife.

[To Dul]: All the necklaces and knives that MDDT gave us we must keep nicely in the corner of our above house. [Apparently another dwelling, not yet known to us.]

DUL: We always keep ours very nicely in our corner.

BALAYAM [to Sindi]: To us we are people of the forest. Tell MDDT that we are good in the inside of our feelings so he will always think of that.

[To Lefonok]: When our companions come back, we will tell them that, now MDDT loves us, we should increase our traps. I had a dream when MDDT was sleeping with us here that I was on my way to look for *biking* and to make a trap. I saw a small white boy on top of the mountain sitting on the stone. He said to me: "Balayam, don't stop making traps and looking for *biking*." I think this was the spirit of MDDT, whose feeling goes with us in whatever we do.

LEFONOK: Tomorrow let us make *natek* again.

BALAYAM: Let's go out now and look for *biking*. We'll help each other in digging and won't go out very far. Help me always to look for food, Lefonok, so that Sindi will not feel hungry.

ADUG: If we go out, we will come back soon. When we go, MDDT might come up here and he won't see us.

BALAYAM: Let the women stay home. [Begins to sing.]

ADUG [jokingly]: Balayam has a good voice now.

[Tekaf and Ginun enter the cave.]

BALAYAM: The deaf and the dumb are arriving.

[Laughter. We learned later that neither of them could speak or hear.]

LEFONOK: MDDT and his companions went to the stream and gathered the things he and his companions brought.

[Laughter. This apparently referred to our cleaning the stream of garbage.]

DULA [to Biking, her son]: Help Siyul [her daughter] and we will go with Mahayag to look for *biking*.

BALAYAM: We will always be happy even though we are different from them [MDDT and his companions] and MDDT will always understand us.

Where is Bilangan? The whole feeling of MDDT is with us now. We must think of him always. If MDDT has only small love for us, he will not let me marry Sindi. Sindi is the daughter of MDDT and Sindi is the sister of Kakay Mafoko.

[Udelen and others arrive. Balayam continues very seriously.]

We must always show our whole good feeling to MDDT. Kuletaw, you must be happy always so MDDT will always see happiness in our faces.

Dul, Dula, Etut, Sekul—we have to combine our feelings together, and when MDDT comes here give him betel. When he is no longer below we will make lots of *natek* and gather much *biking* so when he returns he can see the great work we have done. We must not turn away from MDDT. We must not vary in our united love for him. The love of MDDT for us is more than too much—even when it rains he walks through the rain to visit us. We have been living for long and this is the first time we have experienced a love like that of MDDT, which is even more than the love of our own parents.

Mahayag [who has just arrived], when MDDT is no longer below, we will feel very painful. It is all right if MDDT does not sleep with us every night as long as he stays below. He put us already inside himself because he slept here. MDDT has us in his own insides and we hope that when he leaves he will return soon.

Mahayag, Lefonok, Kuletaw, Adug—we must not make our feelings far from MDDT, because he has put us inside his feelings. We must talk to him, tell him that if he leaves he must return immediately, and if he does not we will have great pain and I will die. To me, if MDDT will stay away very long I will die in the forest and no longer be here when he comes back. We have asked MDDT to sleep with us and he did what we asked, so if we talk to him again he will surely listen.

Lefonok, we forget one thing when MDDT slept with us, we forgot to give him the food we had prepared. Udelen, MDDT must always be with us. Our ancestors have all died and now they have returned to us in the form of MDDT. This is why, Kuletaw, we must never be away from MDDT. I, Balayam, as you know, Mahayag, was brought up by Kuletaw since I was small. To all of you women, and all of us men, and especially you small children, you must not make your own way, you must look to MDDT. Mahayag, what do you say about ourselves before we saw MDDT?

[The session became something of a forum. Sounds of the meeting reached the tents below; the voices were loud and intent.]

MAHAYAG: I can't just say why MDDT comes to love us so much. He even loves the leaves we wear. I understand from what MDDT said to us about the *natek, biking,* and monkey they are all ours here in Tasaday. But who is that person MDDT said we might see in the forest? [Elizalde's warning to avoid strangers.] We have not seen any, and if we did we would run. We must do always what we have been doing in the past. MDDT has given us many knives, and we must always wear our own clothing. We have to combine our feelings and love MDDT.

BALAYAM: We can't say that any more, because it already has been done.

MAHAYAG: When that big bird comes, it cannot see us at once, and this big bird can't see inside our home. He can't make it. We must never forget to love our leaf clothes, because MDDT likes them. Balayam, all of our different foods must be tasted by MDDT and Kakay Mafoko. MDDT will know when all of these *natek* trees are finished what we should do next.

BALAYAM: We will not finish these trees until our hair is white.

MAHAYAG: Dul, all this *ubud* and *natek*—nobody can get it. We can't see any others cutting, and only we can have it all. It has been told by our ancestors that we should never leave this home because it is here that Diwata Tasaday can find us. We have also seen some companions of MDDT with tall noses. Even when MDDT is not here we should not stay out overnight, so that whenever he comes on his big bird he can see us at any time.

Dul, when we go fishing we should go every other day—we must not just sit here without tasting food from the stream.

DUL: Yes.

MAHAYAG: Balayam, we have to stay here always, stay here so MDDT will see us easily at any time. This group of ours, let us call all men one man, and all women one woman. We must combine our feelings together. When MDDT comes to us we must always meet him with good feelings within us. Also the women. And even if they are many that come we will look up only to MDDT. This way that I see things now there seems to be no more night—only daylight. Now that we have many knives, we will make many traps so we can get pigs and deer. We will cook it in bamboo and keep it for MDDT.

BALAYAM: Yes, yes. And we must not get tired from all the questions of MDDT, even until the time that Kuletaw may be dead, because there are still many things MDDT does not know. Our feeling now is not heavy, but light. MDDT has told us that all the *natek* and *biking* are ours, and although he says that, we should also give him some. All fish in Tasaday must be tasted by him. MDDT said all the frogs, tadpoles and fish in the stream are ours. We'll always be happy now that we have MDDT with us —not like before when he was not with us. Have all of you heard what I said? [He calls each person by name and each answers yes.]

MAHAYAG: We are very happy because, although the place of MDDT is very far, he still comes here to stay with us. Our only work [?] is to make deer- and monkeytraps, but they, those people, know so many things. We will tell MDDT the way we live here in Tasaday and the way our ancestors lived. All of us are now the sons of MDDT, including you, Kuletaw. Even you old women. We must always continue to look for the food that we eat so MDDT can see it and taste it. This is what our ancestors had been telling us—it has come true! As our ancestors said it, we should stay in this place of ours and a good man will come to us, and that is MDDT. Now it seems that our fathers are not dead, because the father we have now is more than our fathers because he gives us knives and puts things on the necks of the women. The big surprise we can't understand is the arrival of MDDT in that big bird. When we first saw MDDT he had few companions, now he brings many, which shows his love and gives us more help.

9

Protection and Criticism

THE "rescue" of Lindbergh and
the expedition immediately attracted world-wide attention. Elizalde had
worried this would overshadow and downgrade the positive accomplishments of the trip, but it seemed mainly to heighten interest. The general
response ran enthusiastically favorable, although a negative undercurrent
in Manila characterized the rescue as an Elizalde publicity gimmick and
the whole expedition as some kind of stunt.

Fresh criticism was making the rounds even before we reached Manila.
Some people, reacting to newspaper stories, were skeptical, some down-
right incensed. One argument was that the unique circumstances of the
Tasaday—*if* they were really as unusual as was claimed—required a professional team of scientists exclusive of outsiders, particularly journalists,
to study the people meticulously and quietly. The scientists were outraged
by a news report that the expedition included forty-one persons. (The report failed to mention that twenty-five were tribesmen who carried supplies
and prepared the treetop landing place, saw only one or two Tasaday, and
never once visited the caves; that eight or nine others had seen the tent
camp or caves only two or three times; and that only seven people had
made regular visits to the caves. When I mentioned this later to an American scientist, he moaned, *"Only* seven! My God, that's almost one for
every three Tasaday—they must have felt overwhelmed!")

My wife reported that several people at a party she attended were curious as to why Fox had not gone on the expedition, and why Lynch had
—another American, colonial days were past, weren't they? Why not a
Filipino? The fact that Carlos Fernandez had gone encouraged some, although at least two people pointed out that he did not have his doctoral

degree. A few others challenged Elizalde's interest in tribes, speculating about his family's possible involvement in mining or other exploitative enterprises, and some said they thought the chief objective of the expedition was his personal publicity.

Expressions of approval far outnumbered such complaints. Still, when Elizalde heard the criticism it rankled.

He was triumphant, though, on April 6, five days after the expedition ended, when President Marcos signed a proclamation granting the Tasaday and Manubo Blit 46,299 acres as a reserve, forbidden to outside exploitation, entry, sale, lease, or other disposition. The President also stated anew the government's policy toward minorities, saying, in part, that his administration was committed to "integrating those minorities who wish to join the mainstream of Filipino national life and protecting the rights of those who prefer to remain and preserve their original life ways." Marcos said he would count heavily on Elizalde to implement this.

Elizalde praised the President lavishly, saying that he had cut through possibly many months of bureaucratic red tape in denying the forest to three logging companies who already had claims on it. To people who suggested the President was seeking to get in on the world-wide publicity the Tasaday were generating, Elizalde responded: "He didn't have to go so far if that's all he was after. He went against some pretty powerful people and established that reserve in record time. And the statement about minorities holding on to their traditional life ways—beautiful! I mean, this whole thing is absolutely fantastic. The proclamation, the policy statement—they alone make the expedition worth everything. Forget the critics. It would've taken years for them to get this kind of protection for the Tasaday or anyone else—*if* they could get it at all, and *if* they really wanted to."

The proclamation did not quiet the critics, though. On April 9 I heard caustic disapproval during a dinner given by a journalist friend for a Filipino history professor and a few European diplomats and their wives. The professor, Z. A. Salazar, described Elizalde as a publicity-mad confidence man who staged the whole affair for political gain. He based this accusation on the discovery of the Tasaday during an election year, on subsequent publicity and Elizalde's seeking of a senate seat, and on a deep suspicion of Elizalde, whom he had not met but whose public image and family status were sufficient cause to suspect him of anything. He buttressed these views by attacking the first data paper by Elizalde and Fox as inept and premature. (Salazar had written a critique of early published material on the Tasaday, and Elizalde had recommended it to me, saying he did not agree entirely but felt in some ways it was one of the best articles written on the Tasaday. The historian, who also had degrees in anthropology and linguistics, had written, among other things, that it was impossible to understand Tasaday life without a command of their language.) Salazar recommended that an anthropologist live with the Tasaday for several months, or even a year, in order to learn the language and proceed from basic to more complex data. He challenged all of the early research, questioned claims of the length of their isolation and their lack of metal, and ridiculed the role of Dafal, saying it was incredibly coincidental that everything modern in the Tasaday world had come from him.

One of the diplomats at the dinner suggested that the whole Tasaday discovery had been staged: the Tasaday were merely primitive mountain people who had been put into caves for dramatic effect—perhaps even the caves had been manufactured! Asked why this might have been done, the diplomat said he did not know, but suggested dark and unknown motives and cited unspecific scientific hoaxes in Russia and Germany as precedents.

At this point I mentioned that I had met the Tasaday, visited their homesite, and believed they were authentic. With this the discussion grew heated. Salazar argued that as a newsman I had far less right to have been there than a scientist. He accused Elizalde and Fox of having used the Tasaday and people like me as playthings for self-promotion.

Agitated, I asked what *he* had done in behalf of the minorities? If he was concerned over people's welfare, where had he been? Why had only the Tasaday aroused his deep humanistic concern? Did he think Elizalde and Fox were more dangerous than the frontiersmen who were killing tribesmen and stealing their lands? I argued that it was easy to stand back in a holier-than-thou attitude and recommend what should be done as in a laboratory case study; however, the tribes were not in a test tube, but in a fight for survival. Salazar observed that now I was being self-righteous and as an American journalist I had much more money and time for field work than the vast majority of Filipino scholars.

We argued through much of the evening, bitterly at first and more amicably toward the end, but neither made any substantial changes in the other's views. Significant to me, and almost ironic, as I thought about it later, was that I had put forth arguments similar to Elizalde's; and I was sometimes on the defensive when perhaps I should have stayed impartial. This gave me pause. Was I interpreting matters correctly, or had I been so swayed by Elizalde's rhetoric that I was overlooking negative aspects? I was extremely sympathetic to the Tasaday; I was also becoming increasingly sympathetic to Elizalde.

I did not think I was glossing over things, but I felt a stronger need than ever to see clearly. I needed to know Elizalde better. Although I had an improved understanding and appreciation of him, various matters still puzzled me. To clarify them I needed to establish and sustain a rapport with him. His moods and manners changed constantly; he was invariably surrounded by loyal aides and followers, bodyguards, sycophants, people seeking help, all of whom he could and did use as shields from outsiders.

Most of these people were beholden to him in some way, and his attitudes toward them ranged from the affection of a close friend to the imperious disdain of a grandee.

Once, in the mountains, we had spent a tiring day at an Ubu settlement. He was fussed over by the women, pawed and crawled upon by the children, and pulled here and there by the men who told him their problems. This went on for hours, and he was by turns thoughtful, humorous, playful, serious—but his good humor never flagged. We left by helicopter and twenty minutes later he pointed at something as we circled the Tboli settlement to land. On the ground he walked directly to a white Jeep that was standing ready. (In Manila he always had a chauffeur, but here he drove himself.) Waiting beside the Jeep were bodyguards with rifles and staff aides with papers for him to read or sign (they never knew how long he would stay and caught him as they could). Elizalde nodded at them, muttered something, jumped behind the wheel and in seconds roared away with the guards and aides running in his dust. He screeched to a stop at a house less than seventy-five feet from where he had started and climbed from the Jeep as the others ran up.

"Who's in charge here?" he growled.

"Guevarra," someone answered.

"Get him!"

One man shouted and another raced inside the house, which was used by security guards and aircraft-maintenance men. Guevarra appeared in a few seconds, a snap brim hat on his head, a cigarette in his mouth, and a puzzled look in his eyes.

Elizalde, standing with his hands on his hips, snapped: "You in charge here?"

"Ah, yes . . . I . . ."

Elizalde slapped the dangling cigarette out of the man's mouth and bellowed, "Then what the hell is this?" He pointed down a slope toward a terraced Tboli garden. The slope was sprinkled with paper, tin cans, and other debris.

"I . . . ah . . . well . . . ah," stammered Guevarra, a Manila man from Elizalde's private staff, his eyes blinking rapidly.

"Damn it! No more of that!" Elizalde snatched Guevarra's cream-colored hat and sailed it into the garbage. *"I want it clean!"*

He whirled, jumped back behind the wheel of the Jeep, and quickly shot off to the main staff house. The Jeep had filled with aides and guards during his confrontation with Guevarra and everyone rode in tense silence. At the staff house Manda leaped out of the Jeep and stomped inside. Five minutes later, he was seated with two Tboli children on his lap as he joked with Mai Tuan, teasing him about his wives.

I thought then how misleading it could have been to have seen him in only one of the situations that day. I was reminded of that some weeks later, when I found myself applauding the results of the first expedition to the caves—the reserve proclamation, particularly—and at the same time understanding why there was skepticism. Had I not been on the expedition, I, too, probably would have suspected the rescue was a stunt and that the Tasaday had been overrun by gawking tourists.

Both cases re-emphasized the need of restraint in making judgments about Elizalde; yet I felt that he occasionally led me to draw unfavorable interpretations. Though he was often forceful and decisive, he also could be vague and defensive, sometimes seeming to relish being enigmatic.

There was, for instance, the matter of Sindi, the Blit widow who had become involved with Balayam. Had their relationship developed accidentally, or had it been arranged? When I asked Elizalde about it, he did not answer one way or the other, but suggested that the possibility of Sindi and Balayam getting together had been considered in advance. His worry was that their relationship, however it came about, might be misunderstood by outsiders not acquainted with the circumstances.

I suggested that if he were more open and candid, it would encourage understanding all around, but he felt that being more candid publicly would also mean being much more critical of various people, which would only cause more disputes, and added that openness would not quiet his toughest enemies, who would twist whatever he said to malign him.

This did not apply to the whole scientific community, however, and he wanted the criticism and doubt from that quarter overcome. One major step toward accomplishing this would be the report that Frank Lynch and Carlos Fernandez were preparing about their visits to the forest.

During the second week of April Lynch, Fernandez, and Oscar Trinidad met to discuss this report, and to consider a program of scientific study. I was there as an observer, and also so that my photos and any data I might have picked up would be available to the anthropologists.

Robert Fox and a few others would be asked to read it and comment, then a meeting would be convened to discuss a scientific study program based on Fox's earlier proposals. Lynch said he would like the first phase of the program, covering about five months, to include additional field anthropology by Fernandez, linguistic study by Teodoro Llamzon, and ethnobotanical work by Douglas Yen, of the Bishop Museum in Honolulu. It was hoped that Yen and Llamzon could be in the field at the same time because some of their work would be complementary. After they had finished, presumably about September, Jack Kelso, from the U.S., could do physical anthropology, possibly combining his study of the Tasaday with another group, the Tasafeng or Sanduka, with whom, ideally, contact would have been made by that time.

Lynch's intention was to separate the various studies with a period of no activity so that the Tasaday could rest; if they indicated dissatisfaction with any researcher or his work the program would be revised or stopped at once. Lynch and Fernandez stressed the need to observe the Tasaday without Elizalde present—he was such a powerful influence that the Tasaday presumably deviated from their standard routines and behavior when he was there.

Lynch hoped that the tape recordings of the Tasaday in the cave would soon be available for professional linguistic study. He felt they were extremely valuable and suggested they be copied and one set stored for safe-keeping.

Trinidad reported that concern for the Tasaday was continually being expressed in letters and editorials from abroad and that a not infrequent view, particularly in the United States, was that the Tasaday should be left alone by everyone—not just loggers, but Elizalde, scientists, photographers, and journalists. At the same time more than thirty news organizations, photographers, film makers, and other documentarians from all over the world had asked to visit the Tasaday. Panamin's general reply was that the Tasaday were being cared for, that a research program was under way, and that data would eventually be available to all who wanted it. Inquiries about filming were followed up further, however, because Elizalde believed a film could provide funds and publicity.

This was off in the future, however. For now, Lynch was pleased that the number of journalists and cameramen allowed into the forest would be controlled. He and Fernandez hoped that patience, solid scientific work, and a well-planned program would overcome the criticism. With this in mind, they suggested that more local scientists be included. Lynch said he was considering a board of experts from several universities, including Robert Fox as a chief consultant, to advise on and assess the studies of the Tasaday.

I concluded that Fox would soon be participating. Elizalde had indicated he would not object, and Fernandez had conferred with Fox almost immediately upon returning from the forest.

Elizalde was pleased with Lynch's work and approach, but he knew that Panamin would never be Lynch's major concern, because he had so many other long-standing responsibilities. Elizalde had always wanted Panamin to have its own professional research center—but either it was short of money or personnel, or else he was at odds with the scientists who might have made it work. Fernandez was asked to head the research program, but he was committed to another project; he would, however, be able to spend another two to four weeks with the Tasaday before he had to leave. The responsibility of moving the program along seemed to rest with Lynch for the time being.

During this time, Elizalde had begun planning the next visit to the forest. The proclamation of the reserve created an immediate need to lay out the boundaries. Also he wanted to see the Tasaday again and observe their reactions to the first expedition, and check on the progress of the logging roads—nothing had been heard from loggers, or any other people who had been affected by turning almost fifty thousand acres into a reserve.

About the middle of April, Elizalde flew to Tboli with Norman Certeza, who would head the surveying operation, Ching, Felix, and Toby Pyle, a free-lance photographer. Two days later, I flew to Mindanao and found everything ready. This expedition would have fewer people than the one before, it knew what it had to do from the start, and was expected to be easier and more relaxed in every way.

IO

New Threats
to Tranquillity

WE flew over the forest April 17 under a cloudless sky and golden sunshine that glazed the jungle and made it shimmer with shades of amber and green. There had been no rain for several days and crackling dry leaves skittered across the ridge as we landed.

Sindi, whose parents had agreed to her return, was on the first flight with Igna, Mai, and Elizalde. She flashed nervous smiles while waiting for the helicopter to shuttle in Dafal, Ching, Felix, Lucy, Mila, a Tboli girl named Fao, who was to help in the kitchen, two Tboli boys, Sol and Manuel, who would act as porters and general helpers, radio operator Lopé Tutor, known as Love Tear, Certeza, Toby Pyle, and me. As we headed across the ridge, Bilangan bounded up with shouts and grins. He embraced Elizalde, took a red-colored satchel from one of the girls, and led the way.

Bilangan almost toe-danced down the slope, the bag balanced on one shoulder, while most of us stumbled and slid. We reached the campsite within an hour, and whether it was the dry weather or being more accustomed to the forest, the interior growth seemed less dense than I had remembered, as if there were great splotchy-shadowed tunnels or rooms beneath the many canopies of green. Slightly damp fallen leaves blanketed the campsite. Mai and the Tboli boys collected the orange canvas from the lower cave, where it had been stored, and we began reassembling the tents.

Balayam arrived shortly, spotted Sindi at once, and exploded with glee. He hugged and sniff-kissed Sindi, Elizalde, Mai, Ching, anyone within close range, then hopped about, patting everyone, laughing and emitting little yelps of ecstasy. Udelen arrived a few minutes later, carrying his young son on his back, and greeted us with cooing smiles and gentle hugs.

As soon as the tents were up we visited the caves, which were quiet because many Tasaday were out gathering food. We noticed at once that two platforms of bark lay on the floor of the upper cave and a piece of bamboo had been tied between thick stems of rattan along the steep rocky incline leading to the upper cave. This railing apparently was for visitors, devised after watching us climb so awkwardly during the previous visit. The platforms were to sleep on, Bilangan said, but also could be burned if the firewood supply gave out during the night. Each was about four feet square, constructed of bark that had been removed from a tree in one piece, flattened, and bound with vines to sturdy branches, which kept the platforms about three inches above the cave floor. Bilangan said the Tasaday had seen such things at the tents (the Tboli had made them), liked their looks, and decided to make copies.

Udelen brought *natek* and passed it around, and his wife, Dul, smiled and called out our names. Sindi, beaming constantly and already wearing a leaf skirt in place of her Blit clothes, stuck close to Balayam. Lefonok greeted us, but the only names he could remember were Momo Dakel Diwata Tasaday and Mafoko.

The Tasaday had caught a small hornbill, leashed it with a vine thread, and gave it to Manda, who gave it to Ching, who gave it to Toby. She took care of the big-beaked bird for the rest of the visit; it would perch on her hand as she walked about.

Balayam could not contain his excitement and continually hopped around, climbed trees, sang, or just shouted. Lobo was his exuberant self, and as I walked up a narrow trail beyond the lower cave he sprinted ahead, stopped, and motioned to me to follow. I reached a roomy shelf, but Lobo had vanished. Then I heard a shout, looked up, and saw him holding on to the end of a seventy-five-foot vine, swinging like a pendulum from a towering oak tree. He sailed past me, laughing, head back, hair flying. He swung back and forth three or four times, grinning all the while, then jumped to the ground and sprinted back down the hill.

By the time I reached the lower cave the rest of our party had come down from the upper cavern and were preparing to return to camp. Balayam was up in the sapling in front of his cave, imitating everyone, even himself. *"Akun* Balayam,*"* he shouted, and pretended to play an imaginary mouth harp.

Just before leaving, I removed my glasses to clean them and Mai said he overheard Dul remark to Udelen, "Why, I thought those were Jambangan's eyes. They aren't. He has eyes under those eyes."

The day ended with visits to the tents by Mahayag and Dula and other

Tasaday who had been away, all saying they were happy Momo Dakel had come back. Balayam performed his christening ritual and pronounced Norman "Kakay Malaman" and Toby "Kakay Toefee."

We settled into the familiar routine of visiting two or three hours with the Tasaday at the caves or stream, eating and talking at the tents, walking in the forest. Norman studied the problems of surveying. Tape recordings occupied several of us for inordinate amounts of time because only Ching was consistently able to work the machine. Elizalde and the rest of us frequently got the tape wound wrong or running too fast or backward and had to shout for Ching. A couple of times when the recorder was brought from the cave, there was nothing on the tapes.

One afternoon we joined half a dozen Tasaday adults at the stream. We walked past three or four lines of stones and wood that Dafal said he had taught the Tasaday to make to help catch fish and tadpoles, then stopped and sat on some rocks for a rest. Balayam nibbled on crabs as we talked. The moon came into the conversation, and Balayam said when they saw the moon from the cave it sometimes was round, sometimes a crescent. When it was a crescent, the Tasaday called it a "pig's tooth." Stars were "small things that shine."

Balayam said G strings were worn mainly to keep off itchy vines and insects, but also to protect genitals from *busaow,* an evil spirit or a witch (translation varied).

I doubted that *busaow* was truly his word, because the Ubu told stories of a *busaow* that was a vampirelike spirit creature that preyed on the dead, drank blood, and stirred up violence. It figures in several Ubu ghost stories and myths. I suspected *busaow* was Igna's or Dafal's word. But Balayam insisted that it had been passed to the Tasaday by their ancestors. We asked what the *busaow* was like—a question that would bring shivers and giggles from Ubu children and descriptions of a one-eyed, fanged, blood-sucking beast that flew through the night.

"We don't exactly know what the *busaow* is like," Balayam answered. "We've never seen it. Our fathers told us it was not good, but that's all we know. I guess it is a big ugly person who walks around the forest. I don't know what it might do if you saw it. Our bird [the *le mokan*] warns us if there is any danger around like the *busaow.* That bird is our good friend." His attitude showed very little worry about the *busaow.*

We asked if the Sanduka and Tasafeng wore leaves like the Tasaday. The answer was yes, but Dul and Sekul said they had departed as children and did not remember much about those people. We asked if they lived in caves. Dul said maybe, but she wasn't positive; she remembered sleeping sometimes in buttressed tree roots.

Balayam plucked a bright-red crab the size of a tablespoon from the stream and ate the claws. Then he found a bigger crab, with a brownish-black shell, and offered it around; no takers, so he nibbled at it himself.

Interior of the Tasaday rain forest

Bamboo-and-sapling
platform made to
receive
Tasaday expedition.

Elizalde moves
through trap door
leading to
tree-trunk ladder.

A Tasaday pausing in the stream that ripples along the valley floor

Lobo swinging from a branch. *Opposite,* boy in treetop gathering fruit; Balayam scaling tree under large air plant; men and boys in front of the caves; Udo using tree to enter cave

Tasaday in mouth of main cave; morning scene in the cave. *Opposite,* Lolo snug among vines, rattan, and descending roots in front of the caves

View from a treetop into the Tasaday caves as they were on the first visit from outsiders

Kuletaw

Sekul

Mahayag

Gintoy

Adug

Lefonok

Udelen

Bilangan

Dul and Ogon

Etut

Siyus

Lolo

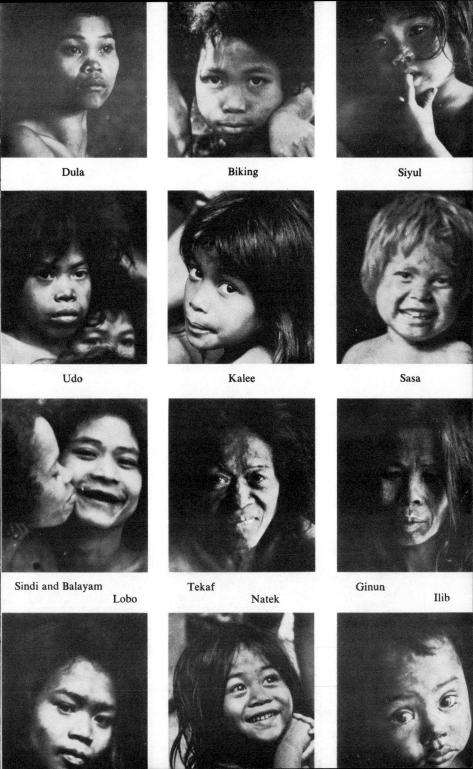

Dula

Biking

Siyul

Udo

Kalee

Sasa

Sindi and Balayam

Lobo

Tekaf

Natek

Ginun

Ilib

Opposite, Tasaday taking turns spinning a wooden drill to ignite dried moss. *Above,* Mahayag proudly displaying the blazing material to his son, Biking

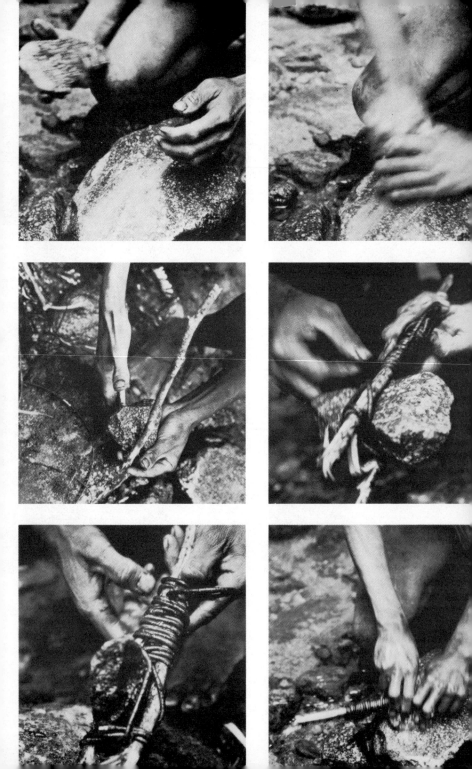

Making a stone tool, with a vine-bound branch handle, which takes the Tasaday about ten minutes

Lindbergh and Kalee listening to Mahayag making birdcalls

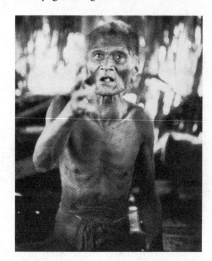

Blind Kasuk

President Ferdinand Marcos signing Tasaday reserve proclamation, with
Manuel Elizalde, Jr., and Imelda Marcos

The children clambered among boulders, playing and looking for tad-poles. Lobo pranced around with Ching's camera, going into contortions and pretending to photograph. Conversation continued for about an hour. When we asked if they minded our questions, the Tasaday said they liked to tell about things they knew.

We asked where the stream began and ended. Balayam said they did not know. They never had been there. It seemed improbable, but per-haps they did not think of its having a beginning or end—it was just there. "Did you ever try to go to the source of the stream?"

"No," Balayam said. "Should we?"

On our second day it rained—for the first time in nearly two weeks, the Tasaday said. It came down briefly but hard. The night was cool.

Sitting in the tents, we asked Igna how much of the Tasaday language she understood. Mai translated that she knew more than 75 per cent and that the Tasaday had learned many Blit words from her and from Dafal. Then she and Sindi said they did not discuss the Tasaday in detail with the Blit, or the Blit with the Tasaday.

Certeza announced that the surveying job would be much more diffi-cult than he had anticipated. He had thought surveyors might cover two hundred meters a day, but the terrain was so difficult and the forest so thick it would go much more slowly. Elizalde was worried about the Philippine law requiring a concrete monument to be placed at regular intervals; he said it would mean tearing up the forest with surveying teams.

As we talked with several Tasaday at the stream again, the subject of death came up. Balayam, continuing as the prime spokesman, said their ancestors told them that when somebody died the spirit stayed near the body, and that it might try to persuade the spirit of the living to join it. So, when a person died in the forest he was covered with leaves or branches or put among buttressed tree roots and left immediately. A death in the caves meant that the most able relative present must drag the body to a faraway place—not an overnight trip, however—where the Tasaday rarely went, cover the body with leaves, and depart at once. They must not go back to that place, Balayam said; it could imperil their spirits. We asked where the spirit of the living resided, but it was not clear whether it stayed within a person or hovered around him. We also asked if bodies of the dead were placed together when possible, as in a burial ground. Balayam said no. Did they mark the place in a special way so that it would not be stumbled upon accidentally? Again, no. Balayam appeared disturbed by the subject. We asked him if he was, and he said, "Yes. We don't like to think about Tasaday who are gone. It makes us hurt inside." We changed the subject.

One morning Elizalde put on a show in the tent. Toy false teeth, fake rubber flowers that squirted water, a wriggly rubber spider, eyeglasses with goggly paper eyes, and a beak nose were the props. A dozen Tasaday gathered around and giggled and guffawed over the jokes. Balayam tried on the false teeth and nose, and Dafal clowned with the eyeglasses. Some scholars might have flinched at the goings-on, but it was fun for the Tasaday—and for the others who participated.

At lunch that day Elizalde and Certeza got into a discussion about minority peoples in general, Certeza remarking that, of course, a major priority was to get them into schools and educated.

"Why, for God's sake?" Elizalde retorted. "Why even educate the head-hunters? Leave them alone. They don't hunt heads much. It would be as expensive as hell to set up educational programs, and unless those programs were really geared to their way of life, their needs, they would be useless. Conventional education would be absolutely wasted. And supposing you did educate them, then what would you do with them? Build cities and factories? Make them like us?

"Why not educate the thugs and beggars in cities like Manila first? Stop crime. Stop pollution from destroying. Get rid of slums. Norman, you've got a colonial mentality that says all people must be educated and Westernized and Christianized—Forget it!"

One afternoon we went upstream with the Tasaday on a food-gathering foray. In less than two hours of playful collecting they had sixteen tad-poles, four crabs, three frogs, one fish about four inches long, two feet of *ubud,* assorted edible flowers and nutty fruits.

Mahayag, Adug, and Gintoy got most of the tadpoles and crabs. Mahayag kept them on a steady pace, but the others played and nibbled as they moved along. Balayam caught two frogs by hopping spread-legged over rocks and stumps, looking much like a frog himself and chortling as he went. He proudly displayed his first frog and waved it for all to see. Then he held it around the thick part of its body with his left hand and popped it gently on the head with the flat palm of his right hand. A few soft blows killed it and he dropped it into a leaf cone held by Dul.

The Tasaday wandered singly or in twos or threes up the stream or off into the forest, taking turns minding the young children as they kept adding to their catch. Dul twisted a claw off a crab and used it to slit the belly of the fish and scrape out the insides. She cleaned a frog the same way, and gutted the slippery gray tadpoles in a flash by flicking back their heads and running her thumbnail along the underside. Dul did all this with one arm crooked around her son Maman, who straddled her hip, watching her work or sucking at her breast. When a leaf cone was filled, one of the men took it, folded the loose ends into a seal, and cached it along the stream bank.

The sun shone alternately bright and dim as puffy clouds floated overhead. During one bright period, I caught a glimpse of Adug sprawled across a large flat boulder, bathing in the sunny warmth.

The stream flowed about six inches deep in flat stretches and made pools up to two feet deep around the big rocks; the highwater mark on the banks showed that a heavy rain could make it more than four feet deep. After about an hour, we turned a bend and saw a silvery waterfall some five feet high. The water poured through a smooth trough in huge boulders and into a pool about fifteen feet wide and twenty feet long. It looked no more than knee deep, but a couple of the boys splashing in front of the fall dropped into a hole up to their necks. Balayam plunged in, followed by Adug and Mahayag. They laughed and bounced up and down in the chilly water for several minutes. Elizalde waded in and Lobo and Adug pulled him head first and laughing into the deep part. He came up shivering.

Balayam bounded into the forest and returned with an armful of leaves. The men and boys changed the old dry leaves in their G strings for fresh ones, modestly ducking under the water to do so or fitting fresh leaves over the old and then pulling out the dry ones.

As I watched Lobo and Adug paddling from the deepest water out to the shallow edge, I recalled that the previous July we had asked about bathing and the answer was that they never had seen water deep enough to cover themselves. Had they not understood the question? Had it been translated poorly? Or had they just wanted to keep this place secret? This was one of many casualties of our early data. And what about recent data? Perhaps much of that also would prove incorrect.

The helicopter flew over and activity stopped as the Tasaday scurried to try and catch a glimpse of it through the trees. Pointing, they shouted, *"Manuk dakel!"* (big bird). It was bringing Oscar Trinidad and Amy Rogel, a Filipina in her early twenties, who was running Panamin's museum in Manila. She had spent many months in the field with Mansaka and Negrito groups while an anthropology student, but had dropped her studies just before getting a degree because of financial problems. Elizalde encouraged her to finish the last phase of her work for a degree, but she kept putting it off.

Amy was pert, plump, and outspoken, and said sir occasionally with a hint of sarcasm, or so it seemed. At any rate, she stood her ground with Elizalde and told him what she thought even though it might not please him. It had become evident that those who would not stand up to him got bowled over and lost in a shuffle of underlings, called upon when needed, but not prized. Mai and Ching, for instance, not only were needed, but were valued because they had ideas and were not afraid to express them.

In the early evening, Dafal returned from having set up the tape recorder in the cave and reported that Tekaf had caught a pig in one of his traps. It apparently had been dead for three or four days and stank. Mai said he and his family used to eat spoiled meat and it did not bother them. "My father still can—but not me. I get sick to my stomach."

The next dawn came like a jigsaw puzzle being assembled from the top down: patches of blue, pink, and white appeared above the dark trees, then green and white and yellow colored the treetops, gradually pushing the browns, greens, blues, and blacks lower into the forest. The first sounds, other than birds and small insects, came from the cave— Balayam's singing, which carried into the valley. He sang and played his harp often, and it was exuberant, cheerful music, perhaps in celebration of Sindi's return. Mai said Balayam made up the songs as he went along and they were about how happy he was. The vibrations of the bamboo harp against his lips made sounds like bung-bung, bee-rung bee-rung, be-bung be-bung, beedle-beedle-bung. He would stop often and break into joyous laughter. His singing was melodic and rhythmic, with a nasal sound at times. A fast "do-dah" and "ah-do-do" often was followed by a quavering passage that slid up and down the scale. Sometimes he ended with an explosive "yeah!" or "ah-yeh!"

Amy Rogel and Trinidad visited the cave that morning and quickly were named Ahnee and Osaka. They helped Norman and Ching measure the caves for Carlos Fernandez, who had requested specific figures. The rest of us chatted with the Tasaday and the conversation was steered toward their ancestors and kinship structure, which we knew little about. Our questions seemed difficult for the Tasaday and they squatted tensely, often looking puzzled. Lefonok and Adug mostly just stared out into the forest with vacant eyes.

Balayam answered the questions at the start; Mahayag, Dul, and others joined later. They said their ancestors told them Bebang, Sidakweh, and Fuweh were the first people, and that Fangul was created by them. But it was hazy. Balayam told a story about some people Sidakweh made with noses so sharply turned up they had to be covered when it rained or the people would drown. Fuweh fixed the noses, and thus Bebang's wives, Sidakweh, and Fuweh, became known as the bad and the good. It had remarkable similarities to an Ubu story and I wondered if Dafal or Igna might have told it to the Tasaday, but Balayam said it came from Salibuku, his father. He complained that he could not remember it very well.

Balayam said Salibuku also told him that Fangul lived in this very same cave. He described Fangul as a powerful man, more like a Paul Bunyan folk hero than a god-spirit, who could carry a large tree by himself and catch many fish. His wife, Balayam said, was Tukful, from . . . "I can't remember where." Fangul was the father not only of Salibuku, but also of the fathers of Bilangan, Udelen, Lefonok, and Tekaf. This meant that Fangul was the grandfather of all the adult males present except Kuletaw and his son, Mahayag. We asked Kuletaw if he knew of Fangul, but the old man said he was cold—*"M'gum-gum"*—and had a chill and could not talk now. We asked the name of his father and he said he could not remember. So we asked Sekul, his wife, and she said she could not remember, either. We persisted and they finally said that Kuletaw's father was Lingao and his mother was Indan; Kuletaw was the only surviving child; an undisclosed number of others had died. Then Kuletaw said his father also was the son of Fangul.

This meant, then, that all the Tasaday males were blood relatives in one way or another. There was some doubt about the accuracy of it all, however. For instance, Sambal was previously cited as Fangul's brother; now he was a son.

I tried to write it all down, but got lost in the various relationships as we tried to link brothers, uncles, cousins. The kinship terms were vague; it seemed that sometimes the Tasaday used the same term for uncle and brother, or brother and father, and at other times different terms. All was jumbled. Amy, who was experienced at this, set to work trying to straighten out the relationships and construct an understandable genealogy. But it required many specific questions, and, as we became more intent, the Tasaday became more uncomfortable.

They said all the men had been born at Tasaday, which included nearby places such as Lambong. We asked about the women, who, we understood, had come from other places—how did they happen to be here?

This was tortuous going. They said Sekul had arrived from Tasafeng long ago when she was young, and had married Kuletaw; they would give no further details. Bilangan had gone with his father to Sanduka and got Etut when she was young. How young? Sekul held her hand about shoulder level.

Udelen had acquired Dul through Sekul, their account seemed to say, after Sekul learned that Dul's parents at Tasafeng had died and left her an orphan. No further explanation was forthcoming, such as how Sekul had known the parents died.

Mahayag, most recently married, except for Balayam, said he had gotten Dula from Ofut, her mother, after encountering a Tasafeng man in the forest. He said they had met by accident; when the subject of women came up, another meeting was arranged. Ofut came to this meeting and arranged to exchange Dula for some *asa* (deer meat), *biking,* and *natek.*

The inclusion of *natek* meant it had occurred since the coming of Dafal, if previous information was correct.

"Was it long ago that you got Dula?"

"Not so long."

"Had you met Dafal yet?"

"Yes, we knew Kakay Dafal."

Manda, who had been quiet for several minutes, suddenly asked, "Did you give Dula's mother some metal also, a knife?"

Mahayag looked up, seeming a bit surprised, and said, "Yes, yes, I did."

"And did the Tasafeng already know how to make *natek?*"

"No, they had not seen it."

"Did you teach them?"

"No."

Dula, in a high, thin voice, said she had a father, mother, sister, and brother living in a cave at Tasafeng when she left. She added that there were more people at Tasafeng than at Tasaday, as far as she could re-member, but that she had not been back and had forgotten a great deal. She thought the Tasafeng were very much like the Tasaday, but that they did not have some things that were here, such as brass earrings. They wore only rattan in their ears as the Tasaday had done before. She added, with giggles, that she had learned to sing by listening to Balayam, but that some Tasafeng sang like that also.

We asked about Lefonok's wife and Balayam said the story was simi-lar to Mahayag's. Lefonok himself did not volunteer any information about his wife—who had died perhaps three years earlier—and had such a faraway look in his eyes that he was not questioned.

Tekaf's wife, Ginun, had been brought from Tasafeng because she was a deaf-mute like Tekaf, Balayam said. He said Sambal, his uncle and Bilangan's father, had heard of Ginun and arranged the marriage. Both of them, who now appeared to be in their fifties or sixties, were gentle, docile people who usually stayed in the background and watched or slept. Tekaf frequently smiled and nodded; sometimes he would embrace us when we looked at him and smiled. Ginun rarely smiled or showed any emotion. Weeks later we learned she had cataracts on both eyes and was nearly blind. Tekaf and Ginun had no children. Older Tasaday took an interest in whatever they did, helping them and advising them.

By now, the Tasaday showed they had had enough questioning about this. They were restless, glum-faced, and silent for long periods, so the subject was changed. Some children had been named only recently and two—Biking and Natek—had food names. We asked if other names had meanings—Balayam, for instance. He said no, it was just Balayam. Mahayag? Yes, that meant a kind of mountain. But Lolo, Tekaf, and Adug had no particular meaning, Balayam said. Maman had to do with "the never-ending search for food."

There was little to conclude from this, except that three younger chil-dren had names connected with food. Perhaps Dafal had had something to do with it, since all had been born after he met the Tasaday.

Elizalde stood up and said the questions had gone on long enough. The Tasaday were pleased, and everyone began stirring and stretching and wandering about. I found myself next to Sekul and called to Elizalde that I would like to ask one more question, to try to establish a better relative sense of the adult ages. Mai came over and we asked Sekul how old she had been when Mahayag was born—was she about the same age as Dul, Etut, and Dula were now, or younger or older?

Sekul looked at me after Mai translated, then broke into a sly laugh. "Why do you ask about that?" she said. "Why do you want to know how old we are when we have children?" Then she laughed and waggled her head at me. It was clear she was not going to say any more on that subject.

The Tasaday regained a measure of gaiety after the questioning stopped and began laughing and talking among themselves. Elizalde asked what was above the cave and the Tasaday asked if he would like to see. Sure, why not? he said.

Lobo and Lolo and Mahayag started straight up the bamboo and rattan that rose in front of the cave and joined with the tangle of roots and vines growing down from above. Bilangan went out the cave's mouth and turned sharply right. We followed him and, about fifty feet away, passed what smelled like a toilet area. He then turned right again and up the mountain. It was overgrown with trees and plants and grass, and had enough niches so that we could find foot and hand support. We made a half circle from the cave and fifteen minutes later stood directly above it.

A lean-to of branches and palm leaves at the edge of an open space held spears, arrows, monkey skulls, and several unidentifiable items. This may have been where they had brought things when Dafal asked them to remove everything new from the caves.

Trees about two hundred feet high encircled the clearing, which was somewhat smaller than a tennis court. Lobo skipped across it and grabbed a vine as big around as a man's wrist. A bar of bamboo was tied horizontally to the end of the vine. Lobo jumped up, put his feet on the T bar and sailed across the clearing, more than fifty feet, and up to the brow of the caves. The vine was attached at least one hundred feet up, out of sight in leaves and branches. Mahayag swung, then Biking, and Udo, then Lobo and Udo at once. The rest of us took turns. It was a thrilling ride, sailing out to where you could see into the valley in front of the caves.

Elizalde walked on up the mountain with Mahayag, passing a four-foot-deep hole that had once contained *biking,* and followed the thin creek that trickled over the mouth of the lower cave. The jungle was thick, but the footing was solid on the narrow rocky paths; the going was easy as the incline leveled near the summit. When they came back, Lobo and Mahayag walked over to the brow of the cave and lowered themselves hand over hand down vines; this was apparently what was meant when they said earlier that their special place was down.

Elizalde decided we should try following them, but when he started out on the protruding brow, the loose dry sod wavered under our weight. We ventured one at a time to the edge, clung to a tree, and peered down through a maze of vines and roots into the cave. The Tasaday were visible on the cave floor, and Lolo lay in a curve of rattan and vines about thirty feet above them, relaxing and swaying as if in a hammock. It was questionable whether the vines would hold Elizalde, or whether he could hold on to them. The whole network might tear under the weight of an inexperienced, heavier-than-usual body. We took the roundabout route back to the cave.

The morning had been mentally and physically tiring, so we stayed at the camp in the afternoon. Igna said the Tasaday were friendly and that nothing she had seen or heard so far was very surprising. Did this mean they were similar to the Blit and Sduff? She said yes, adding, however, that she did not understand some of the questions she relayed—she simply passed along the words as best she could.

Igna said Sindi had been worried her first night at the cave and lay for hours unable to sleep. "She said she was waiting for something to happen, but nothing happened," Igna reported. "Everybody just slept. After that Sindi didn't worry. She likes them."

We asked what was worrying Sindi, and Igna giggled. Did it have to do with sex? Igna giggled harder and jerked her eyebrows yes. Intercourse was "playing together," she said, and it was practiced only by married couples as far as she knew. Their sex life was quite ordinary, she said, adding, "I think they're good people."

Late in the afternoon, the sky darkened and rain began to fall, softly at first, then harder. By four-thirty it was torrential and half an hour later the storm moved in in earnest; thunder rumbled, lightning flashed stunningly close, brilliantly illuminating the forest again and again. The booms of thunder were deafening and the crack of the lightning was like a whip snapping right beside our ears. Between the booms and cracks we could hear the stream raging like a river.

The storm crashed around us for nearly an hour as we sat silently—almost cowering—inside the tents. We had tried to talk, but gave it up. When it moved on we still could see the lightning in the distance, zigzagging through the night sky every few seconds until the storm disappeared southward, deeper into the forest.

Mai later shook his head. "That is the most fearsome thing about the forest . . . that lightning . . . the wind. A storm like that knocks down trees. There is great danger. Falling trees are a terrible fear."

Before the storm, Amy had mentioned some fresh criticisms of Panamin and the Tasaday project that were being circulated by various scientists. Now we picked up the discussion where we had left off, with Elizalde doing most of the talking.

"What the hell right have they to criticize us? What have those guys ever done but go into the field once in their lives to write a doctorate paper and then sit in Manila and pontificate? Why don't they get out, live with the people? Do they really want to? They've got a million reasons why they can't, but the fact is most of them don't really like the people or the outside, don't want to work that hard. They just study them and proclaim their great affection—but if they really are so hot for them, why do they spend so much time in offices talking to each other?"

He cited Fox and Lynch and a few more scientists as exceptions, and said Fernandez seemed very good. But others, some with whom he had tangled, made him bitter. "Don't worry, I know what they all want to do here. Each one has to prove it all to himself. He has got to be a skeptic and challenge us and every other guy that came before him."

Amy interrupted to say that it did indeed seem possible to her, now that she had seen the Tasaday and this place, that the caves were their permanent homes, and that many of the other things claimed about the people were true.

Manda looked at her and said nothing, but later muttered privately, "Good Christ, what did she think? That we had made all this up? And remember, that's Amy, she works for us. What're you gonna do? We can't just bring every nonbeliever in here and let him poke around until he is personally satisfied. I tell you, they better be careful or I'll just shut this thing down—tell the Tasaday to go away and that'll be it—I can do that, you know. . . ."

The group conversation took various turns as suggestions were made for organizing the proper kind of scientific study. Elizalde recognized its importance but added, "One scientist with rude endless questions and nosing around, trying to fit it all into his own pet theories, can do more to upset these people than dozens of the rest of us who just enjoy being with them and like them. I know, I've seen it before."

We ate dinner—rice and chicken, our fare about 70 per cent of the time, except breakfast—with a chill wind blowing into the tents. It warmed during the night, however, and dawn brought an unusually rosy sky. I sat with a blanket around my shoulders and watched the day begin. Lucy and Mila got up first, started a fire, and boiled water for coffee. I sipped a steaming glassful as they cooked eggs and handed out cups of coffee when Mai and the Tboli boys arose, then Toby, then Certeza. The girls were the busiest members of the expedition, cooking, cleaning, laundering, keeping the kitchen and the main tent in order, fetching Elizalde's cigarettes, soda, mosquito repellent. They never complained; in fact, they looked as if they never even had a complaining thought. Their work was somewhat harder this trip because Onto had not come. The girl replacing her, Fao, was a strikingly pretty Tboli teen-ager who had arrived wearing several ankle bracelets and a classic embroidered Tboli blouse and skirt with a wide brass belt adangle with bells. She spent long periods combing and arranging her long hair, fixing her lipstick and her clothes. And, of course, she had to be careful of mussing herself as she helped with chores. While Lucy and Mila worked in the kitchen this morning she labored over her coiffure. Many Tboli girls would have done the same, as would many Ubu. It was important for young women to look as attractive as possible, thereby adding to their family's chances for a rich dowry when they married. The Blit were not so concerned with appearance, much more like the Tasaday, who seemed indifferent to their looks. The Tasaday had no mirrors, of course, and there was no apparent competition for the affection of a man or woman—all the women were taken and, under their rules, there was nobody to compete for.

Of course, we did not know what subtle competition might go on among the Tasaday. We knew so little of how they behaved among themselves. They had told us they said nothing bad about anybody, but how could twenty-four people live together without tension and conflicts? The children showed the egotism one might expect—arguing over a stick, crying for food, slapping at one another. What happened to rechannel that? Lobo was particularly interesting because he was between childhood and young adulthood; if we observed him over a sufficient period we might learn. By continually putting himself in the limelight, Lobo seemed to be showing us competitiveness. Other children had been too shy at first to do much of anything, but recently when Lobo climbed a tree his older brother, Lolo, climbed a tree beside him and went higher than Lobo; there was no fruit up there, so it may have been competitive sport. Another time Udo swung on a vine in front of the cave, attracting attention until Lobo bounded over, grabbed the vine, and took over. Was this due to our presence?

And what about Balayam? Like Lobo, he was outgoing and enjoyed attention. His clowning and mimicry seemed to delight the Tasaday as much as us, but did he perform when we were not there? He occasionally took it upon himself to stir up laughter, working so hard sometimes that his own laugh sounded hollow and forced. He and Mahayag came forward as cheerleaders of sorts if they sensed the mood growing somber. This may have been intended to assure Elizalde that everybody was happy and enjoyed having visitors—but did they all, really?

Elizalde referred to Balayam as the "politician," and we all were aware of his abilities as a spokesman and comedian. Yet, clever as he was in many ways, he was slow in others. One day he kept trying to cut a piece of firewood with a long knife, but fumbled badly. Mai called out to him and Balayam looked down at the knife, laughed, and turned it over—he had been trying to cut with the thick, dull edge. Was he the classic nonhandyman, a poet not a laborer? Did this mean that he always left work to others and therefore had not learned to use the knife properly?

And what about Bilangan? He had been in the forefront during the first meetings, but was reserved and usually fell into the background when Balayam, and now Mahayag, were present. Of course, his family's needs were heavier than the rest and he often worked when others relaxed. Did he mind that? Did he mind that Balayam, who was younger than he, was always in the center of things? It was hard to tell, but I believe Bilangan did not mind.

And what about Udelen, Lefonok, Tekaf, and Kuletaw, the oldest and most experienced? What did Kuletaw think about developments? And the women? How much did we really know about the workings of their society? At times it seemed we were learning a lot; at others, nothing. Sometimes new information seemed to contradict what we thought we had learned before. I had to keep reminding myself that we had known the Tasaday only a short while and should be patient. Still, I could not help wondering about things. For instance, what part did fear play in their lives? The only time I had seen stark fear in any of them—inside the forest, that is—was while Lobo and Lolo were on the stream bank picking bright-red, tart-tasting wild strawberries. Suddenly Lobo froze, shouted, and pointed into a small tree whose branches were just above his head. Lolo hurried over and both boys peered into the leaves. A couple of us joined them and saw a two-foot-long shiny green snake curled around a branch.

The excitement attracted Mahayag from somewhere and he arrived as the boys, open-mouthed and wide-eyed, stood in a half crouch, pointing at the snake. Mahayag parted the leaves to see better and the boys squealed and shouted for him to stop. But he got a stick and poked at the snake. It uncoiled from the branch, raised its head, flicked its tongue, and slithered away. Mahayag laughed and the boys chattered excitedly, turning back to stare at the tree even as they hurried away. They told Igna it was a very, very dangerous snake, could make you terribly sick—or worse.

And what was Elizalde's full significance for the Tasaday? A god? A spirit? That he was extremely important was obvious, but on a day-to-day basis we visitors sometimes forgot this. It was brought back into focus the fourth afternoon of our visit, when we went to the stream so Amy could take notes on the making of stone tools. Elizalde was with us at the start, but then walked upstream with Mai and Felix.

Lefonok, Balayam, Mahayag, and Lolo worked hastily on the tools, and in less than an hour fashioned eight tools of various sizes and shapes. They became aware of Elizalde's absence less than halfway through and thereafter looked around anxiously for him as they worked. Amy's questions were answered perfunctorily or glumly, and they kept asking Igna where Momo Dakel was.

Mahayag went into the jungle to get more thin vines to complete lacing the handle on his second tool, and in his absence the other three Tasaday each finished their second tools, nodded to us, and walked away. Mahayag returned, glanced around, hurriedly completed his work, and left. Lobo and Lolo, who had been playing nearby, wandered over, asked Igna where Momo Dakel was, looked disappointed, and left. The rest of us did not interest them.

Ching, Norman, and I decided to make our own stone tools. The biggest problem was finding stones that did not crumble or chip away raggedly at the edges when we tried to sharpen them; many were conglomerates of small pebbles and soft gray rock with a consistency not unlike cement. We did find some serviceable stones, however, and, using leftover branches and vines for the handles, produced three or four reasonable imitations of the Tasaday's tools in about forty-five minutes.

We returned to the camp afterward. Elizalde had not yet come back from his walk, and none of the Tasaday were present. Pondering the Tasaday's behavior at the stream, I realized that they had been subdued and lackluster the whole day, and the day before, too. Elizalde's absence at the stream accentuated it. He, too, had seemed moody and irritable lately, and so was I. Was I imagining things, or did Toby, Ching, and others also seem uncomfortable?

Perhaps it was tent fever—people confined to a small area getting on one another's nerves. One factor surely was that the sunshiny lightness of the first day had been drenched by rain the past three days. The bright greens and ambers had been dulled by hard downpours that left a dripping grayness. At the same time, perhaps influenced by the weather, irritants that might have been eased aside blossomed into troublesome vexations.

Our mood may have been communicated to the Tasaday, who then came down with their own case of gloom.

Reconstructing the visit, I realized that there had been several small incidents that may have led to an edginess for which I was to blame as much as anyone. It began the first or second morning at the cave when I looked around and realized that Ching, Toby, Certeza, and I were all taking pictures at once. Nobody was behaving badly, but occasionally we bumped each other as we moved around, clicking away. Although the Tasaday were occupied with Elizalde and Mai and paid us no noticeable attention, I felt extremely uncomfortable. I had the sense of doing exactly what I would have criticized others for doing. Ching and Toby were merely taking a picture now and then and staying quietly in the background, but I was poking around with four cameras slung on me. I had acknowledged years ago that pointing cameras at people could be rude, especially if they did not want it or were unaware, but I had justified that as an occupational hazard when taking news photographs; these, however, were not news photographs.

My self-consciousness grew into annoyance; but, instead of proposing a friendly arrangement in which we would take turns photographing, I self-righteously stopped taking pictures completely and sulked. When we reached the tents, I told Elizalde I would like to go to the cave in the morning to sit quietly and take pictures in the early light—*alone*. "Sure," he said. "Any time."

Three days passed and each time I mentioned the morning picture taking, Elizalde put it off. He, Mai, Igna, and Ching visited the caves a few times during this period, and each time but one the rest of us were left behind at the tents. At first it made me only restless, but then I began to feel it was deliberate—Elizalde was putting us in our places! I tried to talk to him about it, but our conversation was stilted and uncomfortable. I became increasingly irritated, and, apparently, so did he.

Around this time Toby—who had won Elizalde's respect when she came from Saigon to join the first news coverage of the Tasaday in 1971— asked loudly if we might "go to the caves without God?" It was a joke directed at Elizalde, of course, and said deliberately so he could hear. But he held a cool silence and we did not visit the caves. Shortly after that, Toby remarked on the possibility of finding brass earrings in the midden in front of the cave. I didn't think much about these remarks at the time, but later Elizalde brought them up to me, surprisingly upset, mostly about the earrings. "Brass in the midden?" he said. "What does she think this is, a hoax? Why, she's just as skeptical as all those others!" I said she had merely been making conversation and was not suggesting the Tasaday had metal before meeting Dafal.

Despite the touchiness that was developing there were enjoyable times, and I did not notice the Tasaday were affected until the day we went to the stream to make tools and the men were so obviously disappointed when Elizalde went for a walk.

When Elizalde returned, he said his hike upstream had been spectacularly beautiful. He had passed several small waterfalls and two forks in the stream. Pig tracks and trails were abundant; in fact, a wild pig blundered out of the jungle, coming for a drink, and almost ran into Manda and Mai. They shouted, the pig grunted and scooted back into the underbrush.

In the late afternoon at the tents, Mai, Igna, and Elizalde huddled together, translating a tape made the night before. The rest of us did not pay much attention. Half an hour later, after a whispered exchange from the huddle, Elizalde turned off the recorder.

"Where's that monkey Dafal caught?" he asked loudly. "Let's take it up to the Tasaday for them to roast." It was fetched and, after another hushed exchange of words, he, Mai, Igna, and Ching left for the caves.

Long after dark they sent down word for the rest of us to go ahead with dinner. Two hours later the radio operator came to me and said I was wanted in Mai's tent, which was below the main one. Mai, Manda, and Ching had come down from the caves in darkness and were talking there.

"Well," Manda said. "What did you think?"

"About what?"

"The tape. Did you hear that? We had to cut it off before it got embarrassing."

I said I had not been listening closely, but had been aware that something must have happened while they were transcribing, because they all suddenly left.

"Yeah. Well, the Tasaday are not too happy with some of us. For one thing it seems Certeza has asked them to make him a special tool, with a haft wrapped with rattan like their heirloom pieces. That got them a little upset, that and some other things. It was coming through on the tapes."

"How serious is all this?" I asked.

"But that's only part of it," Elizalde said. "Just before we cut off the tape, Mahayag told Balayam, 'You must stay in our cave tonight because we must talk . . .' and then he started a speech that sounded very serious. That's when we went up, and as soon as we arrived Mahayag stood up and said to me: 'We want to talk straight to you.' I'm telling you, he looked grim." Manda paused.

"And what was that all about?"

"Several things. For one thing, the last trip—the chopper that came to get us. Mahayag had climbed a tree to watch us leave and saw that big green air force chopper. He told us how he had gone up the tree and saw that strange big bird with the strange thing inside—the guy in the doorway in the flight suit and black eye goggles, remember? Anyway, Mahayag looked at me and said, 'What is that thing? We don't know that thing. We don't like that! If that one comes again we will run. . . .'

"Then they got to talking about this visit and they told about Norman's request for the stone tool and I asked if that bothered them. They paused a bit. Then Balayam said, 'We have little love for Kakay Malaman.' But get that—Balayam didn't say they didn't like him—just that they had little love for him. Then they went on to some other people they had little love for, people with loud voices and sharp looks. I'm not sure who they all are, but apparently a couple of people at the clearing last year and somebody on the last expedition.

"They kept repeating that they didn't like loud voices and hard looks and didn't want them here. And—oh, man—that questioning yesterday morning at the cave, about their ancestors and stuff, that *really* got them upset. Poor Amy took the rap for that one because she had to ask most of the questions. One of the men said, 'Kakay Ahnee has a hard look and asks many questions.' But then another said, 'Yes, but she is new and doesn't know us well, so she must ask many questions. She will learn.' "

"What about me, then?" I said. "They must have been upset with me, too. I was asking questions."

"I don't think so," Elizalde said. "Amy got stuck with all the tough questions and you had the advantage of having been around them a lot before. Remember, they haven't had long to get used to Norman and Amy. They like Ching fine, and Toby and Felix, of course. None of them were asking questions. Mai and Igna were translators, but old friends."

Manda said he told the Tasaday he was glad they were talking straight to him and that they always must tell him as soon as they were bothered or upset. He assured them that the big strange bird with the strange man would not be coming back, adding that it had not been dangerous and had friends inside it. He said Kakay Malaman was new and didn't understand all the ways of the Tasaday yet, but Momo Dakel would advise him not to ask for any more things. He said Kakay Ahnee was simply eager to learn about the Tasaday's beautiful ways, that's why she asked so many questions. Then he told them to go about their daily routines—"Do what you would do if I were not here."

It apparently helped the Tasaday to share their distress and to receive a sympathetic response. They chatted together a while longer and the Tasaday eventually began singing and laughing. Manda, Mai, and Ching left after another hour and the sounds of their singing could be heard at the tents late into the night. It was interrupted occasionally with long loud speeches by Balayam and Mahayag. Elizalde made sure that the tape recorder picked up a good sample of what went on.

We had been in the forest only five days, and had originally planned to stay seven or eight. Now Elizalde was considering leaving the next morning—or that at least some of us should leave. "The Tasaday are not comfortable," he said. I pointed out that none of the rest of us had even seen the caves or gone near them for two days. "Yes, but it's the mood, our presence . . . just being here," Manda said.

It was decided, however, that we all would depart the day after next, and we would leave the Tasaday alone as much as possible in the meantime.

Elizalde mused again about the scientific program. "You can see from this stuff today that it simply has got to be the right kind of scientist. Carlos is good, but he's already talking about his other projects and going abroad. Lynch is busy with too many other things and can't come. What're we supposed to do? I don't know. . . ."

He then told us his theory that an interconnecting system of cave-dwelling peoples had once existed in Mindanao. He believed the Blit,

Tboli, Ubu, and others—including the Higa-onon in the North—probably had ancestors in caves.

Then he disclosed, for the first time to my knowledge, that he knew of other groups still living in remote places who never had met civilization. These were in addition to the Sanduka and Tasafeng. He said he had been accumulating bits of information and evidence for a long time and was convinced of the existence of these other groups, some in this same forest, some elsewhere.

"I bet they live just like the Tasaday," he said. "There may be half a dozen different groups we know of, and I'm certain we could reach three or four of them within a few days if we set out to. But why? What for? They aren't hurting anyone. The only valid reason we should make contact is if they needed protection, or if we were convinced it would help them or the whole Panamin effort in some way."

He wondered what to do about them, and worried that somebody else would reach them first. Then he pondered what to do about the Tasaday. He discussed various ideas with Mai, Ching, and me for nearly two hours. Out of this came a consensus that he must develop a solid plan, or at least the framework of one, into which existing programs and projects, current and future, could fit. No contact with other new groups or tribes should be sought until the Tasaday program was stabilized. It was reasonable for science to have a part in the plan, and to establish long-range studies of the Tboli, Ubu, Mansaka, and Blit, not just the Tasaday. A five- or ten-year program for Panamin was necessary, a broad outline of which would touch on administration, development, research, fund raising, museums, pulling them into a unified effort for whatever goals were decided.

It was agreed that Elizalde's drive, determination, and imagination had made the foundation and accounted for its accomplishments. But unless Panamin became able to function well without his constant nursing—and, furthermore, could avoid total involvement in his enthusiasms of the moment at the expense of its ongoing work—it would never realize its potential. Elizalde was Panamin's greatest strength, but also its potential downfall.

We all thought the same thing about the Tasaday's distress over the strange helicopter and the questions about ancestors: we were compelling them to think in new ways; we asked too many questions, sought too many reasons. Whereas perhaps Dafal had given them their first bite of the Apple of Knowledge, we were dumping the whole applecart on them!

The next morning, however, the Tasaday showed no obvious signs of distress. Balayam arrived at the tents early, eager to show off a new imitation. He had tied a piece of rope to a stick and talked into it: "Go-hed," "Ober." It was Felix's walkie-talkie radio, which Balayam called "Kakay

Fix's kee-totie." Lobo came, too, and the two of them perched by the fireplace to watch Lucy and Mila prepare breakfast.

After breakfast, Sol, one of the Tboli boys, led Norman, Toby, and me on a hike upstream. It was a beautiful morning and we walked steadily, past a dozen small waterfalls, some as high as ten feet, and a series of stepladder falls. We had to help each other up the slippery rocks of the highest falls.

We moved gradually up a slight incline, passing three forks in the stream. When huge boulders blocked the way or pools were too deep to ford, we had to detour into the forest. The sunlight hit the stream in patches, making rocks look like cubist paintings—multidimensional in burnished browns, rust, orange, plum-red, mossy green-black.

The surrounding jungle vegetation was spectacularly lush: purple growths like giant eggplants, orange and pink and violet flowers, white blossoming ground plants, branches festooned with three-foot-long clusters of maroon berries, fruits like apples and green tomatoes, red, rust, and chartreuse berries. Huge rotting tree trunks lay across the stream. Fossil-hard black mushrooms as large as dinner plates clung to trees along the banks. Snails inched across stumps, brown snakes slept on flat rocks, an orange worm squirmed in the sand. Big-winged butterflies flapped in and out of the shadows, yellow and black, aqua and black, ocher, violet.

We passed a cave cut into a high embankment and saw the remains of fire inside; it was large enough to hold four or five people and had a hole in the back that let in light. There were two smaller caves farther on, but neither showed any sign of use.

There were many pools in the stream, some waist-deep or more. Large boulders showed the effects of swift-flowing water: smooth cup-shaped depressions, straight channels, winding alleys.

A pig's skull lay next to a sharpened piece of bamboo alongside a tree —vestiges of a trap. There were several other pointed bamboo stakes throughout the area. Signs of cutting along the banks confirmed recent visits.

But, after two hours of hiking, there were no more such signs. The brush grew so thick that it was a wall on both sides of and across the stream, which had narrowed to three feet; it was now no more than two or three inches deep. The jungle was almost impassably dense. Sol slashed at the growth over the stream and we passed through, only to encounter more brush barriers. There was nothing to indicate anyone had ever been here—no traps or scraps of bamboo, no cut or broken brush.

We stopped to eat a packed lunch about noon and considered whether or not to go on. We had hoped to reach the source of the stream, but it had maintained constant size for the last half hour, and ahead the mountain kept rising steadily. The summit, or what we thought was the summit, looked as far away as when we had started, so we turned back.

We reached the camp in early afternoon, carrying fruits and plant specimens for Amy to take back to the museum for study and display. We had no educated ideas of what plants to gather, so the collection consisted of samples of anything that had appeared exotic.

The mood of the camp was much more relaxed than it had been the past couple of days. In the evening we sat talking and just looking out into the forest. There were what seemed like thousands of fireflies and stars, which were visible even through the canopies of foliage. For a moment I had the sensation of being suspended in the sky; the fireflies blinking in the blackness below us looked exactly like the stars twinkling overhead.

This was our last night and we visited the caves. Light from fires and a bright but unseen moon made it possible to see inside. Balayam put on a show, climaxing it with an imitation of Dafal depositing the black satchel with the tape recorder in it. Elizalde said that they had been told about the recorder but it was doubtful that they understood it well. Balayam's Dafal placed the satchel carefully on a rocky ledge, said effusive good-bys, and departed from the cave. But, outside, he remembered something (he had forgotten to switch on the machine?) and rushed back, greeting everyone en route to the bag. Balayam fiddled with it (turning it on?) and then, with waves and shouts, departed again, walking in Dafal's flap-footed hunched-over style.

The skit had Dafal screaming with laughter and the Tasaday were not far behind him, doubling over and howling. Adug had a convulsive laughing fit that he couldn't stop. Each time the general laughter died down, his roosterlike cackle went on and ignited new rounds of laughter. A full half hour was spent this way; one ten-minute stretch was filled with continuous hoots, guffaws, and chuckles.

Balayam then played his harp and improvised songs using all the visitors' names. Unexpectedly, a head and arms rose beside us as we sat at the lip of the cave. It was Udelen coming in. He crooned Toby's name and draped an arm around her shoulders as we listened to Balayam. Then Adug sat down and gave everyone a hug. They moved on after a few minutes, and other Tasaday stopped by with friendly pats or hugs.

After the singing, Mai shined his flashlight on the ceiling and several Tasaday tried to trap the beam in their hands. Adug and Gintoy seemed certain that they had captured a handful of light when Mai suddenly switched the beam off. They carried their light in tightly cupped hands to the far side of the cave, then opened their hands. No light. All the other Tasaday roared with laughter, and the boys went back for another try. Some Tasaday were so spirited that, despite the dark, they climbed the vines in front of the cave.

As we were walking past the lower cave on our way back to the tents, we noticed a few infants and the oldest Tasaday men and women huddled around a small fire in the wide mouth. It was the first time we had seen this cave used in any way. Perhaps the speeches and singing the past two nights had kept the children and oldsters awake, so they moved below; or, as we so often had to conclude, there was some reason we could not begin to guess.

We departed in the morning, after a brief good-by visit to the caves. There were tears in the eyes of several Tasaday, and many accompanied Elizalde to the landing place. It was mostly out of affection, I think, but they may have wanted to see if the strange big bird would return. Sindi came along, looking happy to be staying this time. Balayam perched on a stump and imitated Bart piloting as the familiar helicopter came in for a landing.

Manda told the Tasaday he would return before long, and, despite a few sad looks, they seemed cheerful. They watched, some imitating our waves, as the helicopter took us away.

II

The Tasaday on Tape:
The Pain of Change

LATER, at Tboli, Manda, and Mai completed transcribing the eight hours of tape recordings made on the second visit. Particularly interesting were the Tasaday's remarks—pointed and seemingly angry on one or two occasions—about the things that had bothered them: questions and sharp looks, their doubts about the intentions of some visitors. They also revealed a steady determination to stay near the caves to please Manda and to receive gifts, although Mahayag insisted, quoting Manda, that it was not necessary to stay home all the time and that they should gather food as usual.

It was impossible to know if the Tasaday said things differently after the attempt was made to explain the tape recorder to them, even though we were never certain how much of the explanation they understood. Did they perform—as dutiful disciples of Momo Dakal, for instance? Or did they express their feelings as freely as they had before?

The reference to Kuletaw raising Balayam and having fed him monkey brains, and Bilangan's providing wild pig posed the question of whether they ate meat before knowing Dafal. Especially interesting among the many personality vignettes are Balayam's rebuke to Mahayag for being absent from the cave, his song of joy over Sindi's return, and his claim that he could live now on only flowers and water; Lobo's bragging about having got a knife while some adults had not. There is conjecture about Elizalde's abilities in the forest, which, despite references to him as a god-spirit, suggest that the Tasaday did not consider him to be supernatural.

These and other details of the tapes nourished a growing sense of the Tasaday as flesh-and-blood fellow humans, in place of the exotic and mysterious forest creatures they had been for some of us. Other aspects of the visit also gave a less romantic, more realistic tone to the experience. The Tasaday's annoyance, upsetting at times, had apparently been overcome; they talked straight about their worries and got positive responses. The vexations among the visitors had faded the last day or so. I left the forest with the impression that we had learned a considerable amount about the Tasaday—and something about how we should deal with them as well.

The following was recorded between April 18 and April 22, 1972, in the upper cave.

Session 6   Morning of April 18

[Recording opens with vigorous singing and playing of the jew's-harp by Balayam.]

DUL [to a child]: Don't hold the knife because it is very sharp. Don't hold that! You don't know how to use it yet.

BALAYAM: Yesterday I was making a monkeytrap, otherwise I would have been the first to meet MDDT. I had to run so fast because I knew the bird was bringing MDDT. I have to make a monkeytrap now because I have a wife. I have to make *balatik,* I have to make mousetraps so my wife—the sister of Kakay Mafoko—can live. [To Sindi]: I have to get you monkey, pig, mouse . . . this is what I can get for you.

SINDI: Anything you can get for me will be all right.

BALAYAM: I have to look for these things for the sister of Mafoko. This Sindi is the daughter of MDDT. I am happy now, I must play my harp. [Plays exuberantly for several minutes.]

BALAYAM: Don't cry, children, because I am making nice sounds.

UDELEN: When that harp is played by Balayam in the afternoon and MDDT is not here, I feel tears in my eyes.

BALAYAM: My inside feeling is very happy because the sister of Kakay Mafoko is back. All you women should be happy. [Singing]: MDDT is back again with us . . .

I don't know why my voice is not improving. My whole inside is very happy MDDT has returned to us. This Sindi is a continuation of MDDT with us. Kakay Mafoko and MDDT always laugh at my jokes. Bilangan went to see his monkeytrap and Tekaf also went to check his monkeytrap. We will wait here to see if they got anything. [Sindi tries to give Balayam some *ubud.*] That's all right, Sindi. I can live by just drinking water and eating flowers. [Baby apparently tries to climb on Balayam.] Don't climb here, I am singing.

DUL: Do not let your wife do the cooking of the *ubud.* You do it for her, Balayam. I want some betel.

BALAYAM [to Lefonok and Udelen]: We have to make more traps

because we have with us a new woman, the sister of Kakay Mafoko. We will look for monkeys, tadpoles, crabs, because we have someone new with us. All the inside of us is known by MDDT, and maybe he does not ask any more questions because he knows everything. MDDT really loves us—imagine cleaning that stream of ours below. And now our MDDT is here with us again in Tasaday. The love of MDDT is not small love like this [probably meaning his little finger, as we had observed him do previously], but his biggest love like this [probably his thumb] because he has returned. It is not good that Kuletaw and Sekul are not here. They should be here by now. We have not been able to ask them where they made their monkeytrap. We have more knives—that is why we are able to make more monkeytraps and pigtraps. Many of our monkeytraps, pigtraps and mousetraps strike but always miss—only seldom do they catch anything. Remember when Dafal told us for the first time about the big man with a big love—MDDT. He is here now because the thin man [Dafal] told us about him. The man with big love—MDDT. We have a very good feeling within us because we now have many knives given by MDDT.

UDELEN and LEFONOK: *Oh-ho.*

BALAYAM: We are very happy because MDDT gave us all these knives.

DUL: *Oh-ho.*

BALAYAM: MDDT is with us and also Kakay Mafoko and Kakay Jambangan. We pity MDDT because of his difficulties in visiting us. We now have the same blood [Sindi] as Kakay Mafoko and all the friends of MDDT. Now, Sindi, you are here again with the big bird of MDDT and with Kakay Mafoko. Sindi, I would not have been able to marry you if it were not for the love of MDDT. But, whatever your brother tells you, you must obey. I have not thought of having a wife before. Sindi, you have to obey MDDT. We have very good sunshine today [meaning they feel very good today]. Sindi, you have to get used to our food and we will get you *natek, biking, ubud* . . .

DUL: You have to be strong, Balayam, in looking for meat.

BALAYAM [to Sindi]: If you do not like our way of life, making traps and things we do, tell us. [She answers that she likes it.]

[To Lefonok]: MDDT's feeling for us is more than love, as shown by his wonderful gift, Sindi. We have to combine our feeling together for MDDT. Because of the great love of MDDT we now have Sindi. I am now the son of MDDT and brother of Kakay Mafoko.

DUL: Maybe I will be getting a knife from MDDT.

[Balayam plays the harp.]

BALAYAM: Wake up Etut, because I found a big *biking* and also a *natek* tree. Maybe Tekaf will get a monkey. I hope he gets a monkey so MDDT can have some. The monkeytrap of Bilangan cannot catch monkeys, because it is very new. We have to make good *natek* because MDDT will like to eat it.

UDELEN: Tomorrow I will make my monkeytraps.

LEFONOK: Udelen, how many spear traps have you?

UDELEN: If we could only catch a pig with these traps, we could show MDDT what a pig looks like.

BALAYAM: Good if we get a pig. The hair of the monkey is somewhat yellow and the pig's hair is black. If Jambangan could see the monkey, the monkey hair is almost the same color [as his].

[Laughter.]

DUL: If Jambangan sees it he will start. . . . [She probably gestures, as if taking photographs.] I thought Jambangan's eyes were not real [because of the glasses], but I have seen his eyes.

BALAYAM: I don't want to go away too far because if MDDT arrives I have to rush back, like yesterday. It is not so good all our companions are not yet here and have not seen MDDT. They should not go too far. In my case, if I go far and leave Sindi, they may think I don't love her. When we cannot see MDDT we have bad feeling inside us. We have to put all our feeling to MDDT. MDDT is so concerned for us he gives us many bolos and beads. These things given to us by MDDT have not been seen by our grandparents and only we have seen them. Further love of MDDT is shown by this thing you push and the rest lights at night [flashlight]. Kakay Mafoko said if you point this at night you can see your way. MDDT gave us the bow and arrow and we have eaten much of his *natek* [rice]. I will ask MDDT for a knife like one with this handle [Tboli-decorated bolo]. Since MDDT has been with us we have seen many things we never saw before. Before this coming of MDDT none of us knew when he was returning, but I dreamed the other night about MDDT. When they [the visitors] look at us they are shiny [smiling?]. I wonder how we look to them. They always come to see us because they like to look at us. Also they like this home of ours. If they like to see our place we should also see their place where Kakay Mafoko is from. When MDDT will sit with us, I will ask him to take me with him, because I can return immediately by the big bird. All of this Tasaday food is for MDDT. All food and animals belong to MDDT. All the rattan and all the things we can see are for MDDT. All of Tasaday is for MDDT. We must unite our feeling for MDDT.

DUL: *Oh-ho.* We always unite our feeling for only MDDT.

BALAYAM: In this visit of MDDT he again brings the extension of his body, Sindi. [Repetition about gifts.] With this visit MDDT will again give us knives, how can we thank him? Tekaf is very happy because he has his own knife. [Repeated about Adug, Kuletaw, Gintoy, Udelen.] Etut, you must have a good feeling, and also Gintoy and Udelen, because MDDT is here—plus all the knives he has given us. [Talks about decorated knife again.] I will tell Kakay Mafoko to whisper to MDDT about one like this for me. If I can get one knife like this, I will not use it but keep it until my hair is white. When we first saw MDDT, we were not fully satisfied because that was not our place [the clearing at the forest's edge], but now that he is here, we are happy.

DUL: If MDDT will give you [Balayam] another knife he also will give me one. Maybe when these children grow up they will be able to have one knife each from MDDT. We do not have to ask MDDT for knives, he knows.

Session 7   Night of April 18

DUL: The *natek* of MDDT [rice] is starting to taste very good.

UDELEN: Where can we fish tomorrow?

MAHAYAG: I was not able to return immediately, because I had to wait on my trap.

BALAYAM [to Mahayag, with an indirect scolding for being absent]: We will talk about where we can find more *natek* and place new traps—you should not go so far away, in case, like now, MDDT comes. We are happy now for gifts from MDDT and should not wander too far. If MDDT always sees us he will give us more metal axes. When MDDT leaves again, we will ask him not to be away longer than the space of time between the last visit and this one. I was asked, Mahayag, by MDDT, how we felt about the length of time he was away. MDDT loves us—you see, he did not stay very long in his place. We are able to get many *biking* because of the knives given by MDDT, and much *natek* with the axes he gave us. We have received many things from MDDT, but what can he expect in return? Only our good feeling. MDDT has meaning in his love because he gives us axes and knives, but we can only give our feeling because we are forest people. What do you have to say, Mahayag? I am sleepy.

MAHAYAG: I have a painful throat. [Pause.] This place of ours here is not owned by us alone, but is owned by MDDT also. We have nothing else to think about except to make more traps [he names different types]. Now that we have the knives, let us not just chop and chop everything—only for useful purposes. Now we are all sons of MDDT and must not chop all the things we see, only the trees we eat. This is all I can say, Balayam. When MDDT asks us again what we want, we do not know what to answer because we do not know what the names are of those things like the ones he gives our women [beads]. Every time we fish in the stream we always see that short woman [Igna] with them. Now that MDDT is with us down below, I wonder what he would like from us. We can always tell that we are children of MDDT, because he does not mind the hardships encountered to reach us. MDDT will love us until the end of his life, and we will do the same. When we get monkey, when we get *biking,* we will reserve some for MDDT even if he is not present. If MDDT comes to us very often, he will be able to eat all the food we get in the forest. He will be able to taste all the fish in the stream. Those are the only things we know, Udelen.

BILANGAN: We will look for more *biking* and more *natek*. MDDT loves this place. We must not stay out long. If MDDT comes up here, you women must not be heavy, you must be light. [Indirectly aimed at pregnant Etut?]

DUL: I am always expecting the face of MDDT coming up here at any moment.

BALAYAM: We are happy now because MDDT is below. We must always be happy here . . . [Long talk praising MDDT, expressing their love for him.] If MDDT likes to eat our tadpole, we will also eat his tadpole. If MDDT likes to eat our *biking,* we will eat his [and so on]. This is what our ancestors said: one day a big good man would come to us, and here he is—MDDT. Our ancestors said that the good man would come to them at this place in Tasaday, which is on Mount Tasaday. His knife is better than the stone tools that our ancestors taught us how to make. MDDT gives us this knife, which our ancestors never had and had never seen. Only we now see them. Our ancestors have never seen the things brought by MDDT. Some are yellow [probably tents], some green. When we look at MDDT's companions, they seem to be shiny to us, and the way they look at us seems that we look very good, this would also include this home [cave] of ours. Our whole self and everything here belongs to him. All the *biking* is his, all the [names other foods, then takes roll call to make sure everyone is still awake and listening to him].

Before we saw MDDT, Dul and Dula were very heavy [unhappy], but now we know and we all are very happy. He loves us so much, he has increased our number. We are thankful to MDDT, Kakay Jambangan, Kakay Mafoko, for increasing our number. It is nice that MDDT, Kakay Mafoko, Kakay Jambangan, Kakay Ting, Kakay Malaman, Kakay Toe-fee [names others] are all here. If it were not for MDDT, we would not have Sindi. [He takes another roll call.] This is all we can say, Bilangan, because this is all we know about. These are the only things we know about which to talk.

MAHAYAG: We have talked about everything we know how to talk about. We cannot be the same as MDDT because he knows many things, flying around in his bird.

UDELEN: We have to unite our feeling to work together.

LEFONOK: This is what we know: making traps and fishing. When they ask many questions my neck becomes stiff because I do not know what they are asking.

DUL: MDDT is here with us, and now each of us has one knife and we no longer have to borrow from one another.

MAHAYAG: Good, because now we have these knives from MDDT. It would be good if MDDT would not go back any more. MDDT has many ideas that would be good for us.

DUL: I like that thing in the ear of the fat woman [Igna].

DUL: MDDT gave one knife to Balayam and one to Lefonok.

MAHAYAG: My body is painful from carrying the wood for my trap.

Session 8   Early Afternoon of April 19

BILANGAN: Next, after MDDT leaves, we will make more traps. MDDT loves us very much because he visits us often and gives us knives. Before MDDT we had a hard life, but after MDDT we have an easy life. Almost all of our women have knives now and all of us have tasted the *natek* of MDDT. The *biking* of Tasaday is owned by MDDT. It is also owned by Kakay Mafoko and Kakay Jambangan. MDDT is very, very good man.

BALAYAM: Where did Mahayag and Dula and Udelen go? I am still waiting for my knife from MDDT.

BILANGAN: Also me.

BALAYAM: MDDT knows what we want. We do not have to ask him. He has also given us cloth and knives. If MDDT has tadpoles of his own, we will try to eat them also so he will not feel bad. MDDT is our father and Kakay Mafoko, Kakay Jambangan, Kakay Dokoto, Kakay Fix, Kakay Ting, and Kakay Toefee are all our brothers and sisters. MDDT has big meaning in his love because he has given us many things and yet we have not given him anything. The love of MDDT is shown through his gifts of his *natek,* his leaves [cloth?], his knives. . . . All these things given us by MDDT we never saw when our ancestors were still alive. What else can we say, Bilangan? This is all that we know.

[Long pause punctuated by children's voices and wood being chopped.]

BILANGAN: I ate plenty of MDDT's *natek.* It is already getting late for making *natek,* so we will eat some of MDDT's *natek.*

DUL: I am happy because I have my own knife and I can look for *ubud.*

Session 9   Early Afternoon of April 21

MAHAYAG: Imagine they can make the climb to the top [above the cave]. Let's put together these knives of ours.

DUL: Ginun has no knife yet.

SEKUL: You go out now and look for our food.

MAHAYAG: After we visit the river, we must bring back *daon* [leaves for G string]. I like the taste of this *natek* of MDDT.

BALAYAM: This is why we must always stay at home.

MAHAYAG: We cannot go out to make *natek* now, because we have MDDT. This *natek* of MDDT is white. We have to get the bamboo tubes to cook our food and also get some wild flowers. We will now again eat the *natek* of MDDT.

SEKUL: Let's not lose the knives!

DUL: It's good that we have the *natek* of MDDT, because we are not getting our own *natek.* If we had our own, we would not eat MDDT's, because he might run out.

MAHAYAG: If MDDT will always stay with us we cannot make our own *natek* and we will have to eat his *natek*. Even if we do not go out, we have MDDT's *natek*. When MDDT is not here, everyone will go out to make traps. We cannot leave MDDT when he is here, because it is to us that he comes. Our small children might become hungry if we do not get *natek* from MDDT, since we don't go out.

DUL: MDDT is very good. He knows that we cannot go out to make our own *natek,* so he gives us his.

MAHAYAG: MDDT is very good.

DUL: We cannot go out to look for *biking.* That's how MDDT loves us, he gives us his own *natek.* And so we must show our love for him by not going out while he is here.

MAHAYAG: We will also eat the tadpole [dried fish] of MDDT's. Now we are eating his *natek.* We only know MDDT's *natek.* The rest of his food we do not know. MDDT has also frogs, crabs, and other things, but we do not know the taste of them.

DUL: When we go out to fish, we cannot get so much because these children of mine go with me and I cannot help so much. Maybe MDDT has a painful body from falling down yesterday. [He slipped on some rocks at the stream.]

[A small boy describes how he missed catching a big frog.]

DUL: Why does Ginun always go out? When MDDT is here he does not know how to talk.

MAHAYAG [to Balayam]: Do not sleep on the other side tonight! We must talk about the questions asked by Kakay Ahnee.

BALAYAM: Kakay Jambangan and Kakay Toefee ask questions from us, but we must not be tired. Those are companions of MDDT, and they also love us. All of the companions of MDDT have love for us. The love of MDDT is shown by Sindi. MDDT might think that our love is very small because we do not give him much *natek* or *biking,* but if we go out to gather he may not find us here.

DUL: *Oh-ho!*

BALAYAM: We will ask MDDT not to bring us people with big voice and sharp look! We will tell MDDT the reason why is because we do not know about that sharp look and big voice. We only know our forest. We are all the sons of MDDT. We will not make our feeling go away from MDDT, because his own feeling is very close to us. We are very happy when MDDT comes to us. Dula, Sekul, and Etut: If MDDT is with us you should always be happy, for he is the only father who has come to us. We must always be happy because MDDT is with us.

DULA: *Oh-ho.*

BALAYAM: This home of ours is the home of MDDT. Aside from this, we only know how to make *natek,* monkey, mousetraps. . . . This is what we know.

DULA: That's right. The monkey, deer, wild pig are also all owned by MDDT.

BALAYAM: I am Balayam, also the son of MDDT. I am the son of MDDT, he gave me Sindi as my wife. We cannot find Sindi if not for MDDT. This is where we know the big love of MDDT to us. We have always to show our love because we have many brothers [mentions all the visitors]. All of these [mentions names again] are our brothers, also the sons of MDDT. Kakay Mafoko and all of us now are the sons of MDDT—all together. We have very good feelings because MDDT is with us. We have to make our feeling to MDDT very good because MDDT is giving us a companion. We also have good feeling now because we have company to talk to. Let us tell MDDT he must bring us only those who could understand us and not those who don't. How we wish to talk to MDDT, but we could not talk because we do not understand what they say. Even the companions of Kakay Mafoko [Sol and Manuel], we cannot understand each other. We only know one way of talking—Tasaday talk. One question asked by MDDT is who made us? As told to me, Dul, by my father Salibuku, the father of Salibuku was Fangul, and the wife of Fangul was Tukful. And what I do not know is the father of Fangul. And this is what I have always been thinking: Who is the father of Fangul? Who made Tasaday are Fuweh and Sidakweh. The ancestor of Fangul made Tasaday. The ancestors of Fangul are the originators of Tasaday. [Fuweh, Sidakweh, Bebang]. Sidakweh and Fuweh made the first Tasaday and also the ancestor of Fangul. And the kind god *le mokan* was included during the making of Tasaday. They made this *le mokan* so that people of Tasaday will know when dangers will come to them. That is why, Dul, we must respect *le mokan,* because from it we will know danger before death comes to us. This *le mokan* was made for us by Sidakweh so we could predict [avoid?] our death.

Why? This has made me feel more than what joy or sorrow would make me feel. Bebang is a man. Sidakweh and Fuweh were women. That is why, Dul, the real owner of this top [the upper cave?] is Bebang and the owner of this [perhaps pointing to the lower cave?] is Sidakweh. I am very happy, Dul, because I am still young and I could still remember.

Session 10   Night of April 21

MAHAYAG: All these things brought here by MDDT for us we do not know the names. We are really true sons of MDDT because he loves us. Kakay Malaman wants *fais batu* [stone tool] with handle and tied with rattan, and we don't have this right here. We will unite among ourselves for MDDT. If we sleep we will always think of MDDT, and when we awake we will always think of MDDT. MDDT has one big love for us and we will also unite our love for him. Even me, Mahayag Bulol [mountain], wherever I go in the forest, I always think of MDDT. When I look for *biking,* I never forget MDDT and always have MDDT inside my feeling. MDDT really loves us very much. When we first saw MDDT our feeling was not yet whole, but now our whole feeling is for MDDT, even though he has companions. We know these companions. Why is it that they ask so many questions from us? Maybe they do not know anything about us here and we do not know how they look at us. This is the only thing that we know; when we go into the forest we only know [names foods, traps]. And when our traps can catch something we look for it. [Shouting]: That is all we know! These are the things we know! All of us in this home of ours! They ask us many questions, yet we do not know of other things! When we do not have anything we bend our heads [to sleep or relax], and when we want food we go out and then come back to this home of ours. We are people of the forest! We only know about going out and looking around to make *natek,* gather *biking,* and make traps. In addition to what we know, MDDT has taught us how to use this knife, and also Kakay Mafoko.

BALAYAM: I also have something to say but I cannot talk with babies crying!

MAHAYAG [loudly]: Listen to what I say! What I am telling you is not bent but straight! I will repeat because all of you—Balayam, and also you children—must remember this when you go out for food. We must not forget and we must always remind ourselves of our love for MDDT in this home of ours. We will always tell our men, women and children and ourselves about MDDT. Children, do not cut trees, because MDDT says this is not so good. Also, all of you women, do not cut trees that we do not want; only cut trees we need. Women and children should also not forget this. Even the rattan must not be cut that is not used for traps. If we will not use trees to make traps, do not cut them if we do not need them, or if they have no use, do not cut them! To us this may not be important, but to MDDT the trees are very beautiful. Keep this in your heart—keep all things said by MDDT. All of what MDDT tells us we must put in our feelings and what we have told him he will put in his feelings. The rattan and also the wood are all his, and if we have no use for them we should not cut them. If we cut these it will be a waste of rattan and wood. We will pity the trees and the rattan, and also the *biking* we do not need. If we do not chop trees, the *biking* can grow under these trees. This we have always to remember: the things told to us by MDDT and Kakay Mafoko. No cutting of trees we do not need. We have soft feeling for two companions of MDDT, Kakay Mafoko and Kakay Jambangan, because they do not get mad. I will go now. Bilangan, you know how to make mousetraps and I must also be good at making mousetraps [perhaps a metaphor]. This we must remember: we can go out to make *natek* and gather *biking* and we do not have to just sit here. MDDT has said so!

BALAYAM: Listen—also you, Kuletaw, you have brought up Mahayag and next myself. You have fed me monkey brains and fed me *biking* of

Tasaday, and Bilangan has fed me wild pig of Tasaday, and you have fed me *biking* of Tasaday. That's why, Bilangan, we must unite all our feelings to make mousetraps [?]. Too bad Udelen is not here, he went to check his monkeytrap. We have seen the big love of MDDT for us. MDDT and Kakay Mafoko are staying long with us now. The *natek* of MDDT is being eaten by us and also the monkey of MDDT is being eaten by us. MDDT now has big love for us, he is not holding us by his small finger but by his big finger, because we have now Kakay Sindi, sister of Kakay Mafoko, who is an addition to Dul, Dula, Sekul, Etut. We are very happy because we have the knives. MDDT says we will not cut trees we do not need and rattan we do not need, only those for *natek* and traps. All these things said by MDDT we must keep with us even if we are sleeping. We have to keep this, Dul, in our feeling when we are gathering *biking*. Do not let your baby cry, Dul. MDDT and Kakay Mafoko have plenty of companions and we must unite our feeling with them. [He names as many of MDDT's companions as he can remember.] Of these companions of MDDT, those who have sharp looks or big words [shouting] we do not like them here in Tasaday! We pity ourselves because they ask us many things we do not know how to answer! We do not know how to answer these things. We know how to dig for *biking*. It is up to MDDT to understand us! All we can do is make our feeling always good to MDDT so he will always see us good. MDDT has continuous love for us—he gives us knives, his own *natek,* and the yellow, the red, the white [beads]. This is his love to Dul, Dula, Etut and Sekul [the beads] . . . Ginun also has that . . . and that is the love of MDDT to them.

DULA: I will take my child out because she is crying.

MAHAYAG: I will go out with my baby, who is crying.

BALAYAM: You must return quickly so you can eat the *natek* of MDDT and we will all share the monkey meat of MDDT. All what we say MDDT loves to hear [perhaps a reference to the tape recorder].

MAHAYAG: All that I have said is all true.

DULA: Hurry, Mahayag, the baby is crying.

MAHAYAG: This is true, what I say. When MDDT was last here, he gave us his *natek* and now again he gives us his *natek*. All he can get from us is our stone tools. Maybe these tools are very new to the companions of MDDT. But if these companions ask for these stone tools we will not give them unless MDDT tells us to do so. Maybe all those companions of MDDT never have small love for us, or maybe they have [don't like us]? Do not let the baby cry, Dula, or MDDT may not be able to hear what we are saying, down below [perhaps referring to the tape recorder]. The way we talk now, is like that of men [a serious talk].

BILANGAN: What is told to us by MDDT, we must believe. Lefonok has chopped down a *natek* tree and we will work on it tomorrow. MDDT said he will visit us when we make *natek*. If all of us were here now, and some not absent, you would see that all I have said is right and true. This is the sign of MDDT's true love for us—his second visit. Do you have a knife yet, Lolo?

LOLO: No.

BALAYAM: If not for Dafal, who told us of MDDT, we would still have only stone tools. In the beginning Dafal gave us few knives that we used, but now with MDDT we have many. Now that we have MDDT here with us, we have many knives and we are no longer thin. We all have good bodies, thanks to the knives. If not for MDDT we could not get more *biking,* catch more wild pig, and make more *natek.* The way I feel, Udelen, with all these knives we have, our bodies will become stronger. [Yes, echo Sekul and Lobo.] The way I feel before these knives, we were very small—but with all these knives our arms will become big and our heads will also grow big. This will be the start of our big arms, big bodies, and big heads —these knives. With these our thighs will become big and this will make them heavy in the forest, but we must be grateful. If it was just Dafal, we would probably get thin because he only has few knives. [Laughter.] If we knew Kakay Dafal only, it would not be enough because he only gave us three. [More laughter.] And none for our women, not even for me. But we must be thankful to Dafal, who taught us about MDDT. We had seen only one man before, Dafal, who taught us about MDDT; but he never saw our home. Kakay Malaman and Kakay Ahnee ask too many questions. Kakay Toefee never asks anything. Kakay Osaka, Kakay Usi, Kakay Miya, Kakay Fao, they don't ask anything. But [shouting] Kakay Ahnee asks too many things! Maybe this is because we are new to her eyes. And the way she looks at Dul! But maybe Ahnee might look good to us in the future. Maybe the reason she asks so many questions is because she does not know anything. We really do not know how she looks at us— whether she sees us as good or bad in this home of ours. [Still very excited]: Maybe this is why Kakay Ahnee asks many things—because she will help MDDT here in Tasaday. The reason why she came with MDDT may be because she has love for Dul, Dula, and Sekul. Maybe Kakay Ahnee has sympathy for us here. All the things she asks from you, you should answer because she might have sympathy for you. Also Kakay Jambangan asks many questions. He asks many questions with Kakay Ting, but their questions are good. Maybe Kakay Jambangan is the brother of MDDT. We must get used to them, even if they ask so much from us—and even if we do not know how to ask these companions of MDDT any questions.

BILANGAN: If they ask us questions, we will answer them with what we know—even if our answers are only very short. If these are bad people who go with MDDT, I am scared! Especially those with sharp looks. Remember that one who followed us at the small creek? If I see good people with MDDT, I will feel good. But if I see those with sharp looks, I might run. All our women have good feeling for MDDT. MDDT has good feeling to see this place of ours. All of us men are happy within us, and all women must feel happy within yourselves. This is all I can say—even if MDDT asks me himself, this is all I can say!

BALAYAM: What do you say, Udelen, and you, Dul?

LOBO: [interrupting Udelen, who had started to answer]: Me, I already have a knife. I will also talk down below [to answer visitors' questions?]. Do you have a knife already, Lolo? I already have mine. Etut has no knife yet. Ginun has none, either. Udo has no knife—but me, Lobo, I have my own knife. MDDT gave this to *me!*

UDELEN: The *natek* of MDDT tastes very good.

LOBO: Yes, it is good. After eating, I will go to sleep. I will sleep in the next cave [apparently said to tease Balayam. Lobo sings.]

DUL: What else should we say? We do not know what else to say. We only know how to fish. If they ask us, we do not know what to say.

[Long pause while eating.]

BALAYAM [Mentions all names of MDDT's companions and that they can all hear this below]: I have a very good feeling within me now because MDDT will leave Sindi. This is now the sound of MDDT's big bird. . . . [Long, fast playing of harp to imitate helicopter, followed by Balayam singing while people make jokes in background. Then he says]:

What is that very shiny thing below? [Perhaps a flashlight from the camp. He continues with his song, a story about digging for *biking* when the *biking* cannot be reached.]

UDELEN: If I could only get one wild pig, I would let MDDT roast it.

DUL: MDDT has not yet tasted *biking* mixed with pig meat—good! Especially the fat.

UDELEN: I would like to bring MDDT to the trap and see if it has hit a wild pig. Then MDDT would pick it up. If we can bring MDDT with us, maybe he will see our monkeytrap with a monkey at the end of it.

BILANGAN: When MDDT was above our cave we were worried he might fall.

UDELEN: We are also expecting a back pack [a small woven bag with a strap, like the one given by Dafal]. The trouble with that one [Dafal's] is when you put something inside you can no longer find it. [It probably has holes.] If we have that pack covering our back, perhaps we will not be cold.

DUL: If you are given a pack like that, we should put worms inside and give it to MDDT to take out. And if we can get a wildcat or wild chicken, we should put it inside also. I would like it if I had my own pack [which is used only by men in other groups]. I would place the tadpoles and fish in it.

UDELEN: I would also have a very good feeling if I had one, and I would get much more food.

BILANGAN: If I had one, I would go out every day.

DUL: If you have a pack and you put crabs inside and do not remove the claws, it will bite your back.

BILANGAN: No, no. I must remove the claws or I will be bitten through the pack.

DUL: If you get a pack, fill it full of crabs and surprise MDDT with the full bag. Before going out [to the stream], tell MDDT that if they ask me anything, I do not know how to answer because we are not used to asking each other these questions.

BILANGAN: I would have difficulty answering also.

12

In the Mind's Eye
of a Blind Tasaday

AT the Blit settlement, after the usual ardent welcome, Elizalde asked for a meeting with an old man whose ancestors were reported to have lived in caves.

Datu Dudim, the Blit chieftain, led us on a twenty-minute walk through cornfields and head-high grass, over knolls and a ridge, down a green slope to a knobby shelf beside a shallow ravine. Scrubby foothills stood in the shadow of the forest and mountains of the Tasaday.

A thatched house on stilts stood alone on the shelf. We climbed a rickety ladder, squeezed through a narrow door, and sat on the squeaking rattan-slatted floor. In the middle of the small main room sat the old man, a faded cotton loincloth the only covering on a body so lean that folds of skin hung from his ribs and bony limbs. His hair was thick and ash-gray. Over high cheekbones and sunken cheeks he wore a mask of wrinkles that spread out from his mouth and closed eyes, blind eyes.

The old man's name was Kasuk. Nobody knew his age; he looked at least eighty and could easily have been over ninety. He sat with bowed head, hands clasped, legs folded into a near-lotus position; his torso rocked slightly and he uttered a soft crooning sound. It was easy to imagine him as an ancient sage, gnarled by time and an awesome knowledge of life's mysteries.

Behind him sat his gray-haired wife and two wide-eyed grandchildren. Manda and Mai, who had met Kasuk only briefly before, said they were glad to see him again. He nodded, his lips parting to emit guttural, almost moaning sounds, which Mai translated to mean he was happy to welcome them to his house.

Manda said he understood the old man's ancestors had lived in caves.

"That is so," said Kasuk in a husky, creaking voice. "I, too, was born in a cave."

This was unexpected news and, after an exchange of surprised glances with Manda, Mai asked Kasuk to tell about the caves.

"It was there," he said, lifting a bony arm and waving it toward the southwest, the forest. "It was a place of beauty. The sun came into the cave in the mornings. There was a waterfall. A stream ran through the valley below."

"What did you call this place?" Manda asked. "Did it have a name?"

"Yes," Kasuk grunted. "We called it Ta-tasadayee."

The quiet, almost solemn atmosphere had become tense when the old man said he was born in a cave, and now the name—Ta-tasadayee—heightened that tension. Mai's eyebrows shot up; Manda gasped. The old man rocked and murmured, rocked and murmured.

"Was that right, Mai, Ta-tasadayee? Did he say Ta-tasadayee?"

Mai asked for the name and Kasuk repeated it exactly the same way. He was asked when he was there last. Why had he left? Had others left, too?

Kasuk's voice seemed to slip even deeper inside him and then rasp out in a hoarse whisper that Mai had to lean down to the old man's mouth to hear.

"I was a boy, a small boy. I had gone to look for *ubud* and met Agun, yes, a boy named Agun. It was somewhere along the creek. This was at Lomung Creek, which flowed from Kakeet on the other side. And Agun asked me to go with him to his place. I went, and his place was near here —but it was all trees then and was not called Blit. It was called Goleet. I met Lindunbong here and he became my good friend. I liked to stay with Lindunbong and go places with him—but I soon became blind."

The low but steady murmur of the old man stopped and he mumbled to himself. Mai asked Kasuk to continue his story.

"I had had bad vision for a long time," he said. "My eyes were running with the sickness and then, one day, I could see no more, I could see nothing!" With this, Kasuk arched his back and spread his fragile arms wide, rolled his head, and opened his lids. Eyes of surprising whiteness and stark blankness, making his face look fierce, stared blindly at us. It was as if an unseen puppeteer had suddenly jerked him out of sleep. His nearly toothless mouth fell open and he remained in suspension momentarily, like a man crucified, then collapsed back into the nodding, rocking position.

"It was not long after I left Ta-tasadayee [that he lost his sight]. I was never able to return," he said.

Kasuk said his father's name was Sambal and that he had had a brother, but could not recall his name or what had happened to him. He said there were three caves at Ta-tasadayee; they had lived in the highest one, where the sun shone in; birds had nested in the lower one, where the people fetched water from a fall. A stream flowed below the caves. Their food was *biking,* which they took from the ground and mashed with stones.

He was asked about the name Ta-tasadayee—what did it mean?

Kasuk rocked forward and back, and made soft moaning sounds. Mai leaned closer to him and repeated the question. Kasuk snorted and mumbled something, Mai thought, about Sadayee being the name of a person he had heard about, a very, very old man. *Ta* was a tall, strong man.

Kasuk then seemed to wake up and become alert. He said he was the only living child of Sambal. Ugat, his sister, had died—and, now he remembered, so had Bilangan, his brother. And his father, too, was dead when he left Ta-tasadayee.

Asked about other ancestors, he said that his grandfather was Sudafon, his great-grandfather was Silifit, and his great-great-grandfather was Mulalan. All of them lived in the caves because the caves had good fortune. They never leaked rain and never were destroyed.

Kasuk named the wives of his father and grandfather, Tabua and Keboy, and said Sambal's sister was Ubao, whose husband was Yu and son was Aya. Did the names Kuletaw, Sekul, Tekaf (the oldest Tasaday) mean anything to him?

"I am not sure. But perhaps I have heard those names before."

He said his playmates had been Aya and Lagoie, the sons of Yu, and their sister, Bitato. She had died and two other girls, Linana and Dayan, had wandered away and were never heard from again. Their mother's name was Etut.

Which place did he prefer, Blit or Tasaday?

"It is good here," Kasuk said. "Even though I could not see, I found friends and was able to get a wife and family. But Ta-tasadayee was so beautiful. It was a good life in the forest. There always was the best fruit and plenty of food. That was when I was there. I don't know if it is still the same . . . if it is still there. . . ."

He nodded and mumbled to himself, then lapsed into a long silence. Mai spoke to him but got no response. Kasuk just sat, rocking and moaning.

Everyone was quiet for several minutes. Mai then tried again to talk to him and Kasuk responded. We asked how the Ta-tasadayee had gotten *ubud.* With tools of stone, he said, or a group of men might bend and break a small *ubud* palm.

Did they have any metal knives, any metal at all?

"No metal . . . stones only."

We questioned him again about their implements, wanting to be certain they used no metal, but it was difficult to hear his response. Mai asked exactly how they had obtained *ubud* with stone tools. He leaned close for the answer and heard him say something about men sawing at a palm with the stone and then pulling the tree down.

Nobody present had heard of that before. The Tasaday had said, we thought, that they had never got *ubud* before Dafal brought knives. So it was suggested to Kasuk that perhaps they actually had some metal with which they cut a tree and stripped away the bark, and *then* men tore it down with their hands.

"Unh," Kasuk grunted, and said gruffly, "I will tell you one more time! Perhaps you can understand this time if I say that our tool was stone and was shaped like the head of a pig! We struck with it so that the snout always hit first!"

With that, apparently weary of our questions, he stretched his lean body on a woven mat and went to sleep. Mai talked softly to him, but Kasuk was through; no more questions.

We talked briefly with his wife, Tudel, who told us she was born at Sala-ubon, near the Ubu's place at Datal Tabayong, and had a sister and two brothers. She said she never had met anyone else who had lived in a cave and that her own home had been in a wooden shelter; she had never slept in tree roots. She said her people ate *camote*, tadpoles, crabs, and occasionally *biking* and *ubud*. She met her husband while on a trip with her father. She was still a child and Kasuk was at an age that we guessed from her description to be about ten or twelve.

We left soon after that. Kasuk was still asleep. At his advanced age, the old man might have forgotten a lot, but his memory seemed extremely clear on the caves and the stream, his description fit the Tasaday's place exactly. On the other hand, his mention of getting *ubud* with a stone tool contradicted what the Tasaday told us. His recollection of ancestors' names was extraordinary, if it was accurate, tracing the Tasaday back through his great-great-grandfather, Mulalan. Putting his own age conservatively at eighty and adding twenty years for each generation of forebears would take Tasaday history back one hundred and sixty years. (Of course, the Bilangan and Etut he had mentioned could not have been the young ones we knew; either they had been named for their ancestors, or it was simply a coincidence.)

We wanted to ask Kasuk much more—about the Tasafeng and Sanduka, for instance, or what stories his father might have told him about the origin of the Tasaday—but he had found the best answer yet to bothersome questions: roll over and go to sleep. We hoped to talk with him again soon.

Back at the main Blit settlement the people were called together. There were more than two hundred, mostly Blit but including perhaps two dozen Sduff. They had fled intruders on their lands and sought temporary refuge with the Blit, who, apparently because of their remote location, had had no direct contact with settlers or loggers—but they had heard many stories about them.

Elizalde and Mai made rousing speeches to explain the proclamation of the reservation. They displayed and explained a large map, the first all but a few people there had ever seen. It showed that Blit land had been included in the reserve area for the Tasaday.

Manda, speaking through Mai, told the Blit to be proud and strong—not like the Sduff, who had sold their lands to loggers and now were beggars (the Sduff bowed their heads and some cried). He told them that President Marcos—whom many had never heard of—was the big leader of all the land and had taken the reserve area from loggers and had promised that the Blit could keep it forever—as long as the Blit themselves did not give it up. "Don't give up your land, no matter what you are offered or told. Your land is your strength, your pride, you must keep it." He said the only way outsiders might legally claim the land was for a Blit to put his thumbprint on a lease or deed—"and any man who does that, we will take his thumb on a stick!"

Manda singled out a Sduff youth who had been living among settlers in Lake Sebu and had lost all his belongings there. "Stand up! You see. He was going to be smarter than any of you. He went to Lake Sebu and was a big man. He took off his Sduff earrings and clothes, because those important people at Lake Sebu laughed at them and ridiculed him. And now what does he have? Nothing. He doesn't even have his original Sduff things any more. Remember your great ancestors, your own greatness, and don't be ashamed. Don't sell or give away that greatness. If you do, you'll be running and hiding like these Sduff here today."

Mai was a gifted public speaker. As he translated, his voice rose and dropped dramatically, trembling and rolling at the right points. His black mustache and thick body made him look tough and powerful. He and Manda had spoken in tandem so often over the years that their pauses in building a speech and putting emphasis at appropriate places were perfectly timed.

Throughout the speech, the Blit roared and shouted. The Sduff were forlorn; later, Manda told them they could be great again and some seemed heartened.

Manda then said that the Tasaday should be their good friends, their brothers, and that it was because of the Tasaday that Marcos had proclaimed the reserve. So, he said, the Blit must protect the Tasaday from troublemakers who would enter their forest.

The Blit yelled their agreement.

We flew the next morning to the Tboli settlement at Kematu, where Elizalde discussed the surveying job in detail with Certeza. The worry was that placement of the concrete markers and creation of required visual clearances from marker to marker would mean cutting down perhaps thousands of trees and plants, which could severely deplete large areas of the forest. Certeza was to study other possibilities.

Afterward, Mai, Elizalde, and I had a long talk at Mai's house about the problems they had foreseen when first contemplating entering the Tasaday's forest. Mai, better than anyone I knew, represented a meeting between the natural and the intellectual worlds. He began the discussion.

"The Tasaday's eyes are beginning to penetrate further. Before, the only things they saw were right before them—the trees, leaves, *ubud*—but now they look beyond that, they themselves are discovering, as we are discovering. They are starting to look ahead, back, left, right, up, down—to learn things they didn't know.

"Is this good or bad? It can be either. But it is good for men to know many things. And now they start to compare the *'natek* of Momo Dakel' with the foods they know. They didn't like the rice at first, but now they are beginning to and they can't find it anywhere in their forest."

Manda spoke up. "That's right. Want is already there . . . now fear may be coming."

We discussed the role of Manda as god to the Tasaday. It created great responsibilities for him. "Well," he said, "on this god business, their ancestors simply told them that one day a good man would come to them. They don't talk about supernatural attributes. We are putting our ideas of that ahead of their ideas, our concept of a god or gods in the clouds, and so on. But rather than explain our concept of god, it would be much better to simply change or adjust the meaning of *diwata* to something closer to what we think they really mean."

Mai suggested the name be changed to "the big man with much love." Love in their language was *key-he-de-wan,* so it would be Momo Dakel Key-de-wan Tasaday.

Manda replied, "Okay. It doesn't make any difference to me. I just don't want to see this god business get out of hand. People on the outside just wouldn't understand it. Of course," he added with a grin, "I am rather godlike."

Mai remarked that he had been to Japan, Indonesia, Hong Kong, Singapore, Manila, and all over the Philippines—"and everywhere there are good people, and some bad ones, too. But the real goodness—the best people I've ever seen anywhere are the Tasaday. Ah, the way they live. Alone. Their home is good. They have clothes easily. They don't argue among themselves. They are truly virgin people. And when they look forward, they look forward together, and they love things together. None tells another that this is not good or that is not good. They seem to forget themselves as individuals, they do not even know themselves as individuals. But competition is coming. Anything we do, everything we do, they will remember. They do not forget. They are great imitators. You'll see."

This could be dangerous. The problem was to deal with them so that they could flourish in their own way.

"How?" Mai said. "Trust them. Join them. Don't tell them what to do. And don't use them. They do not like people who just go to see them to get what they can, learn what they want to learn. The Tasaday recognize this in people, they sense it. The first thing to remember when going there is to admire them, to respect the Tasaday. Forget yourself and be truly interested in them for themselves, not for yourself. And laugh with them, do not laugh at them.

"And, even if you are not in the mood, you must look straight at them. Look them in the face. If you are evasive, if you have worried eyes and a worried face, they know. Then they may worry, too. Enjoy them.

"Their thinking increases little by little already. They think of the Sanduka and Tasafeng; the helipad, the whole forest. They may wonder about the small shacks on the other side [the ones seen at Blit from the helicopter]. And they will think, Where is that place where Momo Dakel goes when he leaves?' You know, I think they could be the ancestors of all of us here [the Tboli]. Perhaps we are not so far from them. Not so long ago, in 1958, my father used to carry us children in the bark of a tree in the forest. . . ."

Manda spoke up. "The Tasaday will lose some of this and some of that, and if they were to come fully into our world they would have to learn to cheat, to be dishonest, to deal in the competitive world. If some sharpie were to ask them to lend him their sister—so he could rape her—they would have to learn to say, 'You should not borrow that one, she is sick.'

"What they would learn mostly in order to survive in the outer world would be to compete and to hide things. Now their life is open. They will tell you anything. How do we avoid the negative change? There are no certain answers. There's not been a situation like this here before.

"I think that the best thing is just to leave them alone and watch. Some think we should educate them, and there is some thinking that they are dying out and must be saved—with schools, clinics, churches, agriculture, construction, religion, and so on. But then they won't be Tasaday, they'll be something else. If we're not pressured to introduce change, they probably won't change too much. They will change some, of course. But they have more food now than they know what to do with. They don't need clothes or shelter. Sindi might introduce new ideas, and it might have been a mistake to let her stay in there. But what could you do? Tell Balayam no?

"Now, what we could do is just stop taking in outsiders, everyone, and maybe just visit once or twice a year to see how they are doing. That's one way. I think we've just got to watch and wait and see, and be careful. The

Tasaday offer a great chance for man to see himself and ask what happened. They are amazing, and it makes one wonder how we have come to where we are. Where did we take the wrong turn?"

We also discussed the causes of the misunderstandings and irritations of the visit just completed. Mainly, the problem had been ignorance on the part of all visitors about how to behave with the Tasaday. In view of this, we devised a list of do's and don't's, summarized Panamin's policy, and worked out a general statement of approach to the Tasaday. The views of Lynch and Fernandez on each matter were later included. The end result was a set of guidelines and conditions for scientists and any other visitors to read and sign before entering the forest. Would-be violators of specific conditions or of the spirit of the guidelines were advised that they would be escorted from the area at once.

The guidelines stressed that anyone entering the area should keep in mind that it was the Tasaday's home and therefore conduct themselves as guests. The Tasaday were to be treated as friendly fellow humans, not as museum artifacts or creatures in a zoo. The Tasaday's discomfort with certain types of questions and their sensitivity to certain attitudes—such as loud voices and sharp looks—were described. Prohibitions included taking stone tools or other artifacts, asking the Tasaday to perform tasks, make tools, carry supplies, guide tours.

The ten-page memorandum was preceded by two policy summaries (given below). A copy was henceforth presented to every potential visitor in the hope that a firm protective policy toward the Tasaday would be established.

POLICY STATEMENT
(GENERAL)
ON THE TASADAY

The Tasaday people enjoy a unique way of life, which they consider happy and fulfilling, and which virtually all observers have noted to be marked by an extraordinary harmony between the people and their environment and one another.

It is the aim of PANAMIN and the Philippine Government to protect the Tasaday so they may preserve and pursue the life they love.

Change is inevitable, however, as the Tasaday have even the most limited contact with the outside world. Indeed, the sporadic contact since 1967–68 with a single man, the Manubo Blit hunter Dafal, has initiated change that is still being evaluated.

PANAMIN and the Government are committed to the principle that whatever change comes to the Tasaday must, whenever possible, be allowed at a pace which the Tasaday themselves can understand and assimilate with the least disturbance to them and their environment. At the same time, the interest of the scientific community and world at large is keen, and PANAMIN believes that, wherever possible within the confines of the aim to protect the people, the life ways of the Tasaday should be documented by and shared with scholars and the public.

Because of the fragile life style of the Tasaday and their sensitive nature, there is danger that, through innocence and ignorance, the best-intentioned visitor may cause harm to the Tasaday, who are unprepared to meet successfully many of the challenges of twentieth-century life that are treated as commonplace by much of mankind.

To many who read these words, we may be stating the obvious, but in the interest of sustaining the well being of the Tasaday people, we seek your indulgence and ask each visitor to their cave home to read and signify understanding of a few guidelines that we hope will benefit both the Tasaday and you in your time together.

PANAMIN
STATEMENT OF POLICY

PANAMIN was founded to assure a continual operation of organized efforts in favor of Philippine minority groups, particularly those who have no other advocate. Its general aims are knowledge, assistance, advice, and protection.

The assistance that PANAMIN offers, whether medical, material, advisory, or developmental, is guided by the principle that every minority group has the right to preserve its traditional way of life or, if it so desires, to change it at the pace and direction it chooses.

To understand these traditional ways of life before they have been irreversibly altered by external influences, PANAMIN feels bound to carry out and encourage scientifically acceptable studies of the culture and environment of the minority groups it serves. It is convinced that this is one of the greatest contributions it can make to the development of a meaningful national identity.

Because minority groups often find themselves helpless in the face of outsiders who encroach on their traditional domains, PANAMIN finds it necessary not only to expose these illegal threats and attacks, but also to assist the disadvantaged minority peoples through appeals to the law and to the government's armed forces, through resettlement activities, through petitions for the declaration of reserved lands, and through the encouragement of responsible reporting by mass media.

In this same spirit of protection, particularly where a minority group's life ways have not yet been observed and recorded, or where the group has had very little exposure to the outside world, PANAMIN feels obliged to exercise the same vigilance toward those well-meaning and competent individuals who wish to visit and observe the members of these groups.

In this regard, PANAMIN wishes to state that it is pledged to assist in every way possible those qualified scientific personnel who wish to spend some time among the people for whom PANAMIN has a protective mandate. PANAMIN will invite such individuals to visit these people under the following conditions:

1. The plan of study that the individual has in mind should be submitted to PANAMIN for a review by PANAMIN'S Research Advisory Council, a board that includes scientists competent in the field in which the applicant wishes to do research.

2. The Research Advisory Council will study the proposal in the light of its intrinsic worth, and in relation to the ongoing PANAMIN research program, asking, relative to the latter, if the study would duplicate what was already under way, and if the people would be unduly taxed by this additional inquiry.

3. If the proposal is approved (with or without suggested modifications), PANAMIN will do everything it can to assist the proponent to arrive at the study site and to accomplish his objectives as expeditiously as possible—it being understood that previous commitments of time and money may require PANAMIN to set a schedule different from that which the proponent had in mind, and to ask him to pay all or part of the expenses involved.

4. In any event, if the project is approved, PANAMIN will require that the proponent subscribe to the "Guidelines for Visiting the Remote Philippine Community" and sign a statement as well that he undertakes the trip at his own risk.

13

Stone Age Revolution

IN Manila Elizalde took up problems of the land survey, Lynch and Fernandez worked on their research report, and I conferred with them and Amy Rogel on Tasaday data and pictures. In early May we matched photographs with the genealogy and found an extra Tasaday face.

The photographs clearly showed twenty-five Tasaday, not twenty-four as had been listed the previous year. It had been difficult to count them because of communication problems and because they were seldom all together and at least four youngsters had no names. Now only Bilangan's youngest son was still unnamed, or so we thought; but the photographs showed two unnamed children. A check would have to be made on the next visit, tentatively set for mid-May, about two weeks away.

The principal purpose of this expedition would be to give Carlos Fernandez an opportunity to study the Tasaday further. Elizalde was to accompany him, explain the plan to the Tasaday, and then leave, thereby enabling observations to be made for the first time without his influential presence. Fernandez planned to stay in the forest at least two weeks, perhaps four. He hoped to have another scientist go along, and he also asked if I would accompany them to take photographs and assist in other ways. I eagerly accepted.

Elizalde was invited by the Philippine Embassy in Washington, D.C., to come to the U.S. and give a speech at the Smithsonian Institution about Panamin and the Tasaday in early June, as part of celebrations commemorating Philippine independence. President Marcos endorsed the idea and Elizalde agreed that it would be worthwhile. There was also to be an exhibit of photographs, which would later move to the gallery of the

National Geographic Society. Elizalde asked me to handle the exhibit, which would involve printing and mounting about seventy-five large photographs and taking them to Washington to set up the displays. I agreed, signed a short-term contract with Panamin, and started immediately to work. Elizalde got to work, too, planning his speech and also investigating the possibility of a Panamin fund drive in the U.S.

In the course of preparing for this trip, I met with three anthropologists, two Filipinos and an American,* who had never worked with Panamin, but had heard a lot about it. Our discussion lasted almost three hours. I present its highlights here as another sample of the continuing criticism of Elizalde and Panamin.

Elizalde was invariably the first target of critics, and the three anthropologists were no exception. They demanded to know why he was keeping the Tasaday to himself, making them his private toys! What right had he to control who went into the forest? Why had he allowed so much news coverage? Why were only American scientists involved? One of the men claimed that no Filipino anthropologists had been included or even consulted.

I responded that some evaluations relied mainly on opinion. In the case of scientific involvement, however, it was simply wrong to say no Filipinos were involved, mentioning the work of Llamson, Peralta, and Fernandez.

One Filipino said he was aware of this, but emphasized that Fernandez was still working toward his doctorate and had been taken along only as Lynch's protégé anyway. He added that he also had learned that Carlos had been denied the use of interpreters, largely because all the journalists were monopolizing them. I replied that Lynch had stayed only one day, Carlos ten, and that apart from me, the only reporters were MacLeish and Reynolds, and they had visited at different times and had not had access to the interpreters except in concert with Fernandez, Lynch, or Elizalde as part of a deliberate effort to minimize interrogation.

When the American interrupted to say that he had talked with Fernandez since his return and understood that he was not being allowed any further field research among the Tasaday, I insisted that was not true. Fernandez was already planning to make another visit, with Llamzon or another Filipino, and that Elizalde was expected to leave them alone.

The anthropologists wanted to know why I was supposedly so well informed when they were not, which, they said, exemplified Panamin's priorities. All three began talking excitedly, claiming that the Philippine people and scientific community were being denied information that was being circulated in many other countries, particularly the United States.

---

* I agreed to present their views but not their names, owing to the sensitivities of the local scientific community and a desire on their part not to get into a public controversy.

One Filipino insisted that it was time to study the Tasaday without Elizalde's interference: "The Tasaday are not his—they belong to the world!" He said he would lead an expedition of his own except that he knew Elizalde had tribal henchmen at the site who would shoot him if he tried.

I mentioned the Elizalde-Fox report. Only one of them said he had seen it; and only one knew Lynch and Fernandez were working on a report. None knew that a research program was being laid out.

The two Filipinos were among the anthropologists Oscar Trinidad had told me were invited to participate early in the program. They had declined. I asked about this and both men said it was true. One argued that the invitation had come with such short notice that it had been impossible to accept, the other that he had not realized what it was all about, since the discovery had not yet been made public and few details had been included with the invitation. I asked if either of them had followed it up later and both said no, that it would be virtually impossible to work with Elizalde, and, anyway, when scientists were already on a project, protocol dictated that the researcher in charge do the inviting.

As the meeting broke up, we agreed there had been misunderstandings all around. I expressed the belief that there would be very few, if any, journalists allowed into the forest for several months and that scientists would have ample opportunity to conduct research. One scientist said he hoped so; if it did not turn out that way, he was going to urge all Philippine anthropologists to make a unified demand on Elizalde, Panamin, and the government.

A week before the expedition was to start, Fernandez introduced Elizalde to David Baradas, thirty-four, one of the most highly regarded Filipino anthropologists. He had a doctorate from the University of Chicago and had spent the last three years teaching at Mindanao State University and studying the Maranaw people. Fernandez proposed that he join him on the expedition. Elizalde agreed, and then gave both of them something of a lecture about how in the past Panamin had been compelled to concentrate on helping people in trouble—"putting out fires," he said—and now the need was for research to catch up with social action.

About this time, a Spanish film maker arrived with an introduction from a relative of Elizalde's. He and his wife were on the way back to Spain from Vietnam, and he wanted to make a film on the Tasaday. He said he was familiar with jungles and primitive peoples and had spent several years with tribes in Brazil. Elizalde enjoyed his company, but told him that there could be no filming of the Tasaday at present. He should come back in several months.

On May 14, 1972, Elizalde flew to Mindanao and spent two days with the Tboli and Blit. On the sixteenth, Fernandez, Baradas, and I caught the dawn plane from Manila and arrived at the Allah Valley Airport about nine o'clock. To our surprise the Spaniard and his wife were there, waiting. They had just flown in from Davao and were going to visit the Tasaday.

The Panamin helicopter soon arrived, and the Spanish couple and I were told to get aboard. We flew directly to the mountain landing pad, by-passing the Tboli and Blit settlements. Baradas and Fernandez arrived next, then Elizalde and his regular party came in from Blit.

Only after Elizalde arrived did any Tasaday appear. Presumably Lobo, Balayam, and Sindi had been watching unobserved, because they rushed up minutes after he landed. Balayam bubbled with excitement. He embraced Elizalde, Mai, and others he recognized. Sindi, more shyly, did the same. Lobo jumped on Elizalde and then Ching.

Immediately after reaching the tents, which had not been taken down at the end of the last visit, Mai walked to the caves. He returned to report that there had been a great deal of construction. We had been gone less than three weeks, but from his description it sounded as if the Tasaday had experienced an industrial revolution.

Indeed, when we saw it for ourselves later, it looked revolutionary. Four wooden stands, one tripodal and the rest four-legged, had been erected beside fire areas to hold wood so it could dry and be handy; next to the stands were platforms for sleeping. And all were in the spacious mouth of the lower cave.

This was the most surprising development—that most of the Tasaday had moved out of the upper cave. Only Bilangan's family remained there; Balayam and Sindi were still in the middle cave. Everyone else was living below, with their platforms and wooden stands, under the arching dome in front of the low-ceilinged dark chamber inside the mountain. Each stand was about four feet high and had two or three tiers. Two stands were flush against the rocky wall; the others had boulders for support. They had been sturdily made by notching limbs together and binding them with rattan strips and vine. The constructions were surprising and impressive, and the Tasaday seemed pleased with them and with our interest in them.

The new arrangement surely gave individuals and families more space and relative privacy, and there were no corners in the ceiling where smoke could hang—but we wondered if something more than convenience was involved. What had the move out of the upper cave meant? Was it a splitting of the group? Perhaps the first step in a move out of the caves entirely, out of the forest?

During the next few days, we asked in several different ways why they had moved; each time the answer was simply that it had seemed like a good idea, they just felt like it. We suggested that perhaps it was better below because it was less crowded. Dul replied, "It is good both places. We like it here and we like it up there."

We subsequently noted that two of the wood racks had beveled edges on the shelves and legs, and that the sleeping platforms, of thick flattened bark, were more solid than any the Tboli had built at our camp and were large enough for several people.

One evening, we observed a major effect of the move on group life: each family unit had its own sleeping platform and space around it, creating several islands of territory. This would have been impractical in the smaller, upper cave.

The construction also caused new sanitation problems. The lower area had an unpleasant odor and there were swarms of flies. This was because some of the urine and excrement of infants soaked into the wood, even though it was being cleaned up as quickly as before, and food particles were getting trapped under the platforms and in the niches and crevices around large rocks, which the upper cave did not have.

Mai and Fludi demonstrated how to lift the platforms and clean beneath them, and explained that it was necessary to extract all garbage that fell among the rocks. They showed how water should be used to scrub away traces of urine and feces. This brought a noticeable improvement; after another demonstration two days later, the problem appeared to have been solved—the odor had disappeared and there were far fewer flies. But flying insects would probably always be somewhat of a problem because the lower cave lacked the upper cave's smokiness, which had acted as a repellent.

Another significant result of the move was that there were more fires to be fueled. The upper cave usually had three fires, with only one burning high. But at least four fires were needed below, plus one for Balayam and one for Bilangan. The fuel requirement was more than doubled because the firesites were more widely separated, which reduced the efficiency of each fire.

There was no significant use of the inner chamber at the lower cave. The most prominent position at the new site was atop several boulders, where Dul and Udelen had established their place. Mahayag and Dula were about six feet below and in front of them. Kuletaw and Sekul were about thirty feet away, against the left wall looking out of the cave. Lefonok's platform was against the same wall. Tekaf and Ginun had a small place but shared Lefonok's much of the time.

Henceforth, whenever we arrived, Dul usually was on her family's platform, which had the best view into the valley and was in direct line with the path from our camp. We were reminded of a tape-recorded remark by Balayam about the Tasaday's creators: Bebang (first man) was owner of the top of the caves, and Sidakweh (one of his wives) owned the lower part. In the ensuing days Dul revealed a surprisingly strong position in the group. From that time on, at least 80 per cent of the time we were at the caves was spent in the lower one, usually around the centrally located platform of Dul and Udelen.

The first day of this expedition Lobo and Udo brought us a tiny bird with a vine thread tied to one leg. Lobo used the thread as a leash; when the bird tried to fly away it fell and dangled helplessly. Lobo set the bird in his hand, held it up for display, then raised it to his puckered lips as if to kiss it. Udo, who was carrying the bird's nest, danced around and asked to have the bird, and Lobo gave it to him. We were told that Lolo had found a bird and shot it with a bow and arrow, then roasted and ate it. This was the first we had heard of them killing and eating birds; it was surprising, saddening.

A soft rain began to fall while we chatted. The Tasaday said they had planned to go fishing but because of the rain would stay home. Balayam sat beside Tekaf and they communicated for several minutes in sign language. Balayam was intent and patient, his motions graceful and precise, as he signed first (we guessed) that they would not go out because of the rain, and then, as Tekaf nodded, that tomorrow he should get Ginun (pointing at her and then at his own chest) and go into the forest (hands together and fluttered away) to dig *biking* (motion of digging with a stick). They could sleep there for the night (one index finger was brought alongside the other, then the touching fingers were laid along his cheek as his head dropped to one side and his eyes closed). Tekaf smiled and nodded and looked at us. We said something like, *"Oh-ho,* Kakay Tekaf," and he smiled more broadly, as if reading our lips. Tekaf was a gentle-looking man with a shy, sweet manner and sad eyes underlined with dark half circles. Ginun was much more retiring and seldom smiled at or even acknowledged anyone, presumably because cataracts had nearly blinded her.

Balayam had told us his uncle had got Ginun from Tasafeng. He seemed to be chief interpreter for the couple, and he acknowledged that he had helped them since he was a boy. Perhaps his gift of mimicry had been nurtured through the learning of sign language. This could explain his facility of perceiving and communicating ideas through gesture, selecting essences of manner and expression as would a caricaturist.

Later that first afternoon we checked our list of Tasaday names with them and found that the group did total twenty-five persons, not twenty-four as had been thought for so many months. Now all the children were named; Bilangan's newest son, the youngest Tasaday of all, was called Ilib, their word for cave. We tried to learn the etymology of *ilib* but were unsuccessful.

The next day Lobo showed up at our camp with a limp. He had

smacked his right big toe with a mallet sometime earlier while pounding a palm trunk to loosen the pith to make *natek*. We had not noticed it the first day; now it was swollen and infected. Dr. Rebong swabbed it with disinfectant and bound it with white gauze and tape. Lobo fidgeted and grimaced during the treatment, but afterward he was proud of the bandage and hobbled around waving his foot like a flag. But, on the third morning when we visited the caves the bandage was off and Lobo's toe looked much worse, puffy and inflamed. Elizalde asked Lobo to come with him to the tents so the doctor could treat it again, but Lobo refused adamantly, saying it would be too painful. Rebong was summoned and Lobo consented to treatment only if he could sit in Elizalde's lap. As the infection was being treated with disinfectant he screamed and writhed in Manda's arms.

Rebong said the toenail should be removed. "It eventually will come off anyway," he said. "It's very loose and the infection will clear up faster and better if I remove the nail now. It's so loose, it won't be difficult."

Manda said to consult the older Tasaday and Mai translated Doc's recommendation to the group that had gathered. Balayam listened, frowned, and looked around. Dul unhesitatingly said, "No!"

"But," Rebong implored, "it would be so much better. Tell them it would be better, Mai."

Mai did, but Dul repeated, "No." The other Tasaday said nothing.

I wanted to ask if Dul had a specific reason for objecting—perhaps it involved a taboo—but Manda shook his head. "No, it's clear what she said. If we keep asking, they'll think we're trying to pressure them. Do the best you can, Doc."

While Doc treated other small cuts and ailments of the Tasaday, the wife of the Spanish film maker sat on a rock in front of the cave rubbing beauty lotions on her face and applying make-up. Her husband was making still photographs, his movie camera having been forbidden; he told Elizalde, in Spanish, that he needed to use flash bulbs. Manda told him not to, that the Tasaday did not like that. Half an hour later, however, at the upper cave with Ching as guide, the man photographed Etut and her children, and used his flash bulbs anyway.

The wife, an attractive blonde of about thirty with smooth pink skin and a shapely plump figure, usually looked lost and miserable. Her troubles had started with the walk to the camp from the landing pad. It exhausted her, and upon reaching the tents she heaved herself onto a folded canvas and lay breathing heavily for nearly an hour. Her husband, a craggy, ruggedly handsome man, spoke to her softly in Spanish; he seemed embarrassed.

Elizalde and the girls were solicitous of her at first, but after a while they became impatient with her complaints about the weather, her feet, the food. She found the Tasaday "cute," comparing them to "little monkeys."

On the second morning, the Tasaday made fire and the woman fussed over the wooden drill—she had to have it. Her husband and Elizalde stepped away to look at something and returned to find she had the drill and that the Tasaday, apparently in response to her acted-out entreaty, had told her to keep it. Elizalde said she could not have it. She insisted that the Tasaday had given it to her. Perhaps so, he replied, but visitors were not allowed such souvenirs; the written rule was that no artifacts, tools, plants, or anything else were to be taken except for scientific or equally valid reasons. She did not have a valid reason, Elizalde said, and looked to her husband to intervene. The husband talked to her in Spanish, and finally she put down the drill and, sulking, stomped off down the trail to the camp.

It was time for lunch, so the rest of us followed. As we ate, the husband half apologized for the incident, but then confided in Spanish to Elizalde that he had searched for years in South America for a fire drill and desperately wanted one. As Elizalde later told it, the man said, "I know the rules, and I know I signed the paper saying I agreed, but still . . . I must have a drill! I've simply got to have one!"

Elizalde told him he would think about it. That evening, he instructed Mai to secretly make a drill like the Tasaday's.

The gray sky turned darker during lunch and clouds hung heavily over the forest. Lobo, Gintoy, and Udo came to the tent and said the Tasaday had again called off a plan to go to the stream for food because it looked like rain.

Lobo and Udo huddled among us and teased and played for an hour. Gintoy stayed all the while but smiled and watched from a few feet away, as usual. He never joined in, possibly because he was self-conscious of his ringworm and fungus conditions. His face looked ghostly, as if powdered, and his skin was crusty to the touch. Gintoy rarely hugged or embraced Elizalde or any others, including Tasaday. Except for his skin and the beginnings of a goiter, however, Gintoy looked healthy. He was between fifteen and twenty years old, slightly younger than his brother, Adug, who was handsome, golden-skinned, and lively, although he, too, had the slight bulge of a goiter on his throat. Like most of the Tasaday men, they had excellent posture, straight bodies and graceful carriage. Doc Rebong said he thought external treatment of Gintoy's skin condition would be futile; it would require daily dosages of special capsules for months if it was to be helped at all. The goiters were the result of insufficient iodine, which iodized salt would have prevented, Rebong said, but it was too late to make the goiters go away. However, treatment might prevent them from enlarging.

Before the boys returned to the caves Manda gave them knives to replace three that had been broken and one for Gintoy, who had not received a knife before.

The boys' prediction about rain was fulfilled soon after they left. It poured all afternoon so we stayed in the tents until it stopped, after dinner. Manda and four or five more of us walked to the caves about seven-thirty and found the Tasaday curled up on their platforms beside fires. The children were asleep, some under rice sacks left from previous expeditions. Balayam and Sindi came down from their cave. Dul, Dula, Udelen, and Mahayag gathered around, then Lobo, Adug, and Gintoy. We sat for an hour, chatting over nothing in particular: How was the *biking* these days? The children? The knives? Small talk. Manda and Mai asked if they had any problems, did they need or want anything?

The Tasaday said everything was fine, thanked Elizalde for the knives; they were not relaxed but subdued, almost sullen. Balayam made an effort to rouse enthusiasm, capering around in the dark, laughing and chortling and *oh-ho*ing. But it was forced, like a cheerleader whose team is fifty points behind with a minute left in the game. Balayam said something to Mahayag, who carried on for a while, too, but without success. Flashlights came out and Balayam went through what had become something of a comedy routine: trying to start a fire, failing, and shaking his head in puzzlement. Mai made shadow animals on the cave wall with his hands and then some Tasaday played the game in which they tried to catch the light's beam in their hands. The atmosphere grew increasingly friendly, but still lacked warmth and spontaneity. Manda asked Mai to talk with Sindi privately to find out if there was trouble of some kind. The rest of us said good night.

Sindi's comments to Mai did nothing to explain the Tasaday's mood. Or was it *our* attitude? Perhaps we had become accustomed to constant playfulness. They might have been perfectly comfortable, and we merely imagined otherwise. Sindi said the move out of the upper cave had not meant anything was wrong. She mentioned that she had helped make a platform to dry wood over fires, and recalled that the Tasaday had said they would run away if Momo Dakel was not around when strangers came—and if the strangers gave chase the Tasaday would use arrows against them. She said the Tasaday liked Fernandez and Baradas but were not happy with the Spanish couple.

The most surprising of her comments was about using arrows against people. That idea, like shooting the bird, was new and surely had come from exposure to us. But how? None of the expedition members had carried bows and Elizalde was unaware of any discussion with the Tasaday on the subject. He suspected that Sindi suggested it. Or perhaps warnings about strangers coming into the forest had inspired the idea. There had been little doubt that loggers would have come someday, if allowed, but supposedly that worry was past; perhaps too much had been made of the danger of strangers.

Later that night, Mai got to the source of the moodiness and reported it at breakfast. Balayam told him that the day of our arrival the Tasaday had planned to go fishing but delayed because we came, and then it rained. They put fishing off until the next day, but then we came to the caves again and, with Lobo's toe treatment and other things, the morning slipped away. Then came the confusing episode over the fire drill. To top it all, Balayam said, while the blonde woman was sitting on the rock by the caves she had twisted off a leafy branch from a tree. This meant trouble, he said, and when it rained again all afternoon, preventing the Tasaday from gathering in the stream, the Tasaday knew that the tree or mountain spirit was punishing them for the breaking of the leaf. The principal result of all this was that they had had very little to eat and they were upset.

Elizalde went to the caves and told the Tasaday again that they should go out whenever and wherever they wished, and if our presence was obstructing them, they must say so. He gave them rice to make up for their inability to gather food, as had been done on earlier occasions, and the Tasaday cheered up at once. They explained about the taboo against cutting or breaking leaves or branches from certain trees or plants in and around the caves; violation would bring punishment such as yesterday's rain. Asked about the Spanish man and woman, the Tasaday indicated, with evasive and glum looks, that they did not have big love for them.

That afternoon, after a discussion with Ching and then over the radio with Bart, Elizalde advised the Spaniards that the helicopter had developed a minor problem but it would require a thorough overhaul, taking several days. They could stay in the jungle with us if they wished, but if they were ready to leave the chopper would make one last trip the next morning. Otherwise it would be at least a week, probably longer, before they could leave. The woman was eager to go; the husband preferred to stay but really had no choice. They visited the caves briefly in late afternoon to say good-by. The woman tried to get Lobo to sit with her for a photograph, but each time she sat beside him he jumped up and ran away. The couple left the next morning, the man proudly clutching a fire drill that he assumed was the Tasaday's, but was in fact the handiwork of Mai.

Later, Elizalde said it had been a mistake to let them come, but that he had been compelled by circumstances. They had arrived with an introduction from a member of the family; he had cabled Spain to double-check their references and was told the man was highly regarded as a film maker. But then another cable arrived from Spain saying that the first report was not exactly correct—the man was known for adequate work but was not very highly regarded. Elizalde said he had then ruled out the visit to the Tasaday, and the couple said they were leaving for Spain. But the day after he reached Tboli, he received word they had flown on their own to Davao City, where they cabled Panamin that they changed plans at the last minute and would take their chances on getting to see the Tasaday, please send a plane.

"So I did. What could I do? You couldn't just let them sit there. And we had to go to Tasaday right away, so we brought them along."

The last evening in camp the Spaniard had called him aside for a confidential talk, disclosing that in the tourist business in Europe he had important friends who arranged high-class tours around the world. He proposed that a small lodge be built—something tasteful and in keeping with the surroundings, nothing cheap or junky—across the stream from the caves; not too close, of course. Small tours—no more than twenty people—could be brought to the Philippines, shown a few sights around the islands, the climax of which would be a two-day visit to the Tasaday caves. It would, he predicted, be a tremendous hit.

Elizalde said no, but, upon hearing of the proposal, others of us agreed it had been a superb idea and suggested several added attractions: Bilangan and his children could set up a small tool factory and sell souvenir stone hatchets inscribed "Welcome to the Tasaday caves"; Sekul and Kuletaw could peddle leaf G strings and skirts; Balayam could give a concert at the upper caves, singing and doing imitations of persons selected at random from the audience. The big event would be the birth of Etut's baby, for which the tour fee would be doubled; only carefully screened tourists would be allowed to watch.

To my knowledge, the couple was never heard from again.

The Tasaday were jovial the next morning, pleased with the rice and a bright sunshiny day. Their living area was freshly swept. Mahayag, Kuletaw, and their wives had gone out, and Dul sat like a Buddha atop the family platform, center stage, with her increasingly excess poundage in folds around her middle and bulging breasts. We noticed that Balayam would glance at her before speaking; once, he waited quite a while before answering a question. Lucy and Mila made one of their rare visits to the caves and Dul scrutinized them throughout their stay. Elizalde was keenly sensitive to her seemingly increased importance—or had it existed all along and we simply had not noticed? He complimented Dul on being a good wife and mother, and then teased her about bossing people around. She laughed, said, "Oh-ho," then looked thoughtful.

The helicopter that had taken out the Spanish couple brought Lindbergh, who had come to the Philippines after a visit to Tonga, in the South Pacific. He reached the caves during a conversation in which the Tasaday were stressing that the leaves in front of the cave were special, never to be cut or broken by anyone.

Then they asked some questions of Fernandez and Baradas: What do you call your place?—Manila; what was it that Felix always carried and talked into, saying "ober . . . ober . . . go-hed"?—the walkie-talkie, which Balayam had called kee-totie but later became known as the *anuk* go-hed, the baby radio. The larger single-side-band radio was the *dakel* go-hed, big radio.

The discussion was steered onto the possibility of strangers' coming. Elizalde was curious about Sindi's report that they said they would use their arrows. He doubted this, suspecting that she had been the one to recommend it. The Tasaday made no mention of using bows and arrows, but they did say they would hide. "When a big bird that is not Momo Dakel's comes here, we will go to a certain place. All of us will go." They asked if we would like to see that place.

Bilangan, Mahayag, Balayam, and Sindi led us up a trail starting at the outside north wall of the lower cave and circling up and around the mountain. We passed the vine swing Lobo had surprised me on one day and continued for about half an hour, following the barest of trails, dropping down from a ledge and through heavy tangles of trees, vines, and bamboo, crossing logs, ducking under an arbor of leafy branches. Just ahead was another cave.

It curved along a rocky incline for more than sixty feet and was about ten feet deep. The sharply uneven ceiling was roughly eight feet high in some spots, twenty feet in others. The cave had a small chamber at one end. Velvety moss greened the rocks and the charred remains of a few fires were the only obvious signs that anyone had been there. Our guides said the cave was used when they were out gathering and got caught by rain or darkness.

We all relaxed in the cave for a while. Lindbergh had some questions he wanted to ask the Tasaday, and it seemed like a good time to do so. Mai, who had acquired considerable fluency in speaking Tasaday, translated.

Lindbergh: "What do you think of our way of life—that which you have seen so far?"

Balayam: "We think the things we have seen are good. The place where you outsiders live must be good."

Mahayag: "Things we like we will copy. If we see things we don't like, we will tell you."

Lindbergh: "What do you like best of ours?" (We predicted the answer would be knives.)

Balayam started to answer and then discussed it with the others. *"Oh-ho,"* they all said in apparent agreement upon a reply.

Balayam: "We like Momo Dakel. We don't like people with sharp looks and loud voices. We like no hard looks and no big talking."

Lindbergh: "But what do you like best of the things we have brought?"

But they continued talking about people—most were good, but not those people with sharp looks and hard voices. One Tasaday also said:

"We seem to get a wound inside us when people are asking, asking, asking. They want us to make answers, but we only know what we know."

This reply might have been taken as criticism of the questioning going on at that very moment, but the Tasaday did not act unhappy. They treated it like a game.

Lindbergh: "Well, then, what do you like best? How would you rank these things—knives, cloth, medicine, bow and arrow?"

They said all were good, they liked all those things. But then they seemed to get confused. There was the possibility that they thought they were being asked to choose among these things—either to receive more, or to give up the least important. Mai tried the question another way and one said: "Dokoto is best."

"You mean medicine is best?"

"Yes, Dokoto and medicine."

Baradas then said, "Carlos and I wish to learn your language. Will that be all right with you?"

"Oh-ho," they said enthusiastically and laughed. Bilangan said: "And we also want to learn the way you talk."

Lindbergh: "Would you like to have a helicopter of your own?"

There was much laughter and giggling, with hands clamped over mouths.

Balayam: "I'd like very much to have a big bird like Momo Dakel Diwata Tasaday. It would give me a very good feeling. But we would need Kakay Ching and Kakay Balat [Bartolo] to make the bird fly for us."

Lindbergh: "What would you do with the big bird?"

They discussed this, then Bilangan said, "We don't know. We would wait for Momo Dakel Diwata Tasaday."

The Tasaday seemed to enjoy the questions, and afterward they laughed and hugged Elizalde. He asked them if they had ever heard of a Tasaday person named Kasuk (the old man at Blit).

Bilangan looked thoughtful for several seconds and then said, "When I was a child, I was told of a person with that name who had lived in our cave. But I don't know what happened to him." He shook his head.

This cave seemed to contradict the Tasaday's earlier statement that they knew of no other caves. Perhaps it was because they had been asked if there were any more caves like the main ones—this cave was much different. Or perhaps they had deliberately kept it secret.

Elizalde, Mai, and I agreed that there must be many caves in the forest. Mai asked Balayam about it and he said, in confidential tones, "Yes, there are other caves. We will show some to you, but we would not want the new ones [apparently meaning Lindbergh, Fernandez, and Baradas] to know about them yet."

We returned to the main caves. Lindbergh continued on to the tents, planning to walk by the stream; Fernandez and Baradas went with

Bilangan to watch him hunt for *ubud* and *biking*. Balayam and Mahayag examined my cameras and indicated they wanted to look through the view finders. Each took a camera from my neck and peered through, laughing and exclaiming *"Ta-suk, ta-suk"* (their word for the sound of the shutter). They wandered around for about ten minutes, looking through the view finders; each time they pressed the release button and heard the click they shouted and came back to me to have the film wound and the shutter cocked again. Eventually they learned to do this themselves and repeated it again and again. They had not seen photographs (except possibly once in the second or third meeting at the forest's edge, Elizalde told me; somebody had a Polaroid camera and may have shown prints to a few Tasaday, but he was not sure), and they did not know the purpose of the camera, but the sound and the unusual views they got through wide-angle and telephoto lenses must have amused them.

Dul asked if we would like to see another cave. She and Udelen, each carrying a child, and Mahayag led us around the other side of the mountain this time. We crossed several small jungled slopes and a low ridge, then followed a narrow stream until we reached a *natek* press below a thin fall of water that slid off a huge table-flat rock imbedded in a hillside. We clambered up the embankment and through a thick growth of bamboo, detoured around a tree with a beehive, and continued upward to a small rock shelter. It was a dark, damp niche under an overhanging rock, big enough for half a dozen people. We saw a large black spider and a bird's nest inside, and pig tracks marked the lower lip. While we rested, Mahayag went back to get honey. He yelped a couple of times from bee stings, causing Dul to laugh, and returned with a chunk of honeycomb. The hive was old and dry and the comb had little honey. Elizalde broke off a piece of the comb and bit into it—and into a dead bee entombed inside. He spat and gagged; the Tasaday guffawed.

Continuing on, we reached a path that took us, in a sweeping rise along a curving, rocky face, past three large niches in soft, yellow stone and up more than one hundred feet. At the top was a shelf and a shallow chamber ten feet deep and high enough to stand in. A trickle of water fell in front of the cave. We rested inside on boulders. Manda gave Dul a bead necklace. Dul was thrilled, beaming as he put it over her head, and when Udelen came back from a short walk she immediately showed him the necklace. He gave a long admiring "ooh," and, standing behind her, tried to reach around to touch the necklace but jabbed her in the breast by mistake. She flung his hands away. Udelen looked surprised, glanced up to see me looking at him, and made an embarrassed giggle. He was a quiet and gentle man. With Dul's strength and big-mama eminence, he seemed doomed to be a henpecked husband.

I asked Mahayag where Lefonok's late wife had come from. He paused a moment and told Mai that he did not know; we should ask Lefonok.

We said that because Dul, Dula, and all the other women came in from other groups, we wondered if that meant Tasaday women went out to other groups. It seemed certain that they did; there were only two females, Kalee and Siyul, both under ten years old, who were born at Tasaday. Mahayag shrugged and said something that Mai took to mean either that he did not know or had no comment. Mahayag remained friendly during this exchange, but it was obvious we would get no information from him.

We returned to the main caves—slipping and falling occasionally, to the delight of Dul, who looked back and laughed as she moved along briskly with Maman on her hip.

Fernandez and Baradas arrived shortly with Bilangan, who carried the edible cores of two *ubud* palms. Mai joined them as they sat with Bilangan on the path leading to the upper caves, and they checked their word lists and the data they had collected on the language. Elizalde stretched out on a platform and napped. Igna and Sindi chatted together beside Dul on her platform.

As I was wandering around taking pictures, I noticed Dul summon Adug and say something to him. He trotted off and spoke to Bilangan, who nodded, resuming talking to the anthropologists for a minute, then walked over to Dul. They had a brief discussion, then Bilangan shrugged and walked past Fernandez and Baradas to the upper cave. A few minutes later he went into the forest.

It seemed unusual, and later at the tents Mai and I mentioned to Igna that I had seen her sitting next to Dul during that talk with Bilangan. Igna nodded and knew immediately to what we referred. She said Dul had sent Adug to tell Bilangan she wanted to talk to him. When he arrived, Dul said, "Why are you talking to those people so long? We don't know them well yet."

"But we are only talking. Kakay Mafoko is there," Bilangan replied.

"Yes, but still we don't know these new ones yet. We must be careful. It would be better for you to get firewood." And he did, Igna said.

We asked if Dul often gave orders like that and Igna said not often, but that Dul was a very important person and was considered by other Tasaday to have good ideas, good thinking. Igna said Sindi confirmed that, then seized the opportunity to change the subject: Sindi would like to go to Blit for one day to visit her mother.

Most of us were scheduled to leave the next morning. Fernandez and Baradas would stay, with Fludi as their interpreter, Dog Love as radio operator, and two Tboli—Manuel and Dad Tuan, the younger brother of Fludi and Mai—to help cook and clean up.

Mai reported to Elizalde Sindi's request to visit her home. At the caves that evening, with about three-fourths of the Tasaday present and in good humor, Manda explained that he would be leaving the next day and that his good friends Carlos and David would stay. They would be learning how to speak Tasaday and would ask questions, but they were friends of the Tasaday and did not mean to bother them. Elizalde asked the Tasaday to please help them and to speak up if they were bothered. If the Tasaday were troubled or wanted anything, they should tell Carlos or Fludi. The Tasaday said, "*Mafeon, mafeon* [good, beautiful]."

Dul, whose youngest son, together with Lefonok's youngest, had been receiving daily medication from Rebong for skin ailments, asked about continuing that. Elizalde told her medicines would be available and the men here would know what to do.

Everyone seemed satisfied and chatted aimlessly in the dark. Balayam and Adug sang and played with flashlights. Mahayag sat on a rock and put his arm around me and murmured my name and *"mafeon"* and *"oh-ho"* over and over. It was all very relaxed and quiet, perhaps too quiet for Balayam, who began his cheerleading. He laughed and laughed, calling upon Mahayag and Adug to join in. Perhaps Balayam got the idea for this hearty, fake laughter from Dafal, who was fond of suddenly, for no apparent reason, letting out a long, shrill, cackling laugh that startled people and then caused them to laugh after him.

As we left the cave Manda, Igna, Sindi, and Balayam conferred about Sindi's wish to visit Blit. She said it was for Momo Dakel to decide if she could go. He said it was up to Balayam. Balayam said it was up to Momo Dakel. Finally it was agreed that Sindi would go but must return as soon as possible.

We talked at the tents until late. Lindbergh was impressed by the Tasaday's choice of medicine as their favorite gift from the outside world. But supposing one of the Tasaday became deathly ill, he asked, what would happen—would Panamin try to treat him here, bring in doctors or surgeons, or take the patient out to a hospital? Of course, doing anything at all would influence the natural order that had long prevailed, Lindbergh said, and wondered if it might pose an ethical-moral problem in certain cases. It was agreed that it could but that the priority would go to the well-being of the Tasaday, which would have to be judged on a case-to-case basis. Mahayag's hernia was cited as such a potential problem.

Elizalde was more concerned this particular evening, however, about going out of the forest and leaving outsiders behind, although he knew Fernandez and Baradas were bright and able. Nevertheless, he was concerned, because he knew a long time in the forest could affect any outsider. He was worried also that the anthropologists might live in the caves; they had told him that the subject came up with Bilangan, who said they would be welcome to stay in the caves. Elizalde was insistent that they not do so at this time. Perhaps later, if at all, he said, and probably not then unless it was with the intention of living just as the Tasaday did for a long time, eating their food, helping them gather it, and so on.

Adding to his specific concern was an uneasiness about scientists in general. Elizalde would be in the U.S. for much of the time Fernandez and Baradas would be in the forest. Fludi had been instructed to help the researchers all he could, but his first priority was the welfare of the Tasaday. Mai, from his base at Tboli, would have over-all authority while Elizalde was away. If the Tasaday complained or seemed upset about anything, Fludi and Mai would have to smooth things out.

The next morning, after bidding the Tasaday good-by and dropping off Sindi and Igna at Blit, the rest of the departing visitors flew to Tboli, where Elizalde worked on matters requiring attention before he left the country, approximately ten days later.

He and Mai also transcribed the one short tape recording made at the lower cave on this latest visit. Recording had been virtually discontinued because the lower cave was so spacious and the people so spread out that reproduction quality was poor; then, too, there was less need, because the Tasaday now expressed themselves more openly.

Elizalde summarized the one taped session in a few sentences: Dul and Dula talked excitedly about their gifts of beaded necklaces. Then Dul said, "The things on Igna's ankles are nice [brass bracelets] but she couldn't chase frogs because the frogs would hear her coming and run faster. If I had those things and chased a frog, and it got away, I'd just throw those things in the creek."

Udelen, apparently overhearing their talk, said he would like to have one of "those sparkling sticks [flashlights]. If I had one of those I could walk around the forest at night."

Dul said firmly, "One of those sticks would not be good for you, Udelen."

They chatted about a variety of things then and Lobo said, "If those other ones [apparently the Spaniards] come again, I'm going to run into the forest."

Dul said, *"Oh-ho"* and added that "if anybody sleeps here [apparently in the cave], I'll go into the forest."

Mai said the rest of the tape was largely a repetition of oft-heard remarks about food, gifts, knives, and Momo Dakel Diwata Tasaday.

Elizalde worried about how to handle the matter of his supposed god role. *Diwata* means "spirit" or "godlike figure" in some Philippine dialects, but Elizalde had not established what special meaning it might have for the Tasaday. Mai talked by radio to Dafal at Blit to see if he could furnish anything about *diwata*. Dafal said he had merely told the Tasaday a good man was coming to them, and that a good man is a good man— not necessarily a god, although this was a particularly special man. At any rate, *diwata* was not his word, Dafal said, it was a Tasaday word. He said he had heard them use it for the first time when he showed them how to make *natek*. They remarked, *"Ig-sekal me-do oh natek diwata,"* which, to Dafal, meant "learning to make this natek is a good fortune." So he suggested that Momo Dakel Diwata Tasaday meant the "important man who brought good fortune or good luck."

In the late afternoon Elizalde insisted on driving a group beyond the south end of the Tboli Valley and into a smaller valley. The Jeep broke down and we had to walk back, but the weather was clear and warm and the setting sun made the sky a fiery red. As we walked and talked, Lindbergh recalled that he had once parachuted into a forest at night in a lightning storm. "I was scared, but there was nothing I could do—just float down with the lightning all around me. I landed on a barbed wire fence. I was wearing a heavy bearskin flying suit—we often wore them in those days—and wasn't scratched a bit."

Elizalde was ahead of us, strolling along and joking happily with Ching and Mai.

Lindbergh then reminisced about his experiences with the Ford Motor Company, when he was a consultant for their aircraft program in 1942 and 1943.

"Oh, we had some experiences in those days at Ford," Lindbergh said with a chuckle. "It was an extraordinary place to work. All kinds of things happening all the time. They even had fist fights among some of the staff. And Ford himself—a genius, a real genius, and an eccentric; those qualities seem to go together—was extraordinary. There never was a dull moment around him. This Panamin outfit is the only one I've ever seen quite like it."

14

Trouble at the Caves

SEVERAL of us spent the following week in Manila preparing for the visit to Washington. I was in a darkroom printing exhibit photographs the afternoon of May 30 when Elizalde telephoned.

His voice was gruff as he said a quick hello, and then, "There's trouble. Somebody's trying to get the Tasaday!"

A few minutes before, Mai had radioed from Tboli, reporting rumors that a group of gunmen had entered the Tasaday's area. Minutes after that, Oscar Trinidad phoned him with a message from Fernandez and Baradas inside the forest that the route to Blit was believed to be blocked by a gang of armed men. They asked that Lynch be informed and requested advice on what to do.

It sounded incredible. "There must be some mistake," I said, "some kind of mix-up. Rumors! Who's the source of these reports? Who says there is an armed gang? What the hell is going on?"

"I don't know, damn it!" Manda snapped. "We're trying to check it out . . . trying to raise Mai on the single-side-band right now. We'll get back to you."

I put down the telephone, assuring myself it was a mistake . . . it had to be. Still, my palms were wet.

The phone rang again a few minutes later. Elizalde said, "I don't know . . . sounds serious. We've . . . Wait . . . here's another message from Fludi just coming in. Says he saw footprints near the stream this morning and—my God!—there's shooting! Shooting going on! Hold on . . . wait . . ."

I heard excited voices in the background as I stood gripping the phone.

I couldn't believe what I had heard. Shooting! It was almost beyond imagining. Who . . . why? Elizalde returned to the phone. He said Fludi's message, relayed by Mai, reported footprints had been spotted this morning, and two hours later men were seen in the stream directly below the tents. Fludi shouted, the men stopped, turned, and ran. Fludi fired his carbine.

"That's all we know. No word yet on the Tasaday, so I guess nobody has been hurt. I don't know what the hell is going on . . . Hold on, we just got Mai on another phone hooked into the single-side-band . . ."

After a minute or two, Ching came on the line and said it would take a while, they would call me back.

I put the phone down and tried to think clearly. It still sounded like a ridiculous, terrible mix-up. Why would anybody want to hurt the Tasaday? My imagination conjured visions of panic and wild shooting in the forest, at the caves, the Tasaday wandering around uncomprehendingly and being blasted down by bullets. . . . I tried to stop thinking such things, but instead I suddenly remembered the story of Ishi, the American Indian, and how thirty-three of his Yahi brethren had been massacred by gunmen as they huddled in a cave in California in the 1860's. . . .

Elizalde called back; he was in direct voice contact with Mai, who was in radio contact with Fludi inside the forest. Fludi said he had received word from Blit that a group of outlaw Ubus who lived about one day's walk from Ma Falen's settlement had been seen entering the forest: eight men, all armed with guns. They were bent on creating a disturbance, or, according to one report, intending to "wipe out the Tasaday."

Elizalde said Mai had ordered Fludi to shoot to kill and that Datu Dudim had immediately dispatched an armed team led by Dafal to the caves. According to one Blit, the intruders were led by a mountain man named Kabayo, a notorious troublemaker. His motives were not known. It was rumored the men sought revenge against Elizalde for unknown reasons, but this was later denied. Mai said the Tasaday were aware of difficulty, but did not know the extent of the danger. Most were at the caves, but Udelen, Tekaf, Ginun, Biking, Lolo, Gintoy, Kuletaw, and Mahayag were out gathering food.

At 6:10 P.M. Mai reported that, although a few Tasaday were still out, the situation seemed to be under control. Dafal had reached the camp with four armed Blit. They apparently had run all the way at an extraordinary speed and made it before dark, taking about four hours over the mountains. Together with Fludi, Manuel, and Dad, they were forming a guard perimeter around the caves; Dudim was to dispatch another team of men to reinforce them. Mai said he understood Balayam and Bilangan would stay at the caves but would help keep watch for strangers.

Elizalde had informed Lynch of the situation. Although the picture had clarified somewhat, it was impossible to predict what would develop.

Mai's confidence and the presence of Dafal and the Blit reinforcements were reassuring to Elizalde. "It may not be as bad as we thought," he said. "Fludi is cool. Very cool. Solid head. He never gets flustered and he's been through some tough ones. Nobody is better to take care of a situation like this, except maybe Mai. It sounds better . . . We can only wait."

A group gathered at his house early in the evening, before he arrived home: Norman Certeza, Ching, Oscar, Bert Romulo, a Panamin executive, and Vince Revilla, a business associate and longtime friend. Some thought the situation was in hand and Elizalde should stick to his plans to leave for Tokyo in the morning, preparatory to flying to the U.S. June 4. Others thought he should go to the caves, or at least wait in Manila until matters were clearer.

When Elizalde came in, he said he thought he should go to Mindanao. But Ching told him that the Panamin helicopter was undergoing repairs; it would take at least three days to be reassembled and ready to fly. Just then President Marcos telephoned, about an unrelated matter. At the end of the conversation, Elizalde asked to borrow an army helicopter. He said only that he needed it badly in Mindanao. Marcos said yes, he would order the helicopter to be standing by at the Davao City airport the next morning.

I went home about ten and later talked to Elizalde by phone. He said Mai reported the situation was stable, guards were in position all around the caves, no more intruders had been sighted, all the Tasaday apparently had been accounted for—although four or five were still out—and supposedly were unaware of the extent of the difficulty; the scientists were safe; Joe Torres had taken a group of Ma Falen's men to Kabayo's place and Dudim also had sent a team there from Blit led by Sut, Igna's husband.

"Mai and everyone thinks we should go to Tokyo as scheduled," Elizalde said. "Maybe we will." Mai would go in as soon as Panamin's helicopter was ready—in about thirty-six hours. Elizalde decided to delay his trip to Japan at least one day—too many questions remained unanswered. Mai would report again to Manila at 6:00 A.M.

Joyce, my wife, voiced my own thoughts: "I can't imagine taking up a gun for anyone outside of our family, but I think I could use one to protect the Tasaday. What have they done to hurt anyone?"

Coincidentally, world news media were reporting on a conference on world disarmament. The world's great powers were discussing how to control nuclear weapons while the Tasaday were facing guns for the first time in their lives.

Mai's messages the next day said all was well. There had been no further trouble, and footprints of the intruders were sighted at the stream heading out of the forest. A group from Blit was on watch for them outside. With Lynch's concurrence, Fernandez and Baradas had decided it was best to come out of the forest for now; the disturbance had made research temporarily impossible.

Matters seemed to be under control, so Elizalde decided to fly to Japan the following day. Mai would maintain guards in the forest, Dudim outside. But about ten that night Elizalde telephoned.

"We're going in. Got to." His voice was tight. "It's worse—more shooting tonight. About eight o'clock there was a lot of gunfire *right at the tents!* Sounds very bad. We're leaving as soon as possible, setting it up now. You with us?"

A transcript of radio communications from Tasaday to Blit kept by Amy Rogel at Tboli gives the following account:

7:50–7:55 P.M. Carlos, David, and Fludi were talking in the tent of Tau Bong. While this was going on, Dafal attempted to boil coffee. Suddenly, while in the process of blowing the fire, he was fired at [from] a distance of less than 30 meters. After immediately taking cover, Dafal fired back towards the direction of the shot. They don't know whether they hit anyone.

8:33 P.M. David, Carlos, and Dog Love took cover in the tent. Half of their bodies were outside tent while maintaining silence.

8:55 P.M. Firing very often . . . many shots, like stars. Bullets were hitting trees where they were taking cover. Via VHF Saro [Mai] has given orders for Manuel to use applegreen [grenades] if possible.

9:05 P.M. Somebody seems to have been hurt from the other side. Heard sound of moaning at a distance from Dida [Fludi] which was less than 30 meters. Shot fired at group believed to have come from a 12-gauge shotgun. After hearing the sound of people from other side, they heard them scampering towards the direction going downstream. Manuel fired. Fludi fired. Toward the direction where 3 shots came from.

Mai was relaying these and other reports to Manila every few minutes. He said there was no word of injuries among the Panamin group, but that there was extreme confusion and some people were unaccounted for out in the darkness.

Over the next few hours, the only additional information from the forest was that no more shooting had occurred, that everyone had been accounted for, and that Mahayag had returned to the caves earlier in the day and then had gone out again.

Ching pushed all night for repair of the Panamin helicopter; it would be able to fly to Davao at first light. Several of us would go by commercial jet, be picked up by the chopper in Davao, and fly directly into the forest.

By 7:30 A.M., June 1, Elizalde, Certeza, Ching, Lucy, Felix, several other security guards, and I were in Davao awaiting the helicopter. When it failed to arrive, Ching phoned Manila and learned it had taken off but had to turn back because of a malfunctioning rotor blade. Elizalde put through an emergency call to the Presidential Palace and arranged for army helicopters. (Two had waited at Davao the day before but left when nobody showed up.)

The Elizalde Company's twin-engine plane arrived shortly from Manila with Johnny Ugarte, and another small fixed-wing plane was chartered in Davao. The army choppers were waiting as we landed in a rainstorm at Allah Valley, and took us to Tboli. Each helicopter had a pilot, co-pilot, and two machine gunners.

We landed at Tboli at 12:15 P.M. A large crowd greeted us in the rain. While the helicopters were refueled, the Tboli danced and sang on the staff-house porch. Rain continued and the sky was dark. The Ubu and Blit radio stations reported bad weather, heavy wind and rain over the forest.

Mai said all had been quiet inside the forest since the shooting. Nobody had been hurt on Panamin's side and all the Tasaday were safe. He said the Tasaday had first heard of Kabayo's coming from Dog Love or Fludi, but had not fully comprehended what it meant. Dul had supposedly said, "If that Kabayo man comes, people should go inside the caves."

About three o'clock, the weather was okay for flying. Just before we boarded the choppers, a local informant ran up to Elizalde and whispered that that morning he had overheard in town that forty thugs "had left General Santos City three days ago in trucks headed for the Tasaday. They belong to—" and he named a powerful logger.

Elizalde nodded and jumped into a chopper. The rain had stopped but the sky was still dark. Our tension was somewhat relieved simply by getting under way.

Within half an hour the helicopters approached the landing ridge from an unusually high angle—the pilots had been instructed to fly as high as possible because of the chance of sniper fire. The first chopper swooped down and hovered over the ridge as we jumped to the ground—Elizalde, Certeza, Ching, Ugarte, Felix, and I. Right behind us, Mai and his group, including Dr. Rebong and Sgt. Roland Daza, of the Philippine Constabulary based at Tboli, leaped from the second chopper. When they were off, Fernandez and Baradas, who had been waiting at the landing pad, climbed aboard and flew to Tboli. There had been no chance to talk with them.

Balayam, Sindi, Lobo, Bilangan, and Adug greeted us on the ridge with their usual warmth and excited good humor, despite the chilly wind and our somber mood.

The Tasaday continued to laugh and chatter as everyone gathered on the landing knoll for the distribution of shotguns, carbines, pistols.

Elizalde checked out each gun and supervised the issuing of ammunition. The M-60 machine gun had been brought for Manuel, and a shotgun was offered to me, but I turned it down. Though I had fired guns, I was not comfortable with them. I was much better qualified to shoot photographs. With a shotgun plus all the camera gear hanging on me, I might accidentally shoot the wrong person, even myself. Norman Certeza had a shotgun and recommended that I take his Spanish .22-caliber pistol: "Put it on safety and into your pocket. If you don't need it, just leave it there. But if you get in a spot, at least you'll have something to defend yourself with." He gave me a quick lesson, loaded the pistol, and I stuck it in a pocket.

Although Elizalde said nothing about it, the last-minute report of a forty-man gang headed this way must have been on his mind. If the men had started by truck three days earlier, they could have taken one of the logging roads and be somewhere in the forest by now. "If there's anybody still here they've got to have seen the choppers," he said. "That may have scared them away—or they may be in an ambush. Keep alert and let's go single file, spread out."

It was similar to a patrol in Vietnam jungles. One man at a time stepped out nervously, cautiously, along the ridge and down into the forest, not knowing what was ahead but expecting trouble. The Tasaday made the most noise, talking and giggling among themselves and clinging to Elizalde and Mai whenever possible. Adug and Lolo even shouldered guns, until they were taken away from them.

The difference between this walk to the caves and all the previous ones struck with depressing effect. Always before, it had been a hike of happy anticipation; this time it was tense and apprehensive, grim.

We reached the tents without incident shortly before five, and it was nearly dark. Rainclouds had closed in again. Fludi, Manuel, and Dad met us. They had deep circles under their eyes. Fludi looked exhausted. All had gone without sleep the past two nights and caught only brief, fitful naps in the daytime. Dafal and his companions had also stayed awake after the shooting.

Soon after we reached camp, a message arrived from Fernandez and Baradas, telling Elizalde that they would have stayed to discuss matters had they known he was coming into the forest. Later, they said they had thought he was out of the country during the first day and night of the trouble, then learned he had not left. When the helicopters came in, they had not expected to see him, and then, because of the confusion, they continued with their plan to leave. They stressed also that during the early stages of trouble one of their messages had been misplaced at Tboli, and when it finally was relayed much later only half of it was sent. This message had proposed a meeting at Tboli of the key people in the project to discuss the situation and plan the next steps. This and other mix-ups heightened the disorder and bewilderment and caused misunderstandings and aggravation.

The party in the forest now numbered thirty men and Lucy, who maintained her usual smiling good nature. A defense perimeter was plotted with two men at each of seven positions leading out from the caves and converging on the opposite bank of the stream. Dafal and his men were posted along the stream. Manuel set up his machine gun at the camp's edge, aiming downhill toward where the shots were believed to have come from the night before.

Lucy set to work over a kitchen fire and prepared dinner—noodle soup, rice, canned squid. The squid was rubbery and tough in its inky sauce, but everyone ate. The guards took turns coming in to eat by flashlight. No lamps or candles were lit, but, of course, whoever was in the forest knew exactly where we were anyway.

Mai peered into the darkness. "Those men are probably out there right now. Waiting. Watching. Watching everything we do."

As we ate we listened to Fludi's account of the trouble. The camp had received a message from Blit that Kabayo and seven others—all named but one—were coming with guns. A lookout was set up and two men were sighted in the stream two hours later. Fludi first thought they were Manuel and Dad. He shouted, the men stopped, apparently startled. Fludi realized they were strangers and fired once. The men ran downstream. He reported this to Blit and Tboli and before nightfall Dafal and his team arrived, making such fast time even Fludi was impressed. It had been quiet the next day, but about 8:00 P.M. Dafal, beside the fire, heard a shotgun cocked nearby in the darkness and instinctively dove to the ground, reaching for his own gun. Fludi, Fernandez, Baradas, Manuel, and Dad were in the main tent. In seconds shooting erupted. Fludi said he thought Dafal fired first but was not sure. A shotgun blasted from somewhere. Manuel fired twice, Dad fired once and then his gun jammed. Nobody kept track in the excitement, but Fludi said he thought two more blasts had come in from the outside and then there was a shout or groan and he heard movement, like running feet. The shooting stopped, but nobody knew how many men were out in the forest. Fernandez and Baradas were unarmed and had flattened themselves on the ground. Feeling exposed in the open tent, they had crawled away from the presumed target area toward the cover of trees outside. Baradas made it before the firing stopped, and then couldn't be found for more than an hour. Everyone was tense and stayed awake the rest of the night.

In the morning Fludi and Manuel found a spent shotgun shell and barefoot prints about sixty feet from where Dafal had been perched by the fire. There were broken branches and tree trunks had scars from buckshot, but the tent was not damaged.

After Fludi finished his account, Dafal, cradling a gun in his arms, told how he had seen Kabayo (a name taken from *caballo,* the Spanish word for horse) once some years ago. He was a big man, strong, smart, and very bad, Dafal said. He had killed, burned, and robbed in the mountains around a place called Lamboling, and *datus* of several tribes wanted to get him. He was a loner but had a band of followers. He hired himself out to lowland exploiters for pay, but also liked to bully people just for pleasure. "Once he decides to move, he does not stop until he gets what he wants," Dafal said sternly. Reports reaching Blit and Datal Tabayong, Ma Falen's place, said Kabayo had told people he had been watching the Panamin helicopter flying in and out all the time and wanted to kill it. "Kabayo himself has two shotguns and his other men are armed. They are good mountain men, good hunters," Dafal said. "The only way to stop this is to get Kabayo."

Some Blit had also heard that Kabayo vowed he was going to "get a taste of the Tasaday," meaning to the Blit that he wanted to kill them. Dafal said he did not know if Kabayo was connected with loggers, but it was possible.

Kabayo lived between the Blit and the Ubu in a remote rocky valley with a high waterfall, and Dafal thought the intruders would go back there and hide until the guards got tired. They might wait for weeks or months. The Blit and Tboli agreed that the only solution was to catch Kabayo. But, as Mai put it, "We can get plenty of volunteers, but only those who are real hunters, real mountain hunters, will be able to get this Kabayo."

Elizalde sent a message to his informant at Tboli to double-check quickly the reported movements of the logging gang from Santos City.

The description of Kabayo eased the sense of mystery somewhat, but the prospect of a long wait while Kabayo relaxed and picked a time to attack created new nerve-racking worries.

"We can get them, sir. We can," Mai told Elizalde.

"Yeah, but time. Time! I was supposed to be in Japan two days ago and in Washington four days from now. We could sit here for weeks trying to get these guys."

"That's right, sir. But once we have a good plan and are prepared, you can go." Mai said that in his view the two key people were the "Mali" boys (not the real name of two brothers known among the Tboli for bravery and cunning and their intimate knowledge of mountains and forests). "That's who I want," Mai said. "With them, Dafal, and a couple of others, that's enough. Other men can guard here, but only a few can go after Kabayo—a few special men."

Mai's plan was for guards to protect the cave area, a team of snipers to deploy along the stream; Sut and his Blit force would wait at Kabayo's home outside the forest; teams of two or three men would then pursue

Kabayo through the jungle. "It will be chase and hunt, chase and hunt. Small teams. We'll either kill him or chase him out. I don't think he'll give up, but if we can get Kabayo, his gang will quit."

Mai explained this plan to Dafal, who said, "Yes, yes . . . good." Then Dafal joined other Blit along the stream for the night.

It was black in the forest; clouds blocked the moonlight. Elizalde said softly, "If they come tonight it will be at about two o'clock, and where we don't expect it. And they'll all come at once. If they are crazy enough to come here in the first place, they're crazy enough to attack us."

Tired from long hours of tension and little or no rest the previous night but still not ready for sleep, several people sat awake in the dark. The mood was heavy with disappointment as well as apprehension. "This may be the end of the Tasaday as we know them," Elizalde said. "Where is the good fortune we brought them?" Nobody responded. In the silence, the events seem to hit with fresh impact and I could almost hear the men thinking: The Tasaday could have been murdered! Would they ever be safe again? Could their life ever be the same as before? Lobo, Balayam, Dul, Udelen . . . innocent people . . . And now, what? Madness!

And with such thoughts came guilt. The argument that loggers indifferent to the Tasaday's welfare would inevitably have entered the forest·was valid—but what if discovery of the Tasaday and the inevitable publicity had speeded up the loggers' reaction? Or had been the inspiration for a gratuitous, cruel attack by outlaws or madmen? The undeniable fact was that Elizalde and Panamin had opened the door. There was no turning back; protection of the Tasaday would be a never-ending responsibility.

When I voiced these thoughts to Elizalde, he shrugged. "Jesus Christ! What have I been saying all this time? You didn't believe it either? Aw, hell, you don't know—you just don't know. What do you think we've been doing down here the last four years? Goddammit! This is nothing yet. Nobody's been killed. Ask the Tboli and the Ubu and the Blaan how many dead they've got. How much blood is on their land? How many of their women have been raped, kids murdered?" His voice was harsh and bitter. "The hell with it! I'm tired of saying it. I've said it enough times.

"Our guilt? Our guilt? Yeah, man, we're guilty because we're supposedly civilized, but we didn't bring those goddamned Kabayo people here. That's bullshit to say that. That's twisted thinking. If we hadn't come, somebody else would have come someday, sometime, somehow, and nobody would have been able to do a damned thing about it. Maybe the world would never have known about the Tasaday, would never have known they even existed. Just be thankful that the scientists happened to be in here when they were. If they weren't here, Fludi and the boys wouldn't have been either. And be glad for the radio. It saved us so far. We've got to give some credit to Norman and Lucky [an engineer Norman had brought in] for that—they've improved our whole communications setup. Imagine what would have happened if Kabayo, or whoever the hell it is, had come in 'to get a taste of the Tasaday,' and there was nobody else here, or only Fludi and his boys and no radio! The Tboli would have got some of them—but these guys are mountain men, mountain fighters. Do you know what that means? They're part of these mountains. They could live in here for weeks, for months, and you'd never know they were around if they didn't want you to. Oh, you might see a footprint now and then, but they're like animals. Live off the land. Can you imagine Lobo or Balayam wandering up to them with an *'Oh-ho, kakay'* and smiling? Blam with the shotguns in the belly!"

After midnight the clouds cleared and moonlight made the tent canvas glow yellow and limned the trees with silver. Those who slept kept their guns beside them.

Dawn of June 2 came gray but by seven o'clock patches of sunshine were lighting the dark green. Lucy was making coffee, rice, and hard-boiled eggs. Elizalde called Dr. Rebong to help her. Men from each guard position took turns coming in for breakfast. None had anything unusual to report.

Roland Daza, of the national police, came in from his outpost, sleepy-eyed in his camouflaged fatigue uniform. Over breakfast, he told us that Kabayo was well known to the police. He was not an Ubu, but a Surallah outlaw, Roland said, and collaborated at times with a former town official who had been kicked out of office and now was a notorious lawbreaker. Roland also mentioned that many stories were being heard about the Tasaday in town. He said an American had been trying to get police escort into the Tasaday forest for some unknown reason, and that some Surallah residents insisted that the Tasaday were actually Tboli that had been trained, undressed, and delivered to the caves, to be shown to visitors as part of a bizarre and sinister scheme. There was a rumor that Panamin had a mining camp in the Tasaday mountains.

While Daza talked, Balayam and Lefonok stepped around the corner of the tent and came inside. They joked with Dad and Manuel, who rattled off a surprising number of Tasaday words. Manuel did an excellent imitation of Balayam's exclamations and laughter. We noticed in the by-play that Balayam used an exclamation new to us: *"Cheet!"* It meant something like "wow," or "oh, boy," or "look at that!" Along with *oh-ho* (yes or okay) and *mafeon* (good or beautiful), *cheet* became a stock exclamatory word for all the Tasaday. Later, we heard more words new to us but never learned whether they were their own or variations of something learned from the Tboli boys, with whom they had developed a lively and close relationship.

Lobo arrived and began a game of hide-and-seek in the unmade beds, poking his head out from under the blankets. Balayam left, but soon passed by again on his way to the caves with a batch of fresh leaves for G strings and skirts—Sindi had returned from a short stay with her mother. The Tasaday's mood seemed far from tense or unhappy.

Elizalde conferred with Mai and Dafal and agreed to send for the Mali brothers. "We can't just sit like this on the defense," he said. "We've got to go out, got to get on the offensive."

He took a dozen men downstream to look for signs of the intruders. Within a mile were two campsites with the remains of fires, half-eaten fruit, and other rubbish. Dafal inspected footprints; they were those of strangers, he said. The group advanced slowly in a formation spread over about fifty yards, with Dudim's son Mafalo and Dafal wading the stream. Three tribesmen were on each side at about ten-yard intervals and ten to twenty yards into the jungle. They were rarely visible from the stream, where I was walking with Fludi, Daza, Felix, Ching, and Elizalde.

A shout came from the left, where a Tboli spotted someone scurrying through the underbrush. The flank men held their positions; the center group moved ahead and saw fresh footprints up a soft embankment. A tribesman scooted up and then, to the left, the greenery rustled. Out walked Lolo with a smile.

He told Fludi several Tasaday were gathering food and had not seen any strangers, but they did notice the unfamiliar fire sites and wondered who made them. Lolo hurried away and returned with Dul, Maman, Tekaf, and Ginun. All greeted Elizalde happily; he suggested they go back to the caves and he would meet them there later. They nodded and strolled upstream.

Dafal found more footprints heading downstream, and followed them until they turned into the forest. About half a mile from camp, Daza and Elizalde selected an ambush site behind heavy foliage on a ten-foot-high embankment, with a clear view along the stream as it rounded a bend. This would be staked out in the afternoon and evening.

Back at the tents the air was warm and muggy with impending rain. Elizalde, working on his speech for the Smithsonian, was interrupted by a message from his informant that the forty-man logging gang had indeed gone looking for trouble, but not here. A double check disclosed they worked for a logger with a new concession on which a rival company was cutting. Much later we were told that the companies had fought and there had been several casualties.

Midafternoon rain turned the stream into a muddy brown torrent. The rain stopped before dusk, and Daza took a three-man team to stake out the ambush site.

Six of us went to the caves and, except for Mahayag's family and Adug, all the Tasaday were there. The mood was playful. Lobo imitated how Fernandez, Baradas, and Dog Love had hurried up the path from the tents and into the lower cave's inner chamber. It was amusing, but sad, too; he was innocent of the danger that lay behind it. Dul contributed to the joking and Balayam clowned, but then he accidentally cut his finger with a knife. He laughed as the blood oozed down his finger and Doc, pistol sticking out of his belt, cleaned and bound the wound.

Etut joined the laughter, too, although she was obviously uncomfortable; she was so big with her pregnancy that her leaf skirt barely covered her belly. Most Tasaday used pieces of rope or string salvaged from the tents to hold up their leaves; Etut had added a second string at the bottom of her skirt to prevent its flaring out. It made her midsection look like a leaf-covered pillow.

Balayam asked for "those things that make the stick sparkle"—fresh batteries for the flashlight. Lobo pranced around, pretending to use a walkie-talkie, saying "Dog Lub, Dog Lub, come in, come in, ober . . ."

Dul sat in her usual prominent position, Udelen beside her grinning and chuckling. Tekaf and Ginun had moved their platform to a spot behind them and communicated there with hand signs.

The sun broke through the clouds, giving the dusk a last flare of light, and the chopper flew over, causing the Tasaday children to scurry for a view, shouting *"Cheet! Cheet!"* It was bringing the Mali boys.

Then, as darkness moved in swiftly and the rain-swollen waterfall splattered down, Elizalde and Mai tried to explain the seriousness of the situation to the Tasaday without frightening them. They described how some bad men carrying dangerous weapons had entered the forest. Balayam nodded and spoke up. "We don't like people with sharp looks and hard voices—we don't want them here. Why should they come here and bother us? We don't have sharp looks and hard voices."

Concern was on his face, but his manner was that of a parent admonishing mischievous children. The other Tasaday chorused, *"Oh-ho! Oh-ho!"* in Balayam's support.

"We will make these people go away," Manda said. "We will use the big bird. Don't worry."

"Mafeon," several Tasaday said. "We are happy that Momo Dakel Diwata Tasaday is taking care of this for us," Dul added.

Manda paused. He wasn't satisfied that the Tasaday understood the danger and that they had to be careful. It seemed impossible to clarify the present danger without terrifying words or examples, which neither he nor anyone wanted to use. "Look, Mai," he said, "tell them that these men can hurt the Tasaday, hurt them badly, so the Tasaday must stay away from them."

Mai translated and Balayam answered. "Yes, these are not good people, but we should not leave the cave. It is better to die here than in the forest. Momo Dakel Diwata Tasaday might come and not be able to find us in the forest."

According to Mai's translation, Balayam had unmistakably mentioned death, a painful subject on some previous occasions, but his manner was not grave; nor was that of any Tasaday. They looked serious, yes, but apparently were not worried, not fearful, because they had no experience of violence, we believed. How much longer could their innocence be preserved? How much longer *should* it be preserved? Elizalde's original intention had been to protect them indefinitely, but if danger worsened they would have to be taught to protect themselves. How much should they be told now?

As Manda and Mai attempted to impress upon them the gravity of the situation, I watched their faces. They listened intently, nodding and blinking, a frown here, a squint there, a hand stroking a chin or cheek, an occasional murmur escaping. But no one trembled, no eyes showed fear or anger. They were being told of danger from evil men, that they could be seriously hurt, yet their reaction seemed to be "Tsk, tsk, that's really not very nice. Rather unpleasant, actually, wouldn't want that sort of thing in here. Awfully good of you to take care of it."

They had responded more deeply to so many other things—the memory of their dead dog, for instance, the one Dafal had given them, had brought tears. Watching them now was like watching children at story hour—and a rather unexciting story hour at that. Some had the look of a very young child who did not believe what he was being told—that his puppy had been run over and would never come home; the puppy had always come home before and, of course, it would do so again. Would anyone be willing to convince the child by showing it the mangled puppy? No. Words had to suffice, as gentle words as were possible.

I felt myself slipping into melancholy as Elizalde and Mai tried to explain matters. To save myself from facing the possibilities that their innocence was about to be destroyed forever, I began to wonder again if I had romanticized their unworldliness. Perhaps they were familiar with warfare and this was merely tame stuff. But, no—we would have noticed signs of hostility and defensiveness by this time. It was no use. I could not believe they knew this aspect of life. Indeed, it occurred to me that children in the sophisticated modern world were far more knowledgeable of violence than these people—how would the Tasaday react to an evening of televised war news, westerns, cops and robbers?

As we left the caves, the Tasaday were again telling stories and chuckling. They gave us hugs and called out good-bys as we walked toward the tents—their tenderness seeming to trail us like a heavy fragrance that was nearly tangible, that could be touched if one just knew how.

This tenderness was even more deeply felt a few minutes later at the camp. We met the Mali boys, who had, it seemed, made a craft of violence.

It was, however, not the Mali brothers who had come, but the elder Mali and a trusted young friend. Mali the younger was, unfortunately, in jail. They joined a meeting in the main tent to discuss how to get Kabayo.

Mali was, in the language of the Old West, a professional gunslinger, a hired gun—what today would be called a contract man. And yet this would not have been entirely accurate, from the accounts I heard. Mali was not for hire to just anyone—he was Tboli and did jobs only for Tboli friends, jobs that usually carried more than a touch of Robin Hood justice.

Mali looked so cool and sinister that it was startling at first, and then strangely amusing. He was probably in his mid-thirties, small, slender, and smartly outfitted in black slacks, black jacket, and black snap brim hat with a wide white band. His smooth brown face was strikingly handsome, with even, sensitive features. A narrow mustache drooped across both corners of his mouth, which seemed always parted in a half-smile that showed the edges of shiny white teeth. His slightly slanted dark eyes at first gave the impression of being heavy-lidded, almost sleepy, but later seemed piercing. They did not dart about, but took in a scene with steady sweeps, as if Mali were memorizing every detail, every face. His hands executed sharp, precise movements, and he sat hunched forward, feet flat on the ground. The only detectable trace of nerves was in an occasional flick of the tongue, which wet his lips.

Mali spoke softly and sparingly to the welcoming group of tribesmen gathered around him. He seemed to have the status of folk hero. Then Mai and Dafal briefly explained the situation and what was needed. It was dark; Mali sat on a sack of rice in the orange light of the kitchen fire, his manner superbly confident as he listened to Mai's explanation and then gave a short nod.

"You must do this with purpose," he replied in Tboli, his tones dramatic and yet evenly measured. "You can never turn back. Turn back or give up against a man like this Kabayo and you are finished. You will die." He made it a simple statement of fact.

"We will take care of this one. I want only two men. And who comes with me will not wear shoes. And [spoken even more deliberately] there will be no talking. No talking . . . until we are through." He smiled soundlessly, passed his eyes over the group before him, and was still.

Mai waited, finally nodded several times, and seemed satisfied. He looked at Elizalde, gave an upward jerk to his eyebrows, and smiled, his teeth glinting beneath his bushy mustache.

At dinner, Mali, like an entertainer answering requests from the audience, recounted one adventure after another. He became increasingly animated, so much so that if the requests had stopped, I would have expected him to give his half-smile and say "Here's one I think you'll like. . . ."

Asked if he thought the present problem would be difficult, Mali shrugged and said, "To hunt a pig—*that* is difficult. A pig knows the mountains and forest like no man. But to hunt a man . . . easy."

He quickly added: "Mali does not fail. Ask people who know. My reputation is good."

Throughout most of this, his partner, a loose-limbed, curly-haired Tboli of perhaps twenty who looked like a juvenile delinquent beside Mali, slouched on a sack of rice, his head down. But his sloppy indifference was only a mannerism; he listened intently to every word that was said. He mumbled incoherently a couple of times, but never spoke out, and a few tribesmen glanced at him, curious. Mali flicked his eyes at the boy once and said he was very, very good to work with. Nobody questioned it.

Several men volunteered to go with Mali. Fludi asked, but Elizalde said no; Mai asked, no again. Dafal would go, and Tennes, a black-whiskered Tboli with a fireplug body who looked like a pirate. Another three-man team would trail them as a backup force.

"Fludi and Mai really wanted to go," Manda said later, "but we need them here with the Tasaday. Besides, this is too risky. It'll take real mountain men who can live in this forest for months without coming out. One little mistake and it could be all over with a guy like Kabayo. Yeah—Mali, Dafal, and Tennes. We can't do any better. Meet only one of those guys in the forest and it'd scare the hell out of you."

Elizalde, Mai, Fludi, Dafal, and Ching discussed plans off and on through the evening. The perimeter guards held their positions all night, but nothing happened. Mai reckoned that Kabayo and his men were still watching from somewhere and would not try something while so many men were present. "They'll just wait. They don't have to hurry. Next week, next month, then they'll come. And they are more sure than ever now that there must be something worth getting in here—if not, why had we all come?"

Guards would be kept in the forest around the caves continually until Elizalde returned. Mai himself would stay at camp to supervise while the teams chased Kabayo, and would keep Elizalde informed of developments by coded messages. He assured him that the primary aim would be to capture Kabayo, not kill him. It would be harder, Mai said, but Kabayo would serve better alive, to tell why he had come in and who, if anyone, had sent him.

Elizalde concluded that the plan was good and that he could not improve it by staying. Ching spent the night beside the radio rearranging plane tickets to Manila, Tokyo, and Washington.

It was gray and cool the morning of June 3 as Elizalde, Ching, Certeza, Lucy, and I said good-by to the tribesmen—their camp looked like a mountain hideout of Castro's guerrillas: bearded young men with knives and shotguns and homemade pistols; bandoliers of bullets hanging from tent struts behind Manuel's machinegun. We walked to the caves, where Manda explained to the Tasaday that Mai and Fludi would stay to make sure the bad men did not return. Then we hiked to the landing pad. Bilangan and Lobo took a short cut and were waiting when we arrived. They made awkward waves as we climbed aboard the repaired Panamin chopper about eight o'clock and flew to Tboli.

At the settlement, Fernandez and Baradas, who had been advised the night before that Elizalde would pass by on his way to catch a plane to Manila, were on the porch of the staff house. The Elizalde Company's plane, however, was due momentarily at the Surallah airstrip, so we stayed only long enough to exchange a few words with them. They each gave Elizalde reports they had written covering their two weeks in the forest.

While waiting at the airstrip, Elizalde leafed through the reports, which covered eighteen pages of legal-size paper. The plane failed to arrive and he grew increasingly impatient. After about forty-five minutes, Elizalde decided we should return to Tboli, where a message said the pilot had turned back because of rain. "That guy," Elizalde grumbled, "wouldn't fly through a lawn sprinkler. Ching, we gotta get another plane somewhere or we'll miss the flight to Japan. See what you can do."

Fernandez and Baradas had friendly smiles as they inquired about the latest developments in the forest, but were somewhat reserved. Elizalde mentioned he had not been able to read their reports. The anthropologists responded that their original intention had been to help him with his speech and with questions he might be asked at the Smithsonian, but they had ended up by giving most of the space to the difficulties in the forest.

It soon became obvious that Fernandez and Baradas were upset. The experience in the forest had been a strange and troubling one, of course, but there was more to it than that. Edginess crept into their voices as they mentioned not knowing Elizalde's whereabouts, mix-ups in incoming and outgoing messages, the delay of their key message proposing a meeting at Tboli early in the Kabayo episode. They also said that they had gathered data that challenged earlier findings and beliefs about the Tasaday.

It appeared the discussion might become heated. Elizalde already knew of difficulties between the anthropologists and the Tboli crew, and although he was sympathetic to both sides, his greater sympathies and loyalty lay with the tribesmen. Thus he did not respond in detail to the scientists, and after a short while excused himself and left the porch. He was scarce for the next hour and told me later that because of everyone's weariness and tension and his momentary departure, he had wanted to avoid further discussion of the trouble. There was no point in having angry words about all that had happened, or to open up lines of argument that would continue while he was away.

Fernandez, Baradas, and I talked for a while. Their two weeks in the forest had been valuable scientifically and they had included in their reports criticisms and recommendations that in their opinion would enable Panamin to strengthen itself and avoid repeating certain problems in the future. They believed that their findings would update Elizalde and help him deal with what they said might be "hostile" questions from the Smithsonian audience. Both men said it was impossible to continue field study at this time—the Tasaday would need to relax and the circumstances must return to normal. They would remain at Tboli a few days to write up their notes; Fernandez indicated he might like to return to the forest briefly to complete some work. I felt the anthropologists were leaving many things unsaid.

Finally Ching announced that a chartered plane was on the way to the airstrip. We hurriedly collected our belongings and left the settlement.

Elizalde read the reports while waiting in Davao City for the flight to Manila. The anthropologists were in rather sharp dispute with Fludi and the other Tboli on several points, one being the Tasaday's behavior during the early stages of the trouble. Elizalde had asked Fludi about that and was told they had been calm. Fernandez and Baradas, however, described some Tasaday as prepared for battle.

"They are not strangers to aggression," Baradas wrote, adding that at least three men were excitedly running around the hillsides with bows and arrows ready. Furthermore, the Tasaday had been unduly alarmed by Tboli who "senselessly" told them too much about the trouble. Fludi had told Elizalde that there was a scarcity of guards in the beginning and that Balayam, Bilangan, and Mahayag had helped keep watch at the caves. Some carried bows and arrows, but he insisted that they were merely walking around with them, that there was no indication they would use them. Fludi had said also that the Tasaday were told only that unpleasant people led by a man named Kabayo were in the area and that everyone must be watchful so as to avoid them.

There was no disagreement that messages had been fouled up—but the Tboli said this was due to the excitement and confusion, while the anthropologists suggested at least some of it may have been deliberate and that they had had disagreements with Mai over who was running things even before the Kabayo trouble began.

There were several other points of disagreement. Fludi had said Tekaf and Lolo stayed away from the caves continuously since Manda had left two weeks earlier, and several other Tasaday had stayed out a great deal. In a message to Manila, Fludi was quoted as saying that maybe the Tasaday "don't like all the questions and being followed around, and are staying in their other caves."

But, in his report, Baradas saw their absence from home as a sign of a natural preference for greater activity and movement outside the cave area. Nobody had realized this before because of the Tasaday's inclination to stay home when Elizalde was present.

Another point of contention had arisen over giving the Tasaday rice. Elizalde had not authorized regular gifts of rice; his radio instructions were for it to be given when the trouble started and food gathering had to be curtailed. But Fernandez and Baradas reported that, without their knowledge, rice had been given regularly and to such an extent from the beginning of their visit that it had distorted their research on Tasaday gathering habits and economy. Baradas estimated that the Tboli had given rice at least twice and possibly three times every day until the anthropologists discovered it. And then it was extremely difficult to stop or even curtail because the Tasaday had become accustomed to the daily ration and knew that rice was plentiful at the tents. Fludi had suggested that giving rice was the only way to keep the Tasaday at the caves, otherwise most of them would have gone away.

Both the scientists and the Tboli crew proclaimed they had enjoyed the companionship and respected the abilities of one another, but that the arrival of Kabayo had brought new considerations and put tough strains on the relationship. As for the messages, they were admittedly not always relayed quickly to the anthropologists, so that they were sometimes not up on what was happening outside the forest; and it turned out that they occasionally did not know what was happening inside either, because the Tboli sent some messages without advising them. These and other mix-ups had fueled the criticisms and differences of opinion—which would have come up anyway, but Kabayo's entry had thrown everything into turmoil and prevented an amicable settlement. The anthropologists felt that Mai had interfered with their work. For instance, they had messaged for fresh medication for the skin ailments of Tasaday children, and, instead of merely sending medicine or Dr. Rebong, Mai himself came in. This upset the whole day, because the Tasaday flocked to the landing pad as if it were Elizalde visiting. The anthropologists said it had been expressly understood that there would be no such disruptions, and that this one, like the giving of rice, had thrown the Tasaday far off their normal behavior. They believed the expedition was, or at least should have been, under their direction; and Mai, while granting that research was under their control, felt the Tasaday were his chief responsibility; and, presumably, remembering Elizalde's stipulation to that effect, he was eager to show the boss that he could do the job.

We discussed the situation on the plane to Manila. I felt it was natural for the Tboli to react as they had when the trouble started. Intruding gunmen made it a fighting situation for them, one totally unfamiliar to either of the anthropologists. If there had been no confusion up to this point, it surely would have developed under these extraordinary circumstances. And while it had been extremely aggravating, I did not think it was surprising and was relieved matters were not worse. Thus far, at least, nobody had been injured. Elizalde hoped it would not leave permanent rifts. He felt there was nothing he could do about it at the moment, however, and so concentrated on the research data summarized in the reports. The major findings were covered in five points.

(1) At least one third of the Tasaday words collected previously were actually Igna's and Dafal's Blit words; therefore all linguistic data gathered before required major revisions.

(2) There was limited basis for the Tasaday's supposed sedentariness —they were on the move more than was thought.

(3) The Tasaday's behavior during the Kabayo crisis revealed that "aggression was there in blunt terms and they did not seem to act as strangers to it."

(4) The Tasaday were no longer strictly food gatherers; they were on their way to becoming hunters.

(5) The "supposed pristine and unspoiled image" of the Tasaday was a thing of the past; "the impact of contact was evident."

In general, the reports re-emphasized how little was truly known about the Tasaday. And now, because of misunderstandings between the anthropologists and Tboli, and the attack by intruders, we had more confusion. It struck me that we knew very little about Kabayo, assuming it was Kabayo. The most we could say with certainty was that the Tasaday had been in danger, and perhaps still were, from persons unknown and for reasons unknown.

Murkiness again. Mysteries. Not for the first time, I wondered what I would have made of these strange events had I not been present and had only heard about them.

We reached Manila about eight that evening. Ten hours later, we were aboard a flight for Tokyo, en route to the United States. If there were fresh developments, good or bad, we presumably would hear about them.

15

Time Abolished: The Blare of Megalopolis

IT took slightly less than one day for Elizalde, Ching, and me to go from the forest and caves of the Tasaday to the neon and steel of Tokyo, from a community of 25 to a metropolis of 10,000,000. The abrupt change, on top of the tensions and weariness of the previous days, was numbing.

We spent one night in Japan and flew the next morning to the U.S. Ching was all over the plane, charming the stewardesses and handing out Panamin brochures to whoever looked remotely interested; several had heard of the Tasaday, and even the pilot stopped by to get a brochure, to Ching's great delight. We landed in Washington, D.C., the afternoon of June 5. Clocks were twelve hours behind those in the Philippines, midnight was noon. That, plus the long flight, the transition from the jungle, the hectic recent events, caused me to have flashes of bewilderment over the next few days. I remotely sensed the "lightning" the Tasaday had felt in their first meetings with the modern world, and wondered how they would react to such a trip as this.

We were met in Washington by Bert Romulo and Oscar Trinidad, who had flown ahead with stacks of Panamin brochures, which detailed the work completed in the Tasaday scientific program, and outlined six more periods of study to be carried out over the next six months, crates of exhibition photographs, and freshly printed copies of an eighty-five-page Tasaday data report by Lynch and Fernandez, which included drawings, photographs, charts, maps, and a section on linguistics by Teodoro Llamzon.

Also waiting at the airport were officials of the Philippine embassy and several American friends of Elizalde's. Within an hour meetings were under way, and over the next several days Elizalde spent many hours with Philippine and U.S. Government officials. He also spent considerable time with a consulting firm discussing a possible fund drive, and attended an honorary luncheon given by the National Geographic Society the day the photographic exhibit opened at their galleries. News reporters phoned him, editors of an encyclopedia flew in from the Midwest to confer about an article on the Tasaday, an editor from an Eastern publisher spent a couple of hours trying to convince him to write a book about himself and Panamin.

Lindbergh visited with Elizalde several times and attended the speech at the Smithsonian. It attracted a few hundred people, who gave it a warm reception and asked many questions at the end. Only one or two in the audience were critical; many people expressed concern over the future of the Tasaday.

There had been no public mention of the recent trouble in the forest. Elizalde and the rest of us thought about it a great deal. Mai sent messages indicating everything was all right; the latest coded report that I knew about said Kabayo and his men had been chased out of the forest. I was not sure whether there had been casualties.

Most of my time was spent with Oscar Trinidad setting up the exhibit at the Smithsonian and later at the National Geographic. We found a surprising awareness of the Tasaday. A truck delivered us and our pictures to the Smithsonian. Guards made us wait at the delivery entrance for clearance. As we stood beside an open box of pictures, two laborers walked by, one glanced down, went on a few steps, stopped, and came back.

"Hey, lookit this!" he said. "Hey, Carl, come here. This must be those people down in . . . ah, where is it? Philippines?" He picked up a photograph of Tasaday in one of the caves. "Wow, what about that! Really something, huh? Boy oh boy, live in a cave. Happier than hell, right? Stone tools, the whole works. Yeah, yeah, I seen about them on TV. I was in the Philippines at the end of the war but never seen anything like this. Been lost in that jungle for a thousand years, right? See, I know all about 'em.

"Well, what's gonna happen now?" he asked, not waiting for an answer. "Their happy days are over, right? We found 'em and you know what we do to people—screw things up, right? Screw up ourselves is bad enough, but now we gotta wreck these people. Yeah, they don't know how lucky they are—were! No fighting, no smog, no high prices, no traffic. Man, that's really somethin'."

As we worked to mount the exhibit during the next two days, hundreds of people passed by on their way from one gallery to another. Most stopped to look at the pictures spread out on the floor and exhibit panels.

There were no captions or titles yet, but up to half of the people recognized the Tasaday, although many could not remember the exact name or whether they were in the Philippines, New Guinea, or Australia.

Oscar and I usually didn't say anything unless we were asked, and the comments we overheard were invariably sympathetic toward the Tasaday. Only one person was openly critical—an American university student whose Filipina roommate had told her the whole thing was a political gimmick. The girl, thinking us museum workers, confided that it was all a stunt, and a shameful one. She explained that her roommate had told her that the Philippines was politics-crazy. We finally told her the pictures were ours, that we had spent considerable time with the Tasaday, and that it was not a stunt. She returned the next day and said she was fascinated with the Tasaday and would come to hear Elizalde's speech, but she still seemed skeptical. Maybe the speech convinced her.

The Smithsonian's scientists who stopped by were interested, but generally guarded in their comments. Laymen were more open. A typical reaction was that of a man who walked by with his family.

"Say, Marge," the man said, "this is that tribe. Kids, look here, these are the people who have no wars or weapons and are very happy in the jungle. Isn't that something? See, they live in these caves and have never been outside the jungle. I wonder what's going to happen to them? They should leave them alone. Those people were better off before they were found."

The discussion on the fund drive took up many hours in Elizalde's suite at the Watergate Hotel, but little was settled. The talks continued in New York, where the party moved the second week, but the only significant accomplishment was the contracting for a preliminary study to determine if a drive would be promising. Bert Romulo would stay in the U.S. to follow through on the drive and to get the foundation incorporated in the States so that funds could be sought.

Another reason for going to New York was to discuss a documentary film with NBC. Several television outfits around the world had proposed making a film, but NBC had the inside track because of their previous filming of the Tasaday, and because Elizalde liked Jack Reynolds and his crew and their manner with the Tasaday. Reynolds had met with Elizalde in Tokyo and confirmed his continuing keen interest. Lindbergh suggested that the film be discussed with all major U.S. television film makers and opened for bids, but Elizalde worried this might look mercenary and also that he might end up with a crew he did not know who would be difficult to work with.

Bert, Elizalde, and I met with Gerald Green, the novelist, who produced documentaries for NBC television, and three of the network's executives. The project was agreed upon in principle, and NBC would donate $50,000 to the foundation for its work with minorities, in return for certain exclusive rights and assistance in making the film.

The day after that meeting, Elizalde flew to Europe, on his way back to the Philippines. Bert stayed behind to shuttle between New York and Washington, following up on the fund drive and contractual details with NBC. I stayed another week in New York.

I thought the pace had slowed considerably in the city. On a visit two years earlier, the winter of 1969–70, I had a continual struggle to understand what was happening. Crime was booming, cities were blighted, suburbs growing too fast; marriage was dying, families were crumbling, schools were a mess; women's lib was shrill, students were marching, radicals bombing; racial stress seemed more acute than a few years earlier; money was tight, construction was down; pollution was a national plague; drugs were sending shock waves through all strata of society.

Yet, despite the confusions and the tensions, many of the challenges to ideas and institutions seemed to promise eventual improvements.

Now, three years later, it seemed less tense and more optimistic. (But, then, we had checked out of the Watergate just before the celebrated break-in.) Of course the improved atmosphere may have been largely due to the warm summer weather, so pleasant in comparison to the ice and snow of the previous visit. It was delightful to walk around New York on a balmy Saturday, looking in shops and museums, watching an endless variety of costumes on long-haired boys and braless girls parading along Fifth Avenue. It looked more exotic—perhaps bizarre is a better word— than anything I'd seen in a long while.

But there was also the impersonal bustle of the streets, the dirty air, the noise and traffic and grimy buildings. One gray, rainy afternoon, I was browsing through a small clothing shop on the East Side. As I stood near racks of wide, bright neckties, I heard a woman's voice, rasping and weary: "Anyway, all I want now is a place with a porch, you know, a porch—out somewhere; I don't care where, just someplace away from all this." She wasn't shopping, apparently, just escaping the rain and chatting with the clerk to pass the time. She looked about forty. Her hair was covered by a scarf and she wore a wrinkled plastic raincoat, the kind that folds into a tiny packet.

The clerk said something I couldn't hear, and the woman went on: "I'd just sit on that porch and listen to crickets. Sure. That'd be all you could hear, just crickets. And I'd sit there and be quiet, no noise, no rush. And the air—it'd be clean, fresh, it'd smell good, you know? That's all I really want now. I'm beat, tired, really beat." She stood gazing out at the rain. After a few moments, she sighed, looked back at the clerk, and said, "You know what I mean?" then pulled open the door and walked out into the drizzle.

Despite scores of conversations with old friends and new acquaintances, that overheard commentary in the small shop stayed vividly in my mind. Modern society was superior in many ways to the rough and perilous existence of the Ubu and Blit and Tboli; yet I felt that this woman's lament touched on a creeping malaise in which life seemed to be slipping away from people day by day.

From New York I went to Portland, Oregon, to visit my mother and father. One afternoon I met an old friend, a businessman my age, who had done extraordinarily well and made a great deal of money. He had read about the Tasaday and was fascinated. "What a life they must have," he said. "Sounds beautiful. And look at us. Progress! Hah. What've we got? Pollution, taxes, prices going outta sight. Brand-new car breaks down, crime and dope all over the place. I'm earning more than I ever did and it's going out as fast as I can make it—and what have I got? More gimmicks and gadgets and clothes, and most of it I don't even need. Insurance costs a fortune. Naw, gimme half a chance and I'd leave this rat race in a minute."

I don't want to make too much of these examples—perhaps the woman was merely having a bad day, and the man surely wouldn't give it all up —and, after all, they were only two people. I realize, too, that many of my observations might seem like tired clichés. But since I had lived abroad for most of the past decade, they hit me with vivid freshness.

From my random conversations and observations, I gathered that a considerable number of Americans felt that they had lost something, something that the Tasaday still had. Of course, we did not and could not have their innocence and simplicity, but even the latter-day manifestations of these qualities had changed so radically for many people that the words themselves were meaningless; we had to romanticize to imagine such values. And in this romanticizing there was a real sense of loss. We were smarter and slicker and more successful, but somehow it wasn't enough.

III

DEEPENING CONTACT

16

Calm Settles and Plants Speak

BY late June the Tasaday had resumed their customary routines in the forest, although three Tboli with a radio remained at the camp as guards. I returned to Manila in early July and Elizalde reported that Kabayo and his gang had been chased out of the forest and captured. He said Kabayo claimed to have gone into the forest on his own, without outside involvement, and Mai described him as terrified, begging that he and his followers be included in Panamin's programs. The Blit were keeping watch on Kabayo in his rocky valley home, and Elizalde said he planned to see him on his next trip to Mindanao.

I inquired about casualties during the chase and was told only that Kabayo had been captured and everything was all right. I subsequently saw the key Tboli and Blit tribesmen involved; if there had been casualties, they must have been on the side of the intruders. Mali had apparently been successful—and also added another story to his repertoire.

Although that difficult situation apparently was taken care of, the distress of the anthropologists remained unresolved. Lynch, Baradas, and Fernandez had indicated they were still upset and wanted to discuss matters with Elizalde and Trinidad. A meeting of the three anthropologists, Elizalde, Trinidad, and Mai was tentatively set for early August.

Lynch, who continued as head of the Tasaday research program, was friendly toward Elizalde and Panamin but annoyed. He told me that an understanding had to be reached about what had happened during the aborted study period, and how the scientific program would proceed. He said Fernandez and Baradas still believed strongly in the foundation's work and goals, but were really bothered by several things, among them that Mai Tuan had usurped their authority throughout the last expedition.

Lynch felt it demonstrated one of the main problems of Panamin itself: everybody wanted Elizalde's approval. Naturally, this affected everything Panamin did, and was especially disruptive in research.

Lynch noted that two months earlier he had requested the tape recordings of the Tasaday in the caves so they could be studied by linguists, but that he had heard nothing further about it. "It seems that I'm the director of Tasaday research in title only," he said. "I hear about things in the most roundabout manner." Some matters pertaining to research had been handled by the Panamin public relations department and he learned that much later, by accident. "Public relations seems to take a higher priority than science," he said. Nonetheless, he was essentially optimistic that things would be straightened out. He was going ahead with the study program and planning a polished version of his and Fernandez's Tasaday report, which had received many commendations.

Elizalde was concerned about Lynch's criticisms but uncertain what to do. He saw the problem chiefly as part of a long-standing difference of approach to minorities between science and Panamin. "It would be nice," he said, "if we could establish laboratory situations in the forest, but it simply can't be done. The scientists don't like me there, don't want Mai there. Now, I can understand that, but, on the other hand, we are the ones who have to take the responsibility for the Tasaday at this point. The scientists forget that, forget that we have a real day-to-day obligation to the people, not to history or science. Science comes second. I've said it over and over, and that's just the way it is."

Meanwhile, David Baradas had joined the Panamin staff. He did not want to resume field work among the Tasaday but was willing to serve as a consultant. He preferred to concentrate on other aspects of the scientific program, which was in great need of direction, and on the Panamin-run museum for minority cultures.

Bert Romulo was still negotiating the contract for a documentary with NBC. Production was tentatively set to begin in mid-August. This would complicate the next phase of scientific study, because Douglas Yen, the ethnobotanist originally expected to start work in the forest about mid-July, was instead coming in late July and might stay a month. When Lynch learned from Baradas that NBC might overlap with the latter part of Yen's field work, he reportedly said that if this happened he would stop all his involvement with Panamin. Lynch was described as extremely disturbed by the possibility that the TV team would be there when Etut's baby was born.

Neither Lynch nor Baradas had favored the TV filming, but they went along reluctantly. They said, however, they would object strongly to such disruptions in the future—the large cameras and recorders and continual surveillance by film makers would have a negative effect on the Tasaday.

Baradas declined to accompany the TV group into the forest, preferring to be as far removed as possible from that part of the Panamin program.

When Elizalde learned of Lynch's distress, he phoned him, later reporting that Lynch had been pleasant and was agreeable to asking Yen to come earlier so he would complete his work ahead of NBC's arrival. Yen replied to this request that he would come as soon as he could, at least a few days early.

Since Elizalde still did not know how long Yen would stay in the forest, he phoned Reynolds in Hong Kong and told him the problem, asking if NBC could delay filming until late August or September. But by this time the contract had been settled and crew members had already been assigned out of New York, Saigon, Tokyo, Korea, and Hong Kong. Reynolds felt it would be extremely difficult to delay until late August. He added that special camera equipment to avoid the use of artificial light had been contracted for use in August and might not be available later. He said NBC could delay a few days, perhaps several, but a month would be too much. He assured Elizalde that if there was an overlap, the crew would take pains to avoid bothering Yen.

In mid-July the German embassy announced that an internationally known ethologist, Irenaus Eibl-Eibesfeldt, was coming to Manila and wanted to meet Elizalde. The scientist headed the research unit on human ethology at the highly respected Max Planck Institute, near Munich. Baradas, the first member of Panamin to meet him in Manila, was impressed, and a few days later Elizalde had a dinner at his home for Eibesfeldt and the Germany embassy's cultural attaché. Lynch, Baradas, Trinidad, my wife, Joyce, and I also attended. Eibesfeldt, an outgoing and articulate man in his forties, had written several books, of which the latest, *Love and Hate,* presented his view that man's aggressive impulses were counterbalanced by impulses toward altruism and goodness. He was anxious to observe the Tasaday.

Elizalde talked at length about them and various other tribes, particularly the Higa-onon. Onto, the young girl who had joined the first cave expedition, had only recently disclosed for the first time that she had been born in a cave. Her Higa-onon family had moved out of the caves about five years earlier, and her grandfather said he wanted to go back to the caves to die. The walls of the caves, she told Elizalde, had once been covered with drawings. When her people left the caves they moved into trees, living high above the ground in houses connected by swinging bridges.

He had always been fascinated by the Higa-onon, long contending that they were an extraordinary subject for scientific study. Furthermore, Onto's story supported his thesis that people throughout Mindanao had once lived in caves. He speculated that it would be possible today to go into almost any village or town of Mindanao and find people whose ancestors had lived in caves.

Eibesfeldt would be leaving the Philippines soon and was committed to several projects over the next few years, but said he would like to fit in something with the Tasaday or another Philippine group.

The interest of Eibesfeldt and the Planck Institute was gratifying to Elizalde, and he was hopeful that a project could be worked out. But he remained worried about Panamin's own scientific program, which was in disarray and for which he was responsible. Neither Lynch, Baradas, nor Fernandez had the time or willingness to undertake over-all leadership of the scientific program.

For the first time in several months, Elizalde met with Robert Fox to discuss matters, particularly the Tasaday. Fox was cordial and helpful, and Manda said the meeting confirmed that Fox was one of the most imaginative and capable social scientists in the Philippines. (Despite this, their former close association did not resume after this meeting.) Among various suggestions by Fox was that either Fludi or another tribesman who had learned the language be used as a researcher's surrogate, living among the Tasaday with a prescribed set of data to record. Such a person would be psychologically and physically much closer to the Tasaday than scientists, and therefore could work with them more easily.

Douglas Yen, who had worked in the Philippines often over the years, arrived July 23 and met with many of the resident or visiting scientists who were old friends. He and Carol Molony, a linguist from Stanford University making a lengthy study of Chabacano, met with Lynch, Baradas, and Fernandez to discuss the Tasaday program. A day later they all attended a dinner at Elizalde's house. Also present was Richard Elkins, a linguist with the Summer Institute of Linguistics, the Protestant organization which translated the Bible into many languages. Elkins was considered the foremost authority on Manubo dialects spoken in Southern Mindanao. He would go to the forest with Yen, who said the co-ordination of linguistics with his own work was important.

Yen, forty-eight, a Chinese born and raised in New Zealand, was described by several scientists as the top ethnobotanist in the Pacific. Presently on the staff of the Bishop Museum in Honolulu, Yen had spent long periods in New Guinea, the Solomons, and Polynesia, as well as in South America, notably Peru. Yen was cool and precise, yet relaxed in his manner. He said he had heard a good deal about the Tasaday and was looking forward to the field work—and he expressed some doubts about the report that before meeting Dafal, the Tasaday's primary food was *biking.*

Yen said that in other forest areas in which he had conducted ethnobotanical studies, the wild yam (*biking*) was not plentiful enough to provide the everyday staple food. And even though the Tasaday were few in number and supposedly sedentary, it would be rather surprising if *biking* was sufficient for them to have relied upon it to the extent reported. "Perhaps *ubud* or something else was used. Of course, I don't know. We'll have to wait and see."

We flew to Tboli July 28, and that evening sat with Yen on the porch, discussing various aspects of the Tasaday project—including the shooting episode with Kabayo, which Elizalde covered in considerable detail. Yen said he knew about it already, but not from Lynch, Fernandez, or Baradas, which was surprising because we thought it was known by only a few people connected with the program. Yen did not say exactly how he knew, only that he had heard it on the grapevine, which obviously meant it was rather widely known. It was disclosed also that Yen had been warned by colleagues in the United States to avoid the project because of intrigues and political involvements in the government and Panamin, and in the Philippines' scientific community.

Mai, who had spent nearly a month with the Tasaday after the Kabayo incident, was asked to brief Yen. Mai said he had learned at least three fourths of the words commonly used by the Tasaday and believed that as a people they were as "good" as when he first met them. When Yen asked about wild yams, Mai said that three or four Tasaday men went out daily in search of them; Mahayag stayed out the longest, sometimes four days at a stretch. Mai said the women gathered food on their own from time to time, usually at the stream. Food was shared equally when it was brought back to the caves, but each family was responsible for its own firewood.

The Tasaday had learned to like rice, Mai said, though it was given seldom, because Elizalde agreed with the anthropologists that the Tasaday should not become dependent on it. They still preferred *biking* over rice because it "tasted better and lasted longer inside." Wet *biking* was inferior to dry, in their view, because watery yams shrank when cooked and did not taste as good. The Tasaday had different kinds of *biking*—hairy and nonhairy, Mai called them—and none was ever too old to eat. Mai told Yen that the Tboli ate the same variety as the Tasaday, and that the plants usually were so widely scattered that you were very lucky to find two close together. Mai added that the Tasaday had two kinds of *ubud*, but only one was found at Tboli.

Mai had observed nothing among the Tasaday he would call magic or religion; no rituals or ceremonies, no talk of spirits or deities. He had not heard much talk about the Kabayo incident after the first few days, and he never heard them discuss the Tasafeng or Sanduka.

Yen and Elizalde discussed the possibility of making contact with one of these other groups, and Yen felt that if it were done at all—and he questioned that it should be—it might be wisest to do all the research possible in one swoop, get it over with, then leave the people alone.

Yen was asked how he would begin his work with the Tasaday. "Well, I suppose we'll start by defining activities and go from there. We'll just have to see how it goes."

The party would include Hermes Gutierrez, a botanist with whom Yen had worked before, and Ernesto Reynoso, assistant to Gutierrez. Both worked for the National Museum. They would stay about two weeks. Richard Elkins, the Manubo language specialist, would join the party in a few days. Dad and Sol would be general assistants, and Love Tear would operate the radio.

The next morning we flew to the forest. Immediately upon landing, Yen and Gutierrez called attention to plants on the ridge with red blossoms and fuzzy plumes like dry dandelions. These plants, named bernonia, were not indigenous to this locale, they said; the seeds must have been brought on the wheels of the helicopter or on someone's clothing or shoes. Bernonia grew quickly and the wind carried the seeds easily.

Balayam, Sindi, and Bilangan were the first Tasaday to reach the ridge. They hugged and sniff-kissed several of us and shouted and laughed with Sol and Dad. It was a happy reunion, a marked contrast to the visit two months earlier during the Kabayo episode.

Elizalde introduced the scientists and the Tasaday received them warmly. Balayam looked Yen over carefully, waggled his head, and said, "*Oh-ho.* Kakay . . . Kakay Mmmmin . . . Kakay Min-ing. Kakay Ming. *Oh-ho!* Kakay Ming!" He laughed. From that moment Yen was Ming. Later, Gutierrez became Filimon and Reynoso was Basitu.

Dad, who had come out of the forest only two days earlier after a long stay as a guard, carried on animated and lengthy conversations with the Tasaday. We heard some new expressions, apparently slang, from the Tasaday. There was *yaoweh* (ya-oh-way), *ah-do-do,* and *bow-gay.* The last two were sometimes used together—"*Ah-do-do, bow-gay,*" which seemed rather like "Good for you, pal."

The etymology of these words was not pinned down, but the Tboli boys may have been responsible for one or two. *Bow-gay* might have come from *pogi,* widely used in the Philippines to mean "good-looking," or from *sige* (pronounced see-gay or siggy), an all-purpose expression that could mean "okay," "good," "let's go," to name just three. *Yaoweh* might have been Tasaday; it could also have come from yeah, which they heard often. It was an exclamatory yes or good or wow in the Tasaday vocabulary. (The sound was close to Yahweh [modern transliteration of Hebrew word for God], but if there was a connection it presumably was a mere coincidence of sounds, meaningless across two languages.) *Ah-do-do* was Tasaday and may have evolved into a spoken expression from the singing of Balayam, who often used a similar-sounding phrase.

As we moved into the jungle, we noticed it was extraordinarily dry. Dad said that it had not rained for the past thirty days. The stream was no more than two inches deep in most places, and the waterfall over the cave was a drip. Because of the dryness and a new, easier route that went farther along the ridge before slanting down into the valley, the hike to camp took only about twenty-five minutes, less than half as long as before.

At the tents, several Tasaday came to welcome Momo Dakel. Adug and Udelen, with tiny Maman on his back, grinned and hugged everyone. Dul, heftier than ever, smiled and then told Mai, "We could not bring a gift of food because our knife is broken." This was not lost on Elizalde and Dul soon had a replacement.

Balayam later brought gifts of the two kinds of *ubud: ubud basag,* crunchy and almost sweet, and *ubud blagun,* smaller and rather bitter, although when cooked it had the texture and flavor of artichoke leaves. Both were from palms.

As more Tasaday moved around and through the tents, Yen noted that they merely glanced at various bags of gear and supplies we had brought, displaying no particular curiosity. "In some places my bags have been practically emptied by the local people—not to take anything, just to see what I had in there," Yen said.

Balayam kept hugging Elizalde, occasionally making the rounds of the rest of us. Lolo and Lobo showed up with their mother, Etut, and bounced around the gathering, which had grown to a rather sizable crowd. Etut had replaced her leaf skirt with a rice bag and said it was much better in view of her pregnancy; she appeared near her delivery time. Her large dark eyes sparkled as she shyly smiled.

In all the hubbub, I noticed that Lobo had sat down and was concentrating on making a sketch with a ballpoint pen and paper. We had never seen any Tasaday do this before. Dad explained that Lobo had learned by watching Carlos Fernandez, who was a gifted drawer. Lobo showed surprising skill, drawing a picture of a helicopter with figures inside it, each of whom he named; the stick figures encircling it were the Tasaday, he said. There was no mistaking it was a helicopter; it even had minor details such as the tail antenna and small rear wheel.

Lobo gave us another surprise a few minutes later when he walked to the edge of the main tent, unhitched a vine from a tree, leaped forward, and sailed across the gully alongside the camp. He rode on one of two wrist-thick vines that had been made into swings. Each rose about one hundred feet into the trees and had a T bar at the bottom that hooked onto a small tree when not in use.

Everybody began taking turns on them; sometimes two Tasaday or Tboli boys rode on one vine together. Balayam, however, had trouble. When he swung back he failed to jump off onto a small dirt ledge at the tent's edge, and so rode back out over the gully again. On the next return the jump was farther; he hesitated, and swung out a third time. Each time he returned, he was shorter of the ledge. Finally he stopped swinging completely, stalled about twenty feet aboveground. He clung to the vine and shouted for help, between giggles, until Lobo and Adug threw him a liana vine and hauled him back to the ledge.

Dad and Sol teased Balayam and joked with the other Tasaday, seeming completely at home. Dad, particularly, spoke Tasaday with ease.

Igna was much gayer than in preceding months. Mai explained that she had been upset for a long while about her husband, Sut, a bright but troublesome man. He wandered away from home frequently for lengthy periods and sometimes returned with a horse or other items the Blit suspected he had stolen. Mai said Sut had been shot and killed in mid-July, apparently while on some escapade in the hills. Igna seemed far from sad about it.

We visited the caves at dusk. Yen, Gutierrez, and Reynoso were introduced as friends who were very interested in plants. The Tasaday remarked on the long dry spell and said it was good, because *biking* was better, and it was easier to gather food and firewood and walk in the forest.

It had clouded over that afternoon and Mai asked Balayam if he thought it would rain the next day, anticipating a sage prediction of the weather. Balayam looked up at the sky and said, "We will know if it will rain when the rain comes down."

Balayam, whose face inevitably mirrored his feelings, then laughed and sang happily in the twilight. Adug sang, too, as darkness closed in and the crickets and cicadas began singing in the forest.

Asked what they did when they saw deer or monkey before they had knives or traps, Balayam said, "The deer came close to us. Now it stays far. The deer did not run from us then."

Did the Tasaday catch them?

"Yes, but we let them go again. They were no use to us."

"Why catch them, then?"

"We just like to touch them sometimes. They were our friends."

We asked what had been their reaction when Dafal taught them how to trap deer, and Balayam said they had been surprised.

"Were you sorry or sad, did you feel anything special, to be trapping and killing animals that used to be your friends?"

"No," Balayam said. "We were happy that Kakay Dafal showed us how to do that. Those things are good to eat."

There had been indications in the tape recordings that the Tasaday had eaten meat possibly before they met Dafal (Balayam said Kuletaw had fed monkey meat to him when he was a youngster). Someone suggested that they may have occasionally found a dead animal, and, since it was so unusual, Balayam had made particular mention of it. We tried to clarify this by asking if they ate meat before meeting Dafal, but Balayam answered that they had not known how to trap animals. We tried the question another way, and Balayam said no, they had not eaten meat. We did not know if they made a distinction between deer and pig and monkey meat; if they had eaten meat, it apparently was uncommon.

How did they like their new living arrangements, now that most of them had been at the lower cave for several weeks?

"We still have one feeling, one feeling together," Balayam said. His answer seemed somewhat defensive, and we asked again *why* they had moved, but Balayam seemed to answer something else—perhaps the question was translated incorrectly. "It is like our life," he said. "When we go out into the forest for food, each of us goes separately, yet we still have one feeling together."

"Is it more comfortable nowadays?"

"It is good, the same as before."

We did not notice any significant changes or new construction since our last visit, except that the wood rack with three legs now had four and other racks had been enlarged.

At the camp, after dinner, Yen remarked that it was evident that the Tasaday were reticent to answer questions. Dealing with them, he said, would require tact and patience.

His general first impression of the situation was that it was a "phenomenon." From the ecology, the conditions of the environment, and the capacity of the caves, he said, it was obvious that the Tasaday were not sharply reduced in number from previous times. "They have not gone from two thousand people down to a population of twenty-odd. So the big question to me is why they are so few. The population is an important question, very important."

As he rode in on the helicopter, he said, the appearance of the forest had struck him as extraordinary. "I wanted to take photographs on the way, but it was so exciting just looking that I couldn't do anything but look. The chopper ride alone was worth the whole trip."

As we talked, Onto, the Higa-onon girl who enjoyed coming into the forest, was working with Lucy in the kitchen. Elizalde asked her to fetch something for him. She did and then walked away, saying loudly, with mock indignation, "What is a child like me doing working so hard?" Manda laughed and then translated her remark into English.

The previous day Onto had told him that her people's diet was similar to the Tasaday's—favoring *biking, ubud,* and *natek*. She also said more people had lived in the Higa-onon's caves than did here.

Manda took this as an opportunity to elaborate, for Yen, upon his theory about the early people of Mindanao having lived in caves all over the island. "I bet," he said, "that if we looked hard enough we would find that the Mansaka [a tribe in eastern Mindanao, some two hundred miles away] came out of caves. Why not? Men walked to the Philippines when the oceans were low, then went to the high ground when the water rose. Mindanao became a bunch of islands. Then, when the water receded again, some people went to the lowlands and others stayed in the mountains. Why not? It's a better idea than any other I've heard so far. Better than that one about *fugu* disease making people flee into the mountains. I heard that and even repeated it myself about the Tasaday, but it's junk, I know now."

Yen nodded and looked thoughtful, but did not say anything.

The next day was sunny again and in the morning a group of Tasaday came to the tents. Balayam noticed a new chromium-plated gas lamp hanging from a tent support and approached it as if it were a strange animal. Then he spotted his reflection and walked goggle-eyed around the lamp, making faces. He pushed his chin up against it and the curving chromium made his face appear long and wavy. He opened and closed his mouth several times, watching his strange reflection with fascination, then let out delighted yips and danced about. He was so engrossed that he seemed unaware of my presence as I took photographs from a few inches away as he peered at himself.

In the afternoon Yen started his ethnobotanical work at the stream, enlisting Lobo and Lolo to study plants. Dad was the interpreter and also gave the Tboli names and uses of each plant. Dafal did the same for the Blit, so three sets of data were collected for each specimen.

The session appeared casual as Yen led the group slowly along the stream, stopping here and there to select a plant, chat about it, and move on. He prevented—sometimes with exasperation—other members of the botanical team from suggesting answers or asking leading questions of the informants, and was precise in phrasing his own questions. Each plant was tagged, numbered, wrapped separately in newspaper, and put in a plastic bag.

Here is a sample of the responses. The Tasaday boys said an orchidlike flower was used for catching frogs—rubbing the petals on the palm of the hand was supposed to attract the frog. Dad said the Tboli also used this plant to catch frogs, but petals were not used; rather, the dried roots were tucked into a person's waist belt, which made the person invisible to frogs. Dafal said the Blit dried the root and wove a trap for frogs.

Lolo showed how to make twine out of a strip of inner bark, or bast, of a wild banana tree. He said that until Dafal taught them to make this, they had no twine, and used a thin green vine to hold up their leaf loin covers. Manda had speculated that the Tasaday had been naked and Dafal taught them to cover themselves, but the boys said otherwise.

Fifteen plants were collected in a couple of hours along perhaps one hundred fifty feet of the stream. According to the Tasaday, fourteen of them had specific uses, none of which, however, were medical. This was significant, Yen said, because some of the species collected were related to some used for medicines elsewhere in the Pacific region. One plant was used by both the Tboli and Blit to treat snakebite.

Lolo said that when a Tasaday was bitten by a snake they summoned Udelen. He added that this had been done recently when Balayam was bitten. He did not know what Udelen did, but Balayam got better.

Lobo, who had stayed quiet a surprisingly long time for one usually so exuberant, rolled a long green leaf into a flute and tooted it. He said this was to call snakes, and then laughed. But why did he want to call snakes, we asked, aren't the Tasaday afraid of them? "Yes," he replied with giggles. "This is just for fun, we call the snakes and then run."

He and Lolo also demonstrated how they cleaned their teeth with a soft leaf that they folded and wedged between the teeth and rubbed against the enamel.

Many of the day's specimens were useful as foods—flower petals, ginger, wild bananas (which, the Tasaday said, were really more valuable as bait in monkeytraps than for people to eat). But one tree, a pandanus, also known as a screw pine, with leaves that swirled up like a spiraling umbrella, was not used for anything by the Tasaday. Elsewhere, Yen said, the tree had several uses.

It was fascinating to watch him work, and to hear the Tasaday, Dad, and Dafal reveal details of their lives through talking about the flora. Yen said he did not want to tire the informants the first day, so he quit while they were still enjoying themselves. He passed around pieces of hard candy once during and once after the session, and Lolo and Lobo were obviously fond of it.

Dad, whose English was excellent, had performed well in his first real try as a translator. He had spent nearly ten of the past twelve weeks with the Tasaday and estimated that he understood about 95 per cent of their everyday words. I had a chance to talk with him about his recent experience.

Dad said the Tasaday had told him the current dry spell was one of the longest they could remember, and the reason it had not rained was that the owner of the caves loved Momo Dakel Diwata Tasaday so much. This came from Balayam, the group's chief storyteller. Dul was the only other Tasaday Dad had heard tell stories, and she did so infrequently. One of Balayam's stories centered on a small cave his ancestors carried on bamboo poles when they traveled. They would stop, set up the cave house, and search for food. But they returned one time to find that the small cave had grown into a large cave, which they could not carry, and it was decided that they must stay there forever. Was this the site of their present home? Dad said he did not know, Balayam had not made that clear.

Another of Balayam's stories was about a man named Oogoo, who carried a stick he swirled in a stream until a hair clung to it. The direction in which the hair pointed led to people, and Oogoo went after them. He pointed his stick at the people and their fingers and limbs fell off. Balayam's father supposedly had a special cure for this, and after that the cave grew big and Oogoo came no more. I asked if this stick made a noise and did it perhaps represent a gun or a spear, but Dad said no, it was just a stick. I pointed out the similar sound of Oogoo and *fugu,* the supposed dreaded disease of long ago, but Dad made no special connection to the Tasaday. In fact, he said, some Tboli told almost exactly the same story, and he was not sure Balayam had truly heard either of these stories from his ancestors; he may have got them from Dafal or the tribal guards. Dad considered Balayam quite inventive, and said he was the only Tasaday to talk at length about ancestors.

Dad and I were alone during this discussion. When I asked about the Sanduka and Tasafeng, he said he had never heard the Tasaday mention them. Even if they had, it was doubtful he would have told me, because Elizalde and Mai had discouraged the boys from discussing these other groups with outsiders; they reasoned that talk about the other people would encourage outsiders to try to find them.

Dad reported that he had never witnessed an argument or disagreement among the Tasaday, although Mahayag had once cut rattan near the caves and later that day there was a lightning storm. Some Tasaday had admonished Mahayag, saying *"N'da* [No], Mahayag," but he merely laughed and nobody seemed seriously bothered.

Food was shared equally among the families when it was brought to the caves, with Dul usually dividing the portions, Dad told me. The Tasaday were always friendly with him, but asked few questions, and those were only about his family—did he have a mother, father, brothers, sisters? The Tasaday had liked Fernandez and Baradas all right, but did not care for some of their questions or for being followed around. He said Dul had counseled the others not to take the anthropologists on walks, although now some Tasaday asked why Kakay Kalow and Kakay Did (Carlos and David) had not returned to the forest—"Perhaps they forgot about us." The Kabayo incident was not mentioned after the first few days, Dad said, and the Tasaday roamed the forest as if nothing had happened.

After dinner on the second day of this visit, Elizalde remarked to Yen that he did not appear to be very impressed with the Tasaday. "What do you really think?" he asked, seeming rather eager for Yen's approval.

"Who, me?" Yen replied. "Well, I guess I'd have to say that this is one of the most exciting experiences I've ever had . . . I mean, it's the first time for me to see, actually see, gatherers like this, people whose subsistence level is so low. There are ripe fruits on the trees, not taken, so they obviously have enough."

"Yes, but how about the caves?" Manda said. "You don't say much . . . haven't said anything, in fact, while everyone else was so excited about them, amazed."

"Well, no, the caves don't amaze me. I mean, I could live in them myself," Yen said, then quickly changed the subject: "Now, something amazing to me is Tboli, the Tboli settlement."

There was a questioning pause and Yen praised the settlement for its organization and attractiveness, specifically citing the handsome Tboli houses—so many such peoples nowadays constructed houses with ugly sheet metal roofing. "And you can't keep them from it, if that's what they want. You can find that metal roofing in some very remote places."

When the subject turned back to the Tasaday, Yen said that so far their knowledge of plants seemed to be good. They could be challenged on only one or two responses, which may or may not be significant. For example, they had been unable to distinguish between two plants that the Blit and Tboli informants had differentiated. If this became a pattern, that is, if the Tasaday frequently got confused over names or identified different plants as the same plant, Yen said, it might indicate they had less knowledge of plants than people outside the forest. Forest dwellers should be the most knowledgeable; if the Tasaday were not, it might mean they had lived in the forest for a shorter time than had been reckoned.

How long did he think the Tasaday had been here and how had they got here? Yen shook his head. "I won't answer that. There is no way you'll get me to even try to answer that." He said continued scientific study could help provide answers and that ordinarily a logical next step after botany and ecology would be physical anthropology—genetic studies, blood sampling, skull and bone measurements, and so on. "But," he added, "I wouldn't do it. I mean, *I* wouldn't. I couldn't—it would be too tough on me and these people. That's a ticklish business—taking blood, for instance—and could cause problems with sensitive people like these. I must admit, though, I'd be very, very interested to see the results of such studies."

He hoped language study would be concurrent with his own work and that of other researchers and was looking forward to the arrival of Elkins, the linguist. Yen believed the language was important not only for understanding present-day Tasaday, but also because it might lead to hypothetical views of their ancestry.

In all areas of study, comparative material on such groups as the Blit, Ubu, Tboli, peoples who might be related to the Tasaday, was scanty. It was possible that studies conducted among those peoples would shed light on the Tasaday, as most assuredly would study of the Tasafeng and Sanduka.

Yen later observed that archeology provided a potentially valuable approach to knowing the Tasaday, but that this could be troublesome. The only evident excavation site of promise was the midden at the mouth of the upper cave, the debris pile that spilled down the mountainside. Its formation and composition would be difficult to work with; there were no uniform layers, refuse was tossed in and stuck or tumbled haphazardly, so that the usual relationship between depth and time would be upset. Also it might mean that significant materials could be recovered only by tearing apart the midden. But the Tasaday's taboo against cutting or breaking leaves and plants, which nearly covered the mound, would make excavation extremely delicate. "That midden is tricky—and, who knows, there may be nothing in it," Yen said. "It'll take a real expert. And inside the cave: nothing. I scuffed at the firesites and they had a thin layer of ashes, that was all."

While talking about archeology, Yen recalled a previous remark of Elizalde's about finding pottery in remote areas of the Philippines, and suggested that finding pottery shards in the Tasaday's midden might indicate the people had been here a shorter time than was surmised.

But supposing they did have pottery at one time, I said, what happened to it, where is it now? There were no signs of anything resembling clay pottery.

"That's right," Yen said. "I'm not saying they did have them, nor do I have any reason to speculate that they did—but it is possible. People can actually lose traits like that. Quite a number of groups in the Pacific had pottery in the earlier stages of their prehistory, only to lose it at a later point in time."

The chance of the Tasaday having had pottery and lost it seemed extremely remote; Yen noted that they apparently did not have even a simple earth oven—a hole covered by leaves or branches and dirt upon which fire was placed. He emphasized that many of his speculations would not even go into his field notes; they were purely for the sake of our discussion.

Had he speculated or conjectured on why the Tasaday were here and for how long? "You already asked me that." He laughed. "I just don't know, and at this point I won't even try to guess."

We returned to his earlier remark that a major question was the Tasaday's small population. If this was a group that had come here relatively recently from another place, or a group from which families regularly split off and moved away, it might explain the small number; but if, as the Tasaday claimed and many observers seemed to believe, this was *the* Tasaday place and they had lived here for centuries—even only two or three—why weren't they more numerous? From the number of children now present, the Tasaday obviously were a fertile people, and it was possible for a small group to multiply to hundreds or even thousands over a few centuries. Disease, high infant mortality, wars, natural disasters could have limited the population, but the Tasaday had made no mention of such things. What did Yen think might explain it?

"Look, I'm fishing around for possible answers, and I've only been here a couple of days, so anything I say may be wild—but I did think about it some before I came and had a few ideas. One idea— It's really too fantastic, I shouldn't even talk about it—but what the hell! Here it is: If the *biking* has been their staple food—and I've got to say that it begins to look like I was wrong, that *biking* was—then perhaps, just perhaps, it has had an effect on their birthrate."

He explained that certain species of dioscorea (a family of plants including wild yams) were a source of some of the ingredients in birth-control pills. If the *biking* eaten by the Tasaday contained a contraceptive agent, it might explain their small population. "This may be way off, totally wrong; I don't know, of course," Yen said. "Just the same, I'm going to want lots of *biking*—as much as twelve pounds of it if possible—for two different labs to analyze. That should tell us if there is anything to the idea."

The fact that the Tasaday were few made it possible for them to live within a relatively small area. It was not known what amount of food they required for subsistence, but their immediate surroundings, presumably a few miles in each direction, were sufficient to support them. Otherwise, they would have traveled farther—and five miles northward would take them out of the forest. But perhaps the Tasaday did not travel northward because of a taboo or territorial limit; perhaps they moved only south, east, and west, deeper into the forest and along its edges. They claimed they not only had not gone outside the forest, but also that they did not even know the outside existed. Was there some special reason why they insisted that they had always stayed near the cave and ventured only short distances?

New questions arose every time we discussed the Tasaday. As our experience with them increased, so did the questions.

One morning Elizalde had to fly to Blit to confer with a lawyer friend from Washington. Yen was curious to see Blit, and I tagged along, too.

As Yen and I wandered among the stilt houses to look at the gardens and farmlands, he remarked that he felt a bit of culture shock because the Blit, compared with the Tasaday, had so many cultivated plants. He had expected a difference, but the contrast was almost startling. He spotted three varieties of gabi (a potatolike vegetable) in the first few minutes and pointed out several other plants, whose scientific names were lost on me, although I tried to write them down as we strolled through patches of corn, tomatoes, lettuce, tobacco.

Ching was passing by just then; he told us that the seeds for many of these plants had been provided by Panamin within the last year or so. Yen acknowledged that but said the most widely planted crops had obviously been present much longer.

Then we walked toward the forest; the peaks marking the Tasaday's place were bright green in the morning sunlight and seemed surprisingly near. We followed a path through high grass and wound around knolls and into small gullies, and each turning opened new vistas. A bluff overlooked the flatland and shallow valley that ran along the edge of the forest—forming the plain that had shocked the Tasaday with its vastness, although it was only a few miles long.

We also could see several hillsides covered with slash-and-burn farms. Yen disagreed with critics who contended that slash-and-burn, or swidden, farming, necessarily destroyed mountains. He believed that farmers usually were careful to leave sufficient trees and plants to hold the soil against erosion. Also, swiddeners did not uproot the growth, but burned it over and planted within it.

However, after surveying the Blit area, Yen observed that the slash-and-burn appeared to be a little too extensive; if it were further expanded, it might cause serious erosion problems. He mentioned this later to Elizalde, who replied, rather defensively, "Well, if that's the case, then it is a recent development, and it's because pressures from settlers in the lowlands have pushed a lot more minority people back in here, where it's still peaceful. Just take the Sduff people [Igna's tribe], for instance. A lot of them have been forced to farm here because they lost their own land." And another reason for the heavier concentration of slash-and-burn plots was that the discovery of the Tasaday had compelled the Blit to stop burning the edge of the forest; they had to pull back and work the adjacent lands more extensively.

As we flew to the Tasaday in midafternoon, Elizalde pointed down to a patch of ground that was haphazardly burned and had a helter-skelter of charred logs and stumps and waist-level grass. He said it must be Dafal's farm. "Dudim gave him a spot to plant his rice, but ol' Dafal just can't seem to keep at it," Manda said with a chuckle. "We went looking for him one day when everybody was out tending their crops, but we couldn't find Dafal. We sent runners out and they finally found him—down in a stream catching tadpoles and crabs. He was all by himself and having a great time."

We visited the caves in the late afternoon and stayed till after dark. It was hard to say later whether we had stayed one hour or three—we rarely consulted wristwatches. Time passed unnoticed. Hours and even days blended together, and sometimes we had to check notes or a calendar to know how long we had been in the forest; four days might be like six or seven like five.

Dul sat in her usual spot on the uppermost platform. Balayam and Adug sang, then Dafal in his shrill loud voice and Igna in her delicate one. General laughter and teasing followed each song. Balayam promoted Adug as the next Tasaday bachelor to get a wife, mentioning this with an eye on Manda, suggesting without saying so that it would be good for Adug to have someone like Sindi. Manda was seated beside Dul, with whom he had developed a rapport similar to that of leaders who share a joshing, friendly respect. He did not respond to Balayam's hint, instead asking him to demonstrate how he communicated with Tekaf.

Balayam and Tekaf went through a dozen hand signs, but then, without a practical reason, the men hesitated. Occasionally, Balayam would glance at Dul after explaining orally what a sign meant, as if he were waiting for her approval. Once, she called him over for a consultation, which ended in giggles; Dul did not understand several of the hand signs herself.

The next morning, about a dozen Tasaday stopped at the tent on their way to the stream to gather food. They waited for us to join up and then moved along the drought-shrunk waterway. They played and chatted as much as they gathered food, except for Mahayag, who worked steadily, foraging ahead with feet and hands in the water, rising only to deposit a tadpole or crab into someone's leaf cone.

The group seemed unaware of our presence most of the time, frolicking over mounds of branches and logs, chuckling over a large crab, shrieking in pursuit of a frog. Balayam came up with a fish about five inches long, the largest we had seen them catch, and held it out proudly in his cupped hands so all could exclaim. Yen remarked that they were more ebullient, more playful and excited, than any group he had seen gathering.

More than half a dozen cones were filled in two hours, but it was difficult to count accurately because some cones were stashed along the bank for pickup on the trip home. The Tasaday had also collected *ubud,* firewood, and leaves for wearing, and one woman carried a fistful of orange flowers for the children to nibble.

The long dry spell had exposed much of the stream's sandy bottom, and several boys found a place where the sand formed soft banks on each side of a shallow, six-foot-wide flow of water. The boys lined up and took turns leaping across the stream with yelps and laughter, landing feet first and spraying sand. Lobo soon tired of this and dunked his head in a pool, rising with hair plastered over his face like a wet black mop. He wrung out the water with both hands, then scrubbed his hair with sand and a yellow-brown bar of clay they called *dolem tanuk*. They used a vine called *kuba* to scrub their bodies.

Dul found a seat on a log and dipped her head in the stream, then rubbed the bar of clay into her great mass of hair. Pieces of the bar crumbled off and she worked the gummy bits through the dripping ropes of hair, rinsed several times, and sat up straight. She parted the curtain of hair hanging in front of her face and peered out, blinking and smiling.

Her son Siyus squatted nearby, stacking stones until he had a tower about eighteen inches high. His toddling brother, Maman, tried to help but knocked over the tower. Siyus waved him away. Maman persisted, however, and Siyus finally discouraged him by tossing pebbles at his feet.

Dula occasionally chatted with Dul and Sindi throughout the morning, but usually stayed near Mahayag. The women searched for food with less determination than the men, generally paying more attention to their children, who were always present, riding on the back or hip of an adult, scampering along the banks and across rocks, splashing in the water. The older boys moved around on their own, but the two girls stuck closer to adults. Kalee, motherless, often followed her father, and Siyul stayed near her mother, Dula. She was about six years old and able to get around quite easily, but Dula still often carried her and she still sucked at Dula's breast. Biking, Siyul's brother and perhaps a year older, was more independent and bounced around on his own, helping his father from time to time.

Lobo still climbed trees and shouted for attention, but seemed to show off less than in the past. Perhaps the other boys played more freely now and Lobo simply did not stand out so much. He sat beside us on some rocks, and we asked what he liked to do best. Lobo said he enjoyed equally going to the stream and accompanying the men to check their animal traps. Asked what he liked to eat, he said tadpoles, fish, crab, meat, *natek, ubud, biking*—everything.

On this day, some of the catch was eaten at the stream, but most was taken to the cave for a late-afternoon or evening meal, as usual. It was eaten with leftover *natek*. Tadpoles and small crabs were mixed together, water added, and the whole put into bamboo tubes. The larger crabs were thrown directly onto hot coals. After the cooking, all the food was divided into family portions and distributed.

The only remains of the meal were fishbones and crabshells, which were tossed into the fire, presumably to be swept away with the ashes. Asked if they had any use for shells or bones, the Tasaday said no; nor did they use the bones of animals. This was somewhat puzzling, because they had used deerhorns as digging tools and bones could be used as implements, too. But there was no sign of such things. We did notice innovation, though: on a tree in front of the lower cave they had recently started hanging the jawbones of pigs and skulls of monkeys. Sindi or Dafal may have suggested this, as it was commonly done at Blit and other communities outside. The Tasaday said they merely hung the bones and skulls for fun, for decoration. It was the first such embellishment we had seen, and we wondered if it might also be some kind of totem.

Yen and his team continued their botanical studies, varying the approach on one occasion by having Gutierrez and Reynoso collect specimens on their own and bringing them to the tents, where Dad, Dafal, and the Tasaday explained their names and uses. The work seemed to be proceeding smoothly. Gutierrez and Reynoso had only ten days to spend in the forest and then would return to Manila. Yen, who was establishing a solid rapport with several of the Tasaday and Dad, said it looked like he would stay another week or two after that.

This meant that NBC would very likely arrive before he had finished his work. Elizalde, somewhat hesitantly, mentioned this possibility to Yen. Yen said he was not in favor of filming, but that he understood the arrangements had already been made and so would not object to the film crew coming in while he was still working. Elizalde was relieved. He said he would send a message to Yen before bringing in NBC and urged him to let him know then if scientific work was under way that might be upset; if so, NBC could hold off a while. He said that Jack Reynolds had given assurance that his crew would take pains to avoid bothering scientific work. "Don't message, just come ahead," Yen said. "I won't bother them, and they won't bother me. We won't have to get in each other's way."

All but the botanical team and the Tboli aides were scheduled to leave the forest the next day. Elizalde would stay in Mindanao and I would go to Manila to meet the arriving NBC crew. I had agreed to assist them by taking still photographs, advising them about the Tasaday, and serving as a sort of liaison between them, Panamin, and Elizalde, with the understanding that my own work came first.

That same afternoon, a message arrived from David Baradas saying it appeared certain that a Tasaday boy was missing. We suspected it was the same mix-up of months past concerning Udo, who had been difficult to recognize in the earliest pictures. Nonetheless, when Lobo and Lolo stopped by the tents to visit, Manda asked them if there was a Tasaday boy who had been there when we first met them but was not there now. Both Lobo and Lolo shook their heads without hesitation and said no, there was no such boy.

This was messaged to Baradas, who replied immediately that there was "proof," photographic evidence, of a missing boy.

I said I was certain that he referred to the photos of Udo; it was agreed that before pursuing the matter further with the Tasaday, the so-called proof would have to be inspected.

We left the forest the next day. Elizalde told the Tasaday he would return soon, and told Yen to expect us in about a week. He was quite comfortable leaving Yen, for whom he had developed a considerable fondness and respect.

17

A Missing Boy
and an End to Peace

ELIZALDE stayed at Tboli, planning to visit several outlying tribal settlements and to confront Kabayo in his rocky valley hideout. I returned to Manila and called David Baradas, who was ready to display his proof that a Tasaday boy was missing. We met at his office in the Panamin Museum. He showed me several photographs I had seen often before and pointed to a boy with short hair and a distinctive arch to his eyebrows. "This one," he said, "simply is not there any more!"

As expected, it was the same boy we had noticed before and ultimately judged to be Udo. As David and I went through at least a dozen photographs made a year earlier, some by Robert Fox and a couple of my own, I kept insisting it was Udo. Baradas insisted it was not and produced a magnifying glass so we could inspect the details of past and recent photographs. I agreed that in the latest pictures the boy whom we knew beyond doubt to be Udo did *look* different, but it was because he was a year older and had longer hair and was shown in contrasting attitudes and camera angles. David still disagreed. I argued that if they were two different boys, why didn't they ever appear in the same photograph? Furthermore, the boy David said was Udo did not show up once in the early pictures.

David would not give in, and he said that Carlos Fernandez was equally convinced a boy was missing.

"Despite the flat denials of Lobo and Lolo?" I asked. "They are shown with him in the photographs—they had to be close friends and playmates of this so-called mystery boy. They didn't hesitate a second, just said nobody was missing."

The photographs were by now scattered all over one gallery of the museum as staff members also took turns looking at them through the magnifying glass. Finally we called off the debate for the day and drove to my house for dinner.

I could not resist going to my workroom to dig out a stack of early pictures of the Tasaday to prove to Baradas that he was wrong. I shuffled through the pile and stopped at a print showing Udo, looking very much as he did at present. I laid it beside recent photographs and there was no question: there were different boys! The other boy simply was not there now.

Of course it was impossible to argue with David any longer. I took the pictures in to him, and we then packaged several and sent them to Tboli, along with an explanatory note, so Elizalde could send them on to Yen to follow up.

Looking over the photographs later, I was embarrassed by my mistake and stubbornness. I blamed it partly on a belief that the Tasaday would not deliberately lie to us or mislead us. The question was simple and clear when we asked Lobo and Lolo . . . why had they denied knowledge of this boy? Without a blink or a stutter, they had said flatly that there was no such person.

What had happened to him? Had he joined another group? Run away? Died? Been traded? . . . killed?

I checked my notes on the March meeting with the Tasaday, after the seven-month break, to see if everyone had been all right, if there had been serious illness or sickness. Balayam had said no, everyone was fine; the only problem had been a storm that knocked trees and branches onto some of their shelters.

If they had deliberately misled us about him, had they deceived us in other ways? Had they withheld things—about the other groups, about going outside the forest? Naturally, they were not obligated or compelled to tell us everything, and it was understandable that they might have secrets, but what unsettled me was that I had come to regard them as absolutely straightforward, guileless. The new information about the boy did not mean they were scheming plotters, but it did suggest that my notions of their ingenuousness and utter purity were rather romantic and foolish.

Having thus admonished myself, it became increasingly intriguing to consider where this information might lead. What had happened to the boy?

On August 5, the first members of NBC's crew arrived in Manila: Gerald Green, the producer, and Bruce Bassett, the unit manager, who looked after film, equipment, schedules, accommodations, transportation. They were followed two days later by Jack Reynolds and five others: Lim Youn Choul and Detlev Arndt, who had covered the Tasaday twice before, cameraman Teruhiko Yashiro, soundman Shunichi Yasuda, and Joung Do Kwan, who would work wherever needed. There were to be two teams; the documentary approach required that events be filmed as they were happening. Scenes were not set up or staged, and if one team was off in the jungle with the Tasaday, perhaps even in search of the Sanduka or Tasafeng, which might take weeks, the other team could still film activities around the caves. They all met with Baradas and Oscar Trinidad at the Panamin offices to read and sign the ground rules for entering the Tasaday's area.

A few days after they arrived in Manila, Trinidad received a letter from Frank Lynch resigning as scientific director of the Tasaday project. This was not too surprising; Lynch had said recently that Baradas, as a Filipino, should be director, and also that his own work at Ateneo University and the Institute of Philippine Culture, plus an upcoming special project, would further limit his ability to participate in the Tasaday program. There was, however, another point that may have hastened his decision: NBC's arrival.

Lynch's letter of resignation did not say this, but he had made remarks to Trinidad and Baradas indicating that he was quite upset. When I talked to him by phone, Lynch said he had formally resigned because of his many commitments, but then added that the arrival of the TV crew was a shock. "I was never told when they were coming," he said, "never told about any of these arrangements. I'm too old to play footsie. And this could hurt Panamin heavily in U.S. scientific circles."

I told him that Oscar had asked me to deliver the letter of resignation when I went south, adding that I would pass on anything Lynch wanted to say beyond the letter.

Although he was concerned about the TV work overlapping Yen's work, the crux of his anguish was over the expected birth of Etut's baby. "They [Panamin] are bringing in cameramen in an off-limits period," Lynch said. "I had absolutely no dream they were going in. They should keep those people out of there the whole month of August."

I mentioned that it had been my understanding right along that NBC was coming in August, and that that had been the reason Yen was asked to come early. "I did not understand that," Lynch said. "I would have objected. You know, the majority of scientists are skeptical about Panamin, and I've failed to change that. I had thought I might help; but no. Now they [Panamin] go right over to NBC. And the birth? Are they going to photograph that? Well, that's apparently the way Panamin wants to run it—okay, I tried and I failed."

I said I did not think they planned to film the birth, and Lynch replied, "Well, I hope not, but we'll see. Word has been broken. Manda has that candy and is sucking on it, won't let go. This is a clear indication of exploitation . . . it has got me very aggravated. Manda simply cannot go on having it all his way in these things. He must trust and give to the scientists who are working with him."

Although Lynch's words were angry, his voice sounded merely firm. I told him I did not think Elizalde had deliberately misled him about NBC's arrival. Lynch replied that he had been misled, deliberately or otherwise, and it was unfortunate for all concerned that not just he, but science in general was being constantly shoved into the background.

He then added, and a smile was audible in his voice, that he really was not *that* disillusioned with Elizalde or Panamin—their work was valuable and meaningful. "Give Manda my regards," Lynch said, "as from a fond but disappointed father."

After we hung up, I thought about that last remark and wondered if Lynch meant father in a paternal sense or a priestly one—perhaps both. He was, of course, a Jesuit priest, a fact I occasionally forgot.

I also wondered about a matter that may have affected his work with Panamin, though we never discussed it, which was that he had stepped in for Fox, which may have strained their relationship. There had been considerable talk in the spring of the two American anthropologists working as joint consultants on the Tasaday program, but nothing came of it.

The eight-man NBC crew flew to Mindanao August 10 aboard a chartered C-47 loaded with film gear, camping supplies, and food. It was a relaxed and pleasant ride, but immediately upon reaching the Surallah airstrip it was apparent something was wrong. An extraordinarily large number of people were waiting, including many local and national police. We wondered if they wanted to search all the NBC goods, but Panamin trucks inched through the crowd and backed up to the plane. Everybody and everything was loaded quickly and driven off to Tboli, with armed guards posted on each vehicle.

At the settlement the Tboli gave NBC a warm welcome, but behind it there was an unpleasant tension. Elizalde, his face stubbled with whiskers, looked worried and said privately that there was serious trouble. My first thought was that something had happened again among the Tasaday.

No, he said, it was among the Tboli. A family of Christians had been horribly massacred not too far from the settlement; eight people, including a pregnant woman, had been hacked to death and their entrails strewn all over their small house, which was in back of a refreshment stand they operated. Police had produced two Tboli youths who named four other Tboli as responsible for the killings. With Manda's concurrence, Mai had helped round up the four suspects for the Surallah police, although each man pleaded his innocence. After they were jailed, the two youths who had implicated them showed up at the Tboli settlement and said they had been tortured into naming the four and that they had no evidence whatsoever that they were guilty. The informers showed bruises and burns on their bodies and asked for protection.

At a pretrial court hearing, Elizalde said, the prosecution had been unable to produce evidence against the accused, but the judge, who would hear and decide the case (there was no jury system), had announced in the presence of the mayor and Panamin lawyers that Tboli were most certainly guilty, because "we all know a terrible massacre like this had to be perpetrated by pagans—Christians simply would not do anything like this."

Elizalde immediately arranged for a team from the National Bureau of Investigation, the Philippines' version of the American FBI, to come from Manila with a lie detector to test the suspects. He also engaged two of the best known and highest-priced criminal lawyers in Manila. "We're going to fight," he said. "If they can be proven guilty, then let the town have them and do what it wants, but if they're innocent we've got to show the Tboli that they can get justice, that they have a chance. Either way, guilty or innocent, it's got to be established that Tboli cannot just be pushed around any longer."

The local settlers were being stirred up, rumors of new troubles circulated daily, and it was risky for Tboli to go into Surallah. Panamin was being accused of skulduggery, so the police at the airstrip that morning probably had wanted to search the cargo for arms and ammunition, which, he admitted, were being brought in because of threats against the Tboli.

When he finished talking about this, I remembered the letter from Lynch. Oscar Trinidad had already messaged Manda about the resignation; the letter merely made it formal. Lynch had written a polite statement that it was because of his many other obligations and that David Baradas was on hand to take over. I added as much as I could remember of my telephone conversation with Lynch, stressing that I thought he had been upset at first and concluding with the disappointed yet fond fatherly regards.

"Yeah, okay," Manda said. "I guess it's my fault. I don't know . . . no, damn it, I don't think so. This one-man show and Manda's lollipop business, I've heard it so many times, the same old banana. Damn it, what would we do if I wasn't doing it? If we had to wait for committees and bureaucrats? Money? Where would we get the money? This trial right now is a perfect example—fifty thousand pesos for the lawyers and twenty thousand for other stuff, flying people down here, getting our own guards to watch the prisoners inside the jail— They doped them, you know, gave them something, so that when they took the first lie-detector tests, they were all goofy; we had to put our own constabulary people in jail to take care of them. And then we had to buy ammunition. The town is upset, the Tboli are upset—supposing somebody gets up a mob and they come looking for Tboli? They've gotta be able to protect themselves."

The fervor that had supplanted his earlier, worried manner intensified as he spoke. "Now, look, where did that money come from? Panamin just hasn't got it. From my pocket, that's where. Seventy-thousand pesos [about $10,000] just like that [finger snap]. I may get it back, or some of it; maybe all, maybe not. But that's not the point. Supposing we had to wait for official allocations—it'd be too late, these guys would have been convicted already. And the helicopter—now, who the hell pays for that? It would take practically our whole annual budget from the government just for the helicopter. What is it? Five or six hundred dollars a day. We spent something like a quarter of a million dollars—dollars, not pesos —on it over a couple of years. I pay for it. And I can't say that all my family or the people in our businesses are exactly pleased by that. Some hate it and they'd love to nail me somehow. Now, I'm not bitching about it, just saying that it's nice as hell to say we should run this like a university—but how? The fund drive in the States? Hell, we gotta spend twenty-five thousand dollars just on research to find out if they think it's feasible—and even then, what? Maybe no, maybe yes. And if we go ahead, there's no assurance what we could collect. Did you hear that fund-raising guy in Washington? Said just to run the campaign might cost at least a dollar for every dollar we got. What are you going to do? One-man show? Well, all right! If that's the way it's got to be, screw it, then that's the way! I'm gonna do what I've got to and that's all I can say. If somebody else wants to come down here and do it, then more power to 'em. If they got a better way, a better idea, let's hear it! But until then, until then, we'll do it the best we can—the only way we know how."

The tirade seemed to spend his anger, and he decided to write a note to Lynch, politely accepting his resignation but trying to word it so the door would be left open for Lynch to work with Panamin in the future. "I'm not glad to see him go, by any means," Manda said. "He's been good, very good. That report he and Carlos did was first rate, first rate. Damn it! The scientists take more handling than the Tasaday."

It had long seemed to me that Panamin operated on such a short-range basis, often on the spur of the moment, that it would be extremely difficult for scientists, who usually planned their programs far ahead, to work with them. I didn't believe scientists were so much at fault, but, rather, circumstances, I said to Manda. "Yeah, right!" he replied. *"Right!* But what the hell am I supposed to do? Tell the police that this massacre and trial simply doesn't fit into our present schedule? Would you mind, gentlemen, putting it on our calendar for, say, July of next year?"

Just before the murders, he had flown into the mountains to meet Kabayo. Manda said he was an extraordinary man of about forty, tough and dirty and weird-looking, strangely impressive. He was wearing short trousers and no shirt, and had refused to go into detail about his venture into the forest, claiming only that he had intended to see what was going on in there after hearing about all the activity. Then he added that the Panamin helicopter always landed at the Ubu and Blit settlements, and now the Tasaday. It had been passing over for years; why didn't it stop even once at Kabayo's place?

"Kabayo was scared," Manda said, "no question of that. The boys had really put the fear into him. He admitted they must be pretty good boys, but insisted they never would have got him if he had been by himself. But he didn't seem angry—and he wouldn't let us leave, insisting that since we finally had come we had to stay the night. I wasn't too hot for it. What a place he had! Filthy dirty . . . people in rags . . . crap all around the houses. And the smell—awful!

"But, I've gotta say this, the guy has guts. He's got 'em. He stood there —ol' Felix and the boys were ready to blast his head off if he made a wrong move—and told Mai: 'Now you tell brother here,' meaning me, 'that I'm going to call him brother and that I talk fast and I move fast and I do everything fast, but tell him not to mind because that's just the way I am.'

"It was a riot. And then, after we agreed to stay the night, he sent out runners and riders on horseback to call 'his people.' Well, a few showed up, but not many, and we sat around in his house after dark, waiting to go to sleep. But then we were called outside. Jesus! The mountains . . . all over the mountain were these lights, torchlights, long strings of them coming down toward us, from everywhere. It was an *incredible* sight. And they just kept coming all night, and by morning there were hundreds of people, Kabayo's people, and they were just as grimy and dirty as he was. And he was the big guy. Yeah, I'll tell you, they looked up to him, they really did.

"He promised us he'd never bother the Tasaday again, said he was sorry and just didn't know what was going on in the forest. He begged us to come and see him and help his people. You've gotta hand it to that guy, he cares about those people and they love him. But don't worry, we warned him that one more mistake and he's dead. We'd chase him next time until we got him. The Ubu from Ma Falen's place and the Blit will keep an eye on him. He moves out of line just once, we'll know it by radio in a minute. But I still can't get over him, those people really love him."

I wanted to ask more questions about Kabayo, but Manda was being interrupted every few minutes by aides or messages. He did add, however, that Richard Elkins, the Manubo language specialist, from the Summer Institute, who was scheduled to work with Yen, had arrived but stayed in the forest only four days. Elkins was on a special medical diet and had asked Panamin for certain foods, but those supplied disagreed with him and he became ill and had to leave. "It was really too bad," Manda said. "He didn't look so hot, but he told us he was very impressed with what he saw and would like to come back."

Elizalde spent the late afternoon and all evening with the NBC troop and the lawyers and the NBI investigators. I talked with the botanists, Gutierrez and Reynoso, who had completed ten days of work with Yen and were returning to Manila with about one hundred eighty plant specimens for further study at the National Museum.

The Tasaday had provided a remarkable experience, Gutierrez said. "We had read and heard about them, but, you know, we wondered if it was really true, what it was really like. I'll tell you, I'm a believer now."

He said the Tasaday had named all the plants and described uses for about one hundred twenty. The Tboli had more uses for the plants than the Blit or Tasaday, Gutierrez said, and this was partly because they had a lot of medicinal applications. The Tasaday used only one specimen as medicine, for treating cuts, which may have been learned from Sindi or Dafal.

The botanist was an enthusiastic storyteller. He recalled that at a considerable distance from the cave a specimen was collected that was similar to the sacred plants at the cave. It rained that day, for the first time in weeks. Bilangan noticed the specimen among many others at the tents and shook his head, saying, "You see, you must not cut that one. It has rained." Gutierrez said they assured him it had been cut away from the caves, and Balayam replied that it didn't make any difference. "But he didn't seem mad," Gutierrez concluded.

Reynoso asked him to tell about the grubworms. Gutierrez chuckled and said the Tasaday had tested them with the grubs—to see if they would eat them. "These grubs had been cooked. I bit into mine; it tasted sort of like mild cheese. Then Yen popped a whole grub in his mouth, chewed, and swallowed. Balayam looked at him strangely, then snapped the head off his grub and ate only the body. Balayam said they *never* ate the heads. Yen just sat there and smiled. He looked sort of odd."

Later that night, Mai reported rumors of an attack being planned by lowlanders against the Tboli or Blaan.

About eight the next morning, the radio at the staff house began to crackle, spewing excited words in Tboli and Tagalog. "Get the boss!" somebody shouted, and a runner was dispatched to Mai's house, where Elizalde had spent the night. By the time he reached the radio, the report was in: as several Tboli boys from a mountain settlement called Datal Kemalas walked to their cornfields at dawn, a group of men opened up on them with automatic rifles.

The teen-agers dove to the ground, rolled over a small ridge, and sprinted back uphill. Nobody had been hurt, but bursts of automatic fire followed them and cut down a line of cornstalks and small trees only a hundred yards below the hilltop settlement.

José Torres, Panamin's man with the Ubu, had moved to this place several days earlier because of increasing troubles between the Tboli and Christian farmers. He reported by radio that the men who had fired this morning could be seen gathering in a grove of banana trees; they looked as if they might have been preparing to attack the settlement, which had about two dozen houses.

Bart was sent to warm up the helicopter and Manda and Mai organized a group to go to Kemalas, only three or four miles north of the main Tboli settlement. Reynolds asked if he and a camera team could come along and was told yes. Manda, Mai, and I, Roland Daza, and another member of the Philippines Constabulary (the national police, together with the Marines, had stationed a few men at Tboli to assist the tribesmen in their problems with the lowlanders) flew in, followed by Reynolds, Lim Youn Choul, Det Arndt, Felix, and another security guard.

Kemalas stood on a ridgeline perhaps fifteen hundred feet above a flat valley that stretched for miles. The ridge was a saddle on the mountain range that separated the lowlands from the rugged country of the Tboli, Ubu, and Blit—and the Tasaday, who were about thirty-five miles east. From Kemalas, terraced shelves dropped like steps to the flatland, which was covered with farms and ranches and dotted with hamlets along the road to Surallah, the largest town in the area. All of this flatland had once belonged to the Tboli and Blaan, Manda said, but now was occupied by settlers—the "Christians," as tribesmen called them. Now the Kemalas tribesmen confined their farming to the shelf-steps of the ridge. They had their corn and rice and vegetable plots there, and also their houses.

West from Kemalas, the view was rice and vegetable farms and plantations of sugar cane and coconut palms spreading to the horizon. In the opposite direction were mountains, jagged peaks rising through mist and trailing off into dragon's-tail ridges right out of an ancient Chinese painting.

Only a few armed men were on the ground as we landed at Kemalas. Torres, wearing a bright orange-green headband around his thick black hair, talked with Elizalde in muffled tones. We could see Manda responding with agitated gestures and frowns. Then he shouted, "That makes sense! Now what happens if those guys below decide to attack? What are you going to do then? Yell at them? Where are your weapons, Torres? Where are your *brains?*"

It seemed that Torres, upon learning by radio that unidentified guests were accompanying Elizalde to Kemalas, surmised they were local politicians or police authorities on a survey of the troubled area. Torres sent most of the armed men into hiding, leaving only a few stationed at lean-to bunkers on a shelf just below the main ridgetop settlement.

After Manda finished screaming at him, Torres looked momentarily sheepish, then ordered runners to fetch the other men. Within fifteen minutes about forty arrived, most of them with spears and bows and arrows;

about a dozen had homemade rifles, and several had homemade pistols. Many of the men wore headbands and all had talismans of yellow ribbon or red cloth tied to their bows, spears, or rifle muzzles.

Elizalde sat on a knoll and peered through binoculars. The corn and small trees shattered by the bullets earlier were about 75 yards directly below him, and some two hundred yards beyond was the banana grove where the attackers had gathered. The people were not visible to the naked eye; Manda, using field glasses, began to count: "two . . . five . . . seven . . . ten . . . there's two more . . . and more behind them, by those coconut trees." Mai and others took turns with the binoculars and the number of men was put at between twenty and thirty. Most had weapons and Mai said a few were wearing police fatigue uniforms, which did not prove they were police, because such clothing was sometimes worn by thugs pretending to be police.

After more than an hour of waiting, during which little happened except that the number of tribesmen on the ridgetop grew to about seventy-five, the men below began to retreat out of the grove in twos and threes. They could be seen without binoculars as they appeared and disappeared in dips and gullies and finally boarded trucks near the base of the mountain.

I visited one of the lean-to bunkers and found half a dozen boys about sixteen years old. Each had a homemade gun, which he kept trained down the slope, and extra bullets tucked into a belt or pockets or wrapped in a handkerchief-sized cloth. We did not speak the same language but did communicate by smiles and nods and gestures. They seemed an extremely friendly but tough group of boys.

After the men below had dispersed, presumably thinking the helicopter had brought armed reinforcements, we returned to Tboli. It was mid-afternoon and the lawyers on the massacre case were on the porch reporting the day's developments. Both nattily dressed Manila attorneys zestfully re-enacted their court appearances that morning, demonstrating how they had established themselves as men not to be trifled with.

At dinner, the four-man NBI team reported that their lie-detector tests had been overwhelmingly favorable to the Tboli prisoners. The problem now was to make that stand up before the judge. The two young men who claimed they had been forced to implicate the other Tboli were possible witnesses for the defense, but they were terribly frightened. They said they had been in the vicinity of the massacre the evening it occurred and had noticed a drunken party of men carousing around the refreshment stand; they didn't know the men, but they definitely were not Tboli.

While we were relaxing on the staff-house porch that evening, somebody spotted tiny bright points of orange off in the distance. At almost the same moment Torres radioed from Kemalas that at least five houses were on fire. Nothing could be done to put out the flames, Torres said, but it was believed all Tboli had escaped injury because the houses—on the slope about halfway between the ridgetop and the flatland—had been evacuated when trouble started several days earlier. Torres added that rumors had reached Kemalas that a group of men was planning to come up a mountain south of the settlement for an assault that night.

Such reports flashed through the region with surprising speed during times of trouble—frequently started as psychological warfare by one side or the other—and it was impossible to quickly determine their validity.

"We're ready as we can be," Torres said. "I think we can handle anything that will happen tonight."

Green, Reynolds, and the rest of the NBC crew took turns peering through binoculars at the fires. The sight was mesmerizing: houses flaring up in bright color, weakening to a soft flickering glow, then dying into faint dots in the darkness. Everyone on the porch, whether from NBC, Panamin, or the Tboli, gazed helplessly, muttering words of anguish and frustration.

We flew the next morning to the site of the burnings. The five houses had stood in line on a shoulder of land with a spectacular view into the valley. Now they were ashes—black timbers, a sooty metal pot, a half-burned wicker basket, odd pieces of broken crockery. There were no signs of life, only wisps of smoke curling from the ruins.

We saw more charred wreckage from the helicopter on the way back to Tboli; we found out later that at least twelve Tboli houses had been burned during the night.

The word from the courthouse that afternoon was that in spite of the defense lawyers' impressive presentation, bail had been set at several thousand pesos for each of eight murder counts against each suspect. The Tboli began taking up a collection, but there was no hope they could bail out even one man. The lawyers reported that the judge, in replying to arguments that no hard evidence had been presented against the accused men, announced to the crowded courtroom: "Evidence will be forthcoming."

Elizalde was alternately furious and depressed. "It looks like somebody is stirring things up for a real fight. What for? It has been more quiet lately than in two years, more peaceful than most of Mindanao. Who is behind this? It's not accidental. Why are they doing it?"

Green was shocked by what was happening to the tribes and impressed by Elizalde. "I thought when we met him in New York he was some kind of rich playboy fooling with this as a hobby," Green said privately, "but no, he's really into this. He knows what it's all about."

In midafternoon a truck drove through the main gate of the settlement and parked at the medical clinic. A clinician phoned the staff house and said three men were there to see Elizalde and to make a film on the Tasaday.

The information was relayed to Manda, who looked confused. "Who are they? What do they want? Find out all you can."

Ching went to the phone and reported back that the men said they were from a television company in Tokyo and were expected here. They gave their names and that of their organization, and said they had been traveling for several days from Japan. Ching added that Dr. Rebong had spoken with them and said they apparently had caught the wrong plane in Manila and ended up in Santos City, a coastal town to the south, where they had rented a beat-up truck, which they then drove here piled with trunks and suitcases.

"This is all new to me," Manda said. "I've never heard of them. Better have them come up here and we'll see what's happening."

The Japanese arrived at the staff house and stood stiffly among the NBC equipment until they were asked to come to the porch, where they stood stiffly under the curious stares of the NBC crew. Then, politely and formally, the Japanese bowed and shook hands all around, stepped back into a line facing us, and announced that they were here to make their film about the Tasaday.

Elizalde said he did not understand.

The leader of the Japanese replied in broken English that he had met Elizalde while covering the elections in the Philippines the previous year and had asked him then about making a film on the Tasaday.

"Oh, really. What did I say?"

"You say talk Panamin office. Talk Mister Trinidad."

"And . . . did you?"

"Ah, yes. Talk much. He know I come. Say, 'Okay.' "

The Japanese were offered seats and refreshments while a rush message was radioed Trinidad in Manila. He replied immediately that he had been reached by the man—several times in recent months, by letter, cable, telephone, all from Tokyo—and that he told him that filming of the Tasaday was closely regulated and arrangements had been made with NBC for the present; perhaps there would be another opportunity next year. Trinidad then urged them to get in touch with Panamin when its TV organization had a man in Manila so they could discuss it in detail. Trinidad's message ended by saying that no contact had been made in Manila and no permission had been given for them to make a film.

Elizalde read this, sighed, shook his head, and asked Ching and me to take care of it. "I don't know what the hell is going on," he said. "Everything is coming apart all at once. Tell 'em something, tell 'em anything, but they can't film, of course. They can stay the night, and film around here, but no Tasaday."

The Japanese were advised that there had been a mix-up and that Mr. Trinidad acknowledged having had contact with them but had not spoken to them in Manila or told them to come here.

"Ah so, umm . . . so. Mister Trinidad not there when we go Panamin office. We talk secretary Panamin who say Mister Elizalde here and okay we come."

"Who? Which secretary? You mean the executive secretary, Mr. Certeza?"

"No, no. Not mister, was woman."

After a confusing and painstaking reconstruction of their visit to the Panamin office, it appeared that in the absence of Trinidad and Certeza, and apparently almost everyone else, the Japanese had spoken with a secretary in the accounting section. It seemed doubtful that she understood what was going on, but supposedly had told these men that Elizalde was at the Tboli settlement and if they wanted to see him and the Tasaday it was perfectly all right with her. And here they were.

It seemed implausible that experienced travelers and news reporters would be so mixed up, but that's the way they told it. And they insisted they were going to film—would not budge from the porch.

We offered them sympathy for their lost time and effort, but told them repeatedly that it would be impossible for them to film the Tasaday at this time. They stuck to their chairs, saying they did not understand, they had come all this way and simply had to make their film, it would take only a few days. As the conversation continued, however haltingly, it was disclosed that they had come to the Philippines to cover another story, and after finishing it decided they might as well do the Tasaday film as long as they were in the country. They remained on the porch for another hour, insisting that they could complete their work in a couple of days. When the answer continued to be no, they turned down the offer of a place to sleep, sighed, shook their heads, and bowed all around. Within a few minutes they were aboard their overloaded old truck, bouncing off into the dusk.

Elizalde, who had stayed out of their way the latter part of the episode, groaned with relief as they drove away. "What is going on? We've got massacres, phony arrests, phony trials, shootings, burning houses—and now we're invaded by a Japanese television crew. It's ridiculous!"

He was asked if anything had been learned from the Tasaday about the missing boy. "Missing boy? I've been too busy to even think about it. The pictures are still here. No use sending them in to Yen now, we'll take them when we go ourselves."

Rumors of impending troubles filtered in from scattered tribal areas the next day, but no incidents were reported. Elizalde hoped the worst of the difficulty was over and told Reynolds and Green that he believed filming of the Tasaday could start soon. The NBC team said they understood the delay and, in fact, had made use of the time in Tboli to film the Kemalas trouble, the burned houses, and the court hearings, which dramatized the dangers the Tasaday might face someday.

18

Television and the Tasaday

ELIZALDE intended to stay in the Tasaday forest throughout the filming, but it appeared that he, and Mai, might be compelled to spend time on the worsening troubles of the tribesmen outside. He delayed entering the forest a couple of days, hoping matters would be settled or at least clarified, but to no avail. He then decided to start the filming as soon as possible. On August 12, he radioed Yen that he and the TV crew planned to arrive the next morning. Yen said come ahead.

The helicopter worked all day, shuttling in people first, then equipment and supplies. Balayam, Bilangan, Lolo, Lobo, Udelen, and Udo were waiting at the landing ridge and swarmed over Manda when he stepped off the chopper. Green and Reynolds arrived on the next flight. Green was visibly impressed by his first meeting with the Tasaday. "It's marvelous just to see them," he said. "There's something different in their faces . . . like they've never been hurt."

Yen greeted us at the tents in excellent humor. His work had gone well and the Tasaday had been extraordinarily interesting. "I'm convinced this is about as close to nature as man can get. They are true gatherers. Their trapping has taken them a step away from that, but it's so new to them that we can reconstruct what it was like before. This has been a tremendous experience."

Yen said that several times he had watched them cooking and dividing the food brought to the caves; everything was shared, and if a family was away, its portion was set aside until it returned.

He had observed also that various individuals were specialists of sorts. Udelen, for instance, was a meat cutter and Balayam said that was be-

299

cause he cut equal portions. Balayam was watcher of the caves, apparently a legacy from his father, and did not venture as far afield as others. Dul continued to emerge as a strong figure and Dad said this was because she was "young, clever, and a stranger"; exactly why this particular combination of qualities was highly regarded had not been learned.

We noticed that Dad and Yen seemed to be almost inseparable. The teen-ager had performed exceptionally well as translator, guide, informant, cook, hiker, camp helper, botanist's assistant, and in any other role that had needed filling.

The NBC crew, minus Yasuda and Yashiro, who had stayed at Tboli with Bassett to film the massacre trial, immediately set to work pitching tents and preparing its accommodations. Three Tboli boys were busy all day portering goods from the landing ridge.

Not long after we arrived, the radio disclosed fresh troubles among the Tboli. Several more houses had been burned during the night and a woman and her son had been wounded by gunfire. The helicopter brought in a Manila *Times,* which carried a story quoting Mayor Sison of Surallah as saying that twenty-six settlers had been slain by Tboli raiders. There was no mention of injuries to Tboli or of houses burned. Manda was furious and radioed Tboli asking the latest information about killings in the area. An hour later Juan Artajo, Panamin's regional director, replied that three tribesmen had been killed and the eight members of the Christian family massacred—that was all. He said the news report was absolutely false.

Elizalde said he had no illusions about the mayor's sympathies, but that he had been publicly quiet in recent months and his statement could indicate an escalation of the troubles. Mai said that a Christian friend had informed him yesterday at Tboli that two town officials and several other residents had met and discussed plans to raise an army of up to five hundred men to raid the Tasaday area, find out what was going on, and kill Mai. He said his informant, an old friend, had attended the meeting.

That evening the radio delivered reports of more Tboli houses burned, and Manda dispatched a lengthy message to President Marcos, informing him of the trial, the house burnings, the killings, and warning that the peace in the area was imperiled.

The next morning Elizalde debated with himself whether to fly back to Tboli, but Artajo reported the situation remained stable, so he decided to stay. He got out the photographs of the missing Tasaday boy and showed them to Igna and Dafal. Both said they did not remember the youngster, had no idea of his identity or what had happened to him. Elizalde said he would check with the Tasaday as soon as it was convenient.

After breakfast Dad reported that the Tasaday had located a *natek* palm and were starting to work on it. Yen had not seen them make *natek* and wanted to observe. The Tasaday said that would be fine and we stopped by NBC's tents, just below ours, and asked if they wanted to film it, presuming the Tasaday would agree.

Reynolds wanted to but, having met the Tasaday twice before, he was aware of their sensitivities and did not want to move too quickly. Green agreed that their first priority was to make a good start with the Tasaday, establishing friendly relations that would carry throughout the expected three or four weeks of filming. There was no script to follow and, as much as possible, events would be treated just as they developed, allowing the Tasaday to set the pace. They decided to ask the Tasaday if they were willing for NBC to film. The Tasaday said visitors were welcome.

We found the Tasaday tipping three large chunks of *natek* palm, each between seventy-five and one hundred pounds, end over end down a sharp grade covered with heavy foliage. They wrestled the chunks to a small dimly lighted hollow that had a shallow creek no more than two feet wide. Within two hours the Tasaday had built their apparatus and pressed the first batch of carrot-colored pith, but apparently not enough of the starch was being extracted and the soupy mixture was too thin. Balayam and Bilangan fussed with the press but could not solve the problem. Dafal, seeming to sense he was needed, materialized out of the jungle for the first time that day. He poked around, adjusted the leaves of the press, added more water to the pith, jumped up and down more vigorously to force the liquid into the bark trough. Whatever he did was just right and batches began rolling through. When it was cooked, hot pieces of *natek* were given to all the visitors.

When we returned to camp, Manda, who had stayed there, said Lobo had stopped by to play. He was shown the photographs of the missing boy and was asked his identity. Lobo looked, frowned, jumped up, and dashed to the caves. Mai followed after a few minutes and met Dul, who already had heard a report from Lobo. She said, "We will tell you about this boy when we are all together, when Balayam and the others are present."

But at the caves that evening, mention of the missing boy caused Dul and Balayam to switch into a strange language. It was almost like a code and sounded similar to children's pig Latin in that each word had a similar ending. The Tasaday's ending was *uff*. Mai and Igna puzzled over this; they could not understand a single word. Soon, other Tasaday joined in the secret conversation.

Manda said they obviously did not want to talk to us about the boy, so the subject would be dropped for the present. "I don't want to force them or trick them into telling us," he said. "We'll just have to wait. It'll eventually come out."

Half an hour later, as we were leaving, Balayam walked over to Mai and whispered something. Mai talked privately to Manda and then we left.

At the tents Manda said Balayam told Mai the boy had died. "His name was Ukan, son of Lefonok. He was the older brother of Udo." That was all Balayam had said.

"I guess we'll just have to wait to see if they'll tell us more," Manda said. "It'll come when they feel like it, *if* they feel like it. What puzzles me now is that code language. Never heard that before."

Mai said he knew tribes that used subdialects, and Yen said he had encountered it elsewhere in the Pacific. But what use would a second tongue have for the Tasaday? They claimed to have seen no other groups for years. Perhaps it was used when adults did not want children to understand. Or maybe it was a kind of game or a holdover from when they had met other groups; perhaps they still met them. Whatever the reason, the mystery of the boy had been partly clarified, but there was a new mystery.

That same day, a message arrived from Oscar Trinidad saying a writer on assignment for the *New York Times Magazine* had come to Manila to prepare an article on Elizalde, Panamin, and the Tasaday. The writer, Peggy Durdin, and her husband, Tilman, a *Times* correspondent in Asia for many years, wanted to interview Manda and spend some time with the Tasaday. Reynolds and Green were worried that any more outsiders would increase the possibility of disrupting the Tasaday. They noted also that NBC had been planning this expedition for many months and had made a sizable donation to Panamin. This contractually granted only television exclusivity, but in spirit it had assured general exclusivity while they were filming. In fact, nobody had mentioned the possible inclusion of other newsmen, because Panamin had not allowed journalists to visit the caves except by prearrangement. Nonetheless, the New York *Times* was the New York *Times,* a fact known to open doors that were closed to reporters of other organizations; and the Durdins were respected journalists.

Elizalde, more concerned by the problems outside the forest, threw the matter to Reynolds and Green, saying that, in view of Panamin's commitment to NBC, he would be guided by their opinion. They said they believed Panamin's story should be told as widely as possible and would not object if the Durdins visited the Tasaday, but only for one day. Elizalde agreed and messaged this to Manila.

Late that evening, a message arrived saying an unusually large number of uniformed men and helicopters were in the Surallah area. This was followed about midnight by a message that the head of the constabulary for Mindanao, Gen. Wilfredo Encarnacion, was planning to visit Tboli and wanted to meet with Elizalde. No time was mentioned, but after breakfast the next morning the general was reported on his way. Elizalde arranged for the helicopter to fetch him at once, explained quickly to the Tasaday that he and Mai had to leave for a while, and hiked to the landing ridge.

The NBC crew said they could use the time to work on their accommodations and would not do any filming until he returned. At Manda's invitation, Yen went to Tboli to take a break from two weeks in the jungle, and I accompanied them to see what was happening.

As we left camp, Lobo and Udo were watching the NBC crew tighten their tents and clear the grounds. Green and Arndt took off their caps, revealing shiny bald heads. Lobo was delighted and could not resist running his hands over the smooth skin, giggling and repeating *"n'da bul-bul"* (no hair). Green and Arndt got as much fun out of it as Lobo; henceforth, one or the other had his head rubbed almost daily by a laughing Tasaday.

Dad, Balayam, and Sindi walked with us to the landing ridge. Yen, as was his custom, studied the vegetation as he hiked and found on the ground a delicate violet-colored flower. It was the only one in sight and apparently had been blown from a tree or a plant. It looked to me like a tiny orchid. Yen was intrigued, called Dad and Balayam, and asked if they had a name for it. Balayam reached out, took the tiny blossom between his thumb and forefinger, and pulled it close to his face, staring almost cross-eyed as he twisted his head this way and that. Then he popped it in his mouth, swallowed, and smiled, indicating it had been rather tasty.

"What!" Yen sputtered. "Oh, no. I wanted to save that. It's the only one I've ever seen." He sighed, then smiled and said that this was an occupational hazard; it was not the first time an informant had gobbled up botanical specimens.

At Tboli, the general already was on the staff-house porch with several aides and local constabulary officers. Elizalde, with a two-week-old beard and grimy clothes, strode briskly up to them, smiled congenially, and then gave a detailed rundown of the troubles at Kemalas, the house burnings, and Tboli casualties.

General Encarnacion said his mission was to get between the opposing factions and stop the trouble. He had a platoon of twenty-one army regulars to be deployed together with an undisclosed number of locally based constabulary troopers.

Manda did not know whether this was a response to his message to Marcos describing the situation, but he welcomed the troops and requested that at least some of the army men be stationed at Datal Kemalas. He said he feared that bands of men known as Ilagas (rats, in the Visayan dialect) had moved into South Cotabato from the north and were stirring up the trouble, either on their own or in the pay of someone else. The Ilagas were notorious outlaws who had been in North Cotabato Province for the past eighteen months, during which, authorities estimated more than two thousand persons had been slain and tens of thousands made homeless. The Ilagas—loosely organized bands of landless settlers, jobless laborers, adventurers, mercenaries, and men bent on revenge for harm done their families—were in the forefront of the fighting. It was often described as a Moslem-Christian war, but religion itself was not the issue. The trouble had started mainly over land, with the formerly dominant Moslems opposing ambitious new settlers, who were primarily Christians. The Ilagas always fought against the Moslems. The charges and countercharges of the opposing sides had their origins in centuries of cultural, religious, and blood loyalties.

The general was eager to prevent similar fighting in South Cotabato and said he wanted to visit the main troublespots during the next few days with Elizalde and the mayor of Surrallah.

Later, Elizalde said that one of the local constabulary officers on the porch had worked actively against the tribesmen, and was linked to politicians and rich landowners. He said several Tboli reported that this lieutenant had been with the group in the banana grove the day we were on the hilltop at Kemalas. Two days after that, a local newspaper had quoted him to the effect that guns in the Panamin helicopter had fired on the police and farmers who were investigating trouble started by tribesmen from Kemalas, that the helicopter had used "Vietnam war tactics" in attacking the investigators, and that the cause of the trouble was Panamin's attempt to steal land below Kemalas to build a private airstrip. An editorial in the same newspaper blamed all the recent trouble on Elizalde and Panamin, who, it said, were stirring up the tribesmen for evil purposes, and added that the Tasaday were fakes being used as a smoke screen for mining and other Elizalde ventures in the mountains. Still another story in the paper claimed that Elizalde was planning to run for congress from the district, and that all his activities were politically motivated.

After the general and his party left, Elizalde met the Durdins, who had arrived from Manila. It was soon clear that Peggy Durdin's magazine story was to focus on the Tasaday and that she hoped to spend considerable time with them. Her husband would accompany her to the caves, but his primary aim on this trip was to prepare articles on Mindanao unrest in general, tribal problems, and the Philippines political situation.

Yen and I spent the afternoon walking around the Tboli settlement. He was keenly interested in it. Elizalde had already described to him how the property had been acquired and improved. The subject of further improvement, a favorite with Elizalde, had come up two weeks earlier, on Yen's first evening in Tboli. "Where do we go from here?" he asked Yen. "Look, Doug, they've got the will to live—that's number one. And now they've got a place to live—number two. But the place isn't big enough, they've got to figure out ways to live on less land than they once had and at the same time learn to make it in terms of the twentieth century—but their own way. The Tboli don't necessarily have to accept Christian methods, that's up to them. But they've got to make it some way. That's the next step, the third step, a way to live. We've got to figure out a way to live."

Various projects had been tried. Technical assistance teams from both the U.S. and Japan had suggested growing peanuts, for instance, and the Tboli had tried. But the soil was not right and the Tboli were not really interested in peanuts, anyway. Ways to develop the whole area had to be discovered. How could the land, water, and man power be best used to establish a co-ordinated system of development that would give the Tboli a foundation for the future? The more Elizalde saw of Yen, the more he became convinced that Yen was the man to direct this development program. Every chance he got, Elizalde presented arguments to Yen as to why he should take it over.

Yen and I discussed this project as we continued our walk. He was impressed with what he had seen of the tribes and Manda, and fascinated and challenged by the idea of developing a whole valley. But it would take a couple of years of intensive fulltime work, and he had many obligations already. Still, he was interested in the possibilities and told Elizalde he would give them serious thought. Did Panamin have the money to do this project right? was one of the questions uppermost in Yen's mind. Experts in agriculture, irrigation, energy would be needed—could Panamin afford to get them? And what about Manda, who was so essential to the workings of the organization? What would it be like to try to get things done with him out of the country or otherwise unavailable, or if you disagreed with him?

We wound up returning to the subject of the Tasaday, with whom Yen was fascinated. He said again that "perhaps the most significant fact is that they are hunters and gatherers, but that their hunting is so recent and undeveloped that we can still see them as when they were only gatherers." He was deeply impressed with their warmth and friendliness. As he talked, it became clear to me that he had become attached to them as people, not merely as scientific challenges.

Elizalde had to remain at Tboli to work on plans for the army and police peace-keeping efforts. The massacre trial was stalled, so Yasuda and Yashiro flew with Yen and me to the forest. Manda asked us to explain to Reynolds and Green that there had been a misunderstanding in Manila and that the Sunday *Times* story was to focus on the Tasaday, and the Durdins would like to spend considerably more than one day with them.

The debate about this went on for two days. Finally, many radio messages later, it was agreed that the Durdins would come in for one night, two days. Neither side was ecstatic about the arrangement, but it seemed to be the most amiable solution.

The Durdins were to arrive the morning of August 17 with Elizalde, but he sent word at the last minute that he would have to stay another day to deal with complications in the massacre trial, meet with another general and the mayor, and investigate more house burnings.

The next morning, we received a message that the tail rotor of the helicopter was not working properly and flying was prohibited; they would be delayed indefinitely.

The television crew had not yet been to the caves and had done very little filming. The men had worked on their camp facilities and the Tasaday stopped by several times to play and watch them. Their small gas stoves fascinated Balayam, Lefonok, and Udelen, who edged forward warily until they were practically on top of the tiny jet flames. Balayam, wide-eyed, crooked his fingers to look like the metal prongs that angled above the flames to hold the pans.

As time passed without substantial work being accomplished, and with the rain making a daily appearance, the tents seemed to shrink a little. Things that otherwise would probably have been overlooked became annoying. Three Tboli boys who were being paid by NBC to help in the kitchen, for instance, were often scarce when it was time to burn garbage, clean up, wash dishes. A pail of dirty dishes waiting to be washed became a symbol of nothing happening. The gray skies and drizzles made the idleness dreary.

On the positive side, Yen and I had pleasant meals and conversation with the NBC group, and Yen, who had been opposed to the idea of television filming of the Tasaday, was impressed with the crew's attitude of concern for the Tasaday. Reynolds, despite his eagerness to start filming, did not want to work around the caves without Elizalde.

Yen was able to continue his plant research. One afternoon at the main tent, Bilangan, who had become an enthusiastic and articulate informant, described to Dad in words and gestures how the Tasaday had made rattan into thin strips before they had metal knives, and how they used these strips to lace handles on stones. They began by dividing a long stem of rattan into pieces about four feet long, bending the rattan over a stone anvil and then sawing it with another stone. They split the ends of the pieces by biting them with their teeth or picking at them with the stone. They then lengthened the splits with their fingers until the separated ends would fit over the crown of their heads, at which point they pulled down on the split ends, causing the rattan to come apart in two long strips.

This was significant. We had assumed that the hastily made crude stone implements we had seen them make were their standard tools, and that the handles of their much superior heirloom pieces had been rewrapped with rattan after the acquisition of metal knives, because the rattan lacings were so neat and uniform.

When Yen asked about this, Bilangan said they had always prepared

Incident in the settlement of Kemalas
Armed tribesmen on ridge above Allah Valley

Guards, with talismen on their guns, crouching in a bunker; José Torres and Elizalde;
Elizalde counting attackers; Dad and Fludi

Lolo leaping onto vine swing, Udelen sailing by. Lobo at end of 100-foot vine, and hanging by his feet. *Opposite,* Lobo climbing as he swings

Balayam and Lolo rolling a palm trunk down a hillside; Bilangan hacking trunk with bolo; Mahayag and other Tasaday using bamboo pounders to mash the pith into *natek*

Dafal supervising press construction; Bilangan treading on pith in press to extract starch, which is later shaped into loaves and cooked

Doc Rebong indicating pill dosage for Balayam's cold

Dad offering water to
Balayam to wash down a pill
as Douglas Yen watches

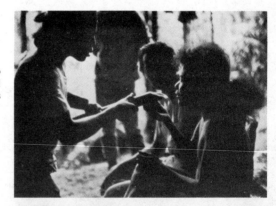

Doc Rebong working on Lobo's infected toe while Elizalde comforts the patient

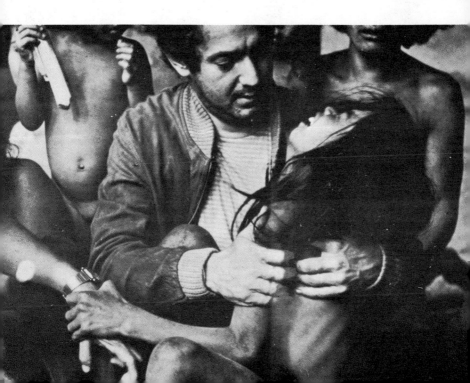

Lobo with his pet bird

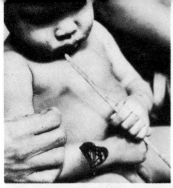

Maman holding stick to which his father, Udelen, has attached a live butterfly

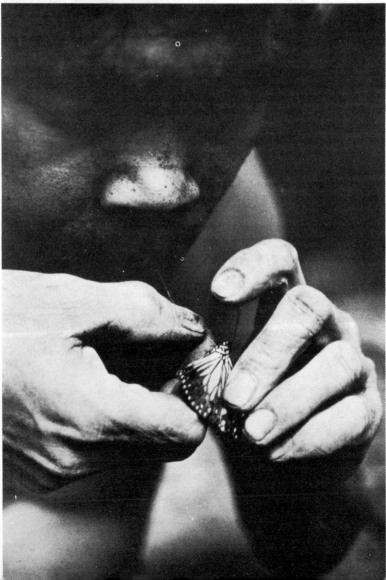

Balayam leaping from the big cave to his own

Lobo on the cave path

Udo in niche with deerhorn diggers

Sindi on broad midden shelf

Balayam carrying firewood

Tasaday peering out of Balayam's cave into the jungle

A boy passing entrance to Balayam's cave

Dul, with Maman, leading others down steep slope to stream

Kalee

Siyus drinking

A frog being killed by soft claps on the head

A full catch from the stream: tadpoles, frogs, crabs, fish

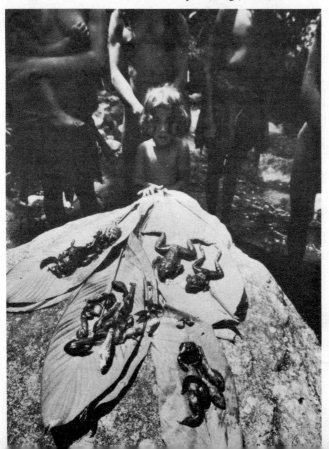

Above and below left, Lolo and Lobo answering questions about a flowering plant as Dad translates and Yen takes notes

Drying slices of *biking* to be tested for a contraceptive ingredient

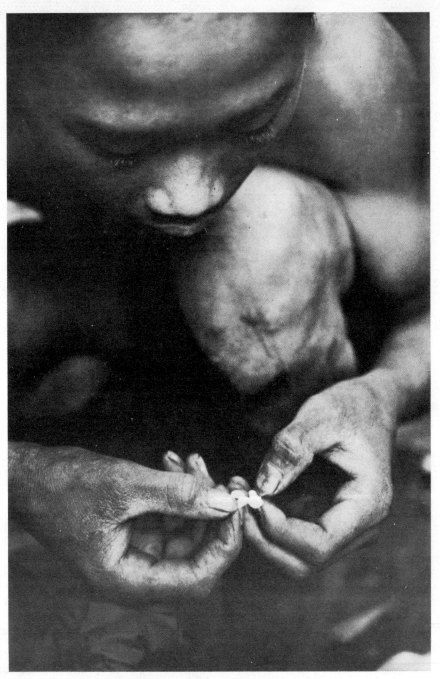

Lolo inspecting a tiny flower

Balayam telling a story; explaining
stone-tool making; using sign language
for Ginun; demonstrating pointed
digging stick

the rattan bindings in the way he had just told us. When Yen mentioned that the stones in the heirloom tools were so much harder, better shaped, and sharper, Bilangan said that was because those stones had not come from the stream, but from a special place in a mountain. Yen asked Bilangan if he would like to demonstrate what he had just described, and also if he would show us the heirloom tools again. Bilangan smiled and nodded. He would do it the next morning.

It occurred to us that it would be an opportunity for NBC to do some filming, undramatic but something, at least, after days of waiting. It would not disrupt the Tasaday's regular activities and Bilangan seemed happy to participate. Yen continued talking to Bilangan. I walked to the NBC tents and, rather eagerly, told Reynolds about it. He seemed pleased. Soon after I got back to the main tent, Balayam stopped by and was invited to join the demonstration the next day. Balayam glanced at Bilangan, looked thoughtful, talked with Dad, then nodded and soberly said yes, he would come.

Just before dinner, however, Dad arrived with word from Dul that the heirloom tools could not leave the caves; perhaps they could if Momo Dakel were present, but not now. Also, Dad said, Bilangan and Balayam would not be demonstrating how they had worked with rattan and the tools.

Yen and I looked at each other. What was this all about? "What's wrong?" we asked Dad. "Bilangan wanted to come. Nobody would have been bothered, and the tools have been out of the caves many times before."

"I don't know," Dad answered. "Dul just said no. That's all, just no."

It was rather obvious that Dul, and probably Balayam, too, was letting us know that we were not to try arranging things. No matter how minor the activity, it would be ruled out. I felt a depressing sense of futility. It was not so much the disappointment about the demonstration, but, rather, the fact that I had been rebuffed. I had flattered myself that they considered me a special friend, but it was obvious that they did not trust me; I had no influence with them, none.

Yen may have had similar feelings. In the past two weeks he had developed a close relationship with several of the Tasaday, and they seemed fond of him.

Minutes after Dad brought word of Dul's decision, a group of Tasaday arrived and surrounded Yen and me. Balayam, Mahayag, Adug, Lolo, and one or two others hugged and petted us, repeating our names and *"mafeon."* It seemed as if they had delegated themselves the job of consoling us with affection, and, after a brief application of it, they said good-by and returned to the caves. There was something dutiful rather than spontaneous about it—Yen and I both sensed this.

We visited the NBC tent for dinner. Reynolds also was disappointed that the demonstration had been called off—not that it was expected to be a terribly important sequence, but it had promised a change from sitting and waiting.

Back at the main tent, my bruised ego and feelings of futility twisted into indignation. What we had asked was of very little consequence, I blurted out to Yen. It meant no inconvenience for the Tasaday, and Bilangan was more than willing. Who in the hell did Dul think she was?

He was more philosophical, saying that we may have unknowingly touched a sensitive point. He agreed, though, that to be shown our impotence was a letdown. It also emphasized the extraordinary role Elizalde played. Manda, Yen continued, was surprising. "I'd heard about him, of course, but I didn't know if I would see much of him, and, if I did, whether I'd like him. But I do, and he has a remarkable way with these people. He's a very complex person—and if what he has isn't a touch of genius, it is still something quite extraordinary." Yen was especially impressed with Elizalde's ability to communicate with the Tasaday even though he knew very few words of their language.

Yen remarked that what other scientists had said about the Tasaday being difficult to work with was correct. This did not mean they were not enjoyable, but that you had to use great care and delicacy in dealing with them. They did not like sustained questioning, they did not understand the purpose of interrogation and observation. With other groups, it was often possible to make questioning into a game, something that was fun rather than traumatic. He felt that one of the most difficult things to arrange on a limited stay with the Tasaday was being with them when significant activities took place. They preferred not to be followed into the forest, for instance. It would take much patient diligence over a long period to learn satisfactory ways of overcoming their resistance and reticence.

This was often a problem for researchers. Yen showed me tattoos on his shoulders that he had acquired in Anuta, in the Solomon Islands, after a long, vain attempt to get responses to certain questions. He was advised that the old men of the society were blocking him; if he could win their confidence, he could get answers. But the old men, after lengthy discussions and deliberations, rebuffed him; so Yen decided to get himself tattooed in the manner of the Anuta men in hopes that it would establish symbolically that he was one of them.

For several painful hours artists with thorns worked on Yen and created on each shoulder three lines of half-inch-high figures representing trees, fish, and wooden pillows. The artists had wanted to go on, next decorating the corners of his eyes and then tattooing fish from the point of his chin down to his chest, but Yen begged off, saying his wife would not like them. The artists agreed that that was a good reason for not having them. The tattoos had the desired result—the old men responded favorably and the research proceeded smoothly.

Yen had, in effect, paid a price the Anutans understood. Usually in such a situation, gifts of tobacco, clothing, or beads produced the same effect. But the people of Anuta had not wanted such things enough to trade the information he had sought.

"Let's face it," Yen said. "You, me, anthropologists, anybody—we're all like missionaries and we have got to pay our way, to buy our way in. At the start, anyway. Every man—from the twentieth century back to the Stone Age, apparently—has some kind of price."

This struck me as overly cynical at first, but the more I thought about it, the more reasonable it became. We all had a price, if not money then an intangible—opportunity, love, pleasure, challenge, power.

And what had we given the Tasaday in exchange for their privacy? Why should they want us to always tag along, to poke and pry into their lives? To watch and cluck and make notes and photographs? What was in it for them? Of course, there was fun sometimes, and they enjoyed that. But when playtime was over and they had to make their living, it was not exactly helpful to be accompanied by stumbling strangers with cameras and notebooks and endless, meaningless questions.

I voiced some of my thoughts to Yen, and he told me that he had given pieces of candy to Lolo and Lobo the first day they had participated in the ethnobotanical work. The boys had liked the candy and readily accepted the second piece at the end of the session. But when Yen offered candy later, they refused it. Dad said they had been instructed not to take it any more. Yen said he thought it was Dul's order; I thought it might have been from Mai. "Well, it's okay with me," Yen said. "It's a reasonable rule, I guess. Of course, it removes a tool that could help in the work. But it hasn't been a real factor this time, because the kind of work I'm doing doesn't need the candy. In some research situations, though, you really might need something in order to get co-operation."

We agreed that the worth of any tool was dependent upon the persons wielding it. In the wrong hands it could be destructive, a hammer in the hands of a maniac, awesomely powerful among people as inexperienced as the Tasaday. Yen and I decided that for the moment there was no point in pushing the matter. Dul had made her decision very clear.

Several days later, after Elizalde's return, I found myself again dwelling on the subject of gifts. I remembered what he had told me about the first time he met the Tasaday. They appeared to be on the verge of flight but were kept from it, at least partly, by gifts of beads and knives. Now they felt considerable affection for him, and his continuing provision of gifts undoubtedly was an influence—the tape recordings clearly disclosed their keen interest in and eagerness for presents.

What licensed these gifts, in my mind, was Elizalde's intention of protecting the Tasaday, and so far he had been successful. Some people did not see that as his purpose, however, and their criticism occasionally nagged at me. One particularly caustic Filipino had argued that the Tasaday were mainly an "ego trip" for Elizalde, a chance to indulge his vanity and flex his muscles, play God. I recalled his remark one dusk at the caves. Manda was sprawled on a platform, surrounded by Tasaday who were literally burying him with their bodies, hugging, kissing, touching, smiling, murmuring. He loves being loved, I thought. But this was not merely an "ego trip," because he accepted the responsibility of being loved: he loved in return.

It was an awful and impossible responsibility to be Diwata or Great Brother or God or Good Fortune—whoever or whatever it was that these people wanted or needed.

Elizalde's response, of course, was bound up in his various resources and in his own values, loves, and needs. And beyond the theorizing about his motives and the toting up of observable results was his statement that he was doing "my thing" with the tribes. He liked it, enjoyed it, loved it—it gave him more pleasure than anything he had ever done or could think of doing. I did not see this as an ego trip strictly in the negative sense. I understood it far better than I did self-proclaimed altruism, better than a righteous commitment to help others, save them, improve them.

To me, then, the crucial questions were: How wisely did he apply that love? How long would it last? What would happen if he lost his enthusiasm?

When I mentioned all this to Manda later, he said I was still trying to judge him. He neither agreed nor disagreed with my view that the wise application and the longevity of his love for the Tasaday and the other tribes were crucial. "Well," he said, "I guess the only thing you can do now is wait and see, isn't it?"

He then gibed at me, saying I had become involved with the Tasaday and the project whether I had wanted to or not. Yet I claimed to be objective, refusing jobs he had offered me with Panamin and declining to make a real commitment to work for the tribes, a cause for which I claimed great sympathy. "This," he said, "is a kind of hypocrisy."

I admitted that now it was much harder for me to be objective, but that I still believed I could report and photograph fairly and that this was the service I could best provide. I did not have the abilities Panamin needed most—I was as poor a day-to-day organizer and administrator as he was.

We discussed this for a while, and then I brought up the matter of gift giving. Elizalde conceded that gifts were important to the Tasaday, but insisted that his relationship with them was not based on gifts. I tended to agree with this, but pointed out that, under present conditions, he was virtually the only person from whom the Tasaday would accept presents. I noted that Yen, for instance, could not even give the Tasaday candy, which limited his influence. When I suggested to Elizalde that this may have been his or Mai's doing, he became somewhat indignant, insisting that he had not instructed the Tasaday to refuse candy from Yen. What he had done was make a strong pronouncement to Mai and Fludi against gift giving after Carlos Fernandez and David Baradas discovered that large amounts of rice were regularly being given to the Tasaday. Of course, he said, sometimes rice had to be supplied because the presence of visitors upset the Tasaday's normal food gathering, no matter how often they were told to go about their business as usual.

Manda said that Yen was authorized to give rice whenever he wished. This was to make up for the considerable amount of *biking* the Tasaday were providing for his future research into the possibility that the wild yam influenced the birth rate. But one evening, Yen had discovered the Tasaday were still getting rice from the tribesmen at the camp: when Dad delivered the rice due them for *biking* received that day, he found that they had already got rice in the morning. It turned out that Dafal and some of the Tboli camp staff helping Yen and NBC had been giving them rice regularly. Yen and Manda asked them again not to do this, but they now realized that it was extremely difficult for the tribesmen to see anything wrong with giving the Tasaday rice—there was plenty, the Tasaday liked it; what harm could it do? I had been surprised that rice doles continued despite the strictures against it, but soon found out for myself that it was not easy to stick to that rule.

The day after our "rebuff," we received a message that Elizalde and the Durdins would be further delayed; the chopper had still not been repaired. Then Blit sent a message that Igna's new husband, Mafalo, a son of Datu Dudim, was very ill. She wanted to join him immediately. I cabled this information to Elizalde and added that filming was at a standstill with no prospect of getting under way without him.

Within a few minutes I was called to the radio tent. It was Elizalde asking what was holding up the filming. I explained, and he said it was his fault because he had left so hurriedly, thinking he would be right back, and neither he nor Mai had explained to the Tasaday what the TV crew was doing in the forest and what all their strange equipment meant. Manda said the helicopter could not fly for at least two more days, and suggested that perhaps he and Mai could explain to the Tasaday by radio.

Dad fetched Balayam, Dul, and several others to the radio tent, with Igna as interpreter. All the Tasaday had seen the single-side-band many times—the path from camp to the caves ran alongside the tent—but this would be the first time that any had spoken on the radio. They brightened immediately upon hearing the voices of Mai and Manda, and were shown how to press the button on the hand microphone so they could talk back. Dul went first; after three or four exchanges, she was flipping the switch by herself and ending her statements with "ober." Balayam could not wait to try it and practiced saying "go-hed" and "ober" to himself as he stood by. Then he took a turn with the microphone, followed by one or two others.

They were told that the big bird was sick and could not fly, that Mai and Manda would be back in a day or two, and that meanwhile the Tasaday's new visitors were anxious to see them gathering food at the stream—they did not have to take the visitors if they did not want to; but if they did, it would make Momo Dakel happy. The men were good friends of his and would try not to bother the Tasaday. If there were problems they should tell Dad, Yen, or me.

Dul and Balayam said they would not mind going to the stream with the new visitors, but had been worried because they brought many strange things and nobody knew what they were. Furthermore, Manda and Mai had gone away saying they would come back soon, but they had not!

The radio conversation put everyone in better spirits. Igna hiked off to Blit with Dafal to see her husband, and in the afternoon Yen, Dad, and I went to the stream with Reynolds, Green, the camera crew, and about ten Tasaday. They gathered tadpoles and crabs for about an hour with the film crew following a short distance away. It was not an exuberant foray, but pleasant enough. When the Tasaday had sufficient food, they said so and returned to the caves.

It drizzled on and off all the next day, and various groups of Tasaday stopped by the camp for short visits. The boys favored the attractions of the NBC area: tan tents with aluminum bars, various shapes and sizes of cans, containers, trunks, suitcases, crates.

About midday, at the main tent, Yen, Dad, and I were chatting with two Tasaday when Balayam popped around a corner, bounded past us with a nod and wave, and unhitched a vine swing. He jumped on, swung out with a long *"cheeeet,"* swung back, jumped off, hitched up the swing, and continued on down the hillside, sending back a few words and a laugh over his shoulder.

It was the kind of silent-comedy sequence that Charlie Chaplin might have done: a handyman waltzes through the parlor during madame's tea party, sits on the piano stool, twirls around a few times, and then dances blithely out through the swinging kitchen door with a kick of the heel and tip of the derby.

We had held up our conversation to watch Balayam's performance and then sat in dumb amusement. Dad laughed as he told us Balayam's departure statement. "He said he just stopped by for a quick swing to give a little fresh air to his *lassu* [penis]."

After that "a little air for the old *lassu*" became something of a rallying cry for anyone taking a ride on the swing.

The mood was happier all around by the time Manda came August 19 with the Durdins. Yasuda and Yashiro moved into other tents so the Durdins could use theirs, and in the afternoon the NBC crew made its first working visit to the caves. They photographed Manda first and then Reynolds arriving to warm greetings from the Tasaday. Then they visited the upper cave, where Etut, her burlap rice bag hugging her pregnant belly, was looking after her youngest sons, Natek and Ilib. Peggy Durdin's dangling earrings and bright-red rain hat and coat intrigued the Tasaday and they fondled them and made admiring noises. She offered to leave the earrings and rain gear with the Tasaday, but Manda said it would be better if she did not.

Bruce Bassett flew in to pick up exposed film so it could be shipped to New York for development. It was his second pickup trip and by then all the NBC group had been given names by Balayam. He was Bee-loo. Jack Reynolds was Kakay Biang, Gerry Green was Sheeling, Det Arndt was Wet, Lim Youn Choul was Leem, Shunichi Yasuda was Shuga, Teruhiko Yashiro was Biro, and Kwan was Kuwan.

In the evening we all talked in the main tent about Tboli problems. Elizalde felt that the present was probably the most promising period in history for minorities; many people were concerned about them, wanted them to have a chance, public opinion was favorable. "Andrew Jackson and a lot of other men killed Indians and were heroes," he said. "Only few people openly condemned it, and if they did, nobody paid much attention. But now we have a chance. President Marcos, for instance, really has done things. People listen."

Later, Tilman Durdin was tuning his small transistor radio to find a news report when Balayam came by. He had never seen this kind of radio and it fascinated him. He sneaked up on it in a half crouch and watched as Durdin moved the selector dial and, finding no news, stopped on music. Balayam was thrilled. The music was new to him and he glued his ear to the small radio, lifting his head only to shout and laugh.

We were always a bit concerned about the Tasaday's reaction to something totally new to them. What would they think? Would they be frightened? Would it have a lasting effect? And, if so, would it be negative or positive? Usually they seemed amused rather than scared. Such exposures could not be prevented entirely, considering the number of visitors and their activities. Playing tape recorders and showing magazines and photographs were forbidden around the Tasaday, but we freely used flashlights, cigarette lighters, forks, spoons, cooking pots, clothes, and shoes as a matter of course. The Tasaday had a flashlight, but they did not ask for other things. And if they were to ask, the policy was to be give nothing unless some overriding need of the Tasaday made it advisable.

Following another visit to the caves the next day, the Durdins left, as had been agreed. They said they would have liked to stay longer, but seemed happy for the time they did have. Elizalde accompanied them to Tboli, to check on the situation, and promised the Tasaday he would return the same day.

Yen, Dad, and Balayam went to the stream with a film crew to demonstrate the procedure of collecting, labeling, and naming plants. The samples selected brought an immediate response from Balayam. "No use, no use," he said, before Dad could even ask if the plants had any application for the Tasaday. They had gone through the routine so often that everyone knew it by heart. "No use" had already become a much-used Tasaday phrase, applied with giggles to anything they thought a waste of time or ineffectual.

Udo showed up, and he was livelier than ever, floating green figs in the stream and then stabbing at them with his bolo as they bobbed along. His first strike usually impaled a fig. Balayam found an *ubud* palm, cut a large chunk and nibbled on it, and gave a piece to everyone.

Late in the afternoon a large party of Tasaday came to the main tent in anticipation of Elizalde's return. Balayam and Mahayag carried on a long dialogue and the others listened. Dad reported that they were saying Momo Dakel owned all the forest and, when he and Mai were not there, Yen and I took care of it. The Tasaday took up all available space, so Dula told her daughter to come and sit on her lap, calling her Dina (pronounced Deena). I asked Dad what the word meant; he spoke to Dula and replied that it was the girl's name.

"But, no. Her name is Siyul. Always has been Siyul," I said.

Dad asked about this, but the Tasaday acted as if they did not know what we were talking about. "This girl's name is Dina," Mahayag said.

It was confusing until we learned later that the name of Fludi's daughter was Dina and that Dula and Mahayag supposedly liked it so much, they substituted it for Siyul. It was possible the name switch had a deeper meaning, but we did not discover it.

Elizalde and Mai returned that day, as promised, and were welcomed as if they had been gone for much longer. Mahayag said to Elizalde, "You should come to our cave. We always come to yours [the tent] and you don't come to ours so much."

He went after dinner, but not before he had reminded Yen about the Tboli development project. He also asked Yen to take a larger role in the Tasaday research, perhaps as head of the scientific part of the project. Yen said he was interested, but had so many responsibilities that it looked impossible. "Well, of course, forget it if you're the kind of guy who can just turn your back on these people—people who really need you," Manda chided. "Who is going to do it? I can't; don't know how. But you, Doug, you're the one. Of course, if you don't care about the Tasaday and Tboli, never mind."

Yen said he would continue to think about it.

It was a raucous evening at the caves. Everyone was in good humor and the Tasaday insisted that each visitor laugh, alone. So we each laughed in turn. Balayam, Adug, and Dula sang songs, and then insisted that everyone sing.

Our repertoire was rather dated, ranging from "Mac the Knife" to "Figaro." Each rendition brought such shouts and hugs as would have gratified an opera prima donna.

Then the Tasaday played the flashlight game of trying to catch the light beam and making shadows on the cave walls. Yen remarked that they seemed to be performing a regular routine created out of similar evenings in the past.

The quietest but most satisfying development of the evening was Gintoy's emergence from his shyness. For the first time, he was not reluctant to sit close to people; he became a laughing, hugging participant right before our eyes. The reason seemed obvious: the special pills that Doc had said would probably clear up Gintoy's ringworm and fungus had been brought from New York by NBC. He had begun taking one a day and the change in the condition of his skin was remarkable. After only one week the white flakiness and the patches of discoloration were disappearing. Rebong had watched for undesirable side effects, but noted none. He said the pills were working exactly as he had hoped.

The next day both camera crews photographed at the caves for about two hours: fire making, Balayam playing his harp, and various activities of families around their platforms. The Tasaday called upon Gerald Green to sing—he had been absent the night before—and he rendered a sprightly "Good Morning Blues."

Lobo climbed trees and ran up and down the paths, counted to ten in English (learned, apparently, from the Tboli boys), walked about with a pretend walkie-talkie, saying "Go hed," "Tank you," and "No use." He even tried a timid "Hello."

Just before we left, Lolo and Gintoy decided to tie all the visitors' hair back as the Tasaday did when going into heavy jungle. They called the ponytail style *fakul*. The boys worked busily over all of us, pulling hair tightly behind heads and binding it with a vine. They even found enough strands on balding Det Arndt's head to make a small tuft.

Bilangan brought out the heirloom stone tools and several of us followed him, Balayam, and Mahayag up a trail beside the caves to see how they had formerly made rattan lacings. Bilangan was not well, complaining of chills, and had draped a burlap rice bag around his shoulders, fastening it beneath his chin. With his erect posture and deliberate manner, the bag became almost a flowing cape.

Mahayag demonstrated how to work with the rattan, cutting a long piece by bending it over one stone tool and sawing through it with another tool. Then he split the ends of the rattan with his teeth and fingernails and pulled off long, flat strips, slightly wider than a shoelace. He removed the bindings of one tool and deftly rebound it with the fresh rattan. The whole process took only five minutes.

Mahayag explained, as had Bilangan, that these stones did not come from the stream but from a special place in the mountain, quite far away. They no longer needed to go there, since they now had knives, he said.

That evening Elizalde described the tours he had taken with the generals. They had visited the hamlet just below Datal Kemalas and also Takonel, near Lake Sebu, and the Tboli community at Lake Sebu. The tribal people had responded affectionately, Manda said, but the settlers had been cool. The generals seemed favorably impressed by the Tboli. Several Manila newsmen had made the tours and the Durdins had gone on one. Elizalde said, "Tilman Durdin told me the mayor of Surallah had confided to him that the Tasaday were fugitive bandits."

Manda, exuberant as he described all this, seemed depressed the next day. He worked for hours, using his cigarette lighter to melt foot-long tapers into empty coffee jars, inserting a string wick as the jars filled. The flickering soft-orange glow of these candle lights was to be our only light from now on. The gas lamps and battery-powered lights used in the main tent had attracted hordes of flying night creatures, including beetles as big as golf balls that buzzed around like tiny helicopters. The bugs attracted by the candles would be singed when they got too close.

Huddled over his candles, Manda muttered that there was a new murder charge filed against Mai by the Surallah police, and a local radio station was broadcasting that Mai and Fludi were wanted dead or alive, rewards offered. "I can't sleep," he said. "Too much going on in my head."

His hair had not been cut for weeks and hung shaggily over his shirt collar; his black beard was ragged and the mustache curled into his mouth, so that when he ate it collected particles of food. He had complained of this and yet he would not trim the mustache.

After a lengthy silence he said heatedly, "It's the same old banana with the scientists all the time. I mean they really don't like having me in here. Damn it! I've got something. I mean . . . it's nothing. I don't know, call it what you want. Maybe I'm no good at business or whatever else, but I'm good at this. This is what I do . . . I know this. I know all these people around these mountains. They know me. I'd like to see any one of those bastards who are always bitching about me try and do a single thing we've done. Just one thing!"

I asked what had brought this on.

"I don't know. It just came into my head," he said and changed the subject. "You know, General Venadas told the Tboli that if any men with uniforms—and he pointed to the fatigues of the constabulary guys with him—come to make trouble, 'you tell me about it.' Can you believe that? When did anyone like that tell the tribes that before? It means something. It's important. Maybe now we can do what we never could have done years ago."

That morning there was about two hours of filming at the stream. According to the pattern that had developed, that was all the shooting for one day. The film makers were happy with two hours, and the Tasaday were left virtually alone the rest of the time.

Lim Youn Choul's camera was connected by a cord to Det Arndt's sound equipment. Dul watched them as they went about their work. "Those men are funny," she said. "They are connected—like a mother and a new baby."

In the afternoon Tboli reported by radio that Surallah officials were claiming that two Christian houses had been burned below Kemalas. Elizalde sent a message to Torres, ordering him to "surrender no one" to the police. The trial for the four Tboli accused of the massacre remained in a muddled state. Elizalde was convinced that none of the four was guilty; he deeply regretted that Tboli had helped the police round them up.

At the caves that evening, Mahayag chopped up a large piece of *natek* and sent portions to each family's platform. The arrangement of the platforms was about the same as when they were first constructed, although Lefonok had built onto his and now it almost joined Kuletaw and Sekul's place along the north wall of the cave. Tekaf and Ginun had moved to a point almost directly behind Dul and Udelen, and were almost inside the dark chamber that extended into the mountain. At night the adults and young children slept on their family platforms, but the older boys moved elsewhere—Adug and Gintoy took their pallets to the top of either Lefonok's or Mahayag's firewood rack. Lolo and Lobo slept wherever they found space.

Dul had handled the division of food the other times we had seen it; now she sat on her platform, paying only casual attention and chatting with Dula. What did this signify about the roles of various individuals and the leadership structure of the group? Yen and I speculated. Dul had a special role; but Dad's reference to her being influential because she was "young, clever, and a stranger" still had not been fully deciphered. Clever was clear enough, but young? Perhaps that was meant to be taken as a description of her vigorousness and strength. And maybe her value as a stranger lay in the fact that she had brought the knowledge and new blood of another place to the Tasaday.

Balayam played several special roles—watcher of the cave, politician, entertainer, spokesman. Possibly because of the responsibility of his new wife, he had shown himself to be a much harder worker than we had first thought. And he was sly; once, he borrowed somebody else's knife when going after *ubud*. Asked why he did not use his own, Balayam chuckled and said he did not want to risk breaking it.

Later on in the evening, Manda again talked with Yen about his possible long-term involvement in the Tboli and Tasaday projects. Yen was tempted by the Tboli development but felt it might be too unsettling to his career and personal life. "If I were thirty years old I'd jump at it, but now, I don't know—I've got a great job, a marvelous job at the museum. I've got field-research commitments over the next couple of years . . . my family is settled in Hawaii. . . ."

He saw the Tboli project as demanding extremely hard work but offering potentially great success. The Tasaday presented different problems. Once the scientific work was finished, they could be left alone. But what did that mean? Friendship and even love had developed between them and some people who had come to know them. "It's the most basic of human ties," Yen said. "There are responsibilities on both sides."

He suggested that if archeological study was to be the next step in learning about the Tasaday, it would be a good idea to explain to them what was intended and see how they reacted. If they were opposed to digging in the midden, then it must be left alone.

As we mused over how much we did *not* know about the Tasaday, Yen said, "You know, there is a saying in anthropology that when you are studying a people, you throw away the first few months of field notes and start from there. There are always confusions and mistakes at the beginning that you can correct only by sustained experience with the people. But with the Tasaday we're keeping the first few months' notes—it's all we've got."

In fact, the total professional field study of the Tasaday—the combined time spent by the scientists Fox, Llamzon, Peralta, Winters, Lynch, Fernandez, Baradas, Yen, Gutierrez, Reynoso, and Elkins—came to only about three months. Manda had spent about fifty days with the Tasaday, and Mai, including the lengthy period he stayed to supervise security, about seventy.

And virtually nothing was known about the Sanduka and Tasafeng; Yen was convinced that a triangular relationship had once existed between them and the Tasaday. In the future it might be advisable to try and connect the triangle, he said, but how? Who would do it?

Our conclusion was the same as it always was when we had this discussion: the first task was to learn more about the Tasaday before seeking out other forest peoples.

We flew to Blit after breakfast the next day so that NBC could record the story of Kasuk, the blind man who had been born at Tasaday. He sat on the ground outside his house, the Tasaday mountain blue-green in the background, and was filmed as he told Mai and Reynolds about his childhood in the forest. He added nothing significant beyond what we already knew, but there was no opportunity to ask him more than a couple of questions. Kasuk embraced Reynolds, saying he liked the sound of his voice, and was quite amiable throughout the visit.

Walking back to the main settlement at Blit, Yen spotted a cluster of millet, its green-amber grain tassels waving above some low-growing shrubbery. He took samples back to the camp, where Adug and Lolo refused to touch it, goggle-eyed and afraid, until Dad demonstrated that it was harmless.

Lim Youn Choul and Det Arndt filmed Dafal on the route he had taken from Blit the first time he met the Tasaday. Dafal was asked to outfit himself exactly as he was then. He showed up with his bolo, spear, and shield, and wearing aqua slacks that Toby Pyle had donated at the end of her visit. Told the slacks did not seem quite right, he switched to a pair of short cloth pants. Manda insisted, though, that Dafal had worn a G string in those days but now wanted to appear more sophisticated.

At the Tasaday camp, a wan Balayam complained of a headache. He moped around, his eyes soulful and his voice a whisper. He looked so ill that it was a wonder he could walk. Dr. Rebong gave him an antibiotic capsule to be taken at once and another for the next morning. After two hours Balayam was hopping about, almost at his usual pace.

We then remembered the problem of Mahayag's hernia. Rebong said that the only way to make sure it did not strangulate—knotting itself around Mahayag's intestines, killing him—would be to operate. He did not think it was necessary at once, but there was no telling when Mahayag might exert himself in such a way as to cause strangulation. The operation could not be done in the jungle, or at Blit. The nearest possible place would be the clinic at Tboli, and better still would be the large hospital at the Dole pineapple plantation farther north. The operation would not take long, but Mahayag would have to be hospitalized a day or two and then should recuperate for at least a week before returning to the forest, Rebong said.

"How do we explain all this to Mahayag?" Elizalde asked. "And to the Tasaday? How can we tell him he's got to go and have this done when the hernia doesn't even bother him? How do we explain taking him out of the forest, that whole outside world, the operation, staying there to recuperate? We'd have to take some Tasaday with him. I don't know. Does it really have to be done now? Right away?"

The doctor said it did not appear dangerous at present, but there was no way to know when it might cause trouble.

Yen felt that Mahayag should be taken to Tboli for the operation. It would simply have to be explained some way. "What is our responsibility here?" he asked. "If it really is as potentially serious as it sounds, I just wouldn't want to see him left here to take his chances."

But Elizalde said the operation should wait until there was evidence the hernia was definitely dangerous or until a more suitable place was devised. He believed the potential trauma of the operation at Tboli or Dole was riskier than Mahayag's present condition.

That evening Manda told the Tasaday that he, Mai, and Yen would be leaving the next day and that he and Mai would return after two nights. (In addition to checking on the trial, Elizalde wanted to take Yen, who was going back to Manila, on a tour of all the Panamin projects in the area and show him the land in the development project that he wanted Yen to direct.)

Dul replied, "Momo Dakel Diwata Tasaday says he will be gone one night and it is two nights. If he says two, it is three or four. Maybe it will be two moons this time."

"No, I'll be back in two nights or Dul can throw me in a deertrap."

Dul gave a little smile and said, "I'll see. If you are not back, I will go out and stay in the forest until the big bird comes."

Manda assured her again that he would return in two nights.

There were interesting aspects of their brief exchange: Dul's chiding of Elizalde, her threat to go away from the caves (taking others?), and her mention of reckoning time by the moon. The chiding and threat were in keeping with her steadily more apparent authority and the teasing-challenging relationship that had developed between her and Manda. The moon time, however, was completely new to us. We asked her about it.

"We count from one moon to ten moons," Dul replied.

"What is a moon?"

"It is when the moon comes and then goes away."

"Where does it go?"

"We don't know."

Was it possible to see the moon regularly? During our visits we had glimpsed it only once. We tried to find out if she reckoned a regular period between moons or if she just counted at the odd times it could be seen, but apparently our questions were confusing, because we could get no meaningful answers.

We then asked how they had learned about counting moons and why they stopped at ten. Dul said her ancestors counted that way. We asked if there was any word that meant the period encompassing all ten moons together. "No," she said. "We have no word like that."

Similar questions drew blanks—not evasive answers, simply no information. It was quite possible that Dul's ideas of moon time had come from the Tboli boys during their many weeks with the Tasaday, but further questioning elicited nothing and the subject was dropped.

Once during the day we heard Dul speak briefly in the strange sub-language, in which each word had a similar ending. She did so again now, laughing, as if it were a joke. We picked up some of the words—*"kanuff," "keenuff," "sakuff," "tekuff"*—but could not guess their meaning, any more than we could figure out why she had chosen to use the "secret" language at this particular time.

The absence of Elizalde and Mai for a day or two posed no worries for the NBC crew. The situation had improved steadily; Reynolds and Green and their camera teams were generally in good spirits. They felt the filming was going smoothly and that a solid rapport had been established with the Tasaday. In the interim they would rest, filming whatever was convenient by the stream or camp. "We don't want to push anything," Reynolds said. "We'll just film it as it happens. We don't need stagy, spectacular kinds of things. The Tasaday just doing what they normally do is dramatic enough."

Elizalde and Yen spent the next day surveying the forest and Tboli lands from the helicopter, stopping at several places. They decided to return to the forest camp rather than stay at Tboli that night. Yen arrived at the tents excited and impressed. "It is magnificent. The forest is beautiful and the Tboli land looks good. The whole thing is a virtual kingdom, and everywhere we went the people treated Manda like some kind of god. It's not just in here with the Tasaday. Not at all. Everywhere we went, the people came out and gave him a tremendous welcome. And they didn't know he was coming, so it had not been arranged ahead. Extraordinary . . ."

The next morning, Manda and Mai went to the caves to advise the Tasaday that they had been delayed a day, were leaving now, and would be back in two nights. Dul nodded patronizingly and said, "I'll wait and see."

Yen went to the upper cave, said good-by to Etut, and came down the path to be embraced by all the Tasaday at the lower cave. Three or four men, women, and children at a time put their arms around him and laid their heads against his body, their faces against his face. The cluster rocked back and forth with croons and soft cries as tears trickled from their eyes. Yen finally turned away, muttered that he would try to come back someday, and, wiping his own eyes, half ran down the trail to collect his belongings and hike to the landing ridge.

Dad already had gathered together the botanist's things—a back pack, a cloth bag, a package of plant specimens, and *biking* that Yen had sliced into poker-chip-size pieces and dried over the fire. Dad's conscientiousness and handling of heavy responsibility—he had headed the camp detail when Mai was away—often made me forget he was so young. But now, as he stood there with Yen's bags in his arms, the pack on his shoulders, Dad looked even less than his sixteen or seventeen years. His slim body had a forlorn slump, making it look small and fragile. He tried to hold back the tears, but they slipped down his high-boned cheeks.

"Now, Dad, none of that," Yen said, but he was blinking his eyes again himself. "Damn it, this is awful," he grumbled. "I'm too old for this. I can't be getting involved this way with all these people. Never again." Then he grabbed a bag, slung it on his shoulder, and hurried away to the landing pad with Dad dogging his every step.

An hour later Dad returned, red-eyed and carrying a mound of clothes and other gear that Yen had pulled out of his pack. Within a day or two, Dad had regained most of his good humor, but he still missed Yen.

From the landing pad Elizalde asked angrily over the walkie-talkie who had given Lobo a cigarette. It was not lighted, but Lobo was dangling it from his lips playfully when he arrived to see Elizalde off. Fludi, who had just come from Tboli to replace Mai, said he would find out.

Lim Choul and Det Arndt spent the morning at the stream photographing the jungle, and hoping some Tasaday would come by. Finally Adug and Lolo came to bathe in a small pool beside a long flat rock. They splashed and laughed and scrubbed their hair and bodies with their special vines and clay, stopping once to leap upon one another for a friendly wrestle in the pool. They finished by scooping up fine sand from the stream bottom and rubbing it with one finger on their teeth to clean and polish them. The young Tasaday took time to make their teeth shiny, yet later they probably would file them flat and stain them with pitch and betel so that they would not have the white sharp teeth of animals. Was the filing part of some kind of coming-of-age or puberty rite? The one time I tried to find out, they simply said they did it because their ancestors had.

As the boys were finishing, Bilangan arrived and bathed quietly and deliberately. Then Tekaf and Ginun walked by, smiled and nodded. They took a few steps off the path to give me a hug, after which Tekaf raised one finger and pointed toward the opposite ridge—the helicopter landing place? Bilangan nodded to him and also raised one finger—perhaps it meant the helicopter would be gone one night, or that Tekaf and Ginun would stay out one night. Nodding, the mute couple continued on their way into the forest.

At lunchtime another message arrived from Elizalde in Tboli, reminding me that there should be no gift giving; rice was permissible, depending on the circumstances. He asked again who had given Lobo the cigarette. Fludi replied that a porter claimed Lobo took the cigarette from his pocket without its being offered.

Groups of Tasaday came by the camp in the afternoon—boys to swing and play, men on their way to check traps, and Bilangan just to sit and talk. He was wearing his burlap cape. At first it had looked rather ridiculous in combination with his leaf G string, the only other thing he wore, but the incongruity was overcome by his natural dignity, which made the burlap bag become a royal robe. He sat with Dad and me and carefully pronounced the Tasaday words for the times of day, showing the appropriate sun position with his hand: *taliwada* (morning), *mafun* (afternoon), *siguf* (night). Then he pointed to me and said, in Tasaday, "Now in your words."

We went through the words several times, Bilangan repeating "moaning," "nun," "afta-nun," "na-eet." A few minutes of this, and Bilangan pointed toward the stream, bid us good-by, and stepped down the slope, a light breeze rippling his gunny robe.

Balayam arrived at the NBC tents at dusk, inspected various pieces of equipment, made jokes about bald heads and *lassus,* then sat with his knees crossed as it got darker and darker. NBC had connected some electric light bulbs to the small generator they used nightly to recharge their camera batteries. Reynolds avoided turning it on when the Tasaday were around. But now it became so dark that we could barely see one another, and Balayam rose and went over for a look at the bulbs. He began talking to Dad, who said Balayam wanted to know when those things would sparkle . . . this was what he had come for, apparently having seen them from a distance. So Reynolds switched on the generator, the lights sparkled, Balayam grinned, danced around happily, and, after a little polite conversation, went to the caves.

It was colder than usual the next morning as I sat with Fludi and Dafal around the kitchen fire drinking hot coffee and smoking cigarettes. I asked Dafal if he thought Dul was a strong figure among the Tasaday. He said she was—"She can command"—because she was intelligent, both quick and wise. Fludi said he knew of Tboli groups in which women were the most powerful individuals.

Bilangan arrived, on his way to gather food and check his traps. He might have to travel far, he said, and would be gone at least one night, maybe more.

We nodded. Then he said he would be taking Lolo, Lobo, and Etut.

"Taking Etut? Why, she's about to give birth. She's so big and slow afoot, she rarely leaves the caves," I said to Fludi. Then it occurred to me that perhaps the birth was imminent and Etut preferred it to be in the forest. Fludi mentioned this to Bilangan, who said there was no sign of impending birth and that the cave would be a better place for it anyway.

Why, then, was he taking Etut?

Bilangan, looking serious, said it would be better for Etut to stay in the cave, but she would have to go with him: "We have no food. We must get some. She must have food, soon."

Fludi looked at me and said, "Should we give them rice?"

"It seems that's what this is all about," I said. "What do you think?"

"I think so," Fludi replied. "If we give rice, Etut probably will stay, and Bilangan will go for *ubud* and come back this afternoon or early tomorrow."

"Okay. Suggest to him that perhaps Etut is too big to walk easily in the forest, and if he would like to have some rice so she can stay home then we would like to give him some."

Bilangan nodded and said, "I'm not asking for rice, but if you want to give it I'm happy to receive it."

We said we would be happy to give it. Bilangan smiled broadly and repeated that he was not asking for it, but would be happy to receive it if we insisted.

That settled, Bilangan put a hand to his cheek as if in thought and wondered aloud if there might just happen to be any of Momo Dakel's tadpoles available. Fludi told me he meant the small dried fish that the Tboli boys often ate with their boiled rice. I remembered that Yen had said he thought some of the boys were giving these fish to the Tasaday. I said the rice was all we could provide.

Bilangan said that was all right, beamed a few more smiles, and returned to the caves. But he did not take the rice. Fludi said the usual procedure was for Dafal to deliver the rice to Dul so she could divide it among all the Tasaday.

After this was accomplished it was time for a group of Tasaday to go to the stream, as they had earlier planned. A film team was waiting there to cover whatever happened. Time passed, no Tasaday came, and Fludi checked the caves. He returned in a hurry to say that Udelen had caught a deer in one of his traps and a party was going to fetch it. Fludi had asked if it would be agreeable for us to go along. The Tasaday said we were welcome; they would collect us on their way. We waited at the stream with Yasuda, Yashiro, Dafal, and Det Arndt.

They were moving fast when they passed by, and we had to run to keep up. About four hundred yards downstream they darted up over an embankment, across a shelf in the jungle, past two spear traps, down into a gully, up to a higher shelf, and deeper into the forest, to a place we never reached. It was only because of Fludi and Dafal that we had been able to keep on their trail at all. The Tasaday party, which included young Dina and gray-haired Sekul, slipped through the jungle so easily and swiftly that after five minutes we had fallen far behind. They met us on their way back to the stream.

Balayam was sweating and bent nearly double under the hundred or so pounds of a young hornless male deer tied with vines to his back. Mahayag, Dula, Dina, Sekul, and Sindi stood on the shelf and shouted greetings to us, laughing and pointing to the deer.

Balayam rested briefly and they were off again, filling the humid jungle with yells and laughter. Single file, we went down the slope and up again, with heavily loaded Balayam falling to the rear with us. We moved carefully past the traps, down the embankment, and into the waterway, at which point the group whooped joyously and raced upstream. Balayam chugged along, sliding across wet rocks and climbing over rotting logs. I thought we were going all the way to the caves, but around a bend we found the Tasaday already gathering wood for a fire. Balayam flopped down, eased the deer off his back, and lay panting. Sekul stood on a fallen tree and laughed hilariously, pointing at Balayam and the rest of us sucking in deep breaths and dripping sweat.

I asked why Udelen was not here—the deer was in his trap. Fludi said Udelen had brought the deer part of the way home and then fetched Balayam, the pack horse of the group. Balayam set no traps because his responsibility for the caves meant he could not leave for long periods, so he carried the game as his share of the work.

A fire was started quickly with a *"tik-tik,"* flint and stone provided by Dafal, and it blazed as Mahayag slit open the deer and pulled out the innards, which Dula and Sindi washed in the rippling stream as Mahayag and Balayam stuffed the vacancy in the deer with green leaves and lifted the animal onto the fire. As the hair singed they scraped it off with sticks, turning and turning the deer until most fur was removed. Then they heaved the scorched carcass out of the fire, and Mahayag cut off the legs and head. Balayam put these into the fire, resting them on green saplings brought by Dafal, who kept busy gathering wood and offering advice on butchering.

Mahayag split the deer's belly from neck to tail and carved the flesh from the ribs. Some slabs and chunks were put into the fire, others, like the intestines and liver, were washed and wrapped in leaves. Balayam poked into the flames and brought out strips of cooked fatty meat, chewed on one, and passed the rest to others. He found the genitalia of the deer, held them up, snickered, and laid them on the saplings to cook. Mahayag collected the deer's blood in bamboo tubes.

A soft rain began to fall and Dafal cut palm fronds, some five feet long, and passed them to Sekul, Sindi, and Dula who held them over their heads and the fire. But the rain became a driving downpour and the fire sputtered. The sizzling venison was jerked from the dying blaze, large chunks were tied together with vines and long blades of grass, smaller pieces were wrapped in leaves. Balayam gave Fludi a slab of meat, the leaf-wrapped packages were gathered up, and the Tasaday ran for the caves, the women holding the fronds as umbrellas.

We trudged behind Dafal, who used his shield as protection from the rain, and reached the tents soaked and dripping. Dafal built a fire and immediately fried the liver, which had been his special gift from the Tasaday, and was gulping down slivers of the meat before the rest of us had even dried ourselves. Fludi cut the slab of venison for the camp into steaks and fried it. We ate the first panful with our fingers as it came off the fire; it was delicious, juicy, and tender with a rich but delicate flavor.

The Tasaday had given us a rather large portion. Fludi said he had tried to refuse it, but Balayam insisted he take the whole piece. We had been amply reimbursed for the rice we had given them that same morning. Whether or not this was a deliberate exchange, we could not tell. The Tasaday had no formalized trade or barter system that we knew of, but they always gave Elizalde *natek, ubud, biking,* grubs, or some food item every time he came. Also, Yen's collecting of *biking* had involved an exchange for rice. Dafal said they had provided him *bui* vine for the items he brought, and the Tasaday said they had given foods in return for women.

Balayam and Lolo visited us after the rain stopped. They were delighted to find that we already had eaten some deer meat. We said it tasted good, and that pleased them more. Balayam then mimicked how he had given us strips of meat from the fire and we had eaten it. He concluded by saying, "We are very happy when you eat our food and do not [with a backward flip of his hand] throw it behind you."

That night, long after we had gone to bed, singing at the caves spilled into the valley. Dafal's shrill voice was unmistakable.

The next morning, Dafal joined Fludi and me as we were sipping coffee around the fire. He told us the Tasaday had been preparing and eating the deer meat most of the night. He said everything except the bones had been cooked for consumption: the eyeballs, sliced up; the hide, cut into strips, which the children would chew for days afterward; the blood, cooked in bamboo tubes; the feet, roasted. I must have seemed surprised, because Fludi quickly assured me the Tboli did the same. Fludi said he liked the hide best; Dafal's favorite was the liver, and the Tasaday's was the intestines.

We asked Dafal what he had sung about at the cave. He said it was a story of a good *busaow,* one who did not hurt people. I asked if the Tasaday had learned of the *busaow* from him, but Dafal said he could not remember exactly what the song was about, because he had drunk some rum before he went to the caves.

While we were talking, Adug and Lefonok strolled up from the stream with two flashlights they had got from Dafal the night before to search for Kuletaw. They said the old man had not come home and they were worried, but they found him in the middle of the night, his body curled under the buttressed roots of a tree.

"He didn't move—we thought he was dead," Lefonok said. "But when we turned the light in his face, he woke up. He's all right."

After they left us, Dafal said that before he met the Tasaday the deer would walk beside them, but then he taught them to make traps. The traps were what had brought him into the forest, he said, and he had more than a hundred placed between the caves and the forest's edge. He had seen strange human footprints but never people, until, one day, he spotted Kuletaw, Mahayag, and another Tasaday digging with a deerhorn for *biking*. "They looked different somehow," Dafal said. He chased them, shouting, and they stopped. "We could hardly understand one another . . . just a few words. And they spoke very softly, very low. And they were so skinny."

After that he always met them at a wide place in the stream. "I just called and called and waited until they came. I never saw the caves."

We asked how he had got the Tasaday to come to the edge of the forest, and Dafal reconstructed the conversation.

Dafal: "Come with me and see Tau Bong."

Tasaday: "We do not know this Tau Bong."

Dafal: "He'll come and you'll see him. He'll come in his airplane [Dafal said he described what the helicopter looked like]."

Tasaday: "What is that? A big tree?"

Dafal: "Just come, you will see it. And if it is your good luck, you'll see him, too. He's a very good man."

"And they all came," Dafal said. "Some were very afraid. Cold in their bodies. Shaking. The strongest were Balayam, Mahayag, and Bilangan. Dul asked if they would all die, but she came, too."

And what did they say after the first experiences at the forest's edge?

"Oh, they said 'Momo Bong is a very good man,' and talked about how their ancestors dreamed a good man would come to them. They laughed and said this was the good man they had dreamed about and it was good they had seen him."

Dafal was expansive as he told all this, clearly enjoying himself. Each time his story varied with accounts I had heard from him before, I asked him about it. But Dafal was not interested in what to him were minor details, and so he would either ignore my question, say he forgot or never knew, or go on to tell something else that interested him.

If the Tasaday had been dreaming of a good man coming to help them, why didn't they think that he, Dafal, who taught them so much, was that good man? I asked. Dafal just laughed and shrugged. Questions about when he first met the Tasaday were answered with a shake of his head and a remark about a long time ago.

Asked about the boy who was missing and had reportedly died, Dafal —who the first time Manda asked him had said that he did not know anything about the boy—now gave a knowing account of how the youngster was lost in a severe rainstorm: All the Tasaday were running from the rain and lightning to reach the caves, and the boy, who, Dafal said, was a brother of Adug—although Balayam and Dul had said he was a brother of Lefonok's son Udo—got lost and was never found.

It was hard to believe that a Tasaday boy simply got lost in the forest around the caves. It was as if a farm boy got lost in his own pasture. Did they search for him? "Oh, yes, they looked, but never found him," Dafal said, and strolled out of the tent.

In a story of Dafal's, it was often difficult to know what he had made up intentionally or mixed in accidentally, and what was fact. It could be exasperating; yet that was Dafal, and knowing that was as important in trying to understand him as it was to know the legend of him as "the man who walks the forest like the wind."

This applied also to the Tasaday. To understand them required that they be seen with their foibles and idiosyncrasies, and not just as simple, loving creatures in a Garden of Eden. This might take years—would the cost to them be worth the knowledge to us? At any rate, incidents of the last few visits had dimmed the aura that once had made them seem so astounding, pure, mysterious. These words still described them truly, but they would be said less in blind wonder, more in appreciation. The Tasaday became more intriguing and endearing as we learned more of their everyday human qualities. They reinforced the idea that one of the best sources of insight into a people is through what they take for granted.

For breakfast we had fried rice and chunks of deer meat that Fludi had smoked in the night. It tasted even better than the day before. As we ate, I read a terse message from Elizalde: *"Life* came out with story. No mention of us or Panamin. Soda."* Evidently, *Life* magazine had published something on the Tasaday, presumably using photographs of mine (and Panamin's).

After breakfast about fifteen Tasaday walked through the camp, all smiling and friendly—even Dul and Dula gave us a sniff-kiss, which was unusual—on their way to the helipad. Dul said they were going to wait for Momo Dakel, who had promised to return this morning.

He arrived about an hour later aboard a small helicopter chartered from the Certeza surveying company; the Panamin chopper had deteriorated beyond patching and was awaiting new parts from the manufacturer. The pilot of the chartered craft, a retired Philippines Air Force officer, apparently was fearful of flying over the forest. He huddled tensely over the controls and landed with such grim-faced caution that it inspired a new pantomime by Balayam, who had a good view of the pilot through the chopper's plexiglass nose. Balayam assumed a position as if at the controls and twisted his body in nervous jerks, craned his head from side to side looking for a place to land, then rolled his eyes and heaved a sigh when his imaginary helicopter was on the ground.

The arrival was otherwise routine. When Manda pointed out he had returned on time, Dul smiled and replied, "I have nothing to say."

I asked about the *Life* article, which, he confirmed, was comprised of photographs and caption material I had provided. "Oh, that," he said with a half-smile. "Man, we are going to ship you out on the small chopper with that terrified pilot"—because, he explained, four pages of photographs had appeared but without a word on Panamin, Elizalde, the reasons for entering the forest, the dangers to the Tasaday, or President Marcos's having established a reserve to protect them.

"Well, that's what it didn't say. What *did* it say?" I asked. "It still might be a good article."

He had not seen the magazine but had been cabled the full text, which apparently was all in photo captions. "I dunno. I guess it's okay," he said. "Fine, I suppose—but, my God, the whole idea of our coming in here was to protect them and then the President did such a quick job proclaiming the reserve. When did that ever happen anywhere before? I mean, *Life* could have at least mentioned some of that—a word or two, anyway!"

The NBC troop was ready to go to work when Elizalde walked into camp. They wanted to film a group at the caves, singing, playing, whatever the Tasaday wanted to do, and particularly including Dafal in some of the activities. Elizalde paused briefly at the tents and then led everyone up to the caves. He and Mai sat on a platform with the Tasaday and said it would be nice to hear them sing. Gerry Green walked up and said, "Okay, Manda, you want to move out of there now? We want Dafal in this one." This seemed reasonable enough but, coming right after the information about *Life,* it apparently rubbed Manda the wrong way; he did not say anything at the moment, just moved out of the way. Dafal put on an exuberant performance, singing, gesturing, laughing, telling stories. Gerry thought it was terrific and said so several times as he pointed out camera angles to Lim Choul and Yasuda and moved around the scene, using an aluminum walking stick to help him negotiate the rocky incline.

Manda sat watching on the sidelines. Three or four Tasaday toddlers came over and began teasing him and pulling his beard. But then he was asked to move again so that the camera teams could photograph some older children who had unexpectedly started sliding down the inclined path. They sat with their heels tucked against their buttocks and scooted down on their rumps, sometimes using big green leaves as sleds. Two children went over by Reynolds and he hoisted them playfully in the air; somebody asked Manda if he would move out of the way, please, so they could get that on film.

The last filmed sequence for the day was three Tasaday calling birds by the small waterfall. It all had taken less than an hour and the crew was very pleased at how well it had gone. Green said the business with Dafal was perfect . . . he was the unsung hero of the whole Tasaday story.

Manda said almost nothing throughout this session. At the tents he slumped down, looked around gloomily, and muttered, "It's depressing in here."

In the early-afternoon quiet, a message arrived that one Tboli had been shot and killed, another critically wounded near Kemalas. "Christ! Damn it!" Manda growled. "Mai . . . Mai . . . where the hell is Mai?"

Mai hustled into the tent and Manda shoved the message at him. "You seen this? Mai, when's it gonna stop? Better find out all you can."

Elizalde was restless; finally he decided to rebuild the kitchen and immediately set to work with bolo and ax, shaping saplings and branches to make a new floor. Half a dozen people were soon working on it, Elizalde in the middle doing most of the cutting and fitting as they brought him the wood.

Udo, Lobo, and Biking watched. Ching made a teeter-totter out of two small logs and showed them how to use it. They were a little leery until they got the knack of it, and then played noisily, shouting *"bow-gay,"* their favorite exclamation that week, and occasionally saying something in the code language, with giggles. Udo and Biking were becoming more open and playful. We had been told that Udo was older than Lobo, but Udo was much smaller, possibly having to do with some sort of spinal defect, which had caused a slight hump in his lower back. Biking was younger than both of them, and impish, scrambling around the stream, the jungle, the caves; his knuckles and knees were like coarse sandpaper, covered with scars, scabs, scratches, and grime. The two smallest toes on his right foot had been webbed from birth; he had curly hair, crooked teeth, a nose that seemed to be continuously running, and a mischievous grin.

Manda stopped work to read late-afternoon business messages, but he had little to say about them or anything else; he had closed himself up. Finally, during dinner, he said it was a shame *Life* had not at least mentioned Panamin or the reserve or the President.

"And now," he continued, "we've got the TV. What is *that* going to be? Green told me today as we walked to the caves that Dafal is the star of the show—the unsung hero. 'The star,' those were his words. Ha! Dafal, the Discoverer—now, that's really something. Hell, Dafal couldn't show them anything about these people. He doesn't even begin to understand why they are significant. I wonder, I just wonder, if they have any idea of the importance of Panamin's role in all this?"

Mai interrupted with the news that the people shot near Kemalas were ambushed and there were no witnesses.

"Damn it, Mai, we gotta stop all this! Those people are going to think we're worthless!"

We got back to the subject of the television film. I said it seemed beyond doubt that it would deal with the security aspects of the whole reserve—if not, why had Reynolds and Green been so keen on covering the trouble at Kemalas? They had said it would dramatize what was happening to the Tboli and could conceivably happen to the Tasaday. And it would be impossible to keep Panamin's role out of the film; it was inherent in the story and could not be avoided even if they wanted to, which they obviously did not.

"Inherent, huh? I didn't notice that it was so inherent in *Life* magazine," Manda snapped.

"Sure, but they weren't even here. National Geographic was here and that was a fair story," I said. "NBC will be the same."

"Yeah, maybe," Manda said. "But you know how these things go: big enthusiasm while they're here, but once back in New York or someplace, it's all forgotten."

I answered that this was highly unlikely because of Reynolds's continuing interest, for more than a year, but Manda brushed it aside.

"Maybe," he said, "if the President was in the film . . . that would tie all this into the reserve, protection, the government's increasing concern for minorities. I'd trade all our coverage in the film for Marcos to be in it."

Did "our" mean his own coverage?

"Well, yes, why not? I mean, I really would."

Manda was wary of discussing any of this with Reynolds, however, for fear that it would seem he was interfering. Reynolds, aware of Manda's gloom and guessing that at least part of it was due to the day's filming, stopped in after dinner to talk. The conversation was oddly formal and stiff with lengthy silences until Manda worked into the problems of the Tboli, pointing out that *Life*'s failure to mention Marcos and Panamin reflected poorly on the work they were doing. Reynolds replied that a script had not even been sketched out yet, but that he was certain those points would be there, including the President's proclamation of the reserve.

"What if the President actually was in the film, would that be good, be possible?" Manda asked.

Reynolds replied that it would be possible if the President was truly part of the story, noting that it was not a news account this time, but, rather, a portrait of the Tasaday.

"Well, if the President was in the area—not necessarily at Tasaday, but checking the situation with the Tboli or Ubu—would that legitimately fit in?" Manda asked.

Reynolds said he thought it might be valid, as long as it were not a staged appearance. At Manda's prodding, he agreed also that if the President did not come to the area, it might be worthwhile to meet with him in Manila to discuss the government's policy on minorities in general and his views on the Tasaday. He noted, however, that there could be no telling in advance how much, if any, of this would appear in the finished film, because that would depend on how the story took shape—they would be shooting about twenty thousand feet of film, of which only about three thousand would be used.

Manda was cheered up by this conversation and worked late into the night composing a message to Marcos, reminding him that he and Mrs. Marcos had mentioned visiting Tboli to inaugurate the museum, and suggesting that this would be an excellent time to do that and also survey the increasingly serious trouble in the area. He said that NBC would like to include him in their film on the Tasaday, preferably while he was on a mission in the general area that did not require a visit to the caves (which Manda wished to avoid because it would mean setting up complex security precautions, cutting down trees in order to provide a ground helicopter landing pad, guards, et cetera). The alternative would be an NBC interview at the Presidential Palace.

The next morning there was to be a long walk up the river with the Tasaday. Balayam arrived first, leaning on a freshly carved staff about five feet tall with a long leaf knotted on its top. He hobbled around a corner of the main tent, seemingly engrossed in his every step.

We puzzled over this sudden strange appearance. What had happened to Balayam? He circled slowly in front of us, ignoring our curious looks. Then it hit us: Balayam was imitating Gerry Green with his aluminum hiking stick. Balayam then shrieked with laughter and shouted, *"Oh-hoo, Kakay Sheeling* [Green's Tasaday name]!"

Balayam acknowledged our appreciation of his imitation with a satisfied smile and an incline of his head that could be described as a modest bow. To make sure we had not missed the significance of the leafy knot—simulating the leather strap on Green's pole—Balayam fingered it subtly and hiked his eyebrows.

No sooner had the laughter subsided into chuckles than it was boosted again by the appearance of Mahayag, hobbling around the same tent corner with a similar staff. Balayam, mastermind of the skit, stood by appraisingly until, no longer able to contain himself, he exploded into gales of laughter. Mahayag, who had striven to keep a serious face, unsuccessfully, then struck a pose with one foot ahead of the other, staff clasped in his right hand and thrust forward, left hand resting on his right bicep, head bowed: Green in contemplation.

While Mahayag held this stance, Adug arrived, also probing the ground ahead of him with a leaf-topped staff. Balayam by now was hopping around in laughing convulsions, Mahayag was snickering, and Adug was giggling and unable to sustain his impersonation.

Green was summoned at once and the Stone Age Marx Brothers went through their act again, causing Green to laugh harder than anyone.

Still chuckling, we made our way to the stream, where a dozen Tasaday scanned the water and played as we trailed along behind them. Lobo had linked himself to Manda by a ten-foot length of rope, in imitation of the camera and sound men. "They [NBC] mustn't think I'm upset for myself," Manda said as we walked along. "It's not my ego that's hurt. I'm just worried about the whole show, the whole idea. I mean it's not my feelings that matter, for God's sake."

I passed this along to Reynolds, in my role as liaison, and he nodded his understanding. Green, who was aware of things amiss the previous day and of a continuing though lessening moodiness, said, "Whew! You gotta tiptoe around this place. It's like walking on eggs."

The Tasaday were generally relaxed and kept busy gathering or nibbling on fruits and flowers and bits of crab. Dul was rather long-faced but followed along. Lobo remained close to Manda, occasionally flitting away briefly to perform some feat to attract attention. He had a new habit of incessantly poking into things—people's pockets, baggage—and of taking hats off heads, tickling people unexpectedly. It had been amusing at first, but as it persisted—apparently Lobo felt the other boys were taking too much of the limelight—it sometimes became irritating. Of course, we were the major cause of this, fawning over him and repeatedly singling him out. He remained brilliant and beautiful, but the calculated coyness and spoiled-child mannerisms detracted from his charm. It certainly was unjust to criticize Lobo when we had been the ones to spoil him. Yet, the fact remained that it was not as much fun to play his games all the time; too many other Tasaday were interesting now.

One afternoon Lobo played on the vine swing and nobody paid any attention. He called out to several of us, teasingly, as we sat in the tent nearby, but nobody came to watch him. He continued to perform, climbing high up the vine, sliding down, hanging by his knees, twirling, twisting, spinning, as he swung back and forth on the vine. Finally I could not resist walking out. Lobo smiled and jumped off the swing at once and sat on the ground with his back to me. I called to him; he stayed silent. After I went back inside the tent, Lobo went back up the vine and called me. I went back out and he climbed down and sat facing away again. We did this another time or two, but I got tired of it and went back into the tent and stayed there. Lobo went home.

With increasing frequency Lobo stayed out of clusters of activity around Manda, waiting until either all the other Tasaday had left or there was a quiet opportunity to throw himself on Manda for a few minutes of private attention.

All this did not diminish our affection for Lobo, in the long run; it merely made him seem more like us: capable of being bothersome at times, a feat I would have found hard to imagine five months earlier when every move he made was dazzling and brought gasps of admiration.

This day at the stream, Lobo contented himself with staying by Manda most of the way, until we reached the pool where the waterfall gushed over the flat wide rock. Lobo was first in, splashing and calling the others. Everybody joined except Sindi. Mahayag and Dula carried in their youngest child, as did Udelen and Dul. Balayam and Adug tried ducking the women and each other, then tunneled underwater between each other's widespread legs. The water was chilly but they frolicked in it for nearly half an hour and emerged shivering.

Manda said they were cold, had done enough for one day, and suggested they go to the caves if they wished. Several did, and Manda went to the camp, but some Tasaday stayed at the stream, sunning themselves on rocks and gathering firewood, leaves for skirts, fruit to eat. As the rest of us were strolling back to camp, they passed us, at least four with new staves to imitate Green; even Dul, packing Maman on her back, went by with a long stick in her hand, chuckling.

The mood at the tents remained relaxed until early afternoon, when we heard the small chopper buzz over, land, and take off again. There had been brief radio contact between the pilot and Dog Love at the radio tent but it was garbled. "It must be Artajo [the Panamin regional director]. He's probably got some problem he doesn't want to discuss on the radio," Manda said.

But an hour went by and nobody had arrived at the tents. A Tboli was sent up the trail to see if Artajo had got lost or fallen. The man reported back that there was no sign of anyone.

A message was sent asking Artajo's whereabouts. He was reported at Tboli. Then what was the chopper doing? Tboli said it had left a couple of hours ago to take a constabulary officer to his headquarters after a meeting at Tboli of various factions involved in the current strife. Who was the officer, Manda asked? The answer came back, Lieutenant Cruz.

"What?" Manda shouted. "Lieutenant Cruz? There must be some mistake."

No, the Tboli station said, the pilot, a retired air force colonel, had taken off with Lieutenant Arturo Cruz (not his real name).

He was one of the arch enemies of Panamin, the suspected leader of various raids against Tboli, and the man quoted in the newspaper article that said Panamin's helicopter had flown "Vietnam tactics" and fired on police and farmers. He was crafty, Manda said, "very smart, very shrewd. He practically never says anything in meetings, just sits and listens, but never misses a thing. He's tough, very tough."

The flight plan of the helicopter was checked; its sole mission was to take the lieutenant to his headquarters, about fifteen minutes from Tboli, and return. That was two hours ago. The pilot had no instructions to fly to the Tasaday area—a one-hour round trip—and had not mentioned any intention to do so. But now nobody at Tboli knew where the helicopter was.

"Well, I'll tell them where it was," Manda said, "it was *here!* Right here with that bastard Cruz, and we don't know *who* else! What the hell is going on, Ching? Did that pilot know not to fly in here without advance authorization?"

"Yes, sir," Ching said. "We made it very clear that no one should ever fly here, because it always attracted the Tasaday and might upset filming or whatever was going on."

"With Cruz in this, there's no telling who or what he brought in here," Manda said. "If they just wanted to look things over, why did he land?"

Ching suggested they might have let people get off.

"Yes . . . yes, that's possible," Manda said quietly. "Yeah. They've got a new warrant out for Mai and Fludi . . . might have brought some police, or maybe just some goons, to get Mai or cause trouble or raise hell—make us look bad! And in our own goddamned chopper. If that isn't something! We're paying for Cruz to go riding around and plot against us. Who would ever believe it!"

The Tboli station was ordered to send an alert the instant the chopper returned, *if* it returned. Then the pilot was to be put on the radio at once for voice communication with Tasaday station. Elizalde, Mai, Felix, Fludi, Dr. Rebong, Sol, and Tennes immediately started checking the loads in their guns and spare clips. Two guards were sent to keep watch at the stream, and Fludi, armed, went to the caves with instructions to be casual and say nothing about this, but to keep his eyes open and try and find out where all the Tasaday were.

Gray clouds blew over and thunder boomed in the distance. Rain began falling and was soon a downpour. Tension increased as the Panamin crew sat puzzling over the unexplained events of the past two hours. Elizalde melted more candles into empty jam jars to make his hanging lanterns; Ching and Felix moved back and forth to the radio tent, but there was no report that the helicopter had arrived. The NBC group, following their usual afternoon pattern, worked on equipment, improved their quarters, and ate, read, or napped.

The cloudburst passed, leaving the jungle dripping but less sticky. Ching shouted from the radio tent that the helicopter had landed at Tboli and the pilot was being brought to the radio room. Elizalde leaped to his feet and charged up to the radio tent.

"Get me that pilot!" he yelled into the microphone.

"Yessir, this is the colonel."

"Where did you go?"

"I . . . ah . . . tested the noontime landing conditions at Tasaday."

"He's already been told something's wrong," Elizalde muttered aside to Ching. "Listen to that: the first damned thing he says is an explanation of why he came here."

"You what?" he said into the mike.

"I . . . I was testing the landing at noon at Tasaday."

"A one-hour trip to do what?" Elizalde muttered to Ching. "Test the landing conditions at noon? You mean he wants to check them every half hour of the day? That's absolutely ridiculous. Never heard of such a thing!"

"Who was your passenger?" he asked the pilot.

"Lieutenant Cruz, sir, of the constabulary."

"Colonel, you stupid son of a bitch! You better get out of that project before I arrive. I better not see you there! Ever! Do you understand?"

"Yessir!"

"I'll be there in the morning and you better be gone! Get out!"

Elizalde put the mike down and said, "I don't like it. That guy is making excuses. Before he even heard the questions, he was setting up excuses. Who ever heard of a noontime landing test? It's not even a good excuse. Stupid! Nah, no use fooling with that idiot, just get him the hell out." He then sent a message to the chopper's owners in Manila that he was sending it back because of the irresponsible behavior of the pilot. After that, he asked to talk to Artajo.

"Johnny, what mistake was this? Why did he fly here?"

"I don't know, sir. His mission was to fly to Surallah only, but he went to Marbel first, he told me, and then to Surallah."

"Get that guy's walkie-talkie," Manda said. "I don't trust him. It doesn't add up. Johnny, I want him to sleep at your place tonight. Find out anything else you can from him."

We returned to the main tent and sat conjecturing about the situation. If the pilot had deliberately done something terribly wrong, why had he gone back to Tboli? He seemed to have been making excuses, but perhaps Cruz had simply tricked him. In the end, we all agreed that that was what had happened; the pilot, unaware of the lieutenant's opposition to Panamin, had simply been responding to a friendly request from a fellow military man. It was unlikely the pilot had conspired, first because he was on Certeza's staff and second because he was so new to the area.

Elizalde, as he occasionally did after losing his temper, began to feel he had been too harsh. He decided to send a message asking the pilot to wait at Tboli so they could talk things over in the morning, but before he could do so word arrived saying the pilot had taken off with the chopper for Davao.

Ching was confident it would take more than one trip for Cruz to be able to find the landing ridge. It had taken half a dozen trips for Bart and himself to be certain of the way. Ching's job now was to find a helicopter and a trustworthy pilot by morning. He spent most of the evening on the radio. (Nothing happened at the camp as a result of the helicopter's unauthorized trip, but a few days later a newspaper story in Surallah said Elizalde had established a secret training base for militant tribesmen deep in the mountains; the "base" had tents and a helicopter landing pad.)

The next day, we got word that the Panamin helicopter would be okay for a few flights, but it would have to be grounded after that for more work. Elizalde wanted to check on the problems among the tribesmen at Lake Sebu, often a difficult place for the minorities. He also had to confer with lawyers, business associates, and some representatives of German government television, all of whom were due at Tboli. He decided to go to Tboli with Mai the next morning.

The helicopter that would be coming in to take out Manda and Mai would also be bringing in my wife. Joyce had never complained of my being away from home, had helped keep track of stacks of notes and photographs, and had joined in countless discussions about the Tasaday. Her one request was that, if the opportunity arose, she would like to visit the Tasaday for a day or two. Elizalde agreed, and it was decided that the best time would be during the latter part of the filming, when the helicopter would make numerous flights and there would be no scientific work.

After dinner that evening, Elizalde said he was not convinced the missing boy was dead; perhaps he was at Tasafeng or Sanduka. There might be a great deal the Tasaday had not revealed to us, he speculated. Perhaps they had even made contact with other forest groups recently. Mai was dubious about this. He felt that there might have been an estrangement between the Tasaday and the others; why else, for instance, had Lefonok not gone back for another woman after his wife died? And why hadn't the other men gone for wives? And then there was evidence from the tape recordings and from what the Tasaday said when questioned that they simply did not know if these other people still existed.

And yet, Elizalde said, the Tasaday seemed to be traveling farther afield now. Dafal had told him that their gathering forays of several days' duration were new to him; when he first met them, it was not their custom to travel so long.

Det Arndt had stopped by to chat, and stayed for dinner. He had spent long periods in Vietnam, as had Reynolds and most of the other TV men. We mused over the fact that in Vietnam, only three or four hours' flying time from the Tasaday, who did not even have a word for weapon, huge B-52 stratoforts were dropping thousands of tons of bombs on targets that often were invisible except to laser beams and other sophisticated equipment that supposedly exemplified man's genius. It was the sort of comparison that had become trite; yet every time, it gave rise to the question of which was the more incredible—the Tasaday world or the modern one? The Tasaday would find our behavior unbelievable.

About four in the morning, I woke to what seemed to be singing and laughter coming from the caves. I wondered hazily what was going on, but then dropped back to sleep. I got up at six, and as I was having coffee Lobo arrived. He was in high spirits, scampering back and forth between the kitchen, where Lucy was working, and the next tent, where Mai and the Tboli boys were getting up. About seven, Manda stirred and sat up. Lobo whispered to Dad, who hurried to Manda and said something.

Manda looked around with a grin and said, "Etut had her baby."

19

A Birth
and New Tension

ITT was August 27, 1972, and the first Tasaday of the new era had entered the world. Everybody converged on Lobo, who pranced around beaming smiles, and asked for details. It was a boy—Etut's fifth son—and Lobo said she had started labor early in the night. She had immediately awakened Bilangan, who sent Lolo to alert the other caves. Then everybody, the smallest children included, came to the upper cave. Sekul, Dula, and Dul assisted Etut while the others sat in a circle and watched. The baby was born before dawn, Lobo said, and everybody was excited and happy—thereby explaining the sounds that had awakened me. Lobo said his mother was tired, the baby was crying, and the umbilical cord had not yet been cut.

Lolo came by the tent on his way to get a special flower with which a drink would be made to help speed the separation of the placenta. Only after it had fallen could the cord be cut, he said.

Bilangan arrived soon after that, smiling but looking tired and nervous. He described the events of the night. The women attended Etut, supervised by Sekul, who held Etut's stomach and helped the infant from the womb. The baby had cried and Sekul put it on the platform between Etut's legs. Everybody then gathered around and said, *"Mafeon, mafeon."*

We also kept repeating *mafeon* to him, and he finally said yes, it was good, but that he would be only "half happy" until the afterbirth had come out and the cord was cut. Then he would be fully happy. He wandered in and out of the tents for a while, then went back to the caves.

Udelen and Lefonok stopped by and said all the men except Bilangan were going out to check traps in hope of finding a deer, pig, or monkey to feed Etut and help celebrate the event.

Manda delayed going to the landing ridge because of the birth. But the helicopter was coming on schedule, so I hurried up the trail to meet Joyce, who arrived shortly with Bruce Bassett, in to pick up the exposed film. Udo and Biking were there, tagging after Felix, who had come to tell Bart to wait for the outgoing party, and gave Joyce shy, giggling greetings. "Oh, just to be here, I can hardly believe it," she said. "To see them, small and fragile—and so bright, it shows in their eyes."

We made good time back to the camp and found Manda and Mai in the tents with Bilangan, Lobo, and Lolo, who were describing the birth again while NBC filmed. Manda and Mai then made a brief visit to the caves, conferred with Dul and Sekul, and glimpsed Etut briefly from the ledge outside her cave. Manda asked if she needed or would like to have the doctor attend her. The women said no, both the mother and baby were well, the placenta would separate soon and then the cord could be cut.

Back at camp, Manda said Dr. Rebong would accompany him to Tboli as planned because he was needed at the clinic. The doctor was ready to check Etut before leaving, but it was ruled out. The Tasaday wanted to handle the birth in their traditional way, so there would be no outside involvement unless they asked for it. There was also the possibility that the doctor or any other outsider might unwittingly cause some upset. Although the Tasaday said they had no set rituals connected with childbirth, it was likely that some rules were attendant upon such an event.

Furthermore, the Tasaday, while welcoming Rebong's care and medicines, had been reluctant to have the doctor check a woman too closely on one occasion. Dul, listless and complaining of a headache and stomach pain, had got so heavy that it was thought she might be pregnant. But, when questioned, she said she had menstruated only a few days earlier. The doctor then wanted to listen with his stethoscope to her stomach, the area of more intense pain, but Dul said no. After lengthy talking and cajoling she consented, but huddled in such a tense half-crouch position that it was impossible for the doctor to check properly. At last, with Manda soothing her, Dul allowed the doctor to apply his stethoscope and press his fingers on her abdomen, which caused her to giggle so much she made him stop. He had been able to rule out a ruptured appendix, however, and said the internal sounds were normal. Then she said the pains had begun not long after she ate the liver of a pig. (We were not aware of a pig caught recently, but that was what she said.) The animal may have had a liver infection that had passed to Dul's liver, the doctor said, adding that this was not uncommon but could be serious. But after further checking, accompanied by more giggling from Dul, Rebong said the usual symptoms of the ailment were absent. He prescribed antibiotic pills for the next few days. After taking only one pill, Dul reported feeling much better and, indeed, appeared so. (Wide spectrum antibiotics were occasionally used with the Tasaday and usually brought fast results.) This was the only instance even approaching feminine internal medicine, so the doctor would wait until asked or until after the newborn's cord had been cut before examining Etut and the baby even superficially.

Photography was ruled out until it was certain all was well. Manda shared Lynch's concern about unnecessary intrusions in the cave for the obvious reasons, and also because if anything went wrong the Tasaday might see it as a result of outsiders' presence, whether it was or not. Of course, if something went wrong anyway—the baby or mother became sick or died, or the child was ill-formed—the Tasaday still might judge it a result of our presence in the vicinity or of our breaking of a leaf or a similar infraction.

The policy of nonattendance stuck, despite an invitation from Bilangan and Balayam to be present at the birth, which they had tendered when asked what the Tasaday did when a baby was born. Were there special preparations before, ceremonies afterward? Bilangan said there were not and added, "You should come and watch." But nobody had.

As Manda was preparing to leave after lunch, intending to speed up his schedule and return early the next morning, Mahayag and Udelen told him that none of the men had found game in their traps. They looked deeply disappointed. Manda asked if they would like him to bring a deer for their celebration. They smiled and nodded vigorously. Asked if they preferred a male or female, young or old, horned or hornless—anything special—Udelen said, "Just a deer, any kind would be good."

Bilangan walked nervously into the tent after Manda left and sat down for a while, but he could not stay still for long and soon was gone again. He was much like the caricature of the nervous expectant father pacing the hospital waiting room.

Lefonok stopped by with Udo and Lobo and made a fuss over Joyce, my *sawa* (spouse). Balayam and Sindi arrived from the forest, and he officially christened her Jee-oos. Then, with chuckles and knowing smiles, they all began to repeat the same joke: *"Jambangan n'da m'gum-gum siguf"*—John will no longer be cold at night.

In a few moments, however, Balayam looked around with a worried frown and asked for Momo Dakel. Fludi said he and Mai and some others had left while Balayam and Sindi were gathering firewood. Balayam's face fell, he blinked and looked as if he would cry. He had known they were leaving but had not said good-by or gone to the landing ridge as was his custom. He murmured to Sindi, mooned about, sighed; his eyes became watery and attempts to joke or even talk with him were fruitless. Finally he wandered off with Sindi to the tent of the Tboli boys. After about half an hour we heard his laughter again, and, half an hour after that, he and Sindi returned, Balayam seeming cheerful and joining in the continuing joke about having a companion to keep warm.

Bilangan made an appearance from time to time, always shaking his head no at our question of whether the placenta had fallen.

Dinnertime talk at the tents concentrated on the birth. Bilangan's nervousness was transmitted to some of us. One view was that the doctor should have attended the birth. Letting nature take its course was fine if there was no alternative, but the doctor had been available. Someone remarked that child delivery was relatively simple and the doctor could merely have stood by to provide minor assistance that might prevent serious damage or death to the mother and child. But, as it was, they lay in the cave still connected, with the possibility of infection and any number of added complications. Others believed that it had been handled right: the Tasaday had been through this many times and they had been told help was available if they wanted it; let them do it their way. But, it was objected, what about their small population? It might be due to a high infant-mortality rate—how would we feel just sitting and doing nothing if the baby or Etut died?

That evening Elizalde sent for a report on their condition. Dad checked the cave and returned quickly, saying the mother and child still were attached and Bilangan was even more nervous; he now said he would welcome medical help from the doctor. I messaged this to Manda with the recommendation that the doctor come in on the earliest possible flight the next day.

We went to sleep about ten, Joyce and I in the main tent, which was strangely quiet; the half dozen other people who usually occupied it had gone with Elizalde. Jungle sounds floated in from the darkness with unfamiliar closeness. We hoped we would not be needed, but discussed what we might be able to do if called upon to help Etut before the doctor arrived.

I awoke suddenly in the night, my sleep pierced by the sound of terrible crying from the cave. It was a wail, a howl—too loud and strong to be that of the newborn baby. It had an edge of desperation and I sat up with a start, listening with held breath for any other sounds. There was a faint murmuring of voices coming from the caves.

The wailing continued for several minutes; it was impossible to sleep. I got up, lighted a cigarette, and checked the time: 2:35 A.M. The crying stopped briefly, then resumed with full intensity. Never had I heard such crying among the Tasaday. It could not possibly be the new baby; perhaps it was an older child, one of Etut's? But Ilib was only about two, Natek perhaps four; it was unlikely they were upset over any ill befalling the new baby. But what if something had happened to their mother? It was not difficult to visualize her lying there, with the baby still attached, weak, perhaps infected, sick—dead! Another child pawing at her still body, screaming . . .

What to do? First, stop jumping to morbid conclusions, it was ridiculous to hear death in the cries of an unseen child. If the Tasaday wanted help they would come. And what could we do, anyway? But the wailing continued. It had lasted more than twenty minutes by now. Maybe we should just check the cave. I pulled on my clothes and boots and called down to Dad in the next tent. Nobody was awake. Was I the only one hearing this? Joyce remained asleep, as did apparently everybody else in camp. Was I hearing things? Dreaming? No, the crying was real. But, just as I finally decided to get a flashlight, wake Dad, and go to the caves, the wailing subsided into sobbing. Then it stopped.

It was just after three. I sat up for another twenty minutes, but all was quiet. Whatever had happened, it was over. We would know soon enough. I fell into a fitful sleep.

I must have been half awake, because I sensed someone coming and sat up as the first faint light of day was slipping into the forest. Bilangan stepped around the corner of the tent. Deep dark lines frayed the corners of his eyes and mouth; he looked exhausted. It was obvious that something had happened.

Bilangan's lips twitched into a small smile, then into a grin. It was good. "Etut is finished? She is fine? The baby is fine?" I asked in fractured Tasaday.

"*Oh-hooooo! Ma-fee-on. Ma-fee-on,*" Bilangan said, tapping his chest to say his inside feelings now were good, all good. I woke Joyce, yelled to Dad, called the radio operator to send a message.

Half asleep, Dad stumbled toward us through the thin light. Bilangan told him he was very happy and very tired. He had not slept at all. The placenta had come out during the night, Sekul cut the cord with a piece of sharp bamboo; no knot was tied, it would heal by itself.

Asked about the placenta, Bilangan said it had been put on the limb of a tall tree so the boy would grow big and live to an old age. Putting it on the limb also prevented a pig or deer from getting it, Dad said.

I asked more about this, but it became confusing. Bilangan was weary, Dad sleepy. They now seemed to be saying that the placenta was not on a tree but would be buried about six inches at the base of the tree. In this revised information the tree was still symbolic of growth and age, but now it was burying the placenta that would protect it from animals. Bilangan was going to do this later at the customary site. Could I go with him? Yes, Bilangan said, I was welcome to go.

Bilangan said Etut was well and happy, but weak. She was looking forward to food, particularly the deer Momo Dakel would bring, of which she would be given the liver because it would rebuild her strength.

We asked Bilangan if he would like to take her some rice in the meantime, since he had not been able to go out for food for two days. Yes, he replied, that would be good . . . and maybe—said in the manner of wondering aloud—maybe there are some of those tadpoles of Momo Dakel's and that white stuff (salt).

Fludi had joined us and said we were out of salt ourselves, but he had asked Lucy to bring a supply when she returned with Elizalde. Dad said all the dried fish had also been eaten. Bilangan was given enough rice for everyone and told that salt would be available, and, we thought, the deer, in a few hours, when Momo Dakel came back. He took the rice himself this time and hurried to the caves. He was back in an hour, spending most of his time at the NBC tents, sharing his good feelings and practicing English words with Reynolds and Green.

Udo, Biking, and Kalee came to sit with Joyce and me. They snuggled against us, Kalee more attentive to Joyce than she had ever been to me. Udo wanted to learn the words for morning, noon, and night; in return, he told us the Tasaday words for midmorning and midafternoon, accompanied by a hand gesture to show the position of the sun. Lefonok and Udelen joined us, Udelen cooing and waggling his head so close that our noses rubbed. Bilangan passed by with a piece of freshly cut *ubud,* nodded, pointed to the cave, and kept going. Udelen smiled and said, *"Oh-ho,* Bee-lawng-aan," in an affectionate drawl.

Elizalde arrived about ten with a deer killed that morning at Blit, and Dafal followed him to the cave with it. NBC was already there to film the arrival, and the Tasaday gathered excitedly around the deer. It was Joyce's first time at the caves; nor had she met most of the women. After a hubbub over the deer, Dul and Dula embraced her and even Ginun came over and stood with her arms around Joyce for several minutes. The women wanted to know how many children we had, and said it was good we had a girl and a boy. "You should bring them to visit us," Dul said. Then the women commenced teasing: "Now you will not be cold at night." Sekul added that we must sleep in the daytime because at night there would be no time for sleeping. She cackled and all the others laughed and added their own comments.

The deer was butchered in the same way as we had seen at the stream, and promptly roasted. It was dark under the dome of the cave where this was done, so Green had the artificial lights turned on for the first time. Manda had said he wanted to explain the lights to the Tasaday first, but many things were happening all at once. The Tasaday looked up when the lights came on, shouted a bit, and continued working. "They don't mind the lights," Green said. "See that? A few *cheeets* and a look, that's all. They like it." They did not seem upset, although those directly in the beam looked away or down.

Mai checked the upper cave and said Etut was sitting up and in good humor; it would be all right to visit her. Despite obvious weariness she looked very well, her hair in ringlets around her smiling face. Dul and

Sekul came along and the younger boys played around her as the newborn baby lay in her lap, covered by a rice bag.

Ilib would not leave Etut alone, constantly crawling over the baby to get at his mother's breast to nurse. I asked about the terrible crying in the night. Dul said Ilib had become enraged when he was not allowed near his mother, apparently at the time the placenta dropped and the cord was cut. He was so violently upset that Dul had taken him to the lower cave, where he howled and howled until he was allowed to return to his mother.

A camera team arrived to photograph; they, too, used lights because the back of the cave was so dark. Lolo, Lobo, and Bilangan joined the rest of the family on the platform. Bilangan was beaming happiness, but Lobo seemed to be crying. I asked why and was told it was over some unspecific family discipline. Lolo patted him consolingly a couple of times, but Lobo looked away, rubbing his eyes, and refused to respond. Ilib continued pawing at Etut's breasts, edging past the new baby, who was asleep. Reynolds asked what she would do now with two babies to nurse. Etut smiled and said they would take turns.

After about fifteen minutes, everyone had had enough. The television crew left after filming a sequence of Green and Balayam with their walking sticks.

At the lower cave large pieces of venison had been roasted and the innards were being chopped and stuffed into bamboo tubes. A cooked kidney was portioned out by Balayam, who sat encircled by leaf plates, one for each family; he dealt out the pieces as if they were playing cards, wrapped the leaves into packets, and handed them out.

Chunks of raw meat were strung onto rattan strips and looked like giant skewers of shish kebab. One of these was prepared for each family to cook at its convenience. Bilangan collected his and walked directly up to his cave, the skewered meat dangling from one hand and a leafy bundle of meat in the other.

It was a happy, sometimes exuberant day, with spirited laughter and roasted deer to celebrate the successful birth. The child was the only Tasaday to have a recorded birthdate. The population, including Sindi, was now twenty-seven.

Elizalde had sent messages to Baradas, now officially director of Panamin research, and Yen, advising them of the birth. Manda's message to Yen—who, at his request, was discussing with other scientists the over-all Tasaday study program—suggested that Yen come to see the new baby. Yen replied that he would like that, and asked if it would be all right to bring Carol Molony, the linguist from Stanford. Elizalde cabled his agreement and they would arrive the next day.

Meanwhile, construction of a rope ladder with wooden rungs was being completed; it would enable an NBC camera team to reach a roost from which they would photograph the upper caves. Elizalde explained to the

Tasaday what was intended: a small platform would be placed in trees (about where I had been to photograph several months earlier). Lim Choul and Det Arndt would sit on the platform and film. Then he asked the Tasaday if they would mind, and they said no.

By midmorning of the next day four Tboli had raised a five-foot-square platform of saplings and rattan about fifty feet and rested it between two trees. The Tasaday watched with interest, and, as the work went on, Green tried out some old vaudeville slapstick routines on them. Sekul laughed so hard, she cried. "That old one," Gerry said. "Now, she's a real Miami matron type. You know, the streak of white in the hair, still trim, lively, lots a laughs, a real swinger." Her tan skin and big brass hoop earrings enhanced that image.

When the platform was secure and the rope ladder in place, Lim Choul climbed up, nodded his approval, and asked for a branch obscuring the view into the uppermost cave to be pulled back. Sol, who wore spiked climbers, tied it out of the way and then descended the tree, bits of leaf and bark fluttering ahead of him. Lim came down, noting that the light was poor and thus the only time to photograph from the platform would be in the early morning, when the sun shone directly on the upper caves.

Before lunch, Joyce and I found a sunny spot around a bend downstream to take a bath. We had just undressed and were wading in the chilly water when Mahayag appeared, nodded, and padded off into the jungle. He returned a few minutes later with an armload of leaves, nodded again, and continued on his way. Ordinarily, upon coming across anyone at the stream, Mahayag would have stopped at least briefly to make some comment; from his deliberate manner this time, I had the impression he was avoiding any possibility of embarrassing us or himself.

The Tasaday assuredly had a sense of modesty, particularly concerning their bodies, but it was difficult to define. The adults kept their genitals covered at all times, whether for protection from bugs or witches, or out of modesty, or, perhaps, in deference to our clothing, we did not know. Even when they bathed the G strings or skirts remained in place. And we never saw anyone above three or four years old urinating or defecating; they always slipped away to a private place. As for sexual relations, they appeared to adhere strictly to the monagamous concept of pairing they had told us about earlier. The boys sometimes rubbed themselves through their leaf coverings, in what anthropologists might describe as "penis play," but this was often a rather absent-minded gesture. The only strong suggestion of activity between sexes was Balayam's nuzzling and hugging of Sindi, which was more playful than sensual; I had not seen any other adults embrace or kiss except in a spirit of camaraderie.

They were, however, quite open, occasionally even ribald, in discussing or joking about sex; and, while they did not treat the subject vulgarly, there was frequently the hint of a snicker. Mai reported that the Tasaday teased and laughed about sex more than any group he had known—witness Balayam's jokes about freshening his *lassu* on the swing. Mai said that during his stay in June, Balayam often sauntered down in the morning at the cave and asked, "Udelen, did you do it last night?" Udelen might nod and answer, "Oh, yes. It was fine, good. I did it three times." Or he might shake his head. "Not so good last night—it wouldn't stand up very strong." Such an answer always brought hoots of laughter from whoever was around. Mai reported that Udelen said once, "No good last night, my back is very painful these days." To which Balayam said, "Well, never mind. Dul doesn't care if you couldn't do it last night—she had Maman [their three-year-old son] instead." This caused riotous laughter, and Dul said, *"Wheet-yuka-yuka,"* apparently a rather mild tsk-tsk, shame-on-you rebuke.

The Tboli boys surely knew more than any of the rest of us on the subject, but they said there was nothing particularly sensational. It was Yen who had witnessed the most unusual behavior. It had happened while he was recording data on plants in the botanists' tent. Balayam was there watching the team busily wrapping plant specimens in sheets of newspaper. Suddenly he let out a cry upon spotting a photograph of a shapely girl in a bikini. Balayam laughed, took the sheet of newspaper, spread it on the ground, and proceeded to make love to the photograph, simulating intercourse and chuckling all the while. Everybody laughed. In the days following, Balayam and Udelen, and even Lefonok and Bilangan, would often indulge in this joke. There were few glamour-girl photographs around, Yen said, but the Tasaday would simply improvise with whatever human picture they saw—faces, figures, women, men, it did not matter.

"We tried not to laugh," Yen said, "but it was impossible."

Joyce and I finished our bath, in privacy, and returned to the camp. Just before lunchtime, the helicopter arrived, bringing Oscar Trinidad, a German anthropologist, and a German TV producer. Elizalde had not been able to meet the Germans on his visit to Tboli two days earlier, because he had returned to the caves sooner than planned, so they had been flown in to talk to him. They were not invited to the camp, however, and waited at the landing ridge for a conference. Elizalde, Mai, and Felix were to hike up there, and Elizalde asked me to come along.

At the ridge we all sat on a log and the Germans talked eagerly about making a film on the Tasaday. Elizalde said it was impossible now—NBC was in the process of filming, and he and the scientific advisers had ruled out any other filming in the foreseeable future.

The German TV producer said he recognized the problems, and insisted that his team would not disrupt the Tasaday. There would be only three men, led by Max Rehbein, whom he described as the foremost producer-director of television documentaries in Germany and the exponent of the cinéma-vérité style, which caused a minimum of disturbance to the subjects. Elizalde said nothing.

The scientist urged the making of the film, saying the Tasaday might be able to teach modern man about himself. He had heard of their fondness for touching and noted that physical contact was being extolled in various group-therapy programs currently enjoying popularity. He also mentioned the Tasaday's inclination to look off or walk away rather than struggle to be attentive or feign interest if something bored them. Their story should be told, he said, adding that a Filipino scientist had told him the discovery of the Tasaday was of greater significance than man's landing on the moon.

Elizalde had remained silent, looking at the ground and frowning. Now he repeated that a film would be simply out of the question.

The visitors offered more arguments, including improvement of relations between the Philippines and Germany—the Tasaday had provided the most popular news from the Philippines to appear in the German press in years.

Elizalde maintained his silence. They cited a letter from an official at the Presidential Palace granting them permission to make the film. "Yes," he said, "but the guy [another cabinet officer] who wrote that really hasn't got a thing to do with it. I just happened to be in the United States when your letter arrived."

Nonetheless, the Germans responded, they had received a letter granting them permission, and that had encouraged them to come all this way to talk with him. They said they had waited several days in Manila and now would be grateful merely for an indication of hope.

Manda mentioned that NBC was making a substantial donation to Panamin for the right to make its film, and several other outfits had made offers. The producer said the film was for NDR (Norddeutscher Rundfunk), a nonprofit government network with not much money to spend, but that they could pay all their own expenses and could also perhaps arrange for the donation of German medicines to Panamin. This did not arouse much enthusiasm from Elizalde, and the producer then suggested that the film did not have to be solely on the Tasaday; a major share could be on other minorities, Panamin, and Elizalde.

That would be better, depending on how much was required of the Tasaday. Only five days, the German said. Impossible, Elizalde said. Three days, then? No, perhaps one day, *if* any time at all, Elizalde responded, adding that he must check with the scientists, who were determinedly opposed to any filming. He cautioned that even one day might not be agreeable to them.

The producer then indicated that he had expected the request for a full-length film on the Tasaday would be refused and had already been considering a film on Panamin and the other tribes. The Tasaday would be a necessary inclusion because it was they who had stirred the interest in Germany, he said, assuring Elizalde that something satisfactory could be worked out. Elizalde told him he was for it in principle, and would advise them definitely before they left the Philippines three days hence. The Germans were then flown back to Tboli. Rain began to fall as we slipped and slid down the trail back to camp.

The rain kept us in the tents most of the afternoon. Yen was firmly opposed to the Germans' proposal to film the Tasaday. He asked me about the apparent money shortage in Panamin and the need for donations—if finances were so limited, how could Panamin pay for the expertise required for the Tboli development project? My only answer to that was that Elizalde always seemed able to find money when he had to.

20

Nostalgia: "The Stump
of Our Old Feelings"

THE next afternoon, Elizalde sat
making candles and seemed to be in deep thought. It was quiet; a soft rain
fell on and off. Yen and Molony had gone to the caves with Dad, Joyce
was napping, I was reading. I heard Elizalde half mumble, apparently to
me: "I'm a worrier, you know that? I worry all the goddamned time. A
lot of it is really unnecessary . . . but I can't help it."

"What brought this on?"

"I dunno, exactly . . . nothing, everything, I guess. I just worry, that's
all."

I thought that he might be trying to set me up for something, a revela-
tion of some major new problem, perhaps; but no—he just talked aimlessly about the tribesmen's troubles, the trial, finances, the scientific
program, the Tasaday, the NBC film. . . . He said that he used to relax
immediately upon entering the mountains or jungle, but it was harder
now.

I remarked this had been a tense, difficult period, a lot of comings and
goings, and also the weather had been gloomy, which had a depressing,
time-stretching effect. Although we had been in the forest only about two
and a half weeks, it sometimes seemed like months.

"Yeah, maybe it's the weather. I've also got a feeling the Tasaday are a
little upset, don't know what it is exactly, just a feeling. I notice the boys
down there [jerking his head toward the NBC tents] are a bit on edge, too.
They seem to have a little tent fever. I warned them about those kinds of
tents. Too closed in. We've tried every damn kind of conventional tent in
the world and absolutely none are any good in this kind of place. You
gotta be open, open up as much as possible—no sides on your shelter.

Then you can see out, get the air, a sense of outdoors. Nope, the standard tent is asking for trouble every time. I don't care if you're with your best friends, or your wife, or your girl friend—especially them—you are going to get some tent fever."

At the start of the expedition there had been a lot of good-natured joking and teasing at the TV tents, touching on the cooking and cleanup chores and the sharing of accommodations. It was all fun for the first week or so, but then the newness wore off, as the daily routine came under the influence of drizzling rain, crowded enclosures, outdoor toilets, wet boots, soaking clothes, insect bites, colds, headaches, fevers, sore throats, upset stomachs, diarrhea, twisted knees, turned ankles—nothing terribly serious, just the usual run of minor irritants the mountain rain forest offered its visitors. Before long, the jokes had barbs and the smiles were pinched.

None of this, of course, touched the Tasaday directly, but they may have sensed our moodiness. The main reservation I had was that while we never spent more than a couple of hours with them at a time, we still occasionally crowded them. Once, for instance, not only were the two TV cameramen and I using cameras, but so were Ching, Green, and, whenever they could, both soundmen, who always had their own still cameras with them. Elizalde said this was just too much photography; it was agreed not to surround them that way in the future. Reynolds and Green said that from their group only the two regular cameramen would shoot. But after a day or two, Green could not resist snapping a shot now and then, and soundmen Det Arndt and Yashiro said that if he could shoot, so could they. I had continued to make pictures, and again we had several cameras in action. It was much more restrained than before, but not ideal.

Later in the afternoon Elizalde, Mai, and Igna went to the caves. Elizalde had decided to ask the Tasaday directly about several questions that had been bothering him. That evening, he told us about the visit.

First, he wanted to know if they were being bothered or upset by any of us, and particularly by the cameras. The consensus of the Tasaday was that they liked all the people but were not pleased by the cameras. Lefonok mentioned that he had not been eager to dig *biking* that day, but it had been requested (so it could be filmed)—"So I took them [the camera team] on a difficult path." Mahayag and Dula remembered an awkward situation at the stream but said it had not been serious. Balayam inquired, with a suggestion of distress, "How much longer will all this go on?" Elizalde told him it was nearly finished, only a few days more.

He then asked for details of what had happened to the missing boy. Dul said he died; he had simply got weaker and weaker and died. "We don't like to talk about it," she said. "It makes us hurt inside. And don't

ask Lefonok [the boy's father] about it—it makes him very very sad."
Widower Lefonok sat nearby as Dul spoke but he said nothing. The Tasaday mentioned that his daughter, Kalee, was nearing the time to be thinking about a husband. That could explain the leafy skirt she had worn since
June; before that she wore nothing. Although she looked only eight or
nine years old, she might be considerably older; her brother Udo, for
instance, was much smaller than Lobo but was said to be older.

Convenient for Elizalde was the mention of Kalee's needing a husband,
for then he could ask why she did not get a mate from the Tasafeng
or Sanduka. And why didn't Lefonok also? Lefonok sat motionless and
silent, and somebody said, "Lefonok doesn't want a new wife. He lost his
first one and is ashamed. He doesn't want another." It was not made clear
why her death was shameful. Perhaps it meant he was a poor provider, or
had been away when she died; or there might have been an accident. And,
of course, there was the ever-present possibility of inaccurate translation;
perhaps they had not meant "ashamed" at all.

Why did they not talk about the Tasafeng or Sanduka? There was a
long silence; then a Tasaday said, "We don't even know if they exist any
more."

Manda waited before responding, remembering that Dafal had told
him that he had met some Tasafeng while hunting not too long ago. In
fact, Dafal said, he had met relatives of Dula but had not talked to the
Tasafeng or Tasaday about each other. Manda had also heard, within the
last month, from two Tboli men who claimed to have encountered, in a
distant area, forest people they described as "strange, with no clothes,
and wearing rattan in their ears."

Manda told the Tasaday that "we know these people exist. Dafal
knows. I know. The Tasafeng are there. You must go out and find wives
and husbands your traditional way, as you always have. We cannot bring
you wives again."

"But . . . we don't know where they are," Balayam said.

"If you have trouble finding them, tell us, perhaps we can help you.
But why don't you go out and look for them? Have you tried?"

"We don't know where they are," Balayam repeated, accompanied by
the assenting voices of others.

"Have you had some trouble with them? Perhaps you don't want to
meet them."

"No, there was no trouble," Dul said. "You asked that before. If you
want to ask again, you should ask Mahayag. He was the last to see them
when he got Dula."

"Mahayag?"

He looked up and said, "There was no trouble."

"And so you all want us to help you get wives," Manda asked, "for
Adug, Gintoy, and, someday, for Lolo and Lobo?"

The Tasaday responded with *oh-ho*'s.

"You must first try by yourselves to get wives, as the Tasaday always have. Try, and if you cannot succeed, tell us. Maybe we can help."

The discussion turned to other matters. Before Manda left, he repeated that all the visitors would be leaving the forest in about three days.

Manda considered it a good discussion—although the Tasaday had been reticent at points, the mood was lively and warm at the end.

While Elizalde was at the caves, Reynolds, Yen, and I had discussed the Tasaday. I remarked, somewhat despairingly, that we had at best a superficial knowledge of their society, its tensions and stresses, rewards and punishments—the web of relationships that held it together, that made it function.

Yen said I was too anxious to know everything in a hurry. He pointed out again that there simply had been neither time nor opportunity to allow all such information to be known. "Remember what I said about throwing away the first few months of notes? At this point we haven't even acquired much valid data—among all of us—to work on."

I had to agree, but still it seemed reasonable to ask how the system worked. How, for instance, did it suppress, repress, or rechannel the kinds of competitiveness and aggression we had seen from time to time in the youngsters—rock throwing at the stream, Lobo's hassling with Udo for a vine and attention, Ilib's jealousy over the new baby, struggles here and there over a stick toy, a piece of food? Might there be some kind of buffer of ritualized politeness that was part of personal relationships as, for example, in Japan? Feelings—specifically hostile ones—were perhaps suppressed or channeled into more acceptable outlets because their undisguised expression in close confines could too easily lead to chaos. It was possible that the Tasaday exemplified the group concept that some anthropologists see as the most egalitarian society in history: individual behavior subordinated to the ideal of group harmony.

And did subgroups exist among the Tasaday? Was Bilangan's family going to become increasingly separate, one day splitting off so that all five sons with their own wives would form the nucleus of an independent group? Within a few generations Bilangan and Etut might be considered the creators as well as physical and spiritual ancestors of a whole nation of people.

The subject was irresistible, and so the questions and conjectures continued, leading, as they always did, to the familiar conclusion: insufficient study had been done to even guess intelligently at any answers. Yen insisted we did not even know enough to correctly formulate many questions—for example: the Tasaday had a seemingly extensive knowledge of a complex plant system. In just one season they had identified at least two hundred plants, for more than half of which the Tasaday had specific uses. The bast of one of those plants, the wild fig, was commonly used to make cloth by hunting-gathering peoples in similar environments, yet the Tasaday had never done so. Did that mean anything?

Yen was cautious about drawing any significance from that, as he was about making generalizations on other facets of Tasaday life. The Tasaday were too few in number, he pointed out, to be able to assign them cultural, societal, or national attributes. Their total population was equivalent to no more than two or three large families in the Philippines, and not extended families, either; merely parents and their offspring. Percentage projections from this group could be grossly misleading. For instance, two deaf-mutes out of a total population of twenty-seven is an incredibly high percentage. The percentage of the population with hernia or albino traits would be equally phenomenal. The ratio of boy children to girl children (12 to 2) would make an astounding percentage if regarded as societal, but in a family or two it would be merely unusual.

Our discussion only reinforced the conviction that the way to get answers to many of the questions was for one or two trained researchers to learn the language of the Tasaday and stay with them for months, perhaps years. This had been proposed from the start, but other matters had taken precedence, and anyway no qualified professionals were part of the program.

For instance, Yen had asked for a linguist to work with him, but Llamzon could not participate and Elkins became ill after a few days. On this visit, Yen had spent several hours gathering data with Carol Molony, a tall attractive American with long blonde hair. She worked on the language and Yen used some of that information to enhance his ethnobotanical work.

Yen felt that the hoped-for future study of the Tasaday would be invalidated by repeated TV coverage of the Tasaday. "That big camera eye peering at them—hell, even I get uncomfortable when it's turned on me. It will force a reaction in them. They are already starting to play roles for us—or at least they seem to be acting a bit."

It drizzled most of the day. At one point, Balayam strode in, his beehive of hair decorated with water droplets and his skin coat of dust and ashes looking like a finger painting—wet swirls and streaks of gray on his tawny brown. He was carrying a log, which he said was for us, for the fire.

For several minutes Balayam played the genial caretaker, explaining that in this nasty weather we should not have to go out—that was why he had brought us firewood. He sat cross-legged and talked earnestly about the dangers of the wind, which seemed to be blowing up: If it got strong—he frowned, shook his head, and waved his hands—and rain poured down and lightning struck, it could topple big trees.

He stood up to describe in gestures and words (with Dad translating) how, as he was walking through the forest minding his own business one windy day, a limb cracked off a tree and hurtled toward him. But he deftly stepped aside (this statement accompanied by a quick toe-dance sidestep—pause for applause) and the limb crashed within inches of him and landed at his feet. "Aha! *Oh-ho!*" he said, and grinned all around. So you see, he continued, if it rains hard and the wind blows hard, you must come to the cave—everyone is invited. Fludi and Dad nodded that it was a good idea.

This completed, Balayam ran through his various laughs: a loud artificial one that started high and ran down the scale—"haw-haw-haw-haw-haw"; a sly, sneaky one—"heh-heh-heh, sheet"; a laugh of surprise or acknowledgment—"ho-haaaow," with rising inflection. He concluded with real spontaneous laughter that combined features of all the others, varying them in pitch, tone, and volume, and ran from a simpering snicker to a great gut-busting belly laugh climaxed with yells and whoops.

He then changed the mood. With a soft, bemused chuckle, he began a serious exposition about *why* it was raining: "There is so much *ta-suk* [camera clicking] at the cave. And when they put up that thing in the tree [the platform], the owners of the cave got angry because someone broke leaves [eyebrows raised for emphasis]."

To tell us of this infraction may have been the main reason for Balayam's visit. He frowned and looked pained, but not for long. For no discernible reason he suddenly began discussing the size of various people's *lassus*. It may have been the arrival of Dafal that brought this on, because Balayam described him first. Dad translated: "Poor Dafal has a *lassu* so big that he gets tired carrying it around the forest." This was accompanied by cackling laughter from himself and Dafal, followed immediately by Balayam's loud conjectures about virtually everybody: So-and-so had a "big body, small *lassu;* that one, small body and big *lassu;* this one, big body *and* big *lassu*—but bent! Haw-haw-haw-haw."

An hour passed in this manner. Balayam seemed to enjoy himself immensely. He was singing his *ah-dah-doo* song when Mahayag, Lefonok, Udelen, and Udo joined the group. They squeezed in and softly patted or caressed each person, saying *"Mafeon,* Kakay Ming . . . Kakay Biang . . . Kakay. . . ."* Balayam continued performing another few minutes and then they all went to the caves.

The next day dawned brightly. The forest was fragrant and fresh, and the mood of the camp improved with the weather. Lim Youn Choul and Det Arndt walked to the caves about six for their first filming from the platform. They were to stay no longer than one hour, and if the Tasaday seemed disturbed by their presence they were to leave at once.

Joyce, Yen, and Carol visited the caves briefly to say good-by before returning to Manila. There was much affectionate hugging. At the land-

ing ridge Yen, having replenished his pack after the last departure,
emptied it again for the Tboli boys—shoes, shirts, sweaters, cigarettes.
Joyce left a shirt for the boys and boots for Lucy. Then they flew off to
Blit in a small Bell 280 HP helicopter piloted by Benny Flores, a trusted
friend who had not been available the week before, when the retired
colonel was brought in.

Joyce, Yen, and Carol were taken out of the forest one at a time because the pilot did not want to overload his small chopper. He made a
high approach each time he came in, turning, backing down, and settling
tail first. He said the landing space was so small that he could not see
it from above—he simply judged by the mountains where it should be and
descended: "It always seems to slide out from somewhere just in time."

Bilangan visited the tent after lunch and practiced English words. He
remembered several and asked to be refreshed on others. Of all the Tasaday, he was the only one who made a sustained effort to learn foreign
words, and he took pride in his success. Lobo knew as many words, but
he had picked them up without trying.

Bilangan showed us the general areas in which traps were placed; each
man had a sector of his own, except Balayam, who was exempted because
of his responsibilities as cave watcher. Even creaking old Kuletaw was
responsible for a sector.

Manda, Mai, Igna, and I went to the caves in the late afternoon while
it was still warm; the sun made deep-yellow and brown patches in the
jungle. Manda, lying flat on his back and staring up through the trees,
said, "You've simply got to relax with these people—it's the only way
to know them, to enjoy them. Take it easy, let them enjoy you, too."

The chopper whirred overhead and all the children ran to get a better
view. Lobo and his younger brother Natek got into a disagreement and
Lobo kicked at him, first gently and then with a slashing movement, like
a karate kick. The foot did not hit Natek squarely but did knock him
backward. He began to cry and ran up to the family's cave. Lobo watched
him, then walked away. No Tasaday commented.

Manda asked, conversationally, if the Tasaday used the caves elsewhere
in the forest.

"Yes, we use them sometimes," Dul said.

"When you get caught in the rain or are too late to get back to the
main caves before dark?"

"Other times, too."

"Why?"

"Because we like to change now and then."

"Do you stay long?"

"Sometimes," Dul said. "But we always come back here. This is our
permanent home. It's bigger, the water is closer."

"Were any Tasaday children born at the other caves?" I asked.

"Yes," Dul said. "Siyus [oldest of her two sons] was born there."

Manda had asked that three teen-age Tboli girls, who had been brought to help Lucy in the camp, visit the caves. When they arrived Dul and Dula asked them to sing. Each girl in turn rendered a fast-paced song that was like a musical chant.

Adug moved in close and perched on a rock beside me. He watched the girls' every move and was so excited that he trembled uncontrollably. When they were through he immediately sang, giving it his best.

Lolo had heard the girls' song in the upper cave and came bounding down. We had seen little of him since the new baby arrived. It was as if this had been the sign for him to put aside his childhood. He rarely played at our tents or on the swing any more, and was often out with his father or by himself gathering wood, looking for food. Bilangan sometimes consulted him now and treated him more as an adult. Lolo was somewhere between fifteen and nineteen; he and Adug could not stop staring at the girls.

At dusk Tekaf, Ginun, Sindi, and Balayam appeared on the trail that wound down from behind the caves. Each had a huge bundle of firewood, bamboo, and leaves on their backs, held by straps of vine that encircled their heads. Their bodies were nearly doubled over to balance the heavy loads, and they walked slowly in single file down the trail in the fading light. The unusual beauty of the scene seemed to reach back to an ancient time; it was a vision we had less frequently now, for the longer we stayed the more familiar the Tasaday became to us.

Balayam's load was largest, almost as big as he was. He flopped it off and grinned, sweat running down his face and body. Then he embraced Manda and nuzzled his cheek, leaving wet streaks on Momo Dakel. Mai commented that Balayam was the comedian of the group, but he was also one of its hardest workers, at least since Sindi had arrived.

We returned to camp after dark and found newspapers brought by the helicopter. Manda was delighted over a story in the Manila *Times* about the trouble between the minorities and the lowlanders. A Surallah official was quoted as saying the Tasaday were imposters, not primitive cave dwellers but fugitive criminals hiding in the mountains, who had been identified from newspaper photographs as the neighbors of local farmers. The rest of the story reported that this view sharply diverged from that of people who had met the Tasaday, and went on to quote some of them, including Yen, Tilman Durdin, Bruce Bassett, and the Lynch-Fernandez report. The Tasaday were variously described as "a group of scientific importance," "gentle food gatherers," "incredible people with no weapons or anger."

As we pored over the newspapers, Balayam and Sindi slipped into the kitchen area about fifteen feet away, apparently having learned about the singing that afternoon and eager to hear what they had missed. The three

Tboli girls were soon off again on their flashy mountain music. Balayam sang next, followed by Dafal and Igna. Then all of us were implored to put down the papers and sing, which we did one by one and off key.

After dinner Elizalde, Mai, Fludi, Felix, Ching, and Dad discussed what manner of security should be established when the expedition ended. Elizalde said the Tboli and Blit boys who stayed at the camp before had a strong influence on the Tasaday. This carried risks, he said, and the boys who stayed must be intelligent and sensitive and must not introduce things such as cigarette smoking or the use of guns.

Someone asked if it was still necessary to keep guns and guards in the forest. Mai said that his informants reported that plans continued for sending armed thugs into the forest. The Blit would watch outside but could not cover all areas, so interior guards would be required. It was suggested that they be posted at the landing ridge, near enough to be readily available, yet not so close as to be continually among the Tasaday. That location was judged better than by the stream, where the rushing water drowned out the sound of anyone approaching.

Mai recommended that some kind of booby trap be set up around the ridge post each night and removed in the morning. "The night is very strange in here," Mai said. "When you are on guard at night, you hear a crack in the forest and it sounds like a footstep. You listen harder, and then you begin to hear many strange sounds. You wonder, Should I alert the others? Then you hear more noises and wake everyone up—and it was nothing."

During the discussion, Det Arndt and I had been sitting on an earth shelf in the big tent but moved closer to hear better. Suddenly there were shrieks behind us. We turned and saw one of the kitchen helpers pointing a flashlight where we had been seated. Creeping along ever so slowly was a huge spider. It had a body the size of a wristwatch and eight hairy black legs two to three inches long. Elizalde jumped up, shouting "Look at that! Look at that! Who ever said there were no tarantulas in the Asian tropics? That's one. That is a tarantula!" He sounded delighted about it.

Elizalde grabbed a pillowcase and he and Dad put the open end over the spider. Dafal nudged it inside the case with a stick and Lucy brought a large wide-mouth jar. The open end of the pillowcase was put over the mouth of the jar and Dafal then tried to prod the spider into the jar with the stick, but it clung to the cloth. Dafal finally poked it with his fingers, causing a chorus of yells, and the spider released the cloth and dropped into the jar. It was harmless there but more ugly than ever—its hairy legs waved in all directions as it tried to walk up the sides of the jar and kept slipping to the bottom. On its underside was a pulsating pink mouth with tiny sharp points like teeth.

Dafal did not know what kind of spider it was, only that it was a killer. Mai said he had never seen one, but that his father had described such a creature and warned that it was deadly. Elizalde, who kept insisting it was a tarantula, said the only time they wandered alone in the open like this was when they were looking for their mates—so, he added, "Where is the other one?"

Every available flashlight was put to use as we poked into corners and boxes, surveyed the edges of the tent, shook out blankets and sleeping bags. Two or three small spiders were sighted, but no mate. It was unclear to me whether such spiders truly traveled in pairs or whether Elizalde, who was forever disclosing lore about spiders or snakes or bats he had had as childhood pets, merely felt the need of a small crisis.

When the Tasaday saw it the next day, they said it was very dangerous. (It was never determined whether the spider was in the tarantula family; on its way to Manila for study by the museum the specimen was lost.)

The first of September started out to be a gray day but cleared up, and NBC set out to complete its filming: Balayam made sign language, Lobo and Lolo practiced their English vocabulary—Lobo counting to forty, something I had not heard him do before—and then taught Reynolds some Tasaday words.

Balayam, Lobo, and a few others took my cameras and ran around peeking through the finders, shouting *"ta-suk!"* and clicking the shutters. Dul and Sekul also took turns, then asked to look through a movie camera. It was ten times larger than a still camera, so they called it the *"ta-suk dakel"* (big camera). They giggled and exclaimed over it, and became excitedly animated when Lim Youn Choul let them look through the lens as it zoomed in and out, making objects seem to come close and then recede.

In this midst of this, Lobo appeared with a large purple butterfly leashed to a vine thread. He let go of the thread, the butterfly fluttered away, and Lobo—calling out *"alibangbang* [butterfly], *alibangbang"*—danced after the creature, finally snatching it from the air. Udelen then caught a butterfly and, with Dul's help, attached a thread leash, working as close as a jeweler would on a watch, nose almost touching the butterfly's wings. Dul held the creature with fingertips and Udelen tied the thread around its body, below the thorax. Then they fixed the other end of the thread to a stick and gave the pet to their younger son Maman.

Filming ended by midmorning and the platform in the trees was taken down. The Tasaday were unusually quiet and seemed somewhat depressed. Several men had gone out to check their traps and returned one by one, each reporting that *again* there was nothing—no pig, no deer, no monkey; not even a mouse or a chicken. Mai said Mahayag had told him that the lack of game might be due to all the photographing at the caves: "Too much *ta-suk* has annoyed the owner of the cave and spirits around the traps. All the traps had been visited by animals, the bait was gone, and the spears tripped. But nothing was caught."

Mai said the Tasaday seemed seriously bothered, annoyed. Manda returned to the cave and said he was sorry for all the difficulties. The Tasaday responded in a friendly way but were reserved and ill at ease. Manda told them that because their traps had been empty he would, if they wished, arrange for a pig to be brought. The Tasaday said that would be good. Manda was considering a large pig from the Tboli piggery and so he told them it would be very big and white and like no pig they had ever seen. It would be brought in dead, like the deer.

The Tasaday said they preferred it to be alive. "We want to see it alive first," Dul said. "If we like it, we will eat it; if we don't, we won't."

Manda agreed and said the pig would be delivered that very afternoon. He added that the next day all the visitors would leave, the filming was over. Then he radioed for a live pig to be loaded aboard the helicopter and flown in.

The animal was strapped into the seat beside the pilot so that it sat upright, belly out, a snorting, squealing, pink-nosed passenger with a curly tail.

A sudden heavy rain blew over and the helicopter landed at Blit to wait it out. Dad, Sol, and Tennes waited at the landing ridge with a walkie-talkie, and when the chopper did finally come in they described the unloading to us in the tents. The Tasaday men and boys listened intently. When the pig let out huge grunts and squeals, the Tasaday laughed and hollered and ran off with Manda, Mai, Felix, and Dafal to meet the animal.

The Tasaday-pig meeting took place on the trail, now muddy and slick from the rain. They had seen only smaller brown wild pigs and were totally unprepared for the sight of the massive white creature. It weighed about two hundred pounds and sent the Tasaday into panic. They scrambled frantically into the brush with shrieks and screams, cowered behind trees and ferns, and watched wide-eyed as the strange beast lumbered on down the mucky path. Then the pig slipped, skidded off the trail, and crashed into wet grass behind a tree. The Tboli boys clung to the rope lead around the animal's neck as it made terrible noises and thrashed to get free. The Tasaday pressed deeper into the foliage.

Manda had already advised them that it would be their pig to handle as they wished—they had asked for it alive and were expected to take care of it, to decide whether to kill it and eat it or not. Mai reminded the Tasaday of this, but only one edged forward—Udelen. He took the rope gingerly and pulled while the Tboli boys pushed the pig back onto the trail. It waddled ahead again, with Udelen clinging to the rope, straining his muscles to keep the leash taut as the pig stumbled down toward the stream. The pig slipped off the trail once more and Udelen held tightly to the jerking rope. None of the other Tasaday would go near it, so Dafal leaped in and, while Udelen pulled, guided the pig down the last fifty steep feet to the stream. Lobo finally joined in and helped push as the beast plowed into the water. It stopped there, heaving and snorting. Udelen still held the rope, tense and sweating from his labors. Most of the other Tasaday were in a similar state from fear. Several danced around the pig, even approached it, bending down so their faces nearly touched the water to get a better look. But when it reared its head and grunted they scattered again, shaking and laughing nervously. Mahayag cut a limb the size of his arm and approached warily. Lobo grabbed the pig's tail and tried to help as Udelen struggled to get it out of the stream. Balayam waded close again, but the pig wheeled in his direction and he frog-leaped onto the bank.

Finally Felix and the Tboli boys helped the animal up the bank, Udelen still in the lead. On the bank the pig snorted and lurched and Balayam leaped onto the nearest tree and scrambled five feet up the trunk. He clung there as the pig passed beneath him. Mahayag grabbed a rock to accompany his club and looked ready to hit the pig, but he did not. His armament was apparently for defense, not offense.

Moving the animal up the steep muddy trail to the caves appeared to be impossible, so Udelen dropped the rope and ran ahead to tell the women to come down so they could see it and help decide if it should be eaten. As the group waited, Mahayag tightened his lips, took the rope, and started up the slope. Up, up, up the slippery incline as Dafal, Felix, and Lobo were joined by several Tasaday in pushing the beast's rear. Past the tents they went, scrambling, falling, and puffing, ever closer to the caves. The pig slid off the trail and mired in a crevice jammed with muddy dead leaves and ferns. The Tasaday shouted for Udelen but he had not returned. Even Balayam jumped in to help this time, and the mass of straining bodies finally heaved the pig back onto the path.

They were near the cave now, and Manda called out to Dafal, "It's their pig, let them take it to their women on their own."

And they did. Stumbling and sliding, they arrived at the lower cave in sweating triumph. The women gasped and stared as if transfixed, then shouted. Children circled the pig at a safe distance.

The panting animal was led to an open space between the platforms of Mahayag, Kuletaw, and Lefonok. It swayed from side to side, rooting its nose in the rocky floor. Lobo sneaked up behind it and crouched under a wood rack for a close-up peek. It was the largest pig, perhaps the largest animal of any kind the Tasaday had even seen. A big pig. A gigantic pig.

Dul kept her eyes on it, murmuring to herself and occasionally nodding. Manda straddled the animal and tried to hold Natek so he could ride, but the boy did not like the idea and wanted off.

Elizalde had speculated at the stream that the Tasaday would not kill the pig after they all saw it, and would keep it as a pet. But no, they said it looked fine for eating. They would kill it. Rattan cords were strung from the animal's neck and forelegs and tied to the platforms, but somebody warned that the pig might lunge and tear the structures into pieces, so the cords were untied from the platforms and Lefonok, Udelen, and Adug each pulled one taut in a different direction and planted their feet. Mahayag discussed the situation briefly with Dafal and walked around the pig, holding a large rock. He put it down and took up his club, then put that down and asked to borrow a Panamin ax. He got it, and then circled and circled.

Manda asked how he planned to kill the pig and Mahayag said confidently he would hit it between the eyes with the butt end of the ax head. Dafal continued to offer bits of advice but Mahayag seemed not to be listening. Manda instructed Sol to stand by with a knife and to quickly slit the pig's throat if it were merely wounded.

The men on the rattan cords strained, curling their toes into the dusty rock. Mahayag raised his ax, paused a second, slammed it down.

The pig stiffened, shuddered, and sank suddenly to the ground without a snort or squeal. Mahayag had delivered a single blow to the right spot and the pig was finished. Shouts rose from the gathering and Mahayag clubbed the pig twice more for good measure. After a minute or two the body began to quiver and jerk and Sol slit the throat, causing blood to flow onto the rocks. Several children scattered ashes to absorb the quickly growing crimson pools.

A fire was soon blazing and Udelen, Mahayag, and Adug lifted the pig onto saplings so the hair could be singed. Balayam went to help them, but joylessly. He had been quiet since reaching the cave and seemed abashed. The pig had terrified—and embarrassed—him.

It was Udelen—Udelen the Meek, we had thought, the henpecked husband—who had taken the lead and challenged the awesome beast when others fled. Manda had praised Udelen to Dul. Mai also had told her how brave he had been, how he had taken command when everyone else ran away. Just as Mai finished, Manda turned to see Balayam and Sindi a few feet away. They had obviously heard the description of Udelen's heroics, for Balayam was standing stiffly, blinking, his face tight.

The huge carcass slumped heavily over the fire, bending the saplings supporting it. Several men rolled it off, and Mahayag and Udelen began to butcher it with their bolos. Dula and Dul and the children watched with unflagging interest.

Heavy dark clouds threatened more rain, so the outsiders walked back to the tents. It rained hard but briefly, and an hour later Det Arndt, Dad, and I walked up to see how things were going. The wood rack by Mahayag and Dula's platform looked like a butcher's display counter. All the parts were laid out—intestines, liver, legs, feet. Bamboo tubes were pulled from the fire and the cooked meat was removed and strung onto rattan strips. Raw meat was also strung. The butchers were careful to keep portions equal, holding up pieces to gauge the size, adding a chunk of leg to this pile, a slice of liver to that one, matching the strings of meat as they dangled side by side like long chains of large, oddly shaped sausages. A name was called and that person came to collect. Bilangan, who had been out gathering food and missed most of the activity, stayed in the background, squatting behind the fire and watching, collecting his share at the proper time and walking quietly up to his cave. There was an air of busy industry but it was not exuberant, not joyful; it was surprisingly glum.

We mentioned this to Manda and Dad confirmed that conversation among the Tasaday was strangely dull, considering the feast ahead of them and the triumphant delivery of the pig. Manda rigged a tape recorder and had it placed in the mouth of the lower cave to try to learn what was wrong. Then he, Mai, and Igna stayed awake past midnight to translate and transcribe the tape. The Tasaday were indeed unhappy. Manda passed along the following.

Balayam, perhaps miffed or embarrassed by his performance around the pig, made a strong statement in an almost belligerent tone while talking about the Tasafeng and Sanduka: "If Momo Dakel Diwata Tasaday and Dafal and the others say they know where they are, then let them go find them! If they know this, why don't they show us?"

They also talked about the outsiders' activity at the caves, and one said the cameras were extremely aggravating. "Before we slept well, but now, every morning—*ta-suk! ta-suk! ta-suk!*"

Mahayag agreed and said, "We will go back to the stump of our feelings, before all this was here."

Dafal interrupted the transcribing to say that the Tasaday had also been profoundly upset when they butchered the pig—upon slitting the belly they found eight tiny piglets. The Tasaday were deeply saddened and said that if they had known this was a pregnant pig, a mother pig, they never would have killed her.

Manda was also disturbed that this particular pig had been selected from the piggery, but he was more concerned about all the Tasaday's complaints and worries. He considered going to talk to them at once, but it was late, and all of us would be leaving the next day, anyway—that was the brightest note. The cameramen had planned to shoot some footage of the dawn light hitting the caves, but it was not crucial material and presumably could be foregone without serious loss. Because it was after

midnight, however, and all the NBC men were asleep, they would have
to be advised early in the morning.

But the cameramen were up long before dawn and already on their
way to the caves before anyone heard them on the trail. Mai shouted
and tried to catch them but they had reached the caves by the time he
caught up. He quickly explained everything to them and then talked to
the Tasaday. Manda arrived and picked up the discussion. The Tasaday
said they had had enough. "We are people of the forest," Mahayag said.
"We don't know all the things people ask us about . . . we know *natek*
and *ubud* and *biking* and traps. Perhaps we should go back to the stump
of our old feelings."

They said they still liked the visitors but were very tired of all the
activity around the caves. And Dul worried that the big camera that went
"in and out, in and out, might reach out and take our flesh."

Mahayag left to fetch something and Manda asked Balayam if Mahayag
was very unhappy. "Mahayag is not so unhappy, but he talks always
about our leaves being damaged here," Balayam answered.

Manda assured them there would be no more filming and that everyone
was leaving this very morning. They asked when he would return and he
said it would be at least ten nights. Bilangan said, with a wry smile, "If
you don't come back, I'll cut my head off."

Dula said, "I'll lie down and die; I'll never get up."

Balayam, Udelen, and others began saying what they would do if he
did not return. Then Dul and Dula got vine strings and tied ten knots in
them and said they would untie a knot each night to keep track of the
time.

Green arrived and was told there would be no more filming. Advised
about the upsets, he said he realized it was a most inopportune time, but,
because the crew was leaving this morning, he would like to get just one
more brief sequence. If the Tasaday would agree, he said, it would merely
require that Balayam call out the names of the various members of the
film crew for a sequence that might run behind the credits at the end of
the show. Balayam was agreeable and it was completed in a couple of
minutes. The cameras continued rolling as good-bys were said and all the
visitors headed for the camp.

Lucy already had Manda's gear packed and he set out immediately for
the landing ridge, a small group of Tasaday trailing behind him. During
the next few hours the rest of us packed our belongings and broke camp,
leaving in twos or threes and timing it to match the helicopter shuttle
schedule. Half a dozen Tasaday came to watch the final packing and
Mahayag asked to play with a camera. He did not focus it, but pointed
the lens on everything, clicked the shutter, and laughed wildly between
each click. He aimed the camera at Adug and Gintoy, who were standing
in heavy shade, but then dropped the apparatus from his eye, said *"N'da*

fuglaon" (no sun), and walked around behind them so that when they turned the sunlight would shine on their faces. He snapped two pictures and laughed some more. I had never seen anyone deliberately instruct a Tasaday to turn in such a way, and had never done so myself; but of course we were always moving around for the best light on a subject and Mahayag had obviously detected this. He seemed delighted to play with the camera, but it was impossible to know what he was thinking . . . perhaps he was satirizing us.

A few minutes later, loaded with pack and bags, I started for the ridge. At the stream I passed Sekul with Siyus and Maman standing in the rippling current. The old woman put a hand to her breast and said, "ooo-ooo-ooooo," the same wavering, high-pitched note we had heard from the Blit. It meant hello or good-by or "I have a feeling inside." And it had a lonely sound, too, like wind in distant trees. It was September 2, 1972. The long visit had come to an end.

2I

Frontier Ethics:
The Mayor of Surallah
Presents His Case

THE Tboli welcomed the party back to the settlement with drums and dancing, and, as we sat on the staff-house porch drinking beer and looking out over the valley, the tensions of the expedition eased. Reynolds and Green believed they had the makings of an excellent film, although they had just learned that the broadcast date might be moved up, which would compel them to do the editing and scripting much more swiftly than planned. Elizalde said the work in the forest had ended "just in time"—the Tasaday were edgy and distressed, but he hoped no serious harm had been done. The best thing was that they would be left alone for several weeks.

Manda again turned his full attention to the problems outside the forest. The massacre trial had been recessed and the four suspects remained in jail; the threat of confrontations between tribesmen and settlers continued to be serious, although the presence of government troops appeared to be an effective check so far. A town meeting of sorts was scheduled for the next day in Surallah to allow settlers, residents of the town, Panamin representatives, and tribesmen to air their views.

The Panamin helicopter had been repaired and early the next morning, September 3, Bart flew Lim Youn Choul and me over the forest for aerial photographs. I had never seen the caves from the air because of the heavy foliage, but Bart knew exactly where to go, and then he hovered, jockeying the helicopter so that we could sight down between leaves and towering trees to see about five hundred feet below the mouth of the lower cave. The figures of at least half a dozen Tasaday speckled the dark space, running, stopping, pointing up at us. We hovered with that flickering view for about a minute; just before we flew away, a couple of Tasaday seemed to wave.

We photographed the slash-and-burn farms near Blit, then cruised southward about ten or fifteen miles along the rugged slopes of the rain forest's eastern edge. Craggy peaks rose above us at many points, and everywhere we looked the green rolled back into the vast unknown land beyond the Tasaday.

As the silver crescent of Lake Sebu came into view ahead, we noticed a snaking yellow-brown road scarring the forest below us. It curled through the foothills toward the forest and then plunged into it, leaving ragged brown patches here and there where loggers had cleared the trees. The road penetrated several hundred yards into the forest. Bart followed to where it disappeared behind a high, sharp ridge and then was visible again farther on. But there were no signs of activity, no trucks or other vehicles, no logging equipment, no logging men—the cutting had been stopped.

Bart swerved down and flew low over the lake, almost skimming it like a sailboat might in a good breeze, rose over valleys checkered with crops, crossed more mountains and then plains with coconut plantations, banana groves, rice fields, vegetable patches. He angled back toward the great forest again, climbed, and there below us, wedged among the foothills, was the valley with the main Tboli settlement.

The chopper landed, picked up Jack Reynolds and Det Arndt, and flew to Surallah, where we hoped to interview the mayor about the situation between the lowlanders and the tribespeople, and about a newspaper story that had attributed to him a claim that the Tasaday were bandits.

At the town hall, Johnny Artajo and other Panamin staffers were among the more than one hundred participants in the open forum. All over town, Panamin representatives were handing out leaflets denying newspaper stories that Panamin was grabbing land and mining and logging in the mountains or that it had claims on land for such purposes, and insisting that the tribesmen sought only to live in peace and dignity on their lands. The leaflet carried an offer of 10,000 pesos to anyone who could disprove its claims.

We met the mayor in the town hall and were shown into a large office whose only furniture was a few straight-backed chairs and a bare wooden desk. The mayor seated himself behind the desk. Lim Youn Choul set up his camera, Det Arndt the sound equipment, and Jack Reynolds said we would like to ask the mayor about the area in general and about the Tasaday. An aide intervened, saying the mayor could not discuss the Tasaday because he was trying to smooth over the unrest at this time and did not want to say anything to embarrass Panamin or Elizalde.

However, the aide added, the mayor—who was nodding and smiling—would not object if we interviewed other people who knew about the Tasaday. He offered to call for them and we accepted.

The mayor, José T. Sison, a balding man who appeared to be in his late forties, said he was born in the central Philippines, lived in Manila as a young man, and had come to Surallah several years ago with a construction firm. He stayed, established the largest pig farm in the area, and ran for mayor. He won his second term in 1971. He told us this in slow, deliberate English, smiling often. He looked the small-town farmer at first glance—a stocky frame, stomach drooping over the belt of denim jeans with rolled-up cuffs. He wore a baseball-type cap, the peak slightly askew over his moon-shaped face. He did not, however, have the plumpness that the description suggests; his body looked solid and his neck was muscular. His dark, heavy-lidded eyes held in a steady gaze.

Sison introduced a companion and the man quickly added, "The name is Spanish, of Spanish origin . . . spelled E-l-l-e-g-a but pronounced Eh-yega." He said he was a farmer and had come to this area from the island of Panay during World War II. When the Tasaday were mentioned, Ellega said abruptly, "There are no such people as Tasaday—that's just a name invented by Elizalde. I know this from a Christian who lives near here. He says he knows some of those people who are supposed to be Tasaday, recognized them from pictures in the newspapers, says they used to be neighbors of his. Of course he knew them—it's some kind of trick."

Reynolds said we would like to talk to this man, and he was sent for.

The discussion turned to the current difficulties between the Tboli and settlers. Ellega said he was a farmer near Kemalas and that ten houses on his property and been burned. He said they were houses of "natives," presumably Tboli—whom the Christians usually called Tagabilli—or Blaan—whom they called Bilan. Ellega said the houses had been abandoned long before they were burned.

Asked why the houses had been burned, Ellega smiled and said, "Well, some say it was because the people who used to live in them wouldn't band together with the Panamin projects . . . wouldn't move into the settlements."

Asked if that meant Panamin was responsible for the burnings, Ellega said, "Well, I wouldn't say *I* was saying that, but some people around here are."

"But why burn empty, long-abandoned houses?"

"Well, this sort of thing happens, you know."

"But why? It isn't clear."

"Well, people around here know why," he said, with a grin at the mayor and a couple of other men who had come into the room.

It was puzzling, but Ellega declined further comment on this, so we asked what the basic cause of the current troubles was. He said it was due partly to land disputes and partly to cattle rustling by the natives. The disputes developed when tribesmen sold their land to Christian settlers and then other tribesmen claimed that it was their land.

Asked if land sales were documented or cleared officially, Ellega said, "Oh, yes. The provincial governor himself and his organization clear all sales and titles. Each case must be approved."

Why were there disputes if each case was documented?

"Oh, well, the natives usually kill anybody who gets in their way. Take Ulos, for instance. He killed Segundo, a native at my place. I don't know exactly why—they fought over something. And, do you know, my nephew on a carabao was shot and wounded in that fight! These things happen *all* the time with these natives!"

We remarked that this had nothing to do with land and seemed a rather lame example of tribal savagery against settlers.

The mayor spoke up to say that nineteen persons had been killed in the area in the past three months—eighteen were murders committed by natives against eleven Christians and seven of their own people.

Asked how many arrests had been made, the mayor said there had not been many arrests yet.

How did he know all the murders had been committed by tribesmen?

"We know . . . we know," he said.

"Then charges have been filed against suspects in these cases?"

"Well, in some cases, yes. Right now, four of the criminals are in jail right here." The mayor went on with Reynolds about the killings by tribesmen, and I turned to a man who had taken a seat beside me, and had been introduced as a member of the city council. I told him that if the four jailed men the mayor mentioned were the Tboli accused of the massacre, then there must have been some very recent development, because we had heard only yesterday that nothing had been established and the judge stuck by his earlier announcement that evidence would be forthcoming.

"Ah . . . well . . . ah, yes," the councilman said. "Ah . . . the mayor sometimes has difficulty expressing himself in English. Of course, he has so much to do, maybe he isn't so clear about all the details in all these killings."

Reynolds asked the mayor about Panamin, and Sison said that after six years here Panamin had not given a single land title to any tribesman —"If they are trying to help those people, like they claim, why not give the titles to the individuals? That's what we would like to know. That's what all of us would like to know."

Reynolds said he had been told there was a security problem for the tribesmen, so they stayed together, and also that it would be unwise to divide the little land they had left into individual plots on which few would make a decent living. They needed a co-operative effort.

"Oh, no," a man said with a shake of his head. "Why not land titles? That's what we want to know? Why not titles? That would clear everything up."

I mentioned hearing that many tribesmen had lost titled land because they didn't know the laws or how to deal with clever men who tricked them and took the land for practically nothing. Did this ever happen here?

"Well, I suppose you sometimes have a case like that," one of the men answered. "But our people aren't like that. No, that's no real problem."

By now, Ernesto Pido, a city councilman and principal of the Allah Valley high schools, had arrived. He said the city had forty-seven thousand residents and three high schools. We asked him what had started the trouble with Panamin.

He claimed it was because Elizalde had not conferred with Surallah officials when he first arrived several years ago; he went directly into the mountains to see the people there. "He did not show respect for the local officials. There were no consultations," Pido said.

What about the mountain people, the Tboli, were they good people?

"Well, yes," Pido said. "But, as you know . . . their lack of education . . . why, you feed them, give them money, and they'll follow anything you say. Do whatever you tell them. . . ."

Did he mean Elizalde was feeding them and giving money? We added that we understood there were tens of thousands of Tboli and thousands of other tribesmen.

"Ah, well, yes. That is, he started to . . . Well, it's not exactly that, but there was that feud between Elizalde and our congressman, and then later a group of geologists came here, from Italy, I think it was, and looked over our area and said it had many useful minerals."

What was the connection—had Elizalde brought the geologists?

"No, the government arranged it."

We noted that it was said that Elizalde had mining claims here, was that correct?

"Perhaps."

Could they confirm that he did? Did they know for a fact if either Elizalde or any Panamin people had made mining claims in this province?

"Well, no. Not yet they haven't."

But if they had been here several years, why were they taking so long if that was their purpose?

"We are waiting to see just that."

But what was it, exactly, that Elizalde and Panamin had done to cause trouble?

Councilman Pido sighed and smiled. "You must understand that there are things we would like to say to you, but we are afraid. He has so much power—radio, television, newspapers, industries; and he's close to the President."

"With all this power and influence," I asked, "why does he spend so much time roughing it in the mountains with the tribesmen?"

"Exactly! That's what *we* would like to know. We don't know what he is up to. You hear that, Mayor? This gentleman just asked what Elizalde is up to. That's *exactly* what we would like to know, right Mayor? What *is* he up to?"

At this point another man entered the office and was introduced as a relative of the mayor. He immediately began talking in a loud voice while standing in the middle of the room and twisting his head almost wildly from side to side. The reason for the twisting apparently was that he had one defective eye, possibly glass, which stared blankly as he turned his good eye on various people. "Look here," he said. "Now these Tagabilli are just uneducated—don't know anything. You never know what they might do!"

The mayor interrupted to say that the local people could handle the problems if outsiders would stop interfering. Reynolds asked if he meant Panamin should get out, and Sison said, "Panamin should go if that is the only way we can have peace, and it appears that it is. Before Panamin came we had no trouble with our minorities—oh, a little but not so much. We worked things out."

If everything was fine before, why had the tribesmen lost so much land? Why had they welcomed Panamin? And why was there trouble now?

"Panamin gets those people excited, upset. That's why we have trouble now," a councilman said.

We asked if house burnings were a problem.

"Yes," the mayor said. "Let's see . . . there have been at least nine or ten. More than that, I guess."

He said all of them had belonged to Christian settlers.

And what about the houses of minorities, any burned?

"None . . . except for those empty ones on Mr. Ellega's property."

We said we had seen five houses in flames one evening, and the wrecked shells of possibly a dozen more. All were in tribal territory, and people who said they were friends and relatives claimed the houses belonged to Tboli.

"We have had no reports of any minority houses burned. Elizalde never tells us. Never reports to us. I wonder," the mayor said, giving us a sympathetic smile, "if there *really* were any. You may have been shown some burned houses, but they probably belonged to Christians."

We said we had talked to neighbors who were Tboli.

"We know nothing about that. But the figures you hear . . . why, they try to say eighty-three—is it eighty-three?—houses have been burned. I just don't know where he gets these figures. He must make them up." The mayor then invited us to move to an outdoor canteen for coffee.

A dozen men congregated outside, including an army officer wearing dark glasses. Conversation continued much as it had, the mayor assuring us that we were hearing the true story.

One of the men who had said he knew that the Tasaday were criminals arrived. He was introduced as Francisco Galaura, former vice-mayor of Surallah, now working for a logging company. His wife was with him and both were nervous. Galaura, as did all the men present, spoke English fluently. His wife whispered loudly to him, "Tell them . . . speak up. Tell these men about those people."

Galaura said that about two years ago he had sent a logging-survey team to the Blit area. The Blit were friendly and told the surveyors that the name of that nearby range of mountains was Tasaday. Galaura continued, "You see—not the people were Tasaday, but the range was Tasaday. And I have relatives who know people around those mountains that *know* the people inside there are Manubo criminals hiding out."

If the Tasaday were ordinary Manubo, we asked, why did they speak a different dialect, one nobody had ever heard?

"Hah!" said Galaura's wife. "It's not different. You just don't know the language. It's Manubo, all right."

But if they were criminals from outside the forest, why didn't they have any weapons or tools, clothes, rice, corn, tobacco?

"Oh, they have those things. They are criminals, all right. Bandits. They go in and out of the mountains all the time," she replied.

Perhaps they were referring to other groups, such as Kabayo's band, we said, adding that we had seen the Tasaday and they . . .

The wife interrupted, seeming very agitated. "Of course, we *know* they are not these Tasaday, as *you* call them. They are Manubo—everybody around here knows that—put in there for some reason, probably hiding from the police."

The gathering had grown to about two dozen people, one of whom was the man with the defective eye. He jumped into the discussion at once and said, "Those people . . . those Tagabilli! We never had trouble before. We could handle it. They're criminals . . . savages. They could come down out of those mountains at any time. We've got to straighten this out once and for all. . . ."

The Galauras looked at him, frowned, and resumed the previous discussion, insisting that we were being fooled, that there were no such people as Tasaday. We said we already had reported the existence of a group by that name, which had aroused considerable interest around the world. Many scientists had seen the Tasaday and had compiled data that confirmed their scientific importance. But if the Galauras and others were correct, and it was a hoax, it was a story that should be told. If they could provide evidence to support their claim, we would report it.

The Galauras began talking simultaneously: "Those people are criminals . . . we know . . . My people used to go there . . . move around freely, but no more . . . Panamin will kill them . . . we are all scared."

Galaura said he was affected directly because he owned more than a thousand acres of land in that area, which might be included in the Tasaday reserve. He was trying to find out, but it was too dangerous. Many people were worried about their land but were too scared to go check now, because Panamin and the Blit and other tribes might shoot them.

If nobody goes there, we asked, then what is the evidence that the Tasaday really are criminals?

"I have relatives who know that area, and they know," Galaura said. "They told us."

Was that the only evidence?

"It's not just us," Mrs. Galaura said. "Everybody around here knows!"

Why was it, then, that scientists were convinced the Tasaday had never been outside the forest? Several journalists believed that, too, and none of these observers owned property here or had any political interests.

"I don't know about all that," Mrs. Galaura replied. "But if it is true, why can't we go and see them for ourselves?"

Who wanted to go?

"All of us. All the people here in the area. If it's true, why can't we go in there and see for ourselves."

We said it might be possible to send a delegation, but that access was limited for various physical, scientific, and humanitarian reasons, so very few visitors were being allowed in.

The army lieutenant, who had been quiet so far, spoke up: "We can penetrate that forest. Our helicopters can penetrate! We can get in there!"

But why was it necessary to "penetrate" the forest? There were only twenty-seven Tasaday and they did not seem to be harming anyone in the world.

"Ahhh," the mayor said. "It's twenty-seven now, eh? They're claiming twenty-seven. Let's see, first it was nineteen, then twenty-one, then twenty-four . . . now twenty-seven. I see. Yes, yes— *How many will it be next?*"

One of the councilmen nodded emphatically and said it was obvious that strange things were going on in the mountains. He cited the special force of armed Tboli—apparently Panamin's security unit, which included men like Fludi, Manuel, Sol, Dad. The man said it was understood that this "army" comprised at least three hundred highly equipped troops. Reynolds replied: "Oh, you must mean those boys that carried our gear in the mountains. There's no question they are tough. They carried load after load of heavy equipment for us and never once complained. Excellent boys. Guns? I don't know. They were so weighed down with our things, they couldn't have used guns if they had them. But, you know, when I'm around here I hardly notice guns, anyway—there are so many, you see them everywhere you go. Like right now, just sitting here—you've got your gun, Mr. Mayor, and you there, and over there on that gentleman. I mean, I get so accustomed to seeing guns in everyone's belt that I get sort of blind to them, hardly ever notice them any more."

At this point the helicopter flew over, on its way to pick us up, and the meeting fragmented into half a dozen different conversations as we departed. The helicopter was to land in a yard alongside the town hall and Jack and I passed through the hall on our way. The concrete jail was beneath the stairway leading up from the main floor, and we peered through the steel-barred door and saw, in the dim light, four beds in a room about the size of a large automobile. We could see small barred windows and figures moving around beyond a partition. A town employee who was passing by told us the jail could handle eight prisoners and that four Tagabilli were in there right now. What he did not tell us was that they had been confined a month and the evidence against them was still to materialize.

Thinking later about the afternoon in Surallah, I was reminded of some visits I had made to small Southern towns in the United States during the Civil Rights movement in the early 1960's. There were similarities, particularly in the mood of the place and in people's attitudes. Some people really believed—or wanted to—that the Tasaday were gangsters; and some truly feared the Tboli might swarm down from the hills to murder and plunder. I mentioned this to Elizalde, saying I thought the townsfolk were more frightened of the mountain people than the mountain people were of them.

"What?" he said. "What the hell do you mean, *more* frightened?"

I answered that several people we had met seemed scared of the tribes, but that their worst enemies were their own ignorance and prejudice.

"Yeah, that sounds great," Manda said. "You remember that the next time they wipe out a bunch of Tboli and steal their land. Don't forget what I told you about this area being where everybody else in the country comes to get its hired guns, its killers. Remember, too, that many officials around here—hell, I can name 'em—are wanted for murder in some other part of the country."

I could not deny what he said, having no evidence to the contrary and later I conceded that I did not know the settlers well, having spent almost all my time with the tribes. But, I said, I still felt that a sizable number of the settlers were more scared than set on destroying the tribes. Elizalde countered that *if* they were scared, it was only because they feared the tribes might retaliate for crimes committed against them, a fear born of guilt. Whatever the case, it seemed obvious that it would take little to inflame their fears and prejudices and turn them into an angry mob. They could become pawns easily enough for the people who had the most to gain by defeating the tribes, the rich and powerful men who had already acquired huge chunks of lowland and now wanted the minerals and timber in the mountains. These were the behind-the-scenes brokers who supplied the rabble-rousers with money and guns and so controlled the frontier. The old American West had such men—what frontier did not? One unusual aspect here was that the champion of the natives was Elizalde, a member of the elite, whom many expected to be on the opposite side. It confused people and that made them more suspicious and angry—just as were those who charged Franklin D. Roosevelt with betraying his own class in the New Deal. Elizalde's defense was the same as Roosevelt's—the country belongs to all the people; to serve the weak is no disservice to the strong.

Not all of the citizens of Surallah were scared of the tribes or angry with Elizalde, however. I met one such man the next morning as we waited for the plane that would take us back to Manila. I had taken a walk from the small airport down a dusty road to what could have been a town in an American Western. Signs over weathered store fronts lining the dirt street said: COLLAR STORE; DR. JOSE TANCO, PHYSICIAN AND SURGEON, PHARMACY; MODERN BILLIARD HALL. Carabaos grazed in a nearby field and three-wheel scooter taxis put-putted down Main Street, raising brown clouds. Next to the Airport Café was a small boxy shack, topped by a yellow-and-red sign that ran the length of the building. The sign was decorated with drawings of half a dozen different kinds of guns, and large-lettered words: CENTRAL ARMS CORPORATION—WE HELP YOU SECURE LICENSES, PERMIT TO CARRY, LICENSE FOR VERIFICATION AND ETC.

It was only eight o'clock but the tropical sun was already searing. As I walked back toward the airport, a chubby little man about fifty, in a battered straw hat, white shirt, tan trousers, and open-toed sandals, shuffled up from behind me.

"You were over there by city hall yesterday, weren't you?" he asked. "I saw you talking over there, you and that other American. You two are observers, aren't you? That's good."

As we walked, I asked his name and what he meant.

"Name is Angel [pronounced Awng-hill]," he said. "I have a farm outside of town. I mean, you two are observers, seeing what is going on here. That is good."

What did he think of the situation with the tribesmen?

Angel had sun-squint lines around his dark eyes. His quick smile revealed at least one gold tooth as he answered, "Well, I think much is bad information in this place. People do not understand each other—some,

I think, do not want to. I have been here since twelve years and I notice that it is maybe some politicians who are making trouble. I mean to say the voters are Christians! Yes? I think you understand.

I mentioned the Tboli.

"Now, the Tboli—I have some around my farm. Never any trouble. Never. But some of my own Christian people? Well . . . I can just say that some people like to make trouble for their own reasons. I think you know what I mean."

I stopped to turn off toward the airstrip and said good-by. Angel jerked an eyebrow in response and then said, "To have observers is good." He shuffled on down the road.

Two days later, NBC interviewed Marcos at the Presidential Palace in Manila. He expressed interest in the Tasaday and sympathy for the minority's problems, and restated his policy of allowing the minorities the choice of joining the mainstream of Filipino society or retaining their own cultures. The government would protect them, he said.

Elizalde, who had remained in Mindanao, returned to Manila ten days later and reported that the burnings and ambushes of tribesmen had tapered off. He said he had talked at length with Dafal, who told him he thought he could visit his cave birthplace in the forest without much difficulty but had not done so for a long time. His people, Dafal said, had been very similar to the Tasaday. If he had revealed their names, the size of the group, and other details, Elizalde did not disclose them to me.

Elizalde had also talked to some Tboli who lived in a remote area at the eastern edge of the great forest, perhaps more than thirty miles from the Tasaday. These tribesmen said that in the last few years they and others had killed about fifteen naked people. They said these people, who were "strange-looking," had attacked them with bamboo spears taken from the Tboli's own traps, and were killed in the fighting. The Tboli said the people did not know how to fight well. Elizalde speculated that one or more of the forest people had been killed or injured in a trap, and had been retaliating. He ordered that there be no further bloodshed, that any people inside the forest must be left alone, and if they were seen again or more was learned about them, he was to be informed.

A week after we left the Tasaday, Elizalde paid them an overnight visit, taking along Jack Foisie of the Los Angeles *Times* and a writer-photographer from the Manila *Times*. Dul had three knots left of the original ten on her vine calendar. The Tasaday seemed as happy as ever and gave no indication that the recent long exposure to many visitors and cameras had caused lasting upsets.

For the past week and a half, Elizalde said, he had been thinking a lot about the Tasaday's supposedly having lost the Tasafeng and Sanduka, and about their attitudes toward life in general. "The Tasaday just may show that man was not always a social animal—that is, he didn't travel in search of other men simply because he wanted to be sociable. He had enough companionship in his own group. When Tasaday men went out with women on their minds and they met other men, the subject of women naturally came up, and, if possible, a deal was made. That's the way it sounds to me. They didn't go out seeking others just for the sake of social contact—nope, they probably would always have stayed in their own group if not for the need to get women."

Meanwhile, the film crew for the German network NDR had gone to Indonesia for a few weeks, after which it would come to Manila to film a documentary on Elizalde, Panamin, and the tribes—*without* the Tasaday. Yen, in Manila, had met the same man who had talked to Elizalde in the forest, and had insisted that there be no more filming of the Tasaday. The Germans were disappointed but said that they understood; they would return in late September to begin the documentary.

Elizalde said he did not know when he would see the Tasaday again; nothing was scheduled. He called several meetings of key people in the Panamin Foundation and started outlining priorities and a plan of activities and goals to cover the next five to ten years. His staff felt that the priorities were largely what he wanted to make them and so he vowed to work out a plan—it was a desk job and he detested that, but he would try to lay down in broad terms what Panamin hoped to accomplish, how, and why.

22

Martial Law and
Another Film Crew

ELIZALDE worked on the long-range program for Panamin, on a nation-wide fund drive, and met several times with the advance man for the NDR TV crew through mid-September. On the afternoon of the twenty-first, he invited Joyce and me to a party at the Panamin Museum that same evening. He said he was inviting all the foreign journalists he could reach.

I asked why newsmen, especially on such short notice—unless he had a special announcement to make. But he insisted there was no announcement, he just wanted to have a party. But why this night, a Friday, when people had probably made weekend plans? It had to be this evening was all he would say. He did hint, however, that the Palace had suggested the party and that Mrs. Marcos might attend.

There was a fairly heavy turnout, considering the short notice, and as preparations were made to show film clips of NBC's coverage of the Tasaday the year before, Imelda Marcos did indeed arrive, accompanied by a small entourage of friends and the usual Palace guards.* A beauty contest queen in the 1950's, Mrs. Marcos was still very attractive and moved with easy assurance through the museum gathering, chatting and answering questions. Many queries were political, for she had played a strong role in her husband's presidency and he was under increasingly harsh criticism in the news media. After the film, Mrs. Marcos stayed for the catered supper Elizalde had arranged. I was seated at her small table, and she spoke animatedly about the Tasaday, the museum, a cultural

* The museum, incidentally, was in the same park complex as the outdoor stage where several weeks later, before a large crowd and a live television audience, a man attacked and seriously cut Mrs. Marcos in an attempt to assassinate her.

forum of Asian nations that she had proposed, and about Philippine social problems and politics. She said she was keeping a close record of the President's decisions and activities and that history would show that the criticism he was receiving these days was terribly unjust. There was nothing, however, in the way of an announcement to explain why the party had been suggested. Sometime after eleven, a uniformed palace guard walked up behind her chair, leaned down, and said something to the effect that the President was trying to reach her. She nodded and continued conversing for several more minutes, until the guard returned and repeated his message with more urgency.

The guard stepped back but did not leave her chair this time. She said that it appeared as though she must leave, the President was calling and it sounded as if he really meant it. Within a few minutes she had departed. Elizalde, who had been rather nervous about the party, was very pleased with the way it had gone.

The telephone got me out of bed about three-thirty that morning. An excited AP man said government troops had entered the AP bureau about midnight and ordered the night crew to leave. Teletype operator Jorge Reyes said he had tried to stay to keep the wire running, but he was compelled to leave. More troops were in the street and it was evident that the Manila *Times,* the largest-circulation newspaper in the country (in whose building the AP had its offices) had been shut down. Reyes asked an officer if this was martial law, which had been rumored as imminent. The officer said he did not know; he was merely acting under orders to lock up the *Times* building.

I switched on the radio and the usual all-night stations were silent. I spent the next few hours on the telephone, including several calls to and from the United States, until all communications outside the country were closed. By dawn it was clear that the media shutdown was total and troops were in position throughout the city. There was no official explanation from the Palace until the morning, when Marcos announced that he had declared martial law throughout the country to thwart communist subversives who were threatening the government and also to make major social-economic-political reforms.

It also was reported that Secretary of National Defense Juan Ponce Enrile had been attacked by gunmen while driving to his home in the early evening; he was not hurt, but his car had been hit by several bullets. Officials said the attack had been mounted by the same group of communist subversives responsible for a recent series of bombings of government facilities, in which there had been damage but few injuries. There had been talk that at least some of the bombings were the work of government agents seeking to provoke public reaction against the communists. This was not proven, however, to my knowledge. It had been established, though, that the old-line communist movement, which had grown weary and ineffectual, had been supplanted in the past two years by a small but tough Maoist-oriented force. Hard-core membership was estimated at a few hundred at best, but it was making itself felt. The ground was fertile. The gap between the few rich and the poverty-stricken masses was widening and an array of complex, debilitating problems had created a climate of wholesale deterioration in the nation's affairs. Widespread lawlessness was marked by violence and criminality in the streets, and by corruption in the courts and other high-government institutions and agencies; bitter and divisive rivalries among politicians and the entrenchment of a privileged rich elite with powerful influence in politics offered a continuing bleak future for the poor. The economy was in serious trouble, social improvement programs were stumbling, and the congress and Marcos were struggling inconclusively over how to correct the situation.

The President's critics contended that the six years of his administration had led the country to this deplorable state; he argued that it had been a much longer time in the making and that he had done the best job possible under the prevailing conditions.

But, despite what was apparently considerable opposition, Marcos, in a single night, was able to claim extraordinary powers for himself and, with surprising smoothness, put martial law into effect.

It was a fearsome and controversial move in a country boastful of its freewheeling democratic system, although few people denied that *something* had to be done. The congress was shut down, political opponents were seized and jailed; news media were closed; journalists arrested, censorship imposed. Hundreds of people were detained. There was, however, little evident bloodshed (the one victim of a firing squad was a man convicted by a military tribunal of heavy trafficking in narcotics). The military presence was not pervasive or heavy—that is, there were no tanks rolling through the streets—and Marcos insisted it was a "democratic revolution" within his constitutional authority when the nation was threatened. Some Filipinos questioned if the threat had been that great, but the immediate net response, after surprise, was a general attitude of wait and see. While critics whispered that Marcos was merely seeking absolute power, a more widely heard comment was that even if he were after greater power, perhaps he could change things for the better.

The martial law affected virtually everything in the country to some degree. Elizalde, as a cabinet officer and also a member of the so-called oligarchy (a class that Marcos had branded as something of a national evil), could be in a particularly sensitive position. I wondered also if he were somehow involved in the martial law declaration. His sudden party had tied up several newsmen the evening martial law was put into effect.

I spoke to him the next morning, and he sounded as surprised about developments as did the general public. He claimed he had no idea that martial law was coming.

Although I was on a leave of absence from the AP, I helped cover the eventful days immediately following the declaration, then returned to my work on the film and notes from the last and longest visit with the Tasaday.

Elizalde was busier than I had ever seen him. His father was on an extended visit to Spain at the time of the martial law declaration and, as the oldest son, Elizalde undertook much heavier business responsibilities than usual. At one point troops surrounded the Elizalde steel plant; the family's newspaper and radio and television stations were shut down permanently; there were new regulations—on imports, exports, foreign exchange, taxes, transportation—with which he had to deal. He also supervised the turning over to the military of his own weapons and those of the Tboli and other tribes—new laws cracked down heavily on firearms; the penalty was death for anyone in violation. Elizalde hoped this would succeed in curbing the power of outlaw bands and private armies of powerful men in Mindanao, and thereby lessen the dangers to the minorities.

Throughout this, the German television crew, which had arrived in Manila a few days after military rule was declared, was waiting patiently. They wanted Elizalde in most of their shooting, but he was constantly on the move. They said fine, they intended a slice-of-life style film and would follow him, but most of his time was spent in meetings and discussions, which always looked the same. The team, headed by Max Rehbein, an energetic and compactly built man in his fifties with a ruddy face and an expansive, volatile manner, trailed him in frustration. After three weeks, only a small portion of the film had been shot and the crew was on the verge of giving up and returning to Germany.

Elizalde, however, wanted the film done, so he arranged to free himself for several days to go to Mindanao. In late October he flew to Tboli with Rehbein and his three-man team. They spent two days with the Ubu at Ma Falen's place, filmed at various Tboli tribal sites, and then began working at the main Tboli settlement. Rehbein, a confident and persistent man—he had spent many months as a tank officer in bitter fighting on the frigid Russian front, where he had suffered the loss of two fingers on his right hand and the hearing in his right ear—still clung to the hope that they would be able to film at least a little of the Tasaday.

Elizalde had given hints of encouragement along the way, but had not made a firm commitment. He finally agreed, partly because he felt guilty at having kept them idle for a month, partly because he wanted to visit the Tasaday himself after being away several weeks. He also felt it could help the film and that it could be controlled so the Tasaday would not be seriously bothered. He invited the film crew to accompany him to the caves and a contract was drawn up whereby they would do no filming the day of arrival, film only on the second day *if* the Tasaday were agreeable, and leave the third day. The Tasaday portion of the broadcast version of the film was not to exceed 25 per cent.

Elizalde invited me to join them. I arrived at Tboli October 28 as the Germans were filming a carabao fight in a large open field below the staff house. The film team—Rehbein, cameraman Eckhard Dorn, soundman Klaus Hilgenfeld, and assistant cameraman Bernd Wilckens—was on the ground, following the action. Carabao fights and horse fights were among the favorite entertainments of the tribesmen, and an excited crowd followed the carabaos as they chased, charged, and slammed together, banging their heads and then thrashing them so that their curved foot-long horns would do the most damage. Sometimes they crashed head on and the horns locked; the huge animals, about the size of a bull ox, snorted and heaved furiously as the Tboli yelled encouragement. The tribesmen said the animals rarely inflicted serious injury upon one another and the victor was decided when one animal broke and ran. One of the mud-gray beasts did just that as the camera was rolling and the crew leaped aboard an open Jeep and continued shooting as the vehicle bounced along behind the animal up and down the bumpy lanes between Tboli houses.

With them gone and the fighting over, Rehbein grabbed Elizalde, insisting he had to talk with him about the scenario for the film and complaining that Elizalde was so busy even here that they had had no chance to really discuss things.

Elizalde guided him to Mai Tuan's house and they sat side by side in a small room to talk. But every minute or so, an inquiry or radio message had to be answered. Rehbein's bad ear happened to be closest to Elizalde and the film maker was so engrossed and animated in outlining his scenario that he seemed oblivious of the fact that Elizalde was so often being interrupted. When Elizalde returned to their discussion, neither man knew what the other was talking about:

ELIZALDE: Okay, okay. But what is that all about? I just told you that the Ubu sequence could be filmed after that—the helicopter will be available.

REHBEIN: The Ubu sequence? The Ubu sequence? Vot do you mean? Dot sequence is finished already.

ELIZALDE: But you just said you wanted to film there again.

REHBEIN: Vot? You are crazy. I said the Ubu sequence was perfect. Exactly right. We vant to shoot again the Blit sequence.

ELIZALDE: Then what the hell has that got to do with filming again at Ma Falen's place?

REHBEIN: Vot? Nothing! I have said nothing about such a thing.

ELIZALDE: Jesus Christ! You just got through saying we had to go back to Ma Falen's.

REHBEIN: No! I have not said this!

ELIZALDE: Then what the hell are you talking about?

REHBEIN: Vot am *I* talking about? Ach! Vot is it *you* talk about?

And so it went for about half an hour, both men occasionally shouting and waving their arms, after which Rehbein would hold his head with both hands and Elizalde would mutter disdainful remarks to bystanders. Both men also laughed a great deal, deriving obvious delight from the exchanges, which finally concluded with Rehbein saying, "Never mind! Never mind! It will be a grrreat film!"

"It better be, Max," Manda said. "After all the trouble I've gone to for you on this, it better be great."

"Vot? Trouble? You? Hah! It is we who have troubles. Since I have met you—troubles only!"

This jocular tone permeated their relationship throughout the filming, so that tensions rarely developed; heat was expended so quickly it had no chance to build up.

I spoke with Rehbein at length that first evening. He said he had been having an exceptionally good time among the tribes. At Ma Falen's place, for instance, the colors were vibrant and rich, the people spirited and warm—"It vas simply fantastic!"

We flew into the forest the next morning. From the air it looked deceivingly soft, luxurious. Velvety moss hung from limbs and tree-filled valleys looked like puffy beds of chartreuse and amber marshmallows. It had often looked so inviting from the air, but on the ground it was a maze of twisted limbs and sharp rocks, jagged cliffs and rough slopes under towering triple canopies of leaves that made shadowy tunnels tangled with thorny vines and bamboo hedges.

The area near the Tasaday caves had familiar paths, but beyond them it was strange, forbidding country. And at night even the Tasaday area was mysterious, with shadowy shapes and weird sounds. As we descended, the forest interior was a dozen shades of yellow and green, mustard, chartreuse, olive, amber. On the ground, we could smell the musky odor of drying grass and humus in the sun; in the deep shade, the odor was of cool moist earth.

Balayam loped toward us as we walked from the ridge. Bubbling with laughter, he said he had heard the big bird as it approached and ran all the way to see if it had brought Momo Dakel Diwata Tasaday. He hugged and sniffed Manda effusively and then greeted Mai and others in similar though less exuberant fashion. Dul, Udelen, and Maman followed close behind him and hugged us gently, rubbing their cheeks against ours. Further along the trail we met more Tasaday as they hurried to greet Manda and join the party.

Balayam sang as we walked, then laughingly clucked: "Klek-klek-klek," imitating the sound of Igna's rattling ankle bracelets.

We headed down the slope without Rehbein, who had made the first flight and was to wait on the ridge for the rest of his crew. When we were out of sight, Balayam smiled and whispered to Mai, holding his hand with two fingers folded into the palm to mimic Rehbein's maimed hand. "I saw that and I had to look," Balayam told Mai. "But I didn't want to look too much—that man might not like it."

Physical infirmities had been a source of Tasaday humor on two or three previous occasions. Ginun and Tekaf had been heralded with "*Oh-ho*. Here come old no-hear and no-talk," accompanied by laughter. Mimicking of Kuletaw's wheezing cough and stooped walk had brought guffaws. It did not seem to be cruel laughter, and they were quite open about it. Lobo, too, immediately mimicked Rehbein, with giggles. But their imitation of Rehbein was covert, presumably because they did not know him yet. I believe Rehbein would have been amused rather than embarrassed; he showed no self-consciousness about his injuries and had given us a fascinating and detailed account of the fighting in which he sustained them and almost lost his life.

When we reached the tents, Balayam and Sindi sat close, nuzzling and petting each other, her arms intertwined with his. He hugged her, laughed, and rocked back and forth. Then, squeezing her, he said, "Momo Dakel took away my cold inside when he brought me Sindi."

The helicopter flew over and hovered directly above us, causing leaves and twigs to shower down. Balayam and Udelen peered up through the trees, and Udelen directed Dul, Sindi, and Maman to crawl under a rattan lath table for protection. Balayam went into a dancing, chortling imitation of how Bart flew the big bird. The helicopter left after a minute or so but Elizalde was furious. He grabbed a walkie-talkie from Felix and demanded to know from Fludi at the ridge what was going on. He was told that Rehbein's cameraman had wanted to photograph the cave from the air and Bart had taken him.

Rehbein reached the tents soon after this, not having waited for his crew after all, and Manda lit into him—the helicopter had hovered overhead at the cameraman's request and could have caused limbs to fall on people, injuring and frightening the Tasaday . . . twigs and leaves had been knocked down and it was lucky no serious harm had been done. This was not the way to get started in here, and if it was a preview of the TV crew's behavior, then everyone would pull out of the forest at once . . . no filming, no visit, nothing!

Rehbein, taken aback at having walked into this barrage, could only blink at first and agree that it had been a mistake. He said he had been on the trail when the crew arrived and did not know what had happened—but surely the cameraman had not realized the problem, since Bart had not refused to fly him in over the tents. Nevertheless, he said firmly, there would be no more infractions.

Manda grumbled and swore but in a few minutes was quite friendly again. I had the impression that a certain amount of this was bluster, part of his brinkmanship with Rehbein.

After tightening up the tents and putting the camp in order, we walked to the caves. At the lower one a group of Tasaday lolled on platforms in the arching mouth. Lobo and Lolo bounded down from the upper cave, whooping and laughing as they vaulted along the dusty path with staves. Udo sat near a fire, his feet curled like grasping hands over a log. The rocky walls were muted amber, gray, and yellow; in the afternoon light the Tasadays' skin had the hue of almonds and light chocolate.

Rehbein seemed mesmerized. He stared in silence as we approached, then peered avidly all around as we stood in the mouth of the cave. When he spoke it was an excited babble. "It . . . it . . . is incredible! It is too much, too perfect . . . like a Hollyvood set. I . . . I . . . it is simply un-be-lievable!"

Bilangan arrived from the forest with one of his young sons and Udelen walked off to announce Momo Dakel's arrival to Mahayag and his family, who, he said, were out searching for *biking*.

Dul seemed content and looked fatter than before; flesh wobbled over the waist of her leaf skirt. Balayam, also with added plumpness, gave Max Rehbein and cameraman Eckhard Dorn their names: Kakay Wak and Kakay Ek-ek.

Manda asked the Tasaday if they would mind if the new visitors brought out their big camera—a *ta-suk, dakel*—the next day. Balayam smiled, looked at Dul, and said it would be all right. "We know they have one of those," he said. "Every time new faces come here they have those. We must not mind it."

As we returned to the tents, we saw Udelen walking back to the cave. About an hour and a half had passed since he'd left to find Mahayag. He said nothing, but looked concerned.

After dinner we sat in the light of Manda's flickering candles and talked. After a while, Rehbein and Eckhard asked Manda what he was trying to accomplish. Why was he doing all this work with the tribes?

He gave his usual reply: he liked it, it was his "thing"; he enjoyed see- ing people happy; he took from the "so-called civilized world" and gave to this one, Robin Hood-style. . . .

"Ya ya, but vhy is it so? Vot makes you do this?" Max asked.

"I told you, I like it."

"Ya, but this is not a reason to . . ."

"It's enough," Manda said, interrupting sharply. "Don't ask any more. What right have you to ask me why? In all these years that we've worked with the people out here, they have never—never—asked me *why* I do this, or why I do that." His voice became loud and intense. "They look and judge. They know I'm not fooling them. They believe I'm a good man. They know it!"

"Don't be angry," Max said. "We only vant to explain to our audience vhy . . ."

"I've told you why. But you don't understand. And you'll never under-stand me or the Tasaday or anyone else in these mountains if you put everything on *your* terms. For once in your life you'll have to think on somebody else's terms, and I doubt if you can."

Eckhard, in an aside to me, said, "We are not saying he is wrong. It is just that we want to understand. I do not disagree·. . . I, too, think he must be a good man. I can see this in his eyes. I am a cameraman, the cameraman always looks at the eyes. When Elizalde talks to different peo-ple his eyes are different. And when he is with these people in the moun-tains, you know he is a good man. I can see this in the eyes."

Eckhard, thirty, was tall and slender, with pale skin, blond hair, and a quiet, decisive manner. He conducted himself with solemn confidence. He said he had been a professional cameraman for eleven years and had made documentaries, full-length feature films, and more than one hundred com-mercials. He said quite frankly that he was an excellent cameraman. "I have very steady hands. Very steady. This is not my fault, of course. I just have them. I can shoot for ten minutes, twelve minutes, and never stop the filming."

Eckhard was in considerable pain at the moment, however, because he had fallen the previous night while filming at Tboli. Manda had shown the National Geographic film to the tribesmen and, although they had seen it many times before, they still roared and yelled throughout the program, seeing themselves on the screen so often. Eckhard had been filming the crowd's excitement when he slipped off a four-foot-high stage and toppled to the concrete floor with his heavy camera on top of him. His ribs were severely bruised, perhaps cracked, and his right leg was badly gashed.

Manda heatedly pursued his discussion with Rehbein. "What you don't understand about all this is that you can't use your ideas or your standards to judge the Tasaday—to even think about them. You must try to think like they do. But you cannot. Your society has corrupted you too much."

"Perhaps . . . ya, perhaps. But it is not necessary to become upset like this."

"What do you mean? I have a right to an opinion that is stronger than anybody else's on this. I really care about these people. Sure, so do other people, but I have put my whole damned life into it. Would you? Will you? Where are all our good and concerned friends when we get into trouble? Nowhere, that's where. But afterward they all come around with plenty of advice. This is my life. That's it! That's enough explanation!"

Rehbein and Eckhard responded simultaneously, their words tumbling together:

"Ya but . . . We accept that, but we don't understand . . . The question now . . . why did you change so? Why change from the life you had . . . you told us about this, no? Yachts, planes, everything . . . Many people would enjoy such a life? Why do you change from this?"

"Who said I changed?" Manda snapped. "Or, at least, who said I changed away? Maybe I just changed back to something I was before. Maybe I just told the world to screw off: 'World, I'm going to do what I want to do from now on. Not what you want me to do.' I told my family, my wife. And that was it."

The conversation ran on for another hour. The continuous bickering seemed to be to everyone's taste. After the Germans retired, Rehbein called us to their tent. Eckhard, covered with blankets, was feverish and in great pain. Manda summoned Rebong, who had wrapped the ribs and leg after the accident the night before. Doc knelt beside Eckhard, felt his forehead, took his pulse, inspected the bandaged ribs. Eckhard's pain seemed to be increasing before our eyes. His face turned whiter and he bit his lip, sweat breaking out on his forehead; he rolled his eyes and groaned but said nothing coherent.

"Hmm, he's in severe pain, all right," Doc said. "Not much we can do here, though. Must be those ribs; can be very, very painful, though not serious. I'll get him some pain capsules."

Rebong stood up and left the tent. Eckhard sighed, gestured toward the lower half of the blanket, and grimaced. He clearly indicated that Rebong had been kneeling on his gashed leg! Why hadn't he spoken or cried out?

Eckhard was much improved the next morning and filming began about eight. He had been told of the Tasaday's dislike of cameras, so he tied leafy branches on top of his, peeking under them as he filmed, which amused the Tasaday.

Balayam sprawled on Dul's platform cradling Sindi, while Dul, Udelen, Adug, and several children sat beside them, chatting. It was a relaxed hour, and the Tasaday, moving steadily closer together until they were a tangle of arms and legs, dozed, played, talked. At one point, Balayam announced from somewhere in the pile of people that he had been cuddling Sindi so much that he had an erection. He howled with laughter and the others snorted and chuckled.

Sasa played nearby, tossing pebbles into the forest. His older brother, Udo, pretended to make *natek,* using a bent piece of bamboo as his mallet. Throughout this visit it was Udo's job to keep an eye on Sasa, who chattered to himself as he played around the lower cave. He was plump and healthy now, and I recalled the first time I had seen him, huddled in his father's arms, sickly pale with patchy straw hair, his swollen face and body pitted with red sores and his slightly slanted eyes running. It was thought that perhaps he was a victim of Mongolism or some other mental deficiency. Now he looked fit and contented, although we noticed that he rarely joined groups of Tasaday or romped and teased with the other youngsters. I remarked about this to Dad, who told me that Sasa was very bright and talkative on occasion but seldom traveled from the caves. Dad said some Tasaday apparently considered Sasa as special in some way, but he could not explain it. The unusual aspects of his first few years of life—his fair coloring, the story of his mother having died of a witch's bite on her breast while Sasa was a nursing infant, his recovery from what many outsiders had termed a fatal illness—these could have special meanings for the Tasaday. Perhaps one day he would become their first shaman or witch doctor.

In the afternoon the Tasaday foraged for food upstream. They were cheerful and bounced briskly along the stream, first looking several steps ahead and then bounding from rock to rock, never quite stopping between hops—bop-bop-bop-bip—rather like the ball in a pinball machine.

At dusk they built a fire on the lip of the upper cave and the flames cast a red-orange glow on the men and boys seated around it. Beyond them, in the jungle, the sun's last rays fringed the leafy treetops with pale yellow and turned the shadowy lower depths aqua and murky blue-green. Balayam sang and played his mouth harp, and Lobo and Udo and other boys played a game similar to follow-the-leader, in which they leaped over the fire.

The forest's muted evening colors were at the opposite end of the spectrum from the bright colors of this unusually sunny day. In the afternoon, we were all gazing at the vivid hues during a break at the tents, and someone remarked that some forest peoples had identified scores of colors, classifying green alone into dozens of different shades. When Balayam and Sindi arrived, we asked him about colors. He said the one he liked best was *mulu-unu,* the color of leaves.

We then pointed to leaves of differing hues—delicate light-green ferns, heavy dark-green oak leaves, shiny yellow-green bamboo. Balayam said all were the same color, *mulu-unu,* simply green. Grass, leaves, plants, vines were *mulu-unu,* Balayam said.

I pointed to an olive-drab jacket in the tent: *"Mulu-unu,"* Balayam said. The same for a pastel-green flashlight, a bright-green plastic water bucket, Igna's blue-green cloth skirt.

The color of a red water bucket was *malala-ga,* Balayam said. An orange cloth also was *malala-ga.* Black hair was *ma-etun;* white shirt, *mabula;* yellow paper, *malu-malala-ga* (Mai said it meant sort of half-red). The sun was *mabula,* the sky was part black and, as Mai understood the word, part blue. Fire was a variation of white.

This introduction to Tasaday color terminology indicated that Balayam used the same word for at least eight noticeably different (to us) shades of green; that red and orange were identified by the same word; yellow was half red (or half yellow); white and black were independent colors (if color was the correct word).

While this was interesting, it revealed little because the questioning was so limited and unstructured. Colors, like the names of plants, places, and other classifiable items, can indicate a complicated, perhaps unique system of values and interpretation. Some forest peoples reportedly included such things as size, shape, weight, even taste in what we might call a color description. To perceive their meanings required thinking about and seeing the objects as they did.

Earlier that afternoon, before Balayam and Sindi arrived at the tents, we had been talking with Mai about religion and mythology. Did he know any Tasaday words that conveyed an idea or concept of a god or gods? He knew of none. What about Tboli beliefs? Mai said Mulu was one of the great figures, the Planter of All Things, but was not exactly a god. The Tboli did not know where Mulu lived, although several other deitylike figures lived in the "eight layers of the sky." Mai said there were three places a person's spirit might go after death: the pleasant place, for people who died naturally and would live after death as they had on earth; the red and bloody place, for those who died violently; and the windy and constantly moving place, for those who committed suicide (suicide, though rare, was usually by hanging oneself from a tree; thus the afterworld for such a person would be forever swaying).

We asked Balayam what happened to the spirit of Ukan, the missing boy, after his death.

"Since he died nobody wants to talk about him any more," Balayam said somberly.

"Well, then, not Ukan. What happens to any person when he dies? What happens to that in him which was living?"

"The *sugoy* [spirit] goes away, goes out—then you are dead."

"And where does this spirit go?"

"I don't know . . . we don't know."

"Where did it come from to start with?"

"We don't know that either."

Balayam avoided further questions on this subject by turning and talking to Sindi, whom he called, laughingly, *"Sawa* [spouse] Balayam," and then nuzzling Manda, calling him *ah-do-do* (pal). He rambled on about various things, at one point saying that the *biking* was too small near the caves these days and so the Tasaday had to go quite far to find mature yams, which was why Mahayag had not come home to see Momo Dakel.

He seemed to mean that Mahayag was so far he could not come; but the day before, we had concluded from Udelen's hour-and-a-half round trip to fetch Mahayag, unsuccessfully, that he was not too far away. We did not say anything about this to Balayam, although it followed an extremely curious report we had heard about Mahayag. Two weeks earlier Dad had visited Manila, staying at Elizalde's house, and I chanced to meet him. In the course of our conversation Dad said that Mahayag had confided to him that he had walked for fifteen days and reached the place of the Tasafeng, where he found people. Dad claimed Mahayag had instructed him to say nothing about this to anyone because the trip had been made in secret. I expressed great surprise and asked when this trip had taken place. Dad said he did not know exactly, but that it was within the past two months.

I asked Elizalde about Dad's story and he said he had not heard it, and did not believe it, suggesting with a shrug that Dad was given lately to telling fanciful tales.

Dad had not made this trip with the Germans into the forest. I only recalled his story after Balayam mentioned Mahayag's absence from the caves and I asked Manda if we could ask Balayam about it. "Yeah, okay, we'll ask him, but I bet there's nothing to it."

So Manda and Mai questioned Balayam: had anyone sought or found the Tasafeng or their place? Balayam said no. Mai cited Dad's report about Mahayag having found them, and Balayam, looking astonished, denied that Mahayag had made such a trip. Balayam said he had never heard of such a thing, and then added that Dul had never heard of it either, he was certain; if she or anyone had, he would have known. And if Mahayag had gone on such a trip, the Tasaday definitely would have known. "We do not know where it [Tasafeng] is!" Balayam insisted.

He looked agitated and was so firm in stating his view that there was no place for the discussion to go; neither Dad nor Mahayag was available, so we dropped the subject. Manda and Mai seemed convinced that Dad had concocted the story. I did not know what to make of it.

A while later, Manda asked Balayam if the names Silifit and Sudafon (the great-grandfather and grandfather of Kasuk, the blind man at Blit) meant anything to him. Balayam paused thoughtfully and said he had heard those names in stories told about Fangul . . . or were they in stories that Fangul himself was supposed to have told? He was not sure. In either case, he said, he understood people with such names had lived at Tasaday and were related to Fangul. Asked about the names Keboy (Sudafon's wife) and Tabua (wife of Sambal, who was Kasuk's father), Balayam said he had not heard of them. "I would have known all these things," he said, shaking his head, "if my father had not died when I was a boy."

The Germans ended their filming that day with the fire on the lip of the upper cave. Later, over dinner, they were exultant, proclaiming the scenes they had filmed were far better and more numerous than they had thought possible in one day. Acknowledging the written agreement that the Tasaday would make up no more than one-fourth of his film, Rehbein said he was, to his own surprise, certain that the single day of shooting had produced more than enough usable footage.

The next morning, our third and last in the forest, we were packing and preparing to leave when Lobo arrived at the camp. He peeked around the corner of the main tent, grinned, slipped inside, and looked around curiously. He picked up Mai's stiff rattan hat and tried it on; walked cautiously across the orange plastic-canvas floor cover, sliding his feet as Tasaday usually did on the strange material, and sat beside Manda. Lobo poked and teased him a bit, then wrapped himself in a blanket so only his head stuck out, pretended to bite Manda on the arm, tickled him, then covered himself completely with the blanket. Poking his head out again, he spotted a plastic insole of a boot and fanned himself with it, hid his face behind it, put it down, picked up a flashlight, switched it on and off, shined it all around and into his own eyes, put it down, grabbed one of my cameras and snapped several exposures, shouting to "Miya" (Mila) and "Usi" (Lucy) in the kitchen to look at him. He put the camera down, stood up, danced around in a circle, picked up a dirty stocking, sniffed it, threw it back; sat down and made a tent of the blanket and crawled under it, holding it high with one hand and, while partly hidden, curling his other hand into an imitation of Rehbein's. He copied the smile of Eckhard, who had just joined us, and said, "Gud-moaning, Ek-ek," burst into giggles, grabbed the camera again, snapped two more pictures, put it down, hurled the blanket aside, leaped up, and darted out of the tent toward the caves. Seconds later he was back, sat beside Mai, draped an arm over his shoulder and listened briefly to his conversation with Fludi, jumped up again, shouted *"M'lekub ilib"* (Going to the cave), laughed, waved, and disappeared. He had been with us about ten minutes, in motion the entire time. Missing from his routine was a swing on the vines at the side of the main tent; they had been cut down by the Tboli boys, who said they were wearing thin and might break loose with someone on them.

We hiked to the landing ridge immediately after a breakfast of hardboiled eggs, crackers, cheese, and peanut butter. Bilangan accompanied us and I asked him what he had done with the placenta following the birth of the baby (who, by our observations and the accounts of the Tasaday, was doing very well, as was Etut). Bilangan had said I could accompany him when he disposed of the placenta, but, despite my two or three inquiries soon after the birth, he took care of it without me. Bilangan said he put it in the same tree as the Tasaday always put placentas, hanging it not too low and not too high, in the junction of a limb and the trunk.

This was a somewhat different procedure than he had described through Dad's translation previously. I asked Bilangan if he had accompanied his actions with any special words or gestures, and he said he had not.

Why did the Tasaday always use the same tree and place it in the way described? "Because our ancestors did it that way. It is our way."

More questions about why it was their way, what did it mean, brought the response that it was simply "the way we do it."

Had he visited the place since? "No." Did he plan to go there again?

"No." Was it the custom for anyone to visit this special tree from time to time? "No," Bilangan said. "Once it is put there, that is all we do."

Further questions brought the barest of information. Dad had translated previously that the placenta was either buried or placed high up in a tree to keep it away from animals, but Bilangan did not mention that today. Nor did he say anything about its being put in a tree so the child would grow big and live long. I could not determine whether Bilangan had changed his story for some particular reason of his own or whether these ideas were not getting through Mai's translation. And there was also the possibility that they had been Dad's personal contributions in the first place. Once more, I felt the frustration of not knowing their language.

It reminded me again of Dad's puzzling report about Mahayag's secret trip. Mahayag had not shown up at all during this visit, nor had his wife and children. When we casually asked Udelen about it, he said, rather haltingly, that he found Mahayag and told him of Momo Dakel's arrival —which Mahayag must have already guessed from the activity of the helicopter—but that he and his family decided to stay where they were for undisclosed reasons.

We spent the rest of the day and the next with the Blit, where Rehbein and his crew photographed a deer hunt. During the hot afternoon, we relaxed in Datu Dudim's long house. Dudim, Dafal, Mai, and Igna discussed their first meetings with the Tasaday. I asked Igna who she thought was the most important Tasaday.

"There is no strongest," she said.

"Who would you say is the smartest?"

"They all are about the same."

"How long do you think they have lived at these caves?"

"Long. Very long, a very long time. Longer than I could know."

The next day was spent among the Ubu. NDR filmed the tumultuous welcome scene. Elizalde was carried from the helicopter across a narrow ridge to a special house that had been made for him several weeks earlier by the Ubu.

The Germans completed their filming two days later, when the four Tboli were finally released after having been held in jail for more than two months, without evidence, for the massacre of the Christian family. Using new regulations under martial law, Elizalde obtained their freedom by having them turned over to a military base, whose authorities then remanded the men to him, as Secretary for National Minorities, with the understanding that he would have them watched by the national police force stationed at the Tboli settlement. The return of the four young men to the settlement was an occasion of such jubilation, dancing, and feasting by the ebullient crowds that Rehbein held his head with pleasure and later described it as "ab-so-lutely in-credible!"

23

The Saving of Lobo
and an Itch to Explore
the Flat World

A month later, near the end of November, Douglas Yen arrived in Manila from Hawaii to complete the first phase of his enthnobotanical work among the Tasaday. Yen reported that skeptical scientific colleagues had questioned him about the group—were they really as exciting as was claimed? Was Dafal really responsible for all that was attributed to him?

Yen said he had expected the skepticism; in fact, he shared some of it, particularly about romantic Garden of Eden notions of Tasaday life. But, more important, he said, he was convinced they were true gatherers who only recently had learned to trap and hunt. Upon leaving the forest in September, he had wondered whether his mass of notes and enthno-botanical data would sift into a report that would stand scientific scrutiny; after long consideration in Honolulu, he now believed that another two weeks of field work might be enough to enable him to write such a report. Perhaps he could construct a model for a broader approach to their ecology; this would not begin to answer all the questions about the Tasa-day, he knew, but it might provide a solid framework for additional work.

Biking's possible contraceptive effect had not yet been investigated, but solid, less sensational points had emerged from his notes. For instance, *biking* was always replanted, the tip of the tuber being returned to the earth; all plants the Tasaday used were perennials, and their beneficial parts were never taken in a way that would kill the plant. Yen suggested the Tasaday were perhaps as close to nature as any men ever known, living in harmony with the environment and practicing the ultimate in natural conservation.

Yen hoped to be able to establish this even more solidly in the next two weeks; further linguistic study was of primary importance, not only for his work, but for the whole range of scientific investigation. He believed that a strong general document should be prepared as a response to the skepticism of the scientific world. His hoped-for report might help, he said, but if all the scientists who already had been involved would combine their existing data, they could, without further field work, produce a meaningful monograph at once. This meant, of course, that somebody had to organize it, arrange for the various individuals to pool their information, agree on an approach. Yen said he could not possibly undertake such a project; he was returning to Hawaii after his upcoming visit to the forest. David Baradas, Panamin's research director, was a likely candidate, but he was involved in reorganizing the museum and various other work, including the joint report by him and Carlos Fernandez on their two weeks of field research that had been interrupted by Kabayo in late May. Fernandez had not been able to go to Malaysia to complete his doctoral work as planned, apparently because of a general travel ban imposed under the martial law. He had remained in Manila, although I had not seen him for months.

When Yen discussed all this with Elizalde, he stressed the idea of a joint monograph; he also got Elizalde's and Baradas's approval for linguist Carol Molony to participate in the upcoming field research. They flew to Tboli in early December and, after a two-day delay (while another malfunction in the helicopter was repaired), were taken into the forest with Dad, Sol, and radio operator Dog Love.

Elizalde went to Tboli a week later, and, on December 13, I flew south to join him and visit the forest for the last three days of the Yen-Molony expedition. On the plane that morning I read a newspaper account of the Apollo 17 mission to the moon. Commander Eugene A. Cernan and Geologist Jack Schmidt, the first scientist to land on the moon, had planted a U.S. flag on the lunar surface. Cernan was quoted as saying "We very proudly deploy it [the flag] on the moon to stay as long as it can in honor of all those people who have worked so hard to put us here and put every other crew here, and to make the country, the United States, and Mankind, something different than what it was."

The statement struck me as ironic, headed as I was toward the Tasaday forest, where scientists were searching not for a way to make life different than it had been, but for better understanding of *what* it had been.

Over the forest, the weather was clear, warm, and windy. Strong gusts made the helicopter buck and shudder. No rain had fallen in weeks. The ground was dry and the foliage even thinner than during the last dry period, sharply different from the usual exuberant tangle of moist, moiling greenery.*

The wind seemed stronger than on any previous visit. On the hike to camp, long breezy drafts made the jungle rustle and undulate. It was like looking through an undersea window: plants, vines, trees wobbled in one direction, then wavered languidly back into place when the breeze died; leaves shaped like ribbons, fans, fishtails, rippled and danced.

Manda's party had arrived in the morning and were with Yen and Molony at the caves when I reached camp, so I dropped my baggage and joined them. The first news was that Dul was pregnant. She smiled broadly at the chorus of friendly comments that greeted this information. Yen said she had disclosed it only a few days earlier and it was uncertain how long she had been pregnant. Doc said it could be more than three months, which might explain her stomach complaint in July.

Rebong had more immediate worries, however, because several Tasaday had colds. Doc had flown in once at Yen's request to treat Etut's new baby and son Ilib for severe coughs and inflamed throats. The treatment had been successful, but then several older boys had caught colds. Doc said he understood that the Tasaday believed these had been inflicted upon them because the boys, particularly Lobo, had played around the lower cave, moving rocks and tossing some of the smaller stones, in the course of which leaves and branches had been broken. The owner of the cave became angry and sent the sickness.

The illnesses did not appear serious, Rebong said; he hoped they would respond quickly to medication.

When we went to our tents, Yen summarized the high points of the past ten days. The caves had been devoid of people when he and Molony arrived. He was concerned, but within an hour Bilangan came in. He was very talkative; then Balayam arrived, followed by several others, saying they had been out collecting food when they heard the helicopter. They seemed pleased to have visitors.

A couple of days later, Yen said, Etut came to the camp carrying Lobo on her back. Dul and Dula carried her three younger sons. Lobo had diarrhea, was feverish, and had been vomiting. Etut said: "He is going to die."

Dad and Sol were at the stream, so Yen and Carol tried, using their

---

* The Tasaday subsequently said it was the driest period in their memory. Combined with the dryness of late June and July, it seemed to have thinned the forest remarkably. On the outside, all of Southern Mindanao was suffering from drought, great cracks split parched lands, and crop losses were severe. The Tasaday were delighted by the dryness, however, saying it made gathering food easier. But I wondered whether, if they had not had knives and consequently food from palm trunks, the drought would have forced them to travel farther from the caves for food.

limited Tasaday vocabulary, to discuss the situation with the women. "We didn't get all the fine points," Yen said. "But one thing was clear: they were going to take Lobo to some place upstream and leave him there to die."

Yen was certain from Lobo's appearance that whatever illness he had was not fatal. The danger was that the Tasaday believed he was doomed and were going to leave him alone in a remote place, where the weakened boy, also presuming his end was at hand, would simply fade away and actually die.

As a scientist, Yen said, he perhaps should have allowed the situation to take its natural course, not interfered; but he could not do that. Instead he told the Tasaday that Lobo would not die. They were unconvinced and said they must proceed as planned to take Lobo to the special place by the stream where he would die.

"I tried again to tell them he would be all right, but remember, we were talking in our broken Tasaday. I finally told them no, they shouldn't leave him to die, Momo Dakel Diwata Tasaday wouldn't like it."

The women pondered this, talked earnestly among themselves, and then, indicating they were going to the landing ridge to wait for Momo Dakel, left the tents. They apparently reasoned that if Momo Dakel didn't like it, then he would come to cure Lobo.

Yen and Carol found Dad and hiked to the landing ridge, where they found most of the Tasaday gathered. Lobo was slumped against a stump, beside a mass of exposed roots that stretched from the trunk to the ground like guys, creating a dark recess underneath. Yen was immediately reminded of the report that Tasaday dead sometimes were buried beneath just such buttressed roots.

Lobo, limp, moved nothing, said nothing. His parents and brothers huddled farther down the ridge, while the other Tasaday sat nearer to him. There was little conversation as they waited for Momo Dakel to arrive; as time passed and he did not come, the mood grew steadily more apprehensive and gloomy.

Two or three hours went by, but the Tasaday showed no sign of leaving. Finally, however, Lobo roused himself, rose lethargically to his feet, and stumbled over to his family. The Tasaday watched, murmured, and walked back to their caves. Lobo and his family remained behind.

Yen, Molony, and Dad returned to camp, and a short while later Bilangan and Etut arrived, carrying Lobo. They lay him where the NBC tents had stood, just below the main tent, and covered him with an empty rice bag.

When Yen mentioned taking Lobo to the caves, Bilangan said something to the effect that "the people wouldn't like it." Yen suggested Lobo stay with him in the main tent, but Bilangan said no, and walked away, leaving Lobo alone. Yen and Molony gave Lobo some medication to combat his diarrhea and some encouraging words. Later, Bilangan returned and carried the boy to the caves.

Lobo appeared slightly improved the next day, and became somewhat more lively with each successive day. When I had joined Manda, Mai, and the others at the caves, Lobo was sitting on a boulder, listless and morose, about thirty feet away from the group. His thick hair was matted and his normally bright eyes were sullen; his head hung down and he would not respond to greetings or attempts to tease or talk. Rebong said Lobo was not in physical danger, although his mental attitude was poor; he hoped the antibiotics he had administered would bring rapid improvement.

Lobo's sickness had been the most extraordinary event of the past ten days, but Yen also reported that the Tasaday had made several unusual requests and comments. First, they asked him to ask Momo Dakel to have somebody stay at the tents all the time, and mentioned the names of some Tboli boys.* The Tasaday told Yen that when they passed by the empty camp it made them feel lonely. Yen suggested to us, however, that it might not be loneliness so much as a longing for rice and other items they had received when the tents were occupied; there was the possibility that the Tasaday wanted a steady supply of goods from outside the forest, which could be the beginnings of a kind of cargo cult.

Second, the Tasaday talked about a deep anxiety they had felt after butchering the pregnant pig in September. They said the spirit that had hovered around the cave watching them all night long had been nerve-racking and fearsome. It departed with the dawn, but the memory of it had remained. Then Carol Molony told us how two Tboli youths had teased Yen about a skin rash that had broken out on his neck. Dad and Sol laughingly had said it must have been caused by a fairy urinating on him. Yen asked the boys if the Tasaday had a fairy such as had caused his rash. The boys said yes, and other fairies, too; they mentioned rock fairies and stream fairies, but Carol said the information was sketchy and unclear.

The third notable disclosure from Yen was that Dafal had apparently known the Tasaday longer than the supposed five or six years. Yen said that in the course of conversation, a Tasaday mentioned that Dafal first met them when Lobo was about Ilib's present age, between two and three years old. Lobo's age had originally been estimated at ten, but this was later revised upward at least a year and now, eighteen months later,

---

* Guards had been withdrawn from the forest after the declaration of martial law appeared to have disrupted the activities of armed gangs in the area and sharply reduced the number of firearms, Elizalde had told me. The government reported that more than 500,000 guns had been collected since the advent of new regulations prohibiting, without special permit, the carrying of any firearms in public and also the private maintenance of a firearm larger than a handgun or .22-caliber rifle. He and Mai believed that the Blit and Ubu, with the aid of their radio link to Tboli, could adequately protect the Tasaday's portion of the forest.

he was considered to be about thirteen. If these estimates were off even by a year or two, it still meant that Dafal had known the Tasaday for at least nine years, possibly twelve, which Yen believed was a much more plausible length of time. It would certainly help explain Dafal's extensive influence.

Supporting this view, Yen and Molony had learned that the pith of certain palms was called *lobo*, which suggested that Lobo was named—as was his younger brother Natek—after Dafal brought knives.

Furthermore, an increased period of Dafal's influence might explain a tape-recorded remark by Balayam that Kuletaw and Bilangan had fed him meat when he was young. This had been puzzling, because, if Balayam was in his early twenties now, as we thought, and Dafal had met them only five or six years ago, Balayam would have then been about eighteen, not so young. But if Dafal had met them eleven years ago, Balayam would have been only about twelve years old.

Among other bits of information, Yen said, was what Balayam told him about his dream: Momo Dakel brought in five *mabula ulu* (white-haired or white-faced) people who took many photographs and asked too many questions; Balayam told Momo Dakel that the people were upsetting the Tasaday, and Momo Dakel stopped the photography and the questioning, and everybody was happy.

There also was a vague discussion, Yen said, in which Sindi was reported by Bilangan as having said that it was not as hard to obtain food at her home place as it was inside the forest. Bilangan suggested that perhaps the Tasaday should visit this place of Sindi's.

From what he had observed lately, Yen now wanted to correct an earlier impression that the Tasaday shared everything. He said they had eaten away from the caves often during the past ten days, and that groups went out for several days without returning because, they said, the *biking* near the caves was not ready to eat and *ubud* was becoming scarce. Each group brought back what Yen regarded as merely a token amount of food to be shared with the rest of the Tasaday. His conclusion was that much gathering *and eating* was done in the forest by individual family units, not collectively at the caves. Yen did not see this necessarily as a new development; it might mean simply that food sharing was considerably more limited than had been thought.

He added that, while there was much more data to collect, he was already puzzled by the seemingly low caloric content of their diet. And, furthermore, if it was low now, what had it been before they had knives to get *natek* and make animal traps? During an exceptionally fruitful conversation with Bilangan (who, Yen felt, was his best informant) while all the other Tasaday were away, Yen had asked how they butchered animals. Bilangan described a carefully ordered step-by-step procedure, which tallied with what Yen had seen them do. When asked how they had devised such a procedure, Bilangan said Dafal had taught them. Then Yen—confessing that he had deliberately asked a loaded question—asked Bilangan how they butchered animals before Dafal taught them.

"And Bilangan said they did it 'any how'—meaning, according to Dad, any way or any method," Yen said. "They just cut it up."

"But," I pointed out, "they've said they didn't trap or eat animals before knowing Dafal."

"Right. But that's what Bilangan said. I've got no evidence to prove they ate meat, but he said it. I wonder. . . ."

The next morning, Yen recounted the high points of his ten days to Manda, who had not been present the night before, adding that he wanted to talk seriously about Manda's status among the Tasaday. Whether Manda liked it or not, and no matter how the Momo Dakel title was translated, his role was as some kind of god figure and had deep and far-reaching import.

Manda said that the Tasaday were not so different in this respect from many other tribal groups. "We do have something special," he said blandly. "But I usually don't like to talk about it, because most people misunderstand, get the wrong idea. But the Tasaday know I really care about them. They know it. So do the others, and they all react the same way."

Yen argued that the Tasaday were more dependent than the others and that they had come to rely on Manda, on medicines, on knives and axes, and—

"But the Tasaday are *not more* dependent," Manda interrupted. "All of them are dependent. I'm aware of this and it troubles me. It troubles me a lot. But what is to be done?"

"I'm not saying it is your fault or that you should be blamed for this," Yen replied. "I'm only saying that you really have to face it, and face the fact that the changes taking place among the Tasaday are more epochal than those among the others. Dafal was a secular change in here, but Momo Dakel Diwata Tasaday is secular *and* religious. This makes bigger waves. In our view Dafal has known them for a period in which the pace of change was rather slow but very significant. But to the Tasaday the pace was very fast, a great leap in their reckoning of time and history."

"Okay, I face that. I face it," Manda said. "For six years we have faced this in various places, not just here. Now just what do you want us to do about it?"

Yen was ready with alternatives: first, leave the Tasaday alone—*everybody* go away and leave them alone; or, second—

"Okay, okay," Manda replied. "I'm ready to do that. But what will it accomplish? I'm spacing out my visits now and we can eventually just stop coming if that is best. But is it?"

"I'm not saying that it is," Yen countered, "but it is one . . ."

Manda interrupted again to say that he was being compelled to spend less and less time in the forest anyway because of the many problems now confronting him in Manila. Also, martial law was having considerable effect on the lawless elements in South Cotabato, so Panamin was no longer required to make fighting them its first priority; now it could expand into other areas, such as research and development.

"What we need to know, Doug," he said, "—and people like you who know and love the Tasaday have got to help us on this—is what is best for them, what is the best next step. We're open on this."

Yen felt it was not possible to recommend any single specific course of action with the Tasaday and be able to guarantee its success; however, there were certain approaches that would tend to maximize the possibilities of success.

"We were forced to come here, you know," Manda said. "We had no choice. We simply had to come before the loggers. And we made mistakes. I know it. Bringing Sindi was a mistake. We realize that now. But an even bigger mistake in terms of effect on the Tasaday was leaving the groups of Tboli and Blit boys in here for so long. They've had greater impact than any of us. But we needed them in here for protection. So, what can you do?"

Manda added that the discoveries of the Tasaday had helped Panamin's work with all the other tribes by calling attention to and gaining sympathy for their problems and their rights.

Yen agreed and felt that Panamin and Manda should use all the influence they could muster to prod legislators into decisive action in favor of the minorities.

"Right. We'll definitely do that," Manda said. "But there are no guarantees, and it will take money and pressure."

The discussion was derailed at this point by a lengthy message Manda had to answer.

Meanwhile, Balayam had been visiting the tents. He told Mai that he and Sindi had been out gathering leaves and fruits recently and, while high up in a tree on a ridge, he had seen a cleared place far away. It occurred to him that this might be where the big bird stayed at night. He considered taking Sindi back to the caves and then walking to this clearing where he might find the big bird and also the cave of Momo Dakel. Then, as he finished saying this, he nodded repeatedly, looking as if this seemed quite a good idea.

Mai told Balayam very seriously that the clearing was not the place of the big bird or Momo Dakel—that he could never walk to those places. They were simply too far away—very, very far.

Balayam put his hand to his mouth, nodded some more, and then smiled. "It is good you have told me this, Kakay Mafoko," he said. "I might have tried to go there."

Talking with Carol and me after lunch, Yen said that this visit had enabled him to tie up loose ends and, perhaps even more important, to formulate questions more clearly. Of course, there was still a lot to be discovered about their food gathering and sufficiency requirements, he said, "but you can't calculate exactly the food intake of these people. You can't pursue them into the forest and measure on a systematic basis the amounts they gather and eat. Well, that's not exactly right—you *could* do it, but it would bother them. And for what? Six months of that kind of thing for what? Another scientific paper? It's not worth it. I wouldn't do it."

Elizalde, sitting nearby talking to someone, caught only the last part of that remark and interjected: "If science is going to be the reason for staying with the Tasaday or leaving them alone, then I say forget 'em. But science is not the key factor. It was not; it is not." Then he turned back to his other conversation.

After dinner that evening Carol told us she had filled a flat box with cards of Tasaday words, and was now able to converse in short sentences. Many words she had collected had meanings different from those on both the original word list, compiled in June and July of 1971, and the corrected list, compiled in April and May, 1972. "I was really surprised when I saw *lola* listed as the Tasaday word for grandmother," she said. "I just couldn't believe it. Now we've found that it isn't *lola,* it's *bebe.*" (*Lola* was widely used to mean "grandmother" among urban Filipinos.)

Linguistics seemed rather like detective work to me, gathering first the obvious facts, then searching for evasive clues, and tracing all the leads, often into labyrinthian hideaways. Carol had encountered one Tasaday word that just might be derived from Chinese, but had come across no words of Spanish or English derivation. A Chinese word could have slipped in over a broad period of time—mainland traders had been coming to the islands for many centuries. But a Spanish or English word would strongly suggest that the Tasaday had been isolated in the forest more recently than had been estimated, Spanish having reached the islands first in the mid-1500's, and English, in significant amounts, not until the Americans came at the end of the 1900's.

Carol had also found a hint of a Sanskrit word, which set her now to leafing through a text on Sanskrit. Suddenly she exclaimed, "Yes . . . yes. Here it is: '*mu-len,* to plant.' Dul used that word, I'm sure, just the other day. It had to do with something we saw up on the ridge. It didn't mean 'to plant,' as she used it, but more like putting something *on* the ground. I'm almost certain it was that word. I've got to check it again tomorrow."

She looked up *sawa* (Tasaday for spouse), saying it might be *asawa* in Sanskrit, but could not pin it down, and then searched through her cards for other kinship terms that might be related to Sanskrit. Yen and I thumbed through some books on Indian influences in the Philippines and came up with the fact that it had been felt from the second to the fourteenth centuries, most strongly during the Sri Vijaya period in the eleventh century.

The idea that Tasaday possibly contained words of Sanskrit origin was exciting, although much more checking would have to be done. Further investigation might coincidentally reveal when the Tasaday or their forest brothers last had contact with outsiders.

The next morning's visit to the caves was marked by the enthusiastic presence of Tico Medina, a journalist from Spain and a friend of the Elizalde family. He was visiting the forest for one day and the Tasaday enchanted him. He particularly liked Balayam's singing and listened raptly, after which Balayam said Tico must take a turn. Medina sang a flamenco ballad from his home near Granada. He had a rough but pleasant voice and sang with great emotion, which the Tasaday loved. Tico said later that he had expected the song would touch the Tasaday, because flamenco transmitted feelings rather than ideas. In the early afternoon, just before he left, Medina was at the stream with Balayam, Sindi, Udo, and Kalee. The children nibbled flowers as they sat beside the rippling water and Medina told Manda that he had been overwhelmed by the beauty and purity of the people. He worried about outside influences spoiling them and what he saw as their idyllic life. "The day the Tasaday put flowers in their hair for decoration instead of eating them," he warned Manda, "will mark the end of the Tasaday." We did not mention that they stuck petals on their faces.

During the morning visit to the caves, Sekul and Kuletaw arrived and rushed over to Manda, weeping and trembling as they hugged him and Mai. They offered long, sobbing testimonies of their affection and proclaimed their happiness that everyone had come. It seemed unmistakably sincere, but Manda remarked later that if they had been so overjoyed, why had they waited a day and a half to greet us? They said they had been nearby, so they surely knew of the arrival.

Mahayag, their son, was present throughout this visit, unlike the previous one, when he had stayed away the entire time. He appeared contented and agreeable now and made no explanation of his absence. This could have been interpreted as a sign of his disenchantment with us, or as evidence that Mahayag, more than any other Tasaday, was complying with Manda's edict that they go about their business as usual whenever he was there. Either view supported an impression that Mahayag was strong and individualistic. Manda had remarked several times that Mahayag was

Tasaday on the main platform in the lower cave, Kuletaw in the center

Udelen, Dul, and Tasaday children

Dul with Ogon

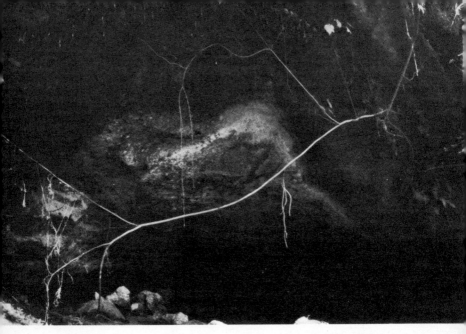

The mouth of the lower cave as it looked in 1972; the same area two years later, showing log-and-rattan sleeping platforms and wood racks

Balayam, Mahayag, Kuletaw, and a sturdier and more mature Lobo, in 1974

Dul, even in late 1972 showing results of pregnancy and increased food supplies, fixing Mai's hair in a Tasaday ponytail; between them, facing camera, Sindi

Lobo, Lolo, Natek, Bilangan, and Etut with family's new baby, the first child born in the new era of Tasaday life

Opposite, Ilib managing to reach his mother's breast despite new baby brother

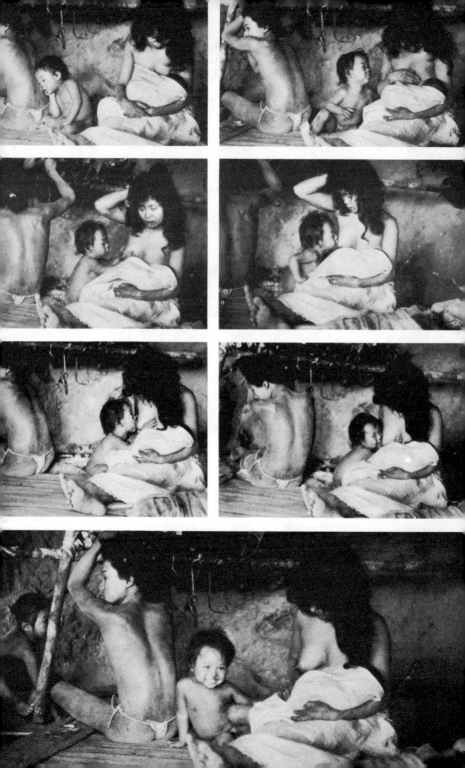

NBC film crew at the upper cave, March, 1972

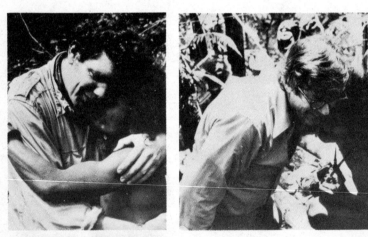

Jack Reynolds, Bruce Bassett, and Teruhiko Yashiro receiving Tasaday affection

The film crew in the lower cave, August, 1972

Gerald Green flanked by mimics Balayam and Mahayag; camera platform

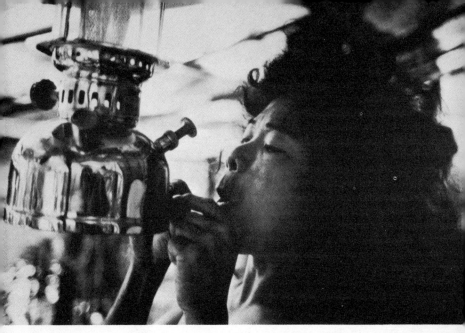

THE IRREPRESSIBLE BALAYAM

Right, pretending to smoke pipe

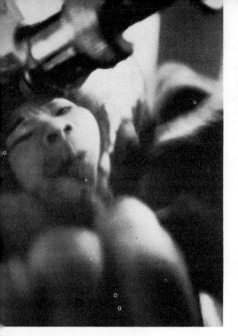

...eflection

...o go *"ta-suk"*

Imitating a photographer

A curious Lobo looking at Elizalde's gift pig

Scraping singed hair from slain pig

Dividing meat equally for each family

Irenaus Eibl-Eibesfeldt and his mirror-lens camera

Mahayag and his daughter looking through telephoto lens

Eibesfeldt's doll: "What is it—a man, a frog, a crab . . . ?"

Children clambering on Ching

Elizalde with Lobo, Balayam, Bilangan

Tasaday women welcoming Joyce Nance

Dafal and Igna greeting Kasuk

Tasaday exclaiming over Hubertus Kuhne's pate

Yen saying good-by

Carol Molony taking notes, Maman peeking around his mother's arm

Lindbergh giving Lobo a ride

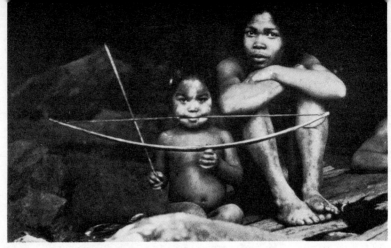

Siyus and Adug

Siyus

Dula and Siyul under palm-frond umbrella

Sasa, 1974

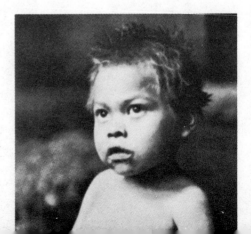

Reynolds presenting picture of Etut and her new baby to President Marcos

Blit defense force drilling near the Tasaday mountains

Mayor José Sison, of Surallah

Udelen in the stream below the caves

the most aggressive member of the group, would be the first to hunt, and would be the most violent defender if the Tasaday were attacked.

After lunch at the tents Sol shouted, calling our attention to a dirty-gray animal slinking through the undergrowth. It was a wolfish-looking dog with a short but shaggy coat, long nose, pointed ears. It sniffed around an area where garbage had been burned and buried. When Sol approached the dog, it whirled away and disappeared in the thicket. It appeared here and there around the tents all day, and Dad and Mai eventually got close enough to see that it was blind in one eye but otherwise apparently healthy. Mai speculated that it had accompanied hunters, chased a pig deep into the forest, and lost its way home.

A debate arose over what to do about the dog. Some people said to kill it. Others said no, the Tasaday had said they wanted a dog so let them have it. The other side objected that the creature might be diseased and have fleas, lice, ticks; or might be fierce; or bring hunters or other dogs —and it would have to be fed. It was finally agreed that the decision should be left to the Tasaday.

Mai's speculation that the dog entered the forest with hunters reminded us of the nearness of the Blit and of the fact that the Tasaday did not go in that direction for food. Yen and Carol reported that Bilangan had told them that the Tasaday's food-gathering trips often ran three and four days since they had met Dafal. It was not clear whether the introduction of knives, which they used to get *ubud* and *natek,* had caused them to venture beyond their usual limits around the caves. Bilangan had also said that the Tasaday did not go west (toward Blit) over the mountain, because there was no *biking* that way. Yen confirmed that the mountain-top altitude was too high for *biking* to flourish. But where, then, did they go? A three- or four-night round trip did not seem a long time, especially if they were making *natek*—the processing alone could easily occupy two days. But if they sought palms for *ubud* and *natek,* rather than *biking,* why not go west over the mountain? And if they traveled only a day or two in that direction and angled north they would reach Blit; Dafal had made it in a few hours the time he ran to head off Kabayo, although he surely took a special route well known to him. Did the Tasaday not travel beyond the mountain because of territorial limits or taboos handed down from their ancestors?

The Tasaday had denied knowing any people in that direction, insisting they did not even know the world extended beyond the forest. And they had said nothing about territorial boundaries, taboos, or equivalent ancestral imperatives—unless the admonition from their forefathers to always stay in these caves, to return each night, because it was safe and would prevent sickness, was in effect a boundary. It might be that their ancestors had known people were out there but had not wanted to meet them, for any number of reasons, and so had lain down limiting strictures without explaining why. Modern-day adults did such things with their children: "Don't cross the street"; "Don't talk to strangers"; "Stay on your own block."

In midafternoon, Dad, Yen, and Carol made one last foray for botanical specimens; all of us would be leaving the next day. I trailed a half hour behind them, photographing the drought-thinned jungle. I met the others as they returned to camp and we sat on the shadowy trail to rest. Carol said she had checked further today and was quite certain that a couple of the Tasaday words had Sanskrit origins. It would take a lot more research in Manila, however, and she added that the Tasaday had a sizable number of words that invited what linguists called "treasure hunts"—searches through etymologies for origins and relationships, grammatical formulations, cognate transfers. "Sometimes you are lucky and find clues right away," she said. "But other times you can look and look and look." The data she had acquired in just the past twelve days could involve up to a year of digging through books and abstruse monographs.

Yen suggested that if the Sanskrit linkings proved true and thus supported the conjecture that the Tasaday had been isolated for up to eight hundred years, it would also negate Manda's idea that the Tasaday or their brothers had been prehistoric forerunners of Mindanao Man. The first inhabitants of the islands probably had walked land bridges that once connected the southern Philippines with Malaysia and the Asian mainland about a quarter of a million years ago. A major influx of people began a few thousand years before the time of Christ, long after the land bridges had disappeared, and continued in trickles and spurts up to Spanish times. These later immigrants came by sea and most were from Melanesia, Polynesia, Malaysia, India, China, and Arab countries. Where and how the Tasaday fitted in could only be surmised, and without much evidence to support the guesswork. Yen was willing to speculate that the Tasaday traveled up the streams and rivers from the lowlands in search of food, to escape invaders, floods, disease, or for whatever reason, found food, shelter, and safety in the high mountains, and stayed.

As we sat talking, the wind breezed along the ridges and valleys in long gusts, making the whole jungle waver. I remarked that the long dry spell seemed to have pruned the foliage; it was much less dense than in many places in Indochina, for instance. Yen said the forest here was higher, cooler, and received less rain. This was a dense growth, but not the impenetrable maze encountered in flat, often swampy, lowland tropical rain forests in which, as in certain spots in Vietnam or Peru, a person could slide into a patch of bamboo and rattan and simply disappear, six feet away.

After we returned to camp, Manda, who had overheard parts of the discussion on linguistics the evening before, nudged our rambling conversation toward linguistics. He warned of the dangers of scientists fitting data into pet theories or patterns with which they were familiar and comfortable. For all anyone knew, he said, Tasaday might be a root language; scientists had been known to claim that Manubo was the parent of many Mindanao dialects and Manubo itself the offspring of a proto-Philippines tongue. But perhaps Tasaday or Tasafeng or Sanduka had been the root of Manubo. He had no idea whether that was the case—he was merely pleading for an open mind on the matter. Yen smiled patiently and agreed that an open mind was desirable.

Later, Manda remarked to Mai and me that he was not so concerned nowadays about what the scientists did among the Tasaday, just so they did not disturb them or hurt them. "We don't have to worry so much any more, Mai. Frankly, things have gone fairly well so far. But remember how worried we were at first? Afraid we might have made a mistake? Whew, man! That was something, wasn't it? Everybody was saying it was impossible the Tasaday had been isolated so long. And then when we thought Dafal had lied—the day Balayam and Mahayag showed up wearing those wooden bracelets—remember? And someone had a basket. . . . That was really something! I thought we might turn out to be frauds."

He explained to me that they had summoned Dafal and asked about the bracelets and baskets: "We got ahold of him and demanded he come clean, threatening that he'd better tell the truth. But ol' Dafal just kept saying, 'I don't lie, I don't lie.' And, thank God, he hadn't."

Manda rambled on, talking long and energetically. Throughout this visit, he was nervous, fidgety, and complained each morning that he had slept poorly. He tried to nap in the afternoons but could not; he was unable to unwind from all the pressures and activities of the last few weeks in Manila. Now he slumped listlessly on the sleeping ledge in the main tent, but after a fruitless attempt to sleep, sat up. "Peace is boring," he said. "I admit it. But it's really much better . . . it's helped us. Maybe if we can raise the pesos we can plan ahead—for the first time." The Panamin plan he had begun to outline in September was no more than a few unfinished notes. He had enlisted the aid of an old friend and highly regarded administrator, Dr. Conrado "Clipper" Lorenzo, Jr., to help restructure Panamin programs and the table of organization, but Lorenzo, like everyone else, had to depend on Manda's vision and decisions to draw reasonable plans for the future; and Manda did not know exactly where he wanted it all to go.

We visited the caves in the evening. It was warm, so there were no fires and we sat talking in the dark. The Tasaday, relaxed and amiable, said everything was fine, they had no problems and were happy. Those suffering from colds were better and even Lobo was showing signs of his usual mischievousness.

Manda inquired casually what was the longest period of time they went out without returning to the caves. Balayam and Mahayag each answered four days. A few minutes later, however, as the conversation continued, Mahayag said he sometimes took his family to a special place that was a three-day-walk away. This meant a six-day round trip, and surely they would stay a day or so at least, which made a minimum of seven or eight days away. Manda and I discussed this during a lull in the conversation, but he said he did not want to bring out the discrepancy because it might make Mahayag feel he was being scrutinized. The same reasoning applied to Dad's story about Mahayag's claiming to have traveled fifteen days and finding the Tasafeng. Manda said he was certain this was untrue, that Dad had made it up; but even if it was true, there was nothing wrong with Mahayag's having made such a trip—they had been encouraged to try and find the other groups. Manda related to the Tasaday instinctively, seemed to have an uncanny ability to sense their moods and feelings, and, except in certain instances, had played down intense direct questioning. (It was something he disliked undergoing himself.)

Asked if they were traveling farther these days, the Tasaday said yes, the *biking* nearby was too small to eat. *Ubud* was still pretty good around the caves, Balayam said, but *natek* was becoming scarce and required longer trips.

But why, he was asked, were roots getting scarce? If they always had sufficient *biking* before, why were they short now? The addition of *ubud* and *natek* to their diet should have lessened their demand for roots. Balayam chuckled and replied, "We eat more now. Everybody eats more. Before we had small bodies, now we have big bodies. The knives are good!"

When the talk about food and traveling ended, I tried to find out if the Tasaday had defined differing roles for males and females. "Do men and women, boys and girls, do all the same things, the same work, the same play?"

Everybody did just about everything, they said, but the men made fires; food gathering was their primary activity, and hunting and trapping were exclusively for men. Women did not make fires or traps, but did gather food and wood, and sweep out the caves, which men did not do. Women collected leaves for clothing, caught fish, tadpoles, and crabs in the stream, and could search for *biking;* but when women found *biking,* they invariably called men to help them. Women had acquired knives, after the men, and also cut *ubud,* but did not cut the much larger *natek.* All heavier work such as carrying heavy wood or animals was for men alone. The Tasaday said both men and women cared for children, with no priority affixed.

We had observed that women took the primary responsibility for child care; or perhaps it appeared so because infants nursed for years, and the chief activity of the men, food gathering, kept them away. It was virtually impossible to generalize beyond the fact that the males' involvement with child care was uneven or to see more definite patterns of male and female roles in child rearing. The inability to be more conclusive was due, of course, to our limited observations, and also because each family unit was unique:

Etut and Bilangan   She had been pregnant or nursing her new baby all the time we had seen them in the forest; he was busy most of the time gathering food and wood for his family of five sons, which gave him twice the number of mouths to feed of any other father; Lolo, the oldest son, had taken increasing family responsibility after the birth of the latest child.

Udelen and Dul   He appeared to spend about as much time tending his two young sons as she did. He was of gentle, affectionate, seemingly passive nature; she was more reasoning, demanding, perhaps ambitious.

Mahayag and Dula   He was strong and independent, an eager and earnest worker; she was gentle and shy. Their daughter Dina stayed mostly with her, son Biking trailed after his father.

Kuletaw and Sekul   The only grandparents in the group, their own offspring were no longer youngsters—Mahayag had his own family, Adug and Gintoy looked after themselves; Sekul, more lively than her husband in all things, took an active role in child care, though Kuletaw, inactive now, apparently had taken part before, because Balayam had mentioned being raised by him after his own father died.

Lefonok   A widower, occupied chiefly by sick Sasa when we first met them, lately was most active gathering food. His three children often attached themselves to another family when he was away or, as we noted most recently, Udo, and sometimes Kalee, looked after Sasa.

Tekaf and Ginun   No children, and, presumably because they could neither hear nor talk, were never observed caring for children.

Balayam and Sindi   No children, but either or both would tend the offspring of others at the stream or around the caves. Dul had remarked once that this was possible only since Balayam had acquired a woman. Sindi, incidentally, was being watched closely by the Tasaday for signs of pregnancy. As months passed and she did not conceive there were mumblings of disappointment. Mai reported that Balayam and Dul had made a point of mentioning this to him on each expedition over the last three months.

The behavior of the children provided scant insight into the differing roles of the sexes. There were only two girls, and both exhibited what some cultures might term feminine shyness, gentleness, teasing coyness;

but, then, so did most of the younger boys. The girls were generally less exuberant in their talk and play, yet it was impossible to generalize because the two lived in such different circumstances within their own family units: Dina clung to her mother; Kalee's mother was dead.

Boys seemed to learn certain male roles by accompanying their elders into the forest and to the stream. I never saw a father actually instruct a boy on how to make *natek,* catch tadpoles, dig for *biking;* rather, the boys watched when they wished, and participated as they grew older.

My overriding impression of the treatment of Tasaday children, whether male or female, was that all of them received love and affection, were given thoughtful attention and made to feel important. They were the first to be fed, always, and frequently were carried and fondled, nuzzled and played with. If they misbehaved, they were disciplined or distracted in a firm but gentle way; I never saw one slapped or struck by an adult.

Following our rather jumbled discussion of the roles of the sexes, Balayam, unexpectedly, asked Manda: "How do you see us now? How do we look to you?" It was rare to hear such questions from the Tasaday; in fact, I could not recall ever hearing them. Manda hesitated only a second or two, then answered: "If you are happy, then you look good to me."

This brought pleased murmurs from the Tasaday, and Manda asked them if they ever talked among themselves about going out of the forest. Several chorused yes, and Dul said Balayam had seen a clearing and considered trying to reach it, thinking perhaps it was the home of Momo Dakel and the big bird.

Manda replied that he had heard of this already, and that Mai had told Balayam that the place he had seen was neither his place nor the big bird's, and that those places were much too far to reach by walking. "But," he added, "if you have questions about those places . . . or about anything at all, you should ask us. Ask now. Ask anything that is in your heads."

Balayam and Dul and Mahayag whispered together in the darkness, and then Balayam said they were interested in looking around outside the forest. Manda said he thought they should not go out alone; they could if they wanted to, of course, but he believed it would be better to go with friends who could guide and help them.

The Tasaday sat quietly in the darkness, listening to each word as it went from Manda to Mai to Igna and into Tasaday, and then waited in anticipatory silence.

"You asked one time if all the people in our world are good," Manda went on. "Well, we have many, many kinds of people. Some are good, some are not so good. If you go alone out of the forest, you might meet some of the people who are not so good."

He paused for this to be translated, then continued. "Of course you are curious about things . . . all of us are. *We* are curious about things we don't know also. It is like the flashlight now makes it possible for you to see at night, and so now you think of finding frogs at night and to see more and more."

He paused for the translation and muttered, "Jesus, this is awful. I can't think of better examples or anything to make this clearer right now. Oh, well, here we go . . .

"Now it is understandable that you want to see more and know more, but I still suggest that you wait before trying to learn about the outside. If you decide, however, among yourselves that you want to go, please tell us before you do go. Please tell us and we can discuss it and decide together how to do it the best way."

Balayam spoke briefly to Dul and some others and responded. "When Momo Dakel Diwata Tasaday decides inside himself that it is time for us to see outside, that will be the time for us."

Quiet followed this. They had thrown the decision back on Manda—for the time being, at least. What was going on in their minds as they sat so still and silent?

Dul then said they would like somebody—preferably Dad and Sol—to stay at the tents all the time. Mai remarked in English that he saw this as a request for a buffer between them and the world they did not know. Manda thought it might mean they had been bothered again by the scientists' questions over the past two weeks and asked Dul about this. She said Yen and Carol had not asked too many questions and that they were their friends.

Then Manda brought up the gray dog that had appeared that day—what did the Tasaday think of it, and what should be done with it? Balayam said Maman had been the first to see it and was so frightened, he ran crying into the cave. They were not happy about this dog, he said. "We don't know where it came from. It is the first time a dog like this has come here—perhaps there are people with it."

Lefonok said maybe they should shoot it with their bows and arrows. Manda said they would not have to do that because he would arrange for the dog to be taken care of and it would not bother them. Not for translation, Manda said he was afraid that if they used an arrow they might only wound it and the dog would cry and thrash around. "It would be terrible to see and hear. They might never forget that yowling," he said. "We'll have Dad or Sol take care of it." (The dog was not seen again, however.)

Back at the tents that evening, we heard loud talk from the caves until midnight. Few words were discernible, but we could not help speculating that the subject was venturing outside the forest.

Mai and Igna spoke to Sindi about Yen's report that she may have suggested going to Blit because food was easier to get there. She insisted she had not encouraged the Tasaday to go to Blit or any other place, and claimed, furthermore, that she had not discussed Blit with them at all.

Early the next morning, Mai visited the caves and returned to report that Dul and Balayam told him the Tasaday had conferred and decided it might be good to just have a look outside the forest.

Mai, frowning as he relayed this information, said, "They say they don't want to stay, just look—at Momo Dakel's cave, perhaps to see where Sindi lived. They say they would just look and then come right back to the caves." Mai added that Dul stressed, possibly aware of his concern, that no matter how far they went for food they always came back to the caves because that is their home.

Mai shook his head slowly. Such a trip, he said, would be only the beginning. "Once they see the outside, of course, they will want to see more. They are curious!" He suggested that teaching them some kind of agriculture might keep them in the forest. (Mai, conditioned to the hard life of struggling against settlers, loggers, and land grabbers, envisioned little good accruing from a visit by the Tasaday to the outside.) He also felt that it might be wise to hold down the entry of new visitors, because they might invite bolder questions from the Tasaday and stimulate their curiosity.

Manda had told the Tasaday we would be leaving this morning. Most of them came to the tents to say good-by, and several accompanied us to the landing ridge. The subject of the journey to the outside world did not come up. But, as we waited for the helicopter, Manda gave Balayam a shiny new ax and said he understood that some Tasaday would like to go out and see his place, and the places of Mai and Sindi. Balayam smiled and nodded.

"Let's discuss it next time we come here," Manda told him. "If that's what you want, we'll see. But please wait until we come again."

Balayam looked thoughtful, smiled, and said they would wait. Then the helicopter arrived and we loaded our bags. As we rose from the ground, Balayam braced himself in the windblast of the rotor blade, waving good-by with his new ax.

It was December 16, 1972—eighteen months and twelve days from that time, ages ago, when five trembling Tasaday stood at the edge of the great forest and fixed their astonished eyes on the plain, that incredible, empty, flat land sweeping away to a faint line of blue-gray mountains on the horizon. All the Tasaday had come, to meet the "good man," but only Balayam, Bilangan, Kuletaw, Lobo, and Adug had ventured the final few yards onto the ridge knoll at the edge of the forest. The others had clung to the jungle, hidden by ferns, leaves, and trees while the five followed Dafal to the brink of the new world, a new time.

In the ensuing eighteen months, some of them recounted that extraordinary day, not in great detail, but their scattered bits and pieces joined with the accounts of Dafal, Fludi, Mai, and others to allow the following reconstruction.

The Tasaday hiked with Dafal from dawn to sundown across trackless mountains, a journey so difficult they had to carry the children—and their dog—much of the way. They spent the night beside a small stream, close by their fires.

Dafal walked off alone the next morning, then returned and left again several times, finally asking them to come. They climbed until leaves and undergrowth thinned and the light ahead was bright, as if a broad stream had cut a great swath through the jungle. But there was no stream and through a fringe of leaves and branches they could see a vast emptiness ahead—the mountains had stopped!

This frightened many Tasaday and as Dafal tried to calm them, urging them on, a huge roaring-screaming creature, visible only in fleeting glimpses, swooped above the trees. Some Tasaday whirled and ran; others gasped and crouched behind plants. Then the noise was gone, as suddenly as it had come.

Dafal assured them there was no danger, soothed them, finally convinced five to step with him onto the knoll overlooking the plain.

Balayam, who had been eager to make this journey, who had encouraged the others, gazed at the strange flatland before him and was troubled, his thoughts spinning, his inside feelings churning. He tried to calm himself, but anxiety increased, his chest heaved and he felt chilled. Half of his inside feelings told him to run, the other half said stay. What should I do? he thought. If Bilangan runs, I will run, too.

Bilangan himself fought against the urge to run, to escape, and finally gave in to it. He rose from his perch on a log and headed back toward the safety of the jungle. Dafal hurried to him and said over and over, "Don't go, don't go. It will be good. Stay. You'll see the good man. He's coming soon. He'll be here soon."

Bilangan heard Dafal's steady voice and stopped, took a deep breath, and turned back toward the plain.

Kuletaw sat on his haunches, staring at the ground, saying nothing, seeming to be made of stone but for the trembling of his skinny body. Lobo and Adug huddled inside a lean-to.

Minutes later Dafal shouted and pointed into the silvery sky above the plain: a dot flitted across the whiteness like a black insect. As the Tasaday followed it with their eyes it grew larger and they heard a thin humming sound. The insect flew straight at them, growing larger and larger, until it was overhead, huge, circling, hovering. It was the black creature that had swooped over the jungle—not an insect, but a terrible, gigantic bird-beast. Its powerful breath shook the trees, so that leaves and twigs showered down. Its shrill screeching whine grew louder and louder, violating their ears. The Tasaday cowered and threw their arms over their heads as the howling beast, whirling and whirling its wing, descended upon them.

Balayam leaped up in terror. His insides churned as if he would explode. He was breathless. He tried to run, too late—fear froze him. He wavered, pitched forward, and crashed onto the ground; his face, eyes shut, was pressed against the damp earth. One thought spun through his brain: We will die! We will die! All of us will die! The Tasaday are dead!

That was June 4, 1971. Now, a year and a half later, as Balayam hugged Sindi and waved his new ax at the departing big bird, the Tasaday wanted to go out of their forest and see more of that strange flat world.

IV
FULL CIRCLE

24

The Terms of
Self-Determination

IT was four months after December, 1972, before any outsiders saw the Tasaday again.

Then, for one day and night in late April, Elizalde visited shortly after Dul gave birth to a daughter, and found all the Tasaday well and happy. In June, Mai and Dad spent a few hours with them, stopping during a helicopter tour of the area, and reported everything was fine. Dafal made an unknown number of visits, apparently to trade for *bui* and as their Panamin-appointed guardian. Reportedly, the Tasaday did not repeat their request to venture outside the forest in any of these meetings. They expressed general contentment but wished Momo Dakel and his friends would visit more often. Dul once said that Momo Dakel and Mai had been away so long "we thought you might have died."

These were the only known contacts with the Tasaday throughout 1973. This was partly deliberate, partly circumstantial. They had been visited so often in 1972 that Elizalde believed the Tasaday needed a lengthy respite. The initial research plans had been completed and the next steps were undecided; the area had the protection of the government and neighboring tribes, and it was unclear what more the outside world could or should do for the gentle forest people. Elizalde felt that both the Tasaday and the outsiders should go slowly. Moreover, in spite of the Tasaday's expressed interest in the outside, he believed they would not leave the forest on their own in the immediate future, perhaps never.

On the circumstantial side, Panamin had begun a time-consuming new settlement project among the Hanunoo on Mindoro Island and was also helping organize a major effort among the Tboli—the formation of their own municipality, a unique humanitarian design which was meant to remove them from the status of powerless wards on a reservation and grant them their own local government; Elizalde had been drawn more deeply than any time in his life into business and government affairs and was compelled to spend much time in Manila (his business efforts, he said, were aimed at establishing a personal financial base that would allow him to retire from business in three years and devote all his time to the tribes).

Within the Panamin Foundation, Oscar Trinidad was made executive director, and David Baradas left as research director to undertake projects for the Ford Foundation and work on a book about the arts of the Maranaw; Charles Lindbergh had kept in touch with Elizalde but had not been able to visit the Philippines since mid-1972. He hoped to make it back before much longer and reaffirmed his support of Panamin's work. Yen, Molony, and Fernandez were preparing papers covering their Tasaday research in 1972. I spent several months with my family in the United States, working on photographs and the Tasaday manuscript. Twice I was notified of an impending expedition to the Tasaday and prepared to join, but each was called off.

When I returned to Manila in mid-February, 1974, Elizalde reported that Panamin had received numerous requests to visit the Tasaday from journalists and others, notably Christian missionaries. "Man, you ought to hear them," he said. "The missionaries want to give the Tasaday a chance to be saved from eternal damnation." Logging companies also had requested rights to cut inside the Tasaday's forest. One company wrote a letter proposing cutting only the largest trees so smaller growths would thrive; the cut timber would be used to build a school and community center for the Tasaday, and, if there just happened to be any cut wood left, the loggers would be willing to remove it from the forest. The whole operation, said the letter writer, a former congressman, was to help the nation's tribal brothers. An American psychiatrist proposed bringing two Tasaday children out of the forest and raising them in the United States to demonstrate the universal qualities of man.

Every request was turned down.

Elizalde also said that the government had ordered that all unexplored land in the country must be surveyed for mineral deposits. "Boy, that's a laugh. After all the accusations that we've been looking for minerals all these years, now we are really going to do it." He said Panamin would have to be in charge of this in the tribal areas or else others who had no interest other than resource exploitation would come in. "At least we can see to it that the tribes get the benefits," he said, "and are not trampled on in the process."

Panamin's major effort in the last months of 1973 and early 1974 was directed toward the establishment of a municipality for the Tboli and nearby tribespeople. It would give them legal borders, their own courts, police force, administration. Weeks were spent surveying the area, conferring with officials of the municipalities from whom the land would be removed. Legal documents, petitions, administrative plans and proposals were drawn up and presented to President Marcos. The new town was endorsed by the mayors of all the eight municipalities from which the land would be drawn, except Mayor Sison of Surallah, whose township would be most severely reduced, almost cut in half. On March 6, 1974, Marcos signed a proclamation creating the municipality, making it an inviolate law of the land. It was named Tboli and had 130,500 hectares on which lived an estimated 163,000 people, about 13 per cent Christians and the rest Tboli, Ubu, Manubu Blit, Blaan, Tirruray, and some 2,000 Maguindanao Moslems.

Tribal leaders were joyous. Difficult and complicated problems lay ahead, but it would be their own place; granting it to them was an acknowledgment that they could and should handle their own affairs. Panamin and the national government would provide money, technical expertise, and advice as long as the tribes wanted them, but the final decisions and work would be chiefly up to the tribes. It promised as much autonomy for them as was enjoyed by any community in the Philippines.

Elizalde was ebullient. "This is absolutely fantastic! This is it—the culmination of eight years of work. When the President signed that proclamation my heart almost stopped. Do you realize what this means? Do you realize? My God! Where else in the world has this happened? Where? Look at what's happening to ethnic minorities in most places, and now Marcos has proclaimed this *municipio* for the tribes. It may be the only one of its kind in the world. . . . We've really got to celebrate! I'll spend my own money on this one . . . got to celebrate. It really means something to me."

The Tasaday's reserve was within the boundaries of the new municipality, which would further ensure their protection. Elizalde planned to visit the Tasaday when he traveled south for the celebration, which would be climaxed by the swearing in of the Marcos-appointed officials, Mai Tuan as mayor, Christian settler Dimas Tanco as vice-mayor, and six tribesmen as councilors.

Elizalde's delight over the municipality was dulled only by streaks of nervous irritability, the result, he said, of many months of confinement in the city, endless meetings, and conventional society. He plunged into preparations for the celebration and in early March a chartered DC-3 transport flew to South Cotabato loaded with supplies, followed the next day by Elizalde and ten Panamin staffers. The Panamin helicopter, a chartered chopper, and a six-seater twin-engine plane he had purchased a few months earlier also flew down with people and goods. Arrangements were made for a circus with big top, acrobats, ferris wheel, and a troupe of singers, dancers, musicians, comedians, and jugglers. Huge tents were raised around the Tboli settlement; together with the museum, school, clinic and every other available building, they would shelter the expected inpouring of tribespeople.

On March 11 Dad and Sol were flown to the Tasaday's forest to make sure the helicopter landing was serviceable. Dafal and Dog Love, the radio operator, went in later that day.

Manda, Mai, and I flew in the next morning with the rest of the usual party. We passed Ma Falen's mountaintop settlement, skirted Blit, and veered over the rain forest. It was dark, thick, dense—no shards of amber and chartreuse this time. There had been plenty of rain and the forest looked solid blue-black-green, as it had on the first visit to the caves in March, 1972, only a week short of two years before.

And now, fifteen months since I had last seen them, my nervous excitement was similar to that of the first visits. The questions, however, were different. Would all the Tasaday be there? Would they be well? Had they changed? How far had the switch from the Stone Age to Metal Age taken them? Were they hunting now with bows and arrows, cutting the forest rampantly with their knives, depleting the environment? Had personal possessions and wooden constructions, the search for *natek* and *ubud,* and the knowledge of an outside world pulled them deeper into the mountains or drawn them closer to the edge? Had they found the Tasafeng and Sanduka? Or had the need for women already lured them outside, on their own? And, if not, did they still want to venture out? Did they want trade? How did they feel about the long time without Momo Dakel's visits? How would they feel about us now?

Dad and Mai had said that on their last visit, ten months earlier, the Tasaday had been happy and said, "Visit us always." Mai said he didn't know how many times Dafal may have walked in since then.

I asked what Dafal had reported or had been doing in there.

"Who knows, who knows," Manda said. "We don't know what he may have taken in, he'll never say. I don't know why. And I don't know what he gets in there—*bui,* I guess, for trading. You can be sure of one thing, though. Dafal is our assurance that the Tasaday will not run out of whatever they want from outside. Want knives? Okay, ol' Dafal can get them. What else? He can get it. They won't have to go out themselves."

Mai said Dafal had cleared a patch of land between the Tasaday and Blit where he was starting a farm so he could be near the Tasaday and keep an eye on them. But this farm would attract other farmers, so Mai told him to stop it. Dafal indicated that he did not particularly want to farm anyway; he forgot his plot and walked to all the groups living on the edge of the forest and advised them not to farm inside. None had, Mai reported.

Dad and Sol waved as the helicopter approached, and guided it onto the narrow ridgeline landing space. It was overgrown with grass. The foliage at the edge, formerly trimmed low, was now shoulder high. Dad said several Tasaday waited at the caves and Dafal had gone to find the rest to tell them Momo Dakel was coming. Dad added that when he and Sol arrived, Balayam had rushed up and hugged them without a word, weeping happily. Balayam then said he had seen the bird that brought them and did not like it. It was the chartered helicopter, bright orange with an uncovered tail section revealing the superstructure; compared with the Panamin chopper it was skeletal-looking.

As soon as Igna and her husband were brought from Blit, the party started down the trail with Manda in the lead. The route showed scant sign of use, no broken branches or trampled grass; a hole marking the site of a recent *biking* dig was the only manmade mark. The forest had hidden the traces of past incursions. Multiple canopies overhead blocked the sun, and vines and air plants twisted into dark knots. Far fewer were the cavernlike rooms and alleys that hollowed the jungle during the long droughts two years ago. We heard the stream long before we saw it, and then waded in the sparkling water. The upward trail to the campsite was barely visible. At the camp's edge, where once had stood small tents, dead leaves and fresh grass and ferns shrouded rotting wooden poles; a forgotten pickax lay half buried and rusting. At the main site, two tents stood surprisingly intact, the earth dusty dry in places underneath the yards of faded plastic canvas, which fallen leaves made sag heavily.

We stopped momentarily to put down baggage and catch our breath, then continued on. Our noise preceded us and as we neared the caves Sindi rushed down the trail and leaped on Manda, hugging him with a strength surprising in one so lean. Then she embraced each of us in turn, tears streaming down her cheeks. Close behind her were Balayam, Udelen, Lefonok, and two youngsters—the foliage was too thick to identify everyone. The men whooped, laughed, and hurled themselves on Manda. They all tumbled into a heap, yelling excitedly. Dul arrived, carrying her year-old baby. The midmorning light through the trees shone on the grinning Tasaday and I realized for the first time what they must have meant when they talked about friends with shiny faces—their smile-rounded cheeks were brightly highlighted.

Restored to his feet, Manda walked with Tasaday arms around him to the caves. Other Tasaday filtered through the arriving party, cooing names and greetings, hugging and rubbing their faces against ours. Some men had scratchy little whiskers and smelled earthy and musky. (There was never any sourness in their odor, because, so it was suggested, they did not eat meat.)

In the mouth of the lower cave, where most had lived, there were fewer constructions, but they were larger and more expansive—almost forming a horseshoe of platforms, racks, fireplaces, and rock niches around the inside of the mouth, and facing out into the small valley where the waterfall spattered down.

The platform of Dul and Udelen had been expanded and dominated the left side of the cave. It rested on logs six and eight inches in diameter that had been notched into large boulders. The platform extended back like a ramp, bridging a gap and connecting with large flat rocks running in front of the low-ceilinged inner chamber. Bark mats and another platform lay across this line of rocks and almost joined another platform and wood-drying rack along the right wall of the cave's mouth. The space in the middle of this u-shape of constructions was empty; formerly it had held the platform of Mahayag, who, the Tasaday said, still spent most of his time here, sharing the larger platforms. He was out now, gathering food with his wife, children, parents, Kuletaw and Sekul, and brothers, Adug and Gintoy. I wondered if that particular unit of eight had made a permanent move out of the cave. We noticed also that Lobo and his family were not present and were told they were coming.

Everyone found a place on the large platform of Dul, which comfortably held a dozen persons, more if squeezed together. The reunion fell into a familiar groove of laughing chatter, Balayam chuckling, others shouting *"Cheet!" "Oh-ho!" "Yaoweh!"* Despite the months that had passed, it soon seemed as if we had been here only yesterday. The Tasaday appeared to be the same as always. Few knives were in sight, no trinkets or salvaged materials from our camp—no tin cans, bottles, sheets of canvas or cloth. The most obvious remnant of our former visits was blue-and-orange nylon rope they had used to lash together the platforms and racks. Beads and most of the knives and other items they had been given were obviously kept elsewhere.

As we sat talking, our ears were assaulted with the shrill chatter of a monkey; the small brown creature was leashed to a platform in a shadowy corner. It screeched and jumped about, jerking at the blue rope encircling its neck. The Tasaday said the monkey was their friend and they had had him for quite a long time.

"Does it have a name?"

"Yes," Balayam said with a laugh, "It is Kakay Ubal [Friend Monkey]."

Conversation turned to the Tasaday, who huddled around Manda— How had they been since we saw them last? Mai had been fluent in Tasaday before, but now had trouble translating, so Igna and Dad handled it. The Tasaday said everything had been well, though they were lonely for Momo Dakel and his friends. Balayam said they cried inside when Momo Dakel was not here. "Sometimes," he said, "I sit with Sindi in our cave in the afternoon and look out and think about our friends who are not here. I become sad. And Sindi becomes sad. Then we play together [make love] to forget our sadness and feel better." He laughed softly and sighed.

Dul, smiling but reserved (Manda had predicted she would be cool, to let him know her displeasure over his long absence), sat cuddling her new child, a sturdy-limbed, healthy-looking girl who nursed at her breast. I asked the baby's name and Dul repeated it three or four times until I got the pronunciation just right: Ogon. Does the name have any special meaning? "No, it's just Ogon," Dul said.

Only eleven Tasaday were present. Balayam said Tekaf and Ginun were on their way home now, as were Bilangan, Etut, and their five boys. Mahayag's group was expected the next day. The Tasaday said they all still made these caves their permanent homes; they were just out gathering food.

As the discussion went on I took photographs occasionally at first, then with increasing frequency—of the people, their smiling faces, their arms and legs tangled together; of the new constructions, the waterfall, the fire-darkened walls and ceiling which were shiny black where they had been patchy brown before. Everything was bathed in a smoky-blue sunlight. I heard one Tasaday say *"Ta-suk"* and chuckle, and Dul made a remark about me and cameras. Then, when Ching snapped a couple of pictures, Manda said, "Ching, I think we ought to take it easy with the cameras. We just got here. Lay off a while."

I suddenly realized that he was really talking to me. I realized also, with embarrassment, that I had been snapping the shutter like a *paparazzo* on the Via Veneto. I stopped taking pictures—but ten minutes later could not resist a few more of those faces beaming out of the soft light.

Manda told the Tasaday he was happy to be here and see them all, but we must go to fix our camp. In the next few hours the site was restored. New tenting was stretched over old, rotting poles were replaced, molding leaves swept away with ants, spiders, centipedes, worms, and tiny crablike creatures who had burrowed into the sandy soil. Gray-white fungus was scraped from tent poles and the crumbling bark of the living trees that formed the main supports had to be removed, revealing thousands of termites, which we burned off with kerosene.

Igna joined us after spending some hours at the cave. She said happily that she had held Dul's new baby, napped, and then talked and joked with the Tasaday. "They are the same as before, the same as always," she said. Asked if they said anything of notable interest, Igna said Lefonok wanted a gift like Momo Dakel had brought Balayam—Sindi, a wife. Igna said Sindi was happy, happier than before, and made no mention of going to Blit to visit her relatives. As for food gathering, Igna said it seemed to her the same as always—they were traveling farther, but apparently still did little hunting and their traps did not catch much.

When Igna ran out of things to say, I asked if the Tasaday had mentioned my rampant picture taking so soon after we arrived. Manda commented about my overzealousness, with a mirthless laugh: "Yeah, you went a little wild up there with the cameras. Nice way to say hello to them. Dul remarked about it." Igna said they did mention it, but did not seem upset. One said, *"Ta-suk, ta-suk.* That is the way of Jambangan. That is just his way. He always does that. We have our ways and he has his ways." Mai agreed that they did not seem annoyed, but I resolved to be less greedy.

We revisited the caves in late afternoon and found that Tekaf and Ginun had arrived and taken a place on a bark mat behind the main platform, against the rocky wall. They embraced Manda, who remarked about Ginun's healthy appearance. This was translated to her in sign language and she smiled. Tekaf hugged and kissed us.

The monkey chattered and screeched, calling attention to itself. The rocks around it were wet and stained with urine and Manda sniffed. "That is a terrible pet for anyone to have," he said to us. "I've had monkeys, they are mainly a nuisance—into everything, smelly, dirty, fleas, lice. Aagh."

We asked if they always kept it tied up and Balayam said no, that it followed without a leash when they went out. It was allowed to go out on its own but it always returned. They had tied the monkey up now, he said, because they thought it would bother us, get into our belongings.

"So they let it go free," Manda mused. "That's extraordinary. Unusual it doesn't run away and join other monkeys. Can they free it now?" he asked. "Why not let it loose?" (He did not like seeing it tied up, especially with the blue nylon rope.)

They did. The monkey screeched and jumped up and down, then leaped from boulder to boulder, supposedly looking for food. It showed no inclination to leave the cave and stayed back near the inner chamber. Finding nothing to eat there, the monkey bounced up and down and screeched more loudly, finally scooting over to some children near a fireplace. It tried to take what looked to be a piece of *natek.* "See how spoiled it is," Manda said. "Demanding to be fed." Lefonok finally intervened, pulling the monkey away and tying it up again. Manda said he wished they would either release it or take it someplace else. Igna relayed this and the Tasaday said they would move it the next morning.

We sat quietly for an hour or so, chatting and relaxing. Dul cuddled her baby constantly and her son Siyus occasionally sat beside her and petted the baby, rubbing his face against hers. Kalee's hair, which had been cut eighteen months ago to treat ringworm, now reached her shoulders. She looked about fourteen and was pretty. She played with the baby, too, cooing and nibbling at its fingers.

Dr. Rebong asked to see Sasa, so his father, Lefonok, hurried over to a platform near the dark chamber and returned with the boy in his arms. Sasa looked strong and sturdy, though his belly was swollen and he had severe ringworm on his arms, legs, and buttocks. Doc examined him and prescribed the daily doses of medicine that was used so successfully to treat the ringworm and fungus of Gintoy.

Felix arrived with a walkie-talkie so Manda could receive a message off the single-side-band. As he spoke, Lefonok tied a vine to the box containing Sasa's medicine and pretended to talk into it like a walkie-talkie. The Tasaday hooted in acknowledgment and then, for no apparent reason other than to continue the entertainment, Udelen began joking about the size and shape of various *lassus*. Balayam joined in, then Lefonok, and they spent about ten minutes in a chortling discussion. The women chuckled from time to time but made no comment.

Evening darkness moved in quickly and the forest fell to dim outlines blending together. Mai strolled around and Manda stretched out on the platform. Dul sat quietly, but then suddenly called Udo and sent him toward the upper cave, behind her. Udo stopped short of the cave and started down the slope in front of it. Dul told Igna that Bilangan was coming.

Igna translated and Manda said, "Where? There's nobody out there. I've been sort of watching out that way, wondering if Bilangan's family would make it before dark. Mai, you see anyone?"

"Nossir. Nobody there."

Udo had stopped on a small bluff. We sat listening to the dusk's chorus of frogs, crickets, cicadas. Then Udo shouted and received an answering call. Soon a figure approached him from below. It was Bilangan carrying a child on his back; then Etut came into view, carrying another child and followed by a boy.

"Bilangan! It *is* Bilangan!" Manda exclaimed. "How did she know? She didn't even look around. I've been sitting right next to her all the time. How did she know? It was a couple of minutes ago that she sent Udo up there to wait."

Igna relayed these questions but the answer, if there was one, was lost in the arrival of Bilangan, who dropped off the child he carried and walked to greet us while the rest of his family continued to the upper cave. He embraced Manda warmly, then Mai and the rest of us in turn, pronouncing each of our names in an almost formal welcome. He took a seat on the platform and said all was well. The *natek* preparation was not quite finished, so Lobo and Lolo stayed behind to complete it. They would be here in the morning.

Bilangan said his family had been at another cave they used frequently. It was, he said, similar to the one Mahayag had. We asked if these caves were their permanent homes now and Bilangan said no, they used them when they went in search of *natek* and *biking;* it was taking them farther now.

Manda distributed gifts—knives to each of the men present and powdered lime, which they favored over that which they made them-

selves from snail shells, to Dul for all their betel chew. Balayam mentioned
that Tekaf had told him he was not going to come to the caves because
he never got an ax. Balayam said he had to promise Tekaf that he could
use his ax in order to get him to agree to come. He added that the Tasaday
had missed Momo Dakel constantly. Then, looking around, he said they
had missed the rest of us, too. "We think of you, we think of you often
and our inside feelings are about you always. We never forget you. If you
were this big [holding up his clenched fist] we would put you inside of us."

We asked if there had been any serious illnesses since we saw them and
they said no. What about hunting, which previously had appeared to be
increasing? Balayam said some of them used bows and arrows. "I shoot
mine at pigs and birds and monkeys."

"And do you hit them?"

"Well, I shoot at them, but I don't always hit them."

All the group was listening intently and a few Tasaday chuckled.

"How often do you hit them?" I asked.

"Not so often," Balayam mumbled with more chuckles in the background.

"Don't keep asking him," Manda said. "He probably makes a hit only
rarely, if at all. You'll embarrass him if he has to confess that he hits
nothing."

Balayam produced his mouth harp and strummed it, making, he said,
the sound of the big bird. He sang a song in which the big bird had a new
color on its belly: "Big bird, big bird, whose belly was blue, blue; now it
is yellow, yellow; the big bird with a yellow belly." (The Panamin helicopter had been repainted.) Then he sang about Momo Dakel Diwata
Tasaday and his friends returning to the Tasaday.

By this time it was so dark that you could not see the person seated
beside you. No fires had been lighted. I even wriggled my fingers in front
of my face but could not see them. We saw only faint lines of treetops
against a dark-gray sky, and hundreds of fireflies. The winking insects
flitted all over the valley in front of us, and some, apparently carried by
wind, made tiny darting lights in the trees.

We returned to camp by flashlight and talked. "What do you think?"
Manda asked Mai, Igna, Ching, me. "Have they changed? I don't think
so. They're the same. I'm actually a little bit surprised . . . thought they
would have changed some; don't know how exactly, but had expected
something. But they're the same, exactly as we left them," Manda said.

The rest of us agreed, based on what we had seen so far.

"The only thing that bothers me," Manda went on, "are those knives
and that damned *natek*. That's going to keep taking them farther and
farther. They must know all the caves around here now. And their
women. They haven't found the Tasafeng or Sanduka. It looks to me like
it'll be necessary to help them find those others. We can't bring them any

more Sindis. And if they're going to get wives, it looks like they'll need our help. But if it wasn't for the women, I bet Dafal would make it possible for them to stay in here and not go out for knives or anything else. He's the link, all they need, with the outside."

Mai said he had talked with Bilangan about his new cave. It was not big, and Mahayag's was large enough only for his immediate family. Bilangan also told him that Dafal had come to visit them seldom—but seldom was not quantified. Dafal was taking his responsibility as forest guardian very seriously, Mai said, and continued to make regular rounds of the area. "He's very proud of that job," Mai said.

The next morning over breakfast we asked Dafal several questions about the forest and his own people, who, he had told Manda, still lived inside. He said they called themselves the Ba'a-na, and they were similar to the Tasaday and other forest folks he knew. I asked the origin of all these people and Dafal said they probably had come from Fangul and his wife Tukful and another woman, whose name he remembered vaguely as Bi. I asked if he meant that all these people were related, and he answered that they were like chickens—Fangul was the rooster and the hens each had different families.

Asked about Tasaday spirits or gods, Dafal said he did not know about such things around here; there were none as far as he knew. What about spirits elsewhere? He shrugged and indicated he did not know, or else he did not want to talk about it. After more questions from Mai, Dafal said he guessed the original people had been only Fangul and Tukful, no other woman. But what about Bebang and his wives, Sidakweh and Fuweh? Weren't they the creators of the Tasaday? Dafal thought these people had nothing to do with the Tasaday. He had doubled back over his own previous stories, and I could not tell what he really thought.

Shortly after nine, the helicopter flew in from Tboli, bringing David Aikman, a thirty-year-old Englishman who was a correspondent for *Time* Magazine based in Hong Kong. Aikman had talked with Manda and other Panamin officials several times during the past year in pursuit of a story about the Tasaday and had been invited to come on this trip. Dad and Sol met him at the landing and guided him to the campsite. Then he, Manda, Mai, Igna, and I visited the caves.

Lobo and Lolo had arrived. They shouted and embraced Manda. Both boys were enthusiastic, but Lobo had a new reserve. About fourteen now, and taller and heavier, Lobo was on his way to manhood. His voice had dropped from its high pitch, and cracked now and then. His arms and legs were fuller, no more the limbs of a child, and his face had lost some of its girlish prettiness. He was still handsome, but not so delicate. He greeted the rest of us with shy friendliness, not the exuberant playfulness we had known. Lolo, always more quiet, took a place on a boulder, while Lobo sat beside Manda.

We noticed the monkey was nowhere in sight, apparently in line with Manda's request to either move it or free it. The Tasaday said they had taken it elsewhere but did not elaborate. "I wonder what they did with it," Elizalde said. "If it was tied up nearby, we'd hear it screeching for sure. And if they tied it up alone way out in the jungle it would attract other monkeys; they might even attack it."

We all went for a walk along the stream. The Tasaday were extremely playful there—Igna said they were more interested in having fun than in finding food—but they still kept adding tadpoles, crabs, ginger, and other edibles to their leaf cones and packets. Dul, her new baby on her hip, collected mushrooms from a mossy stump—the first mushrooms I had seen the Tasaday gather—and wrapped them in a huge flat palm leaf. After an hour Manda suggested returning to the caves, but Dul and Bala-yam said the waterfall was near and they would like to bathe. We reached it quickly and the Tasaday men bounded forward. Udelen sat smack in the middle of the fall, only his head and knees poking out of the foamy torrent of water. Lobo leaped head first into the deepest part of the pool, came up sputtering, somersaulted down again so just his feet were above water; then he twisted and sprang up triumphantly, clasping a large frog, which he delivered gaily to Dul. She smacked it softly with her open palm three or four times until it went limp, then deposited it in a cone.

Udo jumped into the water, followed by Kalee, Lolo, Balayam, Dul, Siyus, and Maman. Even Sindi, who had been shy of the pool previously, splashed around and talked Igna in, fully dressed. Dad could not resist joining and finally Manda stripped off his shirt and shoes, and waded in, and ducked under the waterfall, a Tasaday holding his hands.

The Tasaday took their food to the caves. While a meal was being pre-pared, Balayam sat talking at the tents with Manda, Mai, Igna, me, and David Aikman, whom Balayam had named Kakay Eebid.

Aikman began asking him questions, questions heard often over the past three years—what do you like in the forest? what do you do? what are you afraid of? what do you think of visitors? Et cetera, ad infinitum. I groaned inwardly at the prospect of going over such well-traveled ground, and expected Balayam also to be bored. Instead, I found it fascinating to hear again his simple but somehow still fresh answers. And sometimes Balayam gave different answers than before.

He said they did not fear anything in the forest—except snakes. I men-tioned his remark three years ago that they feared thunder, the "big word," and sometimes covered their ears. But when Mai asked about this, Balayam said no, they were not afraid of thunder. Lightning then? No, not lightning either. Balayam said the only sadness they knew was when Momo Dakel Diwata Tasaday was not with them; and his presence was what made them happiest. His responses were successively more praising of Manda, until Manda snorted: "Ha, this guy is some politician. Listen to him. You'll get better answers if I'm not here." He walked to the radio tent.

I was suddenly put in mind of another occasion when Balayam had displayed his political bent. I had asked if he recalled the dramatic first meeting at the edge of the forest, when the helicopter roared out of the sky and landed in front of them. Balayam smiled and said yes and then recounted his fright and having fallen over, thinking all the Tasaday would die. When did he begin to feel better? With a long look and beatific smile toward Manda, he said the moment he saw Momo Dakel he *knew* he was *the* good man. We nodded, but reminded him that for hours they had trembled and appeared ready to dash into the forest. Asked if anything else that day had persuaded them to stay, both Balayam and Bilangan mentioned the bead necklaces. They had never seen such bright, colorful things, and when Momo Dakel draped them around their necks they were very pleased, and intrigued. They did not know what the beads were for, but it did not matter; they were good to feel and see.

I had then asked Dafal and the Tasaday about the first time they saw metal, a knife. What reactions had that momentous event caused? Dafal shrugged and appeared not to remember it too well; he showed them the knife and they liked it, that was all. One of the Tasaday said, "It was good. We had never seen such a thing and were happy to see it . . . and happier when Kakay Daisuklawa [Dafal] gave us a piece." That was all they had to say about it. Of course, they had no way of knowing then the impact it would have on their lives—it was apparently a much more dramatic moment in my mind than in theirs. . . .

What made the Tasaday happy or sad before Momo Dakel came? Aikman was asking now. Balayam replied to the effect that they did not have sad or happy peaks in those days, that they were generally happy, or the same, all the time. Aikman asked if they feared death and Balayam said not necessarily. What happened when a Tasaday died? They just died, Balayam answered. Did the part of him that had lived go somewhere? "We don't know. We die, that's all we know."

The next questions, on soul and spirit, became difficult to translate. Finally, looking restless and uncomfortable, Balayam said it was time for him to go to the caves.

As we ate lunch, Aikman asked about Tasaday competition and leadership and their ethical and moral values, remarking that Elizalde had apparently introduced the concepts of happiness and sadness, and the idea of getting ahead, progressing. We debated this, and then Aikman suggested that the Tasaday had become dependent on Elizalde and Panamin.

"No, I don't think so. They are not dependent on us," Manda replied. "Balayam particularly talks about me a lot, but that's his style. Now look, if I'm the tin god some people say I am, if I'm making these people my playthings, then why are they now, after a year of not seeing us, still as they were? They're happy. We came in the last time a year ago, but it is just like we had seen them yesterday. Do they seem unhappy? No, they aren't."

After Aikman had gone to the caves with Mai and Igna, Manda was still answering the question. The Tasaday were less dependent than many other groups—"they've got this forest, caves, the whole works. They like us, but as far as they're concerned we're not essential to their survival."

When I joined the group at the caves, Mai was lying on the main platform with his head in Balayam's lap, Igna was seated beside them, and ten other Tasaday were relaxing around them as Aikman asked questions. Balayam was the chief spokesman but everyone appeared interested. The first question I heard was whether they saw other people in the forest. The answer was nobody except Dafal, who brought them things and taught them things. Later, asked about their music, they said Dafal had taught them to sing. This surprised me; I understood that they had sung before knowing Dafal; and Dula had once said that her people at Tasafeng had sung. I mentioned this, but Balayam insisted they had no music before meeting Dafal. It made me wonder if perhaps Dafal had become a convenient solvent to dissolve our questions.

Aikman had read most of what had been written about the Tasaday. He asked who owned the caves. They said Fangul.

"But Fangul is dead."

That's right, they said, and after him the cave was owned by Sambal and Salibuku, and when they died it was passed on to all of them here now—"all of us own it."

And who owns the forest? "We do, all of us." The same for the stream and the things in it. What about snakes? "Nobody owns them." I had heard Carlos Fernandez suggest that they ate snakes. I asked if they did. "No," Dul said. "We don't like snakes."

They answered questions easily, seeming to enjoy them after so many months. Did they mind? Balayam said, "It's all right, you want to know us, that's good. We like Kakay Eebid to know our inside feelings. We think he has good inside feelings."

Aikman remarked to me on the "spontaneous affection" they displayed. But what should he ask now? "This is extraordinary—sometimes I just run out of questions."

"What do you do each day?" was his next query.

They went out for food and sat here together, talking and laughing, and discussing Momo Dakel and his friends and how they first came here. "We don't like it when they are gone."

"And what don't you like about people who come?"

"There is nothing we don't like."

"What means something is good?"

"We say it is *mafeon*."

"And what means something is bad?" Mai said they had no word for bad, only not good—*n'da mafeon*.

What happens, I asked, when children argue or disagree over a stick or toy or piece of food?

"We tell them to stop."

And if they keep arguing?

"We keep telling them to stop."

And what happens if adults argue?

"Adults don't argue."

It went this way for about an hour, the Tasaday laughing among themselves occasionally and remarking—"*Oh-ho* Kakay Eebid [or Kakay Mafoko, or Jambangan], you have good inside feelings. We keep your feelings inside of us always."

We then visited the upper cave, where Etut was with her boys. Bilangan accompanied us and Balayam came later. Bilangan was more talkative in his own place, away from the others, and showed he still was the most outwardly curious Tasaday. He asked Aikman where he lived and, upon hearing "Hong Kong," laughed and beamed. "*Oh-hooo,* Kong Kong. *Oh-ho,* Kong Kong"—repeating it again and again with his hand over his mouth and chuckling. He asked if Kakay Eebid had a wife there.

David said no and then asked Lolo, who was sitting beside his mother, if he would have a wife. "No," Lolo said. "There is no woman for me."

"Would you like to be married?"

"Yes," he said with a broad grin. "But there is no one." Then he dropped his chin into a crutch of hands and stared into the forest. He added that he was tired, had been working hard, and walked home this morning without much rest.

Aikman asked Bilangan if he remembered other visitors and Bilangan named those of us present, then stopped and said he could not remember any others. Balayam, overhearing this, began to tick off the names of almost everyone who had ever come. Then he sat on a rock and craned his neck to look at my cameras, pointing and exclaiming at a new metal neck strap on one of them. "Ohhh, Kakay Jambangan's rattan," he said. He took the camera and peered at it this way and that, clucking "*ta-suk, ta-suk*" to himself as he tried to look through the lens but put the wrong end to his eye. Then he peered through a shiny glass that covered the film counter, then the film rewind knob. He acted as if he had forgotten what to do. Formerly, he had been the ringleader of half a dozen men and boys who would take the cameras and scamper about snapping the shutters. But now Balayam looked at me imploringly. I showed him how and he looked through the lens, exclaiming loudly, as if he never had done that before. Then he felt around for the shutter-release button, still looking through the lens, and pressed every knob and notch on the camera trying to make the *ta-suk* sound. I put his finger on the right button, he pressed, and exploded with loud shouts and wide eyes. I had thought he was teasing me, only pretending not to remember how the camera worked, but it seemed that he truly had forgotten. He had remembered the name of virtually every past visitor but could not remember this device. It must have seemed an odd contraption to him, and my behavior with it even more odd. Although they had seen photographs once or twice, I did not think the relationship of the camera to them had been explained. What strange people we must seem, how strangely we behaved—forever peering through little boxes and making them go *ta-suk!*

We visited the caves again with Manda in the early evening. Adug had come by that time and reported that Mahayag and his group would not return today because Sekul had eye trouble and in midday had lost her sight completely. This did not seem to cause great concern among the Tasaday; Igna learned that Sekul had suffered temporary blindness before. Mahayag had sent word by Adug that she probably would be improved by morning and then they would come to the cave. His group was the only one missing; Adug's arrival made a total of twenty-one Tasaday present.

The evening visit included a session of flashlight games, songs, and laugh contests—led by Balayam and Dafal—and a series of imitations by Balayam. We were to leave the forest the next morning, but Manda said it was better not to tell them, it would merely drag out the farewell.

In the morning we hiked to the caves, and Manda told the Tasaday quickly that it was time for us to go. Faces tightened, brows pinched together; eyes narrowed and swam. "No tears, now. Tell them, Mai: no tears. We'll be back. This isn't good-by for long."

Balayam spoke up. "Don't stay away so long this time. We feel sad when you are gone."

"We'll come back more often," Manda replied. "Okay, Mai, everybody, let's make our move, go quickly. The best way to leave is just to get up and leave . . . before we get into those terrible, sad good-bys." He slipped off the platform and headed down the trail, calling back, "Tell 'em we'll come back more often, Mai. And tell them not to come to the helipad. Dad and the Blit can stay here for a while to see Sekul if she comes in."

Since our arrival I had been expecting the Tasaday to talk about going outside the forest, as they had in December, 1972. But they did not. The subject was not mentioned or even hinted at, to my knowledge. Now the Tasaday's good-bys trailed behind us as we moved into the jungle. An hour later we were aboard the helicopter on the way to Tboli.

We landed amid thousands of tribespeople. Some had walked for days to attend the celebration of this new municipality called Tboli. They roared and waved and surged forward, catching Elizalde as he stepped from the helicopter, lifting him onto their shoulders, shouting, reaching to touch him. He floated above the crowd, grinning.

For three days the gathered folk—which Trinidad said totaled more than eight thousand from a dozen tribes—ate and played, rode the Ferris wheel, watched the acrobats and jugglers from morning to midnight. Then the tribes themselves performed dances and musical numbers as the provincial governor and mayors of nearby towns sat on the stage while Mai and other leaders were sworn into office. Mai spoke, saying it was another great day for the Tboli, a day that had its beginnings when Panamin came "in times of sadness and loneliness."

The tribespeople looked toward the future with more pride and hope than they had had for many years. Few were aware of the complexities ahead, and were exhilarated in the attainment of their own municipality. I saw irony in their jubilation, too: the land granted them had belonged to their ancestors for centuries.

There was irony also in that this extraordinary municipality—perhaps one of the twentieth century's most promising creations for its less sophisticated members—was brought forth during a condition of martial law, which usually raises notions of repression rather than humane innovation.

Near the end of March, Doug Yen stopped over in Manila on his way to Honolulu after four months of field work in northern Thailand, with the news that the laboratory tests on the Tasaday's *biking* samples he had submitted showed no trace of a birth-contraceptive ingredient, and also that, after confirming it with Hermes Gutierrez of the National Museum, one of the plants collected had turned out to be a previously unknown species of lily. He proposed naming the lily after Elizalde. However, Elizalde, who had been playing himself down lately, recommended that it be named after Imelda Marcos, in honor of her support of Panamin.

Yen had completed writing the first of a three-part report on his Tasaday research and had done some rough work on the other two parts; his queries to Panamin about publication plans had never been answered, so he had not finished. The last part of the paper, which would include his conclusions and interpretation, would be troublesome because there were still so many unknowns. "I don't like to speculate on some things," he said. "But if I don't, I won't have anything on them."

Some of the results of the chemical analyses of Tasaday foods were still out but, based on analyses of comparable foods elsewhere in the Philippines and the Pacific, it appeared that *natek, biking, ubud,* fruits and other plant life, and food sources from the stream provided very few calories—conceivably no more than 1,000 to 1,500 calories per person a day. It was possible only to speculate on what the Tasaday intake was before they had knives, when *ubud* and *natek* were not available. Adults in the Western world were generally believed to require about 2,300 calories a day, although they could get by on a few hundred less if they were not too active, and even less than that for limited periods.

Yen thought there might be a connection between the Tasaday's leisure-intensive society and their low caloric intake—perhaps helping to explain why they had not traveled far. But the story was far from complete.

"Now, the low estimates so far would lead you to think that they must be eating something else, something we haven't included," Yen said. "We have not included any meat (because presumably they did not eat it before), but perhaps, if we interpret Bilangan correctly, it was meat."

He had been thinking a lot about Bilangan's reply when asked how they butchered animals before Dafal taught them. (They did it "any how," which Dad, who was translating, said meant they did it without any particular method or procedure.) This had led him to conjecture that they may have eaten meat regularly before.

However, Yen was certain they had not been hunting or trapping before—their techniques in both these activities was simply too poor. But they might have eaten very young animals who could be easily caught by hand; such animals could be butchered with stones and sticks. But Yen wanted to do more checking before making any final statements.

Yen understood that Carol Molony, who had completed her work in the Philippines and returned to California, had written up part of her linguistic data, but was also waiting to find out how Panamin wanted to publish it. (Both Yen and Molony could publish their data on their own, but had agreed to make it available to Panamin first.)

She had produced a list of more than nine hundred Tasaday words and their meanings, but her analyses and interpretations were still to come. And what about the words of possible Sanskrit origin? I had had a brief experience with them myself. When in Portland, Oregon, I had tried to trace the origin of *sawa,* the Tasaday word for spouse that Carol had suggested might be Sanskrit. At Portland's main library, however, the anglicized Sanskrit dictionary was no help to me. Two librarians courteously put me in touch with a local scholar who had assembled a "language bank"—colleagues, friends, and acquaintances, who between them knew some sixty languages. The bank gave me the name and telephone number of a man from India.

I told him only that I wanted to know the meaning of the word *sawa,* which might be derived from a Sanskrit word, possibly something like *asawa.* He telephoned later and said his wife had found *asawa* in her dictionary and that it was a word of dual declension, either masculine or feminine in gender, and meant "we two are."

There was clearly a possible link between that and *sawa* (spouse). I then explained why I was inquiring and the Indian became quite excited, saying that he and his wife had recently watched a television program about the Tasaday (apparently Jack Reynolds's) and had been amazed at similarities between the Tasaday and some people living near the couple's home in Madras, southern India. "Oh yes, indeed," he said. "The singing, for one thing—just like the raga, not the new raga, of course, the old raga. And their mannerisms—the way they sat and moved their hands and heads. Oh yes, quite like our place."

We then checked several more Tasaday words. None were exactly Sanskrit, but two—particularly a Tasaday term for young boy—had glimmerings.

Could the Tasaday's ancestors have come from southern India? It was possible. One word and similarities in song and manner did not establish anything, of course, but who could say? Someday we might know; meantime, I was anxious to know more of Carol's findings.

Elizalde and Trinidad were disappointed over the failure to follow through on the publishing of Yen's and Molony's papers. So many other projects were at hand, and also a research director had only recently been found to replace David Baradas—Carlos Fernandez was going to take the post in June.

Fernandez said his paper on the Tasaday field work he had done in May of 1972 was finished. Yen suggested that his, Fernandez's, and Molony's papers be published by Panamin in one volume, and that I serve as editorial co-ordinator. Elizalde agreed, and plans were set before Yen left for Hawaii.

A week later Manda invited me to join him on another visit to the Tasaday. When I reached Tboli, he said the trip was being arranged at the request of Imelda Marcos for two friends of hers who had been in the Philippines about two weeks and had repeatedly expressed a desire to visit the Tasaday. They were a young Spanish couple, Rafael and Mariola Ardid, whom he had met briefly. The husband was a lawyer and his wife was a granddaughter of Francisco Franco's.

"Now, look, before you make any comments," Manda said to me, "I want to point out that this is the only time, after all this time, that the First Lady or the President has made any kind of request concerning the Tasaday. They could have, you know—every time I'm at the Palace, I hear about requests from all kinds of people to see the Tasaday—ambassadors, foreign businessmen, VIP's, everybody. So this is not too much to ask, considering all they've done for the minorities, the Tasaday particularly."

The Ardids, together with a Filipina friend, Isabel Brias, and two husky young men from the Palace Guard as escorts, arrived at Tboli on April 10. They asked questions about the Tasaday and other groups throughout the evening; the next morning we all flew to the rain forest in a chartered helicopter—the Panamin chopper was under repair again.

The hike to camp was a bit difficult, but the visitors were trim and young; they made it without serious problems. Balayam met us on the way and, after a stop at the tents, we continued to the caves. All the Tasaday were present, including Mahayag's contingent, which was very friendly toward us. We stayed about two hours. The Tasaday proclaimed their happiness that Momo Dakel had returned so soon, and made a fuss over Mariola Ardid's long blonde hair; the visitors took pictures, visited Bilangan's upper cave, watched Doc treat an assortment of cuts and infected scratches on Tasaday arms and legs. Right after a lunch prepared by Lucy, the Ardids and their party, expressing delight over their experience, hiked to the ridgetop and caught the helicopter to Tboli.

The rest of us, who would leave the next morning, spent the afternoon with the Tasaday. Doc observed that Sasa's ringworm had responded very well to the medication and was almost gone. Dul, however, had a case of scabies, which needed treatment, and he examined Sekul's eyes. She could see again, but the doctor said she had a viral infection that inflamed the lids. He gave her antibiotics with instructions for their continued use after he left.

Rebong had no doubt that the Tasaday would follow his instructions exactly; they had learned well the healing power of his medicine. It was a blessing nobody could deny; yet even medical knowledge, like metal and other innovations from the modern world, would deeply change the way they lived. I asked Doc if he believed medical treatment had saved any Tasaday lives, and he emphatically said yes, at least two: Sasa, whose condition had seemed beyond hope in the initial meetings; and Siyus, Dul's oldest son, who two years ago had an infected scratch on his leg that became severely swollen and would have, Rebong believed, developed into fatal blood poisoning without medication. And, if Yen had failed to persuade Lobo's mother not to take him upstream (in December, 1972, when he was ill, supposedly because the owner of the cave was punishing him for breaking a plant), Lobo would have been left alone to die.

Of course nobody could be absolutely certain about what would have happened to each of these boys, but the Tasaday gave no indication that they themselves would have been able to save them. Discounting divine intervention or a spontaneous cure, the fact is that visitors' assistance saved three Tasaday lives. Wonderful, certainly—but it might also herald problems. The three boys represent 10 per cent of the present Tasaday population of twenty-eight. Without them the population would be one short of what it was when they met the modern world in 1971 (twenty-six; two were born since then, and the boy who reportedly did die was replaced numerically by Sindi). Perhaps death was this frequent in the past; if so, it could explain the small number of Tasaday, and therefore their ability to subsist within a small area. But, if the intervention of medicine has added 10 per cent to their population in less than three years, what might ten years mean? A population of forty or fifty? When would it run on to the hundreds? Would the caves still accommodate them? Would their traditional area of forest and stream feed that many? Doubtless not. They would have to split up, move away, perhaps leave their forest sanctuary.

Nature had apparently struck a balance between the people and their environment, but now the scales were being tipped.

I am not suggesting that a Lobo—who can be saved—should lie down and die. But the long range implications of their contact with the twentieth century must be faced. The fact that in their delicately balanced ecology a few Lobos have the weight of millions in the outside world reminds us of the broad range of ethical, moral, and philosophical questions of which the tiny group of Tasaday is the embodiment. For instance, would medicine affect their spiritual life? Would the powers of "the owner of the cave"—who had sent sickness as a punishment—be thwarted, reduced, channeled into other areas?

We noticed that the Tasaday's pet monkey was not present. Balayam said it was dead—a large bird had suddenly swooped down one day and plucked the monkey off a rock where it sat in front of the cave. Balayam said he saw this happen; the bird was so strong and swift the monkey had no chance to escape and barely screeched before it was carried away. We wondered if the bird was a monkey-eating eagle, but Balayam could only tell us it was big, strong, and fast. He seemed almost amused, rather than troubled, by the incident.

Monkey-eating eagles were among the largest eagles in the world, some having a wing span of six feet. It seemed to me that if it could snatch a monkey, as Balayam said, then why not an infant child? We asked Balayam if they worried about that, and if the huge birds came often. He smiled and said no to both questions. (Much later, it crossed my mind that the Tasaday might have eaten the monkey. But I had no evidence of that; no doubt, it was just a delayed reaction of reporter's skepticism.)

We left the next morning, the Tasaday saying they hoped Momo Dakel would not stay away longer than he had since his last visit. Several asked for flashlight batteries. Mahayag complained that his flashlight had not worked ever since he used it to look for tadpoles and crabs under big rocks in the stream. When you put the flashlight under the water, he said, it doesn't make good light.

As before, I heard no mention of the Tasaday wanting to go outside the forest.

We flew to the Blit settlement, where Manda planned to stay at least one night because he had not spent much time there in recent months. I asked to visit Kasuk, the old blind man who two years ago had told us he was born at Tasaday and left as a young boy. Datu Dudim said Kasuk had moved, and it was quite a long walk to his new house. So Dafal, Igna, Dad, and I were flown a little way south of Blit, on the edge of the rain forest. Kasuk was seated on the ground in front of his house when we landed. His wife and grandson joined him as we approached. Dafal shouted and Kasuk raised his head and smiled. Dafal knelt and embraced him, the pair rocking and murmuring. I had thought of him as about eighty or ninety years old, but now he looked as if he could have been one hundred. I was introduced and he stretched out his arms toward me, found me, embraced me. His skin was surprisingly soft; though wrinkled and sunbaked, it felt smooth and delicate, almost velvety, like a butter-fly's wing. His thin body looked fragile, and he wore the same faded loin-cloth as before. As he talked to Dafal and Igna, reaching out to hug them from time to time, the old man smiled and wept, saying he was very happy they had come. He said he had left the other place because honey bees had infested his house and stung him. Igna told him I wished to ask him about where he used to live in the forest, and he said he would tell what he could. He repeated his description of the Tasaday caves, and I asked him where the people had come from. Kasuk said there was a story, a legend, that Bebang planted a bean that grew into a great mountain, and that was the place of the Tasaday. It was the biggest mountain in the area, and Blit and other places were like a stairway leading to that moun-tain. This did not answer my question of where the people had come from so I repeated it, and got a repetition of the story of the bean. I asked if he heard this story when he lived at Tasaday or after he left, but the old man could not remember.

Did he eat meat when he lived at Tasaday? Kasuk said they did not eat meat because they had only stone implements and could not kill animals with them. They ate mostly *biking* and fruits. Asked if the name Sanduka meant anything to him, he said that was a place near Tasaday. Did people live there? No, Kasuk said, he didn't think so. What about Tasafeng? He said he had never heard that name, nor had he heard Talili. Lambong was a stream below the Tasaday mountain.

Did he remember any of the people at Tasaday? No. I mentioned some of the ancestors' and playmates' names he had recited before, and he rocked and shook his head. "I remember the place . . . but now I can't remember the people. I like to remember that place." He said no when asked if he had known anyone else who had lived there and come outside.

Could he remember what the Tasaday wore? G strings made of leaves —they had no cloth.

Did they have music, did they sing? As Kasuk listened to this question, he smiled, started to answer, and then broke into laughter. He kept laugh-ing, harder and harder. Each time he quieted and tried to talk he laughed again, rocking and tossing his head back with such pleasure that all of us laughed. When he finally stopped we asked what was so funny and Kasuk, choking back more chuckles, said, "When I think of myself singing . . . when I think of that . . . it just makes me laugh." Then we all laughed together.

We did not learn why the thought of singing was so funny or get an answer to the question about music; the laughter seemed to have tired him. We left soon afterward. The next morning we returned to Manila.

Late in April, Panamin received word that Irenaus Eibl-Eibesfeldt, the German ethologist from the Max Planck Institute, was arriving at the end of the week to start field work among the Tasaday. Elizalde and Trinidad told me they had okayed it with Eibesfeldt when he came to Manila the previous September, thinking that a new phase of scientific research would be planned before he returned. But it had not.

"I didn't realize how soon Eibesfeldt was due here," Elizalde said. "This is a terrible time for me—absolutely no chance of getting away from Manila, I'm stuck here all of May. Besides, the chopper is still not flying. Ching says it looks too expensive to fix this time. We're thinking about getting a new one. But that's months away."

Trinidad sent a message calling off the field work project for the present, but by the time it reached Eibesfeldt, who had been in the Galapagos Islands, off the coast of Ecuador, he was in Honolulu en route to Manila. He continued on.

When Hubertus Kuhne, director of the German Cultural Center, advised Trinidad of this, a luncheon meeting was arranged for the afternoon of Eibesfeldt's arrival. Elizalde wanted Carlos Fernandez, Panamin's anticipated new research director, to attend, but he was out of town. I attended as part of my commitment to co-ordinate the publication of the Yen-Molony-Fernandez reports; I had agreed to act as a consultant on related matters, particularly concerning the Tasaday.

Eibesfeldt was weary after his long flight but affable. He was accustomed to changes of plans, he said, and still hoped to accomplish something while in the Philippines. Elizalde stressed that Panamin's need was for a research program that covered much more than just the Tasaday— the Blit, the Higa-onon, and other groups who had never been studied at all. Eibesfeldt said the Max Planck unit on human behavior, which he headed, would be interested but he could not make a reasonable proposal without actually seeing the peoples involved. Discussion went on through lunch and for the next two days. It resulted in Panamin's chartering a helicopter for one week to take Eibesfeldt, Kuhne, and me on a tour of remote sites within the new Tboli municipality.

We arrived at Tboli on May 4, and flew to the Tasaday the next day— stopping first at Blit for an hour because of a severe rainstorm inside the forest. Mai accompanied us, but could stay only one day because extraordinary demands were being made on the new mayor's time, including problems arising from a series of gunfights between bands of Moslems and Christians. (They had taken more than twenty lives and had involved Tboli and Blaan families at a place called Barrio Ned, on the western border of the new township.) Fludi would be our interpreter. Igna was not asked to come because Eibesfeldt said he would not be asking many questions and would concentrate on observing quietly, filming if possible. Fludi, Dad, and Sol flew into the forest first, followed by Eibesfeldt, Mai, and me. Kuhne flew in that afternoon.

Fludi had told the Tasaday that Momo Dakel was not coming, but they seemed happy enough to see the rest of us. Eibesfeldt was named Kakay Inky (after Rinky, his nickname). He did not unpack his large movie camera and used only small cameras the first day. The Tasaday inspected them and Balayam asked me, "What about this new friend? Does he have good feelings?" I said he did and that he had come with the knowledge of Momo Dakel, which brought a chorus of approving *oh-ho's*. It was a convivial gathering—the Tasaday especially friendly, perhaps in part because of a bag of rice brought to them by Fludi's team and some powdered lime I gave them as a gift from Manda. Eibesfeldt, who had spent many lengthy periods with primitive groups in Africa, South America, Australia, New Guinea, was competely at ease.

His approach to study usually began with film documentation of social behavior: the interaction between children, parents and children, spouses; the way they gestured, greeted and addressed one another, expressed amusement, disappoinment—the usual everyday exchanges. After our introductory visit to the caves, Eibesfeldt remarked that he had observed some classic aggressive behavior between toddlers—striking at one another or pretending to, tugging at opposite ends of a stick. He noted also a universal laughing gesture: head thrown back, hand covering the mouth. And the baby (Dul's newest child), who cried when he arrived, exhibited a standard reaction. "I think children are innately afraid of strangers," Eibesfeldt said.

"I noticed that the baby was crying," I said. "But how do you know it was because of us? Babies cry for lots of reasons. And this one didn't cry long."

"Yes, but this one began when I established eye contact as we first arrived. I recognized the reaction; it cried upon seeing us."

Kuhne accompanied us to the caves in the late afternoon. His name became Kakay Kooney at first, but soon was changed to Kakay Ayatan, a title referring to his shiny bald head, which the Tasaday boys rubbed and laughed about. He joined in the fun. After some casual conversation, Mai told the Tasaday that he and Dad would leave the next day and that the rest of us would stay until the day after. Balayam, Mahayag, Dul, and some other Tasaday had a brief discussion among themselves and Bala-yam said they had a question.

Mai told me this and I said, "Fine, what is it?"

"Not now," Balayam said. "We will ask tomorrow. We will talk about it among ourselves first."

At the tents that evening I asked Mai, Dad, and Fludi if they had any idea what the Tasaday wanted to ask. No one had any inkling. I wondered if they were finally going to bring up the possibility of going out of the forest.

The Tasaday had noticed Eibesfeldt's small tape recorder and asked if it was a *kee-totie* (walkie-talkie). When we said no, they remarked about those other things we had that made noise, apparently tape recorders. I told Eibesfeldt that because it had been felt that the taping of the Tasaday without their knowledge constituted spying, we had tried to explain the tape recorder to them. "That was ridiculous," Eibesfeldt said. "It is not wrong to do such things. It is dangerous only if the results are used im-properly. Otherwise it is legitimate scientific questing, it is perfectly all right in such circumstances. Could prove very valuable. Telling them all about it has, of course, spoiled it. Too bad."

After Mai and Dad left the next morning, a group of Tasaday men and boys called at our tent. It was a brief, friendly visit, something of a social call it seemed, and they left soon, saying they would see us at the caves.

Sol and Fludi went first to the caves, carrying some of Eibesfeldt's large aluminum cases of camera gear and his tripod. I asked them to place the gear against the cave wall opposite the main platform, but we arrived to find that Sol had put all of them squarely in the middle of the platform. There was room for only a few Tasaday and the rest stood around. Sol spoke little English, so I asked Fludi to have him move the bags to the opposite wall. Sol grabbed the bags and then, it soon became evident, told all the Tasaday to move to the opposite wall as well.

They all moved—very orderly—and sat down on a platform. They looked at us expectantly, presumably wondering what this was all about. I had never seen so many Tasaday gathered so formally. All the fe-males were together in the front row. Twenty Tasaday lined up as if for a high-school-graduation photograph.

"What is going on?" Eibesfeldt asked. "What have you done to them?"

"It's a mix-up," I said. "I only asked Fludi to ask Sol to move the bags and then this . . ."

"Well, this is not good. We should not be telling people where to go, what to do," Eibesfeldt said.

"I know that, I know that," I replied. "It was a mistake. I didn't mean for this to happen. Let them relax there awhile and pretty soon they'll move on their own."

The Tasaday sat quietly, still expectantly, as Eibesfeldt clicked open

his silvery cases, lifted out equipment, and set up his tripod and camera—
a large 16-mm. Arriflex with a special mirror device built into the lens so
he could point it straight ahead but photograph at right angles; subjects
did not know they were being filmed.

Several minutes had passed and the Tasaday hardly moved. They appeared content, watching Eibesfeldt, chatting among themselves. More
time went by and they showed no sign of changing position, so I finally
suggested to Fludi that Sol might tell them that it was not necessary to
stay just as they were, they could stand up, walk around, do anything
. . . whatever they pleased.

Sol spoke to them. The Tasaday nodded, looked at one another, and
began to stand up. Then, with soft laughter and giggles, all went into
motion. Men, boys, girls, women with babies, everybody began walking,
stepping out in all directions—across the cave, to the front, to the back.
Several spun around after a few steps, walked back, turned again, stepped
off a few more paces, spun again—to and fro, to and fro. The Tasaday
were calling out *"Fanaw, fanaw, fanaw. Fanaw, fanaw, fanaw"* (their
word for walking or moving around), which Sol had obviously asked
them to do. Wherever you looked Tasaday were turning, crossing, sliding
past one another, bumping into each other. The cave had suddenly become
a downtown street corner during rush hour.

Eibesfeldt was glaring at me; I would have been embarrassed, except
that the Tasaday's giggles had turned to chuckles and then to guffaws.
It was a game, and their laughter filled the cave.

A few started playing tag and Grandfather Kuletaw, his face split in a
grin, pretended he was a monkey. He chased the boys, dragging his arms
low and scurrying rapidly. He caught two or three and then ran after
Adug, who was laughing so hard he had to hold his sides, and grabbed
him as he tried to duck inside the inner chamber, tugging him out by one
foot. The Tasaday were cheering and Kuletaw was beaming. Never had
we seen him so lively. He then walked around and embraced everyone
within convenient reach.

"I don't know what you are doing," Eibesfeldt said, "but no matter,
they are enjoying themselves. But don't tell them any more what to do,
please."

The Tasaday eventually settled on or around the main platform and
Eibesfeldt set up his camera so it pointed into the jungle but actually was
focused on them. After a while we asked the Tasaday about the question
they had mentioned the night before.

Balayam cleared his throat, shifted to a spot at the front edge of the
platform, and sat with his feet dangling down. Dul, Mahayag, Bilangan,
Lefonok, Udelen, and Dula, with Lobo and other children, sat around
him. Sol translated for Fludi and Fludi put it into English. I wasn't sure

what we would say if they asked us to take them on a visit outside the forest.

Balayam spoke. "Did our ancestors who are dark-haired and dark-eyed know your ancestors who are light-haired and light-eyed?"

We didn't know, I answered. But perhaps, long, long ago, they might have known each other. I added that although we had different coloring and different ways of living, we were in many ways alike, and our inside feelings were the same.

Sol apparently relayed the gist of this reply without much difficulty and the Tasaday smiled and chorused *"Oh-ho"* and *"Mafeon."* Then Balayam said, "Why do our new friends—these here now and the others before—why do they come here?"

Momo Dakel and Mafoko and others of us had told people about the Tasaday and this place, I said, and the people thought it sounded so beautiful they wanted to see it and to meet the Tasaday.

The Tasaday made affirmative noises in response to this and Balayam, following a short conference with Dul and Mahayag, said, "But what do they think is beautiful? Why do you find this place beautiful?"

The trees and the mountains and the caves were good for our eyes to look at, I said, and the way the Tasaday lived together—working together, helping each other—gave us good inside feelings.

This seemed to be satisfactory to them. Balayam hiked his eyebrows, chatted with Dul again, then stretched, lay back, and began to play his mouth harp. Did they have any more questions, I asked Fludi and Sol? Sol spoke to Balayam. No, that was all. Was there any special reason for their questions? Sol answered that the Tasaday had seen several new faces lately and were wondering about them.

A group of Tasaday relaxed on the platform for the next hour or so, grooming one another by picking bugs and chaff from their hair, chatting, playing with the babies, listening to Balayam sing. Eibesfeldt filmed steadily and the Tasaday paid him little attention, since his own interest appeared to be directed away from them.

In the late morning, however, a few adult Tasaday became fidgety, mumbled to each other, and cast furtive glances. They quieted again, but after a few minutes repeated these actions. I asked Fludi if they were disturbed by something, but he did not know. We suggested to Balayam that perhaps our group would go to our tents and eat. Balayam responded with a broad smile and said that that would be good, that the Tasaday would eat also.

Fine, then, we said, it was time for us to go. We would eat and return here later, if that was agreeable.

It was, Balayam said, slipping us a sidelong glance with a sly smile that easily could be described as conspiratorial. "Yes," he said. "That would be good. And after we have eaten we will send Lobo to tell you to come back."

We went below, ate, and pondered their behavior, certain that they did not want us present when they ate. Why? We had seen them eat before. I wondered if it had to do with rice; Fludi had given them rice before the rest of our party arrived and the Tasaday might assume that we did not know about it. Giving rice had become a sore point during an earlier visit, when the anthropologists had disputed with Fludi over rice doles to the Tasaday. This led to a cut in the amount given and also caused antagonism among the visitors. To avoid a recurrence, the Tasaday may have decided that rice was to be eaten in private, at least when people they did not know well were around. There was no real evidence for my theory, but Fludi agreed it was possible. Later, he reported that after we left the cave the Tasaday did eat rice.

Within two hours Lobo fetched us and we spent a quiet afternoon at the caves, the Tasaday strolling in and out occasionally, sprawling on the platforms; some napped, others played with children or groomed one another. Eibesfeldt had brought a six-inch rubber doll of a European boy with painted clothing and one hand raised in a wave. He said he had shown it to many tribes around the world; reactions varied, depending on their familiarity with idols, totems, artifacts, spiritual-religious beliefs, or whatever. Eibesfeldt asked me to offer it to the Tasaday while he filmed. The Tasaday reacted with utter astonishment. They cried out, recoiled momentarily, then crowded forward to look closely. Balayam, eyes narrowed and brow creased, took it in his hand and shouted over its rubbery texture. He smelled the doll, examined it, yelled some more, laughed. Others reached for it—Dul, Mahayag, children, all wide-eyed and exclaiming. Someone called to Sol and he translated: "What is it—a man, a frog, a crab? What is it?"

We said it was not alive and was a man-made thing that children where we came from liked to play with, a toy. The Tasaday stood it on the platform, occasionally touched it, but eventually gave it only cursory glances. I returned it to Eibesfeldt. He also wanted to film their reactions to different tastes—sweet, bitter, and so on—and a stick of chewing gum was offered. But none of the Tasaday would try it. Balayam sniffed and looked very closely but said he did not want to taste it. I mentioned that during the first meetings Igna said the Tasaday had feared such things as sugar and salt, thinking they were poisonous, and also that visitors' random giving of candies and other foods had been discouraged. No further taste tests were attempted.

At the tents in the evening, Eibesfeldt said he had filmed many episodes of interaction: mother and child fondling, cuddling, playing; a father soothing a crying infant by petting it, then trying to distract its attention, finally picking it up and strolling to calm it; rivalries between children—

teasing with a stick, tugging, poking, playing with hair, little jealousies over parental attention in which older youngsters squeezed between a mother and her baby or nagged until their needs were fulfilled. Eibesfeldt said he had observed one example of what he believed was sexual behavior between two teen-age boys. They were seated on the platform, close together, one behind the other and had begun making gentle hip movements. But then I had said something or taken a picture and attracted their attention, causing the boys to stop moving. Eibesfeldt said the hip actions did not signify homosexuality or necessarily even overt sexuality, appearing to be more of an unconscious sexual contact. Whether it might have become more overt was not known, the scientist pointed out with a stiff smile, because I had bumbled in and distracted them. "But never mind," he said. "You really didn't do too badly today . . . once we got started of course. This was the only time you bothered my work. Not too bad . . . not too bad."

He then talked about his work among the Waika of the Upper Orinoco, the Bushmen and the Himber of Africa, the Balinese of Southeast Asia, and various other peoples in Australia, Papua, South America. He said that if the Tasaday were truly what they appeared to be, they would add measurably to his studies of human behavior in various stages of technical and cultural development. The Tasaday might be closest, he said, to the Phi Tong Luang of Thailand, whom he had never seen but had read about in researches done decades ago, and the Schom-pen of Great Nicobar Island, whom he had seen briefly in one of the rare instances they had ever had contact with outsiders.

Obviously the Tasaday were keenly interesting to him, as he had anticipated they would be. He remarked that it was hard to believe, however, that they were not hunters because the bow and arrow was so widely used around the world. I passed along all of the information I had about their lack of a hunting tradition, and Eibesfeldt said he did not necessarily doubt that this was true, but that he simply found it so unusual. Without the bow and arrow and associated cultural items, you might consider them at the stage of development of Homo sapiens fifty thousand years ago, Eibesfeldt said—not that they had been in the forest that long; rather, that they represented a secondary culture. We may assume that they lost culture in the forest, he continued, or "perhaps they came here as children . . . possible? Parents killed or lost and the children were long ago left on their own; we see here now their descendants. Of course, on the other hand, perhaps this *is* an original culture that simply never advanced." Eibesfeldt shook his head. "Yes, well, maybe someday we shall know these things, or at least more about them."

He questioned the idea that they had been living in close harmony with their environment; if they were in such fine attunement, why were they so few in number—were they dying out? If so, or if they had been dying out or just barely subsisting before Dafal introduced metal, then this was not the beautiful harmony that had been attributed to the Tasaday. I mentioned the other groups in the forest and suggested that perhaps people split off from a main group when it reached a certain population. That might explain the small number here.

"Well, yes, we just don't know yet, do we?" Eibesfeldt said. "Yes . . . strange about those other groups. Hmm. Very strange. I think we shall learn a great deal when those others are reached. Yes . . . a great deal."

What he had seen the last two days had appeared to confirm the existence of aggression, or what he would term aggression, as a basic characteristic of human behavior. He cited the rivalries and playing of the children. I said that we had noted this behavior before, but that I had not—nor had anyone I knew—observed a single instance of what a layman would term truly hostile or aggressive behavior between adults. We had seen teasing and joking, but not openly angry or confronting types of hostility. I asked if he expected to find evidence that aggression in children was rechanneled or sublimated so that it would not be overt in mature Tasaday.

"We will see," Eibesfeldt said. "But, of course, you have here a family. The Tasaday are like one family—it is natural that they interact well. Suppose you observed a farm family in, say, Bavaria—healthy, happy, outgoing, co-operative—and you took this family as a sample of Germanic society. Then you'd think, What marvelous peaceful people are these Germans. Ha!"

But just because the Tasaday were a family would not necessarily make them co-operative and friendly, I said. Some families fought bitterly, brutally, were extremely competitive. And suppose the family were short of food, as he had suggested the Tasaday had been, or short of women, as the Tasaday most assuredly were—then competitiveness, jealousy, hostility among family members would not be so extraordinary, would it? "How about Cain and Abel, for one example?"

In this type of situation, as with Douglas Yen and others, my stance was akin to that of a student. Since meeting the Tasaday, I had read a fair amount on anthropology and related matters. I realized that a little knowledge could be misleading, but still I had tried to cover a decent range of views about certain subjects, among them aggression. I had read books by Eibesfeldt and his famous teacher and colleague, Konrad Lorenz, in which aggression was considered instinctive. I also had a beginner's acquaintance with the basic arguments of the environmentalists who contend that behavior is the result of conditioning, that humans were born with a blank slate of emotional potential. I was familiar with the arguments that humans had a great propensity for co-operation, for loving; and of the opposite argument that man was biologically determined to be aggressive, hostile, even murderous.

I mentioned Robert Ardrey, an exponent of the latter view, who was not a scientist but whose writing had given wide circulation to the idea that man was biologically determined to kill, was inherently bloodthirsty. The argument was unacceptable to me, and I believed that the Tasaday could provide evidence against it.

"Well, I have spoken with Ardrey," Eibesfeldt said, "and I would say that he exaggerated his points on biological determinism because he wanted to shake up the environmentalists, to make people think, to challenge them."

Eibesfeldt said that, in his own view, man had become a killer for two reasons: the invention of weapons made killing so easy that, inevitably, man had killed many times without intending to; and propaganda and psychological conditioning had been used to convince whole nations that their enemies were somehow subhuman—gooks, kikes, niggers, wogs, krauts, or honkies—disgusting creatures who did not deserve to live as the protagonists did. In this way, mass killing, wars, were rationalized.

The Tasaday had no known traditions of weaponry or enemies, so the key question about them was how they handled aggressions in their children so that they grew up to be essentially loving adults. Other examples of such behavior were not lacking. The Kalihari Bushmen were well known. Margaret Mead had written decades ago about the warm and friendly Arapesh of New Guinea, whose children were fondled and carried and nursed constantly, were surrounded by loving behavior that both reflected and abetted the affectionate nature of the adults. Many scholars felt that co-operation was common to small isolated groups of peoples: each individual's behavior had consequences for all; sharing was mandatory; the group's well-being had the highest priority. These theorists held that in the Stone Age fighting was rare.

Another interesting question about the Tasaday was to what extent did the "owner of the cave" govern behavior, compel ethical or moral decisions? We had only a few isolated hints of a metaphysical force that served some kind of justice. It appeared to be a "thou shall not" influence—but did it have broader application? Was it part of a religious hierarchy or system, or merely casually invoked when circumstances were coincidentally right?

As we discussed all of this, Eibesfeldt kept nodding enthusiastically, and saying "This is what my work is all about, of course—to study and understand human behavior under varying conditions."

In 1973, when we did not see the Tasaday, virtually everything I read, saw, and heard—books, television shows, the daily news—whether on space exploration or the Watergate scandal, the Mid-East war or the energy crisis—caused me to reflect on the Tasaday, seeking parallels, contrasts. This sometimes left me feeling that the Tasaday were at once unique—because of their isolation—and universal, Everyman, symbols of the natural man we may have been.

This view was supported by the anthropologist Paul Radin, for one, who wrote that simple food gatherers formed probably less than 1 per cent of the existing aboriginal population of the world, but they had been much more common as recently as the fifteenth and sixteenth centuries. And, he added, such small, independent communities of five to ten families, twenty to forty people, "must have represented the normal type of societal structures in the Paleolithic Period"—roughly 100,000 years ago.

Reading Theodore Roszak's *The Making of a Counter-Culture* also brought visions of the Tasaday to mind. He suggested that "people heaping," "touch and tenderness," the expression of "inner feelings" (each a characteristic of Tasaday life) were answers to the "depersonalization, loneliness, estrangement, isolation" of modern man. Roszak quoted the students' motto: "One man, one soul," and I immediately remembered Mahayag's admonition to his fellow Tasaday: "Let us call all men one man, all women one woman."

The miseries chronicled in daily news reports caused many people to wonder about the eroding quality of life, to ask, "What have we wrought?" Again the Tasaday leaped to mind—Mahayag expressing his desire to "go back to the stump of his old feelings," recapture life the way it was before the cameras changed it: nostalgia for the good old days.

There were many parallels in the changes brought by technology. Metal knives, for instance, reduced the status of elders, outdating any sage advice old Kuletaw might have given about food gathering. He could not teach his sons anything about knives; each of those strong young men was far more accomplished with them than Kuletaw had any hope of being. And in post-industrial society, innovations such as computers require technical expertise unknown to older people; the ever-quickening and intensely competitive pace of modern life demands youth and vigor. Science has helped people live longer, but it has also made many feel superfluous.

In all of this, the Tasaday, in my mind, were edging toward a place in Lewis Mumford's outlook for humanity. "The human prospect today is both brighter and darker than it has ever been in the historic ages," he wrote in *Interpretations and Forecasts: 1922–1972.* We had the power and knowledge to eliminate starvation and give every human being on the planet the opportunity for personal development and enjoyment formerly reserved to a small elite, "but at present these happy prospects are heavily overcast by well-justified fear and dismay. The method of thinking that has made these advances possible, and the very technology that has brought them to the point of realization, are at the same time working in precisely the opposite direction."

The Tasaday, even as they took the first and rudimentary steps toward possible contamination, stood in the depths of their forest as an extraordinary example for their more sophisticated fellow man. Although we could not or would not emulate them and may never extract new principles of behavior from them, we could treasure them as reminders of what was humanly possible; as inspiring emblems of social peace and harmony, of, simply, love.

Their love was everywhere—for each other, for their forest, for us— for life. We sometimes overlooked it in our quest for information, for the answers to questions and what *we* considered riddles. Sitting among the Tasaday with Eibesfeldt and Kuhne, Fludi and Sol, I could hear Elizalde's voice from some months back saying "For God's sake, enjoy these people. Quit trying to figure them out. Enjoy them; let them enjoy you. Just relax, that's the way to get to know them."

Only time would tell how the Tasaday's love would be rewarded.

And I still had to wonder if time would also divulge answers to many other questions, particularly about their break with the Tasafeng and Sanduka. That represented, for me, the biggest mystery about the Tasaday. Why had they lost them?

With the Tasaday's taboo against incest (which is almost universal, for reasons by no means clear and still under debate) and their need for outside women, they had to have a relationship with the Tasafeng and Sanduka in order to survive as a people. How could they lose something so crucial?

We could speculate easily enough about why they had lost touch with the others (or had they merely told us that they had?): the Tasafeng and Sanduka had left the forest or been wiped out by disease or intruders; the Tasaday argued with them and became estranged; they avoided contact because either the Tasaday had no marriageable girls or were in debt for women received; some taboo prevented the groups from meeting again; they had moved too far apart and truly forgot how to find each other. The irresistibility of speculating was never dampened by the sobering realization that we simply did not have enough facts, and that to play detective with fragments of clues might even lead away from the truth instead of toward it.

One example of playing with the possibilities—say, the Tasaday and the others had become estranged: suppose Lefonok was a key to this. It had once been said that he was ashamed over the death of his wife and therefore did not want to seek another mate. Why did he feel guilt? Had he done something wrong? Something careless or deliberate to cause her death? But we also had been told that she died because a witch bit her on the breast. Was this witch to be taken as Sasa, the strangely complexioned child who was of nursing age at the time of his mother's demise? Did Lefonok's shame have to do with his fathering of this unusual offspring? Sasa, however, according to Dad's testimony and our observation, carried no stigma among the Tasaday. Perhaps the mother had not died but had run away, gone back to her family, upset over the child or Lefonok, and thereby caused a rupture between the two groups.

Further complicating the theory was the fact that there was no such thing as a partial albino—either you were albino or you were not. So Sasa was not—his skin had a pale-tan pigment, his hair was straw colored, his eyes brown. Such a child was not impossible between Lefonok and his wife, although extremely unlikely; their other children—Udo, Kalee, and Ukan—were the same as all the other Tasaday. I had heard a scientist speculate that Lefonok's wife must have met someone in the forest, a man from another group, or perhaps even a hunter from outside, who had sired Sasa. Perhaps Lefonok's wife had run away with him and that caused Lefonok's shame and the estrangement with her parent group. And what about Ukan—the boy whose existence they had at first denied, then said had died? Perhaps that, too, was not true; perhaps he ran away or was called away to rejoin his mother. Was that the reason for their denial of him and for using the secret language? On the other hand, he may truly have died, as Lobo would have died if left alone to his fate once stricken ill. The family, remember, did have health problems besides Ukan: not only Sasa but also Udo, who appeared to have a spinal defect, was much smaller yet reportedly older than Lobo. Perhaps there were genetic problems between Lefonok and his wife—Ukan dead, Udo stunted, Sasa strangely pigmented. Perhaps other children of theirs had died and Sasa was the last straw for the mother. Despondent, she took herself into the forest and never returned; or Lefonok and the Tasaday decided she must go back to her people, she was a bad link. . . .

Of course, as Yen and many others had pointed out, finding those other groups could answer many questions.

That possibility looked remote, however. Manda had talked of searching for the Tasafeng and Sanduka, but lately did not place it in the near future. When I asked what he thought was the long-range outlook for the Tasaday, he said that if they did not find the other groups, they would probably link up with the Blit; and if they did not do so themselves, then Panamin might help them do so. "It would make sense," he said. "The Tasaday know the Blit, and the Blit know them—Dafal, Igna, Sindi, they all come from there. And the Blit are good people, beautiful people. And Blit is close; the Tasaday could stay in the forest if they wanted to and just trade with the Blit for what ever they needed—knives, cloth, women . . . especially women. Besides, the new municipality is getting started. If the day ever comes—maybe years from now, when we're all gone—and the Tasaday want or need education, well, it may be okay then. The important thing is to make sure the municipality succeeds, that the tribes have got their own thing going."

On our third morning in the forest, Eibesfeldt and the entire party packed gear early and prepared to leave. Balayam asked if he could carry a bag and go with us to the helicopter landing pad. Others wanted to carry something and come too, he said, adding with his conspiratorial grin that we should not tell Momo Dakel Diwata Tasaday about this. (Manda had sometimes forbade the Tasaday from carrying the supplies of visitors because he did not want them to be porters; but he had sometimes allowed them to carry things when they made a special request. They seemed to enjoy helping, participating.) We said they could come along and selected the lightest bags for them.

At the landing pad we waited nearly an hour for the helicopter. Several Tasaday boys played, hurling rocks at a distant stump and shouting each time they hit it, which was surprisingly often.

Then, waving and laughing, the Tasaday scurried off the ridge as the helicopter roared down and picked us up. It was May 7, 1974.

We spent the rest of the day with the Blit, whom Eibesfeldt found almost as intriguing as the Tasaday. "They are an extremely peaceful and affectionate people, I can see that," he said. "They'd surely be scared, though, if we hadn't come with Panamin." Datu Dudim confirmed that the Blit never had trouble and said his ancestors had always been peaceful here. Now, though, there was the fighting at Barrio Ned. During our visit, Dudim called a meeting of a dozen Blit leaders, urging them to move their followers closer to the main settlement.

The next morning we flew to a mountain hamlet of the Tboli, about twenty-five miles south of Blit, on the very edge of the great rain forest. The people there called this place Dumamis ("the place of the lime") and themselves the Dumamis. These, too, were peaceful folk but they had had difficulties with settlers. And as we flew in we could see, behind Lake Sebu, the fresh tracks of logging equipment on roads that had been closed but were evidently open again and curling deeper into the forest.

We flew half an hour to the northeast the next day and landed in a spectacularly beautiful settlement of the Tboli at Kemalas. It was where we had gone early one morning in 1972, when gunmen attacked some boys and then opened up with gunfire on their houses. Now it was quiet and there were at least four times as many houses. They sat atop a ridge, more than a thousand feet above a valley that stretched for miles and was dotted by the farms and towns of settlers. The Tboli knew these settlers and were wary, but in recent months they had been able to go about their daily routines without incident, even trading in the towns.

The following day the helicopter took us to the main Tboli settlement at Kematu, the one usually called simply Tboli. Its huge rectangle of houses in the valley was the most civilized place we had seen in a week. Our travels had each day shown us increasing amounts of technology and cultural sophistication—from the Tasaday's caves to the seat of the new Tboli municipality.

Eibesfeldt was delighted with much that he had seen and talked enthusiastically of returning early next year for longer study, and of outlining a research program for his institute that would include many groups. He said he agreed wholeheartedly with Elizalde that the people themselves were more important than science.

He observed that the tribes here seemed to be receiving more support and opportunities than minorities almost anywhere. "And now this municipality," he said. "That is extraordinary. It is pioneering. I don't know of such a thing anywhere else in the world. Maybe these people here really have a chance."

Yet despite these broader interests, the Tasaday remained the most fascinating, and our conversation repeatedly returned to them. Eibesfeldt looked forward to working at the caves and said, "And then, in a few years, perhaps, we will be ready to meet those other people [the Tasafeng and Sanduka]; now that could be something exceptional, too."

We flew to Manila the next morning and Elizalde arranged for Eibesfeldt to spend two days with the Agta people on Luzon's eastern coast. While he was away, Jack Reynolds phoned me from Hong Kong and inquired about the possibility of another documentary film being made, this one about the search for the other groups. It was very doubtful, I said, that any effort would be made to find them for quite a while, perhaps years.

I mentioned Reynolds's inquiry to Elizalde that evening and told him what I had replied.

"Well, I don't know," Elizalde said. "I've been thinking about that. You know, we just may have to go looking for them sooner than we thought. The logging roads are heading into the forest again—we've got to stop that—and that fighting at Barrio Ned could be big trouble. It's causing the Blit to worry for the first time, and refugees from the fighting could very easily start hiding in the forest. On top of that, Mai tells me that when there is shooting around Ned you can actually hear it at the Tasaday's helipad."

When Eibesfeldt returned from the Agta, Elizalde had a farewell luncheon at his house. The Tasafeng and Sanduka came into the conversation, and Elizalde said it might be wise to try to find them. "I've got a pretty good idea where they are," he said. "We've got information that sounds very reliable."

Eibesfeldt thought it would be an important event, but that he understood it was not likely to happen for a couple of years at least.

"No," Elizalde said. "I think maybe the time is getting close. There are several reasons why we should do this . . . but the main reason is that the wrong people may be getting into that forest."

When did he have in mind?

"Well, we'd have some planning to do, of course," Manda said, looking at Eibesfeldt and then asking "When do you plan to come back here?"

Eibesfeldt said about next January.

"Hmm, January. Okay, let's try to make it then. Yeah, we should have our new chopper by then," Elizalde said. "You want to go with us? I think we can find the Tasafeng and Sanduka. Okay, let's plan on that, then. We'll shoot for January. Okay?"

Eibesfeldt nodded. I nodded. Oscar Trinidad nodded. Ching nodded.

In January.

The seeming finality of this made my heart jump and my thoughts race forward.

Where would this lead us? Nobody knew.

But for that matter, how far had we already gone? I couldn't answer that either—although I knew it had been farther than I had dreamed of going. Somewhere, for me, the journey had a beginning—when I read, skeptically, the first news story about the Tasaday? When we first saw them waiting timidly beside the forest stream? Or were stunned by the sight of their caves? Or was it when I realized their vulnerability, realized an unutterable tenderness, and knew that it was true those hands were gentle and those eyes innocent?

And somewhere, too, there had been a beginning for them—with Dafal? Elizalde?—when their time of no yesterdays and no tomorrows was no more. They began to have a history, a past and future in worldly dimensions. And what could anyone do about the inescapable fact that once in motion—as we of the twentieth century knew—the Tasaday's life could never be as it was. Sad? Possibly. But the world the logging roads would have brought would have made it sadder still.

And perhaps in the Tasafeng and Sanduka the cycle of Tasaday life could be traced. This could be good, for them and for us—as it had been good so far.

Yet even as we looked ahead, something in me lingered in the green heart of the Tasaday forest, where we had touched some kind of paradise —gentle people taking no more from nature than they needed each day, nibbling flowers, playing under the waterfall, laughing over *lassus,* weeping over good-bys, cuddling children, embracing friends, unashamedly expressing their love. Whatever lay ahead, that glimpse of Eden could not be denied. No matter how many centuries of history separated the Tasaday from us, whatever our world and their world would find in each other tomorrow, we had shared feelings and experiences that began a mutual history; that underscored our common humanity; that from their peace invited us to "call all men one man, and all women one woman."

Appendix

SOME HISTORICAL FACTS
ABOUT THE PHILIPPINES

THE land of the Tasaday ranges from about 3,500 to 4,500 feet above sea level in a mountain rain forest that covers approximately 600 square miles of Mindanao in the Southern Philippines. The forest touches the lands of the Tboli, Ubu, Blit, and half a dozen more of some sixty tribes scattered throughout the nation. Among some of these people may be descendents of the original inhabitants of the islands.

It is not really known when, how, or from where those first inhabitants came; nonetheless, scholars have postulated a prehistory and an increasing amount of scientific data supports the following theories.

The earliest inhabitants, a quarter of a million years ago, may have walked across land bridges that then connected what are now Philippine Islands—including Mindanao—with the Malaysian Peninsula and the Asian mainland. Perhaps those early arrivals were distant relatives of Java man and Peking man whom scientists classify as *Homo erectus,* the first true man in the evolutionary process, who walked the earth more than half a million years ago.

Some scholars believe the first inhabitants of the Philippines were Negritos, small, dark-skinned people who arrived from the south many thousands of years later. Several tribes or groups of Negritos are still found in scattered enclaves.

Whether those first Filipinos were direct descendents of *Homo erectus,* Negritos, or some other racial stock—possibly a type of southern Mongoloid peoples out of China or India—little is known about their life ways. Doubtless they were food gatherers and hunters, stayed in small groups, and at least sometimes lived in caves. Evidence discovered in the Tabon caves of Palawan Island, west of Mindanao, indicates that no later than 50,000 B.C. they were using crude stone tools. Significantly improved stone implements had developed in various places by 20,000 B.C., and these became increasingly sophisticated until about 500 B.C., when metal became widely available.

Meanwhile, perhaps about 6,000 B.C., significant numbers of people had started arriving by sea—the land bridges having been submerged under rising oceans. During the next several thousand years these people came in waves and in trickles, as migrants and traders, as seafarers and adventurers, mostly from what is now known as Melanesia, Polynesia, Indonesia, Malaysia, India, Indochina, China, and the Arab world. Of course they brought new ideas and new practices, and the traditional hunting-gathering economy of the islanders changed radically. The period beginning about 500 B.C. saw not only the wide use of metal, but also the spread of agriculture—particularly the cultivation of staples such as rice and millet—the domestication of animals, the manufacture of glass beads and bracelets, and the introduction of weaving and pottery.

In about the eighth or ninth century A.D. began a period of more intensive contact with some of the world's most highly developed cultures. Each had lasting impact. First came Arab traders out of the Middle East and Asia, followed a century or so later by Indians from the frontiers of their empire, which extended into Indonesia. The thirteenth century saw increasing numbers of Chinese traders, and, in 1521, sailing under the flag of Spain, Portuguese explorer Ferdinand Magellan introduced Europeans.

Magellan was slain in a dispute with native islanders soon after he reached what is now the central Philippines, but this did not discourage Spain from sending more men. Some historians say those later explorers and settlers found the native inhabitants mostly in small communities, chiefly near seas, rivers, and lakes. Approximately 60 per cent of the land was forested and the fertile soil and tropical climate, with very heavy rainfall, nourished some ten thousand species of plants. The small communities based their social organization on kinship—the family was pre-eminent; marriage was arranged by parents, and elders were revered—although deceased ancestors beyond two or three generations are believed to have usually been forgotten or merged with godlike spirits. Religion was meshed with social and economic life and featured elaborate rituals for such activities as crop harvesting, fishing expeditions, weddings. The dead were believed to go to one of several sky worlds or underworlds, where they continued to live as they had on earth.

It is still possible today to find in the Philippines tribes living in these same ways, although the Spaniards—who officially colonized the islands in the mid-sixteenth century after naming them for Prince Philip, who later assumed the Spanish throne as King Philip II—succeeded in introducing heaven and hell and other Western religious beliefs to most Filipinos. Roman Catholic friars and missionaries spread the gospel so effectively that presently about 80 per cent of all Filipinos count themselves Catholics, making the Philippines the only predominantly Christian nation in Asia.

The Spaniards turned back the northward expansion of Mohammedism—which had reached Manila—but the Moslems of the deep south successfully resisted all efforts to be conquered or converted, and throughout the three hundred and fifty years of Spanish reign maintained Islam's influence in parts of Mindanao and other islands on the Sulu and Celebes seas. Many smaller pagan tribes also avoided Spanish domination and retained their original life ways.

Among most of the people, however, the Spanish colonizers made major inroads beyond religion. Geographically and politically, the islands became a nation for the first time, and, for many Filipinos, Spanish became the second language—second to whichever of the country's many dialects prevailed in a particular region. The Spanish period also brought heavy commerce with Mexico, the marks of which are evident today in art, architecture, and in certain attitudes. Spanish sovereignty was interrupted in 1762, when the British invaded and controlled Manila—then as now the capital of commerce, politics, culture—but little else. In 1768 Spain re-established her superiority and held it until 1898.

In that year, during the Spanish-American War, Spain lost the Philippines to the United States. Americans held authority for nearly half a century, during which American English supplanted Spanish as the second language; the educational and political systems were organized after those in the United States; commerce and many other aspects of material culture took on a heavy American emphasis.

Japan conquered the islands in 1942, at the start of World War II, and maintained a strong military presence in key areas until 1944, when U.S. troops returned and, aided by Filipino guerrillas, recaptured the country. The United States withdrew its government in 1946 and the Philippines became an independent republic.

All of this created a colorful and richly complicated culture and people—Malayo-Polynesian-Indonesian-Arabic-Chinese-Indian foundations with Spanish, American, and a touch of Japanese overlays.

Not long after the Philippines gained independence, special attention was given to the development of Mindanao. It had been among the first islands to be inhabited but had fallen far behind others in development. By the 1950's Manila, on Luzon, the largest island, was a teeming metropolis with all the trappings, from skyscrapers to slums, of the world's major cities. And on many islands cash crops such as sugar cane, tobacco, and abaca were being harvested; minerals such as gold, copper, and iron were being taken in abundance. But Mindanao remained largely unexplored. Filipinos from more heavily populated areas were encouraged by the government to farm Mindanao's fertile valleys, cut its timber, extract its metals.

By the 1960's the frontiers of Mindanao had advanced notably and the natural resources were being exploited extensively—sometimes ruthlessly. Moslem tribes and many other smaller groups with ancient claims to the land often stood in the way. Tribal people who previously had contended with only an occasional missionary or farmer now faced ambitious businessmen and hungry settlers. Unequipped to deal with these men and their modern ideas and weapons, the tribes inevitably lost, often after bloodshed.

This new situation, analogous to that faced by hundreds of Indian tribes in North and South America in the past, and continuing for many in the present, was the greatest challenge to the life ways of some tribes since their ancestors arrived long, long ago. And some did not even know they were being challenged. The Tasaday, for instance, had lost contact with the outside world, and the world with them. But in 1971 events combined to cause the Tasaday's presence to be revealed.

Index

DATE DUE
